Y0-BQP-387

For Reference

Not to be taken from this room

DICTIONARY
OF FRENCH LITERATURE

Plate 1. Honoré de Balzac (by Gavarni)

Plate 2. Charles Baudelaire

DICTIONARY OF FRENCH LITERATURE

edited by
SIDNEY D. BRAUN

GREENWOOD PRESS, PUBLISHERS
WESTPORT, CONNECTICUT

The Library of Congress cataloged this book as follows:

Braun, Sidney David, 1912–   ed.
  Dictionary of French literature, edited by Sidney D.
Braun. Westport, Conn., Greenwood Press ₍1971, c1958₎
  xiii, 362 p. ports. 23 cm.

  1. French literature—Dictionaries.   I. Title.

PQ41.B7 1971   840'.9   70–138576
ISBN 0–8371–5775–7   MARC

Library of Congress   72 ₍4₎

Originally published in 1958 by Philosophical Library, Inc.,
New York.

Reprinted with the permission of Philosophical Library, Inc.

Reprinted by Greenwood Press, Inc.

First Greenwood reprinting 1971
Second Greenwood reprinting 1977

Library of Congress Catalog Card Number 70-138576

ISBN 0-8371-5775-7

Printed in the United States of America

To my Mother
and
to the memory
of
my Father
and
Hilda and Abraham J. Kadish

FOREWORD

This *Dictionary of French Literature* constitutes, in my opinion, a unique achievement.

First of all, it is, to the best of my knowledge, the only book in which students and teachers of French literature will find so much up-to-date information, in English, on all French authors, from the very first writers of *Chansons de Geste* and *Romans Courtois* to Jean-Paul Sartre and Françoise Sagan.

Secondly, it contains not only summaries of every important French work but also motivated reasons why each work was selected in the first place. It also gives much needed definitions of literary terms such as *drame, enjambement, préciosité,* etc.

Thirdly, it combines the best of collective knowledge with the best of individual research: while some twenty experts have written articles on literary genres, movements, or aspects of literary life, most of the items are the work of *one* man. This last feature makes for a real unity of method and tone and gives to the whole work more homogeneity than is usually found in such an enterprise.

The *Dictionary of French Literature* was conceived and realized as a work of love by a man who devoted to this task the best of five years. Professor Sidney D. Braun, after studying at the Sorbonne, at Columbia University, and at the University of Mexico, received his Ph.D. in French from New York University. He has taught at Long Island University, at the Extension Division of the College of the City of New York and, for the past 22 years, at Yeshiva University: he served there as the head of the Division of Languages and Literature and is now the chairman of the French Department. He is also on the

Faculty of the École Libre des Hautes Études (Université française de New-York). As a scholar, he is known for his "definitive" work on *The 'Courtisane' in the French Theatre from Hugo to Becque* (The Johns Hopkins University Press, 1947), his many excellent articles on Péguy, Zola, André Suarès, Existentialism, his frequent contributions to the P.M.L.A., the *Modern Language Notes,* the *French Review,* the *Modern Language Quarterly, Symposium,* the *Modern Language Journal,* and his bibliographical work, including his current research for the *Cabeen Critical Bibliography of Nineteenth Century French Literature.* He was also a founder of the Yeshiva College French magazine *Le Flambeau.* Professor Braun's scholarship and talent have prepared him particularly well for an undertaking of this sort and he has proved equal to a task which might have discouraged a less dedicated humanist. This remarkable work should be in the reference room of every library for the next generation.

Pierre Brodin
Dean of Humanities,
École Libre des Hautes Études

PREFACE

The aim of the present volume is to provide the reader with essential information relating to French literature. Necessarily selective rather than exhaustive, this work nevertheless seeks to present in compact form an over-all view of this literature; to achieve this end, authors and subjects, many of which are frequently not found in the standard manuals and histories of French literature, are here included. The reader's attention is called, for example, to the entries on the origins of various literary genres, on the development of the French language, and, in the contemporary period, on the literature of the "Resistance." Moreover, since this reference work has been especially prepared for the American reader, an article on Franco-American relations has also been included.

From a chronological point of view, the entries range from the *langues romanes* to Françoise Sagan. In addition to the biographies of authors, which also contain titles of representative works and suggested bibliographies, this volume includes brief summaries of works of special significance—the selection of which obviously has been determined by subjective taste—definitions of important literary terms, and surveys of literary movements, schools and genres. Other articles, such as those on Provençal language and literature and on the cinema, have also been included for the light they shed on French literature. All entries, irrespective of the subject, are arranged in alphabetical order and are cross-referenced. A separate list of terms and topics treated, found at the end of the book, will also serve as a convenient guide for the reader.

In the compilation of this volume, I have found particularly helpful certain sources of literary information. These include: J. Bédier and P. Hazard, *Histoire de la littérature française* (revised by P. Martino), 2 vols., 1949; R. Bossuat, *Le Moyen Age*, 1931; M. Braunschvig, *Notre littérature étudiée dans les textes*, 2 vols. (latest edition); *La Littérature française contemporaine étudiée dans les textes*, 1950; G. Brereton, *A Short History of French Literature*, 1954; P. Castex and P. Surer, *Manuel des études littéraires françaises*, 1946-1953; *Columbia Dictionary of Modern European Literature*, ed. H. Smith, 1947; *Dictionnaire des lettres françaises*, ed. G. Grente (*Le 16ᵉ Siècle*, 1951; *Le 17ᵉ Siècle*, 1954); M. Girard, *Guide illustré de la littérature française moderne*, 1949; D. Mornet, *La Pensée française au 18ᵉ Siècle*, 1956; W. A. Nitze and E. P. Dargan, *A History of French Literature*, 1938; J. Nathan, *Histoire de la littérature française contemporaine*, 1954; V. L. Saulnier, *La Littérature française* . . . (surveys of different periods in *Que sais-je* series), 1942-1945; K. Voretzsch, *Introduction to the Study of Old French Literature* (English translation by F. M. Du Mont), 1931.

I wish to express my sincerest thanks to all those, whose names will be found listed on a separate page, who have contributed articles on the various movements, schools and literary genres. Their work and their scholarship have given substance to this volume. All articles, of course, which do not bear the name of a contributor have been prepared by me.

A special debt of gratitude is due the following—most of whom have also contributed articles—for having read various portions of the manuscript and for having offered helpful criticism: Professors Jean-Albert Bédé and Donald Frame, of Columbia University; Professor Fernand Vial, of Fordham University; Professor Nathan Edelman, of Johns Hopkins University; Professors Germaine Brée and Pauline Taylor, of New York University; Professor Georges May, of Yale University. I have also the pleasant duty of thanking Dr. Seymour Lainoff, my colleague at Yeshiva University, for his aid in stylistic matters. Their suggestions and corrections have contributed immensely to whatever standard of accuracy and completeness has been achieved. For the final form which the material assumes

—except, of course, for the articles contributed—I alone am to be held responsible.

A final word of deep gratitude is due my wife, Miriam Kadish Braun. Without her encouragement, devotion and patience, not to mention her helpful criticism, this volume, several years in preparation, might never have seen the light.

SIDNEY D. BRAUN

CONTRIBUTORS

Douglas W. Alden, *Princeton University*
Anna Balakian, *New York University*
Max I. Baym, *Polytechnic Institute of Brooklyn*
Jean-Albert Bédé, *Columbia University*
Konrad Bieber, *Connecticut College*
Germaine Brée, *New York University*
LeRoy C. Breunig, Jr., *Barnard College*
Imbrie Buffum, *Yale University*
Robert J. Clements, *New York University*
Wallace Fowlie, *Bennington College*
Albert J. George, *Syracuse University*
Jacques Guicharnaud, *Yale University*
Harry Kurz, *Queens College*
Milan S. La Du, *Washington University*
Laurent LeSage, *Penn State University*
Georges May, *Yale University*
Jean Misrahi, *Fordham University*
Alphonse V. Roche, *Northwestern University*
Albert J. Salvan, *Brown University*
Pauline Taylor, *New York University*
Robert E. Taylor, *New York University*
Fernand Vial, *Fordham University*

LIST OF ILLUSTRATIONS

PLATE
1. Honoré de Balzac
2. Charles Baudelaire
3. Albert Camus
4. Paul Claudel
5. Sidonie Gabrielle Colette
6. Pierre Corneille
7. René Descartes
8. André Gide
9. Victor Hugo
10. Molière
11. Michel Eyquem de Montaigne
12. Marcel Proust
13. François Rabelais
14. Jean Racine
15. Jean-Jacques Rousseau
16. Jean-Paul Sartre
17. Voltaire
18. Émile Zola

A

Abbaye de Créteil: or, more simply, "Abbaye," refers to the group of writers and artists who, in 1906, decided to live together at this country house in Créteil, near Paris, where they could work and devote themselves to their vocations. This phalanx consisted chiefly of René Arcos, Charles Vildrac (q.v.), Georges Duhamel (q.v.), Henri Martin and Albert Gleizes, a cubist painter. They bought a printing press and, thanks to Linard, one of their group and a printer who taught them his trade, some books, including Duhamel's *Des légendes, des batailles* (1906), were printed. Jules Romains (q.v.), then a student at the École Normale Supérieure, despite the fact that he was not a member, paid this group several visits and brought them his *La Vie Unanime* (1908), a collection of poems. Although no doctrine, strictly speaking, is associated with the Abbaye brotherhood, it can be said that *Unanimism* (q.v.), under the aegis of Romains, was born here. After fourteen months, the enterprise failed, mainly because of financial difficulties, "but the common spirit of the movement continued to inspire those who had joined it."
    Christian Sénéchal, *L'Abbaye de Créteil*, 1930.

Abbaye de Thélème: The monastery given as a reward to Friar Jean des Entommeures by Gargantua (q.v.) for his valiant attack upon the enemy. The only rule of this monastery, to which both sexes were admitted and which anyone could leave when he so pleased, was *"Fais ce que tu voudras."* Based on the belief that the free, well-bred and well-educated are instinctively impelled to virtuous deeds and restrained from vice, the rule of this monastery reflects the Renaissance ideal as exemplified in Rabelais (q.v.).

Abbé Constantin, L' (1882): See *Meilhac, Henri*.

Abrégé de l'histoire de Port-Royal (p. 1767): See *Racine*.

Académie Française: Begun in 1624 as a small private literary circle that met regularly at the home of Conrart, the king's secretary, it won official recognition in 1635 when Richelieu, sensing the possibility of gaining political advantage through a literary society subject to royal supervision, granted it a charter. Legal recognition of this charter, however, was delayed, because of opposition, until 1637. The society, consisting since 1639 of no more than forty members, is often referred to as the "Forty Immortals." In contrast with the *Académie Goncourt* (q.v.), the members of the Académie Française cannot be elected unless

1

they have first declared their candidacy. Unlike the *Académie Goncourt,* moreover, the Académie Française is not an exclusively literary academy; it is also composed of lawyers, doctors and statesmen. The purpose of the Académie Française, as intended by Richelieu, was to exercise authority in matters of language and, to a certain degree, in literature. At his request, it intervened in the *Querelle du Cid* (q.v) and drew up the famous *Sentiments sur le Cid,* edited by Chapelain (q.v.). More important than performing the function of a literary tribunal, a role it has since given up—it prefers to award literary prizes each year to deserving authors—has been its work on the Dictionary of the French Academy, the first edition of which appeared in 1694. Through this Dictionary, which established standards of vocabulary and syntax, the French Academy contributed importantly to the development of the French language. No grammar, however— the fine *Remarques* of Vaugelas (q.v.) notwithstanding—was published by the Academy until 1932.

G. Boissier, *L'Académie française sous l'Ancien Régime,* 1909.

Académie Goncourt: A literary academy, inaugurated in 1900, consisting of 10 members, all of whom are elected, in contrast with those of the *Académie Française* (q.v.), without declaration of candidacy. In accordance with the provisions of the endowment made by Edmond de Goncourt (q.v.), the members of this academy receive annuities. At their annual dinner held in December, they award the *Prix Goncourt* (q.v.) to the author of the best novel of the year.

Académistes, Les (1650): See *Saint-Évremond.*

Achard, Marcel: (1899-   ) The plays of this dramatist, once a prompter at Copeau's (q.v.) *Vieux Colombier,* belong properly to fantasy, suggesting as they do an escape in dreams from the harsh realities of life; such fantasy, moreover, often recalls the world of Marivaux or Musset (qq.v.). The situations depicted in them are generally improbable, and the characters, who are very much alike, consist of sentimental but ridiculous heroes who are paralyzed with fear by the inconstancy of women. These romantic heroes are spared suffering in the end only because of the moonlit universe in which they live and because of the ingenious talent of the dramatist to bring to these plays a happy ending. Gaiety, wit, irony, and humor, with a free dialogue, enable the dramatist to achieve such endings. The characters in his first successful play, *Voulez-vous jouer avec moâ* (1923), the action of which takes place in a circus, are clowns. In *Jean de la Lune* (1929), probably his most notable dramatic achievement, later made into a film, the perfidious Marceline is finally disarmed and won over by the obstinate faith and love shown her by her husband. Included among his other plays are: *Malbrough s'en va-t'en guerre* (1924), *La Vie est belle* (1928), *Domino* (1931), and *Le Corsaire* (1938).

Acheteuse, L' (1930): See *Passeur, Stève.*

Adam de la Hale (or **Adam Le Bossu**): (*c.* 1250-*c.* 1288) Well-known for his lyric poetry, this *trouvère* (q.v.) from Arras is especially noted for having initiated the secular, comic *jeu* (q.v) in France. His *Jeu de la Feuillée* (*c.* 1276), possibly so called because it was performed during the May festivities under an arbor, is generally regarded as a kind of farce satirizing, in the form of a *revue* or a series of disconnected scenes, those whom he knew or lived with, including his wife and his father. His *Jeu de Robin et Marion* (*c.* 1285) has been called the first of the French *opéra-comiques* since the play includes music and song; more exactly, it is a dramatic *pastourelle* (q.v), its main protagonists being a shepherd and a shepherdess.

H. Guy, *Essai sur la vie et les œuvres littéraires du trouvère Adam de la Hale*, 1898.

Adolphe (1816): See *Constant, Benjamin.*

Adolescence Clémentine (1532): See *Marot, Clément.*

Age d'homme, L' (1939): See *Leiris, Michel.*

Aigle à deux têtes, L' (1945): See *Cocteau.*

Aiglon, L' (1900): See *Rostand, Edmond.*

Alain (pseud. of **Emile Chartier**): (1868-1951) This essayist and philosopher, for many years (1909-1933) a professor at the *lycée Henry IV*, exercised a strong influence on his students, many of whom became important writers and thinkers in their own right. He created the *genre* of the "Propos"—short, aphoristic pieces that, much like a fable or parable, generalize from a concrete fact. His philosophy, not based on a system, and drawing its source from the specific problems of daily life, is founded on an understanding and knowledge of the limitations of the human mind. For this reason, too, he prefers poets and novelists like Homer, Stendhal (q.v.) and Balzac (q.v.)—to the latter two of whom, incidentally, he devoted studies. The various works of this humanist reveal an agnostic attitude in matters of religion (*Propos sur le christianisme*, 1924), a pacifist attitude in politics (*Mars ou la Guerre jugée*, 1921) and a realistic attitude in matters of morality (*Les Propos d'Alain*, 1920; *Propos sur le Bonheur*, 1928). His *Système des Beaux-Arts* (1931) is a work on aesthetics, one of his major interests, while his *Propos de littérature* (1934) deals with various authors.

A la Recherche du temps perdu (1913-1928): See *Proust.*

Albertus (1832): See *Gautier.*

Alcools (1913): See *Apollinaire, Guillaume.*

Alembert, Jean Le Rond d': (1717-1783) As Diderot's (q.v.) chief collaborator and assistant editor until 1759 of the *Encyclopédie* (q.v.), he contributed, in addition to several articles on mathematics, the *Discours préliminaire*, in which he explained its purposes and methods, and the article *Genève*. Natural son of Mme. de Tencin, whose *salon* was a leading one during the eighteenth century, he frequented the *salons* (q.v.) of Mme. du Deffand and Mlle. de Lespinasse. A distinguished *philosophe* (q.v.), too, he wrote such works as *Mélanges de philosophie, d'histoire et de littérature* (1753) and *Essai sur les éléments de philosophie* (1759).

J. Bertrand, *D'Alembert*, 1889; M. Muller, *La philosophie de J. d'Alembert*, 1926.

Alexandre le Grand (1665): See *Racine.*

alexandrine: A twelve-syllable line, one that is most frequently used in French poetry. It derives its name from the twelfth-century poem the *Roman d'Alexandre* (q.v.), the first to be written in it.

Alexis, Paul: (1847-1901) Novelist and dramatist, he was one of the authors of the *Soirées de Médan* (1880; q.v.). An exponent of naturalism, he produced at the Théâtre-Libre three plays. One of them, *La Fin de Lucie Pellegrin* (1888), was adapted from his short story; a typical *comédie rosse* (q.v.), it caused a furor. The other plays are *Mademoiselle Pomme* (1887)—written in collaboration with Edmond Duranty (q.v.)—and *Les Frères Zemganno* (1890). The last-named piece, drawn from the Goncourt novel, was produced with the collaboration of O. Méténier.

Amants (1895): See *Donnay, Maurice.*

Ame et la danse, L' (1923): See *Valéry, Paul.*

Ami des lois, L' (1793): See *Laya.*

Amiel, Denis: (1884-) Adultery, *liaisons*, divorce and matrimonial problems make up the situations in which woman, with her psychological aspirations and emotional conflicts, is studied by this dramatist, for a long while secretary to Henry Bataille (q.v.). In *La Souriante Mme. Beudet* (1921), written in collaboration with André Obey, he depicts the incompatibility existing between a crude, philistine husband and a sensitive, cultured wife; in the end, however, the latter is brought to a reconciliation when she suddenly becomes aware that her husband has a true, loving heart. *Le Voyageur* (1923), however, reveals more clearly the principles and aesthetics of the "school of silence" (cf. *J. J. Bernard*) to which this writer subscribes. The characters here are more eloquent in the silence of their internal drama than they would be had they indulged in grandiloquence or beautifully phrased language. Other plays reveal a changing world in the life of modern woman, portray the sentimental problems of the young girl of today, or else represent an indictment of our mechanistic civilization. Included among the latter plays are: *Décalage* (1931), *La Femme en fleur* (1935), *Ma Liberté* (1936), and *L'Age de fer* (1932).

Ami Fritz, L' (1864): See *Erckmann-Chatrian.*

Amoureuse (1891): See *Porto-Riche.*

Amours (1552): See *Ronsard.*

Amphitryon 38 (1929): See *Giraudoux.*

Amyot, Jacques: (1513-1593) Before becoming the most celebrated translator of the sixteenth century, he was professor of Latin at the University of Bourges and then tutor to the future Kings of France Charles IX and Henri III. His translation of Plutarch's *Parallel Lives* (1559), undertaken at the request of Fran-çois I, won him much success and recognition. Borrowing resourcefully, in accordance with the method recommended by the Pléiade (q.v.), from Latin, Greek, and Italian, as well as from technical and popular vocabulary, his originality lies in the fact that he contributed to the development and the enrichment of French prose by his free, natural, clear, non-literal and unpedantic style. From this point of view, he represents a transition between Rabelais (q.v.) and Classicism. Through this translation, moreover, he introduced to the French the world of antiquity, with its examples of heroism and glory, with its way of life, virtues, and vices and, in general, its wisdom. In addition to his *Vies des hommes illustres de Plutarque,* his translations include *Œuvres morales* (1572) and works of Heliodorus and Longus.

R. Sturel, *Jacques Amyot, Traducteur des Vies parallèlles,* 1909; A. Cioranescu, *Vie de Jacques Amyot,* 1941.

Ancey, Georges (pseud. of G. Mathiron de Curnieu): (1860-1917) This dramatist wrote for the Théâtre-Libre (q.v) *M. Lamblin* (1888), *L'École des veufs* (1889)—a good comédie rosse (q.v.)—*Les Inséparables* (1889), and *La Dupe* (1891). These plays are written in a cynical and pessimistic vein.

Andromaque: This play (1667) is the first to reveal Racine's (q.v.) genius and to establish the definitive type of French tragedy (q.v.). Based on the story of Andromache's misfortunes and final triumph as related by Homer, Euripides, Seneca, and, especially, by Virgil, in his *Aeneid,* its entire action, relatively simple, hinges on a psychological chain of vacillations and reactions, the result of loves temporarily denied or reciprocated. The dénouement is brought about by Andromaque's final decision—a decision that stirs violent passions of jealousy, anger and revenge and that causes murder and insanity. Andromaque, widow of Hector, is the captive of King Pyrrhus. The latter, though betrothed to Hermione, promises Andromaque, with whom he is in love, to spare her son, Astyanax, and not to deliver him to Oreste, sent as ambassador of the Greeks, if only she will marry him. Oreste, too, hopes that Andromaque will consent; in this way, he would be able to marry Hermione, with whom he is blindly in love. When Andromaque, however, true to the memory of her dead husband, refuses, Pyrrhus declares he is ready to hand over Astyanax to the Greeks and to marry Hermione, who is madly in love with him. To save her son, Andromaque, torn between her feelings of conjugal and maternal love, agrees to marry Pyrrhus, but secretly plans, after the ceremony, to kill herself. Hermione, on the other hand, furious, now seeks revenge; at her instigation, Oreste, ready to do anything to please her, assassinates the king at the marriage altar. Pyrrhus dead, Hermione, whose request to Oreste belied her true sentiments, in despair kills herself on the body of her beloved. Oreste becomes insane with remorse and grief.

Anglais tel qu'on le parle, L' (1899): See *Bernard, Tristan.*

Annonce faite à Marie, L' (1912): See *Claudel.*

Anouilh, Jean: (1910-   ) Born in Bordeaux, this writer, who for a while was secretary to Jouvet (q.v.), decided, after being inspired by Giraudoux's (q.v.) *Siegfried,* to write for the stage. His plays, which he himself has conveniently categorized under the labels of "pièces roses" and "pièces noires," are characterized by the struggle they depict between the principles of good and evil incarnated in symbolical characters. Those pieces that are "roses" and that end with the victory of the

good, center upon the young and pure, the intransigent, and those who revolt against the injustices of society and human distress; the "pièces noires," more numerous, in which the wicked triumph, center upon the mean and ugly who are protected by society. Between the two antithetical types, moreover, no compromise is possible. The action in these plays stems from some "romanesque" situation or a modernization of an ancient legend. In *L'Hermine* (1913) and *La Sauvage* (1932), a young woman, in order to satisfy her ideal, refuses to compromise, even at the expense of her happiness. A victim of amnesia—in Giraudoux (q.v.) the amnesiac represents a conflict of nationalities—typifies revolt in *Le Voyageur sans bagages* (1936), Anouilh's first genuinely successful play. Here, in a setting that blends humor with realism, the shell-shocked soldier, when he has regained his memory, refuses to return to his past, to him now an ugly existence, in order to retain his new feeling of freedom and purity. Love and death, in an atmosphere resembling that of Tristan and Iseut, is the theme of the poetic and tragic *Eurydice* (1942). *Le Bal des Voleurs* (1937), on the other hand, a ballet comedy with agreeable buffoonery, is a "pièce rose" with a happy ending, in which love triumphs. The equally happy ending in the gay *Le Rendez-vous de Senlis* (1939), however, leaves the spectator in a somewhat skeptical mood. *Antigone* (1942), a tragedy in modern costume in which the heroine is implacably drawn to death, perhaps out of a desire for purity and liberty, represents an anarchistic transformation of the heroine of old. The pessimism of Anouilh seems to have come to an end with *Médée* (1949). His language, generally mordant and poignant, expressive of his antagonism to the injustices of the era, is relieved by his poetic and idealistic instincts.

More recently, moreover, his "pièces brillantes," including *La Répétition ou l'amour puni* (1950) and *Colombe* (1951) represent a kind of synthesis of his two previous types of plays. Reversing many of his previous ideas, Anouilh at times is disconcerting.

Hubert Gignoux, *Jean Anouilh*, 1947.

Antigone (1942): See *Anouilh*.

Antiquités de Rome, Les (1558): See *Du Bellay*.

Antoine, André: (1858-1943) An early passion for the theater caused him to join, while yet a clerk in the Paris Gas Company, a group of amateur players, with whom he was to organize, in 1887, the Théâtre Libre (q.v.). Though lacking in formal education, and with little experience as an actor, he nevertheless had new ideas about the presentation of drama. As director, he was able to introduce these ideas into this independent theater which was open only to season-ticket subscribers and was free from censorship. Wishing to break with the conventional theater, he launched unknown dramatists, many of whom—Porto-Riche, Brieux, Curel, Lavedan (qq.v.)—were later to become famous and whose plays could not have been produced elsewhere, and presented the plays of Ibsen, Tolstoy, Hauptmann, and other foreign dramatists.

To achieve greater realism, he turned against the play that subscribed to the Scribe (q.v.) formula; instead of the complicated plot, the *raisonneur* (q.v.), and the tirade, he advocated the *tranche de vie* (q.v.), stressed naturalness in acting and verisimilitude in staging. Although in the selection of his first plays Antoine was eclectic, he later yielded to the partisans of naturalism (q.v.) and produced the *comédie rosse* (q.v.), which depicted the lower classes in scenes and situations that emphasized the sordid and the ugly, and which was based on the concepts of heredity, environment, and the instincts. During the seven years of his directorship (1887-1894), he produced 124 new plays. After his resignation, in 1894, because of financial difficulties, he turned its direction over to the actor Larochelle. Two years later, the theater closed its doors. By this time the Théâtre-Libre had left its mark, making play-construction even in the commercial theater less artificial and scabrous subject matter more acceptable. Antoine's influence, moreover, made itself manifest in Berlin and in London, where the Freie Bühne and the Independent Theater, respectively, were modeled after the Théâtre Libre. In 1896 Antoine was appointed codirector of the Odéon theater, but resigned a few months later. At his own playhouse, the Théâtre Antoine, which he directed from 1897 to 1906, he continued the traditions of the Théâtre Libre. In 1906, he became director of the Odéon, in which capacity he remained until 1914. Antoine also served as drama critic on several newspapers.

A. Thalasso, *Le Théâtre Libre*, 1909; S. M. Waxman, *Antoine and the Théâtre-Libre*, 1926.

Antoine de la Sale: (c. 1388-1465?) A prose writer of importance, he is the author of the novel *Petit Jehan de Saintré* (1456) and possibly of the *Quinze Joies du Mariage* (1440?) as well as of the *Cent Nouvelles nouvelles* (1462), which show some influence of Boccaccio's *Decameron*.

J. Nève, *Antoine de la Sale*, 1903.

Antony (1831): See *Dumas* PÈRE.

Aphrodite (1896): See *Louÿs, Pierre*.

Apollinaire, Guillaume (pseud. of Wilhelm Apollinaris de Kostrowitzki): (1880-1918) Son of a Polish mother and an Italian father, this poet, novelist, and dramatist, probably born in Rome, was educated in Monaco, enlisted in 1914 in the French army, was wounded, and died two days before the Armistice. A disappointment in love inspired in 1903 the celebrated "Chanson du Mal Aimé," a poem containing anecdotes, references to friends and much of his personality. In Paris he later met such poets as André Salmon, Léon-Paul Fargue, and Max Jacob (qq.v.), and became the good friend of Braque and Picasso, whose aesthetics of cubism (q.v.) he helped establish when he wrote *Les Peintres cubistes* (1913). The same year one of his two most important volumes of poems, *Alcools*, appeared. In this collection of pre-war poems—among which are "Zone" and the previously cited "Chanson du Mal Aimé"—many characteristics of cubism are to be found, including a chaotic juxtaposition of disparate *motifs*, a spontaneous transcription of a chance conversation heard in all its confusion at some public café or elsewhere, and the use of "modern" images (automobiles, airplanes, moving pictures) that express both the movement and the multiplicity of life. This new poetic composition, moreover, is marked by an absence of punctuation. After this publication, there followed novels, short stories, and *Les Mamelles de Tirésias*, which was written *c.* 1903 and later produced in 1917. The preface of the last mentioned title—a play dealing symbolically with a misunderstood genius—is a kind of manifesto of Surrealism (q.v.), a word Apollinaire was one of the first to use. *L'Esprit nouveau et les Poètes* (1918), an essay in which he favored a synthesis of poetry, painting and music, gave further definition to Surrealism. In his last important collection, *Calligrammes* (1918)—inspired by the war—he made use of a fantastic, humorous typography, one that arranged words in the form of a watch, rain, or even the Eiffel Tower. The purpose of this typography was to suggest visually the object or theme of the poem. In this way, as well as in his nonsensical use of words, Apollinaire was to reject the universe of logic and order, and was to seek, in his "adventure," "new domains" of the subconscious and the unexplored. The Surrealists have rightly acknowledged their debt to Apollinaire, whose poetry is a veritable magic. His last collection of poems and letters, *Ombre de mon amour* and *Tendre comme le souvenir,* appeared posthumously in 1947 and 1952.

André Billy, *Apollinaire vivant,* 1923; André Rouveyre, *Apollinaire,* 1945; Marcel Adéma, *Guillaume Apollinaire le mal-aimé,* 1952.

Après-midi d'un faune, L' (1876): See *Mallarmé.*

Aragon, Louis: (1897-   ) From the very beginning this Parisian-born poet, novelist and essayist set out to shock the bourgeois world. His early prose works, *Le Libertinage* (1924), *Traité du style* (1929), and *Le Paysan de Paris* (1926) are typically surrealistic in style and subject matter. Upon his return from Russia in 1931, Aragon renounced his early surrealistic tendencies, best seen in his poetic collection, *Le Mouvement perpétuel* (1925), and embraced, in his *Hourra l'Oural* (1934), a militant communism. In the novels that followed, *Les Cloches de Bâle* (1934), *Les Beaux Quartiers* (1936) and *Les Voyageurs de l'impériale* (1943), Aragon's sympathies are clearly with the oppressed and the idealistic but not with those whose revolt stems from the cultivation of *self;* against the pharisaism of the bourgeois he opposes the sincerity of the proletariat. The Second World War inspired such anti-German and anti-Vichy collections of poetry as *Le Crève-cœur* (1940) and *La Diane Française* (1945), published clandestinely. Aragon, intent on catching the patriotic enthusiasm of the French, employed in these poems traditional, sonorous, and rhymed verses reminiscent of the popular *chansons* of the Middle Ages. Since 1949 Aragon has undertaken a romanticized chronicle of the communists.

Claude Roy, *Aragon*, 1945.

A rebours (1884): See *Huysmans*.

Argent, L' (1895): See *Fabre, Emile*.

Aristotle (Influence of): Aristotle's influence in French literature, based primarily on his *Poetics*, begins with the Renaissance. A Latin commentary on Aristotle's *Poetics*, by J. C. Scaliger (q.v.), one of France's earliest theorists, was published in 1561, anticipating the strict rules that later applied to French classical tragedy (q.v.). From the same work by Aristotle, the famous passage on the *catharsis* becomes the basis of French tragedy. According to Aristotle, Greek tragedy arouses pity and fear and purges the spectator, who experiences a *catharsis* of these debilitating emotions. What Aristotle meant by a "purgation" of such emotions was not clearly understood; but Corneille (q.v.) was to substitute admiration and heroism in place of pity and terror, introducing in this manner a new motivating force in his drama. Aristotelian rules for the drama were formulated by Jean de La Taille (q.v.), an important critic. But it was because of a misinterpretation, originating in 1570 with the Italian Castelvetro, that the French classical doctrine of the unities (q.v.) as applied to tragedy (q.v.) was accepted by Corneille and other dramatists as binding. The absolute rule concerning the three unities, nothwithstanding the fact that nothing is said in the *Poetics* about unity of place and that Aristotle's notion of unity of time becomes somewhat dis-

torted, was to figure prominently in the *Querelle du Cid* (q.v.), and was to become the key-stone of classical dramatic theory. Respect for Aristotle continued almost until the end of the seventeenth century, and Racine (q.v.) made a partial translation of the *Poetics* [See E. Vinaver's edition of it (1944)]. Many writers, however, including Molière (q.v.), owe nothing to Aristotle, for they did not believe that the "art of pleasing" could be codified by rules and reason. With the *Querelle des Anciens et des Modernes* (q.v.), Aristotle's authority was contested by the Moderns, and his influence began to wane.

R. Bray, *La Formation de la doctrine classique*, 1931; D. Mornet, *Histoire de la littérature française classique (1660-1700)*, 1940.

Arland, Marcel: (1899-) His numerous novels and short stories betray strong humanistic influences and the early influence of Gide (q.v.), which, however, was later tempered by a self-imposed classical discipline. In addition to strong moralistic and psychological characteristics, his writings show a sense of the tragic and of destiny. Included among his better novels are *L'Ordre* (1929) and *Antarès* (1932). His short stories, in which he excelled, include *Terre Natale* (1938) and *Il faut de tout pour faire un monde* (1947). An important critic, too, Arland has published *Essais critiques* (1931).

Armance (1827): See *Stendhal*.

Arnauld, Antoine: (1612-1694) Connected with Port-Royal (q.v.), this theologian—called "the great Arnauld" because he was a leading member of a distinguished family—championed the cause of Jansenism (q.v.) against the attacks of the Jesuits. Author of *De la fréquente communion* (1643), he wrote, in collaboration with Nicole, also a Jansenist, *Logique de Port-Royal* (1661), and with Lancelot, another Jansenist, *Grammaire générale et raisonnée* (1664). A. Gazier, *Histoire générale du mouvement janséniste*, 1922; J. Laporte, *La doctrine de Port-Royal*, 1923.

Artamène ou le Grand Cyrus (1649-1653): See *Scudéry, Madeleine de.*

Artaud, Antonin: (1895-1948) This poet and actor carried Surrealism (q.v.) to unusual lengths when he tried, not by words, but by actual physical identification and integration, to achieve a life of psychic "automatism." These efforts, which had all the appearance of madness, resulted in his being institutionalized for nine years. His remarkable ability to interpret the role of the person with hallucinations was recognized by Dullin, Pitoëff, and Jouvet (qq.v.), with whom he played. His was a case of sincerity carried to the extreme. Two of his collections are: *L'Ombilic des Limbes* (1924) and *Le Pèse-Nerfs* (1927).

Atelier. See *Dullin, Charles.*

Arténice ou Les Bergeries (1618): See *Racan.*

Art for Art's Sake: See *Gautier, Théophile.*

Arthur (or Artus): Legend has transformed this warrior chief into a British King. He is said to have successfully defended his country against the Saxons in their struggles during the sixth century. He instituted the Order of the Chevaliers of the Round Table, who went in quest of the Holy Grail. His adventures have given birth to the *Arthurian Cycle,* also called *Cycle breton, Cycle of the Round Table,* and *romans bretons* (q.v.). The Arthurian legends have also been collected in various chronicles, among them the ninth century Latin version by Nennius, later developed by Geoffrey of Monmouth in his *Historia regum brittaniæ*

(1136), which in turn was translated into French verse by Robert Wace, a Norman poet, in his *Roman de Brut* (1155). R. S. Loomis, *Celtic myth and Arthurian romance,* 1927; *Arthurian Tradition and Chrétien de Troyes,* 1941; J. Marx, *La Légende Arthurienne et le Graal,* 1952.

Art poétique (1674): See *Boileau.*

Art poétique (1548): See *Sebillet, Thomas.*

Assommoir, L' (1877): See *Zola.*

assonance: differs from rime in that it does not take into account consonants that follow the accented vowel or diphthong. It is identified by the last accented vowel as well as by the "mute" *e* that follows, as *âme, âge,* etc. Assonance is used for the most part in the oldest French epics, such as the *Chanson de Roland* (q.v.).

Assouci, Charles Coypeau d': (1605-1677) This Parisian-born poet led a vagabond existence. Writer of parodies that are not dissimilar in spirit from those of Scarron (q.v.), he has been called the "emperor of burlesque." Included among his writings are *Le Jugement de Pâris en vers burlesques* (1648), *Ovide en belle humeur* (1650), *Le Ravissement de Proserpine* (1653) and *Les Aventures de M. d'Assoucy* (1677). P. Brun, *Autour du 17ᵉ siècle,* 1901.

Astrée, L' (1607-1627): See *Urfé, Honoré d'.*

Atala: This tale, published separately in 1801, was originally an episode of *Les Natchez* (q.v.)—a prose epic dealing with the Indians on which Chateaubriand (q.v.) worked while yet in England—but was revised when he undertook to incorporate it as part of his *Le Génie du Christianisme* (q.v.). As a part of the latter work, it was to serve as a picture of the baneful effect of "le vague des passions." This story, the scene of which is laid in Louisiana,

9

on the shores of the Missisippi, relate how Chactas, now an old Indian who during the reign of Louis XIV had once visited France, had been taken, when yet a very young man, prisoner by an enemy tribe, and how he was saved by Atala, a young Indian girl brought up in the Christian religion. While fleeing together through the forest, the two young Indian lovers come upon Father Aubry, a hermit who has come to rescue them. When the latter makes it clear that he wishes to convert Chactas and unite him with her, Atala, believing that the vow of virginity she had taken at the deathbed of her mother was irrevocable, in order not to break that vow by succumbing to her love, poisons herself. The entire story is characterized by much melancholy, revery, luscious descriptions of the exotic, natural setting, and by a poetic prose that is very musical.

Athalie: First produced at the Théâtre-Français (q.v.) in 1716, this tragedy, written by Racine (q.v.) in 1691 at the request of Mme. de Maintenon (q.v.), was later to be hailed by Voltaire (q.v.) as the masterpiece of the "esprit humain." Although classical in form and containing a chorus, it is biblical in source and spirit, reflecting, not an inner conflict, as in *Andromaque* or *Phèdre* (qq.v.), but the invisible hand of Providence. Based on Second Kings of the Old Testament and set in the temple at Jerusalem, it depicts the anxieties of Athalie (Athaliah), because of her wish to destroy every last vestige of Jewish worship, and her final defeat. Unknown to Athalie, who, as queen of Judea, has decreed the worship of Baal, there remains from the family of David, believed to be completely eradicated, a grandson, Joas (Jehoash) by name, who has been saved and reared secretly in the temple by the Jewish high priest, Joad (Jehoida), and his wife, Josabet (Je-

hosheba). Although, moreover, Athalie is unaware of Joas' identity, and of Joad's intention to have the last descendent of David placed on the throne, she comes to the temple after being disturbed by a dream and views the young boy with suspicion. Unsuccessful in her attempt to take him away, she threatens destruction to the temple. At this point, Joas, hitherto ignorant of his true parentage, is told by Joad of his descent from David, is anointed King and placed on the throne, to the joy of the kingdom's faithful followers. When Athalie again comes to the temple to claim Joas, whom she now sees on the throne, she is abandoned by her soldiers, and is assassinated.

Athénée: See *Jouvet, Louis.*

Atlantide, L' (1919): See *Benoit, Pierre.*

Atrée et Thyeste (1707): See *Crébillon, Prosper.*

aube: A type of lyric poem, common during the Middle Ages, whose usual theme is the separation of lovers at dawn.

Aubigné, Agrippa d': (1552-1630) This militant Calvinist and humanist who, as a child, learned Latin, Greek, Hebrew, Italian and Spanish, combined in himself elements of both the Renaissance and the Reformation. In 1576 he helped persuade Henri IV, whose apostasy, however, he never forgave, to escape from court, where he had remained since the Massacre of St. Bartholomew's Day (1572). He also took part in the Protestants' resistance against Louis XIII. In his principal work, *Les Tragiques* (written between 1577-1594 but first published in 1616), an epic-lyric poem in 7 cantos of mingled invective and satire, he reveals at once his hatred for those who persecute and his love for France. Though unequal in inspiration, many of its passages are comparable to the *Châtiments* of Hugo (q.v.). In addition to his other poems, which contain odes, sonnets, *chansons* and *élégies* in the tradition of Ronsard (q.v.), he wrote several works in prose, including *Histoire universelle* (*p.* 1626), *La confession catholique du sieur de Sancy* (*p.* 1660), a mordant pamphlet against Catholicism, and *Les Aventures du baron de Foeneste* (1617), a satirical novel. S. Rocheblave, *La vie d'un héros: Agrippa d'Aubigné,* 1912; J. Plattard, *Une figure de premier plan dans nos lettres de la Renaissance, Agrippa d'Aubigné,* 1930.

Aucassin et Nicolette: A "chante-fable" (or mingled narrative in verse and prose) of the thirteenth century. Written in the Picard dialect, its verses are in seven-syllable assonanced lines. The unknown author has created, in light, graceful verse and in elegant and sophisticated prose, a delightful world of idyllic young love. Aucassin and Nicolette share a love that is young and tender, yet inviolate to the vicissitudes it constantly must face. After their flight from the Count of Beaucaire, Aucassin's father, who is planning a loftier match for his son and who opposes his son's wish to marry Nicolette, a Saracen captive, and after their separation by pirates, their final reunion is effected by Nicolette disguised as a *jongleur.* The author, with much success, constantly intersperses his fantasy with contrasting elements of realism and absurdity. This work presents a complete contrast, both to the rough, bold spirit of the *Chansons de Geste* (q.v.) and the literal realism of the *fabliaux* (q.v.).

M. Lot-Borodine, *Le Roman idyllique au moyen âge,* 1913; *Aucassin et Nicolette, chante-fable du XIIIᵉ siècle mise en français moderne* par Gustave Michaut, avec une préface de Joseph Bédier, 5ᵉ ed., 1929; *Aucassin et Nicolette, trad. du roman d'oïl* par M. Coulon, 1933.

Au-dessus de la mêlée (1915): See *Rolland, Romain.*

Audiberti, Jacques: (1900-   ) The return to rhetoric which this writer proclaimed as a necessity in his manifesto *La Nouvelle Origine* (1942) is seen in his poetry, plays and novels—most of which can be characterized as fantastic. A virtuoso with language that makes one think of Hugo (q.v.), in his poetry—which includes such collections as *Race des hommes* (1930), *Tonnes de Semence* (1941), and *Toujours* (1944)—he uses a torrent of words, with a mixture of all possible rhythms and forms of prosody to express the themes of love, death, and man's destiny. His novels, poetic and fantastic, like *Carnage* (1941), express the vagabondage of imagination. *Le Mal Court* (1947), a philosophical farce which won much success, deals with the moral problem of the Orient and the Occident.

Augier, Emile: (1820-1889) The social theater of this dramatist, whose life was a comparatively uneventful one, represents a reaction against the romantic drama. He arrived at this theater, however, only after having written several plays in verse, whose action, moreover, was historical or exotic in setting. But even in these—*La Ciguë* (1844) and *L'Aventurière* (1848), for example—he already showed the danger in glorifying passion. *Gabrielle* (1849), too, realistic in details of every-day life, but written in verse form, showed that happiness is to be found in legitimate love. With *Le Gendre de M. Poirier* (1854) and *Le Mariage d'Olympe* (1855), both written in prose and both dealing with the contemporary scene, it can be said that Augier contributed his part to the inauguration of the Social drama in France. The first-named piece, based on Jules Sandeau's novel *Sacs et Parchemins,* and a modern version of Molière's (q.v.) *Le Bourgeois Gentilhomme*, ridicules the vain and ambitious M. Poirier, who is willing to sacrifice his daughter's happiness in order to have a titled, though worthless, son-in-law. The second play, written after Dumas *fils* (q.v.) had made Marguerite Gautier morally acceptable in his *La Dame aux Camélias* (1852; q.v.), indignantly protests against the rehabilitation of the courtesan. Combining Scribe's (q.v.) technique in the construction of his plots with a utilitarian view of the theater, Augier was now to become the champion of the family and of the better values of a bourgeois society. Observing closely the society of his day—during the Fifties and Sixties—he exposed, in his comedy of manners, various vices, foibles, and hypocrisies. Many of the problems—to which Augier, unlike Dumas, gives no "logical" solution —involve the nefarious influence of money. Its influence on marriage can be seen in *Ceinture Dorée* (1855), *Les Lionnes pauvres* (1858) and *Un beau mariage* (1859). Speculation and venal journalism are lashed in *Les Effrontés* (1861), and politico-clerical intrigues are exposed in *Le Fils de Giboyer* (1862) and in *Lions et renards* (1869). Augier represents one of the best writers of the comedy of manners during the nineteenth century.

H. Parigot, *Émile Augier*, 1890; H. Gaillard, *E. Augier et la comédie sociale*, 1910.

Aulnoy, Marie-Catherine, Baronne d': (*c.* 1650-1705) The reputation of this writer is based on her charming fairy-tales. These include *La Belle aux cheveux d'or*, *Nain jaune*, *Chatte blanche*, and *L'Oiseau bleu*. She also played a not insignificant part in the important development of the pseudo-historical novel toward the end of the 17th century, as can be seen in *Hippolyte, comte de Douglas* (1690), *Jean de Bourbon, prince de Carency* (1691) and *Comte de Warwick* (1703).

E. Pilon, *Bonnes fées d'antan*, 1909; J. Roche-Mason, *En marge de L'Oiseau bleu*, 1930.

Autre Monde ou Les États et Empires de la Lune, L' (1657): See *Cyrano de Bergerac, Savinien*.

Avare, L' (1668): See *Molière*.

Avenir de la science, L' (*p.* 1890): See *Renan*.

Aventurière, L' (1848): See *Augier*.

Aymé, Marcel: (1902-   ) Showing little or no interest in the philosophical issues debated by present-day authors, this gifted and rather prolific novelist and short-story writer is more concerned with the verisimilitude of his often fantastic story and characters. *La Table-aux-Crevés* (1929), a kind of Gallic, Rabelaisian novel, dealing with peasant life, established his reputation as novelist. In *La Jument Verte* (1933) and *Maison Basse* (1935), Aymé revealed his ability to be a satiric observer; in *Les Contes du Chat perché* (1939 and later) he wrote remarkable stories for children. The Second World War and Occupation left him with a morality of indifference, one that saw chance as the only factor to explain the difference between heroes and traitors. *Le Chemin des écoliers* (1946) and *Uranus* (1948) are good examples of this attitude. Although fantasy and revery go hand in hand with his satire, his work in its totality reveals a real world.

Axël (1890): See *Villiers de l'Isle-Adam*.

B

Bachaumont, Louis Petit de: (1690-1771) This Parisian-born writer of memoirs is the author of *Mémoires secrets pour servir à l'histoire de la République des Lettres*, which appeared after 1777. Containing gossip, anecdotes, witticisms, details concerning Voltaire's (q.v.) influence, Rousseau (q.v.), and the importance of the *Encyclopédie* (q.v.), these memoirs, covering the period of 1762-1771, offer an important picture of the times.

Baïf, Antoine de: (1532-1589) A member of the *Pléiade* (q.v.) group and son of Lazare de Baïf (q.v.). He studied, together with Ronsard and Du Bellay (qq.v.), under the great humanist Dorat (q.v.), at the Collège de Coqueret. His writings, which were prolific, include *Les Amours de Méline* (1552) and *Les Amours de Francine* (1555), collections of love sonnets, mythological poems in which he reveals an extraordinary erudition, translations of Latin comedies and Greek tragedies, and eclogues. His best work is *Les Mimes, enseignements et proverbes* (1576). He is the most audacious of the Pléiade poets, having tried to introduce French versification based on long and short syllables, in the manner of the ancients. Moreover, he invented the *vers baïfin*, a verse of fifteen syllables. He also wished to reform spelling so that it would conform to a phonetic transcription of syllables.

M. Augé-Chiquet, *La Vie, les idées et l'œuvre de Jean-Antoine de Baïf*, 1909; H. Chamard, *Histoire de la Pléiade*, 1939-1940.

Baïf, Lazare de: (?-1547) Celebrated French humanist and father of Antoine de Baïf (q.v.). At his home the Hellenistic scholar Dorat (q.v.) initiated his host's son and Ronsard into the culture of the ancients. Baïf himself translated into French verse Sophocles' *Electra* (1537), in the introduction of which he gave a definition of *tragedy*.

Bajazet (1672): See *Racine*.

Bal des voleurs, Le (1937): See *Anouilh*.

ballade: This French term is not to be confused with the English *ballad*. It refers to a poem of fixed form, composed of three equal and symmetrical stanzas, the lines of which are most often of six or eight syllables, and of a shorter concluding couplet called the *envoi* (which usually begins with the word *prince* or *princesse*, the patron to whom the poet addresses or *sends* the poem), and all four parts of the poem end with a refrain. Charles d'Orléans and François Villon (qq.v.), in particular, have left some unusual poems in the *ballade* form. The *ballade* as a kind of poetry with legendary or fantastic themes has been adopted by such English poets as Robert Burns and Thomas Moore, and such German poets as Schiller, Goethe, Heine. The *ballade* with the fantastic theme has been especially employed by the French romantic poets, particularly V. Hugo (*Odes et Ballades*).

Ballade des Dames du temps Jadis: Written by François Villon (q.v.), it has the famous refrain: *"Mais où sont les neiges d'antan?"* ("But where are the snows of yesteryear?")

Ballades françaises (1897-1924): See *Fort, Paul.*

Ballanche, Pierre-Simon: (1776-1847) Together with Chateaubriand (q.v.), whose friend he was, this writer restored religious mysticism to France. *Du sentiment considéré dans son rapport avec la littérature et les beaux-arts* (1801) exalts sensibility and heralds, even before Chateaubriand, the importance of religious ideas in nineteenth-century France. Many of Ballanche's ideas are presented, as in *Antigone* (1814) and *Orphée* (1827)—poems in prose— in the form of Greek myths. In *Vision d'Hébal* (1831)—a mythical presentation of the conquests and messages of great civilizations—he becomes a precursor of Hugo's (q.v.) *La Légende des siècles.*

Ch. Huit, *La vie et les œuvres de Ballanche,* 1904; A. J. George, P.-S. *Ballanche precursor of romanticism,* 1945.

Balzac, Honoré de: (1799-1850) Born at Tours of a bourgeois family—he had no legitimate right to the *de* he inserted in his name—this important novelist never betrayed any brilliance as a student. At the Collège de Vendôme near Tours, where he spent six years (1807-1813), and to which he refers in his *Louis Lambert* (1832), he read books on spiritualism and on the doctrines of Mesmer and Swedenborg, to the neglect of his text books. Later, in Paris, he took courses at the Sorbonne, and even began the study of law, while serving an apprenticeship in the law firm of M. Guillonet-Merville; but, intent on becoming a writer, much to the chagrin of his father and mother, who had no reason to believe that he had literary talent, and finding law, moreover, distasteful, he settled in Paris, in a miserable attic room, to satisfy his ambition. There, a year or so later,

he completed, despite physical and financial hardships, his tragedy *Cromwell* (1820). Undaunted by the disapproval of his family and M. Andrieux, whose opinion of the play was most unflattering, he next turned to writing, under such pseudonyms as those of Lord R'hoone and Horace de Saint Aubin, cheap thrillers of the blood-and-thunder type, the authorship of which he was later to disown and which brought him neither fame nor revenue. Resolving to make money quickly and to print his own books, he became in quick succession a publisher, a printing-house proprietor, and the owner of a type-foundry. After three years of struggling (1826-1829), he abandoned the enterprise, owing a debt of 100,000 francs which he had borrowed from his family and Mme. de Berny, who assumed the role of both mistress and mother. To pay these debts, he resumed writing. Success came to him first in 1829, when he wrote, under his own name, the historical novel *Les Chouans,* dealing with the royalist rising during the Revolution.

Although Balzac first gave the title of *La Comédie Humaine* (q.v.) to his huge collective work in 1842 in its *Avant-Propos,* which states the scope and purpose of his work, he makes clear that he had conceived his plan as early as 1833, at the time of publication of his *Le Médecin de Campagne,* which had already been preceded by such masterpieces as the semi-autobiographical *La Peau de Chagrin* (1831), *Gobseck* (1830), *Le Colonel Chabert* (1832), *Le Curé de Tours* (1832), and *Eugénie Grandet* (1833; q.v.). The plan, as evidenced by the listed titles, not to mention such later works as *Le Père Goriot* (1834; q.v.), *La Cousine Bette* (1846), *Le Cousin Pons* (1847) and many others, was to portray, in concrete and realistic detail, all of contemporary French society. Under the influence of scientific theories, in which he was interested from his early childhood and throughout his life, he saw a "unity of composition," similar to the doctrine applied by Geoffroy Saint-Hilaire to the animal kingdom, that linked all of humanity together. He added to this notion Lamarck's theory of transmission of acquired characteristics. As he viewed the many different types of man, all of whom, as he was to show, were influenced by their social backgrounds or environments, he decided to divide his *Comédie Humaine* into what he called *Études de mœurs*—studies of social types, his major preoccupation, subdivided into *Scènes de la vie privée, Scènes de la vie de campagne, Scènes de la vie parisienne, Scènes de la vie politique,* and *Scènes de la vie militaire—Études Philosophiques,* and *Études Analytiques,* a study of the causes and principles underlying society. Because of the importance given to the notion that man is a social animal, Balzac characteristically begins his novel, after the typical initial scene, which is short and striking, with a long, detailed description of the *milieu* in which the scene of the action is laid. Having established the habitat to which the characters, whose physical and moral characteristics are also delineated realistically and in much detail, are linked, the action, beginning *in medias res,* then rushes on to the inevitable dénouement. The realism of detail—Balzac was especially gifted with keen observation and the ability to reproduce what he saw—is to be found in such novels as the previously mentioned *Louis Lambert, La Cousine Bette, Le Cousin Pons* as well as in *Séraphita* (1832) and *Ursule Mirouet* (1841), which deal either with mysticism, hallucination, or monomania, all essentially romantic aspects.

From the approximately ninety-seven novels, novelettes, and short stories (he had titles for fifty-one more when he died) constituting the huge panorama of French society of which Balzac was, as he liked to consider himself, the historian or "secretary" during the first half of the nineteenth century, there emerges, in addition to the permanent and universal features in human relationships, the notion that life in society is a constant struggle for existence and that human passions are consumed in this unending battle. This pessimistic, but realistic, view of life and of his contemporary society is heightened by the rôle that Balzac attached to money in his own personal life as well as by the importance he gives it in the lives of many of his characters (see *Eugénie Grandet* and *le Père Goriot*).

Notwithstanding the several romantic features of his writing, including the occasional lapses into mystical or melodramatic subject matter and exaggerations of types, by his penetrating study of society and insight into the various forces that act on human nature, at a time when literature in France was essentially Romantic, Balzac acted as an antidote to Romanticism as well as the main precursor to Realism (q.v.). Not only, as already suggested, did he revolutionize the novel, but through the importance he gave to environment he also contributed significantly to the development of the theater (cf. Augier and Dumas *fils*), although, as a dramatist, he himself did not have much success. Fate dealt him an ironic blow when, a few months after his marriage in 1850 to the Polish Countess Hanska, whom he had pursued for eighteen years and who represented his ideal of wealth and aristocracy, he died, exhausted by constant literary activity.

A. Billy, *Vie de Balzac,* 1944; S.

Zweig, *Balzac* (Eng. tr.), 1947; Ph. Bertault, *Balzac, l'homme et l'œuvre*, 1947.

Balzac, Jean-Louis Guez de: (1597-1654) From his country estate near Angoulême, in the west of France, where he spent most of his life, he corresponded with several of the *Académie Française* (q.v.), of which he was a member, and with those who frequented the Hôtel de Rambouillet (q.v.). These Letters, for which he is known, deal with general, moral, literary, or philosophical problems, and, written to be read in public, betray a carefully polished and eloquent style, with much clarity of expression. As one of the precursors of Classicism, Balzac accomplished for French prose what Malherbe (q.v.) did for French poetry. He is also the author of several treatises, including *Socrate chrétien* (1652).

G. Guillaumie, *Guez de Balzac et la prose française*, 1927.

Banville, Théodore de: (1823-1891) The most naturally gifted of the Parnassian (q.v.) poets, he demonstrates much facility and virtuosity. Included among his 20 volumes of verse are *Les Cariatides* (1842), in which he uses Greek themes, *Les Stalactites* (1846), *Odelettes* (1856), and *Odes funambulesques* (1857), in which his poetic technique owes much to the poets of the Renaissance. Mixing the archeological with the topical allusion, he presents, in complicated patterns, a profusion of muses and lyres. In *Petit Traité de Versification française* (1872), a kind of Parnassian *Ars Pœtica*, he emphasizes the importance of rhyme and reveals the multiple resources of poetic technique, a preoccupation that reflects his own conception of poetry as that of Art for Art's sake. He also wrote several comedies in verse and much occasional prose.

J. Charpentier, *Théodore de Banville, l'homme et l'œuvre*, 1925.

Barbey d'Aurevilly, Jules: (1808-1889) This writer, who once led the life of a dandy, was as uncompromising in his Catholic and royalist views as he was in his literary judgments. In addition to his works of criticism —*Les Œuvres et les Hommes* (1860-1909) and *Le Théâtre contemporain* (1888-1896)—he wrote novels. These, based on historical or legendary scenes, events, and types of his native Normandy, and written at a time when Realism (q.v.) was flourishing, include *L'Ensorcelée* (1854) and *Le Chevalier des Touches* (1864). He is mainly known for *Les Diaboliques* (1874), a collection of six short stories (see *Short Story*), whose central theme, in a modern setting, deals with the diabolical influence on women who are "possessed."

E. Grelé, *Barbey d'Aurevilly: sa vie et son œuvre*, 1904; A. Marie, *Le Connétable des lettres: B. d'Aurevilly*, 1939.

Barbier de Séville, Le (1775): See *Beaumarchais*.

Barbusse, Henri: (1873-1935) His experiences in the trenches during the First World War resulted in a novel, *Le Feu* (1916), which won the *Prix Goncourt* (q.v.). This realistic novel, containing the ugliness of the terrible daily episodes on the Front, is a violent protest against the absurdity of war. It was not long before Barbusse took part in anti-war propaganda and wrote another book, *Clarté* (1918), which further affirmed his convictions.

H. Hertz, *Henri Barbusse*, 1919.

BAROQUE: The baroque style, which flourished throughout Europe during the closing years of the sixteenth, and the greater part of the seventeenth century, was for a long time regarded as a decadent manifestation of the art and literature of the Renaissance. The very name, which some have derived from a Portuguese word meaning a pearl of irregular shape, and others from a term used in scholastic philosophy to describe an unsound syllogism, has unfavorable connotations: and in the popular speech of present-day France it is practically synonymous with strangeness or bad taste. In the field of the fine arts, the rehabilitation of the baroque began with the publication of Heinrich Wölfflin's *Principles of Art History* (1915) which sought to set up precise criteria for differentiating it from Renaissance style. This Swiss art historian's famous categories (linear *vs.* painterly, plane *vs.* recession, closed *vs.* open form, multiplicity *vs.* unity, clearness *vs.* unclearness) are applicable to painting, sculpture and architecture alike; in accordance with the principles of this system, not only such artists as Rubens, Bernini or Caravaggio, but also Vermeer and Rembrandt, must be regarded as baroque. Readers who wish to look at examples of the style are referred to Werner Weisbach's *Die Kunst des Barock,* which contains more than five hundred excellent photographs of baroque painting, drawing, sculpture, and architecture in Italy, France, Germany and Spain. The baroque is, perhaps, seen to its best advantage in Rome, where it is represented by such famous works as the façade and *piazza* of St. Peter's, the extraordinary churches of Borromini, the dramatic chiaroscuro of Caravaggio's St. Matthew pictures, and Bernini's spectacular sculptural group, *Santa Teresa in Ecstasy.*

More recently, scholars and critics have come to realize that the baroque style exists in literature also, and that the concept is helpful for the interpretation of many works of the period 1580-1650 which have hitherto resisted classification. Professor Wellek, in an extremely important article, "The Concept of the Baroque in Literary Scholarship," *Journal of Aesthetics,* 1946,

has traced the history of the word as a term of literary criticism, and has compiled a comprehensive bibliography of the subject from 1888 to 1946.

In general, those literary historians who have attempted to define the baroque, while drawing frequent parallels between literature and the plastic arts, have not attempted to find exact equivalents of Wölfflin's categories. On the other hand, although some critics regard the baroque as a universal phenomenon, recurring at widely separated periods in literature, almost synonymous in fact with undisciplined imagination, a sounder view appears to be that this style is connected with a particular period in history, 1580-1650 approximately, and that it has specific, definable characteristics.

In attempting to enumerate these characteristics, it should be borne in mind that the presence, in a literary work, of one or two of them does not suffice to label that work as baroque; nor is the presence of all of them indispensable; if, however, in a work of the late sixteenth or early seventeenth century, we encounter a majority of them, we may safely term it baroque. The following traits appear to be significant:

1. Moral purpose. Baroque literary works are generally animated by a moral intent, and often by a spirit of religious propaganda.
2. Devices of emphasis and exaggeration.
3. A taste for violence and horror.
4. Extremely concrete expression of abstract ideas.
5. Interest in theatricality and illusion.
6. Both with regard to content and form, a delight in contrast and surprise.
7. The stressing of movement and metamorphosis.
8. Despite all the foregoing—

organic unity and the acceptance of life.

In French literature, the following may be regarded as representative baroque works: the *Essais* of Montaigne (q.v.), because of their concreteness of imagery, their interest in the diversity of phenomena, and their concern with "le passage" rather than "l'estre"; *Les Tragiques* (1616) of d'Aubigné (q.v.), because of the violent tone, the insistence upon horror, and the spectacular scenes embracing both heaven and earth; the *Introduction à la vie dévote* (1608), by St. François de Sales (q.v.), with its florid similes; the religious sonnets of La Ceppède (q.v.), so pictorial, sensuous, and dramatic in their expression; the early comedies of Corneille (q.v.), like *Clitandre* (1632) and *l'Illusion comique* (1636), which their author later toned down in order to make them more classical; and Rotrou's (q.v.) tragedy *Saint-Genest* (1646). A word may perhaps be said about this last play, as it illustrates so many essential features of the baroque. The hero, Adrien, is a famous actor; in a performance enacted before the emperor Diocletian, he plays the part of an early Christian martyr, Saint Genest. In the course of this play within the play, the actor is actually converted by the rôle which he is performing. He then declares himself to be a Christian, and is really put to death by the indignant emperor. Rotrou's tragedy thus depicts a metamorphosis in which illusion suddenly becomes reality, and which culminates in martyrdom.

Baroque literature is by no means confined to France; outstanding English examples of the style may be found in the poetry of Crashaw, Donne, and Milton; and in the prose of Sir Thomas Browne. Although the baroque, in both art and literature, is often closely associated with the Counter Reformation, it is by no means exclusively linked with any single country or religion. It can, rather, be regarded as a form of sensibility which for some three quarters of a century became incarnate in all arts and which transcends specific geographic areas or faiths. The French themselves are probably of all peoples most reluctant to concede its existence, because they feel that the concept impinges upon their own cherished notion of a classical age. As a matter of fact, French classicism, in point of time, immediately follows French baroque; and the argument may be simply resolved by stating that "le classicisme est un baroque dompté."

Austin Warren, *Richard Crashaw, a Study in Baroque Sensibility,* 1939; Imbrie Buffum, *Agrippa d'Aubigné's Les Tragiques: a Study of the Baroque Style in Poetry,* 1951; *Studies in the Baroque from Montaigne to Rotrou,* 1957; Jean Rousset, *La Littérature de l'âge baroque en France,* 1953; Wylie Sypher, *Four Stages of Renaissance Art,* 1955.

IMBRIE BUFFUM

Barrault, Jean-Louis: (1910-   ) Probably the best disciple of Dullin (q.v.), this actor—one of whose fortes in the theater and cinema is the pantomime—and *metteur-en-scene* began his meteoric rise to fame in 1939 when Dullin, who gave him the use of the *Atelier,* offered him the oportunity to direct plays by Knut Hamsun and Jules Laforgue (q.v.). After subsequent success at the Comédie-Française (q.v.), in 1946, together with his wife, Madeleine Renaud, he founded at the Théâtre Marigny his *Compagnie Madeleine Renaud —Jean-Lous Barrault.* His productions of classical and modern plays by French and foreign writers, including those especially by Claudel (q.v.), have won him much success and popularity.

Barrès, Maurice: (1862-1923) This novelist, who was also a philosopher and politician [he had been a member of the *Chambre des Députés* (1889-1893; 1906-1923)], used the novel primarily as a vehicle for his ideas; hence the frequent philosophical digressions in each of his stories. Grouped in *cycles,* his novels reveal the evolution of his thought: the first trilogy, under the general title of *Le Culte du moi* (consisting of *Sous l'œil des barbares,* 1888; *Un homme libre,* 1889; *Le Jardin de Bérénice,* 1891) emphasizes the importance of the development of the *individual* and of *self.* His second series, under the collective title of *Roman de l'énergie nationale,* shows a drastic change of attitude; *Les Déracinés* (1897), the most important novel of this trilogy, points up the mistakes made by seven students from Nancy who, under the influence of a rationalist professor "uprooted themselves" to seek a fortune in Paris. This nationalistic and regionalistic doctrine is made even more clear in his *Colette Baudoche* (1909), one of the novels of the third trilogy, *Les Bastions de l'Est,* which poses the question of the relationship between the *Lorrains* (Barrès himself was from Lorraine) and the Germans who had annexed a part of their territory. Although not a believer himself, in *La Colline inspirée* (1913) Barrès urged a return to Christianity on political and social grounds. During the First World War Barrès was prominent as a champion of *nationalism.*

Albert Thibaudet, *La Vie de Maurice Barrès,* 1921; Pierre Moreau, *Maurice Barrès,* 1946.

Barrière, Théodore: (1823-1877) Following his dramatization, together with Henry Murger (q.v.), of the latter's *Vie de Bohème* (1849), this dramatist wrote such plays as *Les Filles de marbre* (1853), *Les faux Bonshommes* (1856), and *Les Jo-*crisses de l'amour (1865). These plays portray many of the evils of his contemporary society.

E. C. Byam, *Théodore Barrière: Dramatist of the Second Empire,* 1938.

Basoche: An association of law clerks (*basochiens*) in Paris, organized in the beginning of the fourteenth century, which produced the French medieval *farces, soties,* and *moralités* (qq.v.), and which had the privilege to present dramatic performances on certain feast days. Similar societies existed also in the provinces.

Bataille de Dames (1851): See *Scribe.*

Bataille, Henri: (1872-1922) Following in the tradition of Porto-Riche (q.v.), this writer, who began as a romantic poet and dramatist, wrote psychological plays that depict the loves of impassioned and frequently abnormal women. Woman as a creature of instinct is seen in *Maman Colibri* (1903), *La Marche nuptiale* (1905), *Poliche* (1906) and *La Femme nue* (1908)— a title symbolic of those who follow the forces of nature— and *La Vierge folle* (1910) in violent and brutal situations that are often portrayed in an excessively lyrical style.

P. Blanchart, *Henry Bataille; son œuvre,* 1922; G. de Catalogne, *Henry Bataille, ou le Romantisme de l'instinct,* 1925.

Bateau ivre (1871): See *Rimbaud, Arthur.*

Baty, Gaston: (1892-1952) Unlike Jouvet and Dullin (qq.v.), this theatrical director and producer was not an actor and was not influenced by Copeau (q.v.). His conception of the theater gives as much importance to staging as it does to the text; the magnificence of his stage setting, costuming, lighting effects, accessories, and music, made the "inner drama" visible and the text alive. His company, "Les Compagnons de la Chimère," was formed in 1922, first settled at the Studio des Champs Elysées (1924) and later at the Théâtre Montparnasse (1930), and performed such expressionistic plays as J. J. Bernard's (q.v.) *Martine*, S. Gantillon's (q.v.) *Maya*, J. V. Pellerin's (q.v.) *Têtes de rechange*, and H. Lenormand's (q.v.) *Le Simoun*. These plays, true to Baty's ideal, are expressionistic, reveal the unuttered between the lines, fuse the world of make-believe with reality, making the partnership of the dramatist and the stage manager an indispensable one.

P. Blanchart, *Gaston Baty*, 1939.

Baudelaire, Charles: (1821-1867) After completing his studies at the *lycée* Louis-le-Grand in Paris, the city of his birth, he was sent off by his mother and step-father (whom he particularly disliked because the latter had replaced him in his mother's affections which he sorely needed and desired) on a voyage to India. He returned, after short stays at the islands of Mauritius and Bourbon (Réunion), to Paris, where he was to spend most of his life, filled with exotic memories and visions. Instead of settling down, he quickly spent the patrimony he inherited, and lived in miserable conditions in the artistic and literary quarters of Paris. Meanwhile he wrote the poems that were finally to appear in 1857 under the title of *Les Fleurs du mal*. For this publication Baudelaire was brought to trial and condemned as an offender against public morality. A second edition of this volume, including thirty-five additional poems but excluding six previously published poems suppressed as immoral, came out in 1861.

Although Baudelaire retains in *Les Fleurs du mal* many romantic tendencies, confessing as he does his personal struggle, one between the spirit and the flesh, he is at once a precursor of the *Parnassian* and *Symbolist* schools. Like the Parnassians, he is an advocate of art for art's sake, aiming at perfection of form; unlike the Romantics, who liked long poems and much rhetoric, he employed short verse forms almost exclusively, especially irregular sonnets. In one of these sonnets, "Correspondances," he expressed the idea, basic to Symbolistic poetry, that the different sensations of sound, color and perfume become "associated" with each other, creating images that instead of being descriptive, are evocative or suggestive. Assisted by such an aesthetic, Baudelaire makes poetry an exploration of the most hidden recesses of the human soul and its macabre visions; hence, the integration into his poetic universe of the abnormal and evil.

Other works by Baudelaire include translations of Edgar Allen Poe (1856-1865) by whom he was strongly influenced, and some original works in prose, notably *Les Paradis artificiels, opium et haschisch* (1861), and two posthumous volumes of criticism, *Curiosités esthétiques* (1868) and *L'Art romantique* (1869).

Ch. Asselineau, *Baudelaire, sa vie et son œuvre* 1869; A. Ferran, *L'Esthétique de Baudelaire* (1933); M. Gilman, *Baudelaire the Critic* (1943).

Bayle, Pierre: (1647-1706) Born of a Protestant family, this scholar and critic re-converted to Protestantism after having embraced Catholicism. Because of his liberal views, he sought refuge in Geneva; most of his life, however, he spent in Holland, where he was professor of philosophy and history. A rationalist devoted to the principle of tolerance, he attacks, in *Pensées sur la comète* (1682), authority and superstition. His major work, *Dictionnaire historique et critique* (1697), is an attempt, through its discussions of ethics, theology and philosophy, to break down many traditional concepts; through his systematic use of the *renvoi*—which refers the reader to related discussions—he suggests the relativity of truth. This device, incidentally, was also to be used by the *Encyclopédie* (q.v.); the articles themselves were to inspire many of the writings by D'Alembert, Diderot, Helvétius, d'Holbach, and Voltaire (qq.v.). His struggle against absolutism and his search for freedom of thought are also manifest in *Nouvelles de la république des letttres* (1684-1687), a philosophical and literary periodical. A seventeenth-century writer, Bayle influenced much of eighteenth-century thought, and, more particularly, the *Encyclopédistes* (q.v.).

J. Devolvé, *Essai sur Pierre Bayle*, 1906; H. Robinson, *Bayle the Sceptic*, 1931.

Bazin, Hervé: (1917-   ) Grandnephew of René Bazin (q.v.) and scion of a conservative family in the western part of France, this writer gained celebrity with *Vipère au Poing* (1947). This novel, which concerns itself with hatred of one's mother, is an attack on the family as the basis of society. Cruelty is again seen in *La Tête contre les Murs* (1949), which, like the previous novel, betrays a lively style and narrative skill. Less hostility, however, and greater family affection are to be found in *L'Huile sur le Feu* (1954). Bazin, merciless in his caricatures, frequently tends to moralize and to indulge in reflection.

Bazin, René: (1853-1932) In addition to his novels of country life, he wrote: *La Terre qui meurt* (1899), dealing with the threatened desertion of the land for industrial life; *Les Oberlé* (1901), a portait of the miserable conditions of the French in Alsace under the German regime; and *Le Blé qui lève* (1907), which dramatizes an agrarian program for the working man. A Catholic writer, his *Magnificat* (1931) shows his concern with morality, both individual and collective.

François Mauriac, *René Bazin*, 1931.

Beaumarchais, Pierre-Augustin Caron de: (1732-1799) A bourgeois who assumed the title *de Beaumarchais* from the name of his wealthy wife's estate, this Parisian-born dramatist led an adventurous life. His talent as a watchmaker resulted in an appointment as *horloger du roi* at the court; his ability as a harp player gained him the position of music teacher to the King's daughters. Enterprising, he acquired, through intrigue and speculations, a considerable fortune; he even furnished arms to the American colonists during the American Revolution. Involved in law-suits, however, he lost much of his fortune; to recover some of his loss, he wrote a series of polemical tracts. His *Mémoires* (1773-1774), in which he discredited the judge Goëzman, made him, moreover, popular as an opponent of corruption and privilege.

Upon his return in 1765 from Spain, this man of varied talents ventured into the drama in the hope of quickly gaining the success which he sought. After *Eugénie* (1767), a *drame bourgeois* (q.v.) conforming to the Diderot (q.v.) formula, he wrote *Le Barbier de Séville* (1775). The latter play, unlike *Eugénie*, is a comedy of intrigue; Figaro, as resourceful and intelligent as Beaumarchais himself, helps his master, Almaviva, win the hand of the beautiful Rosine. In *Le Mariage de Figaro* (written in 1778, produced in 1784), a sequel to *Le Barbier de Séville*, Figaro has to struggle against his master because the latter, now weary of his wife, tries to seduce Suzanne, his fiancée. Containing, as in *Le Barbier de Séville*, a well-constructed plot and intrigue, this comedy, his masterpiece, is more militant than its predecessor in its satire of existing social abuses. Figaro, in his celebrated monologue, reflects Beaumarchais' sympathies

and antipathies, not to mention his experiences, as he boldly lashes out against the privileged classes. Scintillating with wit, this play also crystallizes public opinion against the *Ancien Régime* and presages the French Revolution. Representing, from a dramatic point of view, a fusion—which marks Beaumarchais' originality—of the Molièresque comedy of character, comedy of manners, satire, farce and serious comedy, both these plays also anticipate the comedy of intrigue and the social theater of Scribe, Sardou and Dumas *fils* (qq.v.). Included among his other plays are *Les deux amis* (1770) and *La Mère coupable* (1792), and also *Tarare* (1787), an opera.
L. de Loménie, *Beaumarchais et son temps*, 1855; A. Hallays, *Beaumarchais*, 1897; A. Bailly, *Beaumarchais*, 1945.

Beau ténébreux, Un (1945): See *Gracq, Julien.*

Beauvoir, Simone de: (1908-) This essayist, novelist and dramatist, friend and disciple of Sartre (q.v.) and his existentialist (see *Existentialism*) philosophy, expresses in *Pyrrhus et Cinéas* (1944) the problem of means and ends in all action; in *Pour une Morale de l'Ambiguïté* (1947) she defines the existentialist ethic; and in *Le Deuxième sexe* (1949-1951) she poses in historical and philosophical terms the problem of woman in her various functions: marriage, maternity, and work. *L'Invitée* (1943) is one of the most original existentialist novels; *Le sang des autres* (1945) is a story that develops the thesis that everyone is responsible for everything and for the lives of all; *Tous les Hommes sont mortels* (1946) is a kind of philosophical tale. In her drama of action and ethic, *Les Bouches inutiles* (1945), Simone de Beauvoir concludes that to sacrifice the "useless," the very young or the very old, in order to have the cause of

justice triumph, would be committing an act contrary to this very ideal. For her novel *Les Mandarins* she received in 1954 the *Prix Goncourt* (q.v.).

Beck, Béatrix: (1914-) This novelist, who had served as the secretary of André Gide (q.v.), is the author of *Barny* (1950), *Une Mort irrégulière* (1951), and *Léon Morin, prêtre* (1952), which was awarded the *Prix Goncourt.*

Beckett, Samuel: (1906-) This French novelist, an Irishman, influenced by Joyce and Kafka, has affinities with those contemporary French writers who stress man's anguish and depict the absurdity of love and life. Scoring a literary triumph with *Molloy* (1951), despite, or rather, because of, its obscurity, he attracted readers to his earlier *Murphy* (1947) and to *Malone meurt* (1951). Beckett's reputation is perhaps as much due to his successful play *En attendant Godot* (1953) as to his novels.

Becque, Henry: (1837-1899) Impoverished most of his life, this Parisian-born writer launched his dramatic career with a libretto for the opera *Sardanapale* (1868), a *vaudeville* (q.v.)—*L'Enfant prodigue* (1867)— and *Michel Pauper* (1870), which dramatized the struggle between capital and labor. His first genuine masterpiece, *Les Corbeaux* (1882), following his two successful short plays, *La Navette* (1878) and *Les Honnêtes Femmes* (1880), failed to win theatrical success; its three performances at the Théâtre Français, however, aroused a controversy reminiscent of that surrounding Hugo's *Hernani* (q.v.). Without the claptrap of Scribe's *pièce bien faite* (q.v.) and the social preoccupation of Augier (q.v.), emphasized even more by the *pièce à thèse* (q.v.) of Dumas *fils* (q.v.), this play, with a minimum of plot and devoid of the *raisonneur* (q.v.) and the long tirade, depicts, in a detached manner, cynical "vultures" who prey on their helpless victims, a widow and her daughters who are hounded by their creditors and who are at the door of starvation as a result of the sudden death of their husband and father. For its realism, this play marks a date in the history of the French theater, just as Flaubert's (q.v.) *Madame Bovary* (1857) did for the novel. Becque's new dramatic technique is further seen in *La Parisienne* (1885), produced at the Renaissance Theatre. This play, which had a stormy career, can hardly be said to contain a plot; it ends exactly where it begins, with a *ménage à trois*. More important is its psychological dissection of the amoral wife and mistress who, unconscious of her own vileness, preaches to her lover. With this play, as well as with *Les Corbeaux*, Becque becomes the creator of the *comédie rosse* (q.v.) which was to become a fashionable *genre* at the Théâtre Libre (q.v.). The Théâtre Libre, which never produced Becque's plays, was, however, to be influenced by his realism in subject matter, his gloomy and cynical view of life, and, more particularly, by his technique, de-emphasizing plot and rhetoric and portraying, with a naturalness of language, precisely observed character. Included among his other plays are *L'Enlèvement* (1871) and the unfinished *Les Polichinelles* (1910).

E. Dawson, *Henry Becque, sa vie et son théâtre*, 1923; A. Arnaoutovitch, *Henry Becque; sa vie et son œuvre*, 1927; P. Blanchart, *Henry Becque*, 1931.

Becquée, La (1901): See *Boylesve, René*.

Bédier, Joseph: (1864-1938) A disciple of Gaston Paris (q.v.), whom he succeeded at the *Collège de France* (q.v.), he devoted himself to the study of philology and especially to the Old French epic (or *chansons de geste*). His major contribution on this question is the four-volume *Les Légendes épiques* (1908-1913). His fame, however, was earlier established as a result of his adaptation in modern French of *Roman de Tristan et Iseut* (1900). F. Lot, *Joseph Bédier*, 1939.

Bel Ami (1885): See *Maupassant*.

Belleau, Rémy: (1528-1577) One of the poets of the *Pléiade* (q.v.) and close friend of Ronsard (q.v.). In addition to his translations from Hebrew (*Églogues sacrées prises du Cantique des Cantiques*, 1556; *Discours sur la Vanité*, 1566) and Greek (*Les Odes Anacréontiques*, 1556), he is the author of three poetical works: *Petites Inventions* (1556), in which he describes various objects of nature (Ronsard called him "le peintre de la nature"); *Bergeries* (first part appeared in 1565), consisting of odes, sonnets and hymns); and *Amours et nouveaux échanges des pierres précieuses* (1576), inspired by an eleventh-century *lapidaire* (q.v.). He also composed a comedy, *La Reconnue*, published in 1577 after his death.

Em. Hinzelin, *Livre d'or de Remy Belleau*, 1900; H. Chamard, *Histoire de la Pléiade*, 1939-1940.

Benda, Julien: (1867-1956) This philosopher and essayist, guardian of logic and champion of nationalism, attacked Bergson's (q.v.) intuitive metaphysics in his *Le Bergsonisme ou une Philosophie de la Mobilité* (1912). With a similar perspective, he denounces in *La Trahison des Clercs* (1927) those writers who have allowed themselves to become politically involved, and in *Belphégor* (1912), those who represent emotional tendencies. Contemporary writers who show a leaning toward the irrational or an opposition to logic are again taken to task in *La France byzantine* (1945).

H. E. Read, *Julien Benda and the New Humanism*, 1930; R. J. Niess, *Julien Benda*, 1956.

Benoit, Pierre: (1886-   ) Adventure

fills the books of this world-travelling novelist, who was born in Albi, Tarn, and who spent his childhood in Tunisia and Algeria. In his novels, moreover, are to be found the *femme fatale*—whose name always begins with the letter A—and depressed male characters. Both fantasy and observation characterize his descriptions of exotic and picturesque scenes. *Koenigsmark* (1918), his first novel, deals with Germany; *L'Atlantide* (1919) is an adventure story that takes place in the desert; *Pour Don Carlos* (1920), which takes place in Spain, is fantastic, although the incidents of the adventure have an historical basis. Other novels deal with Ireland, the Far East and the New Hebrides. All his stories are well constructed and easy to read with an exciting plot.

Benoît de Sainte-Maure: (?—*c.* 1175) This poet is especially remembered for his *Roman de Troie* (*c.* 1154), a *roman antique* (q.v.) which relates the tale of Troy from the landing of the Argonauts until the return of the Greeks after the siege. Reflecting the influence of Ovid, this poem of more than 30,000 verses contributed to the conventions of courtly love (q.v.). Benoît de Sainte-Maure is also probably the author of the *Chronique des Ducs de Normandie* (completed *c.* 1175), a work in verse commissioned by Henri II which gives details on Norman customs.

Benserade, Isaac de: (1612-1691) A *précieux* poet (see *Préciosité*), whose sonnet *Job* gave birth to a controversy (1649-1650) in which its merits were compared to those of Voiture's (q.v.) *Uranie*, he is especially known for the verses he wrote for Lulli's ballets composed for the entertainment of Louis XIV.

C. Silin, *Benserade and his 'Ballets de Cour,'* 1940.

Béranger, Pierre-Jean de: (1780-1857) From 1815 to 1830 this Parisian-born *chansonnier* became the great national and popular poet of France. His songs, many of which, like *Le Roi d'yvetot, Le Vieux Sergent, Le Dieu des bonnes gens, La Grand'mère,* remained popular for a long time, possess qualities of literary value. Ranging from the gay and bacchanalian that sing of love and youth, to those in the political, or satirical vein that attack priests and nobles, they reflect the currents and feelings of the period. In them Béranger expresses a patriotic ideal. If, moreover, he celebrated, on the one hand, Napoleon's military glory, and on the other, the "principles of 1789," it was because he felt no discrepancy between these two ideals; both aimed at the glory of France. It is in this light that his struggle against the Restoration must be understood. This "friend of the people" and defender of liberty published several volumes of *Chansons.* Because they were deemed seditious under the Restoration, Béranger was jailed and fined on at least two occasions.

Lucas Dubreton, *Béranger: la chanson, la politique, la société,* 1934.

Bérénice (1670): See *Racine.*

Berger extravagant, Le (1627): See *Sorel, Charles.*

Bergson, Henri: (1859-1941) This Parisian-born philosopher, professor at the *Collège de France* (q.v.), was elected to the *Académie Française* (q.v.) in 1914 and was awarded the Nobel prize in 1927. His philosophy, later attacked by such rationalists as Julien Benda (q.v.), was "intuitive," anti-intellectual, anti-rationalist. His major works include *Essai sur les données immédiates de la conscience* (1889), his doctoral dissertation, *Matière et Memoire* (1896), which ascertains the existence and preservation of past recollections within the mind, *L'Evolution créatrice* (1907), which establishes the genetic impulse or the *élan vital* of the mind, and

Les Deux Sources de la Morale et de la Religion (1932), a kind of testament. His notions of time and duration and of memory entered literature through Charles Péguy (q.v.), who considered Bergson his master, and Marcel Proust (q.v.). His most notable disciple in literary criticism is Albert Thibaudet (q.v.). A. Thibaudet, *Le Bergsonisme*, 1924; André Henry, *Bergson, maître de Péguy*, 1949; Floris Delattre, *Bergson et Proust*, 1948.

Bernanos, Georges: (1888-1948) He is one of the most important contemporary Catholic writers (cf. *Claudel* and *Mauriac*). In *Sous le Soleil du Satan* (1926), his first novel, he describes a priest's struggles with the devil. The writings that follow, novels and pamphlets, are written in the same vein: *La Grande Peur des Bien-Pensants* (1931), a pamphlet, attacks the bourgeoisie that is conformist and Catholic merely through habit; *Journal d'un Curé de campagne* (1936), a novel, depicts a young priest's tragic revolt against the pharisaic formalism of his parishioners, whom he wishes to transfigure by evoking in them an internal spiritual drama and by breaking down their long-worn indifference. Other novels of Bernanos worthy of note are his *Nouvelle Histoire de Mouchette* (1937) and *Monsieur Ouine* (1946). Proclaiming what he believed to be the truth, he wrote a pamphlet, *Les Grands Cimetières sous la Lune* (1938), against Franco, and another one, *Scandale de la Vérité* (1939), denouncing the Munich pact. During the Second World War he wrote several impassioned manifestoes against the Vichy regime.
Gaëtan Picon, *Georges Bernanos*, 1948.

Bernard, Jean Jacques: (1888-   ) Exponent of the "school of silence" as a dramatic theory, this dramatist, son of Tristan Bernard (q.v.), represents a reaction to the rhetoric and false lyricism of the earlier part of the century. The eloquent realism of the true and the sincere, according to this representative of an "intimiste" aesthetics, is to be found not in verbalism, but in the feelings extracted from a look, a sigh, a gesture, a half-uttered remark, or a momentary silence. *Martine* (1922) —produced one year after the war-inspired *Le Feu qui reprend mal* (1921), in which a returning soldier suffers anguish and jealousy because of his wife's hospitality to an American officer—is the classic example of this art that evokes the secret passions and unexpressed sufferings of the soul (cf. *Gaston Baty*). A few brief words expressed by a simple peasant girl suggest the depth of her feelings when her romance, encouraged by the voluble young man from Paris to whom she has given her heart, is put an end to by the sudden appearance of the latter's sophisticated fiancée. The tragedies of various other frustrations are similarly depicted in *L'Invitation au Voyage* (1924), *L'Ame en peine* (1926), and even in *A la Recherche des cœurs* (1934).

Bernard, Tristan (pseud. of Paul Bernard): (1866-1947) A melancholy humor permeates the works of this writer. His novels, including *Les Mémoires d'un jeune homme rangé* (1889) and *Le Mari pacifique* (1901), show a fundamental pessimism and strong traits of observation. Essentially, however, a popular dramatist, his plays, which are hilarious, range from those, like *L'Anglais tel qu'on le parle* (1899), based on intrigue or devices of concealment and mistaken identity, to those that depict familiar human types. *Triplepatte* (1905) is one such comedy of character that portrays a man of indecision when faced with the possibility of marriage; *Monsieur Codomat* (1907) reveals a petty thief who would be a respectable bourgeois; *Le Prince Charmant* (1914) is the picture of an impecunious hero who, though he borrows from everyone, is forgiven by his wife. The success or failure in life of these ordinary souls seems to depend upon the strength or weakness of their characters. The merriest of all his farces, however, is probably *Le petit Café* (1911). More recent plays include *Jules, Juliette et Julien* (1929) and *Le Sauvage* (1931).

Bernstein, Henry: (1876-1953) This Parisian-born stage craftsman first produced plays that were violent, brutal and tense, and that were often plotted around a love triangle. The women in these plays, which include *La Rafale* (1905), *La Griffe* (1906), *Le Voleur* (1906) and *Samson* (1908), either marry for or are only interested in money, at times causing financial ruin. *Israël* (1908), inspired by the effects of the Dreyfus case, gained Bernstein international renown. After 1913 his plays became more psychological and stressed character delineation more than situation. *Le Secret* (1913) is a study of a woman who takes pleasure in hurting those she pretends to love; *La Galerie des glaces* (1924) depicts jealousy and a case of inferiority complex. Most of his plays were produced in his own playhouses, the Théâtre du Gymnase, from 1918 to 1940, and the Théâtre des Ambassadeurs, after 1940.

L. Le Sidaner, *Henry Bernstein,* 1931; Pierre Bathille, *Henry Bernstein, son œuvre,* 1931.

Béroul: A twelfth-century poet from Brittany or Normandy whose version of the legend of *Tristan et Iseut* (*c.* 1180?; q.v.) we still possess today.

Bertaut, Jean: (1552-1611) A disciple of Ronsard and Desportes (qq.v.), whose poetic traditions he continued. His *Élégies* and *Épîtres* have more sentiment, however, than does the poetry of Desportes. Some of his occasional poems and love poetry have a melancholy that is rare in his time. He also translated the *Psalms.* At his death he was Bishop of Séez, to which he had been named by Henri IV.

G. Grente, *Jean Bertaut,* 1903.

Bertin, Antoine de: (1752-1790) Born at Reunion Island, off Africa, this poet is noted for his love poetry, which he expresses with much sincerity of sentiment. Many of his poems also reflect his love of nature.

E. Faguet, *Les Poètes secondaires du 18ᵉ siècle,* 1935.

Bertrand, Aloysius: (1807-1841) Credited with having inaugurated the prose poem, he exercised a certain influence on Baudelaire (q.v.). *Gaspard de la Nuit* (1842), a posthumous collection, reveals a choice of rare words and suggestive imagery, and transports the reader into the limitless world of the dream.

bestiaire: Poem reciting the characteristic peculiarities of various animals which were then interpreted in the light of Christian morality. Very widely read during the Middle Ages, the *bestiaires* exercised a considerable influence on literature, frequently also on the plastic arts, particularly with regard to the representation of animals in the churches. A good example of this kind of poem is Philippe de Thaon's *Bestiaire* (*c.* 1125).

Bête humaine, La (1890): See *Zola.*

Bêtes, Les (1953): See *Gascar, Pierre.*

bienséance: An important feature of seventeenth-century French society, especially among the upper classes, it exemplified both conduct that did not shock good taste and a strict code of morality. Its severity was manifested in modes of demeanor, dress, speech and action. As a literary principle, part of the classical doctrine, it served as a basis for one of the criticisms of Corneille's (q.v.) *Le Cid* (cf. *Querelle du Cid*).

R. Bray, *La Formation de la doctrine classique*, 1931.

Blanchette (1892): See *Brieux*.

Blanchot, Maurice: (1907-   ) A contemporary critic of repute, this writer is also the author of such Kafkaesque novels as *Thomas l'obscur* (1941), *Aminadab* (1942), *Le Très-Haut* (1948) and *L'Arrêt de mort* (1948). Philosophical in their preoccupation with such themes as man's loneliness and death, these works reflect an important current of the present age.

Bloch, Jean-Richard: (1884-1947) Social thinking as well as aesthetic interests dominate the writings of this Paris-born novelist, essayist, and dramatist. His first works—*Lévy* (1912) and *Et Cie* (1918)—are novels that deal with a study of the Jew in modern society. More of a revery is his *La Nuit Kurde* (1925), an oriental tale. Proletarian propaganda is found in *Sibylla*, a lyrical novel, and in *Le Dernier Empereur* (1926), a drama concerned with a revolutionary reformer. His critical studies—*Carnaval est mort* (1920), *Destin du Théâtre* (1930), and *Naissance d'une Culture* (1936)—stress the principle that art emanates from the sufferings and hopes of the people.

Bodel, Jean: (?—after 1202) This *trouvère*, born in Arras, is the author of the *Chanson des Saisnes* and the *Jeu de Saint-Nicolas* (q.v.).

Bodin, Jean: (1530-1596) On the side of the Catholics during the time of the religious wars in France, he gave expression, in his *Six livres de la République* (1576), to political views that vested authority—with limitations—in the French monarchical state. Other views here expressed—his condemnation of slavery and religious persecution, the relationship he establishes between climate and the political institutions of a country—make him a precursor of such great political theorists as Montesquieu and Rousseau (qq.v.).

R. Chauviré, *Jean Bodin*, 1914.

"Bohême": Used in a geographic sense in the Middle Ages, this word was applied, in the eighteenth century, to one who led a "bohemian" or vagabond existence. After 1830, this term designated a certain number of artists and writers living in Paris who had come from the lower classes and from the provinces and who wanted to have their share in literature, now that the writing profession was no longer limited, thanks to the Revolution of 1830, to the nobility and the upper bourgeoisie. The first such group, known more commonly in the Thirties as the *Jeune France*, included Gautier, Gérard de Nerval (qq.v.), Arsène Houssaye, Ed. Ourliac, Célestin Nanteuil, Jéhan du Seigneur, and Pétrus Borel. They were relatively poor, adopted pseudonyms, wore bizarre costumes, and enjoyed their eccentric life. The "real" *bohème* group, thriving from 1848 to 1855, and identified with Realism (q.v.), came from the lower classes; perpetually in need of money, they led a life of misery in Paris, living where they could, and spending much of their time at the cafés. Included among them were Murger, Champfleury (qq.v.), Courbet—whose artistic doctrines, interest in contemporary subject matter, and depiction of all classes were to have much influence—Barbara, Delvau, Bonvin, and Chintreuil the artist. The writers of this group, together with Henri Monnier (q.v.), an important precursor of realism (q.v.), described in their work the life they led, were obsessed with the question of money, and revealed a contempt for the bourgeoisie.

P. Martino, *Le Roman Réaliste sous le Second Empire*, 1913.

Boileau-Despréaux, Nicolas: (1636-1711) Generally considered the theoretician of classicism (q.v.), this Par-

27

isian-born poet and critic, with the fortune he had inherited upon his father's death (1657), was able to devote himself entirely to literature. In 1666 the first seven of his *Satires*, composed between 1657 and 1665, appeared; the eighth and ninth of these satires followed in 1668; and the last three were written between 1692 and 1705. Criticizing in them the *précieux* (q.v.), *burlesque* (q.v.) and mediocre writers, not to mention the mores of his times, Boileau also reflects in his polemical disposition and frankness a familiarity —as the son of a lawyer—with lawsuits. At about the same time—that is, from 1669 to 1698—Boileau wrote a series of twelve *Épitres* in which he attacks human follies, praises as well as advises the King, and in which his literary doctrine takes more definite shape. His ambition to become the Horace of French literature becomes even more evident in his *Art poétique* (1674). In this didactic, but harmonious, poem, he not only discusses the history of poetry in France and enumerates the different poetic forms, but also sets down the rules pertaining to tragedy and comedy (qq.v.). The guiding principles for him, in both genres, are truth and beauty. To achieve this ideal, he advises the close study and imitation of nature—that is, human nature as seen, for example, by Molière (q.v.)—the adoption of reason, and the cultivation of the Ancients as models; the survival of the latters' works is evidence of the fact that they have imitated nature and are founded on reason. The cause of the Ancients he further champions—together with his friends La Fontaine, Racine and La Bruyère (qq.v.)—in the first stages (1687-1694) of the controversy known as the *Querelle des Anciens et des modernes* (q.v.). His views on the Ancients and his other critical doctrines are also seen in *Réflexions*

sur Longin (1694), a work in prose. In 1677, Boileau, together with Racine, was named historiographer to the King, and in 1684 he was elected to the *Académie Française* (q.v.). Included among his other writings are: *Dialogue sur les héros de romans* (published in 1687), a work in prose ridiculing the *précieux* novels, and *Le Lutrin* (1674), a mock epic poem relating an ecclesiastical quarrel over the placing of a lectern.

More than Malherbe (q.v.), Boileau defined the classical spirit, without, however, inspiring its masterpieces; most of the latter were written before his *Art poétique*. An excellent judge of the great writers of his own age, he failed, however, to appreciate the true merits of many great poets before his time. His own merit as a poet is essentially that of a satirist.

G. Lanson, *Boileau*, 1892; D. Mornet, *Boileau*, 1941; R. Bray, *Boileau*, 1942.

Boisrobert, François Le Metel de: (1592-1662) One of the first members of the *Académie Française* (q.v.) and secretary to Richelieu, he is remembered for his *La belle plaideuse* (1654), a comedy that may have inspired several scenes in Molière's (q.v.) *L'Avare*.

E. Magne, *Le plaisant abbé de Boisrobert*, 1909.

Bonjour, tristesse (1954): See *Sagan, Françoise*.

Bordeaux, Henri: (1870-   ) For this prolific writer—he has written more than fifty novels, various monographs, essays, and several volumes of dramatic criticism—the family, considered as the basis of society, is the main theme. In most of his novels, as in *Les Roquevillard* (1906), *La Croisée des chemins* (1909), and *La Maison* (1913), the setting is his native Savoie. In these novels he continues the Catholic, bourgeois traditions of a Paul Bourget (q.v.); however, he is no doctrinaire, and his traditionalism is tempered by a realistic view of life, as can be seen in *La Neige sur les pas* (1912).

Jules Bertaut, *Henry Bordeaux et son œuvre*, 1924.

Bosco, Henri: (1888-   ) This author, born in Avignon, paints his native Provence with an austere mysticism in such books as *Pierre Lampédouse* (1924), *L'Ane Culotte* (1936) and *Le Mas Théotime* (1944). The last work won him much success.

Bossuet, Jacques-Bénigne: (1627-1704) Renowned for his eloquence as a preacher, this theologian, ordained a priest in 1652, was appointed Bishop of Condom in 1669. Residing in Paris, his influence was particularly felt at the court, and he became in 1670 tutor of the Dauphin. In this capacity, he wrote for his incorrigible pupil his *Discours sur l'Histoire Universelle* (1681)—an exposition of history as the work of Providence—and his *Traité de politique tirée des Écritures* (begun in 1678; first published in 1709), in which the doctrine of the Divine Right of Kings is affirmed. Notwithstanding the merits of these works, his reputation as the greatest orator of his century is based particularly on his sermons (*Sur la Providence*, 1662; *Sur la Mort*, 1662; *Sur l'Unité de l'Église*, 1681) and on his funeral orations, the best-known of which are those on *Henriette de France* (1669), *Henriette d'Angleterre* (1670) and the *Prince de Condé* (1687). Following his appointment in 1681 as Bishop of Meaux, near Paris, Bossuet took part in several controversies that reveal his ardent and orthodox Catholicism. In his *Histoire des variations des églises protestantes* (1688), he criticizes the Protestants for the lack of unity that characterizes their church; affirming the authority of Catholic dogma, in his *Relation sur le quiétisme* (1698) he attacks Fénelon (q.v.) for the posi-

tion taken by the latter on the question of Quietism (q.v.). As a writer and as a preacher, Bossuet possesses the qualities of a lyrical poet. His meditations on life and death, expressed in a biblical style, become, in the final analysis, one of the most important contributions to the development of French prose during the seventeenth century.

G. Lanson, *Bossuet*, 1890; A. Rébelliau, *Bossuet*, 1900; J. Calvet, *Bossuet*, 1941.

Boubouroche (1893): See *Courteline*.

Bouches inutiles, Les (1945): See *Beauvoir, Simone de*.

Boule de Suif (1880): See *Maupassant*.

Bourdaloue, Louis: (1632-1704) A Jesuit preacher, he is noted, much like Bossuet (q.v.), for his eloquence. His sermons, more preoccupied with ethics and morality than with dogma, are characterized by logical precision and psychological analysis.

A. Feugère, *Bourdaloue, sa prédication et son temps*, 1874.

Bourdet, Édouard: (1887-1945) The comedies of this dramatist, which combine psychological and social characteristics, are set in the middle classes; his attitude is realistic, but not reforming. In a typically postwar spirit, Lesbianism is analyzed psychologically in *La Prisonnière* (1926); the cynicism of authors and publishers is satirized in *Vient de paraître* (1927), and that of industrialized bourgeois society is satirized in *Les Temps difficiles* (1934), in which the moral consequences of the economic crisis are also depicted: a family seeks financial security through their daughter's marriage, one that offers wealth without happiness. In these and in his other plays, Bourdet reveals a mathematical precision in dramatic construction, a keen ability to observe and an ear for natural dialogue.

Bourgeoises de qualité, Les (1700): See *Dancourt*.

Bourgeois gentilhomme, Le: A comedy-ballet, for which Lulli wrote the music, this play, written in 1670, is one of the most popular by Molière (q.v.). Combining characteristics of the *comédie de caractère* and of the *comédie de mœurs* (qq.v.), it revolves around the comic character of M. Jourdain and is filled with amusing situations that reflect the ambitions of this wealthy *bourgeois*. Monsieur Jourdain, a wealthy *bourgeois* wishing to transform himself into a person of quality—a "gentleman"—engages teachers of fencing, dancing, music and philosophy. Obsessed by the idea of acquiring the manners of the nobility, he is easily taken in by flatterers and by the Marquise Dorimène, whom he thinks he loves. As a result of his obsession, living with him becomes well-nigh impossible: he refuses to allow his daughter to marry, despite the good sense and advice of his wife, her young suitor, Cléonte, who does not spring from nobility. Covielle, Cléonte's valet, and Nicole, Jourdain's cook, decide, however, to take matters into their own hands. Taking advantage of the fact that Jourdain is dazzled only by titles, Covielle, himself disguised as an interpreter, disguises Cléonte and presents him to Jourdain as the son of the Grand Turk. Pleased, the gullible Jourdain, upon whom, moreover, the fictitious title of *Mamamouchi* is conferred, now consents to the marriage of his daughter with Cléonte.

Bourget, Paul: (1852-1935) Following the publication of such early collections of poetry as his *La Vie inquiète* (1875), *Edel* (1877) and *Les Aveux* (1882), he made his literary mark with his *Essais de psychologie contemporaine* (1883) and *Nouveaux Essais* (1885), in which he studied what he thought were the unsalutary influences on his generation of such writers as Baudelaire (q.v.), Renan (q.v.) and Taine (q.v.); however, the studies themselves evidence that he had adopted Taine's method. His early novels, including *Cruelle Enigme* (1885) and *Mensonges* (1887) are psychological analyses of characters moving in the upper circles of society. *Le Disciple* (1889), a novel that combines analytical with moralizing elements, and that poses the author's and teacher's responsibility to the generation whose mental and moral formation they help mold, is an important date in the literary history of France, as well as in Bourget's evolution; for here Bourget stands as an ardent adversary of the scientific positivism of Taine and of the deterministic theories represented by the naturalistic (see *Naturalism*) school. With *L'Etape* (1902) Bourget began a cycle of social novels consisting really of inquiries and dissertations on the contemporary moral, social, political and religious questions with which he was concerned.

F.-J. Lardeur, *La vérité psychologique et morale dans les romans de P. Bourget,* 1912.

Boursault, Édme: (1638-1701) This dramatist, an adversary of Molière (q.v.), wrote several comedies, including *Le Mercure Galant, ou la Comédie sans titre* (1683), *Esope à la ville* (1690) and *Esope à la cour* (1701).

H. C. Lancaster, *History of French Dramatic Literature in the Seventeenth Century,* 1929-1942.

bovarysme: The disposition among many, like Emma in *Madame Bovary* (q.v.), to regard themselves as different from what they really are.

J. de Gaultier, *Le bovarysme,* 1902.

Boylesve, René (pseud. of **René Tardiveau**): (1867-1926) Born in Touraine, this writer is essentially the novelist of provincial life and of sensitive creatures whose passions are frustrated. In *Mademoiselle*

Cloque (1899), the heroine is frustrated by the forces of opportunism and hypocrisy. *La Becquée* (1901) portrays an authoritarian woman whose only passion is to safeguard and increase the family property. In the end she dies without any sense of real victory. The penetrating psychology the author uses in his analyses of these characters explains, in part, why he has been considered a precursor of Marcel Proust (q.v.).

Gérard-Gailly, *Le souvenir de René Boylesve*, 1931-1935; André Bourgeois, *René Boylesve, l'homme, le peintre de la Touraine*, 1945.

Bradamante (1582): See *Garnier, Robert*.

Brantôme, Pierre de Bourdeille, seigneur de: (1540-1614) Physically incapacitated as a result of an accident in 1584, after a life of military adventure, he devoted his remaining days to recording, in an anecdotal fashion, incidents relating to the people he knew at the court of Marguerite d'Angoulême (q.v.) and to the social customs—both good and bad—of his times. The cynicism and licentiousness to which he owes much of his reputation are largely based on *Vies des dames illustres*, which is characteristically impressionistic and full of gossip. This work, like his *Vies des hommes illustres et des grands capitaines*, makes up only part of his *Mémoires*, published posthumously in 1665-1666.

L. Lalanne, *Brantôme, sa vie et ses écrits*, 1896; F. Crucy, *Brantôme*, 1934.

Breton, André: (1894-   ) This poet, critic, and novelist, once a medical student and devotee of Freudian theory, broke, in 1921, with Dadaism (q.v.), with which he had previously associated himself. Founder and theoretician of Surrealism (q.v.), which followed on the heels of Dadaism, he expressed its doctrine in his *Trois Manifestes* (1924, 1930,

1942) as well as in his *Qu'est-ce que le Surrealisme?* (1934) and *Position politique du Surréalisme* (1935). Because of his intransigence and his wish to protect the autonomy of the movement, the Surrealistic group suffered much internal dissension, with the result that several original members left, although new recruits were added. As time went on, Breton became more and more convinced of the importance of investigation into the subconscious and the world of dreams. His poetry, a kind of automatic writing, dictated by hallucinations of the subconscious, includes *Les Champs magnétiques* (1921), which he wrote in collaboration with Soupault (q.v.), and *Le Revolver à Cheveux Blancs* (1932). His most remarkable book, however, is *Nadja* (1928), a novel that deals with a strange woman of marked psychic powers. Julien Gracq, *André Breton*, 1948; Claude Mauriac, *André Breton*, 1949.

Brieux, Eugène: (1858-1922) This Parisian son of a cabinet-maker, elected in 1910 to the French Academy, was first brought to public attention as a dramatist by Antoine (q.v.), who produced at the Théâtre Libre (q.v.) his *Ménage d'artistes* (1890) and *Blanchette* (1892). The latter play, realistic in its psychology and use of language, is the portrait of a daughter of peasants who, after having received a university education which she cannot put to use, becomes a "déclassée." Other pieces, all of which, like the previous one, treat social problems, are more frankly moralistic. Following in the tradition of the thesis play of Dumas fils (q.v.), *Les trois Filles de M. Dupont* (1897) is an indictment of a society that makes marriage possible only for those with sufficient dowry and that brings unhappiness to others, and *La Robe rouge* (1900) is a satire of ambitious prosecutors whose success and pro-

31

motion are often obtained at the expense of some innocent victim. The *théâtre utile* of Brieux is much broader in scope than that of Dumas *fils*, treating as it does political abuses (*L'Engrenage*, 1894), divorce (*La Déserteuse*, 1904), the evils of playing the races (*Résultat des courses*, 1898), syphilis (*Les Avariés*, 1902), and birth control (*Maternité*, 1903). Other problems studied by this dramatist include those related to science and religion. In all, the moral principles of this reformer and former journalist, who chastens more than cures, are those that emanate from a charitable and compassionate mind and heart. He excels in the realistic portraiture of the bourgeoisie. Despite an unpolished language, in his realistic depiction of life, of every-day people, he shows a remarkable dramatic talent, a fact which, added to his sincerity, explains the interest extended to him by the public.

P. V. Thomas, *The Plays of Eugène Brieux*, 1913; W. H. Scheifley, *Brieux and Contemporary French Society*, 1917.

Britannicus: Written by Racine (q.v.) in 1669, this tragedy, unlike most of his others, is based, not on Greek sources, but on an incident in the career of Emperor Néron (Nero) as related by Tacitus in his *Annals* of Roman history. Essentially psychological, it depicts the inability of Néron to free himself from the criminal tendencies he has inherited. Agrippine (Agrippina), his mother, through evil machinations, has succeeded in making him Emperor. In depriving Britannicus, her stepson, of his legitimate rights to the Empire, she has been moved by her desire to be the power behind the throne. When, therefore, she learns of her son's secret passion for Junie (Junia), the fiancée of Britannicus, she is much concerned, seeing her own power imperilled. Although she reminds Néron of the crimes she

has committed for his sake and points to his ingratitude, and though Néron hesitates during three acts—torn between the opposing influences and advice of Burrhus and the perfidious Narcisse (Narcissus)—in the end, condemned by his own perversity, he has Britannicus, his rival in politics and love, poisoned, and seizes Junie. The latter, however, leaves him helplessly outraged by becoming a vestal virgin.

Brueys, David-Augustin de (1640-1723) **et Palaprat, Jean** (1650-1721): This team of dramatists wrote in collaboration several *comédies de caractère* (q.v.), including *Le Grondeur* (1691), *L'Important* (1693) and *L'Opiniâtre* (1722), in which they continue the type of play that was inaugurated by Molière (q.v.).

Brunetière, Ferdinand: (1849-1906) Born in Toulon, this professor and director of the *Revue des deux mondes* became, after the death of Taine (q.v.), the outstanding literary critic in France (see *Criticism*). Opposed to Naturalism (q.v.), he was nevertheless dogmatic in his Darwinian and evolutionary approach to literary criticism. His doctrine maintained the evolution of literary "genres," which, like other living organisms, are born, develop, and die, only to give birth to new types. To understand the evolution of the "genres," therefore, requires a close adherence to the historical method. Included among his writings are: *Le Roman naturaliste* (1883), *L'Évolution de la Poésie lyrique* (1894). His later works betray more of a moralizing tendency, a greater emphasis on Christian apologetics and religious propaganda, and a decidedly conservative point of view.

E. Faguet, *Ferdinand Brunetière*, 1911; E. Hocking, *Brunetière*, 1936.

Brut, Roman de: This chronicle by Wace (q.v.), a French translation in verse (1155) and expansion of Geoffrey of Monmouth's *Historia* *regum Brittaniæ,* makes mention for the first time of Arthur's Round Table. It relates how Brut, or Brutus, son of Silvius, having inadvertently killed his father, first flees to Greece, then lands in Britain, where, according to legend, he becomes the first King. This chronicle may also be considered a source of Thomas' (q.v.) *Tristan et Iseut.* I. Arnold, ed., *Le Roman de Brut de Wace,* 1938-1940.

Brutus (1730): See *Voltaire.*

Budé, Guillaume: (1468-1540) A humanist and one of France's first great hellenists, he persuaded King François I to found the *Collège des lecteurs royaux* (later *Collège de France;* q.v.), so that the study of Hebrew, Greek, and Latin could be pursued free of the traditional authority of the University of Paris, then dominated by its Faculty of Theology. He was also the author of *Commentarii linguæ Græcæ* (1529), a philological study of the Greek language, and of *De Asse* (1514), a treatise on Roman money. L. Delaruelle, *G. Budé,* 1907.

Buffon, Georges-Louis Leclerc, Comte de: (1707-1788) Natural historian, he became in 1733 an associate member of the Academy of Sciences, and in 1739 curator of the *Jardin du Roi* (now the *Jardin des Plantes*) in Paris. In the latter capacity, he devoted himself to scientific observation and investigation and, more particularly, to his monumental *Histoire naturelle* (1749-1804). This work, consisting of forty-four volumes, and prepared with the aid of collaborators and assistants, contains mostly historical and descriptive monographs on the earth, man, animals and minerals. Of especial interest are the two volumes *Théories de la terre* (1749) and *Époques de la nature* (1779), in which he is probably the first to give a history of successive geological stages. In other volumes (*Les Quadrupèdes,* 1749-1767; *Les Oiseaux,*

1770-1783), he laid the foundations for zoölogy and comparative anatomy; and his theories of transformism and evolutionism foreshadowed Lamarck, Darwin and Spencer. Although Buffon, as a scientist, is linked to the eighteenth century, and although he helped pave the way for nineteenth century natural science, he differs from his contemporary Encyclopedists in that, unlike them, he does not view science as a means of antireligious propaganda; he pays lip service to Biblical tradition, and does not show disrespect toward his government.

In his *Discours sur le style* (1753), delivered at his reception to the *Académie Française* (q.v.), he expounds the importance of a good style, which he defines as a logical or orderly plan of one's ideas; in his own words, *"le style est l'homme même."*

D. Mornet, *Les sciences de la nature en France au 18e siècle,* 1911; L. Dimier, *Buffon,* 1919.

Burgraves, Les (1843): See *Hugo.*

burlesque: Characterized, in literature, by a tendency toward parody, travesty and caricature of noble characters, sentiments, customs, institutions, or literary works, it flourished in France from 1640 to 1660 and represents the antithesis to the *précieux* (see *Préciosité*) movement. In a sense, it may be said that this spirit, whether interpreted as the *esprit gaulois* (q.v.), or as realism (q.v.), has always existed, side by side with the idealistic current, in French literature. As seen in the novels of Charles Sorel, Scarron and Furetière (qq.v.), it manifests itself in the depiction of the vulgar and the ordinary, in a style that lacks distinction. A prime example of *burlesque* poetry is seen in Scarron's mock *Æneid* or *Virgile travesti* (1648-1659). Other parodies of epic poems show legendary or historical characters accomplishing ridiculous or unimportant actions and expressing themselves in vulgar and inelegant language.

Th. Gautier, *Les Grotesques*, 1844; V. Fournel, *La littérature indépendante et les écrivains oubliés du XVIIe siècle*, 1862; P. Morillot, *Scarron et le genre burlesque*, 1888.

Bussy-Rabutin, Roger de: (1618-1693) Cousin of Mme. de Sévigné (q.v.), this epistolary writer, not always discreet, was for a long time exiled from the court of Louis XIV. In his *Correspondance*, the first complete edition of which was published from 1858 to 1859, many valuable literary criticisms are to be found. He also wrote interesting *Mémoires* (1696); his novel, *Histoire amoureuse des Gaules* (1665), contains indiscreet references to the early love-affairs of Louis XIV.

E. Gérard-Gailly, *Bussy-Rabutin, sa vie, ses œuvres et ses amis*, 1909.

C

Cahiers d'André Walter, Les (1891): See *Gide.*

Caillavet, Gaston Armand de (1869-1915): See under *Flers, Robert de.*

Calligrammes (1918): See *Apollinaire, Guillaume.*

Calvin, Jean: (1509-1564) Before becoming the great Protestant reformer and founder of Calvinism he was, until 1533, a student of law. His humanistic leanings at this time are shown by his studies of Latin, Greek and Hebrew, and by the publication in 1532 of a commentary on Seneca's *De Clementia.* Other influences—those of Lefèvre d'Etaples (q.v.) and Nicolas Cop, whom he helped prepare a speech which had Protestant tendencies and because of which he had to flee from Paris (1533)—brought about his conversion and preoccupation with religious matters. At Basel he published, in Latin, his *Institutio christianæ religionis* (1536), later translated into French under the title of *Institution de la religion chrétienne* (1541). Apart from the fact that this work established the new theological doctrine, it is important as the first theological treatise to be published in French. The relative clarity and preciseness of its style represent an important contribution to the development of French prose.

Settled in 1541 in Geneva, where he remained until his death and which became the citadel of the new faith, Calvin became in effect a dictator and was merciless with those whom he considered heretics. Religious eloquence, as exemplified in Bossuet (q.v.) in the seventeenth century, was to profit from Calvin's method of basing his arguments on biblical texts; and questions relating to man's problems and destiny, important to Calvinism, were to become the great preoccupation of Pascal (q.v.).

H. Y. Reyburn, *Jean Calvin, his life, letters and works*, 1914; D. Méréjkovski, *Calvin*, 1942.

Campistron, Jean Galbert de: (1656?-1723) This dramatist wrote a number of tragedies, including *Arminius* (1684), *Andronic* (1685) and *Tiri-*

date (1691)—his best—and some libretti, for which Lulli wrote the music.

H. C. Lancaster, *A History of French Dramatic Literature in the 17th Century*, IV, 1940.

Camus, Albert: (1913-   ) This leading figure of the present generation of French writers, born in Algeria, where he remained until 1940, is at once novelist, dramatist, essayist and journalist. A careful examination of his works makes his self-involvement evident, since they reflect either his Algerian background, or his participation in the Resistance, or his general philosophy. *Noces* (1939) contains sketches of Algerian life; *L'Étranger* (1942), his first important novel—one of the best from this generation of writers—is laid in Algeria. Written in a classical, lucid style, as are his other works, this novel, almost completely lacking in action, depicts a detached and indifferent "stranger" in an absurd universe, who is finally condemned to death for a crime gratuitously committed. Except for the immediate pleasures of his instincts, life for him is devoid of any sense until the last moment, when he suddenly clings to that very existence which he had not helped the gods of destiny to fashion for him. The absurdity of human life, seen in this book as well as in his philosophical essay, *Le Mythe de Sisyphe* (1942), is an argument against those who would link Camus with the Existentialist (See *Existentialism*) school and its doctrine of free choice and responsibility. *La Peste* (1947), however, the action of which is placed in Oran, is a revolt against the notion of the absurdity of life, which, as Camus shows, can be abolished by fraternal solidarity and by values that are a prefiguration of universal unity. Together with the somewhat existentialist Dr. Rieux, all the characters in this parable of our world eventually come to understand that they are responsible for their fellow men and for the maintenance of the struggle against the pestilence that has come to plague the inhabitants of this North African city.

In his plays, *Le Malentendu* (1944) and *Caligula* (1946), Camus further illustrates the absurdity of life. *L'Etat de Siège* (1948) is an allegorical play in which the myth of *La Peste*, previously referred to, illustrates the tyranny of fear.

Other works of Camus include his philosophical essays, *L'Envers et l'endroit* (1939), *L'Homme Révolté* (1951), and his more recent *La Chute* (1956), a "récit" (in monologue form) which suggests a new stage in his development. The symbolism in the last named volume is that of self-flagellation; a defeated generation, repenting of its morals and politics, wishes to have a new start. In *L'Exil et le royaume* (1957), a book of short stories, Camus continues the search for values.

During the days of the insurrection of Paris Camus founded the underground newspaper *Combat*. His entire work, basically a revolt against absurdity, is a quest for a positive ethic; it suffers, however, from occasional abstraction.

Camus was awarded the Nobel Prize for Literature in 1957.

Robert de Luppé, *Albert Camus,* 1952.

Camus, Jean-Pierre: (1584-1652) Disciple of Montaigne (q.v.), friend and biographer of François de Sales (q.v.), this bishop is the author of many amusing novels in which love, fully analyzed, is an important ingredient in the cause of religious edification. The emphasis, however, that Camus gave to the novel as a vehicle for moral predication, makes him a forerunner of Fénelon (q.v.) and of many 18th century novelists. Included among his novels are *La*

Pieuse Jule (1625) and *Palombe* (1624).

Boulas, *Camus*, 1878; P. Villey, *Montaigne devant la postérité*, 1935.

Candide: Published in 1759 by Voltaire (q.v.), this philosophical novel, one of his most popular, is a retort to Leibnitz's philosophy of optimism as well as to Rousseau's (q.v.) belief in Providence. A vehicle for his ideas, this tale is a satirical demonstration of the triumph of evil, of man's vices and stupidities, and of the absurdity of life, as the main protagonists experience untold disasters. Candide, an illegitimate son of a noble German family, has been brought up at the castle of Thunder-ten-Tronch. When he falls in love with Cunégonde, the latter's daughter, with whom, incidentally, he has learned from the philosopher Pangloss the Leibnitzian doctrine that "all is for the best in this best of possible worlds," he is expelled from the Baron's household. Pressed into the army when war breaks out, he soon deserts, goes to Holland, where he again meets Pangloss, who, despite his present miserable state, is still an optimist. Together they start out for Lisbon; as they arrive, however, after having experienced a shipwreck, the city is shaken by an earthquake. Arrested and accused of having brought on by their wickedness this disaster, they are tortured by the Inquisition. Not long afterward, Candide finds Cunégonde, who has also, in the meantime, experienced misfortune; together they flee to South America. Losing Cunégonde again, Candide travels on to Eldorado, where life is supposed to be simple and perfect. After many new adventures, as a result of his search for Cunégonde, Candide arrives in Venice, and learns, through Cacambo, his servant, that Cunégonde is now a slave in Constantinople. Starting out immediately for Constantinople, Candide finds his old teacher Pangloss —the unchanged optimist—and Cunégonde's brother, whose lives have been miraculously saved. Finally, Candide ransoms Cunégonde, now become very ugly; he marries her, however, and, on the advice of an old peasant, settles with the whole group on a little farm. Like the peasant, each one of the group finds a certain satisfaction in work. Candide himself now expresses the motto *il faut cultiver notre jardin,* believing that it points toward the best way of life and toward the only remedy to pessimism.

cantilène: More like a song or a ballad than a poem, it celebrates in lyrical rhythm the exploits of a hero. Repeated by soldiers in times of war, it is spread in times of peace by the *jongleur* (q.v.). It is perhaps from its development that epic poetry arose. Cf. *Cantilène de Sainte Eulalie* and *Epic Poetry.*

Cantilène de Sainte Eulalie: Written at the end of the ninth century, this poem—the first French work of any literary value—which consists of 28 assonanced lines (see *assonance*), sings the martyrdom of this Spanish virgin Saint (martyred in 304).

Capitaine Fracasse, Le (1863): See *Gautier.*

Caprice, Un (1847): See *Musset.*

Capus, Alfred: (1858-1922) The average man, interested more in the ordinary things of life, which include food, love, and money, than in ideals, is portrayed in his plays, with the happy endings that are typical of this dramatist. The characters in these amusing pieces trust to luck, and most frequently, the women, as in *Brignol et sa fille* (1895), *La Bourse ou la vie* (1900), *La Veine* (1902)—his most popular play—and *La Petite Fonctionnaire* (1901), in the end make very successful marriages.

E. Quet, *Alfred Capus,* 1904.

Caractères ou les mœurs de ce siècle, Les (1688): See *La Bruyère*.

Carco, Francis: (1886-1958) This novelist and poet was born in New Caledonia of Corsican parents. Although a sentimental and melancholy poet, as in his *La Bohème et mon cœur* (1912), the novels he wrote describing the bohemian life of the Montmartre marginal society before the First World War—novels of mores replete with argot—have contributed to his somewhat dubious reputation. In his sad evocations of twilight life, however, he has shown a compassionate understanding for the social offenders. These novels include *L'Homme traqué* (1921), *Perversité* (1925), *Rue Pigalle* (1928), and *Morsure* (1949). The author recounts his own adolescence in *De Montmartre au Quartier latin* (1934).

Philippe Chabaneix, *Carco*, 1949.

Carmen (1845): See *Mérimée*.

Carmontelle (pseud. of **Louis Carrogis**): (1717-1806) Artist, engraver and dramatist, he is the author and creator of amusing *Proverbes*, most of which were written for the amusement of the Duc d'Orléans and his associates. These comedies, which appeared between 1768 and 1781, were "dramatizations," including songs and dances, of proverbs, a genre in which Musset (q.v.) was later to excel.

Carte de Tendre, La: The best-known part of Mlle. de Scudery's (q.v.) novel *Clélie* (1654-1660), it represents, as a map of the different roads leading to true love, the *précieux* spirit (See *Préciosité*) of the seventeenth century.

Cassandre (1612-1645): See *La Calprenède*.

Cassou, Jean: (1897-) This Spanish-born writer has written novels, criticism and poetry. *De l'Etoile au Jardin des Plantes* (1935), a collection of short stories, was followed by *Les Massacres de Paris* (1936) and the rather long novel, *Centre*

du Monde (1945), written before the German occupation. His critical essays include *Éloge de la Folie* (1925), *Harmonies viennoises* (1926) and *Pour la poésie* (1935). His *Trente-Trois Sonnets écrits au Secret* was written in prison during the Second World War. Several of his works deal with Spanish literature.

casuistry: A part of theology and ethics that takes into account the *cas de conscience,* i.e. the intentions and mental restrictions involved in a crime or sin. For their over-indulgence in casuistry, which attenuated sin, the Jesuits were attacked and ridiculed in the *Lettres Provinciales* (1656-1657) by Pascal (q.v.).

Cathédrale, La (1898): See *Huysmans*.

Causeries du Lundi (1851-1862): See *Sainte-Beuve*.

Caves du Vatican, Les (1913): See *Gide*.

Cayrol, Jean: (1911-) Even before the publication of his famous *Poèmes de la Nuit et du Brouillard* (1945), the expression of his experiences in prison during the Occupation and in a concentration camp, he had established for himself a reputation as a poet. Although he has continued to write poetry, he has since published *Je vivrai l'amour des autres,* a novel trilogy whose main protagonist is a *clochard,* a kind of deportee from society who assumes the misery of the world and personifies Charity, and other, less successful novels.

Céard, Henri: (1851-1824) Novelist and dramatist, he was one of the authors of the *Soirées de Medan* (1880; q.v.). An exponent of naturalism, he wrote *Terrains à vendre au bord de la mer* (1906), probably his best novel, and several plays—*La Pêche* (1890), *Les Résignés* (1889), and *Tout pour l'homme* (1887)—that were produced at the Théâtre-Libre.

Céline, Louis-Ferdinand (pseud. of **Louis F. Destouches**): (1894-) This Paris-born physician, turned novelist, reflects in his personal life as well as in his writings elements of an unidealistic and uninspiring gloom; his betrayal of his compatriots during the Second World War was accompanied in his writings by outbursts of contempt for the human race. His novel, *Le Voyage au bout de la Nuit* (1932), foreshadows the pessimism and despair of that part of contemporary French literature which emphasizes the absurdity of life. In his evocation of this journey through the darkness of human catastrophe, including crime and death, Céline recalls Sartre (q.v.). As in the fiction of the latter, a close relationship is established between the absurd and the obscene; the language used·is the "spoken language" too often marred by a monotonous combination of slang and filth. This work is a *témoignage* of a world in crisis. His other novels, *Mort à Crédit* (1936) and *Bagatelles pour un Massacre* (1938), are written in a similar vein, but without the vigor and evocative power of the *Journey*.

Robert Denoel, *Apologie de Mort à Crédit*, 1937; Milton Hindus, *The Crippled Giant; a Bizarre Adventure in Contemporary Letters*, 1950.

Cendrars, Blaise: (1887-   ) This Parisian-born, widely travelled bohemian poet and novelist exemplifies the view that ours is a chaotic, insensitive world dominated by money and machinery. His poetry, which exercised an influence on Apollinaire (q.v.), includes *Dix-neuf Poèmes élastiques* (1919) and *Du monde entier* (1919) —collections that reveal a catalogue of quick, frantic visions and images, unorganized impressions. The same conception of the modern world is seen in his novels—a documentary of the thirst for escape and adventure common to those of his generation. Included among these novels are: *L'Or* (1925), *Rhum* (1930), *La Vie dangereuse* (1938), and *L'Homme*

foudroyé ⟨1945)—a kind of lyrical autobiography.

T.-H. Levesque, *Blaise Cendrars*, 1948.

Cent Nouvelles nouvelles (1462): See *Antoine de la Sale*.

Chamfort, Sébastien Roch Nicholas: (1741-1749) A friend of Mirabeau who during the Reign of Terror committed suicide, he is known as a moralist and dramatist. As a moralist he is witty, mordant, and, at times, profound, as is evidenced in his *Pensées, maximes et anecdotes* (p. 1803). His comedies include *La jeune Indienne* (1764) and *Le Marchand de Smyrne* (1770). He also wrote literary criticism, including *Éloge de Molière* (1766) and *Éloge de La Fontaine* (1774).

J. Teppe, *Chamfort, sa vie, son œuvre, sa pensée*, 1950.

Chaminadour (1934-1941): See *Jouhandeau*.

Champfleury (pseud. of Jules Husson): (1821-1899) Son of the townhall secretary of Laon, where he was born, he joined, together with Murger (q.v.), the Bohème (q.v.) group in Paris. Not unaffected, in *Chien-Caillou* (1847), he caricatures Bohemian manners; his *Les Aventures de Mariette* (1851) is a documented portrait of the same *milieux* and characters found in Murger's *La Vie de Bohème*. In the novels that were to follow, his identification with realism (q.v.) becomes manifest, especially in his desire to present the times, places, situations, and types of the contemporary life he knew so well. The provincial life of his native town is seen in *Bourgeois de Molinchart* (1855), *Monsieur Boisdhyver* (1856), *Les Souffrances du Professeur Delteil* (1857), and in many other novels. These novels are characterized by a constant preoccupation with truth, by the faithful depiction of manners—especially of provincial manners—and of characters. Equal attention and the most minute detail are given to the most trivial subjects and to the most humble characters, and humor and irony exploit the ridiculous in people—particularly of the bourgeois—and things. *Le Réalisme* (1857) contains his theories of the novel and represents a formula of realism, of which "school" he is one of the leaders.

M. Clouard, *L'Œuvre de Champfleury,* 1891; P. Martino, *Le Roman réaliste sous le Second Empire,* 1913.

Chamson, André: (1900-   ) This student of art, geography, history, politics and archeology was born in the Cévennes region; this fact explains in large part his interest in Mistral (q.v.) and the poems he wrote in Provençal (q.v.). The Cévennes region serves as the background and inspiration of such novels as *Roux le Bandit* (1925), *Les Hommes de la route* (1927) and *Le Crime des justes* (1927), the characters of which, however, are more broadly universal in their concerns. Chamson's later interest in political and ethical problems, following a rather pacifist attitude, resulted in his becoming a writer of the *Résistance* (q.v.); his concern with these problems can be seen in such novels as *La Galère* (1939), *Le Puits des miracles* (1944) and *Le Dernier Village* (1946), a series of gloomy contemporary portraits of the period from 1934 to 1944. More recent novels include *La Neige et la fleur* (1952) and *Le Chiffre de nos jours* (1954).

chanson courtoise: A form of poetry of Provençal origin, popular during the Middle Ages, in which the poet expresses his own feelings, which are often delicate, in matters of courtly love.

chanson de geste: A French national epic poem which tells of the heroic deeds of medieval knights. The *Chanson de Roland* (q.v.) is one of the oldest. The epic knight shows strength, zeal, valor, pride, courage, generosity and fights for his king

and in defence of the church. Most epic poems have some historical basis, but in general they are pseudo-history. They were written in strophes or laisses, usually in lines of ten syllables and in assonance, and were sung to the accompaniment of the *vielle,* generally a three-string musical instrument. In the thirteenth and fourteenth century, they are written in rhyme, and prose versions appear in the fifteenth century.

Jessie Crosland, *The Old French Epic,* 1951; Martin de Riquer, *Los cantares de gesta franceses,* 1952.

CHANSON DE GESTE, ORIGINS OF:
Gaston Paris (q.v.) in his *Histoire Poétique de Charlemagne* (1865), convinced that French epic themes existed some three centuries before the manuscript form, consolidated various theories prevalent at the beginning of the nineteenth century. These theories, briefly, stated that after great battles, lyric poems or cantilenæ arose and were sung by soldiers and jongleurs (q.v.) and later on became the bases of the French chansons de geste as we know them. Léon Gautier in the *Epopées Françaises* (1878-1894) adopted this theory maintaining, in addition, that the cantilenæ were composed in German. Pio Rajna in *Le Origini dell'epopea francese* (1884) supported this belief in the Germanic origin of the French epic. Paul Meyer and Voretzsch insisted on a prose tradition rather than a poetic tradition. Godefroy Kurth in the *Histoire Poétique des Mérovingiens* (1893) reconstructed along these lines a Frankish epic of the sixth century. Philip A. Becker, opposing this view, argued that chronicles were the bases of the chansons de geste and that the French epic poems did not exist before the time of their manuscript appearance. Joseph Bédier (q.v.) in the *Légendes Épiques* (3rd ed. 1926-29), published

at the beginning of the twentieth century, developed Becker's thesis in four volumes based on the documents available. Briefly this is his contention:

Saints' and martyrs' relics gained for the monastery and city that harbored them protection and prestige. The local clergy permitted and encouraged the singing of saints' lives, since this brought fame to the shrine and material advantages. The chansons de geste, with their heroes replacing the saints, were an extension of the saints' lives. In a number of monasteries are found relics of well-known heroes, and these monasteries were situated for the most part on roads frequented by pilgrims, like Saint Jacques de Compostella in Galicia. Local legends were attached to these relics. Poets gave form to the legend, the jongleur sang the poem and the monastery encouraged this, for the latter was the custodian and often the inventor of epic tradition. In order to attract pilgrims to the shrine monks collaborated with the jongleur in the development of the epic poem. This exploitation and collaboration resulted in mutual advantage to both. The pilgrim listened to the jongleur sing the chansons de geste on his vielle, the monastery attracted pilgrims who remembered and transmitted them. It was a form of advertising. Formed in the bosom of the church and taking as their theme chivalrous exploits, the chansons de geste bear witness to the strong link existing between the church and feudalism. Thus, said Bédier, these epic poems were born in the eleventh century, written down in the twelfth, and represent the spirit, customs and psychology of those centuries. They are not to be explained by the cantilenæ. First, he said, came the sanctuaries and the routes, then the poems.

Joseph Bédier's epoch-making study has, since its publication, received much criticism as well as support. Emile Mireaux believes that a first epic poem (the *Chanson de Roland;* q.v.) was composed about the year one thousand and written for the glory of the dying Carolingian dynasty, thus making the *Roland* a poem of lineage. This theory of lineage has been accepted by the historians Ferdinand Lot and Robert Fawtier. Edmond Faral, an adherent of the Bédier theory, emphasizes the classical and clerical tradition of the chansons de geste. Maurice Wilmotte likewise points out the literary Latin tradition. Albert Pauphilet sees in Charlemagne the reincarnation of the war against the Moslems.

Raoul Mortier (*La Chanson de Roland. Essai d'interprétation du problème des origines,* 1939) has traced in detail all theories concerning the origins of the chansons de geste; Itala Siciliano (*Les Origines des chansons de geste,* 1951) has evaluated them critically. At present Bédier's remarkable interpretation still stands and will endure. However, legendary traditions based on historical fact gave rise to popular songs which in turn may have inspired the first short epic poems which developed into the chansons de geste under the inspiration of poets. It is likely that the date of composition of the first epics was around the year one thousand. Pierre le Gentil (*La Chanson de Roland,* 1955) has summarized in very convenient form in Chapter V the history of the question and weighed the evidence. At the back of this excellent little book is found a most useful bibliography on the question. Martin de Riquer (*Los cantares de gesta franceses,* 1952) gives convenient résumés of the chansons de geste.

PAULINE TAYLOR

chanson de mal mariée: A form of lyric poetry (q.v.) in the Middle Ages in which the unhappily married woman sings of her sadness.

Chanson de Roland: Oldest extant and most celebrated of the *chansons de geste* (q.v.), it is the great French national epic (*c.* 1100). Of uncertain authorship, this poem, based on historical fact idealized by the poet's imagination, relates the destruction of Charlemagne's rearguard, including Roland, as it was crossing the Pyrenees after its victorious expedition in Spain. Caught in the narrow pass of Roncevaux, the French were massacred by the Saracens. The sentiments that inspire the actions of Roland, Olivier and Turpin, the heroes of this battle, are those of loyalty to Charlemagne, their feudal lord, and religious zeal against the infidel. The sole manuscript of the oldest version extant is now in the Bodleian Library at Oxford. *La Chanson de Roland publiée d'après le manuscrit d'Oxford et traduite* par Joseph Bédier, 1921.

chanson de toile: A narrative song with a refrain that women would sing while weaving or spinning and which was popular during the Middle Ages. *Belle Doette* is a good example. See *Lyric Poetry.*

chant royal: A fixed form of lyric poetry, popular in the fourteenth century, consisting of five stanzas of eleven lines each, generally in decasyllabic verse, and ending with an *envoi* (cf. *ballade*) of five lines. Hence it is a more complicated form of the *ballade*, with more difficult rhymes.

Chants de Maldoror, Les (*p.* 1890): See *Lautréamont.*

Chants du crépuscule, Les (1835): See *Hugo.*

Chapeau de Paille d'Italie, Le (1851): See *Labiche.*

Chapelain, Jean: (1595-1674) As Richelieu's minister of letters, this Parisian-born critic and poet was, from its very inception, the guiding spirit of the *Académie Française* (q.v.). Most influential, as critic, in the formation of classical theories and doctrine (cf. *Classicism*), he edited, at the request of Richelieu, the *Sentiments de l'Académie sur le Cid* (1638) (cf. *Querelle du Cid*). He accomplished, through this document, the definite triumph of the rule of unities (q.v.) in tragedy (q.v.). His influence on classical poetry, through his criticism, was exercised during the period between Malherbe and Boileau (qq.v.). The latter discredited him, however, mostly because of his *La Pucelle d'Orléans* (1656-57). Although this poem, about Jeanne d'Arc, observed the rules Chapelain himself had set for the epic, it was lacking in interest and bored almost everyone. In 1663, commissioned by Colbert, he drew up a list of writers to be pensioned. G. Collas, *Jean Chapelain*, 1912.

Char, René: (1903-) This poet from the Vaucluse, his birthplace, in the *Midi*, has lived in communion with his native land and with nature. His first tendencies, as can be seen in his collection *Le Marteau sans Maître* (1934), were surrealistic (see *Surrealism*). Later, however, painfully aware of those children who were victims of the Spanish Civil War, he wrote poems with a social and more broadly human theme, as in *Placard pour un Chemin des Écoliers* (1937). Some of his finest poems are *Seuls demeurent* (1945) and *Feuillets d'Hypnos* (1946), which reflect the part he played in the *Résistance* (q.v.). His latest collections, *Le Poème pulvérisé* (1947) and *Fureur et Mystère* (1948), have no longer that element of *engagement* found in his Résistance poetry.

Conscious of the anguish of his fellow men and of their relationship to him, Char teaches the lesson of courage while directing his dream towards a future of justice and liberty. His poetry, however, is difficult, because of his use of elliptical images, of short, dense phrases. Al-

though he has employed free verse, in his more recent work he has used more frequently the form of the prose poem, with almost regular rhythms.
Gilbert Lély, *René Char*, 1947.

Chardonne, Jacques: (pseud. of Jacques Boutelleau): (1884-   ) This novelist, born at Barbézieu (See his *Le Bonheur de Barbézieux*, 1938), was the son of a French father and an American mother. His first novel, *L'Epithalame* (1921), shows how a young couple finds in marriage—through which the secrets of complex personalities are revealed—peace and refuge from a cruel society. His other novels, such as *Eva* (1930) and *Romanesque* (1937), also written in a poetic yet lucid style, deal with the same theme of married love and its conflicts. His outstanding work, *Les Destineés sentimentales* (1934-1936), is a trilogy dealing with the problems of a family.

Charles Demailly (1860): See *Goncourt*.

Charles d'Orléans: (1394-1465) Of royal blood, this poet was the nephew of Charles VI and one of his sons succeeded to the throne of Charles VIII under the name of Louis XII. A good part of his life was filled with misfortune, including his father's assassination and his own imprisonment—after the disastrous battle of Agincourt—in England for a period of 25 years (1415-1440). During this captivity, he composed poems in which he expressed his nostalgia for France or in which he sang of nature or love. When liberated and returned to France, he withdrew to his chateau in Blois, where he established a court for artists and poets. All of his poems, whether they be *rondeaux* (q.v.), *ballades* (q.v.) or *chansons*, are written in a highly polished, graceful and exquisite style; his language is subtle and delicate; his verses are charming and artistic. His *rondeaux*, for which he is particularly noted, include the famous one on the Return of Spring, with the well-known refrain "Le temps a laissé son manteau." Above everything else, however, Charles d'Orléans is a *courtly* poet; his poetry belongs to the thirteenth more than to the fifteenth century. Not a bourgeois, and not writing the kind of poetry that his contemporaries indulged in, he represents a curious anachronism.
Beaufils, *Étude sur la vie et les poésies de Charles d'Orléans*, 1861; P. Champion, *Vie de Ch. d'Orléans*, 1911.

Charles IX (1789): See *Chénier, Marie-Joseph*.

Charron, Pierre: (1541-1603) Theologian, preacher and, above all, friend and disciple of Montaigne (q.v.), he wrote *De la Sagesse* (1601), a philosophical treatise in which he carried the latter's skeptical tendencies to an extreme. His views, which anticipate Descartes (q.v.), represent, in the final analysis, an attempt to find a rational basis for religion and tradition.
J. B. Sabrié, *Pierre Charron*, 1913.

Chartier, Alain: (1385-1429) "Father of French eloquence," as his contemporaries called him, he became secretary to Charles VI and Charles VII. Author of the celebrated "La belle dame sans mercy," his abundant poetic output is marked by sensitivity and occasionally by a real patriotic fervor, as can be seen in his *Le Livre des quatre dames*—a kind of courtly and patriotic *débat* (q.v.) on the battle of Agincourt. His finest prose work is the political *Quadrilogue invectif* (*c.* 1422), filled with violent reproaches, and his *Le Curial*, or the Courtier, is a vigorous satire of the Courts.
P. Champion, *Histoire poétique du XV* siècle*, 1923; E. J. Hoffman, *Alain Chartier; his work and reputation*, 1942.

Chartreuse de Parme, La: Written by Stendhal (q.v.) in 1839, this novel, one of his best, reflects the author's cult of energy, ambition, adventure, and individualism, his pursuit of happiness through love, and his love of Italy, where he himself was to spend several years. If, in addition to these features, the novel gives evidence of a melodramatic plot, it shows, on the other hand, keen observation of political intrigues, penetrating psychological analyses of characters, and sobriety of style. A novel that represents the transition between romanticism and realism, it becomes, in the final analysis, a forerunner of the modern psychological novel.

Set in Italy, it traces the adventures of Fabrice del Dongo from his early youth until his death. Dreaming of glory and love, Fabrice, dazzled by Napoleon's prestige, leaves home to join the latter's army; his ambition to become a real soldier is satisfied when, retreating from Waterloo, where he rode by accident, he kills a Prussian officer. Later, returned to Italy, he meets with many difficulties arising from the politics at Parma; fortunately, these difficulties are settled thanks to his aunt, the beautiful Duchess of Sanseverina, who exerts influence through the powerful Count Mosca, prime minister of Parma. She succeeds in having her nephew sent to the theological seminary in Naples. After three years of studies, Fabrice is appointed alternate for the archbishop; but he very soon becomes involved in a duel, and kills his rival. Imprisoned in Parma, Fabrice is nevertheless happy, for he sees from his window Clélia, the daughter of his jailer, with whom he falls in love and with whom he is able, by means of alphabet cards, to hold long conversations. Thanks to Clélia and to the well-laid plans of his aunt, Fabrice manages to escape from prison, and is acquitted. Later, Fabrice becomes archbishop. When Clélia, who in the meantime had married a rich marchese, dies, Fabrice, saddened, gives up his office and retires to the Charterhouse of Parma where, a year later, he too dies.

Chateaubriand, François René de: (1768-1848) This prose writer, who was to have one of the most important influences on the Romantic movement in France, was born in Saint-Malo, Brittany, of a noble but not wealthy family. Of a melancholy bent, made progressively more so by a stern and pessimistic father and a sick and superstitious mother, he preferred to spend most of his early childhood and young manhood in the sole company of his sister Lucile, whose character was much like his; he indulged much in revery as he wandered along the bleak shores of his native town or in the forest of Combourg. His longing for travel and adventure was satisfied when, in 1791, he sailed for America; here he sojourned several months (July-December), in the course of which he visited Baltimore, Philadelphia, Niagara Falls, probably going as far west as Ohio. The news of the arrest of Louis XVI resulted in his quick return to France, where he was to join the army of the émigrés (1792). Wounded at the siege of Thionville, he fled to England seeking refuge (1793). There, for several years, he managed to eke out a miserable existence; there, too, in 1797, he published in London his first serious work, *Essai sur les Révolutions,* in which are suggested many parallels between ancient and modern revolutions, particularly as they relate to the French Revolution, and which reflects basically the attitude common to the eighteenth-century "philosophes." The following year, when he learned of the deaths of one of his sisters and of his mother, his emotional upheaval, under the stress of the double sorrow, caused him to make a sudden return to faith and religion. *Le Génie du Christianisme* (q.v.), which appeared in 1802, two years after his return to France, was to be the expression of this newly found faith. This publication, moreover, dedicated as it was to Napoleon, at a time when the latter aimed at reconciling France with the Catholic Church, explains in large part the diplomatic career assigned Chateaubriand by Napoleon. In 1803 Chateaubriand was appointed secretary of the embassy to Rome, and in 1804 he was made minister plenipotentiary in the Valais. When he learned, however, of the execution of the Duke of Enghien (1804), he refused to serve any longer under Napoleon, and decided instead to travel through Italy, Greece, Constantinople, Palestine and North Africa in preparation for such works as *Les Martyrs* (1809; q.v.) and the *Itinéraire de Paris à Jérusalem* (1811; q.v.), both inspired by his religious faith. With the restoration of the Bourbons under Louis XVIII, in 1814, he resumed his political career, for, as can be seen in his anti-Napoleonic *De Buonaparte et des Bourbons* (1814), his political faith found itself in accord with the principles of legitimate monarchy. He thus became in turn minister to Berlin, ambassador to London, minister of Foreign Affairs (1823-1824), ambassador to Rome. It should be added, however, that when the application of the constitutional principles of legitimate monarchy, which he expressed in *De La Monarchie selon la Charte* (1816), appeared to be betrayed by the ministers of the Restoration, he sometimes found himself in violent opposition. In 1830 he retired, once again, from public life, because he refused to accept the bourgeois monarchy of Louis Philippe. Spending his last years in retirement, he revised his biographical *Mémoires d'outre-tombe* (q.v.) which was to appear posthumously in 1849. Other works

of this latter period include *Essai sur la Littérature anglaise* (1836) and *Vie de Rancé* (1844), a biography of the seventeenth-century abbé de Rancé.

The publications in 1801 of *Atala* (q.v.) and in 1802 of *René* (q.v.), both inspired by his stay in America, are at the base of Romanticism; through them, Chateaubriand set in vogue exoticism, renewed the feeling for Nature, which the Romantic poets were going to treat lyrically and subjectively, and created the perfect type of the romantic hero, who is somber and melancholy. Through his *Génie du Christianisme* he not only broke with the antireligious tradition of the eighteenth century, but also brought back an interest in the Middle Ages, and, with it, the importance of history—as can be testified by his *Les Martyrs*. His style, except when he draws concise portraits, is poetic and musical, lyrical and oratorical, and therefore appealed to the emotions rather than to the mind—an appeal which set in motion not only the final break with the eighteenth century, but also made of him the principal precursor of Romanticism.

P. Moreau, *Chateaubriand*, 1927; H. Gillot, *Chateaubriand: ses idées, son action, son œuvre*, 1934; L. Martin-Chauffier, *Chateaubriand et l'Obsession de la pureté*, 1943; M. Levaillant *et al.*, *Chateaubriand: le Livre du Centenaire*, 1948.

Châtiments, Les (1853): See *Hugo*.

Chatterton (1835): See *Vigny*.

Chemins de la liberté, Les (1945-   ): See *Sartre*.

Chemin des écoliers, Le (1946): See *Aymé, Marcel*.

Chénier, André: (1752-1794) Probably the greatest poet of the eighteenth century, he was born in Constantinople, the son of a French consul and of a mother whose family came from the Greek islands. Brought to France at a very early age, he cultivated, under the influence of his mother, constantly surrounded by her Greek compatriots and Hellenic scholars, a love for ancient Greece. His earliest poems—*Bucoliques* (including *L'Aveugle, Le Mendiant, Le Malade* and *La Jeune Tarentine*)—many of which he composed at the age of sixteen, reflect his cult of antiquity; they contain ancient myths, picturesque tableaux drawn in plastic beauty, and classical phrases, evoking an idyllic Greece. His *Élégies*, first begun when he was nineteen, are inspired by feelings of love; many of these poems, though sincere and melancholy in tone, are pagan, epicurean, and voluptuous in spirit. In *L'Invention* Chénier reveals greater poetic aspirations and a new conception of poetry; the oft-quoted line in this poem—*Sur des pensers nouveaux faisons des vers antiques*—epitomizes his wish to express the new scientific and philosophic ideas of his Age while striving to imitate the ancients. This ideal he projected in the epic *Hermès* (begun in 1783) and *L'Amérique;* these poems, however, which were to have synthesized modern learning, were never completed. His enthusiasm for the new ideas of the Revolution resulted in his declamatory *Ode au Jeu de Paume* (1791). When the excesses of the Revolution no longer coincided with his views of justice, liberty and moderation, however, Chénier was thrown into prison; while there, waiting to be executed, he lashed out indignantly against the revolutionaries in his *Iambes* and wrote his celebrated *Ode à la jeune captive*. The lyrical satire of these closing poems represents a marked contrast with the calm aloofness of his earlier classic verses. The diversity of his poetic forms—idyls, elegies, epistles, epics, odes and iambics—makes it difficult to place him in any one school. Nevertheless, while belonging, through many of his ideas, to the eighteenth century,

he was recognized, thanks to the first collected edition of his poetry published in 1819 by Henri de Latouche, as a kindred spirit by the Romanticists; in these poems they found melancholy, love of nature, satire of a personal character, and, most important, metrical innovations similar to their own. But Chénier's influence is seen best, perhaps, in the Parnassians (q.v.), who imitated his quest for plastic beauty and his use of science as a source of poetry.

E. Faguet, *André Chénier*, 1902; P. Dimoff, *La Vie et l'œuvre d'André Chénier*, 1936.

Chénier, Marie-Joseph: (1764-1811) Younger brother of André Chénier (q.v.), he is known for his *Chant du Départ* (July 14, 1794)—second in importance to the *Marseillaise* (see *Rouget de Lisle*) for its Revolutionary spirit—and for his tragedies. These, including *Charles IX* (1789) —which inaugurated the theater of the Revolution—*Jean Calas* (1791), *Caïus Gracchus* (1792), *Fénelon* (1793) and *Timoléon* (1794), attacked religious fanaticism and appealed for tolerance and liberty; their subjects are inspired by antiquity and French national history. A. Liéby, *Étude sur le théâtre de Marie-Joseph Chénier*, 1901.

Chéri (1920): See *Colette*.

Chevalier à la mode, Le (1687): See *Dancourt*.

Choderlos de Laclos, Pierre Ambroise François: (1741-1803) This author, toward the end of his life a general in Napoleon's armies, owes his literary reputation to *Les Liaisons dangereuses* (1782; q.v.). This epistolary novel, written in a style that is clear and dry, is a psychological portrait of a depraved aristocratic society during the years preceding the French Revolution. The account of the cynical and carefully planned seduction of a young girl and of a married woman of high principles, as a means of revenge sought by diabolical characters, is Machiavellian in its analysis. In many ways, it foreshadows the novels of Stendhal (q.v.). Unlike Rousseau's (q.v.) *Nouvelle Héloise* (1761), love is here depicted without virtue; viewed as a pamphlet against a depraved nobility, this novel can be regarded as the work of a moralist. In addition to his works on military strategy, Laclos wrote *De L'Education des femmes* (p. 1903).

E. Dard, *Le Général Choderlos de Laclos*, 1905; F. Caussy, *Laclos*, 1905.

Chouans, Les (1829): See *Balzac*.

Chrétien de Troyes: (1135?-1190?) Although little is known of his life, he was one of the most celebrated poets of the Middle Ages in France. For more than twenty-five years he moved within the aristocratic circles of the Court of Marie of Champagne, daughter of Eléonore of Aquitaine. In addition to his translations from Ovid and a lost poem on King Mark and Isolt (See *Tristan et Iseut*), he wrote five Celtic romances or *romans bretons* (q.v.) which center more or less about the court of Arthur (q.v.), including *Erec et Enide*, *Lancelot* or *Le Conte de la charrette* (qq.v.), *Yvain* or *Le chevalier au lion* and *Perceval* (q.v.), the last of which, incomplete, was several times imitated and continued by others, especially by the German poet Wolfram of Eschenbach (d. 1230). Full of imagination, these poems, in contrast with the *chansons de geste* (q.v.), were primarily concerned with courtly love (q.v.) and with gallantry.

G. Cohen, *Un grand romancier d'amour et d'aventure au XII* siècle, Chrétien de Troyes et son œuvre*, 1931; R. S. Loomis, *Arthurian Tradition and Chrétien de Troyes*, 1949; J. Marx, *La Légende Arthurienne et le Graal*, 1952.

Christianisme dévoilé, Le (1767): See *Holbach*.

Christine de Pisan: (1365-1431?) Born in Venice, this highly educated woman spent most of her life in France, a life marked by various turns of fortune. Shortly after the battle of Agincourt she died after celebrating in song Joan of Arc, whose triumph she had lived to see. Besides her early lyrics and the poems in which she defended her sex against the attack of Jean de Meung (cf. *Roman de la Rose*), she left three poems of a meditative nature and a prose life of Charles V entitled *Livre des faits et bonnes mœurs du roi Charles V*. All her works, with the exception of the last, have a marked personal or autobiographical touch. Among the shorter lyrics, her *ballades* (q.v.) are among the best.

Marie-Josephe Pinet, *Christine de Pisan, étude biographique et littéraire*, 1927.

Chronique des Pasquier, La (1933-1945): See *Duhamel*.

Chronique du règne de Charles IX, La (1829): See *Mérimée*.

Chroniques (*c.* 1373-1400): See *Froissart*.

Chute, La (1956): See *Camus, Albert*.

Chute d'un ange, La (1838): See *Lamartine*.

Cid, Le: This very popular tragicomedy (1636 or 1637) by Corneille (q.v.), a drama of love and honor (*gloire*) in five acts and in alexandrine verse, inaugurated French classical tragedy. Set in Seville, southern Spain, it is based on the Spanish *Las Mocedades del Cid* (1621) by Guillén de Castro. It depicts the inner conflicts of Rodrigue and Chimène, two young lovers who are about to be married, but who, because of a quarrel between their fathers, must choose between their love and honor. Don Gormas, Chimène's father, has slapped Don Diègue, the father of Rodrigue, because Don Diègue, and not he, has been chosen by the King to be the preceptor of the crown prince. Too weak to avenge his insult, Don Gormas calls upon his son to save his honor and that of the family. Rationalizing, in a dramatic monologue, a decision he has already instinctively made, Rodrigue hearkens to his father; to safeguard his *gloire*, without which he would be unworthy of Chimène's love, he challenges the latter's father to a duel and kills him. Now, Chimène, who undergoes the same kind of conflict previously experienced by Rodrigue and who, like him, cannot love without honor, demands that the murderer of her father suffer punishment. Only after Rodrigue has repulsed the Moors and been the victor in a trial by combat—in accordance with the code of honor of the time and the consent of the King—with Don Sanche, the champion of Chimène, is the possible planned marriage agreed to. Accepting the final judgment of the King, Chimène leaves the impression that, in time, she will wed Rodrigue. Cf. *Querelle du Cid*.

CINEMA: The first public showing of motion pictures in France was given on December 28, 1895. It was made up of shorts produced by Louis Lumière (1864-1948). The first production company in the world (The "Star-Film") was founded by a Frenchman, Georges Melies (1861-1938), who had also constructed the first studio in 1896. A true poet of the motion picture, his ideas were widely copied by Edison. Today, Melies films (*Le Cabinet de Mephistophélès*, 1897; *Le Voyage dans la Lune*, 1902; *Les Aventures du Baron de Munchausen*, 1911, etc.) are considered priceless early motion pictures.

Since the time of these pioneers, the French cinema has continued to develop on both economic and artistic levels. And today France produces about a hundred full-length motion pictures a year, has a graduate school ("l'Institut des Hautes Études Cinématographiques"

or I.D.H.E.C.) devoted to the creation of technicians and directors, a motion picture museum ("la Cinémathèque Française"), innumerable film clubs and many magazines which specialize in the art and technique of the motion picture.

The lasting works of the French cinema during the period of the silent films were those of René Clair (1898-   ): *Un Chapeau de Paille d'Italie* (1927), *Entr'acte* (1924); Marcel L'Herbier: *L'Inhumaine* (1923), *L'Argent* (1924); and Abel Gance (the French Cecil B. de Mille): *La Roue* (1921), *Napoléon* (1926). When the "talkies" came into being, these directors went on with their work. Today, René Clair is still the great master of the French cinema. All his films, from *Sous les Toits de Paris* (1931) to *Les Grandes Manœuvres* (1955), are characterized by technical perfection and a mixture of humor, tenderness, and ingenuous cruelty which place them in the great French comic tradition of Molière, Marivaux and Musset (qq.v.). Of almost equal importance, Jean Renoir (1894-   ), more turbulent and spontaneous, represents the naturalist tradition with its zest, violence, and generosity in *La Chienne* (1931), *La Grande Illusion* (1937), *French Cancan* (1954). These directors have also achieved international fame: Jacques Feyder (*La Kermesse héroïque*, 1935); Marcel Carne (*Quai des Brumes*, 1938; *Les Enfants du Paradis*, 1945); and more recently: Jacques Becker (*Goupi Mains-Rouges*, *Casque d'Or*, *Touchez pas au Grisbi*); René Clément (*La Bataille du Rail, Monsieur Ripois, Gervaise*); Robert Bresson (*Les Anges du Péché, Les Dames du Bois de Boulogne*); Henri Georges Clouzot (*Le Salaire de la Peur, Diabolique*), and Claude Autant-Lara (*Le Diable au Corps, Le Blé en herbe*).

As the French public, critics and

motion picture world consider the cinema a true art, French productions are often characterized by a freedom and a search for personal expression only surpassed by the Swedish cinema.

In productions of the 1930's, the naturalist—even "populist"—style predominated. The 1940's brought about a revival of poetic and fanciful films: Jean Cocteau and Delannoy's *Eternel Retour*, Marcel Carné and Jacques Prévert's *Les Visiteurs du Soir*. Under the combined influence of the American and neo-realistic Italian cinema, the 1950's are particularly marked by the rise of the "gangster film" and by a search for an expression of everyday realism. France also produces historic films, frequently in conjunction with Italian companies, and light comedies in which Gallic humor is combined with American "gags." The production of animated cartoons is only slight and appears in the forms of publicity strips and in some shorts and average length films—the most famous of which are produced by Paul Grimault, often with Jacques Prévert's scenarios.

French literature and the cinema have always been closely related and are becoming increasingly so. In fact, most of the great French novels have been adapted to the screen: the works of Victor Hugo, Stendhal, Balzac, Flaubert, Zola, Maupassant and Daudet (qq.v.) have been more or less successfully transposed. *Nana* and *La Bête humaine* by Jean Renoir, *Gervaise* (*L'Assommoir*) by René Clément, and *Le Rouge et le Noir* by Claude Autant-Lara, are among the better adaptations. And contemporary writers with few exceptions (Georges Duhamel, q.v., for instance) are interested in this new means of expression. Some were satisfied to supervise the adaptation of their own works by others: André Gide (q.v.) and *La Symphonie pastorale*, Colette (q.v.) and *Gigi*, for example. Others have written directly for the cinema: Jules Romains (*Donogoo-Tonka*), Jean Giraudoux (*Les Anges du Péché*), Jean-Paul Sartre (*Les Jeux sont Faits*), Jean Anouilh (*Pattes Blanches*), François Mauriac (*Le Pain Vivant;* qq.v.). Still others have devoted part of their careers to activities exclusively in the motion picture field: Jacques Prévert, Jean Cocteau (who as early as 1932 produced *Le Sang d'un Poète*), Marcel Pagnol (*Marius, Fanny, Cesar* and the adaptations of Jean Giono's novels and tales; qq.v.).

The French cinema has had a profound influence on literary techniques as well: film "cutting" is reflected in the works of novelists as different as Marcel Aymé and André Malraux (qq.v.). (Malraux's film, *L'Espoir,* was almost contemporaneous with his novel.) Moreover, many literary works reveal the motion picture myth and vision that have penetrated the modern consciousness: the fantasies of René Barjavel and Marcel Aymé, and Raymond Queneau's (q.v.) *Loin de Rueil,* for example.

Maurice Bardèche et Robert Brasillach, *Histoire du Cinéma,* 1953; Pierre Leprohon, *Cinquante ans de cinéma français 1895-1945,* 1954; Nicole Védrès, *Images du Cinéma français,* 1956.

JACQUES GUICHARNAUD

Cinna: Written by Corneille (1640-1641; q.v.), this classical play, sometimes described as a tragic, sometimes as a heroic, masterpiece, is based on the chapter *De Clementia* by Seneca, which deals with the clemency of Emperor Augustus. Urged on by Emilie, the daughter of Toranius, who promises to marry him if he will kill the Emperor Auguste (Augustus), who has put her father to death, Cinna, a trusted friend of Auguste, plots against the life of the Emperor. In this conspiracy, he is aided by Maxime

Plate 3. Albert Camus

Plate 4. Paul Claudel

(Maximus), another trusted friend of Auguste, who also loves Emilie. Cinna is shaken, however, by a moral conflict; he wavers between his love for Emilie and his admiration and respect for the Emperor, who has shown him much confidence. When Cinna, after some hesitation, begins to put his plot into operation, Maxime, jealous of his rival in love, and fearful of the possibility that the latter's plan may succeed, has him denounced before the Emperor. At the discovery of the conspiracy, the latter, in a celebrated monologue, deliberates upon the course of action he must take. In the last two acts, psychologically the most revealing and interesting, the Emperor is seen struggling against his natural inclination to punish the culprits. Thanks to a sublime heroic effort, he overcomes his instincts and shows clemency to the conspirators. The action in this tragedy, as can be seen from the summary, is simpler and more concentrated than in *Le Cid* and *Horace* (qq.v.).

Cinq Mars (1826): See *Vigny*.

Civilisation (1918): See *Duhamel*.

Civilisés, Les (1905): See *Farrère, Claude*.

CLASSICISM: The numerous problems connected with the understanding of French classicism are rendered particularly confused by the indiscriminate way in which the word classicism is used to refer to more than one notion or phenomenon. One may, for instance, call classicism the esthetic tendency, originally illustrated by works of art belonging to Greco-Roman antiquity. Far from being, however, historically or geographically limited, this particular variety of classicism may justifiably be detected anywhere and at any time. One may, therefore, also talk about the classicism of Aristotle or Virgil, of Prosper Mérimée or Paul Valéry (qq.v.), of Dr. Johnson or T. S. Eliot, or again of Ingres or David, of Couperin or Ravel, of the Palace of Versailles or the Paris Opera House. No attempt will be made here toward a definition of this very broad notion. Let us merely remark that the features common to these works and artists—if they exist—would tend to define classicism as one of the several esthetic tendencies existing permanently in man. When these hypothetical features are predominant in the artistic output of a given period of the history of a given national culture, one speaks of a classical period. Under the reign of Augustus, for instance, there was a classical Roman period. Likewise under the reigns of Louis XIII and Louis XIV, there was a classical French period.

Literary history shows that this period was really made up of two successive and distinct moments. First came a group of literary critics, philologists, theorists, and scholars who, roughly between 1625 and 1655, collected ideas borrowed from various sources and, more particularly, from Italian and Flemish commentators of Aristotle's *Poetics,* and put them together in a more or less coherent body of criticism. This doctrine, mostly speculative at this stage, contained dogmas, which we shall enumerate later on, and which eventually earned it the qualification of classical. The early years of the Académie Française (founded in 1634-35; q.v.) coincide with the active and productive period of these classical theorists, the best known of whom are Chapelain, Balzac, Vaugelas and Ménage (qq.v.).

Then followed in their wake, roughly between 1665 and 1685, a group of creative writers whose masterpieces came out in rapid succession and seemed to illustrate many of the critical pronouncements of the theorists who preceded them: 1665, La Rochefoucauld's *Maximes;* 1666, Molière's *Misan-*

thrope, and Boileau's first *Satires;* 1667, Racine's *Andromaque;* 1668, La Fontaine's first *Fables;* 1669, Bossuet's *Oraison funèbre d'Henriette de France;* 1670, Pascal's *Pensées* (qq.v.), etc. These and some others (Corneille, La Bruyère, qq.v.; etc.) are the great French classical writers, *les grands classiques.* Their period of activity is, properly speaking, the classical period.

In recent years, some aestheticians and literary historians, dissatisfied with the confusion inherent in the word "classicism," have attempted, as had done before them the historians of music and of the plastic arts, to affix more discerning labels on the different notions and events which, until then, had gone by that name. Some have suggested distinguishing the literary works once labeled "irregular" of the Louis XIII era, from those more "regular" of the Louis XIV era, by calling the first baroque (q.v.) and restricting to the second the term classical. Others again preferred to call the second baroque, and the first manneristic. Numerous arguments, largely drawn from analogies with the other arts and with the other contemporary European cultures, have been brought forth to defend these new conflicting vocabularies. Until the dispute is settled it seems wise to retain the traditional terminology and, in spite of the obvious looseness of the word, to keep referring to this particular event in the history of French letters as classicism.

In fact, the word itself is easily justified by recalling that it obviously refers to a body of literary works deemed worthy of being read and studied in the classroom. The French classics are those writers who, rightly or not, have been presented, at an early date and uninterruptedly since, to the admiration of French school children. Louison, the young daughter of

Molière's Imaginary Invalid, offered to recite to her angry father one of La Fontaine's fables which had then been in print for less than five years.

The fact that these works are still thought well adapted to classroom use is in itself indicative of two very important features of the French classics: their immediate intelligibility, and their universality or universal applicability. They are easy writers to understand, in part because they were bequeathed a remarkably adequate language in which to express themselves. Rich, mature and versatile, thanks to the linguistic experiments of the adventurous Renaissance writers, the French language (q.v.) had recently been almost definitively regulated and fixed by the philological efforts of the early 17th century purists. Now, if the classical writers chose to cast this language in a style famous for its clarity and simplicity, this was due in part to another historical factor. For the recent formation of a fairly broad and diversified public of non-scholars, interested in a wide range of subjects in which it was in no way specialized, had oriented writers toward an artistic and clear presentation of matters which had previously needed no such care, since they had been presented almost exclusively to specialists. As for the universal applicability of classical works, it is due to the writers' emphasis on general qualities which are likely to be common to all men and to all times. It is, therefore, the sign of a tendency in classicism away from the particular, the concrete and the transitory, toward the general, the abstract and the eternal, in other words toward the highest and the most timeless of human problems. At this stage, French classicism can therefore be tentatively defined as an intellectualistic humanism.

The name classicism can be

further explained by the following observation. Long before the Renaissance, and for a long time after, the classical literary works most often studied in the schools had been certain masterpieces of Greek and Roman antiquity carefully selected for their intelligibility and universal applicability. Now the French classics sought to resemble the original classics at least in that they often chose, with more or less sincere modesty and humility, to present themselves to the public as mere disciples and imitators of certain writers of classical antiquity.

This in itself was no novelty: many poets of the 16th and early 17th centuries, such as Ronsard and Malherbe (qq.v.), to name only the best known, had actually and openly endeavored to emulate Pindar, Horace and a few other ancient poets. Clearly there are in their works unmistakable classical features. Yet, in the times of Ronsard or Malherbe several other aesthetic tendencies coexisted, which more often than not oriented literature in directions other than classical. During the classical period, however, the outward docility to the principle of imitation was but an additional force pulling in the same general direction as the others.

This principle of imitation, however, is indicative of two more essential features of French classicism: impersonality and formalism or conformity to rules. The first is closely connected with a very particular conception of literary originality which, far from being incompatible with imitation, is on the contrary often dependent on it. It implies further—and this characteristic is one which permits perhaps the sharpest differentiation between classicism and romanticism (q.v.)— that classical writers were to avoid, so far as feasible, giving the impression that they were in any way writing about themselves, their lives,

experiences, or ideas. As for the second feature—conformity to rules —it is in fact directly related to the first one, since the principle of literary imitation is clearly acceptable only when the imitable and imitated masterpiece reveals some esthetic qualities of wide application and validity which, in turn, can fairly safely be set up as universal rules.

This inductive process of rule making implied in extreme cases the belief in the existence of absolute values in matters pertaining to taste and art. Such a belief is apparent in the pronouncements of some of the classical theorists. As for the artists themselves, they were understandably reluctant to admit such a dogmatic view. Pascal, for instance, though assuming that there were universal principles governing *l'art d'agréer,* declared himself unable to unearth and formulate them. La Bruyère, on the other hand, strongly asserted the existence of absolutely good and bad taste and went on saying that, in the evolution of art forms, there is a point of perfection which can be convincingly recognized. This extreme position explains how and why one of the most unfortunate by-products of French classicism was a notion that literary art had, with the French classics, reached its apex, and, therefore, that the chief mission of their successors was to keep it at a standstill by means of complying blindly and automatically with the rules of composition which could be abstracted from the study of classical masterpieces. This crippling notion of literature prevailed in some quarters until the beginning of the 19th century.

This, in turn, brings us back to the distinction already mentioned between the classical theorists and the classical writers. The first, mostly concerned with doctrines, had completed by the middle of the 17th century the building up of their corpus of literary dogmas. The belief that rules were justifiable and even necessary, coupled with the persuasion that ancient literatures had provided mankind with universally valid literary models, led these theorists to differentiate and classify in a rigorous manner the various literary genres (epic, tragedy, lyrical poetry, etc.), within each of which a specific set of rules were to apply —for instance, that of the unities (q.v.) in tragedy (q.v.). On the general rules, which were to govern indifferently all the genres of literary composition, a fairly universal agreement was soon reached among the theorists: beyond complying with the rules of imitation and of genre distinction, writers were told to be in their works respectful of reason, naturalness, propriety (bienséances; q.v.), and morality. As soon, however, as the theorists began proclaiming more specific rules governing the actual creation of individual literary works, they became hopelessly lost in a maze of dissensions, feuds, quarrels, and petty disputes. These controversial and debated rules retained, however, from their theoretical, scholarly and sometimes pedantic origin, lasting prestige for subsequent critics, theorists, historians and teachers of literature. They cast a long shadow on a large segment—the most formal, dated and inane—of the literary output of the 18th century. They also bear the heaviest burden of responsibility for the disrepute in which French classicism was eventually to fall during the romantic age, and in which it is still held in some quarters in and outside France.

Yet, these very rules were never wholeheartedly accepted nor granted prime importance by the classical writers. All of them (Corneille, Pascal, La Fontaine, Molière, Racine, Boileau, etc.), to a man, invariably claimed that the real rule,

the rule of rules, was for the writer to insure the enjoyment of his public. The goal toward which they all consistently and avowedly strove was expressed by the word *plaire*. They went as far as to substitute this pragmatic notion for the theoretical principle of the moral utility of literature, a principle staunchly upheld by the theorists, but with which the writers were in basic disagreement. It is true that they were often compelled for strategic reasons to pay lip service to the principle of morality. This was especially true in the case of dramatic literature. Sharply attacked by religious thinkers, playwrights sought a shield in Aristotle's mysterious pronouncements about the *catharsis*, with which they were led to struggle halfheartedly and uncomprehendingly. The pleasure of the public was of course of peculiarly great importance to the playwrights, but it seems to have been judged just as cogent by writers specializing in genres other than the drama, including Christian apologetics, as is evidenced by Pascal's reflections on *l'art d'agréer*.

The consequence of this was that the public, whose taste was thus the all-important criterium, became a matter of unprecedented concern for the writers. Historical factors, which need not be discussed here, had brought about the formation of a small but sufficiently enlightened general public (*la ville et la cour*) entirely worthy of the masterpieces which were submitted to its judgment. This affords an obvious explanation for the outward analogies one can detect between the various works of art produced during this era, in literature as well as in architecture, painting, music, landscaping, etc. There is a family likeness among them, not because of their common origin, but because of their common destination. The temptation to draw too rigorous parallels between the various forms of art is, therefore, to be resisted, for it would, among other things, be a nonsensical anachronism to ascribe to artists of the classical age that feeling of solidarity which our contemporaries have inherited from the artists of the romantic age.

The function of the public as supreme and final judge of the ultimate value of literary works explains how and why the rule which was most universally accepted and respected by the classical writers, in the fields of both literary forms and ideology, was that of propriety (*les bienséances*). In general terms it meant that the public was not to be puzzled, offended or shocked by the works of literature composed for its enjoyment. It was not until later that shock was raised to the level of an enjoyable experience. This explains, for instance, how the classical writers respected the distinction of literary genres as a mere pragmatic consequence of *l'art de plaire,* rather than as an absolute dogma, as the earlier theorists had presented it. This also explains the stylistic efforts made by classical writers to express themselves so clearly and straightforwardly as to be immediately intelligible, even if admittedly the deeper sense of some of their works could be probed and sensed only through prolonged and less pleasant study.

On the level of ideology, the *bienséances* forbade shocking the readers or spectators by questioning those institutional or dogmatic forms of their world which by nature were for them beyond questioning. This clearly reveals a connection between the stability of classical art and that of the established society in which it throve. Between the upheaval and aftermath of the religious wars on the one hand, and the premonitory pangs of the *crise de conscience* on the other,

French society accepted for some years the coercion and restrictions which insured its stability. The same illusion, however, was to blind those later literary critics who believed that literature could be indefinitely kept in the state of stable balance wherein resided perfection, and those social and political thinkers who, satisfied that Louis XIV and Colbert had given France a perfect government, felt that the golden rule in politics was to keep things exactly as they were. One may even push the parallel further and wonder whether the interval of thirty years or so, which separated the theorists of classicism and the artists, would not have been appreciably shorter if the Fronde sedition and the troubled years of the Regency of Louis XIV had not for some time jeopardized the stability and even the existence of the indispensable and all-important literary public.

On the ideological level the *bienséances* may seem to have sentenced writers to an abject conformism on all matters related to the taboo domains of religion and politics. That it was not so is abundantly evidenced by the fact that there never was a time when religious controversies were more lively and more openly publicized, than in the period which witnessed the growth and downfall of Port-Royal (q.v.), the struggle of Molière and the *cabale des dévots*, the quarrel over Quietism (q.v.), the proclamation of the freedom of the Gallican Church, and the fight of Bossuet (q.v.) against Protestant thinkers, to recall only a few historical events.

More particularly, the *bienséances* may well have silenced many demands for reforms, but they never implied any amount of conformism on the part of the writers on the more ageless problems, those that affect and confront mankind in

53

general, and transcend the ephemeral outward forms of Church and State. In fact the same classical writers, who may well appear to have been timid in creating and experimenting with new means of literary expression, never felt it necessary to restrain their extreme boldness when it came to investigating old and new territories in the fields of morals and of the knowledge of man. Indeed they were pioneers. After the debate on divine grace which divided religious thinkers around 1650, came quite logically the debate on human nature, in which all of the classical writers had their say. Complete freedom prevailed in this debate, as well as in the investigations which were conducted around it. The same public taste, which restricted classical writers to certain subjects—chiefly Man—permitted and encouraged a greater depth in the treatment of these subjects. One might rightly argue that Corneille, La Rochefoucauld, Pascal, Molière, Bossuet, Racine, La Fontaine, La Bruyère, etc., probed deeper than ever before into the mysteries of the human heart, and discovered or rediscovered in the process some shocking truths, which never had to be censored on account of the *bienséances*.

Bye and bye, these writers' disciples and followers, whose sequence is well nigh an endless one, chose to retain from classicism only the restrictions imposed by the rules. Without being themselves endowed with the genius for discovery, nor with their predecessors' talent for charming the public, they quite logically produced a vast and hollow body of pseudo-classical literature, of which the shell looked classical only because of passive obedience to rules now transformed into arbitrary and mechanical devices. Many of the now forgotten literary figures of the 18th century, and some of the best-known ones—including Vol-

taire (q.v.) for a large bulk of his works—belong to this group. They seemingly failed to see that, along with classical forms, there were also classical fields of investigation, that, if a literary form may under certain circumstances be considered as stable, an investigation cannot ever be so, and finally that, in the field of art, as in that of economics, stability means stagnation.

The elements which entered into the notion of French classicism are so numerous and so diversified that one may well claim that French classicism ought to be considered only as an ideal, as a dream. No one writer was ever a pure classic. No one masterpiece was ever exclusively classical. A large number of thoroughly non-classical writers—some of them quite talented—always coexisted with their more classical brethren, who, for a time, happened to outrank them by their greatness and their genius.

Nevertheless, the relatively brief period which came closest to fulfilling this ideal, which gave the clearest, the most faithful and the highest picture of what the classical dream was, remains, to say the least, a worthy subject of study and attention for those who sit in today's classrooms. In the heart of many French writers and readers who knew it and lost it, and in the heart of many non-French writers and readers, who had a taste of it from behind the borders of space and time, the French classical moment remains a source of nostalgia not entirely unlike that for the Garden of Eden.

René Bray, *La Formation de la doctrine classique en France*, 1927; "L'esthétique classique," *Revue des Cours et Conférences*, 1929; J. E. Fidao-Justiniani, *Discours sur la raison classique*, 1937; Daniel Mornet, *Histoire de la littérature française classique (1660-1700)*, 1940; Henri Peyre, *Le Classicisme fran-*

çais, 1942; Gonzague de Reynold, *XVIIe siècle; le classicisme et le baroque*, 1944; Georges Mongrédien, *La Vie littéraire au XVIIe siècle*, 1947; Henri Busson, *La Religion des classiques*, 1948; Paul Bénichou, *Morales du Grand Siècle*, 1948; E. B. O. Borgerhoff, *The Freedom of French Classicism*, 1950.

GEORGES MAY

Claudel, Paul: (1868-1955) This poet, dramatist, and essayist, who comes from the old province of Champagne, travelled as consul, minister, or ambassador (1893-1934) to many corners of the globe—the United States, South America, China, Japan, Italy, Germany, and Belgium. Influenced by Rimbaud (q.v.) and his symbolistic (see *Symbolism*) conception of the universe, as well as by Catholicism, which he discovered on Christmas night, 1886, his work reflects the Christian drama and spirit. His lyrical poetry, an inspired creation and act of faith, is religious in tone and theme; all that exists in the world, man, animal, plant or mineral, is seen as an harmonious whole, and is admired as the handiwork of God. His principal collections are *Cinq Grandes Odes* (1910), *La Cantate à trois voix* (1913), and *Poèmes et Paroles pendant la guerre de Trente ans* (1945).

In his plays as well as in his lyrical poetry Claudel made use of the "verset," which resembles a kind of scanned prose, written in accordance with the natural rhythm of breathing. It contains occasional alliteration and assonance without, however, being sustained by rhyme. His plays, written in this biblical verse—much like a hymn or prayer —were first written at a time when a reaction set in against the Naturalistic drama. In these plays, moreover, Claudel, who had much knowledge of Greek and Latin sacred and profane literature as well as of the Bible, borrows from all dramatic sources—primitive Greek tragedies,

mysteries (see *mystères*) of the Middle Ages, and Spanish religious dramas. Among his earlier plays are *Tête d'Or* (1889), *La Ville* (1890), *L'Échange* (1893)—which reflect the influences of Symbolism and the author's conviction of man's despair without Grace—and *Partage de Midi* (1906), which presents the conflict between human passion and divine love. A dramatic trilogy— *L'Otage* (1911), *Le Pain dur* (1918), and *Le Père humilié* (1920)—deals with the history of the church in France during the nineteenth century. His two masterpieces, however, are *L'Annonce faite à Marie* (1912)—which in its fifteenth century setting evokes the conflict between human love and heavenly aspirations—and *Le Soulier de Satin* (1930), an unusually long play, in four cycles—a summation of the author's poetic and dramatic life— that stresses, through the life and achievements of a Spanish conquistador, the sacrifice of love and happiness for the reward of God's grace. The latter play, incidentally, was first produced in 1943 by Jean Louis Barrault (q.v.).

His prose publications, dealing essentially with metaphysics and aesthetics, include *Art poétique* (1906), and *Positions et propositions* (1928-1934).

J. de Tonquédec, *L'Œuvre de Claudel*, 1927; J. Madaule, *Le Génie de Paul Claudel*, 1933; Claudine Chonez, *Introduction à Paul Claudel*, 1947.

Clélie, Histoire romaine (1654-1661): See *Scudéry, Madeleine de.*

Cléopâtre (1552): See *Jodelle.*

Cléopâtre (1647-1658): See *La Calprenède.*

Cloches de Bâle, Les (1934): See *Aragon.*

Clovis (1657): See *Desmarets de Saint-Sorlin.*

Cocteau, Jean: (1892-   ) Versatility characterizes this prolific writer, who has distinguished himself in poetry, the theater, the novel, and the essay. His contributions to the cinema, his talent as an illustrator, his interest in music, ballet and the mime, his acquaintances with stage designers, artists, musicians and writers, including Picasso, Chirico, Radiguet (q.v.), the "Groupe des Six" (Georges Auric, Louis Durey, Arthur Honegger, Darius Milhaud, Francis Poulenc, Germaine Tailleferre), Stravinsky, Christian Berard —all this added to the legend that this Parisian sophisticate was conceited and an eccentric. Because of this legend, perhaps, he was a solitary figure. Since the Second World War, however, he has been better understood and appreciated.

His seriousness as an artist, his poetic vision of the universe, the incommunicable but moving, magical quality of his writings—reflecting his conception of all art as poetry— explain, no doubt, why he has been given greater recognition. After fluctuating between the Surrealists (see *Surrealism*)—whom he has paralleled but not emulated—and the Humanists [Gide (q.v.) and Claudel (q.v.)], he evolved an original position, the influence of which is now being felt.

His aesthetics of language consists in deforming speech in such a manner that what normally is associated becomes dissociated, resulting in a synthetic image of the poet's consciousness. The myriad moods revealed show Cocteau as one in whom the sentiment of the tragic is ever alive and whose explorations of the subconscious suggest the ominous. Themes of solitude and death are prominent in his work. The world most often evoked by Cocteau is that of adolescence and childhood. This world, moreover, is somnambulistic and vertiginous.

Although he entitles all his work "Poésies," his poetry, properly called, includes *Poésie 1916-1923*,

Opéra (1925-1927), and *Poésies* (1948). The poetic quality is also seen in his novels, the most notable of which are *Le Potomak* (1919), *Thomas l'Imposteur* (1929), and *Les Enfants terribles* (1929), his masterpiece. Among his many plays, which include adaptations of Sophocles, Shakespeare and Tasso (*Roméo and Juliette*, 1924; *Orphée*, 1926; *La Machine infernale*, 1934) may also be cited *Les Parents terribles* (1938), a study of bourgeois life, and *L'Aigle à deux têtes* (1945), a romantic drama. The latter two plays were adapted for the screen; other scenarios include *Le Sang d'un Poète* (1933), *Eternel Retour* (1944) and *La Belle et la Bête* (1946). Thanks to Cocteau, certain new artistic forms have become acceptable to wider audiences. In 1955, Cocteau was admitted to the *Académie Française* (q.v.).

Claude Mauriac, *Jean Cocteau, ou la Vérité du mensonge*, 1945; Roger Lannes, *Jean Cocteau*, 1945.

Cocu magnifique, Le (1921): See *Crommelynck, Fernand.*

Cœlina (1800): See *Pixérécourt.*

Colette, Sidonie Gabrielle (pseud. of **Colette Willy**): (1873-1954) The work of this remarkable novelist is semi-autobiographical. Such novels as the *Claudine* series (*Claudine à l'école*, 1900; *Claudine à Paris*, 1901; *Claudine en ménage*, 1902; *Claudine s'en va*, 1903) written in collaboration with *Willy*, the pen-name of her first husband, reflect her childhood and first years of marriage. *Les Vrilles de la Vigne* (1908), a swan-song to her youth, followed by *La Vagabonde* (1910), *L'Envers du music-hall* (1913), and *L'Entrave* (1913), are novels inspired by her career as a music-hall dancer and mime following her divorce and search for happiness. Her love and understanding of nature and animals—in which she seems to have more faith than in human beings—

can be seen in such novels as *Dialogues de bêtes* (1904) and *Sept Dialogues de bêtes* (1905). *Chéri* (1920)—incidentally a model of neoclassical literature—shows a woman abandoned by a younger lover, and *La Chatte* (1933) describes the tortures of jealousy. In all the above novels one finds an author with an extremely fine sensitivity: she is equally bewitched by the fragility of a flower, the grace of an animal and the charm of a landscape; with her womanly instinct she seizes on the most delicate sensations, especially those of suffering and loneliness, caused by love's deceptions. Her descriptions, moreover, reveal, even when most lyrical, a classical purity of style. Among her more recent publications are *Le Képi* (1943), *Gigi* (1945), *Paris de ma fenêtre* (1944)—moving recollections of the German occupation—and *Le Fanal bleu* (1949), intimate confidences of her old age. Colette was president of the *Académie Goncourt* (q.v.) and a member of the Belgian Academy of French Language and Literature.

Jean Larnac, *Colette, sa vie, son œuvre*, 1927; Claude Chauvière, *Colette*, 1931; Margaret Crosland, *Colette: A Provincial in Paris*, 1953.

Colin Muset: (?—?) A popular French poet of the thirteenth century, whose poetry, full of charm and wit, and whose frequent appeals to the generosity of his protectors suggest an affinity to Clément Marot (q.v.).

J. Bédier, *Les Chansons de Colin Muset, avec la transcription des mélodies,* par Jean Beck, 1912.

Collé, Charles: (1709-1783) Dramatist and song-writer, he composed for the Duc d'Orléans and his associates the greater part of his *Théâtre de société.* Staged in private theaters for the amusement of a bored pre-Revolutionary upper class, these plays, that occasionally "dramatized" proverbs, a dramatic form that was to foreshadow the *comédie-proverbe* of Musset (q.v.), include songs and dances. Collé's first and best comedy was *La Vérité dans le vin* (1747) and his last best play was *La Partie de Chasse de Henry Quatre* (1774). Besides his songs and plays, Collé wrote his *Journal et Mémoires* (1748-1772) which have much literary and personal interest.

Collège de France: Also known as the *Collège Royal* (or *Collège des lecteurs royaux,* or *Collège des Trois Langues*), it was founded (*c.* 1530) by King François I, at the suggestion of the Hellenist Budé (q.v.), to counteract the reactionary influence of the Sorbonne. Its professors, called *lecteurs royaux,* taught Hebrew, Greek and Latin. Enjoying almost complete autonomy today, its courses, no longer restrictive, embrace all phases of knowledge and are open to the public.

A. Lefranc, *Histoire du Collège de France,* 1892.

Collin d'Harleville (pseud. of **Jean-François Collin**): (1755-1806) Poet and dramatist during the Revolution, he is the author of such comedies as *L'Optimiste* (1788) and *Le vieux célibataire,* his masterpiece. His plays, full of verve and wit, represent a reversion to classical comedy (q.v.).

H. Welshinger, *Le Théâtre de la Révolution,* 1881.

Colomba: Written by Mérimée (q.v.) in 1841, this *nouvelle* (q.v.), probably his best, represents, by its delineation of primitive passions and exotic setting on the one hand, and use of precise detail and concise style on the other, a transition between romanticism and realism. It relates how Colomba, a Corsican girl, forces her Europeanized brother, Orso, to follow the law of the vendetta and to kill the Barriccini family, suspected of having murdered their father.

Colonel Chabert, Le (1832): See *Balzac.*

comédie à ariettes: Developed by the *théâtres de la foire* (q.v.), it is a type of comic play that includes entirely original songs. Out of it grew the *opéra-comique* (q.v.).

comédie de caractère: Found especially in several of the plays by Molière (q.v.), this type of comedy emphasizes the psychological characteristics of universal types, revealing their secrets of the heart and soul. In such a play, the action derives from the predominant motivating forces in the main characters; but the plot, of necessity, becomes secondary. Good examples are: *L'École des Femmes* (1662; q.v.), *Tartuffe* (1664-1669; q.v.), *Le Misanthrope* (1666; q.v.) and *L'Avare* (1668).

comédie de mœurs: Found especially in several of the plays by Molière (q.v.), this type of comedy satirizes manners observed in contemporary society. Good examples are Molière's *Les Précieuses ridicules* (1659), *Le Bourgeois gentilhomme* (1670; q.v.) and *Les Femmes savantes* (1672).

Comédie de la Mort, La (1838): See *Gautier.*

Comédie des Champs Elysées: See *Jouvet, Louis.*

Comédie-Française: Also known as the *Théâtre-Français*, this theater, subsidized by the State, is located on the Rue de Richelieu, adjacent to the Palais-Royal, in Paris. Often referred to as the *Maison de Molière*, its early history reflects the vicissitudes of Molière's (q.v.) career and those of his company. After the failure in 1643 of his *Illustre Théâtre* troupe, Molière returned in 1658 to Paris, obtaining the Petit Bourbon theater. In 1661, after this theater was demolished, he was given permission to produce his plays in the Palais-Royal, which Richelieu had constructed. Following Molière's death in 1673, Lulli occupied the Palais-Royal, and Molière's troupe, led by the actor La Grange, installed itself upon the Rue Guénégaud, joined by the company of the disbanded Théâtre du Marais (q.v.). In 1680, it merged, as a result of a royal order, with the actors of the Hôtel de Bourgogne (q.v.), becoming the still flourishing *Comédie Française* theater. Before occupying the present location in 1799, it had occupied three other sites. Its repertoire is essentially classical. The first appearance of the *Comédie-Française* company in New York and Canada in 1955 proved a momentous theatrical event.

Comédie humaine: The general title given by Balzac (q.v.) to his project of presenting in his novels a complete picture of French society of his day.

Comédie-Italienne: Although the Italian troupes, who brought with them into France the *commedia dell'arte* (q.v.), made their first regular appearance in Paris during the reign of Henri III (1574-1589), they had no permanent theater for almost a century and had to perform alternately at the *Hôtel de Bourgogne* (q.v.), the *Petit-Bourbon* and the *Palais-Royal.* Only in 1680, when the *Comédie-Française* (q.v.), as a result of a fusion of the then-existing theaters, was created, did the Italian troupe, headed by Scaramouche, establish itself as the sole possessor of the *Hôtel de Bourgogne.* Here they remained until their expulsion in 1697, as a result of a satirical play—*La fausse prude* —against Mme. de Maintenon. Returned to Paris in 1716 following the death of Louis XIV, they met with competition from the *théâtres de la foire* (q.v.), where the musical interlude, following the example they had set, was being offered since the time of their banishment from Paris. In 1762 they negotiated a merger with the *Opéra-Comique* (q.v.), which had also been opposing the use of music by the popular theaters. The *Comédie-Italienne,* it should be noted, was also a rival of the *Comédie-Française,* giving its plays, from 1718 on, entirely in French; on its boards, moreover, were produced many plays by Regnard, Dufresny and Marivaux (qq.v.).

N. Bernardin, *La Comédie italienne et le Théâtre de la Foire*, 1902.

comédie larmoyante: Popularized by La Chaussée (q.v.), this dramatic form, an intermediary genre between comedy and tragedy, presents ordinary people in distressing situations, which, however exaggerated, made audiences weep. Virtue, in the end, is rewarded. Paving the way for Diderot's (q.v.) *drame bourgeois* (q.v.), this dramatic genre, which also contains much moralizing, was to have an influence on the social theater of Augier and Dumas *fils* (qq.v.).

G. Lanson, *Nivelle de La Chaussée et la Comédie larmoyante*, 2nd ed., 1903.

comédie rosse: Created by Becque (q.v.) and continued by the Théâtre Libre (q.v.), this kind of play is cynical in its observation of life and society and in the shameless viciousness of its characters. In time, this term came to imply a nonchalant delight in the sordid and corrupt.

COMEDY: A comedy is a play in which the characters, carefully drawn in general, are led towards a happy ending. This definition makes it possible to distinguish comedy from tragedy and "drame," both characterized by a catastrophic denouement, as well as from farce, the characters of which are extremely sketchy and subordinated to purely physical comic effects. True, in the development of a comedy, the ludicrous characters or amusing situations are supposed to make the audience laugh or at least smile. Yet comedy can be serious or even moving, if the characters come up against certain dangers during the action; but the danger is never really frightening, for otherwise the play would be more of a tragicomedy, or if the danger is itself magnified and isolated, a melodrama.

The comedy, in its true sense, appeared in France during the Renaissance, in the form of an imitation or adaptation of the Latin comedy and particularly of the Italian comedy belonging to the genre of the "commedia dell'arte," whose troupes first came to France about 1570 (cf. Pierre de Larivey). At the beginning of the XVIIth century, the tragicomedy, influenced by the Spanish "comedia," was dominant: the action is rich in adventure and romantic rivalries; the characters are often in danger of death; and, by a sudden recognition or a final glorious deed, the denouement is a happy one. In many ways, the comedies of Corneille (q.v.) belong to this genre (*e.g.*, *Clitandre*, 1632); yet they are original in style and construction, in their analysis of proud love (*e.g.*, *La Suivante*, 1634), in poetic inventions (*e.g.*, *L'Illusion Comique*, 1636) and in their treatment of characters (*e.g.*, *Le Menteur*, 1642). This "baroque" (q.v.) period also witnessed the development of a genre of picaresque and grotesque comedy in which the comic aspect of the situation is supported more by effects of language (heroic-comic style, parodies of the "précieux," and of tragic and epic styles) than by the consistency of the characters. Typical of the period was the "burlesque" comedy, represented by Scarron (1610-1660), whose animation and wit served as a source of inspiration for romantic writers of comedy (*e.g.*, *Don Japhet d'Arménie*, 1647). Nevertheless, the medieval farce continued to be presented in various forms—the mountebank Tabarin and his patter on the Pont Neuf, the theatrical clowns at the Hôtel de Bourgogne (q.v.).

Molière (1622-1673; q.v.), under

the triple influence of classical culture, farce and Italian "commedia," succeeded in developing a genre of comedy rich in popular spontaneity and yet highly literary. His scope extended from farce (e.g., *Monsieur de Pourceaugnac*, 1669) to the great "comédie de caractère" (e.g., *Le Misanthrope*, 1666). A comedian by profession, he was capable of constructing a play according to the specific requirements of the stage. Always a keen observer, he created convincing characters to whom he generally subordinated the intrigue. Taken from traditional French, Italian and Spanish characters or "masks," his heroes live independent of the sources from which they were drawn (e.g., *L'Avare*, 1668; *Don Juan*, 1665). As comedian of the King, he also wrote elegant court comedies and, with the collaboration of the musician Lulli, comedy-ballets (e.g., *Le Bourgeois gentilhomme*, 1670).

After Molière's death, French comedy followed in his footsteps: the comedy at the end of the XVIIth and beginning of the XVIIIth century fundamentally consisted of a plot built around a character afflicted by a ridiculous vice or passion [e.g., *Le Joueur*, 1696, by Régnard (q.v.); *Le Glorieux*, 1732, by Destouches (q.v.); *Le Méchant*, 1747, by Gresset (q.v.)]. But, as a result of the gradual transformation of society and the uncertainties of the Regency and of the reign of Louis XV, the comedy began to paint the portrait of social customs more than of characters. In Lesage's (q.v.) *Turcaret* (1709), for example, the characters, although vigorously drawn, are presented in relation to an analysis of a social phenomenon: money. At the same time, the literary mode of sensibility brought with it the development and even the invention of new themes in comedy. Although he had but small success at that

time, Marivaux (1688-1763; q.v.) expressed the subtlety of love as no other playwright had done before him, except for Racine (q.v.) on the tragic plane. His characters are both attracted by and suspicious of love; the resulting mixture within them of hesitations, calculations and sincerity makes up the subject matter of his often cruel comedies (e.g., *Le Jeu de l'Amour et du Hasard*, 1730; *L'Epreuve*, 1740). While Marivaux's comedies represent an effort at lucidity that foretold the novelist Choderlos de Laclos' mathematics of love (e.g., *Les Liaisons dangereuses*, 1782), the "tearful comedy" or "comédie larmoyante" (q.v.) of Nivelle de la Chaussée (q.v.) expressed another tendency of the century: the taste for sentimentality and for the "pathetic" (e.g., *Le Préjugé à la Mode*, 1735).

As a result of the rising importance of the bourgeoisie and the advent of a non-aristocratic taste, comedy in the second half of the XVIIIth century tended to become serious and moralizing. It was no longer a question of causing amusement by means of a ridiculous character nor of inciting interest through love conflicts. Close to the "tearful comedy," the serious comedy of the day sought to move the audience by representing domestic difficulties and to instruct it by the presentation of virtuous characters. It is sometimes difficult to distinguish between the "serious comedy" and the "drame bourgeois," both of which tended to represent a compromise between the comedy, in its true sense, and the tragedy: *Le Philosophe sans le savoir* (1765) by Sedaine (q.v.), with its melodramatic suspense and paradoxically happy ending, is a case in point.

The end of the XVIIIth century also witnessed the return of a joyous comedy of movement: the comedies of Beaumarchais (1732-1799; q.v.). The traditional characters of farce and comedy were picked up again and enriched by songs mixed in with the plot and by frenzied action. Beaumarchais' three leading plays form a trilogy based on the character of Figaro, the barber, man of the people and valet of the count Almaviva. In the first play (*Le Barbier de Séville*, 1773) Figaro helps the young Almaviva conquer Rosine (in a plot which recalls situations in the Latin farce or in certain Molièresque comedies); but in the second (*Le Mariage de Figaro*, 1784) he is in conflict with the count. This conflict between a valet and his noble master made it possible for Beaumarchais to create a vigorous satire of certain institutions and customs of the Old Regime. The third play, written in 1792 (*La Mère Coupable*), is very different in tone and belongs clearly in the category of the moralizing "drame."

The history of comedy in the XIXth century follows the general movement of literary history. The Romantic period produced a sentimental and poetic genre of comedy, often close to the "drame romantique." This genre is best represented by some of Alfred de Musset's (q.v.) *Comédies et Proverbes* (1840). These plays, written to be read, present a delicate mixture of romantic reverie and subtleties in the manner of Marivaux (*e.g., Fantasio; Le Chandelier*). Moreover, as the "drame" is by definition a mixture of the "sublime" and the "grotesque," the romantic "drames" contained numerous frankly comic scenes or acts. One of the best examples is the fourth act of Victor Hugo's (q.v.) *Ruy Blas* (1838), in which a character *à la Scarron*, Don César de Bazan, is presented in epic proportions. Moreover, in *Le Théâtre en Liberté* (published in 1886) Victor Hugo really gave free play to his comic vein, a mixture of burlesque and poetic fantasy.

During the same period, the bour-geois comedy developed with either satirical (*e.g. La Camaraderie*, 1837, by Scribe, q.v.) or "domestic" overtones (*e.g. Gabrielle*, 1849; *Le Gendre de Monsieur Poirier*, 1854, by Emile Augier, q.v.).

In the second half of the XIXth century, the mixture of genres stemming from the theories of Diderot (q.v.) and the Romantics, the influence of Scribe's (q.v.) "la pièce bien faite" and the tendency toward realism make it often difficult to distinguish between the social drama and the comedy of manners. Yet, it is possible to isolate the realistic comedy and to consider it as true comedy. Objective, it presents a slice of life, satirically portraying the hypocrisies of the bourgeois milieu, and is frequently accompanied by a deep psychological analysis (*e.g. La Parisienne*, 1885, by Henri Becque, q.v.; and even some of the plays of Georges Courteline, such as *Boubouroche*, 1893).

A farcical genre also developed from the domestic comedy. Because of its relation to musical plays, it was called "vaudeville" (q.v.). Brought to perfection by Labiche (q.v.) and his collaborators (*e.g. Le Voyage de Monsieur Perrichon*, 1860; *Un Chapeau de paille d'Italie*, 1851), it used increasingly daring situations, such as infidelity in love and actual adultery (cf. Georges Feydeau), sometimes accompanied by the satire of certain milieus and institutions (*e.g. L'Habit Vert*, 1913, by De Flers, and Caillavet, qq.v.).

In general, laughter, at the end of the XIXth century, was provoked by the presentation of conjugal unfaithfulness—still the most frequent situation on the stages of the "Boulevard."

In the first half of the XXth century, the transformation of the theater brought new life to the poetic comedy (*e.g. Intermezzo*, 1933, by Jean Giraudoux, q.v.) and inspired the creation of surrealist farces (e.g. *Les Mamelles de Tiresias*, 1917, by Guillaume Apollinaire, q.v.; *Les Mariés de la Tour Eiffel*, 1921, by Jean Cocteau, q.v.). Today, although most of the comedies belong more or less in the category of XIXth-century bourgeois comedy and "vaudeville," they are often marked by a poetic style (cf. Marcel Achard's *Jean de la Lune*, 1929) or by a spirit of revolt against the sordid aspects of society (cf. Jean Anouilh's *Pièces Roses*).

The most important innovations in comedy since World War II are the two politico-philosophical comedies of Jean-Paul Sartre (*La P . . . Respectueuse*, 1946, and *Nekrassov*, 1955; q.v.), and the violent and destructive humor of the avant-garde plays, the strange and often nightmarish farces of Ionesco and Jean Tardieu.

Gustave Desnoiresterres, *La Comédie satirique au XVIIIᵉ siècle*, 1885; Eugène Rigal, *De Jodelle à Molière: tragédie, comédie, tragicomédie*, 1911; Louis Allard, *La Comédie de Mœurs en France au XIXᵉ siècle*, 1923-1933; P. Kolher, *Autour de Molière: l'esprit classique et la comédie*, 1925; Marie Delcourt, *La tradition des comiques anciens en France avant Molière*, 1934.

JACQUES GUICHARNAUD

comedy of character: See *comédie de caractère*.

comedy of manners: See *comédie de mœurs*.

commedia dell'arte: First presented in France by Italian professional actors who flourished from about 1574 to 1589, it consisted of improvised dialogue based on a written plot and of clowning. The roles of the actors were fairly well fixed; they were thus identified as the Doctor or Pedant, as Scaramouche, Arlequin, Pantalon, or Colombine, as fitted the plot. Molière's (q.v.) early formation owes much to this kind of farce. A permanent troupe of these actors, headed by Scaramouche, was

established in Paris in the middle of the seventeenth century. From 1680 until 1697, the date of its expulsion, it established itself at the Hôtel de Bourgogne (q.v.), where previously Racine's (q.v.) tragedies had been produced. Returned to France in 1716, it eventually merged into the Opéra-Comique (1762).

Commentaires (1592): See *Monluc, Blaise de*.

Commines (or **Commynes**), **Philippe de:** (1445-1511) Author of *Mémoires*, the first six parts of which, written between 1488 and 1498, recount the struggles of Charles the Bold and Louis XI, and the last two parts of which contain the account of Charles VIII's expedition to Italy (1494-1495). He is the first French writer who really deserves to be called *historian:* not only does he relate events, as do the chroniclers who preceded him, but he also searches for their causes and is aware of their consequences. However, he frequently passes judgment based on moral principles; he never fails to bring God into his explanations of events. His occasional cynicism, however, explains why he has at times been called the Machiavelli of France.

G. Charlier, *Commynes*, 1945.

Compagnie Madeleine Renaud—Jean-Louis Barrault: See *Barrault, Jean-Louis*.

Compagnie Pitoëff: See *Pitoëff, Georges*.

Compagnons de la Chimère, Les: See *Baty, Gaston*.

Comte, Auguste: (1798-1857) Founder of Positivism—a philosophy that renounces metaphysical reasoning and that recognizes only the evidence of facts—he laid the foundations in his *Cours de philosophie positive* (1830-1842) for *sociology*, a word of his own creation, which was to apply science to social phenomena. Positivism was to win over not only Marcellin Berthelot and Emile Littré, but also such literary critics and historians as Hippolyte Taine and Brunetière (qq.v).

L. Lévy-Bruhl, *La philosophie d'Auguste Comte*, 1900; H. Gouhier, *La Vie d'Auguste Comte*, 1931.

Comte d'Essex, Le (1678): See *Corneille, Thomas*.

Comte de Monte-Cristo, Le (1845): See *Dumas* PÈRE.

Concorde des deux langages (*c.* 1510): See *Lemaire de Belges, Jean.*

Condillac, Étienne Bonnot, Abbé de: (1714-1780) Friend of Rousseau and Diderot (qq.v.), to whose *Encyclopédie* (q.v.) he contributed articles on philosophy, he is the author of *Essai sur l'Origine des connaissances humaines* (1746) and *Traité des Sensations* (1754). As a disciple of Locke, he shows in these works that all thought is derived from sensations and experience and not from innate qualities. As head of the sensationalist school, he had a considerable influence on eighteenth-century philosophy in France, and more particularly on the *Idéologues* (q.v.), whose psychological approach was to be followed in the nineteenth century by such a writer as Stendhal (q.v.).

F. Picavet, *Les Idéologues*, 1891; R. Lenoir, *Condillac*, 1924.

Condition humaine, La (1933): See *Malraux.*

Condorcet, Antoine-Nicolas Caritat, Marquis de: (1743-1794) Devoted essentially to political and social reform, this mathematician, economist, philosopher—and one of the first *Idéologues* (q.v.)—is the author of *Esquisse d'un tableau des progrès de l'esprit humain* (1794). This work, a veritable synthesis of philosophical thought during the eighteenth century, which traces man's progress toward the ideal of truth, justice and happiness, was written before his imprisonment during the Reign of Terror. In addition to his *Vie de Voltaire* (1787), a philosophical work, he published *Réflexions sur le commerce des blés* (1776) and *Vie de Turgot* (1786), works which link him as an economist to the *physiocrat* school of Quesnay and Turgot (qq.v.), according to which "all wealth is derived from the land."

J. F. E. Robinet, *Condorcet, sa vie, son œuvre*, 1893; F. Buisson, *Condorcet*, 1929.

Confessions, Les (1781-1788): See *Rousseau, J. J.*

Confession d'un enfant du siècle, La (1836): See *Musset.*

Confidences, Les (1845): See *Lamartine.*

Confrérie de la Passion: A dramatic society granted a charter by Charles VI in 1402 giving it the exclusive right to perform all religious dramas in Paris and its environs. This grant was nullified in 1548 by a decree of the Parliament of Paris, forbidding the performance of the *mystères* (q.v.), which had degenerated into unwholesome and indecent abuse. However, the *Mystère de la Passion* (q.v.) continued to be presented in the provinces up to the beginning of the 17th century.

Conquête de Constantinople, La (*c.* 1205-1213): See *Villehardouin.*

Considérations sur les causes de la grandeur des Romains et de leur décadence (1734): See *Montesquieu.*

Constant, Benjamin: (1767-1830) Born in Lausanne of a French family, this writer, a liberal opposing the abuse of power in all political forms, occupied an important position during the Restoration. With Madame de Staël (q.v.), with whom he had had a long relationship, he shared the exile imposed by Napoleon, and remained with her during her stay in Germany. His major literary work is *Adolphe* (1816), a semi-autobiographical novel inspired by his *liaison* with Mme. de Staël. Written in a sober and precise style, reminiscent of a classical tragedy, it analyzes psychologically the inconstancy of the human heart as Adolphe, victim of the romantic *mal du siècle* (q.v.), tries to free himself from a tyrannical mistress. His other works include, in addition to *Cours de politique constitutionelle* (1817-1820) and *De la Religion considérée dans sa source, ses formes et ses developpements* (1824-31), the posthumous *Le Cahier Rouge* (1907), a cynical account of his youth, *Le Journal intime* (1887), a summary of the principal events of his life from 1814 to 1816, and the recently discovered *Cécile* (1951). G. Rudler, *La jeunesse de Benj. Constant* (1909); E. W. Schermerhorn, *Benjamin Constant*, 1929, Paul -L. Léon, *Benjamin Constant*, 1930.

conte: See *Short Story.*

Contemplations, Les (1856): See *Hugo.*

Contemporaines, Les (1780-1785): See *Restif de la Bretonne.*

Contes (1665-1674): See *La Fontaine.*

Contes à Ninon (1864): See *Zola.*

Contes cruels (1883): See *Villiers de l'Isle-Adam.*

Contes de ma mère l'Oye (1679): See *Perrault, Charles.*

Contes d'Espagne et d'Italie (1830): See *Musset.*

Contrat Social, Le (1761): See *Rousseau, J. J.*

Copeau, Jacques: (1879-1949) After having been a drama critic (1904-1910), and while yet editor of the *Nouvelle Revue française* (1909-1914), he reacted vigorously against the decadence of the French drama and its cynical industrialization. To breathe new life into the theater and to restore its inherent beauty, he acquired, in 1913, in the Saint-Sulpice section, the *Théâtre du Vieux-Colombier.* In this playhouse, together with Louis Jouvet and Charles Dullin (qq.v.), his disciples, to whom he had taught his aesthetics of the theater, he started a venture that was to have lasting influence on other groups who, until practically the present day, have followed his inspiration. The dramatic répertoire included plays by Shakespeare, Molière (q.v.), Gide (q.v.), Mérimée (q.v.) and Vildrac (q.v.). The "cul-tured public" that was won over to this theater witnessed productions that presented not the realism of the Théâtre-Libre (q.v.), against which it reacted, but a poetic interpretation of life. Although Copeau advocated no doctrine, he sought, through bare stage accessories that included neither mechanical nor electrical contrivances, to evoke, and not to describe, to appeal to the imagination, and not to the senses. The effect of sincerity he also tried to instill in his actors, who were not to regard their efforts as a personal achievement; all the members of the group had to synchronize their talents to obtain "pure theater." The deeper truth suggested by this kind of acting, one that stressed sincerity of sentiment and action, represented a reaction against the traditions of the *Comédie Française* (q.v.). Although the Company was dispersed for a while during the War, it reopened in 1917 at the Garrick Theater in New York, where it remained for two years. When it returned to Paris in 1920, its repertory was enriched with classical and modern plays, French and foreign. Copeau himself established a school where he taught the art of sincere interpretation. By 1922 both Dullin and Jouvet had left this company to found their own theaters, and Copeau's theater finally closed in 1924. But, as already suggested, Copeau's yeoman service was not in vain; the contagion of his example eventually infected even the *Comédie Française* and the *Odéon.*

J. Copeau, *Souvenirs du Vieux-Colombier*, 1931; R. Brasillach, *Animateurs du théâtre*, 1936.

Coppée, François: (1842-1908) A contributor to *Le Parnasse contemporain* (1866, 1869, 1877), this Parisian-born poet shows many of the Parnassian (q.v.) characteristics in *Le Reliquaire* (1866), his first collection of poetry. In later collections—*Les*

Intimités (1868), *Les Humbles* (1872)—he falls short of the Parnassian ideal, betraying as he does a sentimental note and pity for the suffering poor whose daily life he evokes. He also wrote several plays —including his famous *Le Passant* (1869), a one-act piece in verse presented at the Odéon—and novels. L. Le Meur, *La Vie et l'œuvre de François Coppée*, 1932.

Corbeaux, Les (1882): See *Becque*.

Corinne (1807): See *Staël, Madame de*.

Corneille, Pierre: (1606-1684) The life of this great writer of classical drama was relatively uneventful. At Rouen, where he was born, he received his early education in a Jesuit school. Later, following the tradition of his family, he studied law, in which profession, because of a speech defect, he had a short-lived career. He launched his dramatic career with *Mélite* (1629), a comedy inspired by an unrequited love affair. Other comedies, including *La Galerie du Palais* (1632), *La Place Royale* (1633), and *L'Illusion comique* (1636), were to be followed by *Le Menteur* (1643). This play, one of the best comedies of intrigue before Molière (q.v.), is an adaptation of Alarcon's *La Verdad Sospechosa;* because of its success, Corneille produced, the year following, *La Suite du Menteur* (1644), which was to be his last comedy.

In tragedy, after his initial *Médée* (1635), he wrote the famous but controversial *Le Cid* (1636 or 1637; q.v.). The tremendous popularity of this play aroused the jealousy of Georges de Scudéry and Mairet (qq.v.), his rivals, and led to the *Querelle du Cid* (q.v.). Notwithstanding the validity of some of the criticisms levelled at *Le Cid,* and despite the fact that it is not a true tragedy, Corneille, by having concentrated on the heroic qualities of its leading characters and on the strength of their emotions, and by

having established a new style, form and tone, inaugurated French classical tragedy.

The plays that followed—*Horace* (1640), *Cinna* (1640-1641) and *Polyeucte* (1641-1642; qq.v.)—all considered his masterpieces, represent a decided improvement over *Le Cid* and a deliberate attempt to strictly observe the unities; unlike *Le Cid,* moreover, which is based on the Spanish *Las Mocedades del Cid* (1621) by Guillén de Castro, they depict three different periods in Roman history. Most characteristic of Cornelian drama, their action is largely psychological; the characters struggle heroically to fulfill themselves and are moved by pride, self-respect and reputation; without their *gloire,* which emerges as they overcome the various obstacles, they would be unworthy of love.

The plays that followed were generally inferior; after the failure of *Pertharite* (1652) Corneille temporarily renounced the theater; with the complete collapse even of *Suréna* (1674), one of his better plays, he permanently abandoned it. During the intervening periods, however, he wrote several tragedies, including *Rodogune* (1644-1645), *Nicomède* (1651), *Œdipe* (1652), *Sertorius* (1662) and *Tite et Bérénice* (1670) which were not without merit. But the tendency in these plays is toward more and more complicated plots. The heroism of his main protagonists, who are masters of their destiny, becomes more and more improbable.

Corneille's contribution to French tragedy, on the whole, is the most important one after the *tragi-comedy* of Hardy (q.v.), but his star was to be eclipsed by Racine (q.v.). Other works include *L'Imitation de Jésus-Christ* (1651), a poetical translation, and treatises on dramatic poetry and tragedy.

G. Lanson, *Corneille,* 1898; H. C. Lancaster, *A History of French*

Dramatic Literature in the 17th Century, II, 1932; R. Brasillach, *Corneille*, 1938; G. May, *Tragédie cornélienne, tragédie racinienne*, 1948; O. Nadal, *Le Sentiment de l'amour dans l'œuvre de Corneille*, 1948.

Corneille, Thomas: (1625-1709) Younger brother of Pierre Corneille (q.v.), he wrote comedies, tragicomedies (q.v.), tragedies, and several opera libretti for Lulli. *Timocrate* (1656), a *tragi-comedy*, was the most successful play of the century; *Ariane* (1672) and *Le Comte d'Essex* (1678)—based on the relationship between Queen Elizabeth and Essex —are two of his better tragedies. His comedies—including *L'Amour à la mode* (1653), *Don Bertrand de Cigarral* (1653) and *Le Geôlier de soi-même* (1655)—are largely based on Spanish models.
G. Reynier, *Thomas Corneille, sa vie et son théâtre*, 1892.

Cornet à dès, Le (1917): See *Jacob, Max*.

Coup du deux décembre, Le (1928): See *Zimmer, Bernard*.

Cours de littérature dramatique (1843): See *Saint-Marc Girardin*.

Cours de philosophie positive (1830-1842): See *Comte, Auguste*.

Course du flambeau, La (1901): See *Hervieu*.

Courteline, Georges (pseud. of Georges Moinaux): (1860-1929) From his experiences in the army, which he hated, and from those in the civil service, where he was a clerk, he acquired a strong dislike for all bureaucracy, and drew material for many of his dramatic caricatures of the soldier, the railroad clerk, the magistrate and policeman. Included among these short *saynètes* are: *Les Gaietés de l'escadron* (1895), *Un Client sérieux* (1897), *Le Gendarme est sans pitié* (1899), *L'Article 330* (1901), and *La Paix chez soi* (1903). In *Boubouroche* (1893), presented for the first time at the Théâtre Libre (q.v.), Courteline created high comedy of character, in the Molièresque (see *Molière*) tradition, with tragic overtones. The psychological depiction of Boubouroche, the over-credulous cuckold taken in by his crafty mistress, while mirthful, is a study of the foibles and stupidities of human nature that cause suffering. Everywhere, Courteline shows close observation as well as a philosophy of life.
J. Portail, *Georges Courteline, l'humoriste français*, 1928.

courtly love: Flourishing during the Middle Ages in the literature of aristocratic, chivalric society, this code of love-making, whose origins have at various times been attributed to Ovid, Arabic poetry in Spain, the social conditions of feudal society, and the cult of the Virgin Mary—which gave religious overtones to the worship of women—held as its principal tenet the complete devotion of the lover to the lady with whom he was in love. This devotion required deep veneration, great deeds, heroism and strength. Demanding loyalty, in spite of all obstacles, true love was held to be, however, incompatible with marriage; often, therefore, courtly love was illicit and sensual. Its ideals are best exemplified in many of the *romans bretons* (q.v.), in the works of Chrétien de Troyes (q.v.), and especially in the first part of the *Roman de la Rose* (by Guillaume de Lorris).
M. Lot-Borodine, *La Femme et l'amour au 12° siècle d'après les poèmes de Chrétien de Troyes*, 1909; C. S. Lewis, *The Allegory of Love: A Study in Medieval Tradition*, 1936.

Cousin Pons, Le (1847): See *Balzac*.

Cousine Bette, La (1846): See *Balzac*.

Crébillon (fils), Claude-Prosper Jolyot de: (1707-1777) Son of Crébillon *père*, the dramatist, he is the author of such licentious tales and novels as *L'Ecumoire* (1733), *Le Sopha* (1745) —his best-known work—and *Le*

Hasard du coin du feu (1763). They reflect the vices of contemporary high society.

O. Uzanne, *Les Conteurs du XVIII° siècle*, 1879.

Crébillon, Prosper Jolyot de: (1674-1762) One of the two great writers of tragedies (q.v.) during the eighteenth century—the other one being Voltaire (q.v.)—he chose mythological or ancient subjects characterized by the horrible and the brutal. In *Atrée et Thyeste* (1707), a father drinks the blood of his own son; in *Rhadamiste et Zénobie* (1711)—his masterpiece—a father kills his son and then himself. Based on the *romanesque* (q.v.), moreover, the plots, which are complicated, contain much physical action, foreshadowing the melodrama (q.v.) of the early nineteenth century. Included among his other plays are: *Electre* (1709), *Xerxès* (1714) and *Sémiramis* (1717).

M. Dutrait, *Étude sur la vie et le théâtre de Crébillon*, 1895.

Crève-cœur, Le (1940): See *Aragon*.

Crevel, René: (1900-1935) Until his suicide, a result, from all appearances, of his despair at seeing his Surrealist and Communist friends separated, this member of the original Surrealistic (see *Surrealism*) group wrote many works. Included among his poetic novels are: *Mon corps et moi* (1925) and *La Mort difficile* (1926). *Êtes-vous fous?* (1929) and *Les Pieds dans le plat* (1933) satirize the bourgeoisie.

Crime de Sylvestre Bonnard, Le (1881): See *France, Anatole*.

CRITICISM: For four hundred years literary criticism has been an integral part of French literature. Critical theory has evolved with literary forms. The poets themselves have often been critics: Ronsard, Malherbe, Hugo (qq.v.). In a few instances, with Baudelaire, Mallarmé and Valéry (qq.v.), the poets have been the leading critics of their day and of their century. The tradition of criticism is one of the most cherished and one of the most respected in France. From generation to generation, critics, who are often writers themselves, have defended the rigorous observation of rules and have maintained the excitement of aesthetic theory. French criticism originated in Italy of the Renaissance, but it lost almost immediately its Italian characteristics of erudition and pedantry.

The first important book of criticism in France was *Défense et Illustration de la langue française*, of 1549. It was written by a young man, Joachim du Bellay (q.v.), who treated the ancients with a fanatical respect. Yet, the principal purpose of the treatise was to prove the dignity of the French language equal to the dignity of Greek and Latin. This young poet and critic advised a break with the mediaeval tradition and a deliberate effort on the part of the new writers to imitate the genres of the classical authors. Tragedies and comedies, following their ancient models, should replace the *mystères* and *miracles* (qq.v.) of the "Gothic" period. Du Bellay was somewhat responsible for the love sonnet which was to have such abundant success in the 16th and 17th centuries, and for the Horatian and Pindaric odes. This early book of criticism was wordy, ill-organized, contradictory, but it provoked enthusiasm and served as a manifesto for two centuries of French poetry.

La Poétique of Jules César Scaliger (q.v.) appeared in 1561 and enjoyed as much popularity as Du Bellay's *Défense*. His work, written in Latin, was the compilation of treatises from antiquity. He compares one with the other, provides examples and definitions, and organizes the vast matter of rhetoric: the rules of tragedy and comedy, the meaning of synecdoche and metonymy, the comparative values of Homer and Virgil, Scaliger's predilection went to the Latin authors rather than the Greek, and this determined to some degree the shift from the marked Greek influence on the earlier French poets of the Renaissance (Baïf and Ronsard; qq.v.) to the almost exclusive Latin influence on later writers (Montaigne and Malherbe; qq.v.).

The humanist critics were scholars. The tone of their writing was doctrinal. Their comments on literary forms were rigorously compressed into laws. The critics were unsure of their objectives. They were enthusiastic readers of the masterpieces of antiquity, but they seldom went beyond the cataloguing of impressions produced by these works. They composed treatises which were the necessary basis for future literary criticism, treatises which were inventories of signs by which ancient masterpieces might be recognized and which might guide the writing of future masterpieces.

The influence of Malherbe dominated the first half of the 17th century. His work as grammarian and poet and critic helped to define the precepts of a French art which was to be called "classical" and which occupies the central place in the history of French culture. In a celebrated passage of his *Art Poétique*, Boileau (q.v.) was later to hail the advent of Malherbe and the authority of Malherbe in all things poetical: *Enfin Malherbe vint* . . . Malherbe was the first craftsman in the history of French poetry who discussed analytically and pontifically the rules of his craft. The criticism of Malherbe is to be found in his *Commentaires sur Desportes* where he shows himself the specialist in grammar and the use of words. He denounced erudition in poetry and the unrestrained outburst of lyricism. He purified the French language by narrowing its range and by making it into a language ca-

pable of enunciating truths rather than personal passions. Ronsard and the poets of the Pléiade (q.v.) had insisted on loftiness of theme and diction. Malherbe was the first in France to claim ordinary speech for poetry.

Cardinal Richelieu participated in the quarrel over *Le Cid* (1636), but his loyal friend and spokesman, Chapelain (q.v.), is thought to have been responsible for the writing of *Les Sentiments de l'Académie sur le Cid*, of 1638. This work, which occupies an important place in the evolution of French criticism, raises fundamental questions, such as the trustworthiness of the public in judging a literary work. Chapelain develops the theory that the quality of the public's enjoyment of a tragedy, for example, depends upon the author's conformity to the rules of tragedy (q.v.). His *Sentiments* established the authority of the Académie Française (q.v.) on literary matters and offered the model of a kind of criticism which attempts to base judgment on general principles.

The tendencies toward bombast (*emphase*) and preciosity (q.v.) which developed in France during the 16th and 17th centuries, largely because of the Italian and Spanish models, were opposed by Boileau, whose authority was strong under the reign of Louis XIV. He was a bourgeois of Paris, like Molière and Voltaire (qq.v.), and thus interrupted the central tradition of French literature which before his day had been largely aristocratic. Boileau, Molière and Pascal (q.v.), in their critical attitudes, represent a strong reaction against the spirit of the *salons* (q.v.) and *ruelles*. Boileau attacked the pedantry of Chapelain, and the French imitation of Italian models. He was backed by La Fontaine and Racine (qq.v.) and Molière. Eventually he won over to his side the public and the king himself. Imitation of nature is the highest rule for Boileau: *Que la nature donc soit notre étude unique.* But this imitation must be carried on rationally, and only in so far as nature conforms to itself, only in so far as nature is universal. Hence, the law of the three unities (q.v.) is applicable because it is natural and reasonable. Preciosity should be condemned because it is unnatural to obscure willfully one's thought by language. Boileau was an artist as well as a bourgeois. He was a craftsman and a painstaking theorist. His defense of reason (*Aimez donc la raison*) established a bond of agreement between himself and his century.

The Quarrel of the Ancients and the Moderns (q.v.) was a complicated affair which transpired during the last years of the reign of Louis XIV. The fundamental issue is still one of controversy: is man's progress in science and industry perceptible also in the realms of art and letters? In France, this "Quarrel" was the first string opposition to the Renaissance belief in the need to imitate the Ancients. Boileau himself was the principal advocate for the Ancients, and Fontenelle (q.v.), nephew of Corneille and bitter enemy of Racine (q.v.), was, with the four Perrault (q.v.) brothers, defender of the Moderns. For the first time, literary criticism was concerned with the concept of progress. The Quarrel provoked sophistry and polemical writings on both sides. Its conclusions centered about the belief that there are other literary models than those of antiquity, that French authors have surpassed Latin authors in the tragedy and the novel, and that they may one day hope to surpass them in the ode and comedy.

The controversy stimulated critical opinion not only in France but in all of Europe. It has been claimed that literary criticism in its modern sense originated with the Quarrel of the Ancients and the Moderns. Traces of the leading arguments are found throughout the 18th century, in novels and plays. The founding of many newspapers helped to prolong the debate. Bayle (q.v.), first of the 18th century philosophers, and to whom Voltaire will owe many ideas, is the free thinker (*libre penseur*) who analyzed for his century the impossibility of reconciling reason with faith, and who preached the religion of tolerance. He occupies no clearly defined position in French literary criticism, but his genius is critical in the highest sense and his method, which is his century's, is the search for factual truth.

Voltaire was, without question, the authority in the 18th century on literary matters. He was enrolled on Boileau's side and was governed by his deep respect for the rules and examples of French classical art. He praised the English to his countrymen, it is true, but his imitation of *Othello* in *Zaïre* was very limited. After revealing Shakespeare to France, Voltaire became jealous of the glory he had created for the English poet. The 18th century demonstrated its major preoccupations in Bayle's *Dictionnaire,* in Montesquieu's (q.v.) *Lettres Persanes* and in Voltaire's *Lettres Anglaises.* These interests were political, religious and social. They were not literary or aesthetic, and such works as Voltaire's *Commentaire sur Corneille* remained conservative. During the long course of his career, Voltaire maintained literary criticism approximately at the same point where he had found it.

In a sense, Diderot (q.v.) did more for criticism. At least he attempted more. He seriously questioned Boileau's doctrine of imitation of nature by claiming that what is natural is not always good. The *Encyclopédie* (q.v.) came into existence largely because of the energy and

69

enthusiasm of Diderot. All of his ideas, from the origin of music to the meaning of the universe, are rehearsed brilliantly in his novel, *Le Neveu de Rameau.* This book is a succinct treatise on the 18th century's belief in reason and humanity.

The critics of the 17th and 18th centuries argued about the application of literary rules but never doubted that the rules existed. Rousseau (q.v.), who was not a critic by profession but whose literary judgments are everywhere in his books, enunciated the fallibility of criticism and the doctrine of "relativity" which Fontenelle had almost developed at the beginning of the century. The advent of Rousseau helped to bring about the shift from the study of universal or common ideas to the expression of personal or private ideas. He abolished the concepts of literary models, literary recipes, literary rules. His influence was predominant in Mme. de Staël (q.v.), the energetic theorist of romanticism, and in Chateaubriand (q.v.), one of the great stylists of the new movement.

In *De la Littérature,* Mme. de Staël studies the multiple relationships which exist between literature and all phases of civilization: religion, government, customs. In her analysis of national and racial characteristics, the concept of "relativity" in literary judgment grows in importance. *Le Génie du Christianisme* of Chateaubriand is not only a work of apologetics, it is a landmark in the history of criticism. It rehabilitated the Middle Ages as a glorious past in French national life. In the wake of Rousseau and Bernardin de St-Pierre (q.v.), it called attention to the color and movement of exterior nature. Chateaubriand claimed that he had replaced the sterile criticism of faults by the fertile criticism of beauty.

Under the influence of Mme. de Staël and Chateaubriand, criticism began to examine works of art not so much in themselves but as products of a culture. The danger of their kind of criticism was dillettantism or an expression of personal preference. This was true of Hugo's (q.v.) famous *Préface de Cromwell,* a kind of manifesto of romanticism (q.v.) and whose ideas were earlier defined to some extent in Mme. de Staël's *De l'Allemagne.* This book, with Chateaubriand's *Génie du Christianisme* and the systematic historical criticism of Villemain (q.v.), instituted in France the study of foreign literatures. But the methods of criticism underwent the most significant transformation in the work of Sainte-Beuve (q.v.), who in his analysis of literary works combined psychology with physiology.

The goal of Sainte-Beuve's gigantic work, which today is contained in approximately seventy volumes was to infuse new life into criticism, to enlarge its scope and transform it. In his short critical papers, collected under the title, *Causeries du Lundi,* and in his long solid works, such as *Port-Royal,* he produced criticism which was a review of French literature in all its forms and which was guided by a desire to understand rather than to judge. He attempted to give as full a portrait as possible of the writer under consideration and raised questions about him which had hardly been thought of in previous systems of criticism. Such questions included physical and anatomical characteristics of the writer, his educational background, his psychological traits, his temperament as explained by provincial or city mores.

The hope of making literary criticism into a science is more apparent in the works of Taine (q.v.) than in those of Sainte-Beuve. His theories of criticism systematized and developed the earlier theories of Mme.

de Staël and Chateaubriand. As all the parts of an organism maintain necessary connections, so all the parts of a work, or of a man, of a period, of a people, form one system. Each of these systems has an essential or dominant characteristic. Taine proposed to study all the variations of given literary data as influenced by what he called race, environment and period (*race, milieu, moment*). He looked upon literature and art as the expression of society, as documents awaiting the scholar and the philosopher and the historian.

During the last twenty years of the century, three academic critics exerted considerable influence. Ferdinand Brunetière (q.v.), who taught for several years at the École Normale Supérieure, stressed the moral and social values of works of literature, and studied the evolution of literary genres. Jules Lemaître (q.v.) was perhaps the most brilliant of the subjective impressionistic critics. Emile Faguet (q.v.), who lectured at the Sorbonne, was particularly concerned with elaborating and explaining the ideas of the authors he chose to study. Literary history, during the past one hundred years, has maintained its place beside literary criticism. The rigorous scientific method of Gustave Lanson (q.v.) was adopted by a generation of university teachers and scholars.

The poets themselves of the 19th and 20th centuries unhampered by an organized system like that of Hippolyte Taine, were critics in their own right. Three at least, Baudelaire, Mallarmé and Valéry, produced literary criticism which appears today the most vital and profound of their age. Baudelaire's revelation of poetry revindicated belief in the spiritual destiny of man. His example and his art convinced his readers that man has the right to ask of poetry the solution to the problems of human destiny. His famous poem on symbolism, *Les Correspondances*, reassigned to the poet his ancient role of *vates*, of soothsayer, who by his intuition of the concrete, of immediately perceived things, was led to the idea of these things, to the intricate system of "correspondences." The experience of the poet is the participation of all things invading him, with their harmonies and analogies. They bear the sign of the First Word, of their original unity. In his passages on beauty and on the distinction between art and morality, Baudelaire often speaks of the very special privilege given to beauty to survive moral deficiencies. He certainly believed, with many modern aestheticians, that a blasphemous idea in a line of poetry did not necessarily diminish the formal beauty of the line.

More implicitly than did even Baudelaire, Mallarmé placed his highest confidence in the sole aesthetic value of a work of art. By this faith, he was the real literary model for such writers as Valéry, Proust and Gide (qq.v.). Of the necessary solitude of a poet he made almost a religion. No poet more steadfastly than Mallarmé, believed that the subject of all poems is poetry, that the reason for every poem to be written is to become engaged in the creation of poetic language. He saw language as a force capable of destroying the world in order to rebuild the world so that it might be apprehended differently. The title of hero he ascribed to Verlaine (q.v.) might be granted to him in his brave assumption of the state of poet. To be a poet, in Mallarmé's sense, is to engage in a perpetual warfare with oneself. It means the daily destruction of convention, the repudiation of dogma, the removal of all the various assurances which life offers. Being a poet forces a man to a constantly increasing degree of self-consciousness, self-awareness, to

71

a willful exploration of the unknown in himself. The poet is one of those men who each day learn more about their human impermanence without which nothing permanent can be created.

During the years between the two wars, Albert Thibaudet (q.v.), who died in 1936, and Charles Du Bos (q.v.), who died in 1939, made significant contributions to that kind of literary criticism which lies just outside of the purely scholarly and historical type. Thibaudet was called by Bergson the greatest French critic since Sainte-Beuve. He was strongly influenced by Bergson. His studies of Mallarmé and Flaubert (q.v.) seem today somewhat less valuable than the collections of separate articles which appeared first in *La Nouvelle Revue Française.* The essays of Du Bos, called *Approximations,* of which there are seven volumes, and his studies of Gide and Benjamin Constant (qq.v.), are characterized by a deep spirituality, by a wealth of allusions and comparisons, by an exceptional abundance of quotations from the author studied which reveal the essence of the literary work.

André Malraux (q.v.), in his volumes on the psychology of art, now collected in the volume, *Voix du Silence,* refers to the arts of all ages and all worlds. The prehistoric cave drawings coexist with Braque and Picasso. His work is really on the subject of human genius, on an extraordinary awareness of man and his destiny. He insists on convincing the reader that an artistic creation is the justification of the mystery of our life. Because of the vigor and the perceptiveness of this hymn to art, Malraux has been chosen by many younger minds in France as a critic and a spiritual guide. His eloquence is always the most vibrant in the passages dealing with the relationship between man and the sacred. One thought above all others

he never tires of reiterating, namely that art does not imitate life, but that it imitates art and reveals life. The great apology he makes for art is its immortality; if not its literal immortality, at least the breath of immortality that permeates it.

Such subjects as the Resistance (q.v.) movement and the concentration camp world have not in any way created a literary school. In fact, 20th century literature, despite the significant programs of surrealism (q.v.) in the 30's and existentialism (q.v.) in the 40's, is characterized by an absence of strongly organized and formulated literary movements. Nothing today is comparable to the romantic or the symbolist schools of the 19th century. Twentieth century literature in France may well be as rich as that of the 19th century, but it is far more confused and anarchical. In its search for an order of intellectual and formal values, contemporary literature has grown into an art of critical assessment. The four masters who have dominated the half-century: Proust, Valéry, Gide and Claudel (q.v.); André Breton (q.v.) and surrealists in general; Sartre (q.v.) and existentialists in general, Mauriac (q.v.) and other Catholic writers, have all devoted large portions of their work to critical statement and theory, to a serious effort of explaining and justifying the more purely creative part of their writing.

A. Principal Works in French Literary Criticism (1550-1950):

1549 Du Bellay, *Défense et Illustration de la langue française*
1561 Scaliger, *La Poétique*
1638 Chapelain, *Sentiments de l'Académie sur le Cid*
1674 Boileau, *Art Poétique*
1687 Fontenelle, *Oracles*
1697 Bayle, *Dictionnaire historique et critique*
1734 Voltaire, *Lettres Anglaises*

1764-67 Diderot, *Les Salons*
1800 De Staël, *De la Littérature*
1802 Chateaubriand, *Le Génie du Christianisme*
1827 Hugo, *Préface de Cromwell*
1851-70 Sainte-Beuve, *Les Lundis*
1863 Taine, *Histoire de la Littérature Anglaise*
1868 Baudelaire, *L'Art Romantique*
1897 Mallarmé, *Divagations*
1924-44 Valéry, *Variété* (5 vol.)
1924 Breton, *Manifeste du Surréalisme*
1947-49 Sartre, *Situations* (3 vol.)
1951 Malraux, *Voix du Silence*

B. Histories and Methods of French Literary Criticism:

F. Brunetière, *Evolution de la Critique*, 1890; G. Lanson, *Méthodes de l'histoire littéraire*, 1925; Albert Thibaudet, *Réflexions sur la Critique*, 1938-1941; Henri Peyre, *Writers and their critics*, 1944.

WALLACE FOWLIE

Critique de l'École des Femmes, La (1663): see *Molière*.

Croix de bois, Les (1919): See *Dorgelès, Roland*.

Crommelynck, Fernand: (1888-) This Belgian-born dramatist, the author of several plays, is especially known for his *Le Cocu magnifique* (1921). The scandalous and farcical plot is not as important, however, as the psychological analysis of the jealous husband, ever suspicious of his wife's faithfulness. *Tripes d'or* (1930) is a social satire depicting the vanity of wealth and capitalistic grandeur. Carine, in *Carine, ou la Jeune Fille folle de son âme* (1934), is a romantic and symbolic character who prefers death to seeing her dream of love blemished. A Maeterlinckian (see *Maeterlinck*) approach is seen in *Le Sculpteur de Masques* (1911), in which, as a result of love, the husband is driven to insanity and the wife takes her own life. Often a mixture of different drama-

tic moods makes some of his plays disconcerting. Included among his other plays are: *Le Marchand de regrets* (1913), *Les Amants puérils* (1923), and *Une Femme qui a le cœur trop petit* (1934).

Crusades (1096-1270): Under the patronage of the Pope, eight official expeditions were organized by the Christians of the Occident in order to deliver the Holy places from the hands of the infidels and to defend the Christian Kingdom founded in Jerusalem. Among the results of these crusades was the creation of a certain *cosmopolitanism*. The first two French historical works, those by Villehardouin and Joinville (qq.v.), show the influence of these Crusades.

cry: The announcement or proclamation that made known, a few months in advance, a forthcoming presentation of the *mystère* (q.v.) play. During this announcement people were asked to contribute money, and volunteer actors were solicited since there were no professional actors, strictly speaking, during the Middle Ages. In the *chansons de geste* (q.v.), this term also refers to the announcement of a battle about to start.

CUBISM: A movement in art and also in poetry which flourished in France in the second decade of the twentieth century. Coming on the heels of fauvism (*c.* 1905) which had already declared the independence of art from reality, cubist painting attempted primarily to abstract or break up objects of nature and to regroup the basic geometrical forms or fragments in independent two-dimensional patterns. Pablo Picasso's *Les Demoiselles d'Avignon* (1906/7) is generally considered the earliest example. The meeting of Picasso and Georges Braque in the autumn of 1907 provided the nucleus around which the movement rapidly grew, although it did not receive a name until the art critic Vauxcelles referred disparagingly in the *Gil Blas* of November 14, 1908, to the "cubes" in the landscapes which Braque had painted the previous summer. In the spring of 1911 the first large-scale exhibit was held at the Salon des Indépendants and included works by Robert Delaunay, Marcel Duchamp, Albert Gleizes, Marie Laurencin, Roger de la Fresnaye, Jean Metzinger, Francis Picabia and Alfred Reth. The violent reaction of the public to this and the ensuing exhibits from 1912 to 1914 prompted a series of polemics which made cubism perhaps the most controversial advanced guard movement in pre-war Paris. Although crippled considerably by the outbreak of the war it continued throughout the rest of the decade as the dominant modern style, reaching perhaps its highest point in the works of the Spaniards Piccasso and Juan Gris, who were free to paint during the war years.

A distinction is customarily made between "analytical" and "synthetic" cubism. In the former phase, which lasted until 1911, the painters, although stressing the deformation of nature, never entirely lost sight of their point of departure. Because of the emphasis on form, however, color was reduced to a minimum with green, ochre and earth colors creating an austere effect. The tendency also prevailed to present facets of the same object from numerous different points of view. This feature of "simultaneity" elicited widespread discussion because of the supposition by theorists that it represented a daring attempt to overcome the limitations of time in painting.

In 1911 and 1912 first Braque, then Picasso began adding new plastic elements to their paintings such as letters of the alphabet, *papiers collés,* imitation grained wood and real or imitation textures. These innovations reflected a desire to incorporate the most familiar, everyday objects in new and surprising combinations, quite apart from any utilitarian function which they might represent. The stress thus shifted from "analysis" or the portrayal of broken-up objects of nature to "synthesis" or the building up of new, original combinations from disparate elements. This new period which dominated the movement from 1913 brought into prominence the concept of the "tableau-objet," i.e., the belief that a painting should become an organic piece of reality, quite as intrinsic and as autonomous as nature itself. Concurrently the stress on bright colors, larger planes and less rigorous composition contributed to a style quite distinct from the more ascetic disciplines of the analytical period.

As an adjective the term "cubist" pertains also to a group of French poets closely associated with the painters and, by extension, to a poetic style of the second decade of the twentieth century in France. Guillaume Apollinaire, Max Jacob (qq.v.) and André Salmon, who lived in or frequented the "bateau-lavoir" studio of Picasso on Montmartre, not only witnessed but actually assisted in the elaboration of the cubist doctrines. Apollinaire and Salmon served regularly as apologists in the Paris press, and all three poets, along with Pierre Reverdy (q.v.), were listed as the literary collaborators of the first issue of the cubist Bulletin of the *Section d'Or,* October 9, 1912. Beginning in 1917 they also contributed to the review *Nord-Sud,* a cubist organ under the direction of Pierre Reverdy. Blaise Cendrars, Jean Cocteau, Léon-Paul Fargue (qq.v.) and Pierre-Albert Birot have also been listed on occasion as cubist poets although with perhaps less historical justification. The poets themselves rarely used the term in reference to their own work, and Apollinaire in fact, as the acknowledged leader of the group, preferred the expression "l'esprit nouveau" to characterize the poetic innovations of his generation. Nevertheless certain common traits have justified the use of cubism as a literary term. Both painters and poets shared the idealistic concept that the real is not independent of mind and that the artist is therefore less concerned with things than with his reaction to them. The corollaries to this belief, namely that nature should not be imitated, that the subject as such no longer counts, that the work of art has its own autonomy, are basic to both groups. Moreover, a similar concept of structure and composition united the two. The typical cubist poem is an arrangement of independent, highly imagistic, elliptical lines or groups of lines which create an initial effect of discontinuity since they are not held together by a discursive framework. The unity of the poem derives more from the analogies and interplay of the various segments, whether contiguous or not, than from any logical sequence and development of ideas. It would seem closer, therefore, to the structure of a Symbolist (see *Symbolism*) poem of the type perfected by Stéphane Mallarmé (q.v.) than to a classical sonnet or other traditional forms. It differs sharply from the Symbolist style, however, in its preference for hard, abrupt imagery and for a block-like rather than a web-like composition. As a matter of fact, the cubist painters and poets, in their search for clear-cut, sharply juxtaposed outlines based upon simple everyday objects, felt a greater affinity for each other than did either group towards what they felt to be the more tenuous or amorphous styles of the Symbolists and Impressionists of the previous generation.

Many of the experiments of Apollinaire's circle were based upon an effort to find poetic equivalents for the cubist doctrines. Thus Apollinaire's own "calligrams," poems typographically arranged in the shape of the objects they evoke, exemplify a principle similar to that of the painting-as-object of synthetic cubism. The omission of punctuation, the rapid shifting of personal pronouns, the telescoping of syntax, the widespread use of the present tense, the abrupt changes of locale and the suppression of connectives and of transitional phrases are all features of cubist poetry which, like the principle of "simultaneity" in the painting, reflect the heroic effort to break down the barriers of time and place and to elicit an immediate, total response on the part of the reader.

On the whole the experiments in cubist poetry were less successful than in painting. The stress upon immediate sensations and an attitude of almost willful negligence often prevented the poets from achieving the structural unity and the balance of tensions essential to a perfected cubist work. If Apollinaire has emerged as one of the great poets of the twentieth century it is because of qualities much too exuberant and varied to be contained within the cubist aesthetic. The purest cubist poet of the group, often considered the counterpart of Juan Gris, is undoubtedly Pierre Reverdy. In his best pieces of the period—the short ones in particular—all the lines, despite their syntactical independence from each other, combine to communicate a single mysterious impression which in turn, upon a second reading, illuminates the meaning of each line alone.

Notable examples of the cubist style may be found in Apollinaire's *Alcools* (1913) and *Calligrammes* (1918); Jacob's *Le Laboratoire central* (1921); Salmon's *Prikaz* (1919); Reverdy's *Les Ardoises du toit* (1918) and *Cravates de chanvre* (1922) and Cocteau's *Ode à Picasso* (1917) and *Poésies* (1920).

Alfred H. Barr, *Cubism and Abstract Art*, 1936; Georges Lemaître, *From Cubism to Surrealism in French Literature*, 1941; D.-H. Kahnweiler, *Juan Gris, His Life and Work*, 1947; Winthrop Jenkins, "Toward a Reinterpretation of Cubism," *Art Bulletin*, Dec., 1948, pp. 270-278; *Art d'aujourd'hui*, sér. 4, no. 3-4, mai-juin, 1953; *Le Cubisme* (Musée Nationale d'Art moderne. [Exposition] 30 jan.-9 avril 1953. Paris, Ed. des Musée Nationaux), 1953; Christopher Gray, *Cubist Aesthetic Theories*, 1954.

LeRoy C. Breunig, Jr.

Curé de Tours, Le (1832): See *Balzac*.

Curel, François de: (1854-1928) This wealthy nobleman, descended of a family from Lorraine, began his career as dramatist under the auspices of Antoine (q.v.), who accepted for the Théâtre-Libre (q.v.) three plays which he had sent him under different pseudonyms. These, *L'Amour brode* (1893)—previously entitled *Sauvé des eaux* (1889) and later called *La Danse devant le miroir* (1913)—*L'Envers d'une sainte* (1892), and *La Figurante* (1896), are basically psychological, and portray the conflict between pride, hate, and jealousy as aspects of love, on the one hand, and reality, on the other. *L'Invitée* (1893), too, depicts a heroine who is frustrated in her search for an ideal love. Ideas that are thought-provoking, but that, unlike those of Dumas *fils* (q.v.), are given no "mathematical" solution, provide the themes for the rest of his plays. The problems posed in these plays stimulate passions, and with them long, frequently oratorical monologues, that reflect more the language of the dramatist than of the characters themselves. In *Les Fossiles* (1892), the problem relates to the duty of nobles in a world that no longer is aristocratic, in *Le*

Repas du lion (1897) to that of industrialists toward the working class, and in *La Nouvelle Idole* (1899) to the progress of science when the life of a patient is at stake. In all these plays, the philosophical content appealed to cultivated readers; however, these plays did not have a popular appeal.

Ernest Pronier, *La Vie et l'Œuvre de François de Curel*, 1934.

Curtis, Jean-Louis: (1917-   ) Depicting in *Les Jeunes Hommes* (1944) the moral experience of the generation of 1940, this writer portrayed in *Les Forêts de la Nuit* (1947) a French province under occupation. The latter novel, awarded the *Prix Goncourt*, is a valuable social and historical document. Preoccupied with the theme of the young of the present generation, this author— who is also a teacher—depicts in *Gibier de potence* (1949) the amoral and delinquent youth of post war Paris, and in *Les Justes Causes* (1954) four young Parisians whose espousal of just causes ends in disenchantment with politics.

Cuvier, Le: One of the two most celebrated farces (q.v.) of the fifteenth century, of unknown authorship, it deals with a submissive husband who attends to all the domestic and household chores prescribed for him on a *rolet* or parchment by his dominating wife. When his wife, while preparing her laundry, falls into a large vat and pleads for his help, he takes advantage of the situation and refuses to come to her rescue unless she promises to tear up the list of his duties.

Eug. and Ed. Adenis, *La Farce du Cuvier, adapt. en vers*, 1897.

Cyclone, Le (1923): See *Gantillon, Simon*.

Cyrano de Bergerac (1897): See *Rostand, Edmond*.

Cyrano de Bergerac, Savinien: (1619-1655) Rendered famous by Rostand (q.v.), in the play *Cyrano de Ber-*

gerac (1897), in which, however, he was idealized, this author devoted himself to study and writing after having served in the army, been wounded in battle, and participated in several duels. A minor prose writer, his burlesque and fantastic *L'Autre Monde ou Les États et Empires de la Lune* (1657) and *Les États et Empires du Soleil* (1662), inspired Swift's *Gulliver's Travels* and Voltaire's (q.v.) *Micromegas.* His bold views, reflected in these "voyages" by bizarre scientific theories, can also be seen in the religious and political theories expressed in the tragedy *La Mort d'Agrippine*

(1653). His comedy, *Le Pédant Joué* (1654), furnished Molière (q.v.) with the famous *"Que diable allait-il faire dans cette galère"* scene. His independent spirit ran counter to the doctrinaire Malherbe (q.v.) and his indulgence in the *burlesque* (q.v.) represented an important reaction against the preciosity of seventeenth-century literature.

Th. Gautier, *Les Grotesques,* 1844; P. Brun, *Savinien de Cyrano de Bergerac, sa vie et ses œuvres,* 1893; R. Pintard, *Le Libertinage érudit dans la première moitié du 17ᵉ siècle,* 1943.

D

DADAISM: An international nihilistic movement in poetry and painting founded by a group of young artists and intellectuals during the First World War; also known as Dada. Revolting violently against all accepted canons of art and social behavior Dadaism proclaimed the supremacy of the arbitrary and illogical aspects of the individual mind. Its principal means of expression, in addition to a series of intentionally scandalous public manifestations, consisted of abstract painting and collages, derived in part from cubism (q.v.), disjointed and nonsensical poems, incoherent aphorisms, typographical disorder and numerous iconoclastic tracts stressing the meaninglessness of the word "dada" itself and the totally anarchical outlook of its members. The strong sense of wry, often malicious, "black" humor which pervaded the movement reflected a

deeper attitude of despair generated by the destructiveness of the war and the seeming triumph of chaos over order in Western Europe.

Dadaism was founded in Zürich in 1916 by several youthful middle-class pacifists and expatriates: Hugo Ball, a German poet; Richard Huelsenbeck, a German medical student; Tristan Tzara (q.v.), a Roumanian poet; and Hans Arp, an Alsatian painter. They congregated regularly at a beer parlor, the Cabaret Voltaire, where Ball, a friend of the painter Kandinsky, had already organized in 1915 an exhibit of modern paintings, readings of contemporary French poetry and a recital of African negro chants. The name of the movement, according to Huelsenbeck, derives from the accidental discovery of the word "dada" in a German-French dictionary while he and Ball were looking for a stage name for a chanteuse in

77

their cabaret. This account is probably more authentic than the widespread but apparently apocryphal story of Arp, according to which Tzara "at 6 P.M. on February 8, 1916" opened a Larousse dictionary at random with a paper cutter and found "dada." In any case, the word, which is French for "hobby horse" and "hobby," first appeared in print with its new meaning (i.e., "Dada means nothing"), in the only issue of the review *Cabaret Voltaire,* June 15, 1916.

On July 14, 1916, the French national holiday, Dada gave its first public performance, at the Zürich Waag Hall, where Tzara read the first of numerous Dada manifestoes. From then until the end of the war the young nihilists shocked the good citizens of Zürich with a series of blasphemous demonstrations which included primitive masked dances, subversive charades, "bruitist" poems (containing a cacophonous mixture of words, inarticulate sounds and mechanical noises), and "simultaneist" poems (made up of different texts read aloud, often in different languages, at the same time). In July, 1917 Tzara issued the first number of the review *Dada,* through which he came in contact with two Paris advanced guard magazines *Nord-Sud* and *Sic,* thus paving the way for his arrival in Paris in 1919.

Meanwhile a similar anti-aesthetic movement was evolving independently in New York under the two former cubists, Marcel Duchamp and Francis Picabia, both of whom were showing their disrespect for art, Duchamp through the exhibit of "ready-mades," i.e., ordinary objects in everyday use, and Picabia through the painting of complex but utterly useless machines. In 1918, during a visit to Switzerland Picabia discovered the Cabaret Voltaire and worked a merger between the two groups, which continued into the Paris period when Duchamp was to achieve considerable notoriety by the exhibition in 1920 of a reproduction of the Mona Lisa which he had adorned with a moustache.

With the end of the war the German Dadaists, returning to Berlin and Cologne, felt obliged to direct Dada along more definite political lines. By allying themselves with the Communist party they committed the movement to a more positive program than would ever have been allowed by Tzara, who, from 1919 on, was to lead the Paris group. Even before Tzara's arrival in Paris three young French poets, André Breton, Louis Aragon and Philippe Soupault, later to be joined by Paul Eluard (qq.v.), had founded a periodical, considerably more destructive than *Nord-Sud,* and *Sic,* which they ironically named *Littérature* (March 1919). Under the influence of Rimbaud, Lautréamont, Jarry and Apollinaire (qq.v.), and more directly of a young nihilist, Jacques Vaché, who committed suicide in 1919, these poets denied the validity of all literary and artistic standards and attempted to use words either in a totally arbitrary manner, divorced from accepted meanings, or as a means of exteriorising the most irrational and incoherent substrata of the individual mind.

The alliance of this *Littérature* group with Tzara, who was already well versed in effective publicity methods, produced the most sensational phase of Dada, during the winter and spring of 1920. Beginning with a matinée at the Palais des Fêtes on January 23 they staged a quick succession of scandalous performances which provoked a wave of public curiosity and indignation in Paris and culminated in the well organized pandemonium of the Dada Festival at the Salle Gaveau on May 26. The very success of this manifestation created a dilemma for the Dadaists: in order to remain faithful to their program of total negation they must go on repeating themselves, at the risk of becoming stereotyped and thus lessening their shock value, or else they must find a more positive program, the search for which would in itself constitute a negation of Dadaism. The plethora of little reviews in the spring of 1920, each one with its own program, had already made the members realize how fragile was their unity. In addition to *Littérature*, Tzara's Dada bulletin continued to appear as well as Picabia's *391;* Eluard meanwhile founded the shortlived *Proverbe,* Picabia published two issues of *Cannibale,* and Paul Dermée one issue of *Z.*

The dilemma in which the group found itself inevitably resulted in dissension which crystallized around Tzara on the one hand, who wished at all costs to maintain the absolute nihilism of the Zürich days, and Breton on the other, who viewed Dadaism more optimistically as only a preliminary stage in the liberation of the human spirit from traditions and conventions. In May of 1921, when Breton and the *Littérature* group staged a mock trial of the nationalist writer Maurice Barrès (q.v.), Tzara and Picabia objected violently, not in the name of good taste or because of any affection for Barrès, but because the serious moral implications of any judgment upon Barrès were bound to be inconsistent with the spirit of Dada, which "means nothing." In 1922 the cleavage became an open break when Breton once again stole the initiative from Tzara by proposing a grandiose "Congress of Paris," a serious gathering of all modern art and literary movements "to establish new directives for the modern mind." Tzara refused all adherence in the name of Dada, and although the Congress was never held rela-

tions between the original Dadaists and the *Littérature* group became so acrimonious that despite the success of the Salon Dada, an international art exhibit in June, 1922, the history of the ensuing months is almost exclusively one of squabbles and personal attacks. The majority of the group eventually rallied around Breton who, choosing the new name "surrealism," (q.v.) issued a manifesto in 1924 which marked the official death of Dada in Paris.

If surrealism was successful in persuading most of the Dadaists to change their allegiance it was because the new movement, with its stress on the rich poetic possibilities of the subconscious mind, provided a more positive creed than the totally iconoclastic program of Dada. By its very nature Dada was bound to die young and through self destruction. It was an impulse, an "intensity," as Tzara said, rather than a creed, and it was so all-inclusive and indiscriminate in its negation that it was quickly spent. In the few years of its life, however, it served as a powerful irritant in Western European thought, conveying through its shock treatment a deep realization of the crisis in social and aesthetic values in the post-war world. At the same time it provided an apprenticeship for a generation of very gifted artists and poets, those born around the year 1900, and thus affected profoundly the direction of later developments in modern painting and literature.

Robert Motherwell (Editor), *The Dada Painters and Poets.* An Anthology, New York, 1953.

LeRoy C. Breunig, Jr.

Dame aux Camélias, La: Written by Dumas *fils* (q.v.) and produced at the *Vaudeville* on February 2, 1852, this play, easily the most popular of French dramatic pieces of the midnineteenth century, marks the foundation of the modern comedy of manners. It is the romantic story of Marguerite Gautier, a contemporary courtesan, who falls in love with Armand. For love of him, Marguerite gives up her former way of life and leaves her friends to go away with him to the country. Her happiness, however, is short-lived; in the absence of Armand, who has gone to Paris to arrange some business matters, M. Duval, Armand's father, calls on Marguerite and entreats her, for the sake of his son's future and as a proof of the sincerity of her love, to leave him. Agreeing, though with difficulty, Marguerite writes Armand a letter, making him believe that she dislikes her present life and intends to return to Paris. Back in Paris with some of her former companions, Marguerite, still very much in love with Armand, longs to see Armand before she dies. Her last wish is granted when Armand, who has finally been told the whole truth by his father, arrives, broken-hearted and humbled. Marguerite, now worn out by her emotions and by her consumptive cough, dies in Armand's arms.

Dancourt, Florent Carton: (1661-1725) A successor of Molière (q.v.), this actor and director, born of a family of English origin, was the author of some sixty plays. His comedies, most of which are written in prose, reflect the manners of his day and the importance of money in the lives of the impoverished nobility, who enter into marriages with ambitious, but wealthy, bourgeois. The types depicted, unlike those in Molière, are local and contemporary, with especial emphasis on the middle and lower classes. Included among his plays are *Le Chevalier à la mode* (1687)—his masterpiece—, *Les Bourgeoises à la mode* (1693), *Le Mari retrouvé* (1698), *Les Bourgeoises de qualité* (1700) and *Le Galant jardinier* (1704).

C. Barthélemy, *La Comédie de Dancourt*, 1882; J. Lemaître, *La*

Comédie après Molière et le théâtre de Dancourt, 1903.

Danse devant le miroir, La (1913): See *Curel.*

Daudet, Alphonse: (1840-1897) The spirit of Provence, where he was born and for which he was to have a life-long nostalgia, stamps the short stories and novels for which he is particularly known. The semi-autobiographical *Le Petit Chose* (1868) contains many details of his early childhood and of his unhappy experience as a teacher at the Collège d'Alais, a position he had to accept when his father failed in the silk business; this failure also explains why the family had to leave Nîmes, Daudet's native town, and move to Lyons. *Les Lettres de mon moulin* (1866), a collection of tales, evokes the charm and legends of Provence. These books, it should be stated, were written under the influence of his friend Mistral (q.v.) and other members of the Félibrige (q.v.) movement; they follow the publication of *Les Amoureuses* (1857), a collection of verse written in Paris, where he had rejoined his older brother Ernest. In the humorous *Aventures véritables de Tartarin de Tarascon* (1872) is seen the character of the *Méridional*, the caricature of which is continued in *Tartarin sur les Alpes* (1885) and in *Port Tarascon* (1890).

In 1874 Daudet wrote *Fromont jeune et Risler aîné*, a portrait of the business world and of unsuccessful actors. This novel is considered to be his first naturalistic venture. Other novels, based on contemporary events and individuals he knew personally, were to follow. The world of high finance, which he got to know when he was secretary to Duc de Morny, is depicted in *Le Nabab* (1877); that of bohemian society in Paris and of the *demi-mondaine* is seen in *Sapho* (1884); political life is portrayed in *Numa Roumestan* (1881). In these and

Plate 5. Sidonie Gabrielle Colette

Plate 6. Pierre Corneille

other novels, including *Les rois en exil* (1879), *L'Immortel* (1888), and *Jack* (1876), Daudet, like other naturalists, makes use of careful documentation and shows concern for the poorer classes. Unlike them, however, he is not guided by any deterministic philosophy; nor are his pathetic and tragic tales consciously pessimistic. Other qualities, moreover—tenderness, sensitivity, pity, and a sense of humor—set him apart from the naturalists. He is, in some respects, the French Dickens. Included among his other works are *Les Contes du Lundi* (1873), which deals with the Franco-Prussian war, and *L'Arlésienne* (1872), a tragedy for which Bizet wrote the music.

Y. Martinet, *A. Daudet, sa vie et son œuvre*, 1940; J. E. Clogenson, *A. Daudet, peintre de la vie de son temps*, 1946.

débat (or **disputaison**): A moral or satiric poem in dialogue, popular during the Middle Ages, in which diverse views are discussed either by personified characters or by real persons. Hence such titles as *Le Débat du vin et de l'eau, Le Débat de l'hiver et de l'été,* and *Le Débat du corps et de l'âme.*

Défense et Illustration de la langue française: See *Pléiade.*

De la littérature (1800): See *Staël, Madame de.*

De L'Allemagne (p. 1813): See *Staël, Madame de.*

De la Monarchie selon la Charte (1816): See *Chateaubriand.*

De l'amour (1822): See *Stendhal.*

De L'Angelus de l'aube à l'Angelus du soir (1888-1897): See *Jammes, Francis.*

Delarue-Mardus, Lucie, Madame: (1880-1945) This novelist, poetess, dramatist and short-story writer was born in Normandy. Her poetry is voluptuous, full of the joy of physical life. *La Monnaie de singe* (1912), one of her best novels, reveals her preference for primitive, as against conventional, or artificial, life. Other novels include *Le Roman des six petites filles* (1909), *Tout l'amour* (1911) *L'Inexpérimentée* (1913), and *L'Ame aux trois visages* (1919).

De la Sagesse (1601): See *Charron, Pierre.*

Delavigne, Casimir: (1793-1843) Achieving fame in 1815 with his *Messéniennes*—patriotic odes inspired by Waterloo and other real events—he gained success also as a dramatist when his tragedy *Les Vêpres siciliennes* (1819), classical in composition and style, was produced at the Odéon theater. Although the language in *Marino Faliero* (1829)—an historical tragedy produced a few months before Dumas *père's* (q.v.) *Henri III et sa cour* and a year before Hugo's (q.v.) *Hernani*—is classical, the play's changes in scene and its local color in costume and decoration, together with its humorous elements, are more typical of the romantic play. In two other tragedies, *Louis XI* (1832)—probably his masterpiece—and *Les Enfants d'Edouard* (1833), Shakespearian influences are discernible. Another romantic feature in Delavigne, who represents, in the final analysis, a compromise between classicism and romanticism, is his attempt to avoid Roman and Greek subjects. In his comedies—*Les Comédiens* (1819), *La Princesse Aurélie* (1828), and *Don Juan d'Autriche* (1835)—Delavigne remained faithful to the conventional aristocratic types of the seventeenth and eighteenth centuries.

A. Favrot, *Étude sur Casimir Delavigne*, 1894; R. Wetzig, *Studien über die Tragödie Casimir Delavigne*, 1900.

De l'Esprit (1758): See *Helvétius.*

Délie, objet de plus haute vertu (1544): See *Scève, Maurice.*

Delille, Jacques: (1738-1813) Excelling in the descriptive and the didactic poem, he wrote *Les Jardins* (1782), *L'Homme des champs* (1802), *Les*

Trois règnes de la Nature (1809), which reflect his impersonal attitude before Nature. He also translated Virgil's *Georgics* (1769), Milton's *Paradise Lost* (1805), and Pope's *Essay on Man* (1805). L. Audiat, *Un poète oublié: J. Delille,* 1902.

Delphine (1803): See *Staël, Madame de.*

Démocratie en Amérique, La (1835-1840): See *Tocqueville.*

Dépit amoureux, Le (1656): See *Molière.*

Déracinés, Les (1897): See *Barrès, Maurice.*

Desbordes-Valmore, Marceline: (1786-1859) Even before Lamartine (q.v.), this poetess, sorely tried in life, expressed in verse emotions characterized by much sincerity. Her lyricism is essentially romantic in its ardor and individuality; she sings of the disquietudes and torments of love, of the joys of maternity, and of religious fervor. Her principal collections include *Elégies et Romances* (1819), *Pauvres Fleurs* (1839), and *Bouquets et Prières* (1843).

Jacques Boulenger, *Marceline Desbordes-Valmore. Sa vie et son secret,* 1926.

Descartes, René: (1596-1650) Born in Touraine, educated at the Jesuit College of La Flèche, this philosopher enlisted in the army of Maurice of Nassau in Holland and fought in the Thirty Years' War before devoting himself entirely to study and writing. After spending twenty years in Holland, where he wrote *Le Discours de la Méthode* (1637), *Les Méditations métaphysiques* (1641) and *Le Traité des passions* (1649), he went, at the invitation of Queen Christina, to Sweden, where shortly thereafter he died. *Le Discours de la Méthode* (q.v.), one of his most important works, had much influence on French literature and language. As the first important philosophical work writ-

ten in French, it represents, by its clear, precise, though somewhat abstract, style, a landmark in French prose. By recognizing, moreover, in its scientific search for truth, *"le bon sens"*—the faculty of reason or the ability to distinguish the true from the false, which is shared by everybody—it suggested the study of universal man that was to become an integral part of French literature during the seventeenth century. The mathematical method of reasoning and evidence that it formulates in place of the scholastic syllogism and medieval authority, which it rejects or finds inadequate, initiated the spirit of rationalism that was to characterize most forms of literature during this century and that was to find free expression in the philosophy of the eighteenth century. In *Le Traité des passions* he establishes the relationship between passions and mind and body, and shows how reason, enlightening the *will,* can govern these passions. Descartes also wrote *Principes de la philosophie* (1644), a treatise on the physical universe.

J. Chevalier, *Descartes,* 1921; L. Brunschvicg, *Descartes,* 1937; H. Gouhier, *Essais sur Descartes,* 1938; J. Laporte, *Le Rationalisme de Descartes,* 1945.

Deschamps, Eustache: (1346-1407) Prolific author of *ballades, rondeaux,* and *virelais* (qq.v.), his most interesting output is his historical poetry, most celebrated of which is his *ballade, Sur le trépas de Bertrand du Guesclin.* Many of his poems are directed against the English, whom he fought at the side of Charles V and Charles VI. Others, including his celebrated *Miroir du mariage,* are satirical or moral, with attacks on the Church, State, financiers and women. The personal element of his poetry can be seen in his many allusions to facts pertaining to his daily life.

A. Sarradin, *Eustache Deschamps*, 1878; E. Hoepffner, *Eustache Deschamps Leben und Werke*, 1904.

Désert de Bièvres, Le (1936): See *Duhamel*.

Desmarets de Saint-Sorlin, Jean: (1595-1676) To justify the Christian inspiration of his epic poem, *Clovis* (1657), he attacked, in the preface to this work and in several other prefaces and works of criticism, the use of pagan myths in literature. His stand set off, in the seventies, a controversy—the first phase of the *Querelle des Anciens et des Modernes* (q.v.)—in which Boileau (q.v.) became his adversary. In an earlier quarrel—this time with the Jansenists (q.v.)—he was called *"un empoisonneur public . . . des âmes des fidèles"* by Nicole, who alluded in 1666 to the novels and plays— *Les Visionnaires* (1637) in particular—he had written. *Les Visionnaires*, a comedy, anticipated Molière (q.v.) in its attack upon preciosity (q.v.). He also composed several *tragi-comedies* (q.v.) and such novels of adventure as *Ariane* (1632) and *Aspasie* (1636).
R. Kerviler, *Desmarets de Saint-Sorlin*, 1879.

Desmoulins, Camille: (1760-1794) Probably the most noted journalist during the Revolution, he ended his days on the scaffold. In his *Les Révolutions de France et de Brabant* (1789-1791), he expresses, with eloquence and passion, his hatred of all despotism and his concern for the popular welfare.
J. Clarétie, *Camille Desmoulins*, 1908.

Des Périers, Bonaventure: (*c.* 1510-1544) In 1538 this Latin and Greek scholar published *Cymbalum mundi*, a theological satire in four dialogues. Parliament ordered the book burned, and Des Périers himself was spared probably because of the intervention of Marguerite d'Angoulême (q.v.), whose friend

and secretary he was. In *Nouvelles récréations et joyeux devis* (1558), a posthumous collection of short stories, he follows in the tradition of Rabelais (q.v.).
A. Chenevière, *Bonaventure des Périers, sa vie, ses poésies*, 1886; P. A. Becker, *Bonaventure des Périers als Dichter und Erzähler*, 1924.

Desportes, Philippe (1546-1606) Uncle of Mathurin Régnier (q.v.), this poet is a precursor of Malherbe (q.v.), by whom, however, he was ill-esteemed. Although his four collections of *Amours* (*Amours de Diane, Amours d'Hippolyte, Amours de Cléonice, Amours diverses*) give evidence of a poetic inspiration that finds its source in Petrarch and in Italy, his ideal was to strive for clarity and ingenuity. His *sonnets* gradually gave way to popular *chansons* that were set to music. In his later years (1592-1595) he composed a famous verse rendering of the Psalms.
J. Lavaud, *Philippe Desportes*, 1936.

Destinées, Les (1846): See *Vigny*.

Destouches, Philippe Néricault: (1680-1754) During the early part of his career, this dramatist, a follower of Molière (q.v.), wrote such comedies of character as *Le Curieux Impertinent* (1710), *L'Ingrat* (1712) and *L'Irrésolu* (1713). His best plays, however, reflect the influence of his stay in England, where he was on a diplomatic mission (1717-1723), and where sentimentalism was advanced in the philosophy of Shaftesbury and in many of the English tragedies. The "philosophic" (see *philosophes*) spirit in France, moreover, made it possible for him to add a moralizing element to the tearful and the pathetic that are already found in such plays as *Le Philosophe marié* (1732) and *Le Glorieux* (1732), his masterpiece. The latter play, in particular, represents an important contribution to the development of what was later to be known as the *comédie larmoyante* (q.v.). J. Hankiss, *Philippe Néricault Destouches, l'homme et l'œuvre,* 1918.

Deuxième sexe, Le (1949-1951): See *Beauvoir, Simone de.*

Deux sources de la morale et de la religion, Les (1932): See *Bergson.*

Deval, Jacques: (1894-   ) *Tovaritch* (1934), his most successful play, one that combines elements of vaudeville and comedy and that deals with the misfortunes of grand Russian émigrés symbolic of the confusion of classes and manners of the times, testifies that this dramatist could have become one of the outstanding writers of comedies of his generation. Further examples, such as *Une faible femme* (1920), confirm that fact. *Étienne* (1930), a portrait of an adolescent obliged to have contempt for his father, and *Mademoiselle* (1932), about an old maid who has generous motherly instincts, suggest, however, that Deval was also tempted by melancholy obsessions. These are especially evident in *Prière pour les vivants* (1933), an implacably distressing picture of contemporary bourgeois who are pitiless toward the weak.

Devaulx, Noël: (1905-   ) The writings of this author, untouched by Existentialist speculation, assume poetic qualities and suggest mystery, as can be seen in *L'Auberge Papillon* (1945), a collection of short stories, and in *Le Pressoir mystique* (1948). *Sainte-Barbegrise* (1952), a more recent novel, contains at once a combination of the supernatural and reality, of comedy and parody.

Dhôtel, André: (1900-   ) The success of this novelist marks a survival of surrealism. Poetry, mystery and elusiveness characterize such novels as *Le Plateau de Mazagran* (1947), *David* (1948), *Les Chemins du long Voyage* (1949) and *L'Homme de la Scierie* (1950). *Bernard le paresseux*

(1952), however, is more psychological.

Diable au corps, Le (1923): See *Radiguet, Raymond.*

Diable boiteux, Le (1707): See *Lesage.*

Diaboliques, Les (1874): See *Barbey d'Aurevilly.*

Dialogues des Morts (1683): See *Fontenelle.*

Dialogue du langage français italianisé (1578): See *Estienne, Henri [II].*

Dictionnaire de la langue française (1863-1872): See *Littré.*

Dictionnaire des Précieuses (1661): See *Somaize.*

Dictionnaire français-latin (1539): See *Estienne, Robert.*

Dictionnaire historique et critique (1697): See *Bayle, Pierre.*

Dictionnaire philosophique (1764): See *Voltaire.*

Dictionnaire universel (1690): See *Furetière, Antoine.*

Diderot, Denis: (1713-1784) Famous as the editor of the *Encyclopédie* (1751-1765; q.v.), this prolific writer, born at Langres, was also to distinguish himself as a dramatic and art critic, novelist and dramatist. Early in life he chose to lead, because of his independence of mind, the bohemian and difficult existence of a hack-writer in Paris rather than adopt, as his father wished, a regular profession. His first significant publication, the *Lettre sur les aveugles* (1749), earned him, because of its sensationalist view of the universe, a term of imprisonment. Freed, he resumed work on the *Encyclopédie,* with whose compilation he had been entrusted. Other literary interests were also to claim his attention during the period of its preparation. In all the genres that he used, however, his ideas, more than his creative ability, are prominent. In the struggle for enlightened thought, he expresses atheistic and materialistic ideas in such philosophical works as *Le Rêve de d'Alembert* and *Le Supplément au voyage de Bougain-*

ville (both written in 1769, but published posthumously); the latter work, moreover, emphasizes the happiness found in nature by Tahitian islanders. Long discussions of ideas, and wit, rather than good character development and construction of plot, are also to be found in such novels as *La Religieuse* (1760)—an anti-clerical tale condemning celibacy—*Jacques le fataliste* (1773), and *Le Neveu de Rameau,* which reflects, in its description of bohemian life, Diderot's early years. The last-named novel, incidentally, though written in 1762, was first published in 1821 after having been translated into German by Goethe in 1805. It was as a theorist of the drama, however, that Diderot's importance, aside from the significance of his contribution to the *Encyclopédie,* was to be established. Seeing in the theater a means of social reform, and convinced that man is naturally good and, unlike Rousseau (q.v.), that man's happiness is dependent upon social institutions, he formulated, in various works, including *Entretiens sur le fils naturel: Dorval et moi* (1757) and *Paradoxe sur le comédien* (written in 1773), the theories of the *drame bourgeois* (q.v.) which he tried to apply in such plays as *Le Fils naturel* (1757) and *Le Père de famille* (1758). Although he was less successful as a dramatist, his theories, rooted in man's natural predisposition to virtue and emotional response to distress and suffering, were also to have a strong influence on the social and moral theater of the nineteenth century. The same principles inspire his *Salons,* articles of art criticism—a genre he is said to have inaugurated —which he wrote (1759-1781) for Grimm's *Correspondance littéraire,* a kind of political, social and artistic journal that was sent to various courts of Europe. The friend of such philosophers

and writers as J. J. Rousseau, Condillac and d'Alembert (qq.v.), not to mention the Empress Catherine II of Russia, Diderot revealed in his *Correspondance* (1759-1774) with his confidante Sophie Volland, whom he met in 1755, a sensitive soul, a temperamental character, and an encyclopedic mind. This many-sided genius, enthusiast of life and of mankind, sought to bring about the triumph of progressive thought. A leader of the philosophical movement of the eighteenth century, he synthesizes in his interests as well as in his views the aspirations of the Age of Enlightenment (q.v.). Included among his other writings are *Pensées philosophiques* (1746), a philosophical work, and works of literary criticism.

L. Ducros, *Diderot,* 1894; L. Cru, *Diderot as a Disciple of English Thought,* 1913; J. Le Gras, *Diderot et l'Encyclopédie,* 1928; A. Billy, *Vie de Diderot,* 1932; *Diderot Studies II,* ed. by O. E. Fellows and N. L. Torrey, 1952; L. G. Crocker, *The Embattled Philosopher,* 1954.

Digression sur les Anciens et les Modernes (1688): See *Fontenelle.*

Dingley (1902): See *Tharaud.*

Disciple, Le (1889): See *Bourget, Paul.*

Discours de la Méthode: This philosophical work (1637) by Descartes (q.v.), the first important one to be written in French, represents an attempt to break away from the scholasticism of the Middle Ages and to recognize man's inherent faculty of reason. In the search for scientific truth, Descartes establishes a mathematical method of reasoning based on intuitive evidence. To find this "evidence," he first begins with a *tabula rasa,* that is, with a discarding of all acquired knowledge and a doubting of everything, even mathematics. But from the fact that he can doubt he derives his basic philosophical principle, *cogito, ergo sum*

("I think, therefore I am"). With this method he also proves the existence of God and arrives at the idea of infinity; on man, therefore, in whom Descartes places the origin of all true knowledge, depends, as has been said, the existence of God Himself. Not foreseen, however, by Descartes, his "method" was to become a weapon in the hands of the 18th century *philosophes* (q.v.), who saw in it a means of revolutionizing human thought and of fostering religious skepticism and political unorthodoxy.

Other principles or maxims establish a code of morals to govern conduct; conclusions are offered relating to the notion of the heart and other anatomical problems, and a program is outlined for a further investigation of nature. His philosophy separates the mind from the body, although he attempts to explain how they work together.

Discours sur l'Histoire universelle (1681): See *Bossuet.*

Discours sur la servitude volontaire (*c.* 1553): See *La Boétie.*

Discours sur le style (1753): See *Buffon.*

Discours sur les sciences et les arts (1750): See *Rousseau, J. J.*

Discours sur l'inégalité parmi les hommes (1755): See *Rousseau, J. J.*

Discours sur l'universalité de la langue française (1784): See *Rivarol.*

dit: Essentially a didactic or descriptive poem popular during the Middle Ages. Many of the *dits* are satirical, their satire being directed against monks, different professions and women (See *Le Dit des Cornettes*).

Divorçons (1880): See *Sardou.*

Docteur amoureux, Le (1658): See *Molière.*

Dominique (1862): See *Fromentin, Eugène.*

Don Juan (1665): See *Molière.*

Donnay, Maurice: (1859-1945) Love is the principal theme in the plays of this dramatist, who once wrote satirical *saynètes,* or dramatic sketches, for the famous cabaret *Le Chat Noir. Amants* (1895), his masterpiece, is a romantic love idyl with psychological significance, treated with wit and sentiment. Although *Le Retour de Jérusalem* (1903) broaches a racial issue, in the end it, too, turns into a problem of love. Other plays cast in the same mold, and which involve such questions as communism and feminism, include *La Clairière* (1900; with Lucien Descaves), and *Les Eclaireuses* (1913). In them all, sophistication is the main note.

P. Bathille, *Maurice Donnay; son œuvre,* 1933.

Dorat (or Daurat), Jean: (1508-1588) One of the poets of the *Pléiade* (q.v.) who wrote remarkable poetry in Latin. Engaged at first as tutor of Antoine de Baïf, the son of Lazare de Baïf, and of Ronsard (qq.v.), he drew them later as students at the Collège de Coqueret, where he was principal and taught Greek. In 1556 he was named Professor of Greek at the *Collège Royal* (see *Collège de France*).

H. Chamard, *Histoire de la Pléiade,* 1939-1940.

Dorgelès, Roland (pseud. of R. Lécavelé): (1886-) Inspired by Barbusse (q.v.), this novelist first achieved success with his war novel *Les Croix de bois* (1919). Its tone was one of disillusionment. Other books dealing with war or war-devastated regions include *Le Cabaret de la belle femme* (1919) and *Le Réveil des morts* (1923). The theme of bohemian life—which he knew very well and in the treatment of which he is at his most original (cf. *Carco*)—is to be found in *Le Château des brouillards* (1932) and *Quand j'étais Montmartrois* (1936). *Carte d'identité* (1945) depicts the German occupation.

A. Dubeux, *Roland Dorgelès,* 1930.

Double veuvage, Le (1702): See *Dufresny.*

DRAMA:

I. MEDIEVAL PERIOD

The French theater of the Middle Ages appears in two generally independent forms: religious drama and comic drama; the latter form is almost entirely secular.

A. *Religious Drama.* As early as the Xth century, "tropes," or paraphrases in dialogue form of the Holy Scriptures, appear in the Christian ritual and constitute a preliminary sketch of the dramatization of religious history. In the XIth century, liturgical dramas (q.v.) were given by the clerics in cloisters, under the church porches or even in the churches themselves. The themes borrowed from the Scriptures were stirring or merely serious. Certain realistic episodes and some of the characters, however, occasionally introduced a comic element.

These dramas, first in Latin and closely bound to religious worship, became gradually separated from the church itself. *Le Jeu d'Adam* (end of the XIIth century; q.v.) is written in French verse and was played by laymen on the "parvis" in front of the church. In the XIIIth century, legend tended to replace the purely biblical or evangelical episodes. But even though these plays increasingly took on the aspect of true drama, they remained essentially religious in inspiration. Because of the supernatural intervention of the Virgin and the Saints, they were called "Miracles" (q.v.). The most significant works of this period are: *Le Jeu de Saint Nicolas* (q.v.) by Jean Bodel d'Arras (beginning of the XIIIth century; q.v.) and *Le Miracle de Théophile* by Rutebeuf (12??-1280; q.v.).

During the XIVth century, religious brotherhoods appeared with the intent of producing the Passion of Jesus in theatrical form, accompanied by the episodes connected with it. In 1402, the brotherhood of Paris received a licence from king Charles VI, and thus was founded the first permanent and paying theater. It was to last until 1548, when a decree of Parliament forbade its performances. The Passion plays were called "Mistères" (from the Latin *ministerium:* divine service, performance), a term which from early times was confused with "mystère" (mystery). The Mistères (q.v.) are very long plays in verse, divided into days: the *Passion* of Jean Michel d'Angers, written in 1486, has 45,000 lines and is divided into ten days. The most famous *Mistère de la Passion* (q.v.) was written by Arnoul Greban (q.v.), an organist at Notre Dame of Paris; it has 35,000 lines and calls for 224 actors. [An abridged version of this *Mistère,* which only lasts one evening, is now played every Spring on the "parvis" of Notre Dame. In spite of the use of modern methods, this production respects the essentials of medieval staging; the church serves as a background; between Paradise, at the extreme left, and the mouth of Hell, at the extreme right, the sets or "mansions" are lined up on a large stage and represent the different places of action.]

Extremely popular, the religious drama was all but killed by the decree of 1548. The XVIth and XVIIth centuries saw the creation and development of the tragedy, radically different in its inspiration, its structure and the public to which it appealed.

B. *Comic Drama:* Its origins are complex: the few comic aspects of the religious drama, the dramatic recitations of jugglers (the "jeux partis"), probably the Latin comedies played in schools, and principally the patter of the peddlers and quacks at the fairs.

As early as the XIIIth century, one finds short comedies which were either satiric (*La Paix aux Anglais*) or frankly farcical (*Le Garçon et l'Aveugle*). The "Jeux" of Adam de la Halle (123?-128?; q.v.) also date back to the XIIIth century: *Le Jeu de la Feuillée* (1276; q.v.) is a kind of satiric review; *Le Jeu de Robin et Marion* (1288; q.v.), a dramatic pastorale, is considered to be the first French comic opera.

The comic drama developed in great abundance, particularly toward 1450, as a reaction of the people to the misfortunes of the Hundred Years War. It was sponsored by numerous brotherhoods such as the "Clercs de la Basoche" (q.v.) and the "Enfants sans souci" or "Sots." The comic genres became richer and more individual, with monologues such as *Le Franc Archer de Bagnolet* (about 1470); "sermons joyeux"—parodies of religious speeches; "moralités" (q.v.) such as *La Condamnation de Banquet* by Nicholas de La Chesnaye—edifying works which, by means of allegories, illustrated moral precepts or criticized corruption; "soties," (q.v.) frankly satirical, in which the "sot," behind the mask of a court jester, criticized the politics and customs of the times; and "farces" (q.v.)—realistic and entertaining plays in which trickery prevails over stupidity or naïveté and of which *La Farce de Maître Pathelin* (1464; q.v.) is the most famous, the best constructed, and the most amusing to a modern audience.

II. THE RENAISSANCE AND XVIITH CENTURY

Although the theater of antiquity was not totally ignored by the clerics of the Middle Ages, the development of humanistic studies during the Renaissance (q.v.) caused the knowledge of Greco-Latin comedies and tragedies to become widespread among those interested in classical genres. At the same time the theater —until then mostly a popular art— was taken over by great literature and became the concern of scholars and grammarians.

Many theoreticians at that time studied the plays of antiquity and the *Poetics* of Aristotle in order to find the formulas and the rules without which dramatic art could only, according to them, be barbaric. In borrowing their subject matter from Greco-Latin antiquity (or occasionally from biblical sources), dividing their plays into five acts, using a small number of protagonists and a chorus, and writing in verse, the tragic poets of the Renaissance sought to give France a dramatic literature similar to that of Athens or Rome and thus exemplified in their genre the theories of the Pléïade (q.v.).

It would seem, however, that at the end of the XVIth century and beginning of the XVIIth century— the period currently called "baroque" (q.v.)—the most fashionable genre was that of the tragi-comedy (q.v.): a play of intrigue with numerous peripeties—"tragic" because of the heroes being constantly threatened by death, "comic" inasmuch as the denouement is happy or at least not wholly catastrophic. From the time of Garnier's (q.v.) *Bradamante* (1588) to that of Corneille's *Le Cid* (1636; q.v.), the tragi-comedy was in great favor. It was not until 1640 that the true French tragedy (q.v.), independent of antiquity and foreign influences (except in the choice of subject matter) and stripped of heroic peripeties, emerged, meriting the designation of "classical tragedy." Many aspects of Corneille (q.v.) after *Le Cid* and the entire works of Racine (1639-1699; q.v.) illustrate this genre, which, in most respects, was original. Few characters, almost always chosen among heroes of historical or mythological antiquity, are united in a single setting and act out the last day of their story—that is to say, the climax of the conflict which sets them one against the other, and its denouement; the essentially inner motivation may be a question of moral intransigence or irremediable self-love, as in Corneille, or an irresistible passion (love), as generally in Racine. Limited in time and space, with the action mostly dependent on psychological developments, the French tragedy is, above all, a "theater of language": the dramatic tension is expressed less in gestures or movements of staging than through a lyricism of words and verse.

Medieval farce not having fallen under the same parliamentary decree as the religious "plays," the formation of the classic comedy (q.v.) is more complex. While at the theater of the Hôtel de Bourgogne (q.v.) in the beginning of the XVIIth century clowns such as Gros-Guillaume and Guillot-Gorju were perpetuating the Gallic farce, the literate public was reading Plautus and Terence. The effort to refine customs and human relationships, which was to result in the society of the "Précieuses" (q.v.), tended to clear the comic genre of verbal or scenic vulgarities. Moreover, the influence of the Spanish "comedia" led to the play of intrigue. Closely related to the tragi-comedy, a complicated comedy of intrigue was thus to develop, in which the entire subject matter was made up of imbroglios and the maneuvers and subtleties of impassioned lovers, and of which the most intellectualized form is to be found in the comedies of Corneille (*Mélite*, about 1625; *La Suivante*, 1634). Otherwise, verbal play and the taste for parody being pushed to the extreme, the comedy was to go in the direction of the "burlesque" (q.v.) of Scarron (1610-1660; q.v.), whose *Don Japhet d'Arménie* (1653), among others, seems to have partly inspired the comic scenes of Victor Hugo (q.v.)

and Rostand's (q.v.) *Cyrano de Bergerac* (1897).

Molière (1622-1673; q.v.) broke away from the comedy of intrigue and "burlesque" and rediscovered the farce, drawing from it a number of masks and raising them to the level of characters, constructing an inner action and underlining it with scenic plays inspired by the Italian "commedia" and thus creating, on the comic level, a worthy counterpart to the classical tragedy. Furthermore, in order to satisfy Louis XIV and his court, he was to integrate the ballet with comedy, creating the genre of "comedie-ballet" with the collaboration of musicians such as Lulli and Charpentier.

If one considers the dramatic genres in the second half of the XVIIth century, including farce, tragi-comedy, ballet comedy, ballet tragedy, heroic comedy, love tragedy, etc., not to mention comedy of character (q.v.) and tragedy, which dominated the period, one is struck by the abundance and richness of the production of the classical age.

III. THE XVIIITH CENTURY

Following the brilliant success of classical tragedy, XVIIIth century dramatists felt obliged to preserve its form and spirit. They tried to put through a few weak reforms: either by accentuating the horror of the circumstances (Crébillon, 1674-1762; q.v.) or by introducing sly audacities meant to be Shakespearean, as in Voltaire's (q.v.) tragedies (*Zaïre*, 1732), in which "philosophy" is mixed with truly tragic analysis.

After Molière, comedy tried to exhaust the catalogue of characters: *Le Chevalier à la mode* (1687) by Dancourt (q.v.), *Le Joueur* (1696) by Regnard (q.v.), *Le Glorieux* (1732) by Destouches (q.v.), etc. But even these comedies were being directed away from the study of character to the study of manners. The masterpiece of the comedy of manners (q.v.) is *Turcaret* (1709) by Lesage (1668-1747; q.v.), which presents a financier practicing his profession and surrounded by swindlers of every class, of whom he is finally the dupe.

The most original comic writer of the first half of the XVIIIth century is undoubtedly Marivaux (1688-1763; q.v.). The importance of his comedies lies less in the study of characters or manners or even in the "philosophy" by which certain are permeated, than in the analysis of love—the most subtle and, with that of Racine, the most ruthless analysis ever presented on the French stage. Marivaux' characters, thrown into amorous but never scandalous adventures, incessantly engage in verbal combat, in which each makes every effort to catch the other in the game of love without being caught himself (cf. *Le Jeu de l'Amour et du Hasard,* 1730, and *Les Fausses Confidences,* 1737). In many respects, his plays are typical of the refined and subtle culture of the XVIIIth century and may be related to the aristocratic art of the painter Watteau (who died in 1721).

The end of the century was to be dominated by an adventurer, Beaumarchais (1732-1799; q.v.). His masterpiece, *Le Mariage de Figaro* (1784), merits its subtitle: *La Folle Journée.* A vast imbroglio in frenzied rhythm, filled with "mots d'auteur," a continuous satire on the institutions and manners of the Old Regime, both ballet and indictment, it is perhaps the most sparkling play of the French repertory. *Le Mariage* is a revolutionary play, for comic devices are not used, as before, in order to amuse the audience with the satire of individual shortcomings, but as weapons against society as a whole.

During the XVIIIth century a serious effort was also made to transform both comedy and tragedy in order to create a "bourgeois theater," intended to satisfy the taste of the rising bourgeoisie. Diderot (1713-1784; q.v.) urged dramatists to abandon the study of character for that of conditions, and the heroes of antiquity for men of the XVIIIth-century bourgeoisie. These theories were illustrated by the dramas of Diderot himself, but more successfully by Sedaine's (1719-1797; q.v.) *Le Philosophe sans le savoir* (1765)—a drama with a happy, touching, moralizing ending, which hails the glory of the tradesman (a "citizen of the world") and of bourgeois virtues. Indeed, a constructive genre at a turning point of history, the bourgeois drama ("drame bourgeois," "tragédie bourgeoise," "comédie sérieuse," etc.) seems today extremely boring, if not ridiculous, when compared with the destructive gaiety of *Figaro* or the aristocratic refinement of Marivaux.

One might add a long list of writers to those few already mentioned, in a century in which the theater was so much a part of the customs that everyone was more or less an actor or a playwright; in which all dramatic genres were fashionable; in which there was a new flowering of French farces at the fairs (some harlequinades were written by Lesage); in which "proverbs" and short, dissolute comedies were constantly played in the salons; in which classic forms began to break down, creating not only the bourgeois drama but also the "tearful comedy" of Nivelle de La Chaussée (1692-1754; q.v.) and the "melodrama," (q.v.) developed particularly during the Revolution by Loaisel-Tréogate and Pixérécourt (q.v.), paving the way for the Romantic "drame" (q.v.).

IV. THE XIXTH CENTURY

Although classical tragedy retained its supporters and writers and though the moralizing bourgeois drama, in verse or in prose, filled the theaters (encouraged perhaps by the imperial and royal censorship), satisfying the mediocre appetites of the bourgeoisie then in power, the first half of the XIXth century witnessed the explosive beginnings, the triumph and then the decline of a new genre: the Romantic "drame." These bombastic plays shattered the classical frameworks. They enriched the general spectacle. They established the solitary, misunderstood, "different" hero, whom circumstances, a vague destiny or simply his own aspirations isolate from the society of his time: the bandit (*Hernani* by Victor Hugo, 1830) or the poet (*Chatterton,* by Alfred de Vigny, 1835; q.v.). Victor Hugo's (q.v.) "drames" are less disturbing today (in spite of a dazzling versification and a whirlwind of images) than Alfred de Musset's (q.v.) *Lorenzaccio* (1832), a play in prose and the most profound and modern of the French Romantic "drames."

During the second half of the century, theatrical productions, for the most part, were portraits of the bourgeoisie of that time. Plays like *La Dame aux camélias* (1852) by Alexandre Dumas *fils* (q.v.) act as intermediaries between the romantic "drame" and the modern bourgeois play. Constructed on the romantic theme of love as a regenerator of the sinful woman, Dumas' play is a tableau of the world of pleasure, a demonstration of the bourgeois mentality of the period, as well as a plea for a victim of society.

The second half of the XIXth century was the period of the "well-made play," perfected by Scribe (1791-1861; q.v.) at the beginning of the century. Although the characters were often petty and the inspiration lacked grandeur, the plays were skillfully constructed. Scribe's methods enabled writers to artfully build up plots and suspense: they could be used in "vaudeville" (q.v.) as well as in the play of historical intrigue (Victorien Sardou: *La Tosca,* 1887; *Madame Sans-Gêne,* 1893; q.v.). The portraits of the bourgeoisie, built around these principles, were written in various styles: *Le Voyage de Monsieur Perrichon* (1860) and many other comedies of Labiche (1815-1888; q.v.) and his collaborators were gay and apparently inoffensive, yet very innocently reveal the mediocrity of the characters; the works of Emile Augier (*Le Gendre de Monsieur Poirier,* 1854; q.v.) were moralizing and conformist; Meilhac and Halévy's (qq.v.) joyous operetta librettos, put to music by Offenbach (*La Belle Hélène,* 1865), disguised the appetite for pleasure with the costumes of antiquity—which fooled no one.

These plays were carefree, unconscious or steeped in good conscience. They became hardened by the end of the century. Henri Becque (1837-1901; q.v.), concerned above all with accuracy of observation and with the elimination of convention and facile effects from his plays, produced *Les Corbeaux* (1882)—an austere drama of financial rapacity—and *La Parisienne* (1885)—a restrained and bitter comedy of manners. Related to the general trends of realism and naturalism (qq.v.), this often cynical return to a clinical study of the manners and characters of bourgeois society was encouraged by the creation of the "Théâtre Libre," (q.v.) founded in 1887 by André Antoine (q.v.), who enlisted the services of writers, actors and directors in order to stage an uncompromising picture of reality and to thus present the public with true "slices of life."

At the end of the century, presented with the techniques of the realistic or naturalistic drama, the great problems of the times and of modern society filled the stage: not only love and finance, but also science, patriotism, feminism, antimilitarism, hygiene, etc. *Amoureuse* by Georges de Porto-Riche (1894; q.v.) is still a "love-play," but *La Nouvelle Idole* (1899; science) by François de Curel (q.v.), *La Robe Rouge* (1900; justice) by Eugène Brieux (q.v.), or *Les Affaires sont les affaires* (1903; business) by Octave Mirbeau (q.v.) and many others are all more or less problem plays (*pièces à thèse;* q.v.) with realistic façades—and all are considerably dated today.

In contrast to these plays, in which the search for truth often led to shocking novelties or in which the expression of ideas often killed dramatic interest, were the gay "vaudevilles" at the Palais-Royal (Georges Feydeau: *La Dame de Chez Maxim's,* 1899; *Le Dindon,* 1896; *Occupe-toi d'Amélie,* 1908; q.v.). These unrealistic and often scandalous comedies of intrigue are constructed as impeccable machines and are carried along in a frenzied rhythm.

Another reaction, of greater consequence, was the "symbolist" theater. An art of mystery was opposed to both the mathematics of vaudeville and the realism of the "Théâtre Libre"; the poetic theater was opposed to the problem play. Among others, Maeterlinck (1862-1949; q.v.) and Paul Claudel (1868-1955; q.v.) sought to reintroduce lyricism, symbolism and incantation into the theater. At the inception of this reaction one might mention the combined influences of French romanticism (as reflected in Rostand's *Cyrano de Bergerac,* 1897; q.v.), Ibsen and Wagner.

Thus, around 1900, three forms of theater were evident in Paris: the "Palais Royal"—the bed-room farce or "vaudeville"; the "boulevard" or bourgeois comedies—more or less serious, and with or without problems; and the "Avant-garde"—which was divided into the successors of the Théâtre Libre and the promotors of symbolist principles.

V. THE XXTH CENTURY

The XXth century continues the genres of the preceding century. "Vaudeville" flourished until the '40's (Jean de Létraz), when it lost some of its mathematical purity, but has been revived by the tenderness and Pirandellism of André Roussin; after Henri Bataille (*La Marche Nuptiale,* 1920; q.v.) and Bernstein (*Le Voleur,* 1906; q.v.), the boulevard comedy (sometimes serious or melodramatic, sometimes frivolous, sometimes poetic) owes its better productions to Edouard Bourdet (*Le Sexe faible,* 1930; q.v.), Sacha Guitry (*Mon père avait raison,* 1919; q.v.), Jacques Deval (*Tovaritch,* 1933; q.v.), Steve Passeur (*L'Acheteuse,* 1930; q.v.), etc. Special mention must be made of Marcel Achard (*Jean de la Lune,* 1929; q.v.), lighthearted and sensitive, as well as Marcel Pagnol (*Topaze,* 1928; *Marius,* 1929; q.v.), the dramatist of the Marseilles myth and of good satire.

However, the first half of the XXth century is characterized by the overwhelming activity of the avant-garde theater, as well as by a literary theater much superior to that of the end of the XIXth century.

The avant-garde theater has been infinitely variable, originating from Alfred Jarry (q.v.), the author of that huge, cynical and poetic farce, *Ubu-Roi* (1896), which demolished a good number of established values, and from Guillaume Apollinaire's (q.v.) *Les Mamelles de Tirésias* (1917). A more or less surrealistic theater followed in which dream, the absurd and the "non-sense" of magical worlds were mixed with a violent criticism of traditions and bourgeois society (Charles Vildrac: *Victor ou les Enfants au pouvoir,* 1928, q.v.; Raymond Roussel: *Poussière de Soleils,* 1926; Georges Neveux: *Le Bureau central des rêves, 1930*). The name of Antonin Artaud (q.v.), author of *Le Théâtre de la cruauté* (1935), whose influence today is felt in the whole of French Theater, remains attached to this dramatic genre.

More easily accepted by the public was the related theater of dream and strangeness (see *Simon Gantillon; Henri Lenormand; Jean Sarment*). The 1950's witnessed the creation and development of a new avant-garde theater, disturbing and pessimistic, half-way between surrealism (q.v.) and the world of Kafka, which takes the form of farce—scenic metaphors in several dimensions, intended to represent the tragic aspects of human destiny. This genre has produced at least one masterpiece: Samuel Beckett's (q.v.) *En attendant Godot* (1954) in which two tramps pass the time as well as they can while awaiting a certain Godot who never comes.

Although less obviously revolutionary, the "literary" theater has renewed the general style of the French drama. This regeneration is due in part to the activity of the great directors of the 1920's and 1930's: Jacques Copeau, Charles Dullin, Louis Jouvet, Gaston Baty (qq.v.), who have revived masterpieces of the past, introduced a large number of foreign plays and given opportunities to audacious contemporary writers.

Several writers, freed from the conventions of the bourgeois theater, from realism at any price and from the bedrooms of vaudeville, surprised and finally conquered a public that was tired of the eternal comedies concerning adultery. Among many, one might mention: Jean Giraudoux (1882-1944; q.v.), whose plays were primarily staged by Louis Jouvet; poetic, ironic, they are highly intellectual, with a subtlety which sometimes hides a depth of thought (*Siegfried,* 1928; *La Guerre de Troie n'aura pas Lieu,* 1935); Armond Salacrou (1899-   ; q.v.) who, following his surrealistic beginnings, wrote increasingly lucid plays in which one discovers the problems of the times and of humanity in general, and whose masterpiece is still *La Terre est ronde* (1938)—staged by Charles Dullin—a play concerning the dictatorship of Savonarola in Florence; Jean Cocteau (1892-   ; q.v.), the most versatile playwright of the XXth century, whose works often seem to be a pastiche of the works of others as well as of his own, and in whom the tragic element is sometimes a mixture of surrealism and melodrama, annoying or enchanting, according to one's taste (*La Machine infernale,* 1934; *Les Parents terribles,* 1938); Jean Anouilh (1910-   ; q.v.), whose plays, whether "roses," "noires," or "brillantes," all seem variations on the theme of purity in conflict with the sordidness of reality (*La Sauvage, 1933; Antigone, 1943*).

The plays of these writers have at least two features in common: in content, a refusal to compromise when faced with the spiritual poverty of the modern world; in form, the frequent use of Greco-Latin myths, already drawn upon by the classical writers of the XVIIth century on a psychological level and reintroduced by modern writers in order to bring out a moral, philosophical or social significance in situations of the XXth century.

These devices are also found in

Jean Paul Sartre's (q.v.) *Les Mouches*, staged by Charles Dullin in 1943; the legend of Orestes and Electra is used as a metaphor of the search for both personal and political freedom. The dialectic of this search is, of course, presented in terms of existentialist philosophy. The '40's were marked by the appearance of this "existentialist" theater. After *Les Mouches*, Sartre was to write *Huis-Clos* (1944), *Les Mains sales* (1948) and *Le Diable et Le Bon Dieu* (1952), among others. The plays of Albert Camus (*Les Justes*, 1949) are also considered as existentialist.

In addition, the public of the '40's witnessed the revival of the symbolist and religious theater of Paul Claudel (*Le Soulier de Satin*, staged in 1943) as well as the production of a large number of plays written by novelists (François Mauriac's *Les Mal Aimés*, 1945; Henry de Montherlant's *La Reine morte*, 1942; Marcel Aymé's *Clérambard*, 1950; qq.v.).

In the '50's, the French theater has been brilliantly alive, not only in the abundance of talented writers, such as Beckett, Sartre, Anouilh or Aymé, but also of creative directors, such as Jean Vilar and Jean-Louis Barrault (qq.v.).

E. Lintilhac, *Histoire générale du Théâtre en France: La Comédie*, 1909; F. Gaiffe, *Étude sur le Drame en France au XVIII⁰ siècle*, 1910; A. Le Breton, *Le théâtre romantique*, 1927; L. Petit de Julleville, *Le Théâtre en France, des origines à nos jours*, 1927; Gustave Cohen, *Le Théâtre en France au Moyen Age*, 1931; Louis Allard, *La Comédie de mœurs en France au XIX⁰ siècle*, 1923-1933; Henry C. Lancaster, *A History of French dramatic literature in the XVIIth century*, 1929-1942; Edmond Sée, *Le théâtre français contemporain*, 1950; Jacques Schérer, *La dramaturgie classique en France*, 1950; René Lalou, *Le théâtre en France depuis 1900*, 1951.

JACQUES GUICHARNAUD

drama, liturgical: The first manifestations of "drama" originated within the medieval church, where Catholic ritual was dramatized in order to bring religion to an unlettered populace. At first, in conjunction with the liturgy, there were antiphonal responses between the priests and the congregation. In the tenth century these were enlarged by chanted dialogues, or *tropes*, which were inserted into the *sequences* of Easter morning mass. The next step was the elaboration of related material from the Bible and the Apocrypha. Soon short plays in Latin were supplied by priests and were presented with music specially composed for the dialogue. By the twelfth century the evolution of the *trope* into what may be called liturgical drama was complete. Gradually, too, French replaced Latin, verse was substituted for prose, and the dramatizations took place outside of the Church, usually on the *parvis*, where the actors now were from the laity. The first extant play represented outside the Church was *Le Jeu d'Adam* (q.v.) in the 12th century.

G. Cohen, *Le Théâtre en France au moyen age*, 1928; G. Frank, *The Medieval French Drama*, 1954.

DRAME: The word "drame," in its broadest sense, indicates all physical or inner action, or any conjunction of circumstances, which causes the misfortune of one or many individuals or at least implies dangers which these individuals must combat. In the strictest sense of the word, a "drame" is a particular genre of theatrical play.

In France, the "drame" came into being during the XVIIIth century. According to Diderot (q.v.), the "drame bourgeois" (q.v.) was to represent contemporary man, in the background, costumes and with the speech of his milieu and his profession. In no longer presenting the public with Greeks and Romans but with the bourgeoisie of the century faced with the problems of that period, the bourgeois "drame" was destined to replace the tragedy of the 17th century. The pathos of difficult situations was to point up a moral lesson which would lead the spectator to virtue, tolerance, honesty in commerce, respect for the family, *etc*. The works which illustrate these theories are often tearful and declamatory: Diderot's *Le Fils naturel* (1757) and *Le Père de Famille* (1758); Beaumarchais' (q.v.) *Eugénie* (1767). The most important bourgeois "drame" of the XVIIIth century is Sedaine's (q.v.) *Le Philosophe sans le savoir* (1765) in which the virtues of the Old Regime are contrasted with bourgeois virtues, and the conflict between an archaic conception of honor and natural ethics is sometimes skillfully treated, but in which the dramatic effects are often melodramatic and the eulogy of the merchant as "citizen of the world" is a bit ludicrous today.

The most significant contributions of the bourgeois "drame" were the introduction of a certain outer realism in staging and the conception of the bourgeoisie as something other than a subject of pure comedy.

The romantic period witnessed the creation of the romantic "drame," the theory of which is partly given in Stendhal's (q.v.) *Racine et Shakespeare* (1823) and particularly in Victor Hugo's (q.v.) preface to *Cromwell* (1827).

Under the influences of Shakespeare, Schiller, and Goethe, the romantic "drame" was to be a kind of historical chronicle, in which the double face of man appeared: God and Satan, the tragic and the comic, the sublime and the grotesque, meditation and action. The concern for truth was to prevail over the

classical "rules": numerous and varied sets, fictional time lengthened at will, and physical violence on stage. Turbulent and rebellious, the romantic writers chose periods which were—or at least which they imagined to be—colorful and excessive: the middle ages, the Italian Renaissance, the XVIth and beginning of the XVIIth century in France, *etc*. Against these picturesque backgrounds, to which they liked to give symbolic significance, they drew a few tormented, troubled and solitary heroes, imbued with Byronic satanism mixed with humanitarian ideals.

The best known romantic dramas are those of Victor Hugo. In 1830, the performance of *Hernani* (q.v.) at the Comédie Française caused great disturbance in the theater, because of its bold disregard of classical rules. A riot began between the advocates of classic art and the "jeune France" partisans of this new form of theater—an outbreak which has come down into history as the "battle of *Hernani*." *Ruy Blas* (1838), less successful at the time but considered today as Hugo's best drama, is moving and has a remarkably comic fourth act, but also includes moments of melodrama.

In addition to the bandits, rebels, and victims of the machinations of history which are found in Hugo, there were also Vigny's (q.v.) misunderstood poet in *Chatterton* (1835) and, in particular, the both idealistic and depraved hero of Musset's (q.v.) *Lorenzaccio* (1833), considered the best French romantic drama: standing out against an extraordinarily vivid background which evokes the Florentine Renaissance, is the figure of the young murderer, who, in order to rid his city of a corrupt tyrant, becomes the favorite of this tyrant, loses his own purity and finally carries out his murder for reasons which he no longer understands. Less literary, but, at the same time, more popular, the dramas of Alexandre Dumas *père* (*La Tour de Nesle,* 1832; q.v.) must be mentioned.

The year 1843 witnessed the failure of Hugo's *Les Burgraves,* and with the help of the actress Rachel, the return of classical tragedy. Nevertheless, the romantic drama was to survive [*e.g.,* Rostand's (q.v.) *Cyrano de Bergerac,* 1897; Cocteau's (q.v.) *L'Aigle à deux têtes,* 1946]. The reintroduction today of *Lorenzaccio, Ruy Blas* and *Marie Tudor* by the "Théâtre National Populaire" proves that, in spite of its inflated style and general limitations, the romantic "drame" is still good theater. However, in the use of physical effects, surprises, historical mysteries and exaggerated contrasts between the purity of the victims and the wickedness of the "villains," the romantic "drame" is often close to "melodrama" (q.v.), by which it was somewhat influenced.

During the XIXth century, the "drame" became increasingly "bourgeois." The historical past gave way to the contemporary world. The allegedly eternal themes (the people against tyranny, the poet against society, *etc.*) gave way to less imposing considerations such as the family and illegitimate love. This turning point was marked by *La Dame aux Camélias* (1852) by Alexandre Dumas *fils* (q.v.).

Having become bourgeois, the "drame" took various forms (comedy of manners, problem play, *etc.*), some approaching comedy, some tragedy, and, with the symbolist movement, at the end of the century, was led to the lyric, magical and poetic play (Paul Claudel; q.v.).

Today, with the prevailing confusion of genres, it is the writer who decides whether or not to call his play a "drame." Generally, the term "drame" is used to describe any serious play in which one or several of the likeable characters struggle against dangers for which they are not responsible and thus evoke emotions of fear and sympathy in the spectator.

Denis Diderot, *Entretiens sur le Fils Naturel,* 1757; Pierre Caron de Beaumarchais, *Essai sur le genre dramatique sérieux,* 1767; F. Gaiffe, *Étude sur le drame en France au XVIIIᵉ siècle,* 1910; André Le Breton, *Le Théâtre romantique,* 1927.

JACQUES GUICHARNAUD

drame bourgeois: A modification of the *comédie larmoyante* (q.v.), this dramatic genre, whose theories were formulated by Diderot (q.v.) in his *Entretiens sur le Fils naturel—* better known under the title of *Dorval et moi* (1757)—and in *Discours sur la poésie dramatique* (1758), represents an intermediary form between the languishing classical tragedy and comedy of character. Portraying bourgeois domestic life, it stresses, contrary to what is found in seventeenth century comedy and tragedy (qq.v.), social conditions and situations, to which characters, their by-product, are subordinated. It becomes, in the final analysis, a vehicle for the dissemination of social reform with a moral basis. This new type of serious play, written in prose, advocates, for an effect of greater realism, the frequent use of pantomime instead of declamatory speech, *tableaux,* or stage pictures —a kind of mute pathos—and stage settings and costumes which conform to its context. Although such plays as *Le Fils naturel* (1757) and *Le Père de famille* (1758) reveal that Diderot was more successful in the realm of theory than in actual practice, and though the principles of the *drame bourgeois* were to be better realized by such a dramatist as Sedaine (q.v.), Diderot's theories were to have a lasting influence on the social theater of the nineteenth century, especially on Augier and Dumas *fils* (qq.v.).

F. Gaiffe, *Étude sur le drame en France au XVIII° siècle,* 1910.

Drieu La Rochelle, Pierre: (1893-1945) This novelist and critic personifies the intellectual, artistic and moral bankruptcy of his generation. In a fruitless but sincere search for a personal orientation toward life, he moved from Communism to Surrealism (q.v.) to Fascism. His political essays—*Mesure de la France* (1923), *Genève ou Moscou* (1928), *Avec Doriot* (1937)—and his novels —*L'Homme couvert de femmes* (1925) and *Gilles* (1939)—reflect his intellectual journey from nihilism and disillusionment to a desire for action and violence. His collaboration with the Germans during the Second World War and his final suicide mark a dramatic and futile end.

Pierre Andreu, *Drieu, témoin et visionnaire,* 1952.

Druon, Maurice: (1918-   ) In *Les Grandes Familles* (1948), for which he was awarded the *Prix Goncourt,* this novelist depicts a decadent, bourgeois French family. Other titles include *La Chute des Corps* (1950) and *Rendez-vous aux Enfers* (1951).

Du Bartas, Guillaume (or **Guillaume de Saluste):** (1544-1590) This Protestant poet from Gascony was attached to Henry of Navarre, who sent him on various missions, including one to England and Scotland. His writings, at a time when pagan sources and mythology were much in vogue because of the influence of the *Pléiade* (q.v.) poets, reflect in contrast the inspiration of the Bible. In 1573 he published *Judith,* an epic in which Judith liberates Jerusalem from Holofernes. His *magnum opus,* also drawn from the Bible, *La Semaine* (1578), relates, in seven cantos, or "days," the genesis of the world. A *Seconde Semaine,* begun in 1584, in which he had hoped to enlarge his subject and bring it up to the time of the birth of Christ, was never completed. His reputation, which rivalled that of Ronsard (q.v.), spread to other countries, where his works were translated, and he is said to have been imitated by Tasso, Milton, and Byron, and admired by Goethe.

G. Pellissier, *La vie et les œuvres de du Bartas,* 1882.

Du Bellay, Joachim: (1522-1560) Born at Liré in Anjou, western France, this writer was, next to Ronsard (q.v.), the greatest poet of the *Pléiade* (q.v.). Together with Ronsard, whom he had met at the age of twenty-five, he studied under the great humanist Dorat (q.v.) at the Collège de Coqueret. Inspired by the study of Latin and Greek, and influenced by his fellow-student and friend, he launched in 1549 the *Défense et Illustration de la langue française.* This manifesto of the Pléiade group argued that the French language was capable of expressing the loftiest poetic feelings and thoughts, and demanded for its enrichment a new poetic system based on classical and Italian themes and forms and a rejection of the medieval traditions. In accord with its program, Du Bellay published at the same time *L'Olive* (1549). In this collection of 115 sonnets (in 1550 ed.), the first sonnet-sequence in French, he sings, much as Petrarch did for Laura, his love for Olive, his muse and ideal woman. Later, while spending four years (1553-1557) in Italy as the secretary of his famous uncle, the Cardinal Du Bellay, in which post he felt humiliated, he wrote *Les Regrets* (1558), a collection of sonnets in which the poet expresses his unhappiness and his nostalgia for France, and *Les Antiquités de Rome* (1558), sonnets in which he points up the contrast between the past grandeur of Rome and its present ruins. Other works by him are the lyrical *Jeux rustiques* (1558) and the satirical *Le Poète Courtisan* (1559).

H. Chamard, *Joachim du Bellay*, 1900; R. V. Merrill, *The Platonism of Joachim du Bellay*, 1923; H. Chamard, *Histoire de la Pléiade*, 1939-1940; V.-L. Saulnier, *Du Bellay, l'homme et l'œuvre*, 1951.

Du Bos, Charles: (1882-1939) This critic, whose mother was English, studied at Oxford, and travelled through Europe. Interested not only in French but also in English and German authors, this voracious reader, as a result of investigation and study, was familiar with Stendhal, Proust, Gide, Claudel, Valéry (qq.v.), Shakespeare, Goethe, Byron, Shelly, and many others. He seriously tried to penetrate the spirit of each work, and inevitably made comparisons which he thought shed light on the mystery and source of inspiration of each literary creation. Thus by intuition he seized the heart of each masterpiece. Included among his writings are *Approximations* (1922-1937), in seven volumes, *Dialogue avec André Gide* (1929), and *Byron et le besoin de la fatalité* (1929).

Du Cange, Charles du Fresne, seigneur: (1610-1688) One of the outstanding scholars of the seventeenth century, he is the author of several historical works and of a notable Latin dictionary (first published in 1678), which has since been expanded and is still in use.

L. Feugère, *Études sur la vie et les ouvrages de Du Cange*, 1852.

Ducange, Victor: (1783-1833) As a successful melodramatist (see *melodrama*), he produced such plays as *Trente ans ou la Vie d'un joueur* (1827) and *Il y a seize ans* (1831). His plays foreshadow somewhat the prose drama of the romantic school (see *drame*).

Ducis, Jean-François: (1733-1816) Following Voltaire (q.v.), he was the first to make adaptations, from the translations of Letourneur, of Shakespeare. These include *Hamlet* (1769), *Le Roi Léar* (1783), and

Othello (1792). The adaptations, however, are very poor, and have a ludicrous effect. Unity of time (see *unities*) is preserved, neo-classic language replaces Shakespeare's lines, but the scenes are freely shifted and much talk of liberty and equality—a tendency conspicuous in the plays of the Revolutionary era—is to be found.

Duclos, Charles Pinot: (1704-1772) In addition to his *Considérations sur les mœurs de ce siècle* (1751)—reminiscent of La Bruyère's (q.v.) *Caractères*—this moralist wrote licentious novels and short stories, including *Histoire de la baronne de Luz* (1741) and *Les Confessions du comte de . . .* (1742). He also published *Mémoires secrets sur les règnes de Louis XIV et de Louis XV* (1791), full of wit and irony.

L. le Bourgo, *Duclos, sa vie et ses ouvrages*, 1902.

Du Côté de chez Swann (1913): See *Proust*.

Duel, Le (1905): See *Lavedan, Henri*.

Dufresny, Charles Rivière: (1654-1724) Though this Parisian-born dramatist produced no masterpiece, his comedies follow in the tradition of Molière (q.v.). Original situations, lively dialogue and wit—characteristics, however, that do not always appear together in the same play—are to be found in such plays as *L'Esprit de Contradiction* (1700), *Le Double veuvage* (1702), *La Joueuse* (1709) and *La Réconciliation normande* (1719).

Duhamel, Georges (pseud. of **Denis Thévenin**): (1884-) This Parisian-born physician and son of a physician started his literary career writing poetry as a member of the *Abbaye de Créteil* (q.v.). Although he wrote some plays (*La Lumière*, 1911; *L'Œuvre des Athlètes*, 1920), his reputation as a writer was first established by his two very moving books, *Vie des Martyrs* (1917) and *Civilisation* (1918)—the latter one receiving the *Prix Goncourt* (q.v.)—

in which he describes the human tragedies and the suffering of the wounded he observed in hospitals during the First World War. His several volumes of essays include: *La Possession du monde* (1919), in which an idealistic program of happiness to be found in the "Kingdom in our hearts" is advanced to replace current nationalistic values; *Scènes de la vie future* (1930), written after his trip to the United States, a denunciation and a satire upon the role of the machine in this industrialized civilization; and *Querelles de famille* (1931), a polemic against the unsalutary influences of the machine, symbolized by the automobile, radio and cinema, on French life. All foreshadow, in their warnings against the dangers that threaten the individual's security and happiness, the humanism and fraternal generosity of his two later cyclic novels.

In his *Vie et aventures de Salavin* (*La Confession de Minuit,* 1920; *Deux Hommes,* 1924; *Journal de Salavin,* 1927; *Le Club des Lyonnais,* 1929; *Tel qu'en lui-même,* 1932), Duhamel describes the life and adventures of Salavin, a pitifully weak and impulsive character, who suffers because of his weakness of which he is conscious, but who seeks a personal grandeur in life. Duhamel shows sympathy for this creature who cannot adapt himself to life; as a matter of fact, in a lecture given in 1934, he interpreted Salavin as both the eternally suffering human being and the twentieth-century man exposed to the difficulties caused by the machine age. *La Chronique des Pasquier* (1933-1945), the more important series of the two, is not only the history of a family under the Third Republic, but also an attempt to reconstruct an epoch in the history of French society. Laurent Pasquier, a professor of biology at the Collège de France conceived in the image of the author, at the age of fifty undertakes to write his memoirs, which constitute the chronicle of this Pasquier family. When a man of middle age, his father undertook to prepare himself for the medical profession, which he later practiced; his mother sacrificed herself for the sake of her egoistical husband. Of the many autobiographical episodes depicted in the ten volumes of this cycle—each one of which possesses a complete unity—that of the birth and death of the *Abbaye de Créteil* (q.v.) enterprise as seen in *Le Désert de Bièvres* (1936) is the most important. In this cyclic novel—which represents a total experience—Duhamel has championed an idealistic ethic of tolerance, of a civilized individualism, in his true portrayal of average humanity. He has shown special talents in creating life-like creatures, in his irony and in his humor. His meditations often take on the quality of the classical moralist; his style, marked by much clarity, repudiates the obscure.

André Thérive, *Georges Duhamel ou l'intelligence du cœur,* 1926; Pierre-Henri Simon, *Georges Duhamel ou le Bourgeois sauvé,* 1946.

Duhautcours (1801): See *Picard.*

Dullin, Charles: (1885-1949) The early life of this actor, theatrical director, and *metteur-en-scène* was fraught with financial difficulties. In 1921, after leaving Copeau (q.v.), with whom he had been associated, he founded his own theatrical company at the *Atelier.* Like Copeau (q.v.), his ideal was one of sincerity, of a harmonious, synchronized effect to be obtained by all the actors together—without any single one as the star. The interpretation achieved thus becomes a poetic one, and is aided by the accompaniment of music. Not only did the *Atelier* become a school for actors, but one also for young dramatists; to the latter Dullin wished to make it understood that in the theater life draws its substance, not from a bald copy of reality, as in the Théâtre-Libre (q.v.), but from the world of fancy. His répertoire, an eclectic one, included not only the French classical plays and the modern plays of Jules Romains, Bernard Zimmer, Marcel Achard, Stève Passeur, and Armand Salacrou (qq.v.), but also those of Aristophanes, Calderón, and Pirandello. His greatest success, however, was the adaptation by Stefan Zweig and Jules Romains (q.v.) of Ben Jonson's *Volpone*.

R. Brasillach, *Animateurs de théâtre*, 1936.

Dumas fils, Alexandre: (1824-1895) The unhappy experiences he suffered as an illegitimate child—even though he was the son of the famous Dumas *père* (q.v.)—brought up in the *demimonde* milieu of Paris are reflected in the themes and views expressed in his plays. He launched his dramatic career in 1852 with the very successful *La Dame aux Camélias* (q.v.), adapted from a novel he had written in 1848. Although this play, which is also based on Dumas' personal experience with Marie Duplessis, depicts the romantic love of a courtesan, it is realistic in background; in a contemporary setting in Paris, the environment of a courtesan is here portrayed for the first time in detail. Dumas gave further evidence, in *Le Demi-Monde* (1855), of his particular interest in the social types, conditions, and problems of his day. His originality, however, was less evident in his observation and description of the manners of society than in his *pièce à thèse* (q.v.). As seen in this type of play, which he inaugurated, the function of the theater is not merely, as in Augier (q.v.), to satirize vices or foibles, but to reform. Such a play, which makes use of Scribe's (q.v.) technique of the well-constructed plot as well as of the *raisonneur* (q.v.), tries to impose

or to prove, much like the logic used in a geometrical theorem, the justification of a point of view that society has not accepted. A prime example is *Le Fils naturel* (1858), in which society is taken to task for unjustly visiting the sins of a father on the illegitimate offspring. Other such plays include *Les Idées de Mme Aubray* (1867), which points to the duty of society toward respectable women who have been seduced, and *La Question d'argent* (1857), a demonstration of the corrupting influence of money on marriage. These and other problems, incidentally, are also discussed in several of his prefaces. Especially preoccupied with questions of marriage, money, divorce, adultery and prostitution, Dumas is at once didactic and rhetorical. The remedies he sought for many of the evils he exposed resulted in the change of several institutions or laws, including those pertaining to divorce.

As a social moralist, he represents a reaction against the romantic theater. To a large extent, many of the more modern dramatists, such as Brieux and Hervieu (qq.v.), who have made use of the thesis play, are indebted to him. Included among his other plays are: *Un Père prodigue* (1859), *L'Ami des femmes* (1864), *La Femme de Claude* (1873), *L'Étrangère* (1876) and *Denise* (1885).

H. S. Schwarz, *Alexandre Dumas fils, Dramatist*, 1927; P. Lamy, *Le Théâtre d'A. Dumas fils*, 1929.

Dumas père, Alexandre: (1803-1870) Grandson of a Negress, this novelist and dramatist, born in Villers-Cotterets, came to Paris at the age of twenty to seek his fortune. His swashbuckling novels, *Les Trois Mousquetaires* (1844) and *Le Comte de Monte-Cristo* (1845), for which he is especially known, draw their subjects, as do most of his novels, from the history of France; they

were written after he achieved success as a dramatist. The historical *Henri III et sa Cour* (1829), presented at the Comédie-Française, inaugurated the romantic theater in France, and, except for the fact that it was written in prose and not in verse, would probably have had the impact that *Hernani* (q.v.), produced one year later, had for Romanticism. This play is based on the assassination in 1578 of Saint-Mégrin, one of Henri III's minions; its action is swift and melodramatic; its plot, centering around Saint-Mégrin's love for the duchess and her husband's jealousy, is simple, and serves as a good pretext for the unfolding of historical scenes. *La Tour de Nesle* (1832), based on the Middle Ages, is another one of his several successful plays, and is the prototype of the swashbuckling dramas. Of his approximately one hundred plays, *Antony* (1831) was the one that initiated, in a contemporary setting, the modern drama of passion. It depicts a literary descendant of René (q.v.), whose gloom, ego, and passion make him a typical, and perhaps worthy, representative of romanticism. But the melodrama and imagination reflected in Dumas' own life were also the dominant characteristics of his prolific output. Dumas' influence on his son was indeed significant (cf. Dumas *fils*).
H. Parigot, *Le Drame d'A. Dumas*, 1899; H. Clouard, *Alexandre Dumas*, 1955.

Duranty, Louis-Emile-Edmond: (1833-1880) This Parisian-born novelist and theorist of realism (q.v.) was the editor of the short-lived journal *Réalisme* (1856-1857), in which he popularized the theories of Champfleury (q.v.), with whom he waged a campaign against the Romanticists and their conception of art. *Le Malheur d'Henriette Gérard* (1860) is the best of his six novels published between 1860 and 1878. A portrait of provincial life that also contains psychological analysis, this novel reproduces, in accordance with his theories, the social milieu of the Gérard family with their speech, mannerisms, and physical traits; his antipathy to the bourgeois, with their meanness and obsession for money, is here also revealed. His technique, different from Flaubert's (q.v.), is generally closer to that of Zola (q.v.) and the Naturalistic School.
P. Martino, *Le Roman Réaliste sous le Second Empire*, 1913; Louis Tabary, *Duranty, étude biographique et critique*, 1954.

Durtain, Luc (pseud. of **A. Nepveu**): (1881-   ) Before 1919 this Paris-born novelist was a poet and allied with the Unanimist (see *Unanimism*) group. Later, widely travelled, he related his experiences in such works as *L'Autre Europe, Moscou et sa foi* (1928), a book on Russia, and *Dieux blancs, hommes jaunes* (1930), a study on Indo-China. In both books the author's basic humanism is perceptible. Although he shows concern over the excesses of an "Americanized" civilization, his attitude toward the United States, as can be seen in such novels and stories as *Quarantième Étage* (1927), *Hollywood dépassé* (1928), *Captain O.K.* (1931), and *Frank and Marjorie* (1934)—grouped under the general heading of *Conquêtes du monde*—is friendly and sympathetic. His style in these novels—modern at its best and worst—is nervous and hurried. A play by him, entitled *Le Donneur de Sang*, was written in 1929.

Du Ryer, Pierre: (1605-1658) With the exception of Hardy (q.v.), this dramatist did more than any other author to revive interest in tragicomedy (q.v.) and to make it popular between 1628 and 1630. In addition to his pastoral comedy, *Les*

Vendanges de Suresnes (1633), he wrote two biblical tragedies, *Saül* (1640) and *Esther* (1642).
H. C. Lancaster, *Pierre Du Ryer dramatist,* 1912.

Du Vair, Guillaume: (1556-1621) Long a member of the *Politiques* during the troubles of the League, and finally Bishop of Lisieux, this humanist was opposed to intolerance and refused to take sides in the religious struggles between the Catholics and the Protestants. His works, which include *De la sainte philosophie* (1580?), *De la constance* (1593), and *De la philosophie morale des Stoïques* (c. 1585), reflect the importance he gave both to stoic philosophy as a guide to conduct and to reason as a guide to faith. His *Discours pour la maintien de la loi salique* (1593) helped save the throne for Henry IV.

R. Radouant, *Guillaume du Vair, l'homme et l'orateur,* 1909.

Duvernois, Henri: (1875-1937) The qualities of observation and analysis evidenced in his depiction of the middle class in his novels and short stories are also seen in his plays. Although as a dramatist he composed three-act pieces, he excelled in one-act sketches of characters and manners, at once ironic and sentimental, that reveal a natural dialogue, gaiety, and verve. Included among the latter are: *La Dame de bronze et le monsieur de crystal* (1921), a portrayal of a husband's unsuccessful ruse; *Jeanne,* a picture of plans indulged in by selfish would-be parents; and *Rouge* (1935), a satire of those living in luxury who spout radical ideas.

E

École des femmes, L': Written in 1662 by Molière (q.v.), this play, the first example of "high comedy," is the result of realistic observation and depicts a psychological study. Arnolphe, the main protagonist, is the guardian of Agnès. Hoping eventually to marry her, Arnolphe believes that the best way to achieve this goal is to isolate her from the outside world and to keep her ignorant of the ways of life. A young man, however, named Horace, unaware of the fact that Arnolphe, an old friend of his father's, is Agnès' guardian, ingenuously relates to him how he has succeeded in winning the girl's heart and how he intends to carry her off. Although Arnolphe now takes new precautions, he receives from Agnès the confession that she loves Horace. His scheme to thwart Horace's plan comes to nought; Agnès, moreover, now braves the anger of the old suitor, making clear that she hates him and intends to escape with Horace. Arnolphe's answering plea, in which he reveals the tragic intensity of his passion and tenderness for her, is of psychological interest, reflecting, at the same time, characteristics which, more and more, Molière was to use in his *comédie de caractère* (q.v.). In the end, of course, love wins out and

Agnès and Horace are united. This play, attacked for religious and other reasons, resulted in *La Critique de l'École des Femmes* (1663) which Molière intended as a reply to his adversaries.

Écoles des veufs, L' (1899): See *Ancey, Georges.*

École Romane: Founded at the end of the nineteenth century by Jean Moréas (q.v.), Raymond de la Tailhède (1867-1938), Maurice Du Plessys (1864-1924), Ernest Raynaud (1864-1936) and Charles Maurras (q.v.), this literary school rebelled against the abstruse in Symbolism (q.v.), and stressed logical clarity. They sought inspiration from the poets of the Renaissance (q.v.), and turned generally to the followers of the Greco-Latin or Classical (see *Classicism*) traditions.

Écossaise ou Marie Stuart, L' (1605): See *Montchrétien, Antoine de.*

écriture artiste: A nervous, jerky style used by the Goncourt (q.v.) brothers in the attempt to convey, impressionistically, the sensations produced by external objects. When used by them felicitously, it resulted in picturesque and colorful descriptions.

Éducation sentimentale, L' (1869): See *Flaubert.*

églogue: Although once used to indicate any lyrical, pastoral, satirical, or epigrammatic poem, this term has been applied, ever since the time it was used in connection with Vergil's eclogues, only to pastoral poems written in dialogue form or which at least present some dramatic movement. See *Marot.*

élégie: In Greece, where it originated, the elegy was characterized by its distinctive poetic form rather than by its varied themes. Despite the strong influence of classical form during the Renaissance, its chief characteristic in France was not its form but its theme—unrequited love, or love that is aborted because of infidelity or death. In the *Élégies*

à Genèvre by Ronsard (q.v.) one finds the modern tone of melancholy which also found expression in the poems of Bertaut (q.v.). Except for the elegiac sentiments, the 17th century gave little importance to it as a genre. In the 18th century, however, it appeared as a form for the expression of pagan or erotic sensualism, even in some of the *Élégies* by A. Chénier (q.v.). In the 19th century it became once again melancholy and somber, the characteristic tone of the elegies of Lamartine, Vigny, Hugo and Musset (qq.v.).

Elle et lui (1859): See *Sand, George.*

Eluard, Paul: (1895-1952) First associated with Dadaism (q.v.) and with Surrealism (q.v.), this poet, in his earlier collections *L'Amour la Poésie* (1929) and *La Vie immédiate* (1932), reveals himself as the poet of love and of woman, whom he celebrates for her mysterious charm. His poems are generally short and stripped of eloquence. Composed "automatically," with images that seem created naturally, they nevertheless leave the reader with a clear impression, doubtless because of their simple vocabulary and the focal points around which they are unconsciously organized. Even in his *poésie engagée,* in such collections inspired by the war as *Au Rendez-Vous Allemand* (1945) and *Poésie et vérité* (1942) or in his clandestine poetry and *Poèmes Politiques* (1948)— poems that sing his political passion for liberty—Eluard, unlike Aragon (q.v.), who broke brusquely with his past, retained generally his surrealistic characteristics. For Eluard, moreover, shifting from a personal love to communion with all humanity, is a natural transition. In *Poésie ininterrompue* (1946) he gives his most complete expression of his parallel loves for his wife and for humanity. He is the poet of love; his praises of individual and collec-

103

tive happiness become spontaneous songs or hymns.

Louis Parrot, *Paul Eluard*, 1947.

Émaux et Camées (1852): See *Gautier*.

Émile (1762): See *Rousseau, J. J.*

Emmanuel, Pierre: (1916-   ) Somewhat influenced by Pierre Jean Jouve (q.v.), this young writer from the Pyrenees, who spent his early years in the United States, has the makings of a great religious poet. *Tombeau d'Orphée* (1941) is a literary achievement; it marks a revival of eloquence and of oratorical poetry. *Le Poète et son Christ* (1942) established his reputation as a poet. Several collections—*Jour de Colère* (1942), *Combats avec tes défenseurs* (1942), and *La Liberté guide nos pas* (1945)—are inspired by the tragic circumstances of the Second World War. Other collections—*Memento des Vivants* (1946) and *Sodome* (1946)—are a passionate and eloquent interpretation of ancient and Christian myths. Of a different vein are his brief, charming, and humorous *Cantos* (1942) and *Chansons du Dé à Coudre* (1947). Emmanuel is also known for his outspoken autobiography, *Qui est cet homme?* (1947).

Empreinte, L' (1896): See *Estaunié, Edouard*.

En attendant Godot (1953): See *Beckett, Samuel*.

Encyclopédie: First conceived as a business venture when the publisher Le Breton asked Diderot (q.v.) to translate the English *Cyclopedia, or an Universal Dictionary of the Arts and Sciences* (1728) by Chambers, it developed into an entirely original work, inspired by Bayle's (q.v.) *Dictionnaire historique et critique* (1697) and by an unorthodox attitude towards religion and government. Entrusted with the direction of this huge enterprise, Diderot enlisted the aid of D'Alembert (q.v.), the celebrated mathematician, and of such other distinguished collaborators as Voltaire, Montesquieu, Rousseau, Condillac, Helvétius, d'Holbach, Marmontel, Turgot and Quesnay (qq.v.), to mention but the most prominent, all of whom contributed articles in the fields of their special competence or interest. The first volume of the *Encyclopédie* (also called a *Dictionnaire raisonné des Arts et Métiers*), which appeared in 1751, included a *discours préliminaire*, written by D'Alembert, which contained an explanation of its purposes and methods: Exposing the order, relationship and history of human knowledge, which, he shows, is acquired through the senses or perceptions—a philosophical principle borrowed from Locke—D'Alembert calls attention to the growth and progress of knowledge, especially in natural sciences. In reality, however, the *Encyclopédie* was much more, as it turned out, than a mere summation of knowledge; it became an instrument of warfare against ignorance and prejudice as well as a means of spreading liberal ideas. Not without complete justification were the Encyclopedists or *philosophes* (q.v.) attacked, because of their views, by the combined efforts of the Jesuits and Jansenists, enemies during the preceding century. Because of various attacks, moreover, publication of this collective work met several times with serious difficulties, and Diderot, after D'Alembert's defection after the appearance in 1757 of the seventh volume, was left with the task of bringing out alone the remaining volumes; in this task, however, he was considerably aided by the indefatigable Jaucourt (q.v.), who did much of the hack work. To bring his work to fruition, which meant, among other things, overcoming the obstacles arising from civil and religious censorship, Diderot was helped by such influential friends as Mme. de Pompadour and the Marquis d'Argenson and by the various ruses he resorted to. These included specious defenses of religion, skeptical arguments and the use of an elaborate system of cross references. With the appearance in 1765 of the seventeenth volume, the *Encyclopédie* was completed; eleven supplementary volumes of plates, however, illustrating the trades and mechanical arts which were hitherto neglected, appeared in 1772. These were followed in 1780 by four additional volumes, the work of other editors, and by two volumes of index.

By emphasizing the notion of progress, especially as seen in the sciences, and by undermining respect for authority and tradition, the *Encyclopédie* encouraged, as did Voltaire (q.v.), social and political reform. Representative as a collective work of the ideal of the second half of the eighteenth century, it prepared the spirit of the French Revolution.

J. Morley, *Diderot and the Encyclopedists*, 1897; L. Ducros, *Les Encyclopédistes*, 1900; J. Le Gras, *Diderot et l'Encyclopédie*, 1928; D. H. Gordon and N. L. Torrey, *The Censoring of Diderot's Encyclopédie*, 1947.

Énéide travestie (1648-1653): See *Scarron, Paul.*

Enfants-sans-souci (or **Sots**): A Parisian association of the fifteenth century mostly composed of young idlers or poor students, whose first presiding officer was named *Prince des sots* and the second *mère sotte,* which was given recognition by Charles VI. Although they played buffooneries and *farces* (q.v.), as did the *Basochiens,* with whom they were later confused, the type of play they particularly presented was the *sottie* (q.v.). They also acted the comical parts in the plays of the *Confrérie de la Passion* (q.v.). Their presentations continued until the end of the 16th century.

Enfants terribles, Les (1929): See *Cocteau.*

enjambement: An over-run line in a poem that continues the sense and grammatical construction beyond the end of an Alexandrine (q.v.) verse. An example, in *Hernani* (q.v.), is the end of the opening line, *C'est bien à l'escalier,* followed in the next line by *Dérobé.* . . . Although its use is not entirely absent in French Classical poetry, Malherbe (q.v.) condemned it. Hugo's (q.v.) innovation of its use in the above-named play threw the audience into a tumult the night of its *première.* The *enjambement* became a characteristic of Romantic versification in general.

ENLIGHTENMENT, AGE OF: The significant revolution in the philosophic, religious and social ideas which characterizes the century of Enlightenment, that is the eighteenth, may be traced to both French and foreign origins. The ideas of rationalism, *naturism,* stoicism, epicurism, tolerance, expressed more or less boldly by Rabelais, Montaigne, Charron, Du Vair (qq.v.), even more perhaps by lesser writers such as Bonaventure Des Périers (q.v.) and Ramus, had found few followers in the well-organized, officially Catholic and monarchical literature of the 17th century. Only some secondary authors, like Théophile de Viau and Gassendi (qq.v.), the libertines, theoretical and practical, whose existence is known to us only through the vituperations of some voluble preacher, such as Père Garasse, had dared express views opposed to those of the King and of the Church. Yet the pompous edifice of orthodoxy and conformist ethics was shallow and would soon offer only a weakened resistance to the blows from within and from without. The very excesses of an authoritarian regime, often clumsily calling upon all the resources of the law to defend religious beliefs and a code of ethics, the quarrels within the Church itself, of the Jesuits against Jansenists, of Bossuet against Fénelon (qq.v.) (setting against each other with an unvaunted bitterness the two most famous figures of Catholicism), the ill-advised Revocation of the Edict de Nantes, the social unrest and misery, here and there turning to actual starvation, of the last years of the reign of the Sun-King—all contributed to undermine the social structure. The death of the monarch in 1715 released pent-up energies and let loose forces hitherto hidden under the mask of hypocrisy. They were to sweep away, almost completely and by a variety of means, the patterns of thought imposed and maintained by a vigilant censorship. Censorship itself was not dead, of course. But new, devious, clever, effective ways were found to contrive its defeat, by innuendos, by exaggerated declarations of respect masking subversive ideas, by the introduction in literature of "le bon sauvage," of even the Oriental, who, under the guise of a perfidious innocence and a seeming ignorance of contemporary customs, was able to criticize with the utmost freedom, the more so since authors were always careful to disassociate themselves from the extreme views expressed by their literary creations.

At the same time, from England, a veritable wave of translations, a constant infiltration followed later by an invasion of new concepts, offered additional support, and in some cases an apparent practical substantiation to the philosophical and political creeds emerging in France. England elicited the admiration of the "philosophes" (q.v.) because of its prestige as an advanced nation, creating no doubt an exaggerated image of progress. Voltaire (q.v.), in his *Lettres philosophiques* (1733), originally *Letters on the English nation*, the fruit of his observations and meditations during nearly three years of an enforced exile in the British Islands,

was the most enthusiastic apostle of English ideas. But many around him shared the same views, acquired either through the now fashionable "pilgrimage" to England or through contacts with English thinkers. Among these were Montesquieu, the Abbé Prévost, Saint-Evremond (qq.v.), who lived and died in England, and, later on, Beaumarchais (q.v.). From England came the most sweeping philosophic system, that of Locke, which would soon supercede the spiritualistic system of Descartes (q.v.); and Newtonianism, which would, around the middle of the century, invade even the sacred halls of the Academy of Sciences.

Thus France was introduced to the vigorous and dominant theory of sensationalism. Indeed, Descartes's method had unwittingly prepared the way for its mortal enemy in basing all truth on the rule of evidence. For, if in Descartes's thought, the first evidence is that of the thinking soul, so for Locke, the first, the only evidence is that of the sensory origin of ideas. No idea is ever born independently of perception and of sensation; hence the existence of a spiritual entity to account for the spiritual nature of knowledge is no longer a prerequisite of metaphysics. The consequences of such a premise are overwhelming. They affect first of all metaphysics, where they render superfluous the spirituality and therefore the immortality of the soul. They required a new theory of knowledge, and spread to religion, to society and even, with J.-J. Rousseau, to the theories of education. From sensationalism to materialism, to theism and atheism, to rationalism and religious tolerance, the road was now open and the French "philosophes" trod it with alacrity. In various measures, and taking also into account other influences, Montesquieu, Diderot, Voltaire, Rousseau, Helvetius, and d'Holbach (qq.v.) may all be situated in the lineage of Locke. Voltaire devoted an entire letter of his *Lettres philosophiques* to the English philosopher. Later, he would become bolder and proclaim, with an assurance belied by the mediocrity of his philosophic thought, that God may have given matter the power to think, thus precariously maintaining his teaching of a divine creator and of divine providence with his professed materialism.

Rationalism has more remote sources. In France its first expression occurs in the philosophers of the 16th century—Des Périers, Rabelais —who themselves received it from the teachers of the University of Padua, exponents of a form of aristotelianism quite foreign to the Christianized aristotelianism of Thomas Aquinas. Rationalism, in fact, is not incapable of an orthodox interpretation, and Thomas Aquinas himself has been rightly dubbed a rationalist. As understood in the sense of the 18th century philosophers, however, it means the supreme dominion of reason over all matters of knowledge, not excluding those so far reserved to faith. Bayle (q.v.), in this matter as in many others, was the initiator, and his *Dictionnaire historique et critique* (1697) may well be considered as the arsenal where most of the ideas subsequently brought into the fight were stored with a superb disdain as to their future use. Following Bayle, and armed with reason alone, to which they would add the light of experience, Diderot (q.v.), Voltaire and the Encyclopedists attacked Christian dogmas and traditions. They unanimously rejected miracles, which they conveniently explained by the ignorance of the people, the cunning of the priests, and, more scientifically, by hitherto unknown forces of nature.

A theory of progress emerges quite logically from this rationalistic consciousness. Pascal (q.v.) was, historically, the first to have formulated a moderate theory of progress in his preface to the *Traité sur le vide* (1654). But the deeply Christian writer of the 17th century includes in it only those disciplines which do, in fact, come within the purview of reason or of science. Other truths are based on authority, namely, those pertaining to faith, and there is in that realm no progress nor modification. No such restriction, of course, was to be brooked by the philosophers of the 18th century— all, besides, bitter enemies of Pascal. Guided by the light of reason, proud of the not inconsiderable latest scientific discoveries, persuaded that religion stands only for stagnation and backwardness, their theory of progress was most sweeping. They hinted, or they proclaimed, that the world is in a state of constant and unlimited progress, of which the measurable scientific progress is only the image and the preamble. Further scientific developments, it was confidently expected, would narrow down more and more the area of mystery, of the unknowable which is the domain of religion; and when, finally, science will have found the secret of life, of death, of matter, of creation, religion will be devoid of its *raison d'être,* and condemned to oblivion.

Such an optimism, so completely belied by subsequent events, found an ally in the development of *naturism,* a theory which asserts the fundamental goodness of human nature. Philosophical, religious (in the negative sense), and social ideas concurred in the formulation of that theory, which is not unrelated, in the 16th century at least, to the utopian concepts expressed by Plato, Campanella in his *De Civitate Solis,* Sir Thomas More in his *Utopia,* reinforced by the discovery of a new continent. There lived on the new continent, according to the reports of perhaps over-enthusiastic travelers, happy people in an idyllic state, where innocence, courage, righteousness reigned supreme in the total absence of formal religion and social organization. Montaigne had already given expression to these disturbing thoughts, without, however, integrating them into a system, in his essays on "Les Cannibales" and "Des coches." The curiosity about America and its inhabitants had not slackened in the 18th century, but was, on the contrary, enlivened by an extraordinary abundance of tales, relations of travel, relations of missionaries, particularly the Jesuits, who thus unwittingly lent arms to their enemies. For still more spectacular demonstrations, savages were occasionally brought to France, there not to admire her civilization, but to compare it unfavorably with their own primitive status. In the writings of the *naturists,* Christian civilization had no more bitter and sweeping critic than the "bon sauvage," for it favored or tolerated inequality in social conditions, poverty coexisting scandalously with extravagant luxury, oppression, avariciousness, hatred, servitude. In sharp contrast, absolute equality existed in his own land, based on the community of goods and of possessions, along with universal kindness, liberality, and freedom. This theme was recurrent in French literature of the 18th century, in the *Lettres persanes* (1721) of Montesquieu, where, however, the protagonists are Persians rather than Indians; in the *Supplément au voyage de Bougainville* (1796) of Diderot, situated in the ideal setting of Tahiti; in *L'Ingénu* (1767) of Voltaire, where a Huron having come to France experiences the usual, and some unusual, difficulties. The implications of such pictures of primitive peoples, the open or hidden criticisms that they elicit were devastating both for religion and society. For how could one reconcile with traditional teaching and beliefs the spectacle of men in the natural state who, instead of being evil, are good, innocent and virtuous, while baptized Europeans are culpable of cruelty; of men deprived of all the so-called advantages of civilization who are so much happier than the French or the Spaniards? The philosophers, eager to seize these handy arms against religion and an autocratic regime, never questioned the accuracy of the descriptions so profusely offered. They did not make, either, the necessary distinctions between natural goodness and supernatural merit which is basic in theology. Thus the "bon sauvage" became a living condemnation of the Christian and even of the citizen.

The idea of *religious tolerance* is, of course, the logical and necessary consequence of rationalism, and more remotely, of *naturism.* There are historically two aspects to the idea. Tolerance became an urgent problem in the 16th century with the advent of the Reformation and the Wars of Religion. But it was posed almost universally on a political basis by writers such as Montaigne, Michel de l'Hospital, chancellor of Catherine de Medicis, and Jean Bodin (q.v.). They preached the doctrine of tolerance not because Protestants have a fundamental right to their opinions but because it served as a practical measure of pacification. Even that concession was withdrawn by the autocratic regime of the 17th century, a measure approved, incredibly enough, even by the enlightened opinion of the times. The Revocation of the Edict of Nantes, which was soon to be considered an abominable abuse of power as well as an irreparable blunder in the political and economic fields, won unanimous acclaim when it was promulgated. Bayle is probably the first who voiced the theory of tolerance as an inalienable right of the minority rather than as a political concession. In his *Commentaire sur le Compelle Intrare* (1686), he enunciated the right of conscience, even in error *("Les droits de la conscience errante")*, to adhere to and to preach its beliefs. Religious persecutions continued during the eighteenth century, but the "philosophes" were unanimous in denouncing them. Voltaire, here again, was the leader of the movement. He effectively took up the defense of Protestants unjustly condemned, of Calas and Sirven, and obtained either their rehabilitation or their freedom. His *Traité sur la tolérance* (1763) contains the theoretical and historical justification of the position he had assumed and already represents the established position of the age of enlightenment.

This tableau of the major currents of ideas of the eighteenth century would not be complete without mention of the *scientific spirit* which pervaded the thinking of the period. Science then was both an achievement and a fashion. It was the ally of reason in the struggle against tradition and religion; and even in the absence of solid scientific background or accomplishment, the "philosophes" were eager to appear either proficient or at least informed in that field. Fontenelle (q.v.) was the initiator, not, of course, of scientific research, for his contributions were devoid of originality, but of the method to link subtly the progress of science with the regression of religion. His work of popularization, the *Entretiens sur la pluralité des mondes* (1686), combats the theocentric and geocentric concepts of the world, showing the earth not as the center of the uni-

verse, but only as a minor planet lost in its immensity. Montesquieu, former pupil of the scientifically-minded Oratorians, was more genuinely interested in physics and natural history, and his short treatises read at the Academy of Science of Bordeaux bespeak serious intent and authentic discoveries. Diderot was a mathematician; Jean-Jacques Rousseau, the least scientific of the great writers of his age, discovered late in life an interest in botany. Voltaire, however, was the great apostle of Newtonianism, on which he wrote a treatise. More inclined towards poetry than towards science, he nevertheless entered the laboratory to conduct experiments in the charming and learned company of Mme. du Châtelet. Perhaps a less sincere adept of science than many of his contemporaries, Voltaire made the most consistent use of that argument, often in conjunction with the argument of common sense, to wage his own particular fight against what he called superstition.

Such are, briefly and incompletely presented and without any attempt to discuss their validity, the main currents of thought which dominated the age of enlightenment. One would mistake their real nature, however, in considering them as merely speculative ideas, conceived in the calm of meditation. They were essentially combative ideas, injected with the passions, the prejudices, the visions also of the time. They were in turn generous and selfish, grandiose and narrow, sometimes sound, often distorted. Considered as a whole, they conjure up a picture of a society in revolt, impatient of old restraints, of an ascending bourgeoisie and a decadent aristocracy. They heralded the approaching revolution, which would show, alas! how illusory were many of their hopes, and would demonstrate that human nature cannot be radically changed, neither by fervent exhortations towards civic virtue nor still less by the utopian dreams of a state from which all injustice will be banished.

Jules Barni, *Histoire des idées morales et politiques au dix-huitième siècle*, 1865-73; John Morley, *Rousseau*, 1878; *Voltaire*, 1878; *Diderot and the encyclopedists*, 1886; Lucien Lévy-Bruhl, *History of modern philosophy in France*, 1899; Jules Delvaille, *Essai sur l'histoire de l'idée du progrès jusqu'à la fin du XVIIIe siècle*, 1910; Mario Roustan, *Les philosophes et la société française au XVIIIe siècle*, 1911; J. P. Belin, *Le mouvement philosophique en France de 1748 à 1784*, 1913; J. B. Bury, *The idea of progress*, 1920; Henri Sée, *Les idées politiques en France au XVIIIe siècle*, 1920; André Cresson, *Les courants de la pensée philosophique française*, 1927; Daniel Mornet, *French Thought in the Eighteenth Century*, 1929; A. Tilley, *The Decline of the Age of Louis XIV*, 1929; Daniel Mornet, *Les origines intellectuelles de la Révolution française, 1715-1789*, 1933; Paul Hazard, *La crise de la conscience européenne (1680-1715)*, 1935; R. R. Palmer, *Catholics and Unbelievers in Eighteenth Century France*, 1939; Fernand Vial, *Voltaire*, 1953.

FERNAND VIAL

Entretiens sur la métaphysique et la religion (1688): See *Malebranche*.

Entretiens sur la pluralité des mondes (1686): See *Fontenelle*.

Entretiens sur le fils naturel (1757): See *Diderot*.

EPIC: See *chanson de geste*.

épigramme: A short, satiric piece in verse ending generally with a cutting phrase. Clément Marot (q.v.) was especially successful in this literary form, the one most suitable for his expression of malice. The eighteenth century, a century of "bon mots" and witty impromptus, produced an incalculable number of *épigrammes*, the most notable writers of which were Piron, Voltaire and J.-B. Rousseau (qq.v.).

Épithalame, L' (1921): See *Chardonne, Jacques*.

épître: A poem in which the author, addressing himself to a real or imaginary person, discusses subjects the variety of which can be compared to that found in letters written in prose. In France it was cultivated during the Renaissance by Saint-Gelais (q.v.), Jean Marot, and especially by Clément Marot (q.v.), who is characteristically witty either when making some sort of request or when flattering somebody. Essentially didactic in the 17th century, in the hands of Voiture (q.v.) it is light, serious or elevated by turns. Curiously, Boileau (q.v.), who neglected to mention this genre in his *Art Poétique*, was a master of this form. Eighteenth-century writers like J.-B. Rousseau and Voltaire (qq.v.), in particular, made frequent use of it as an instrument of polemics or personal attack. Marie-Joseph Chénier (q.v.) was the last important writer to indulge in this literary form.

Épitres (1669-1698): See *Boileau*.

Époques de la nature (1779): See *Buffon*.

Erasmus, Desiderius (Influence of): This Dutch scholar and humanist (1466?-1536), a dominant force during the Renaissance, influenced much of the intellectual and moral history of the sixteenth century. His influence in France, greatest before that of Calvin (q.v.), is especially evident in the thought and works of Rabelais (q.v.) and, to a lesser degree, in Guillaume Budé and Montaigne (qq.v.). His pagan, humanistic writings, including his *Adages* (1500), spread his literary fame and gave added impetus to those who turned their interests to classical learning. In *The Praise of Folly* (1508), also written in Latin, he satirizes theologians, monks, and the ignorant. His criticism of political and social institutions and his appeal to reason reflect a current in France that is epitomized in Montaigne and that leads to modern liberalism. Finding, moreover, no conflict between pagan and Christian truth, he initiated in his Greek New Testament (1516) Biblical textual criticism. His method was to leave its mark on the teaching of the "lecteurs royaux" (see *Collège de France*), instituted in 1530 at the urging of Guillaume Budé. Toward the end of the seventeenth century, Erasmus' work was for the first time summarized intelligently in Bayle's (q.v.) *Dictionnaire;* in the nineteenth century, his exegesis was to be an important source in the work of Renan (q.v.).

A. Renaudet, *Humanisme et Préréforme à Paris pendant les premières guerres d'Italie, 1497-1517,* 1916; M. Mann, *Erasme et les débuts de la Réforme française, 1517-1536,* 1933.

Erckmann-Chatrian: (joint pseud. of **Emile Erckmann,** 1822-1899; and **Alexandre Chatrian,** 1826-1900) In their collaboration lasting over forty years —and ending in an unfortunate quarrel—these writers from Alsace represented the historical and patriotic novel and short story (see *Short Story* (q.v.) was flourishing. Included among these novels and short stories are: *L'Invasion ou le Fou Yégof* (1852), *Madame Thérèse* (1863), *Histoire d'un conscrit de 1813* (1864), *Waterloo* (1865), and *Le Blocus* (1867). *L'Ami Fritz* (1864), probably their best "regional novel," the scene of which is in Alsace, was dramatized in 1877. Their faithful devotion to Alsace-Lorraine and understanding of the role of France in the Rhine Valley give their work a special significance.

L. Shoumacher, *Erckmann-Chatrian,* 1933.

Erec et Enide: In this first Arthurian romance extant (early in the 2nd half of the 12th century), the poet, Chrétien de Troyes (q.v.), shows how a Knight at the Court of King Arthur, whose honor and prestige have suffered because of his love for a lady, aims to recover his reputation. Erec, in search of adventure, meets Enide, with whom he falls in love, and marries her. Enjoying his wedded life, Erec forgets his knightly duties. When Enide laments his fallen prowess, Erec decides once again to set out in search of adventure, forcing Enide to accompany him. Through these adventures, full of danger and humiliating to Enide, Erec proves his valor, also becoming reconciled with his wife.

Espoir, L' (1938): See *Malraux.*

Esprits, Les (1579): See *Larivey, Pierre.*

Esprit des Lois, L' (1748): See *Montesquieu.*

esprit gaulois: Opposed to the feudal spirit, this is characterized by satire, raillery, cynicism, gaiety, malice or licentiousness. This spirit has inspired a good part of French literature. During the Middle Ages, it often manifested itself as an expression of revenge on the part of the weak against the more powerful. See *Roman de Renart* and *fabliaux.*

Esquisse d'un tableau des progrès de l'esprit humain (1749); See *Condorcet.*

Essais: Written by Montaigne (1588; q.v.), who invented the title and the genre, these prose pieces represent the personal impressions of a mind that ceaselessly studied and scrutinized itself in order to better understand humanity. Conceived without apparent unity of plan, the individual essays deal with sundry subjects, from insignificant gossip or details to lofty discussions on life and education. Montaigne's psychological self-portraiture and basic preoccupation with a study of the human condition make him the forerunner of Classicism (q.v.).

111

Essais de psychologie contemporaine (1883): See *Bourget, Paul.*

Essai sur les mœurs (1756): See *Voltaire.*

Essai sur les Révolutions (1797): See *Chateaubriand.*

Essai sur l'indifférence en matière de religion (1817-1823): See *Lamennais.*

Essai sur l'origine des connaissances humaines (1746): See *Condillac.*

ESSAY: There are many definitions of the essay; most agree that it ought to be short rather than long, in prose rather than in poetry, and personal or reflective rather than scientific in approach. Some critics, like Jules Bertaut, define the essay as a literary work that defies classification and that cannot be called anything else. According to Dr. Samuel Johnson, who was thinking of Montaigne (q.v.) when he wrote this definition, "An essay is a loose sally of the mind; an irregular undigested piece; not a regular and orderly performance." Indeed, if definitions of the essay vary, its origin is perfectly clear. The word was first used as a title by Michel de Montaigne in 1580; but it was when he wrote the opening lines of the 50th chapter of the first book that he first stumbled upon the new concept: We must use as much judgment in all things as possible, but when they surpass our understanding, we must then try them out; we must essay them.

Others had presented their thoughts in short prose form before Montaigne. Among his immediate French precursors was Jacques Tahureau, gentilhomme du Mans, whose *Dialogues* appeared in 1565. But Montaigne did more than set his thoughts down on paper. He reached out for thoughts as he went along, more as if to shape his own judgment than to convince others. Thus he invented a new genre and a new title. Richly read, deeply introspective, and born at a time of disorganized public activity which invited introspection, Montaigne was ideally suited to create the new genre.

Villey and Lanson observe that while the essay began in France it found its wider development in England. True, Bacon borrowed Montaigne's title (if not his free, personal spirit) and he was followed in the genre by a long list of English authors. But too many articles on the essay regard it "as a peculiarly English thing" and, except for Montaigne, mention no Frenchman at all. The rarity of this term in France after Montaigne (except for the *Essais de morale* of Pierre Nicole which began to appear in 1671, inspired by Montaigne's *Essais*) can be explained in part by its strangeness as a title: French writers continued to use such titles as *discours, traité, réflexions, considérations,* and even *maximes, caractères,* and *portraits,* in all of which, moreover, they stressed form and composition rather than substance. Nevertheless, though not completely preoccupied with inner questioning, many of their works bear certain characteristics of the essay. In the maxims and portraits of La Bruyère and La Rochefoucauld (qq.v.), for example, one finds a stylized variety of the essay; Guez de Balzac's (q.v.) letters, carefully composed pieces, are essays even if they lack Montaigne's intimate trial and error, for their chief interest is the author's own thoughts. In many *observations,* Saint-Evremond (q.v.) wrote critical and historical essays rich in personal reflections, though he usually attempted to clarify for others rather than to probe for a personal philosophy, as Montaigne had done. But no writer during the 16th and 17th centuries could claim all the qualities of Montaigne.

Lanson and others state that the word "essay," as title, returned to France in the 18th century largely under the influence of Bacon and Locke. The word took on new meanings; it became synonymous with "histoire" or "traité" and as such was applied to long, well-knit, though personal, studies. To mention but a few examples: D'Alembert's (q.v.) *Essai sur la société des gens de lettres* (1753), Diderot's (q.v.) *Essai sur le mérite de la vertu,* D'Holbach's (q.v.) *Essai sur les préjugés* (1770), Montesquieu's (q.v.) *Essai sur le goût dans les choses de la nature et de l'art* (1757), Bernardin de Saint Pierre's (q.v.) *Essai sur Jean-Jacques Rousseau,* Voltaire's (q.v.) *Essai sur les mœurs et l'esprit des nations* (1756). Usually thought of in connection with the theater or the novel, Marivaux (q.v.) must here be spoken of apart; a full fourth of his total work is made up of sparkling, original essays, sometimes resembling those of Addison; his *Spectateur français* (1722), his *Indigent philosophe* (1728), and his *Cabinet du philosophe* (1734), are all collections of essays. The essay was also to be used by many critics; Diderot (q.v.), who wrote much art criticism in essay form, is a case in point.

The essay continued to be throughout most of the 19th century what it had been in the 18th. Edmond About and Charles Baudelaire (qq.v.) carried on the essay of art criticism: the latter's *Salon de 1845,* among others, the former's *Voyage à travers l'Exposition des beaux-arts* (1855).

Countless writers, out of modesty, pride, or perhaps habit, persisted in calling their long historical, philosophical, or scientific treatises essays. In their chronological order, a very few of the more important ones are: the *Essai historique, politique et moral sur les révolutions anciennes et modernes* (1797) of Chateaubriand (q.v.), the *Essai sur le principe générateur des constitutions politiques* (1810) of Joseph-

Marie de Maistre (q.v.), the *Essais sur l'indifférence en matière de religion* (1817-23) of Lamennais (q.v.), the *Essai sur l'amour* (1822) of Stendhal (q.v.), the *Essai sur . . . l'instruction en France* (1816) of Guizot, the *Essai sur la guerre sociale* (1841) of Prospère Mérimée (q.v.), the *Essai sur les fables de La Fontaine* (1853) of Hyppolyte Taine (q.v.), and other historical or critical essays by Victor Cousin, Ernest Renan (qq.v.), and others.

Toward the latter part of the century, however, a number of authors began to write short, personal pieces, somewhat like the shorter probings of Montaigne, though less wandering. Rarely called "essays" by their authors, they must be accepted as such: *Du dandysme* (1845) of Barbey d'Aurevilly (q.v.), the *études morales* (1855 and 1869) of Caro, some of the *Actes et paroles* (1872-) of Victor Hugo (q.v.), and numerous bits by Mme. Louise Ackermann, Léon Bloy, and Remy de Gourmont (q.v.). The word "essayiste" itself came into the French language from English toward the end of the century.

With the advent of the 20th century the essay began to be treated as a distinct genre in the major histories of French literature; coincidentally, Florian-Parmentier could even complain in 1914—as many critics have done since—that authors were no longer writing anything but essays, however disguised the outward forms of their writing. Most critics today feel that the essay owes its present enormous popularity to the fact that authors have become more independent and are giving wider, freer range to their thinking. But the increasing popularity of the essay may also be due to the decreasing popularity of the fixed form. Critics have noted for some years that the novel was swallowing up other forms; instead of writing tragedies or satires, for example, young writers were producing tragic or satirical novels. But the novel itself tended to become a fixed form. André Gide (q.v.) revolted against fixed form in his *Faux Monnayeurs*. Except for Gide's simple tales, most of his books tended to be entirely or mostly without plot, vehicles for a wide range of ideas about man, life, morals, and customs. *Corydon* (1911, enriched in 1920), Gide's personal view of man's physical condition, is an excellent example of the modern essay that springs or claims to spring from a series of scientific facts into a world of far-reaching moral and philosophical speculation. In the same way, but from different facts to a different kind of speculation, Jean Rostand (q.v.) created the *Pensées d'un biologiste*.

The springboard for speculation may be a set of economic, political, or social facts, as well as the biological or physical. From the *États-Unis d'aujourd'hui* (1927) to the *Aspects de la société française* (1954) —to begin and end quite arbitrarily —André Siegfried, professor of political science, has probed into the nature of man and into his future. Such was the springboard that sent André Suarès (q.v.) into a speculative state of optimistic nihilism just after the turn of our century, in his *Sur la vie* (1909-13). In a somewhat similar way, but perhaps less optimistically, Jean-Paul Sartre (q.v.) speculates on man's proper place in the dangerously divided world of the 1950's, in his *Les communistes et la paix* (1952).

Other great essayists today have based their speculations on religious (particularly Catholic) premises. The attack on education by Henri Massis, called the *Esprit de la Nouvelle Sorbonne* (1911), is a fine example.

Travel has been the inspiration for many essayists. One of the most charming examples is the *Autre Amérique* (1931) of Madeleine Cazamian. Equally stimulating, but vastly more annoying for the American reader, is the vitriolic account by Georges Duhamel (q.v.), in his *Scènes de la vie future*, wherein our addiction to vitamin pills, brutality, and pointless spectacle serves as the springboard for foreboding thoughts.

Some of the finest essayists have found their inspiration in academic philosophy or literature. In the best liberal, humanistic tradition Jean Guéhenno recorded his love of man in the *Journal d'un homme de quarante ans* (1934); similar examples by Alain fill the shelves of every thoughtful reader of the essay.

Gustave Lanson, *Les essais de Montaigne. Étude et analyse*, n.d.; Florian-Parmentier, "Les essais" in *Histoire de la littérature française de 1885 à nos jours*, n.d.; H. V. Routh, "The origins of the essay compared in French and English," *Modern Language Review*, XV (1920); Jules Bertaut, "Les essayistes et les voyageurs," *Causeries françaises*, 4⁰ année, 3ᵉ causerie, January 22, 1926; *Anthologie des essayistes français contemporains*, 1929; Pierre Villey, "La Nouveauté de l'essai," in *Les essais de Michel de Montaigne*, 1932; *Les sources et l'évolution des Essais de Montaigne*, 1933; Henri Clouard, "Essaistes français contemporains" in *Larousse Mensuel*, XII, August, 1950; Norman Birkett, "Essay," in *Cassell's Encyclopaedia of Literature*, ed. by S. H. Seinberg, London, 1953; Jacques Nathan, *Histoire de la littérature française contemporaine*, 1954.

ROBERT E. TAYLOR

Estang, Luc: (1911-   ) Reflecting the influences of Claudel, Péguy, and Bernanos (qq.v.)—to whom he devoted a study—the writings of this Paris-born poet represent a non-conformist Catholicism that withdraws from all pharisaism. His poetry, to a large degree rhetorical, melodious and regular—he has made frequent use of the alexandrine (q.v.)—is a veritable dialogue between man and his Creator. His principal collections are: *Transhumances* (1939) and *Puissance du Matin* (1941).

Estaunié, Edouard: (1862-1943) In *L'Empreinte* (1896), his best-known novel, the author, remembering his own experience as a pupil of the Jesuits, studies the effects of this kind of education on one of its former pupils. *Le Ferment* (1899), on the other hand, is an analysis of the effects of a purely rationalistic or anarchistic training. In his later novels, he was to combine strong psychological analysis with precise observation. These characteristics are especially to be seen in *La Vie secrète* (1908), *L'Ascension de M. Baslèvre* (1920), and *L'Appel de la Route* (1919)—novels concerned with the secret sufferings of unhappy souls.

Camille Cé, *Regards sur l'œuvre d'Edouard Estaunié*, 1935.

Esther (1642): See *Du Ryer*.

Esther (1689): See *Racine*.

Estienne, Henri [II]: (1531-1598) Son of Robert Estienne (q.v.), who, too, was a humanist (see *Humanism*), he published *Thesaurus Linguæ Græcæ* (1572), the first Greek dictionary. His other works, those essentially of a grammarian and a philologist, represent a defense of the French language (q.v.). In *Traité de la conformité du français avec le grec* (1565), he shows that French, bearing the closest resemblance in vocabulary and syntax to Greek, is superior to other languages. The Italian and Latin influences, on the other hand, he berates in *Dialogue du langage français italianisé* (1578), while in *Précellence du langage français* (1579), he demonstrates the perfection of the French language. In *Apologie pour Hérodote* (1566), generally considered his best work, he criticizes oppression of belief and conscience.

L. Clément, *Henri Estienne et son œuvre française*, 1899.

Estienne, Robert: (1503-1559) Father of Henri [II] Estienne (q.v.), he printed several editions of the Bible in Hebrew, Greek, and Latin. His *Thesaurus Linguæ Latinæ* (1532) and his *Dictionnaire français-latin* (1539), the oldest French dictionary, represent an important contribution to the development of Humanism (q.v.) in France.

A. Renouard, *Annales de l'imprimerie des Estienne*, 1843.

Étourdi, L' (1655): See *Molière*.

Étranger, L' (1942): See *Camus, Albert*.

Études de la Nature (1784): See *Saint-Pierre, Bernardin de*.

Eugène (1552): See *Jodelle*.

Eugénie (1767): See *Beaumarchais*.

Eugénie Grandet: Written in 1833, this novel, one of the best by Balzac (q.v.), portrays the tragedy of a devoted daughter, victim of her father's incurable avarice despite his considerable wealth. When M. Grandet becomes aware of the budding romance between his daughter Eugénie and her cousin Charles, who is penniless as a result of his father's bankruptcy, he sends off the young man to the West Indies. Before the departure, Eugénie gives Charles, whom she hopes to marry, the birthday gold-coins she received as gifts and which she had hoarded. Charles accepts these savings, hoping to make his fortune, while pledging his everlasting love. When M. Grandet learns that his daughter no longer has the gold, he chastizes her. After Mme. Grandet's death, the result in part of her mistreatment by her husband, the latter tricks Eugénie into signing over to him her share of the property. M. Grandet soon dies, however, and Eugénie comes into a huge fortune. Unaware of her wealth, Charles in a letter asks her for his liberty, ex-

115

plaining that he wishes to marry a certain heiress. Resigned, Eugénie enters into a loveless marriage with M. de Bonfons but is soon left a widow. The rest of her life is spent in philanthropy and self-abnegation.
Eurydice (1942): See *Anouilh.*
Évolution créatrice, L' (1907): See *Bergson.*

EXISTENTIALISM: The term "existentialism" became popular in Paris at the time of the Liberation, and attracted world-wide attention. When Sartre (q.v.) launched in 1945 the new literary-political magazine, *Les Temps Modernes,* he grouped a team of hitherto unknown writers under the common banner of existentialism. Designating a new literary "school," it filled the gap left by the dispersed Surrealists, and seemed to reflect a post-war mood.

It soon became evident, however, that existentialism was by no means a recent, a superficial or even a peculiarly French phenomenon. It had a long and respectable philosophical past which could be traced back to the Greeks. It claimed more immediate ancestors: Pascal (q.v.) and Kierkegaard, Nietzsche and Chestov, Husserl, Jaspers and Heidegger. More than a philosophical "system" existentialism is a philosophical attitude which led philosophers in different directions. There were two main branches: Christian existentialism and atheistic existentialism.

In France itself there were as many shades of existentialism as there were existential philosophers. The Christian existentialism of the Catholic convert Gabriel Marcel (q.v.) could be distinguished from the more prolific atheistic brands; but only specialists could follow the divergencies of thought which distinguished Jean-Paul Sartre and Simone de Beauvoir (q.v.) from their friends Merleau-Ponty (q.v.) or Francis Jeanson. Albert Camus (q.v.), hailed as one of the leaders

of the "Paris school," claimed that his thought had developed partly in opposition to existentialism and that never, at any time, had he belonged to the group. As the forties moved into the fifties, there was hardly a branch of human thought that existentialism left untouched: literature, literary criticism, philosophy, ethics, psychology, sociology, and political theory in particular. By the mid-fifties the principal French existentialist thinkers were fully engaged in vigorous and often bitter political controversies which raged within their own ranks opposing Sartre to Camus to Jeanson to Merleau-Ponty to Simone de Beauvoir. The storm center of the controversy was a hotly-debated evaluation of dialectical materialism in its relation to the policies and attitudes of contemporary Russian communism, (*See* Albert Camus, *L'Homme Révolté,* 1952; Jean-Paul Sartre, "Les Communistes et la Paix," *Les Temps Modernes,* July, October, November 1952; April 1954; Maurice Merleau-Ponty, *Les Aventures de la Dialectique,* 1955). Existentialist literature as such seemed a thing of the past.

It is clear, therefore, that the word "existentialism," like the word "romanticism" can have different connotations. Essentially, however, it designates a literary "mood" prevalent between the thirties and the fifties. Fostered by certain emotional and mental attitudes, it favored the development in literature of recognizable, dominant themes. Unlike the term "romanticism," however, existentialism also refers to a philosophical trend. Existentialist philosophers, like all philosophers, examine the complex problems of human life in the universe. They use a given method and speak a technical vocabulary. Their aim is to give complete and logically satisfying descriptions of the problems they raise.

116

The originality of French existentialism as it appeared in the forties was that it succeeded in integrating the emotional mood of the moment with the intellectual structures of existentialist philosophy. Had Sartre, Camus and Simone de Beauvoir not shared the latent anxieties of their contemporaries and had they failed to express them in their fictional worlds, existentialism might never have been familiar to any but the professional philosophers. However, the fictional worlds of these writers proved all the more challenging because they formulated and attempted to answer coherently the problems which were implicit in the mood of the time.

The method these writers used as a point of departure, both in their fictional works and in their essays, was the phenomenological or descriptive method common to all existentialist philosophers. It was peculiarly well designed to arrest the attention of people whose bewilderment arose in great part from the wide discrepancy which existed between reality as they experienced it and the various traditional religions or intellectual structures which were supposed to account for and order that experience. The rapid evolution of scientific theories and technical innovations, global war, social revolutions and concentration camps had swept away most of the basic convictions on which French civilization, more or less consciously, rested. Existentialism had an initial advantage; it started from the premise that man's presence and action on this earth are inexplicable rationally and cannot be justified. Existentialists accept that fact and proceed to describe, not to explain.

The existentialist, like the Marxist, studies man only as he exists in relation to a concrete, individual "situation." Each individual is "engaged," committed, one might say, to a certain period of time, a geographical location, a social class, a profession. The existentialist philosopher refuses to dissociate the individual and his "situation" in order to consider abstract, ideal "Man." The idea of "Man" or "human nature" is a result of the lives and actions of individual men; it cannot govern their decisions, nor set a pattern for their lives, nor explain them; existence precedes essence. The existentialist philosopher, therefore, cannot start thinking about men by means of a set of basic abstract principles from which he can build, by deduction, a unified rational structure which satisfies his intellect. He does not admit a priori the hypothesis that there is any unifying principle, any God, governing man and the universe according to a preordained plan. His point of departure is strictly limited to the one thing he can grasp, the closed subjective world of individual consciousness, nothing more.

The Christian existentialist moves from this starting point toward a direct apprehension of God. The atheistic existentialist cannot relate the closed subjective world of individual consciousness to any absolute. He cannot, like the Marxist, find a path toward objectivity by referring to the development of man as it is revealed in a man's recorded history. For the existentialist, man's history is not determined by any laws; there is no fatality in history. Each individual merely knows himself as "situated," his situation has no meaning as such, it can be referred to no context. It is the individual alone who through his acts gives a human significance to the situation in which he is "engaged." To act is to choose one's relation to a situation and to modify it and oneself concomitantly. To choose is to evaluate. Each individual in each successive situation in which he is engaged is free to make his choice and so to create his values. In so doing he determines what he shall become. "Human nature" is the sum total of the choices made by millions of men. It is perpetually in the making. Each man's responsibility, therefore, is as complete as his freedom. There are no alibis. The burden of existence is heavy indeed for the frail being the existentialist describes, inexplicably thrown into an alien universe, the strange product of a blind chance, a being who can find no recourse or appeal in anything outside himself. His first reaction when confronted with his position is understandably enough a sort of terror, a "nausea," anguish. Existentialist psychology describes at length the many ways by which men evade the necessity of coming to terms both with their position and with their responsibility. "Nonauthentic" modes of behavior are signs that a human being is acting in "bad faith," attempting to dissimulate from himself and even more from others the real nature of his relations with the world.

These basic assumptions of existentialist philosophy as expressed by Sartre, for example, in the forties, were already quite familiar to the French in the thirties even though the word seemed new. The dominant mood of much French literature in the thirties was "existentialist" in so far as it attempted to come to grips with a reality which it stripped bare of all interpretation. It quite often described the strange "absurd" quality of the most familiar aspects of living when they are merely observed and noted from the outside, as it were. Everyday life could then be seen as fantastic, frightening, poetic even, but in the same manner as one sees the existence of a strange species of insect. It could also be felt as tragic if the endeavors of the human insect to give its life a meaning and signifi-

cance were seen in relation to their essential insignificance. The positive existential ethics of freedom and responsibility emphasized by Sartre was keyed to the heroic mood of the forties, of the Resistance years when many individuals discovered that they were willing to act against great odds so that systematic disavowal of certain human values would not go unchallenged. Freedom, responsibility, action were words which carried weight in that decade.

One may well wonder whether the somber color of much of the literature of the thirties and the forties reflected the tragic aspects of existentialist thought or whether both had a common source in the anxiety caused by the alarming trends visibly developing in Western civilization. It seems that, in France at least, an "existential" state of mind was manifest in the arts and particularly in the theater, the novel, before existentialist philosophies as such had reached any but a few initiates.

In 1932, a powerful and chaotic novel by Louis Ferdinand Céline (q.v.) set the mood. *Voyage au bout de la Nuit* (1932) lyrically describes what is in fact the basic existential experience of life. Bardamu, Céline's pitiful "hero," tells the meaningless Odyssey of dereliction and inanity which constitutes his existence. It is the record of insignificant episodes in a nightmarish décor, and the sum total is nothingness, night. There is a kind of bitter beauty in Bardamu's journey but no fulfillment, no rest, no hope; only a perpetual bafflement, a permanent exile in fear, hunger and slavery. Bardamu can refer to no religious, rational or social structures for any explanation, meaning or cause. In this respect he appeared to many of the younger Europeans as an embodiment of the pure anguish or "nausea" caused by the consciousness that one's existence is a sort of nothingness.

Many of the outstanding French writers of the thirties—a generation of novelists—start from the desperate view of life which is implicit in Céline's novel. The most significant of these is André Malraux (q.v.), a novelist who later became an art critic and whose life is a saga of adventurous action. Malraux's name is connected with political revolution in China and in Spain and with war and resistance in France. In his books, as in his life, Malraux is in search of the values which are absent from Bardamu's universe.

Malraux uses the novel as a medium by which he develops the themes that preoccupy him. He takes as a setting the violent revolutions and wars so characteristic of the Twentieth century. *La Condition Humaine* (1933), the best known of his novels, is a highly fictionalized account of an episode in the Chinese Revolution. But Malraux is not interested essentially in political action and doctrines as such. What he describes is the revolt which, according to him, is at the root of all creative activity of human beings. Thrown by chance on a small planet, his characters perpetually defy and seek to transcend the limitations imposed on them by the natural order of the cosmos or by other human beings. In the three volumes of his *Psychologie de l'art* —*Le Musée imaginaire* (1947), *La Création artistique* (1948), *La Monnaie de l'Absolue* (1949)—Malraux examines all forms of art, the plastic arts in particular. The artist, according to him, is the man who within the limitations of his "human condition" creates an image understandable to all men, thereby freeing us from the limitations of space and time and the anguish of solitude and death. The world of art is a human world through which man imposes his own order on matter according to his own values. Art reveals and forever moulds an image of man drawn from man himself.

One might quote other names, that of the playwright Anouilh (b. 1910; q.v.) or that of St. Exupéry (b. 1900; q.v.) whose works are essentially lyrical meditations on the nature of man. Even in poetry, Francis Ponge (b. 1889; q.v.) and Guillevic (b. 1907; q.v.), breaking with the surrealist attitude towards the world of objects, experimented with purely descriptive forms of poetry, phenomenological in its method and approach to a universe from which the human being is generally absent.

The existential pattern was well set and its basic themes familiar to the public when systematic existentialism appeared in the forties. Christian existentialism had almost no repercussion in French literature. Gabriel Marcel, its principal exponent, was converted to Catholicism in 1929. Neither his philosophical meditations nor his two-dozen-odd plays he produced ever reached a wide audience; he cannot be compared to Claudel, Péguy, Maritian, Mauriac or Bernanos (q.v.). A philosopher by training, Gabriel Marcel chose the theater as a medium because he thought of it as the concrete replica of a metaphysical, existential situation: within a limited universe, that of the stage, a recognizable middle-class set of individuals engaged in a well defined set of relationships are called upon to act, to transform their initial situations. As they move toward their decisions they reveal the inner values to which they unconsciously adhere or which they seek. One of the characters is generally en route toward the discovery of the hidden Christian God. Unfortunately, even the best of Marcel's plays, *Le Monde Cassé* (1933), *Rome n'est plus dans Rome* (1951), are dull. They tend to become abstract demonstrations. Marcel's "metaphysical theatre" is too cerebral to be convincing. Atheistic existentialism had a far greater impact on French literature.

Jean-Paul Sartre is without doubt both the most prolific among French existentialist philosophers and one of the most vigorous writers of the mid-century. Between 1936, the date of his first important publication, *L'Imagination,* and 1955, he had published, besides many scattered essays and articles, twenty-six volumes covering the widest range of subjects as varied in form as in content. Sartre is a philosopher, a political theorist, a journalist, the director of a monthly magazine, a literary critic, a novelist, and a playwright who occasionally uses the movies as his medium of expression. *L'Etre et le Néant* (1943) is a seven-hundred-fifty page essay on "phenomenological ontology"; *Saint Genêt, comédien et martyre* (1952) is a much too bulky example of existential psychoanalysis applied to the personality of the minor writer and petty criminal Jean Genêt (q.v.). It is an introduction to a future Sartrian ethics which is in preparation.

Sartre's literary production is only a small part of a work which is still in the making. In the realm of literature proper he published a first novel *La Nausée* (1936), a volume of good short stories, *Le Mur* (1937), and three volumes of an unfinished work *Les Chemins de la Liberté* (1945-49). But it is through the theater, not the novel, that Sartre has reached his public. His first play, *Les Mouches* (1943), was an unqualified success. The seven plays which followed are uneven in quality, the last, *Nekrassov* (1955), though far from negligible,

being generally considered a failure. But his *Huis Clos* (1945), *La Putain Respectueuse* (1946), and more particularly *Les Mains Sales* (1948), and *Le Diable et le Bon Dieu* (1951), had long runs and provoked lengthy discussion, which is just what Sartre intended them to do. Literature, Sartre explains in his essay "Qu'est-ce que la litterature?" (*Situations II,* 1948), is a form of action. Sartre is a man who, like any other man, is "situated." As a writer he continues to bear the full weight of his responsibility as a man. The work he produces must bear directly on the problems of his time. It must give them significance. A book is not primarily a work of art although it may also be a work of art. It is an objective description, according to existentialists perspectives, of a concrete situation and characters whose "choices" interest us all. It is directed toward the largest immediate audience, not the "happy few" nor to future generations.

The position is not without its dangers. But in many respects the literary medium was particularly well suited to communicate a view of the world concerned first with metaphysical experience in its "subjective, singular, and dramatic aspects." (*See* Simone de Beauvoir, "Littérature et Métaphysique," *Les Temps modernes,* April, 1946.) Rejecting the old forms of drama, Sartre announced that his theater was a "theater of situations." Sartre's characters are men who are free within a given situation and who choose freely, through an act, what they shall become. Sartre's plays deliberately illustrate the basic themes of existential thought and in many ways recall the discredited "pièce à thèse (q.v.)." But Sartre has a real sense of the theater. The characters he creates, though simplified, do not become merely "types." The situations chosen are schematic, but clearly delineated. They are not in the least bit subtle, therefore they are easy to grasp. The language is simple, direct, everyday language. The play goes over well as a play. Sartre's novels are less convincing. *La Nausée* is the fictionalized account of a metaphysical experience. Antoine Roquentin carefully notes in a journal the various stages of his changing relationship with the world; he slowly and reluctantly begins to apprehend his existence and the existence of the world according to existential perspectives. The "nausea" which comes over him even more pervasively is a physiological form of metaphysical anguish: the need to vomit the world, to empty oneself of all existence. *Les Chemins de la Liberté* takes Europe and more particularly Paris as its setting. It describes the collective experience which carried Europeans from Munich to World War II. Sartre follows the itineraries of a small group of Parisian intellectuals. Since the novel has remained unfinished, it is difficult to tell what the "paths of freedom" are that the main characters in the book must find. In spite of Sartre's concern for man, Sartre's novels disconcert the reader by his systematic refusal to describe human beings in general except in terms of a sort of animal baseness; the world in which they move seems incomplete.

Simone de Beauvoir's thought is very close to Sartre's. She has published four novels—the last of which, *Les Mandarins* (1954), won the Goncourt prize—a play, essays, articles and a long study of the situation of women, *Le Deuxième Sexe* (1949). Her fictional world is limited: the world of the small group of Parisian intellectuals which Sartre also portrays in *Les Chemins de la Liberté*. Her first novel, *L'Invitée* (1943), is also her best. In spite of the cold efficacity of the story it does not tend toward the "metaphysical novel" which Madame de Beauvoir wanted to write, but toward the "roman à thèse." The novels which followed and the play *Les Bouches Inutiles* (1945) were far less successful. The existential theses concerning responsibility, freedom, authenticity of choice, and ambiguity in action are too apparent and limit the appeal of Madame de Beauvoir's work: it is frequently both stiff and dull, but it is generally intelligent and thought provoking.

Albert Camus is not one of the existentialists, yet his work is closely related to theirs. An essayist, a novelist, and a playwright, the winner in 1957 of the Nobel Prize for Literature is still in mid-career. His thought developed steadily between 1938, the date of his first book of essays, and 1954, when he published another quite remarkable collection of essays *L'Eté*. *Le Mythe de Sisyphe* (1942) and *L'Homme Révolté* (1954) describe two stages in this development. *Le Mythe de Sisyphe* analyses the "absurd" quality of the life of all individual human beings, inexplicably condemned to death which makes all their enterprises insignificant. And yet, human beings, on the whole, do not commit suicide. Life, therefore, is a value in itself, although logical thought may deny it. Man is comparable to Sisyphus, the Greek hero whom the Gods condemned forever to roll a rock up a steep slope, a rock which, having reached the top, inevitably rolled down. But "absurd" though this situation may be, Sisyphus finds satisfaction in the accomplishment of his task; like Sisyphus, man must shoulder the burden of his "absurd" human condition. For Camus life with that appeal is sufficient unto itself and human beings will cease to evade their immediate responsibilities.

In *L'Homme Révolté*, Camus, like Malraux before him, seeks for positive human values in man's refusal to accept the conditions imposed upon him by the physical world or by other men. Revolt is a form of creativeness; it is the refusal to accept as definitive any religious, political or other abstract ordering of man's life. Camus considers all "systems" as inhuman. Revolt, therefore, is the sign of a living force that refuses to be stifled by abstractions. Camus' two novels, *L'Étranger* (1942) and *La Peste* (1947), were very widely read. They rank among the few contemporary French novels whose success was world-wide. Of his four plays, only one, *Caligula* (1944), was successful. In all these works Camus shows individuals who in one way or another are brought face to face with the "absurd" nature of life. Their reaction brings them into conflict with others as they attempt to escape from the absurdity of living. The hero of *L'Étranger* discovers the value of life only when he is about to die on the guillotine. The emperor Caligula and other heros attempt to impose around them an absurd or amoral order. *La Peste* describes the stubborn fight of a small group of men who in the plague-stricken city of Oran unite to fight the plague. In this tense, strange novel, Camus proposes his ethics: man's greatness consists in his persistent resistance to all the forces that kill men—the "Plagues" that destroy them. *La Chute* (1956) and a book of short stories *L'Exil et le royaume*

(1957) continue the search for values. Camus' work, though far less abundant than Sartre's, has a certain quality of style which Sartre's lacks. Camus is a more careful, more polished writer. Both men, however, stand out from the ranks of their contemporaries.

In the early fifties one could detect a reaction against the attitudes, concepts and terminology of existentialism as expressed in literature. The epigones of Sartre often turned out heavy, obscure works written in a pretentious, abstruse vocabulary, devoid of imagination, and solemnly charged with existential "anguish" and "significance." French literary historians of the future will probably equate existentialism with the work of Sartre, the only literary work of value that systematic philosophic existentialism has produced to date.

L'Existentialisme Chretien: Gabriel Marcel, 1947; Kenneth Douglas, *A Critical Bibliography of Existentialism* (The Paris School), 1950; James Collins, *The Existentialists: A Critical Study*, 1952; R. M. Albérès, *Sartre*, 1952; Iris Murdoch, *Sartre, Romantic Rationalist*, 1953; Pierre Henri Simon, *L'Esprit et L'Histoire* (Chaps. 4, 5 and 6— Marxism and Existentialism), 1954; Francis Jeanson, *Sartre par lui-même*, 1955; Henri Peyre, *The Contemporary French Novel*, 1955.

GERMAINE BRÉE

F

Fables (*c.* 1690): See *Fénelon*.
Fables (1792): See *Florian*.
Fables (1668-1694): See *La Fontaine*.

fabliau (Picard form; sometimes written *fableau*): A short tale in octosyllabic verse whose purpose is to amuse or to satirize: (a) women (e.g., *Le vilain mire:* this inspired Molière's *Le Médecin malgré lui*); (b) husbands (e.g., *Le mari qui fit sa femme confesse*); (c) priests (e.g., *Le curé qui mangea des mûres*). Some of the *fabliaux* have a moral character (e.g., *La Housse partie*), while others are licentious. Drawing their themes from everyday incidents and situations, these poems, representative of the *esprit gaulois* (q.v.), were written essentially for the *bourgeois* and the people. Dating from the 12th through part of the 14th centuries, the 150 extant fabliaux find their origins, according to the most recent theories, for the most part in popular sources.

J. Bédier, *Les fabliaux*, 3d ed., 1893.

Fabre, Emile: (1869-1955) A ready disciple of Becque and Brieux (qq.v.), this dramatist poses in his plays social problems that relate to finance, administration, and colonization. Domestic unhappiness as a result of greed for money is portrayed in *L'Argent* (1895); the corruption of officials willing to take desperate measures to maintain their positions is viewed in *La Vie publique* (1902). The influence of large financial enterprises on the mechanism of modern society is portrayed in *Les Ventres dorés* (1905), while *Les Sauterelles* (1911) depicts the exploitation of French colonies by their functionaries. His theater, in general, mirrors the contemporary society of his times.

Fabre d'Eglantine (pseud. of **Philippe Fabre**): (1755-1794) Noted as the author of the republican calendar, this writer, also a dramatist, ended his life on the scaffold. *Le Philinte de Molière ou la suite du Misanthrope* (1791), his best comedy, rehabilitates Molière's (q.v.) misanthrope Alceste at the expense of Philinte, who is presented in an unfavorable light.

L. Moland, *Théâtre de la Révolution,* 1877.

Factums (1685): See *Furetière, Antoine.*

Faguet, Emile: (1847-1916) For many years professor at the Sorbonne, this critic was prolific in his output of books and articles that won him much distinction. In addition to the dramatic criticism that he wrote for the *Journal des Débats,* he published *Seizième Siècle* (1894), *Dix-septième Siècle* (1885), *Dix-huitième Siècle* (1890), and *Dix-neuvième Siècle* (1887), a series of studies of individual writers that reveal their character and ideas. Perhaps his best and most characteristic work is *Politiques et Moralistes du XIX*^{e} *siècle* (1891-1899), wherein he displays his intellectual brilliance. In all his writings, his approach is more logical and analytic than aesthetic.

A. Bélis, *La Critique française à la fin du 19*^{e} *siècle,* 1926.

Famille Benoîton, La (1865): See *Sardou.*

Fanny (1858): See *Feydeau.*

farce: Originally this term, derived from the Latin *farsa* and *farcire,* which meant "stuffing," referred to the interpolation of comic scenes into the *mystères* (q.v.). Later, farce developed independently of the *mystère.* Of the more than 150 extant farces, all composed between 1440-1560, the most celebrated are *La Farce du Cuvier* and *La Farce de Maître Pathelin* (qq.v.). Related to the theater in much the same way that the *fabliau* (q.v.) is to poetry, the *farce,* in contrast with high comedy or comedy of character, provokes laughter through caricature, gestures, buffoonery, action or situation. It exercised a considerable influence on seventeenth-century comedy (See Molière's *Fourberies de Scapin* or his *Médecin malgré lui*). The farce, continued to the present day, has more recently been represented by such dramatists as

Labiche, Feydeau, Courteline, and Tristan Bernard (qq.v.).

Fargue, Léon Paul: (1876-1947) Student and friend of Mallarmé (q.v.), this poet started out as a symbolist (see *Symbolism*), as can be seen in *Tancrède* (1894), a confession of the young man as an artist, reflecting the influence of Gide (q.v.). The imagery in his *Poèmes* (1902) is reminiscent of Rimbaud (q.v.). In *Espaces* (1928) and *Sous la Lampe* (1929), the poet, already influenced by the dream quality of the surrealists (see *Surréalism*), employs fantastic visions. Essentially, however, the poet of Paris, where he was born, in *Le Piéton de Paris* (1927) and *D'après Paris* (1931)—a veritable poetry in prose—he evokes, in tones of amusement and tenderness, memories of his childhood and youth in this city of mystery and charm. In the final analysis, Fargue is an escapist, and seeks in dreams a remedy for his sorrow and solitude. He represents a link between symbolism and surrealism.

Farrère, Claude: (1876-1957) His experiences as an officer in the Navy served as the inspiration for his novels—which in their adventure and especially in their exoticism recall Pierre Loti (q.v.). *Fumée d'Opium* (1904), his masterpiece, is a collection of tales which reveals great originality and imagination. *Les Civilisés* (1905)—which won him the *Prix Goncourt* (q.v.)—is an Indo-Chinese novel. His sea stories— *Dix-sept Histoires de marins* (1914) —are amusing and appeal to the imagination. *La Bataille* (1909), a work of unquestioned literary merit, is the result of personal experiences, youthful recollections, and imagination. The perfect novel of adventure is *L'Homme qui assassina* (1907), a description of life in Constantinople. Farrère is not obsessed, as is Loti, by fleeting time; his stories contain gaiety, irony, and action.

Faux Monnayeurs, Les: Written in 1925, this "novel"—the only book of his to which Gide (q.v.) assigned this characterization—is the most complex, if not the most interesting, of his works. Compared, because of its elaborate and careful composition— a composition that calls to mind the orchestration of various movements —with such other great works of the Twenties as Proust's (q.v.) *A la recherche du temps perdu*, Joyce's *Ulysses* and Mann's *The Magic Mountain*, it is perhaps his most characteristic work, containing most of his aesthetic and moral theories. In accordance with these theories, each succeeding chapter is not the continuation of a central plot, but rather a new beginning or departure in a series of separate stories. Viewed in its ensemble, however, this novel is given its basic unity through Edouard, the chief character, who is writing a novel about everything other people's lives as well as his own teach him. Edouard, through whom the book becomes the novelists' novel, alternates his personal observations with a description of the lives of those who confide their secrets to him. The account of the experiences of Vincent and Olivier, Edouard's nephews, of Bernard, Olivier's friend, of Laura, Vincent's lover, and of others, becomes, in the final analysis, a portrait of the characters' progressive self-discovery. In his delineation of the various characters, Gide shows a special interest in the psychology of adolescents; through them he is able to bring into bold relief the question of sincerity as they influence each other and reflect the influence of older, disingenuous people with whom they come into contact. Those characters who show a determination to be true to themselves stand in direct contrast with the "counterfeit" souls who conform for the sake of conformity. From this point of view, the novel reflects the mentality of the young who, after the first

World War, wished to free themselves from convention and tradition.

Felibres: See *Provençal* (literature).

Felibrige: See *Provençal* (literature).

Femme libre, Une (1934): See *Salacrou, Armand.*

Femme nue, La (1908): See *Bataille, Henri.*

Femmes savantes, Les (1672): See *Mo-lière.*

Fénelon, François de Salignac de la Mothe-: (1651-1715) A theologian, mystic, educator and writer, known because of his eloquence as *Le Cygne de Cambrai,* he was entrusted in 1686, upon the recommendation of Bossuet (q.v.), then his friend, with missions to win Calvinists back to Catholicism. His first pedagogical work, *Traité de l'éducation des filles* (1687), was written at the request of the Duc de Beauvilliers, father of eight daughters. The same nobleman subsequently appointed him tutor (1689) of the Duc de Bourgogne, grandson of Louis XIV. For his pupil, a potential heir to the throne, Fénelon wrote *Fables* (*c.* 1690)—consisting of fairy tales, animal tales, and adventure stories similar to those of ancient times—*Les Dialogues des Morts* (*c.* 1692) and *Télémaque* (1699). The last-named work, for which he is espe-cially known, is a kind of sequel to Homer's *Odyssey.* As Télémaque, in search of his father, visits different countries, he has the opportunity to observe and study their respective governments. This book, intended as a pedagogical novel, thus be-comes didactic in its indirect criti-cism of Louis XIV and in the politi-cal ideal it suggests. Throughout the eighteenth century, it should be added, this book, tremendously suc-cessful, had a lasting influence in and outside of France. By the time *Télémaque* was published, Fénelon had already been exiled to his dio-cese of Cambrai—to which in 1695 he had been named archbishop—

the result of having espoused the mystic doctrine of *Quietism* (q.v.). For his un-orthodox Catholicism, Fénelon was attacked by his former friend Bossuet. Following his de-cision to submit the controversy to the Pope, by whom he was con-demned, he fell into disfavor at the court. Despite his genuine respect for authority and an admiration, not unlike that of Racine (q.v.), for the Greeks, Fénelon, because of his inde-pendent religious views and ideal of human fraternity and political jus-tice, is regarded as a transitional author and as a precursor of the eighteenth century *Enlightenment* (q.v.). In his *Lettre à l'Académie* (1716), moreover,—a work of liter-ary criticism—his views are not dis-similar, since he flatters both the Ancients and the Moderns.

J. Lemaître, *Fénelon,* 1910; H. Brémond, *Apologie pour Fénelon,* 1911; A. Cherel, *Fénelon ou la reli-gion du pur amour,* 1934; E. Car-cassonne, *Fénelon,* 1947.

Fermina Marquez (1911): See *Larbaud, Valery.*

Feu, Le (1916): See *Barbusse.*

Feuilles d'automne, Les (1831): See *Hugo.*

Feuillet, Octave: (1821-1890) Offering a striking contrast with the writers of the Second Empire, this novelist and dramatist depicted, much like a Victorian, the aristocratic society of his day. In *Le Roman d'un jeune homme pauvre* (1857), virtue is re-warded after much suffering. *Mon-sieur de Camors* (1867) ends with a reconciliation between a straying husband and his wife. Other novels written in a similar vein include *La Petite Comtesse* (1857) and *Julia de Trécœur* (1872). In the theater, too, virtue triumphs, as can be seen in *La Tentation* (1860), a triangle play, and in *Le Sphinx* (1874), in which the heroine, enamored of her friend's husband, dies after having taken the poison she originally pre-pared for her friend. Other plays include *Le Pour et le Contre* (1853), *Dalila* (1857), *Montjoie* (1863), and *Julie* (1869). The sentimentalism and sensitivity of Feuillet endeared him to many of his female readers. L. Deries, *Octave Feuillet*, 1902; H. Bordeaux, *La jeunesse d'O. Feuillet*, 1922.

Feu qui reprend mal, Le (1921): See *Bernard, Jean Jacques.*

Feydeau, Ernest: (1821-1873) Father of Georges Feydeau (q.v.), the dramatist, this Parisian-born writer launched his career with *Les Nationales* (1844), a collection of poetry, and was a devotee of art and archeology. He gained his reputation as the author of *Fanny* (1858). This novel, in a contemporary setting, of a lover tormented by his jealousy of his mistress's husband, bears a resemblance to Flaubert's (q.v.) *Madame Bovary*, written one year before. In contrast to the latter novel, however, its descriptions are much shorter and more imprecise; its style is romantic as are the characters themselves. Its claim to "distinction" is based primarily on the immorality which the critics saw in it and which they equated with realism (q.v.); like *Madame Bovary*, too, it excited the wrath of many. Other novels include: *Daniel* (1859), *Catherine d'Overmeire* (1860), and *La Comtesse de Chalis* (1867). His reputation as a realistic novelist later declined.

P. Martino, *Le Roman réaliste sous le Second Empire*, 1913.

Feydeau, Georges: (1862-1921) In rollicking and witty farces, the plots of which leave much to be desired morally, this dramatist, who is rarely interested in character development, contrives chance meetings between those trying to evade one another and deceptions planned on each other by husbands and wives. These situations developed by the author have little or no connection with real life and thus have a charm all their own. The hilarious difficulties built up in these *vaudevilles* (q.v.) make Feydeau a follower of the theater of Labiche (q.v.). Included among his plays are: *On purge bébé* (1910), *Occupe-toi d'Amélie* (1911), *Mais n'te promène donc pas toute nue* (1912), and *La Dame de chez Maxim* (1914). Such plays were popular with Parisian audiences from 1894 to 1914, and have had a slight revival in the early Fifties.

Fille Elisa, La (1877): See *Goncourt.*

Fils naturel, Le (1757): See *Diderot.*

Fils naturel, Le (1858): See *Dumas* FILS.

Fin de Lucie Pellegrin, La (1888): See *Alexis, Paul.*

Flaubert, Gustave: (1821-1880) The life of this novelist, born in Rouen, where his father was a noted surgeon, was generally uneventful. Brought up in the gloomy atmosphere of the medical environment, sent to Paris to study law, which he found most uninspiring, he turned to literature as an escape. Afflicted in his twenties with a nervous disease which may or may not have been epilepsy, he decided to devote himself entirely to literature. After his father's death, in 1846, he went to Croisset, near Rouen, where his family had an estate. Here he remained most of his life, and, except for his occasional trips to Paris and his journeys to the Near East and Tunis, led pretty much of a hermitic existence, consecrated to the world of letters as an art.

Viewed in its ensemble, the work of Flaubert, relatively small, and composed laboriously, reflects the struggle of two distinct beings, one the romantic, the other the realist, within the author. Of a distinctly romantic temperament, which he tried to overcome, Flaubert struggled piously to achieve the Parnassian (q.v.) ideal of perfection of form as well as of scrupulous documentation. His preoccupation with detail, his obsession with the *mot juste*, his doctrine of truth and beauty, are to be found even in his historical fiction. These include *Salammbô* (1862), a resurrection of ancient Carthage and Punic civilization, *La Tentation de Saint-Antoine* (1874), a symbolic review of ancient religions, *La Légende de Saint Julien l'Hospitalier* and *Hérodias*, two of the *Trois Contes* (1877). The picturesque scenes and tableaux in these imaginative evocations of the Middle Ages and Antiquity contain precise details of background and much careful documentation. His other novels and stories—*Madame Bovary* (1857), *L'Éducation sentimentale* (1869), *Un cœur simple*, and the unfinished *Bouvard et Pécuchet* (1881)—contain contemporary settings and deal with ordinary, insignificant individuals, who are involved in prosaic, vulgar affairs. Of these, *Madame Bovary* (q.v.), his first published novel, which first appeared in the *Revue de Paris* (1856), is considered the realistic novel *par excellence;* it is an exact record of contemporary bourgeois society, faithfully portrayed. Written in an impersonal style and impeccable form, this novel combines the plastic qualities of Gautier (q.v.) and the observation of Balzac (q.v.). Its publication, like that of Baudelaire's (q.v.) *Les Fleurs du Mal* (1857), led to a lawsuit; in contrast to the latter's condemnation, however, Flaubert was acquitted of any attempt to scandalize. The lawsuit, which brought to the fore the whole question of Realism (q.v.) and the author's right not to attenuate truth, assured the success of *Madame Bovary* and made Flaubert, who did not entirely approve all of its ideas, head of the Realistic School.

R. Dumesnil, *Gustave Flaubert; l'homme et l'œuvre*, 1932; E. Maynial, *Flaubert*, 1943.

Fléchier, Esprit: (1632-1710) Bishop of Nîmes, this orator, inferior to Bossuet and Bourdaloue (qq.v.), on numerous occasions preached at the court. He is known especially for his funeral orations on the *Duchesse de Montausier* and *Turenne*, the latter of which has been compared to that by Mascaron (q.v.).

E. Lacombe, *Fléchier à Nîmes*, 1932; G. Grente, *Fléchier*, 1934.

Fleg, Edmond: (1874-   ) Finding the main source of his inspiration in his Jewish origins and in the Bible, this writer, born in Geneva, exhorts the Jewish people to fulfill its ideal of universal peace. Included among his major poetic works are: *Le Psaume de la Terre promise* (1919) —a song of joy—, *Le mur des Pleurs* (1919), the epic *Écoute, Israël* (1922), and *Et tu aimeras L'Éternel* (1948). Famous for his *Anthologie juive* (1923), Fleg is also the author of several plays, including *Le Juif du Pape* (1925), and of the novel *L'Enfant prophète* (1926).

Flers, Robert de (1872-1927) and **Caillavet, Gaston Arman de** (1869-1915): The first of this dramatic team was the husband of Sardou's (q.v.) daughter, and the second was the son of Mme. de Caillavet, whose famous salon and friendship for Anatole France (q.v.) made her a well-known figure in literary circles. Their collaboration, which began in 1900, recalls that of Meilhac and Halévy (qq.v.), whose general tradition they followed; unlike the latter, however, whose theater portrayed the society of the Second Empire, they depicted that of the Third Republic. In scintillating dialogue, they constructed comedies that were at times sentimental, at others satirical; *Miquette et sa mère* (1906) and *Primerose* (1911) are good examples of the former. Of the latter, *Le Roi* (1908) derides the escapades of visiting royalty; *Le Bois sacré* (1910) pokes fun at those who worship titles bestowed by the Légion d'Honneur; *L'Habit vert* (1912) satirizes, ironically enough, the French Academy, to which Flers was elected in 1920! The good humor and wit produced by these literary partners entitle them to be called the masters of Parisian Comedy.

Francis de Croisset, *Le Souvenir de Robert de Flers*, 1929; *La Vie parisienne au théâtre*, 1929.

Fleurs du mal, Les (1857): See *Baudelaire*.

Florian, Jean-Pierre Claris de: (1755-1794) Through his *Fables* (1792), written in verse, he has won the reputation as the successor to La Fontaine (q.v.). In addition, he is the author of such pastoral novels as *Galatée* (1783) and *Estelle et Némorin* (1788)—which describe peasant life in the Cévennes—and of such comedies as *Le Bon père* (1783), *La Bonne mère* (1785) and *Le Bon fils* (1785).

L. Clarétie, *Florian*, 1891; G. Saillard, *Florian, sa vie, son œuvre*, 1912.

Foire, théâtres de la: Beginning toward the end of the sixteenth century, small farces were produced at the fairs in Paris in the Saint-Germain section during the winter, and in Saint-Laurent during the summer. These theaters, taking advantage of the expulsion of the *Comédie-Italienne* (q.v.) in 1697, developed the *comédie en vaudevilles* and the *comédie à ariettes* (q.v.), comedies with song and music. These plays were themselves subterfuges to evade the edicts forbidding first the use of dialogue—the sole privilege of the *Comédie-Française* (q.v.)—then of monologue, then even of pantomime; the dialogue, instead of being spoken, was now being sung. In 1716, upon its return to Paris, the Italian troupe opposed—as did the *Opéra*—the use of music by the *théâtres de la foire*. Eventually, the problem was resolved when in 1762 the *Comédie-Italienne* negotiated a merger with the *Opéra-Comique* (q.v.), which theater effectively absorbed the functions of the *théâtres de la foire*. Among those whose plays, it should be noted, were pro-

duced at the *théâtres de la foire*, are Lesage and Sedaine (qq.v.).

M. Albert, *Les Théâtres de la Foire*, 1900.

Folle de Chaillot, La (1945): See *Giraudoux*.

Fontenelle, Bernard le Bovier de: (1657-1757) Scholar, literary critic and popularizer of science, this centenarian, nephew of Corneille (q.v.), launched his career as a writer of verse, tragedy and opera libretti. It is as a prose writer, however, that he distinguished himself. In perhaps his best known work, *Entretiens sur la pluralité des mondes* (1686), he captures the interest of a marquise as he discusses with her, in easily understandable terms, the solar system. The success of this book, following the imaginary philosophical dialogues in *Dialogues des Morts* (1683), encouraged him to use the same scientific, rational, and yet un-pedantic, method in his *Histoire des oracles* (1687), a subtle attack against religious orthodoxy and superstition. Devoted to the principle of tolerance, skeptical of dogmatic truth, in his *Digression sur les Anciens et les Modernes* (1688) he champions the cause of the moderns in the *Querelle des Anciens et des Modernes* (q.v.). Advancing the notion of progress, while disseminating knowledge of philosophy and science, Fontenelle is an important precursor of eighteenth-century thought and of the *Encyclopédistes* (q.v.). In 1697 he was made perpetual secretary of the *Académie des Sciences*.

L. Maigron, *Fontenelle*, 1906; F. Grégoire, *Fontenelle*, 1947.

Forêts de la nuit, Les (1947): See *Curtis, Jean-Louis*.

Fort, Paul: (1872-) Since 1897, this poet from Champagne has published some fifty volumes of verse. In 1905 he founded and became editor of *Vers et Prose*, a neo-symbolistic review, partly as a result of which he was elected in 1912 "prince of poets." Despite his connection with this review and in spite of his even earlier *avant-garde* role in the founding of the anti-naturalistic (cf. *Naturalism*) *Théâtre d'Art* (1890) which staged "idealistic" plays, he himself owes little to Symbolism (q.v.); his poetry has a clarity and simplicity unknown to the Symbolists. In his more than thirty volumes of *Ballades françaises* (1897-1924), poems presented in the form of prose but which contain rhyme, rhythm, and alexandrines (q.v.), he becomes the national poet; he sings of the provinces and of their folklore, of their legends and traditions, of nature and mythology.

Fourberies de Scapin, Les (1671): See *Molière*.

Fourier, Charles: (1772-1873) Writer of pedantic and obscure works, this philosopher and sociologist is better known for his advocacy of voluntary association in small groups (*Phalanges*). Life lived in this manner would make it possible for each member (*phalanstérien*) to pursue those tasks he is most eager to do. Fourier's doctrine of a utopian socialism was popular in France around 1840. According to the economist Charles Gide (1847-1932), from a practical point of view Fourier is the father of co-operatives. His ideology exercised a strong influence on such writers as George Sand, Leconte de Lisle, Baudelaire (qq.v.)—who was not unaffected, as can be seen in his poem "Correspondances," by his theory of "universal harmony"—Emile Zola (q.v.), and, more recently, André Breton (q.v.).

Fournier, Alain (pseud. of **Henri Fournier**): (1886-1914) This novelist owes his reputation to *Le Grand Meaulnes* (1913),—his only completed novel—in which he transposed real episodes of his childhood and adolescence, and especially that of his hopeless, idealized love for a girl whom he had once met for a min-

ute. The story is a conflict between the dream and reality—the internal adventure of a young adolescent—and suggests nostalgically the impossibility of preserving the youthful ideal. The author died in action. Robert Gibson, *The Quest of Alain-Fournier*, 1954.

France, Anatole (pseud. of **Jacques Anatole Thibault**): (1844-1924) The humanistic training he received at the *Collège Stanislas* in Paris is reflected in his early writings, *Les Poèmes dorés* (1873) and *Les noces corinthiennes* (1876), composed in the Parnassian (q.v.) tradition. His early prose productions—novels, fairytales, short stories—including *Le Crime de Sylvestre Bonnard* (1881), *Le Livre de mon ami* (1885), *Balthasar* (1889) and *Thaïs* (1890), reveal not only a tendency to lean heavily on his knowledge of the Classics but also, more important, his attempt to use this learning as a weapon against all dogmatic ideas in both religious and secular domains. His early philosophy of skepticism, punctuated by irony and by strong doses of sensualism, is tempered, however, by pity for the human condition and its inconsistencies. A follower of Renan (q.v.) and of his *dilettantism*, he placed himself in the position of the completely dispassionate student of history.

With the *Affaire Dreyfus*, however, and urged on perhaps by the inspiration of Madame de Caillavet, he abandoned his arm-chair philosophy as a spectator of the universe and evolved a more positive position toward life; he took an active part in politics, signed manifestoes, made speeches and undertook the writing of the *Histoire contemporaine* series (*L'Orme du mail*, 1897; *Le Mannequin d'osier*, 1897; *L'Anneau d'améthyste*, 1899; *Monsieur Bergeret à Paris*, 1901), in which he presented, in a contemporary setting, a picture of the different sections of the upper class which because of vested interests had lost their critical spirit and their ideals of truth and justice. Political and social issues also make up the central theme in *L'Île des Pingouins* (1908).

Other writings of his worthy of note are *La vie littéraire* (1888-1892), four volumes of criticism, and his monumental *Vie de Jeanne d'Arc* (1908). In all his writings, what stand out as his essential characteristics—characteristics that do not belie what his name suggests—are the classical clarity, simplicity, and wit of his style. Such qualities explain, at least in part, his election to the French Academy. In 1921 he was awarded the Nobel Prize for Literature.

Gustave Michaut, *Anatole France; étude psychologique*, 1913; Haakon M. Chevalier, *The Ironic Temper: Anatole France and His Time*, 1932; E. Preston Dargan, *Anatole France, 1844-1896*, 1937.

France byzantine, La (1945): See *Benda, Julien.*

FRANCO-AMERICAN LITERARY RELATIONS: The initial interrelationship between France and America is traceable to the sixteenth century when Jacques Cartier touched the American continent and when the exotic appeal of a savage El Dorado found expression in the pages of Rabelais, Montaigne, and the poets of the Pléiade (qq.v.). It was not, however, until about 1750 that French literature began to reach the Eastern seaboard of the Colonies; though in philosophy and science Descartes (q.v.) had already been absorbed into the synthesis of seventeenth-century New England thought, along with Calvin (q.v.). The mutual literary fructification becomes apparent in the documents that issued from the American and French Revolutions.

But there was a decided acceleration of interest in French literature after 1770. In 1780, the founders of the American Academy of Arts and Sciences had gone on record that they desired "to give it the air of France rather than that of England." For like reasons, Guérard de Nancrède, appointed instructor in the French language at Harvard in 1787, launched *Le Courier de Boston*. His anthology, *L'Abeille française* (1792) contained selections from Helvétius and Fénelon (qq.v.), but devoted most space to Rousseau (q.v.). He also edited (in H. Hunter's translation) *Études de la Nature* (1784) by Bernardin de Saint Pierre (q.v.). By this time, Montesquieu's (q.v.) *Spirit of the Laws* had become an American classic; while Franklin's French disciple, Jacques Barbeau-Dubourg, was, presumably, the first to conceive of a journal for the exchange of ideas and good will between France and America. Besides the farces of Pathelin (q.v.), the American public enjoyed English adaptations of the dramas of Corneille, Racine, Molière, Voltaire, Regnard, Dancourt, Le Sage, Diderot, Beaumarchais, Fontenelle, Destouches, and Chénier (qq.v.).

After Franklin and Jefferson, the Adamses form a cultural bridge between the United States and France in the eighteenth and nineteenth centuries. John Adams's interest in Descartes and the philosophers of the eighteenth century is now well known. John Quincy Adams, a friend of Mme. de Staël (q.v.), had read and studied Rousseau, Condillac, Diderot, Helvétius (qq.v.), Lalande, Montesquieu, Vattel, Voltaire (q.v.), Cousin, and Chateaubriand (q.v.). Henry Adams, the descendant of the two presidents, is perhaps the most important figure in Franco-American literary relations between 1860 and 1920. *Mont-Saint Michel and Chartres* (1904, 1913) is the monument to that relationship.

Franklin's stay in France had promoted a respect for American democracy. The outstanding report of this new order was Alexis de Tocqueville's (q.v.) *De la Démocratie en Amérique* (1835) which appeared in Henry Reeve's translation in two parts under a New York imprint in 1838 and 1840. The work declared that while America had no poets, it was not wanting in vast poetic ideas and that while Descartes' principles were least studied here, they were most applied.

The exotic dream of America was promoted by Chateaubriand, who visited our shores at the dawn of the nineteenth century. During the same decade, however, the veil of illusion was disturbed by other visitors like Charles Pictet, Ferdinand M. Bayard, and Jacques Pierre de Warville. But the poetic vision of Chateaubriand in *Atala* (1801; q.v.), *René* (1802; q.v.), and *Mémoires d'Outre Tombe* (1848-50; q.v.) prevailed. Incidentally, in drawing a parallel between Napoleon and Washington, Chateaubriand exalted the latter over the former.

Three decades after *René* and *Atala*, the hero of Sainte-Beuve's (q.v.) *Volupté* (1835) speaks of America as the hope of the world. The author of that novel recalled the vivid descriptions of American scenes in *Manon Lescaut* (1731; q.v.) and corresponded with Henry Harrisse, who later wrote on the *Abbé Prévost* (q.v.) and became one of the most important cultural intermediaries between France and America. In the *Causeries de Lundis* (1851-62) and the *Premiers Lundis* (1874-75) there are fine pages on Franklin and Jefferson and references to Washington, John Adams, Gallatin, Madison, Monroe, John Paul Jones, Gouverneur Morris, William Penn, *et al.* Sainte-Beuve (q.v.) was acquainted (through translations) with the work of Cooper, Longfellow, Bryant, Harriet Beecher Stowe, Melville and Emerson. He also knew the literary essays of Washington Irving and had read Poe's stories in Baudelaire's (q.v.) translations.

Between 1830 and 1840, middle-class America was introduced to "doctored" versions of French letters calculated not to offend the mores of some 150,000 subscribers to *Godey's Lady's Book* (1830-98), which tried hard to erase the notion that all French fiction was gross.

In 1841 Eugene A. Vail published in Paris *De la littérature et des hommes de lettres des États-Unis d'Amérique*. In it he introduced the figures of Jefferson, John Adams, Sparks, Bancroft, Washington Irving, Brackenridge and William Ellery Channing. The last writer had written *Observations on the life and Character of Napoleon Bonaparte* and *Observations on the Character and Writing of Fénélon*. By 1851, readers of the *Revue des Deux Mondes* were made acquainted with the work of James Fenimore Cooper, Bryant, Longfellow, Melville, Emerson and Harriet Beecher Stowe. Twenty years earlier *Leather Stocking* had fired the imagination of Balzac (q.v.). Men like Philarète Chasles, E. D. Forgues and Émile Montégut were responsible for spreading in France the fame of the above-mentioned Americans.

Shortly before the mid-nineteenth century France found a new source of poetic inspiration in Poe and Emerson. It was Baudelaire who derived from them the concepts of the *indefinite* (or the *undefinable*) as allied to music and the *universal analogy* as revelatory of the relation between poetry and science. Following Baudelaire's translations of Poe's stories, Mallarmé (q.v.) translated the poems. Thus, Poe had prefigured French Symbolism (q.v.). Paul Valéry (q.v.) later wrote some interesting pages on him in a preface to a new edition of *Les Fleurs du Mal.* Jules Verne's (q.v.) scientific popularizations have echoes of *Pym* and *The Balloon-Hoax*. Vance Thompson said in his *French Portraits* in 1900: "Once I wrote 'Modern French literature is largely a creation of Poe.' I should have no qualification to make, had I said: 'Modern French literature is largely a creation of Poe and Whitman.' " (p. 202). He should have added: "Neither can Emerson be neglected."

Soon after the publication of the First Series of Essays in 1841, the *Revue des deux mondes* carried articles on Emerson by Émile Montégut. To be sure, Philarète Chasles was the first to mention Emerson's name in that magazine (Aug. 15, 1844), and the first French estimate of the Transcendentalist appeared over the pseudonym "Daniel Stern" (Comtesse d'Agoult, wife of Richard Wagner) in the *Revue Indépendante* for July 25, 1846. But it was Montégut who, in 1851, first translated the First Series of *Essays* (*Essais de philosophie Américaine par R. W. Emerson*). This translation elicited Baudelaire's first mention of Emerson by name, in his notes on Poe (*c.* 1852). His two direct references to Emerson are found in *Fusées* and in *Mon Cœur mis à nu*. One is to the effect that necessity, not inspiration, is the prompter of the Muse; the other, that Emerson had forgotten to include Voltaire among his *Representative Men*. In "L'Œuvre et la vie d'Eugène Delacroix" (1863), he talks of "l'hygiène du travail et la conduite de la vie" and quotes from the *Conduct of Life*: "The hero is he who is immovably centred"; also, "The one prudence in life is concentration; the one evil is dissipation." Emerson himself was predominantly impressed by Montaigne.

We turn next to Whitman's influence in France. In an unpublished Harvard dissertation (1943), Oreste Francesco Pucciani has discerned three periods in Whitman's impact on French opinion: (1) the "Polemical" (1861-1888) during which he was denounced for his materialism and was defended for his pantheistic union of flesh and spirit; (2) the "Period of Incubation" (1888-1908) during which his poetry was translated, with Symbolists taking the leading role and Gabriel Sarrazin publishing a study in *La Nouvelle Revue* (May 1, 1888) which inaugurated a new phase of Whitman's reputation; (3) the "Period of Acceptance" (1908-present), initiated by Léon Bazalgette's biography (1908), followed by a complete translation of *Leaves of Grass* (1909) and a study, with the critical analyses of the poems, in his *Le "Poème—Évangile" de Whitman* (1921). The *Œuvres Choisies* (1918) contained translations by Laforgue, Gide, Schlumberger (qq.v.), Fabulet, Vielé-Griffin (q.v.), Valéry Larbaud (q.v.). In *Walt Whitman, la naissance du poète* (1929), Jean Catel, using psychoanalytic concepts, sees Whitman as a forerunner of the symbolists.

Through Baudelaire, France repaid its debt to American inspiration. Our interest in the French poet has been traced in the critical reactions of Henry James, J. B. Perkins, H. McCulloch, F. S. Saltus, B. W. Wells, Joel Benton, Lafcadio Hearn, Park Barnitz, James Huneker, T. S. Eliot, Edna Saint-Vincent Millay and others. The first American article on the Symbolists, from the pen of T. S. Perry, appeared in the July 1892 number of the *Cosmopolitan*. Aline Gorren's "The French Symbolists" (*Scribner's*, Jan.-June, 1893) recognized the debt of Symbolism (q.v.) to Baudelaire's *Correspondances*. For the first time outside of France, she related the term "Decadence" to Verlaine's (q.v.) line: *Je suis l'empire à la fin de la décadence.* She also gave what might be the first English translations of poems from Rimbaud's (q.v.) *Les Illuminations.* Vance Thompson's articles on Symbolism which appeared in 1895 in *Mlle New York* were expanded later to form a portion of *French Portraits* (1900). Throughout its 15 issues (1895-97), *Mlle New York* printed numerous poems in French as well as in translation. Thompson focussed attention chiefly on Mallarmé. In the February *Bookman* of 1900 Thurston Peck called Thompson's explanation of Mallarmé's theories "really valuable." Morrissette feels that with Thompson and the first year of *Mlle New York,* the high point of American criticism of French symbolism was reached, not to be touched again until the period of Amy Lowell and the Imagist School and the appearance of Huneker's essays and the critical writings of the Imagists. According to René Taupin, interest in Symbolism reached its peak from 1910 to 1920.

Just as Symbolism plays an important rôle in the aesthetics of poetry, Realism and Naturalism (qq.v.) occupy a place of paramount importance in the art of prose. (Morrisette points out that Hovey somehow thought of Symbolism as a synthesis of the other two literary movements.) Balzac (q.v.) was widely read from the eighteen forties through the rest of the century. Among the noteworthy readers were Motley, Melville, Hawthorne, and Henry James, for whom Balzac was the "father of us all." Beginning in the early eighties, Katherine P. Wormeley made a new translation of Balzac's works. The impact of naturalism on American critical opinion has been discerned in a progression from the French naturalists (Flaubert, Maupassant, Zola,

the Goncourts; qq.v.) to Dreiser and Lewis, through Frank Norris, Hamlin Garland and Stephen Crane. There were moral reservations about Zola around the years 1879-'83. Henry James's chapter on Flaubert, in *French Poets and Novelists* (1878), tended to cement a better understanding. That same year, the *Atlantic Monthly* (February) introduced Americans to the Goncourts in an essay by Reclus. In the eighties Henry James referred to Goncourt, Zola, and Daudet (qq.v.) as "the most celebrated men in modern French literature," and the critic J. W. Davidson strongly indorsed Zola in a speech before the Concord School. This was quoted in the *Literary World.* In 1887-'88 *The Critic* supported Howells in his defense of veracity in fiction and in his praise of Zola's *La Terre.* It was not until 1899, when Frank Norris's *McTeague* appeared, that a fair reception was accorded to a naturalistic work.

Between 1900 and 1920 James Huneker performed an important cultural service in stimulating American interest in French culture. Inspired by his friend Vance Thompson, Huneker had the talent of creating an appetite in America for French literature and art. His books are crowded with the figures of Chopin, Balzac, Stendhal (q.v.), Baudelaire, Anatole France, Huysmans, Zola, Villiers de l'Isle-Adam, Maeterlinck (qq.v.), the Impressionist and Post-impressionist painters, and Maupassant (See Huneker's *Overtones, Iconoclasts, Egoists, The Pathos of Distance, Ivory Apes and Peacocks, Unicorns, Bedouins, Steeplejack*). Of Huneker's own writing, Benjamin de Casseres has said: "A forbidden and blasphemous beauty lies over his work—the borderland nuances and moonmad hallucinations of Baudelaire, Laforgue (q.v.), Poe and D'Aurevilly (q.v.)." We must not overlook Lafcadio Hearn, Bliss Carman, Richard Hovey, and especially Stuart Merrill and Vielé Griffin (qq.v.) as literary intermediaries between the two countries.

Edmund Wilson underlines for us an idea which we have previously encountered in Richard Hovey, namely, that "the literary history of our time is to a great extent that of the development of Symbolism and its fusion or conflict with Naturalism" (*Axel's Castle*, p. 25). Entailed in this history is Imagism with such figures as Ezra Pound, T. S. Eliot, Amy Lowell, John Gould Fletcher, and before them the so-called American Symbolist school with Richard Hovey and William Vaughan Moody.

In the winter of 1914 Amy Lowell delivered a series of lectures, published the following year as *Six French Poets: Studies in Contemporary Literature*. They were Émile Verhaeren, Albert Samain, Rémy de Gourmont, Henri de Régnier, Francis Jammes, Paul Fort (qq.v.). Her prose translations of the poems were accounted excellent. Four years later, Ludwig Lewisohn published *The Poets of Modern France* (N. Y. 1919) with a 70-page introduction and verse translations of poems by 30 poets, beginning with Mallarmé and running through Duhamel (q.v.) and Émile Despax.

Between 1909 and 1914 American literature was presented to France only by the translations of some portions of Whitman, Emerson, Poe, and Lafcadio Hearn. There were brief notices in French magazines of Henry James, Jack London, and Ezra Pound. The only translations in volume-form "from the American" was a collection of stories by Jack London printed by the *Nouvelle Revue française* publishing house. In those years and continuing, with interruptions, until 1940 the *NRF* magazine was extremely active in behalf of American literature.

The First World War set into motion new intellectual crosscurrents between France and America. Thus Edith Wharton's novels, generally published in French and English simultaneously, employed the French method of psychological analysis and revealed her indebtedness to Stendhal, Paul Bourget (q.v.), and others. Hamlin Garland's short stories have appeared in a French weekly and Jack London's novels of adventure were very popular, perhaps as an antidote (says Cestre) to love intrigues and psychological analysis. *L'Humanité* (French socialist newspaper) published *The Jungle* as a feuilleton. Frank Norris followed in the steps of Zola, while Whitman was a source of inspiration to the vers libristes. Some of Eugene O'Neill's early plays were performed in Paris. After World War I, professorships of American literature were established with Cestre at the Sorbonne and Mlle. Léonie Villard at Lyons, Marcel Clavel at Aix-Marseille, Le Breton at Lille, and Jean Catel at Grenoble. Bernard Faÿ became professor of American history at the Collège de France. In 1923 the *Revue Anglo-Américaine* was founded. In December 1925 and January 1926 the *Navire d'Argent* carried a bibliography of American literature translated in French. A. Levinson presented eighteen studies of contemporary writers in his *Figures Américaines* (Paris, 1929). That year studies of the American detective novel as well as of Negro literature appeared. M. Le Breton wrote on the personality of William James, while F. Delattre studied him in relation to Bergson. Between 1927 and 1931 there appeared numerous dissertations on Poe, Cooper, Henry James, Whitman, and others. Contemporary authors received notice in the *Revue Anglo-Américaine* and studies of Frost and E. A. Robinson were made available. Tauchnitz editions of Willa Cather's *Obscure Destinies,* John Dos Passos' *Manhattan Transfer,* Faulkner's *Sanctuary,* and Hemingway's *In Our Time* were issued. L. C. Powells wrote a French doctoral dissertation, *An Introduction to Robinson Jeffers.* The rôle of the *Nouvelle Revue Française* in promoting interest in American literature after the First World War is inestimable. Translations of Ambrose Bierce, Thoreau, and Waldo Frank appeared. Dreiser's method was analyzed by Ramon Fernandez, who also had an article, "Le Classicisme de T. S. Eliot" (*NRF,* Feb. 1925). Maurice Coindreau introduced and translated Faulkner. During the decade preceding World War II, *NRF* published translations of many more American books than books from other countries. Besides Hemingway and Faulkner, Caldwell, Steinbeck, and Farrell had been introduced to the French public. André Malraux (q.v.) had written a preface to Faulkner's *Sanctuary* (Nov. 1933). Jean Prévost (q.v.) published in May 1939 a long biographical and critical study, *Robert Frost, le Poète et le Sage;* and in June and July of that year Sartre (q.v.) contributed "A propos de *Le Bruit et la Fureur:* la temporalité chez Faulkner." Jean Giono (q.v.) wrote on Melville and was, at the same time, under the spell of Whitman.

Recent American poetry had been brought to the attention of the French public in 1928 by Eugène Jolas in his *Anthologie de la nouvelle poésie américaine.* (In September 1935 Coindreau had made a detailed analysis of Ludwig Lewisohn's *Expression in America*—translated as *Psychologie de la littérature américaine.*) In July 1939,

the quarterly *Mesures* devoted a thick volume chiefly to modern American poets. It contained excellent translations of Emily Dickinson, Vachel Lindsay, Hart Crane, James Weldon Johnson, Edwin Arlington Robinson, Robinson Jeffers, Archibald MacLeish, Marianne Moore, John Dos Passos, John Crowe Ransom, Wallace Stevens, Allen Tate, William Carlos Williams, and others. By the end of the 1930's, then, American literature had assumed a prominent place in France.

As to French influence in American fiction, critical opinion saw now the strain of Zola, now that of Flaubert in the novels of Farrell, Hemingway, Steinbeck, Dreiser, Thomas Wolfe, and Dos Passos. Hemingway's own declaration of devotion to Flaubert has been cited as well as Farrell's insistence of indebtedness to Zola. After the Second World War, novelists like Albert Camus, Sartre, Simone de Beauvoir (qq.v.) were attracted by Faulkner's treatment of Time, a preoccupation also seen in Proust (q.v.), Joyce, Dos Passos, Virginia Woolfe, and Gide (q.v.). The expression of violence in the American novel could not fail to impress them. Anguish as a common source of literary and intellectual creation is reflected in an article by Sartre, "Qu'est-ce que la littérature," in the *Partisan Review* for January 1948.

According to Jean Bruneau, Existentialism (q.v.) is the first French literary movement on which the modern American novel has exercised a strong and acknowledged influence in a "fundamental emphasis on action." Jean Paul Sartre and Simone de Beauvoir have enrolled in the school of Faulkner, Dos Passos, Hemingway, Caldwell, and Steinbeck. The *act* as the basic unity of the American novel seemed to reflect, for Sartre and the other

Existentialists, the unity of life. With this came a shift from analysis to synthesis, for example, in Malraux's (q.v.) *La Condition Humaine* (1933) and *L'Espoir* (1937).

In *Imaginary Interviews* (Malcolm Cowley's translation, 1944), Gide maintains that he was one of the first in France to admire Melville long before Giono undertook his translation of *Moby Dick*. He also recalls the day when Flaubert told him of an extraordinary book and one that nobody in France had heard about, namely *Walden*. "It happens," says Gide, "that I had a copy of it in my pocket." Besides Hemingway's and Faulkner's works, to which Malraux introduced him, he read Steinbeck and Dos Passos in the translations of Maurice Coindreau and Michel Tyr. The picture of America revealed in all of these novels made him feel that "the American cities and countrysides must offer a foretaste of hell." Actually, he believed that each of these novelists achieved "a consciousness of his own nature by reacting."

During the last five or six years (1949-1956), the French attitude towards American literature, though not less enthusiastic, has become more cautiously critical. Nonviolence has become a religion with Camus. This has been regarded as a reaction against violence in American literature.

The Partisan Review and *Yale French Studies* have been particularly active of late in presenting French literature *vis à vis* American letters. In the first, a series of significant articles have appeared on Proust, Sartre, Malraux, Cocteau, Simone de Beauvoir, Camus and others. In the second, a valuable rapprochement has been made between certain American and French thinkers, particularly between French Existentialism and American fiction. We witness the American theater presenting in the recent seasons not only Molière but Sartre, Anouilh, Giraudoux, Cocteau (qq.v.) and others. Everyone is busy reading the English version of *Bonjour Tristesse* (q.v.). All those who care two cents about art in any of its forms are under the spell of Malraux's 3-volume *La Psychologie de l'Art* (1947-50) (translated by Stuart Gilbert. Copyright, 1949).

In retrospect, we may join Cestre and others in viewing France as the ideal place for the confrontation of ideas and the convergence of two civilizations which, if far from identical, reinforce and complement each other, especially in an age when technology needs to be tempered by humanism.

Gilbert Chinard, *L'Exotisme américain dans la littérature française du 16ᵉ siècle*, 1911; *L'Amérique et le rêve exotique dans la littérature française au 17ᵉ et au 18ᵉ siècle*, 1913; Bernard Faÿ, *Bibliographie critique des ouvrages français relatifs aux États-unis (1770-1800)*, 1925; *The Revolutionary Spirit in France and America* (Tr. by Ramon Guthrie), 1927; Howard Mumford Jones, *America and French Culture, 1750-1848*, 1927; Louis P. Waldo, *The French Drama in America in the 18th Century and Its Influence on American Drama, 1701-1800*, 1942; Adrian H. Jaffe, *Bibliography of French Literature in American magazines in the 18th Century*, 1951.

Margaret M. Gibb, *Le roman de Bas-de-cuire: études sur F. Cooper et son influence en France*, 1927; Benjamin Griffith, *Balzac aux États-Unis*, 1931; Charles Baudelaire, "E. A. Poe: sa vie et ses ouvrages," *Rev. de Paris* (mars-avril) 1852; "Ed. Poe: sa vie et ses œuvres": *Histoires extraordinaires* par E. Poe, 1856; Léon Lemonnier, *Éd. Poe et la critique française de 1845 à 1875*, 1928; *Les traducteurs d'Ed. Poe en France*,

1928; *Ed. Poe et les Poètes français,* 1932; Charles L. Young, *Emerson's Montaigne,* 1941; Harold E. Mantz, *French Criticism of American Literature Before 1850,* 1917; Sidney Lamont McGee, *La littérature américaine dans la Revue des Deux Mondes (1831-1900),* 1927. Vance Thompson, *French Portraits,* 1900; Charles Cestre, "American Literature through French Eyes," *Yale Review,* Oct. 1920; René Taupin, *L'Influence du Symbolisme français sur la poésie américaine (de 1910 à 1920),* 1929; Bruce A. Morrissette, "Early English and American Critics of French Symbolism," *Washington U. Studies* n.s., no. 14, 1942; Carlos Lynes, Jr., "The 'Nouvelle Revue Française' and American Literature, 1909-1940," *French Review,* Jan., 1946, No. 3; J. P. Sartre, "American Novelists in French Eyes," *The Atlantic Monthly,* Aug. 1946; Jean Bruneau, "Existentialism and the American Novel," *Yale French Studies,* spring-summer, 1948; William C. Frierson and Herbert Edward, "Impact of French Naturalism and American Critical Opinion, 1877-1892," *PMLA,* Sept., 1948; Edmund Wilson, *Axel's Castle,* 1948; Max I. Baym, *The French Education of Henry Adams,* 1951; Thomas M. Smith and Ward L. Miner, *Transatlantic Migration: The Contemporary American Novel in France,* 1956.

MAX I. BAYM

François de Sales, Saint: (1567-1622) Bishop of Geneva (1602), he tried, in reaction against the influences of Protestantism and Humanism (q.v.), to strengthen Catholicism in France. In *Introduction à la vie dévote* (1608) and the complementary *Traité de l'amour de Dieu* (1616), he attempts, in a style that is at once amiable, flowery and seductive, to make Catholicism attractive by appealing to the heart through his psychological treatment of divine and profane love. His work anticipates much of the religious literature of the seventeenth century.

F. Strowski, *Saint François de Sales,* rev. ed., 1928.

François le Champi (1850): See *Sand, George.*

French Academy: See *Académie Française.*

Fréron, Elie: (1719-1776) This critic founded *L'Année littéraire* (1754-1790), a literary review reflecting contemporary tastes and opinions. He attacked the *philosophes* (q.v.) and was, in turn, the butt of many of the satires by Voltaire (q.v.), his life-long enemy.

Froissart, Jean: (1337-1404?) Great traveller, this historian gathered, much like a reporter, the facts and events which he had heard related during his voyages through France, England and Italy. These details, with animated descriptions, are recorded in his *Chroniques* (c. 1373-1400), a kind of history of the 14th century with particular emphasis on the Hundred Years' War between France and England.

J. Bastin, *Jean Froissart, chroniqueur, romancier et poète,* 1941.

Fromentin, Eugène: (1820-1876) Melancholy characterizes the early youth of this painter, traveler, and novelist, born at La Rochelle. After the death in 1844 of a young married Creole woman, with whom he had been secretly in love, he sought distraction in travel. His descriptions, in *Un Été dans le Sahara* (1857) and *Une année dans le Sahel* (1859), of his visits to the African countries, are unsurpassed in detail and color. One of the finest art critics of his century, he expresses his ideas on painting and on aesthetics in general in *Les Maîtres d'Autrefois* (1876), written after his voyage to Egypt, Italy, Belgium, and Holland. As a novelist, he is known for *Dominique* (1862), a semi-autobiographical re-creation of his youthful idyl. This work makes of him one of the creators of the modern psychological novel, and follows in the traditions of Constant's (q.v.) *Adolphe* and the earlier novels of analysis, including *La Princesse de Clèves*, *La Nouvelle Héloïse* (qq.v.), and Sénancour's (q.v.) *Obermann*. In a sense, *Dominique* represents a reaction against the realistic tendencies of the age.

P. Dorbec, *E. Fromentin, biographie critique*, 1926; C. Reynaud, *La genèse de Dominique*, 1937; V. Giraud, *E. Fromentin*, 1945.

Fromont jeune et Risler aîné (1874): See *Daudet*.

Fumée d'opium (1904): See *Farrère, Claude*.

Furetière, Antoine: (1619-1688) Novelist, poet and critic, this scholar, a member of the *Académie Française* (q.v.), was the author of a *Dictionnaire universel* (1690), which appeared posthumously, but which he had tried to publish, against the wishes of the *Académie* that no dictionary appear before its own, in 1684. For this "crime," he had the dubious honor of being the first to be expelled, the following year (1685), from the society of the "Forty Immortals." He avenged himself in his *Factums* (1685), in which he satirized certain academicians. In *Le Roman Bourgeois* (1666), a realistic novel the scene of which is laid in the Maubert section in Paris, he satirizes members of the legal profession and of the literary world and, in general, portrays the "bourgeois" society of the seventeenth century. This novel is part of the same current that attacked the excesses of preciosity (q.v.).

G. Reynier, *Le Roman réaliste au XVIIe siècle*, 1914.

Fustel de Coulanges: (1830-1889) Parisian-born historian and professor, he is especially noted for *La Cité antique* (1864) and *Histoire des Institutions politiques de l'ancienne France* (1875-1892). Written in a precise style, they reflect the author's passion for truth and the scientific method, and bear characteristics that relate him to Realism (q.v.) and particularly to Flaubert (q.v.) in *Salammbô*.

J.-M. Tourneur-Aumont, *Fustel de Coulanges*, 1931.

G

Gabrielle (1849): See *Augier*.

Gantillon, Simon: (1890-   ) In his experiences at sea, this dramatist found the central theme for his plays, that of the tragedy of departure, of voyages, and absence. *Le Cyclone* (1923), his first play, depicts a storm at sea, whose presence is felt, and which suggests, in the destiny of each of the sailors on the boat, the tragedy of life. *Maya* (1924), his masterpiece, which also takes place at a seaport, combines a naturalistic portrait of a prostitute with the different illusions she creates in the minds of different men (cf. *Gaston Baty*). Bella becomes the symbol of the eternal "Maya"; she represents pleasure and inspires dreams. *Départs* (1928) once again shows imagination at work in two adolescents, whose dreams of travel and adventure carry them to Japan. The mysteries of the beyond become the subject of *Bifur* (1931). The theater of Gantillon, in short, expresses not the reality of naturalism (q.v.), but the poetry of the mind, which drives one away from reality and into the poetic universe.

Gargantua: A hero of gigantic proportions with an enormous appetite who appears in the book of the same name (Book I, 1534) by Rabelais (q.v.). In this book the author relates Gargantua's birth, childhood and education, the aid he extends to his father, Grandgousier, who is at war with Picrochole, and finally his gift of the *Abbaye de Thélème* (q.v.) to Friar Jean des Entommeures as a reward for the Friar's valiant attack upon the enemy.

Garnier, Robert: (*c.* 1545-1590) The oratorical declamations and lyrical pathos that characterize his plays reflect the training in eloquence and argumentation he received as a lawyer. Probably the greatest dramatic poet of the sixteenth century, his tragedies, following the humanistic precepts of the *Pléiade* (q.v.), draw their inspiration from Greek and Roman sources. Included among these tragedies, which reveal the role of fatality, are *Porcie* (1568), *Hippolyte* (1573), *Cornélie* (1574), *Marc-Antoine* (1578), *La Troade* (1579) and *Antigone* (1580). His masterpiece, *Sédécie ou les Juives* (1583), though based on the Bible, projects the Greek concept of destiny; the chorus, like those of the other plays, owes something to Greek tragedy. *Bradamante* (1582), the first *tragicomedy* (q.v.) to be set in the time of Charlemagne, has a happy ending. Garnier is an important precursor of Corneille (q.v.).

Bernage, *Étude sur Robert Garnier*, 1880; R. Lebègue, *La Tragédie française de la Renaissance*, 1944.

Gary, Romain (pseud. of **Romain Kacew**): (1915-   ) This Russian-born novelist first won public attention when he won the *Prix des critiques* for his *Education Européenne* (1945), a novel dealing with the Resistance of Polish partisans against the Germans who had overrun their country. Following the Kafkaesque *Tulipe* (1946), *Le Grand Vestiaire* (1949) describes the chaos of the modern post-war world in which an adolescent comes of age. In 1956, Gary won the *Prix Goncourt* (q.v.) for his *Les Racines du Ciel*. Combining diplomatic and literary careers, he is at the present writing French Consul in Los Angeles.

Gascar, Pierre: (1916-   ) In 1953 this writer was awarded the *Prix Goncourt* (q.v.) for *Les Bêtes* and *Le Temps des Morts*. Consisting of several short stories, inspired by the experiences of war and mirroring man's destiny, *Les Bêtes* is at times reminiscent of Albert Camus, of Loti, or of Maupassant (qq.v.). Like Maupassant, although not to the same degree, Gascar is a master of the short story; like him, too, he tries to be objective and documentary.

Gaspard de la nuit (1842): See *Bertrand, Aloysius*.

Gassendi, Pierre: (1592-1655) The chief philosopher of the *libertins* (q.v.) group, he opposed his empiricism to Descartes' (q.v.) concept of "innate ideas." Representing a liberal current that ran counter to the idealism and dogmatism of the seventeenth century, his epicureanism is believed to have had an influence on Molière (q.v.).

G. S. Brett, *The Philosophy of Gassendi*, 1908; R. Pintard, *Le Libertinage érudit dans la première moitié du 17ᵉ siècle*, 1943.

Gautier, Jean-Jacques (1908-   ) Awarded in 1946 the *Prix Goncourt* (q.v.) for his *Histoire d'un Fait Divers*, this writer continues the realistic tradition in the novel. Included among his more recent works are *M'auriez-vous condamné* (1951) and *La Demoiselle du Pont aux Anes* (1951), a satire of theatrical manners and of a writer who falls in love with one whose ambition is the stage.

Gautier, Théophile: (1811-1872) Born in Tarbes, in southern France, this poet and prose writer, who began his career as a painter, remained essentially the plastic artist in all his writings. At first a romantic, he was among those who hailed Hugo's *Hernani* (q.v.) at its *première*, Feb. 25, 1830. His early poems, in such collections as *Poésies* (1830), *Albertus* (1832), and *La Comédie de la Mort* (1838), contain macabre and fantastic elements; several descriptions, however, here foreshadow the artistic realist he was later to become. In *Les Jeune-France* (1833), tales of irony and fantasy, Gautier pokes fun at romantic exaggeration; in the preface to *Mademoiselle de Maupin* (1836), a novel of erotic passion and pagan beauty, he has already become the advocate of Art for Art's sake. His cult of art and beauty, further developed as a result of his travels as a journalist to Spain, Italy, Greece, Russia, and Turkey, which he objectively described in several works, is revealed in *Émaux et Camées* (1852). The title of this poetic collection is significant, implying, as it does, delicate workmanship, and *L'Art*, the last poem, added to it in 1857, sums up his poetic creed. The exponent of the carefully chiselled poem, Gautier tried to make poetry—and literature in general—a plastic art. The un-romantic impersonality of his poems, the tendency towards accurate and vivid description of the external world with emphasis on impeccable form in the last named collection, make him an important precursor of the Parnassian (q.v.) school of poetry. Even his tales and novels, where the fantastic element,

imagination and the dream play an important role, become a plastic art; much description, elegant and decorative, is here to be found. Included among them are: *Arria Marcella* (1852), *Jettatura* (1856), *Le Roman de la Momie* (1858), *Avatar*, *Le Pied de momie*, and *Spirite* (1866). *Le Capitaine Fracasse* (1863), an historical fantasy, is his most delightful novel. The paucity of ideas notwithstanding, his plasticity of style and emphasis on the fantastic mark him as an important transitional author between romanticism and realism (q.v.). Gautier also wrote many works of dramatic and artistic criticism.

Maxime du Camp, *Théophile Gautier*, 1890; L. B. Dillingham, *The Creative Imagination of Théophile Gautier*, 1927; R. Jasinski, *Les années romantiques de Théophile Gautier*, 1929.

Gémier, Firmin: (1869-1933) This actor and *metteur-en-scène*, who started his career at the Théâtre-Libre (q.v.), where, as Antoine's (q.v.) collaborator, he tried to bring natualism (q.v.) of speech and gesture to the stage, became in 1906 director of the Théâtre Antoine, and later, of the Odéon (1922-1930). Into this nationally subsidized theater he tried to breathe new life by a simple, stylized staging which, instead of being photographically realistic, was, with the aid of gesture and movement, evocative or suggestive. The desired effect was facilitated also by the importance he gave to lighting, reflecting somewhat the influence of the impressionistic painters. The use, moreover, of mounted steps on the stage, which "intensified" it, brought the audience and actors closer together. This spiritual communion between the spectator and the stage recalls somewhat the theater of antiquity, and that of the Middle Ages; it also explains why Gémier, in his appeal to the audience, chose a repertoire whose motivating themes were social and moral and that showed the complexities of modern life. In the final analysis, his staging was an attempt to create a theater for the masses, for the people.

Gendre de M. Poirier, Le (1854): See *Augier*.

Genêt, Jean: (1909-   ) His autobiographical *Journal d'un Voleur* (1949), his plays and poetry, his novels, including *Le Miracle de la rose* (1946)—all not easy to procure even in France—were created out of his own life, one of crime and pederasty. The criminality and sexuality of his work seek no justification and express no remorse. Although the finger of accusation seems to be pointed at society, Genêt's fate is self-determined, and Evil, which is his subject as well as his life, represents his revenge upon society, his own creation of opposition to the Good. This world of vice Genêt transfigures, however, by his prose, which is at once supple and ornate, simple and beautiful; with his rejection of our common language he implies a rejection of our moral concepts.

Génie du Christianisme, Le: The purpose of this work in prose, published in 1802, was, according to Chateaubriand (q.v.), its author, to demonstrate the poetic, social and æsthetic values of the Christian religion. As a justification for Christianity, it bases its arguments not on the dogma of Christianity, but on its artistic beauty (cf. *Atala*). Through this work, Chateaubriand introduced the art of medieval Christianity into literature, and at the same time exercised a considerable influence on the renaissance of religious sentiment in France which was to react against the spirit of the eighteenth-century "philosophes."

Géorgiques chrétiennes, Les (1912): See *Jammes, Francis*.

Géraldy, Paul (pseud. of **Paul Le Fèvre**): (1885-   ) Before the First World War, this writer was the author of *Toi et moi* (1913), sentimental poems that show concern for the psychological aspects of love. This general theme he was subsequently to treat in his major plays, including *Aimer* (1921), *Robert et Marianne* (1925), and *Christine* (1932), which revolve around the secret barriers or inner complexities of love which bring man and woman closer together or cause their separation. These plays, moreover, are classical in structure, consisting of simplicity in plot, of analysis of conflict, and of very few, two or three, characters. Unlike the Classical theater, however, the characters here are of the lower middle-class, and are studied within the framework of their daily existences. *Les Noces d'argent* (1917), another typical example of the regular occurrences in the lives of average people, reveals a crisis brought about when children wish to be liberated from parental ties.

Germinal: Written by Zola (q.v.) in 1885, this novel, considered to be one of his best, is a good example of his careful documentation and study of group life. It deals with the struggles of Étienne Lantier, the illegitimate son of Gervaise Macquart, to emancipate the working class. The strike by the miners, led by Étienne, is broken when hunger drives them to desperation, and several of them are killed. Étienne, driven away, goes to Paris, where he hopes to find a more successful means to achieving his socialistic ideals.

Germinie Lacerteux (1865): See *Goncourt*.

Geste de Charlemagne (or du Roi): A cycle of the *chansons de geste* (q.v.), which constitutes a poetic history of Charlemagne, and which includes *Berte aux grands pieds* (13th century), relating to his mother; *Mainet* (12 century), the story of Charlemagne as a child; *La reine Sibile*, devoted to his wife; *Le Pèlerinage de Charlemagne* (early 12th century), the story of a pretended trip of his to Jerusalem and Constantinople, told to amuse; *Huon de Bordeaux* (end of 12th century), the story of his son's murder by Huon, whom he condemns, but who is aided by the dwarf Oberon, later used as a character by Shakespeare in his *Midsummer Night's Dream*. In this same cycle are those *chansons de geste* which refer not to him nor to his family, but to his conquests or struggles against certain vassals. They include *Les Saisnes* (12th century), by Jean Bodel (q.v.), relating to his expeditions against the Saxons, and, most important, *La Chanson de Roland* (q.v.).

Geste de Doon de Mayence: This cycle of *chansons de geste* (q.v.) recounts the struggle of the barons against Charlemagne, who is here depicted as weak and unjust and is vanquished by the more powerful vassals. An example of this cycle is *Renaud de Montauban* (13th century), also known as *Les Quatre fils Aymon*.

Geste de Montglane (or de Guillaume d'Orange): A cycle of the *chansons de geste* (q.v.) which deals generally with Guillaume d'Orange (*d.* 812) and his struggles against the Saracens, and includes, among the most important, *Girard de Vienne* (13th century), from which V. Hugo (q.v.) drew his theme for his *Mariage de Roland* in his *Légende des siècles; Le Charroi de Nîmes* (12th century), which relates Guillaume's conquest, through a strategy, of Nîmes; *Aliscans* (12th century)—the finest epic work, after the *Chanson de Roland*, of the Middle Ages—which relates Guillaume's combat, in the plains of Aliscans, with a Saracen army of great size.

Geste de Raoul de Cambrai: A twelfth-century *chanson de geste* (q.v.) which deals with the strife during the tenth century of the feudal barons among themselves. Raoul is depicted as the most accomplished feudal type, at once courageous and brutal.

Geste des Loherains: Epic cycle composed of four branches, Garin le Loherain, Gerbert de Mez, Hervis de Mez, Anseïs de Mez. Tells of the long feud between the Lorrains and the Bordelais. No historical basis. Remarkable because of numerous precise geographical data, a realistic, rapid style, precious details on feudal customs.

Russel K. Bowman, *The Connections of the Geste des Loherains with other French Epics and Mediaevel Genres*, 1940; Pauline Taylor, *Gerbert de Mez*, 1952.

Ghil, René: (1862-1925) Born in Tourcoing, French Flanders, this symbolist poet (see *Symbolism*), in *Traité du verbe* (1886), systematized his scientific conception of poetry, according to which each consonant and vowel possesses a particular timbre, or musical value. According to this principle, a variety of emotions can be evoked. His poetic work, including his first collections, *Légendes d'âmes et de sang* (1885)—which reflects the influence of Mallarmé (q.v.)—and *Œuvre* (1889-1909), to which he applied his scientific concepts and musical technique, represents but a curious example of experimentation, and he left no disciples.

Gide, André: (1869-1951) His early rigid Protestant and puritanical upbringing created a conflict within him between his intense religious propensities and his natural ardor for life. Reacting violently against his *milieu*, and obsessed by the desire to be liberated from family ties and from social and sexual conventions, he soon decided to "follow his penchant," to live without hypocrisy, and to construct a personal ethic in accordance with his nature —however abnormally regarded by society. His first trip to North Africa in 1893 and the ensuing contact with the Arab world and its different standards of morality represented the first decided manifestation of his revolt and of his will to conquer his hesitations in living the diabolical and unconventional life. *Nourritures Terrestres* (1897), which appeared after his return from North Africa, is written in a poetic prose that is violent in its lyricism and that reflects Gide's personal liberation from sin and his triumph in sincerity; in breaking with the past he also broke with *Symbolism* (q.v.), in the tradition of which he had written *Les Cahiers d'André Walter* (1891), *Le Traité du Narcisse* (1892) and *Le Voyage d'Urien* (1893); in his desertion of these earlier tendencies he abandoned the cerebral life for the life of the flesh, to whose passionate outcry of revolt he hearkened. Several of his novels [Gide himself considered only his *Les Faux-Monnayeurs* (q.v.), written in 1926, as a "roman"], such as *L'Immoraliste* (1902) and *Si le grain ne meurt* (1926), reveal more directly than others the basically autobiographical or semi-biographical character of his entire work. Other representative works are *La Porte étroite* (1909), *Les Caves du Vatican* (1913) and *La Symphonie pastorale* (1919).

Gide's literary output of some fifty volumes includes, besides his novels, poems, plays, translations, criticism, travel books and his journals. His influence has been especially felt since the end of the First World War. His "inquiétude" expressed the uneasiness of the younger generation living in a society which it considered insincere. To the post-war young, his repudiation of moral and social conventions, his preoccupation with the "authentic life," his probings of the individual conscience in search of self-fulfillment, made a powerful appeal. His complex themes, expressed in a pure and classical style, won him the Nobel Prize for Literature in 1947 and have brought him recognition as one of the most original and brilliant French writers of the twentieth century.

Leon-Pierre Quint, *André Gide*, 1932; Jean Hytier, *André Gide*, 1938; Justin O'Brien, *Portrait of André Gide*, 1953; Germaine Brée, *André Gide, L'Insaisissable Protée*, 1953.

Gigi (1945): See *Colette*.

Gilbert, Nicolas-Joseph: (1751-1780) Romanticized in Vigny's (q.v.) *Stello*, this poet is especially known for his *Adieux à la vie*, a poem which by its melancholy foreshadows Lamartine (q.v.). An adversary, too, of eighteenth-century rationalism, he wrote the satirical poems *Le Dix-huitième siècle* (1775) and *Mon Apologie* (1778).

E. Laffay, *Le poète Gilbert, étude biographique et littéraire*, 1898.

Gil Blas: Also known as *Histoire de Gil Blas de Santillane* (1715-1735), by Lesage (q.v.), this is the first important novel of manners in France. Consisting of a series of disconnected episodes, this picaresque novel, the action of which takes place in Spain, relates, in a style that is at once dramatic and natural, the adventures of Gil Blas, a lad of seventeen, who leaves home to study at the University of Salamanca. On the way, he encounters a band of thieves who steal his money. Finally escaping, he becomes a lackey, and soon serves a variety of masters, including Doctor Sangrado, a surgeon, and the archbishop of Granada. Eventually rising to high political power, he becomes the secretary and confidant of the Duke of Lerma, prime minister of Spain. Not long after, he loses position and wealth, but again acquires a fortune and becomes secretary to the new prime minister, the Count Olivarez. Retiring to his *château*, after having contracted two marriages, he lives, in the end, a peaceful existence. The various social classes and professions with which the vicissitudes in his career bring Gil Blas into contact are a faithful and realistic, though oblique, portrait of French society during the period depicted.

Giono, Jean: (1895-) A native of Provence, he exalts, in such early works as *Colline* (1929) and *Regain* (1930), the joys of nature and of living in the country. In other rustic novels, *Que ma joie demeure* (1935), *Les vraies richesses* (1936), *Batailles dans la montagne* (1937), he reveals a preoccupation with the cosmic forces that link man to the soil. Advocate of a pastoral life, of a utopia that is the ideal of an æsthete, Giono condemns modern civilization, the machine age and war. His plays, *Le Lanceur de graines* (1932) and *La Femme du boulanger* (1944), which present on the stage peasants whose gestures and speech are natural and simple, are similarly inspired. More recently, however, Giono has turned to imagining, as in his *Un roi sans divertissement* (1947), what might have or could have been.

Christian Michelfelder, *Jean Giono et les Religions de la Terre,* 1938.

Giraudoux, Jean: (1882-1944) Born in Limousin, he was a student at the École Normale Supérieure. Later, he became a diplomat and traveled to many countries including the United States, where, for a while, he taught at Harvard. Until the age of forty-six, when he first tried his hand as a dramatist, his writings consisted of groups of short stories (in these he cannot be called, strictly speaking, a novelist) of one kind or another—*poetical divagations,* as they were called—and essays. Among these books—all written in an impressionistic, poetic style, with an endless flow of figures of speech— are *Les Provinciales* (1909), *L'École des indifférents* (1911), *Simon le*

Pathétique (1918), in all of which can be seen his love for the little provincial towns, the simple life, children and animals. After the War and his mission to the United States (resulting in his book *Amica America,* 1918), most of his fiction— except for a few, as, for example, *Siegfried et le Limousin* (1922), which deals with a Frenchman who has lost his memory and is made a German statesman—are characterized by charming female portraits: hence such titles as *Suzanne et le Pacifique* (1921), *Juliette au pays des hommes* (1924), *Bella* (1926), and *Eglantine* (1927). Beginning with 1928, when he produced *Siegfried,* based on the novel *Siegfried et le Limousin,* Giraudoux wrote only for the stage. The same qualities that had marked his novels were to be found in his plays. These include his love for allusions and paradoxes, his humor, a certain *preciosity*—which was attained, however, not laboriously but spontaneously—irony, and unexpected points of view. Moreover, in his several plays based on ancient myths, history and the Bible, he makes use of anachronistic situations, often strange; the conflict of interest is placed in his characters' opposing philosophies, expressed in torrential dialogues, which become a kind of poetic revery. Intelligence and fantasy are to be found side by side; in this way, several of his plays are rich with suggestions of the complexities of modern life. Among those plays that transport the problems of our time to antiquity are *Judith* (1931), *Sodome et Gomorrhe* (1943), *La Guerre de Troie n'aura pas lieu* (1935), which deals with the fatality of war, and *Electre* (1937), which centers around the fatality of revolution. His subtle comedies include *Amphitryon 38* (1929), *Intermezzo* (1933), and *Ondine* (1939)— based on a German legend. A posthumous play, *La Folle de Chaillot*

Plate 7. René Descartes

Plate 8. André Gide

(1945), deals with the problem of contemporary civilization and may be considered as a summary of all his ideas. Another posthumous play, whose meaning is less clear, is *Pour Lucrèce* (1953). Giraudoux's theater breaks with the traditional formulas of intrigue and psychological conflict. As he embroiders upon his myths and legends, he creates an ideal humanity. To give the theater its dignity, he awakens the spectator to serious problems and eternal truths. He utilizes reflection as the main device in treating broad themes, such as life and death, peace and war, the destiny of man and woman. In this world of ideas, the spectator forgets about daily contingencies. All this is achieved by his style—a poetic prose—that sets one's imagination and sensibilities in motion. Finally, the theater of Giraudoux restored, during a time of tragic situations, the climate of tragedy on the stage. No wonder, then, that Sartre (q.v.) has shown interest in this dramatist, whose principal themes deal with man's struggles against God and against his destiny.

Claude-Edmonde Magny, *Précieux Giraudoux*, 1945; Jacques Houlet, *Le Théâtre de Jean Giraudoux*, 1945.

Glorieux, Le (1732): See *Destouches*.

Gobseck (1830): See *Balzac*.

Gombauld, Jean Ogier de: (*c.* 1570-1666) A member of the small literary circle that met at the home of Conrart and that was to develop into the *Académie Française* (q.v.). Furthering in his works the spirit of preciosity (q.v.), he is the author of *Endymion* (1624), an allegorical novel, and *Amaranthe* (1631), a pastoral play. Other works include *Les Danaïdes* (1658), a tragedy, *Sonnets* (1649), and *Epigrammes* (1657).

R. Kervi!er, *J. Ogier de Gombauld*, 1876; L. Morel, *J. Ogier de Gombauld*, 1910.

Gomberville, Marin le Roy de: (1600-

1674) His novels, like those of La Calprenède (q.v.), deal with adventure, and mix gallantry with heroism, subjects that could not fail to please the *précieuse* society (see *Préciosité*) of the seventeenth century. Unlike those of La Calprenède, however, the novels of Gomberville stress the exotic, staged as they are in Mexico, the Middle East, and in other distant lands. Included among these novels are *Polexandre* (1629-1637) and *La Jeune Alcidiane* (1651).

R. Kerviler, *Marin le Roy de Gomberville*, 1876; M. Magendie, *Le Roman français au 17ᵉ siècle*, 1932.

Goncourt, Edmond de (1822-1896) and **Jules de** (1830-1870) The collaboration of these two unmarried brothers, the younger one of whom was born in Paris, and the other in Nancy, ceased with the death of Jules. Until then their common interests and communion of spirit made their work one. They became novelists after having first written monographs—well-documented with precise details taken from the most insignificant sources—dealing with the history of art and manners of French society during the eighteenth century (*Histoire de la société française pendant la Révolution*, 1854; *Portraits intimes du XVIIIᵉ siècle*, 1859-1875). The same documented method they applied to their novels, each one of which becomes a portrait of a different contemporary social class. *Charles Demailly* (1860) — semi-autobiographical — depicts the world of letters; *Sœur Philomène* (1861) offers hospital scenes; *Renée Mauperin* (1864) shows the modern young woman; *Germinie Lacerteux* (1865) reveals the life of a servant; *Manette Salamon* (1867) studies the life of artists; and *Madame Gervaisais* (1869) analyzes religious fervor. Based, as are the other novels mentioned, on personal experiences or on those of their acquaintances, the already-mentioned *Germinie Lacerteux* is the biography of their own servant; the tale of her pitiful life and loves was not to leave Zola (q.v.) unimpressed and was to influence, to a certain degree, his naturalistic (see *Naturalism*) orientation. These novels, preoccupied with morbid, pathological cases and with the lower social classes, and employing a clinical approach that gives emphasis to detail and observation, support the claim that the Goncourt brothers were precursors of Zola's scientific naturalism. Although several of their novels, by their exaggerated attention to detail and to detached scenes, show a carelessness of plot and composition, they give evidence of a style, sometimes called "impressionistic," sometimes called "écriture artiste" (q.v.), that sets the Goncourt brothers apart, in their emphasis on artistic form, from the Naturalistic School. The famous *Journal,* begun in 1851, a mine of observations and anecdotes on the society of their time, and used as raw material for the novels, was continued by Edmond.

After the death of his brother, Edmond published *La Fille Elisa* (1877), a monograph on prostitution and the penitentiary, *Les frères Zemganno* (1879), a study of the life of the circus, and *La Faustin* (1882), a portrait of the life of the theater. The Sunday receptions inaugurated in 1885 by Edmond, which brought together Daudet, Zola (qq.v.), and younger writers, resulted in the founding and endowment of the *Académie Goncourt* (q.v.), the purpose of which was to encourage younger writers.

P. Sabatier, *L'Esthétique des Goncourt,* 1920; M. Sauvage, *J. et Ed. de Goncourt,* 1933; F. Fosca, *Edmond et Jules de Goncourt,* 1941.

Gourmont, Rémy de: (1858-1915) This critic and essayist enjoyed prestige among the poets of the Symbolist school (see *Symbolism*). As one of the main contributors to the *Mercure de France,* he was one of its most ardent champions and theoreticians. His erudition, which was encyclopedic, showed a catholic taste with, perhaps, a preference for the esoteric. Among the subjects that interested him were philology, literature, history, philosophy, sociology, and biology. His principal works include *L'Esthétique de la langue française* (1899), *Promenades littéraires* (1904-1928), and *Promenades philosophiques* (1905-1909).

Graal (or **Saint-Graal**): Varying interpretations have been offered of the nature and origin of the *Graal* (Holy Grail). In Chrétien de Troyes' *Perceval* (q.v.), the earliest version of the Grail stories extant, it is some sort of magic object, the symbolism of which is not very clear. In any case, the Christian tradition is not applicable here, for Perceval, in quest of the Grail, was not a pure knight. According to later Christianized versions, it is identified with the chalice or cup used at the Last Supper, then given to Joseph of Arimathea, who preserved in it the last drops of Jesus' blood at the Cross.

J. Marx, *La Légende Arthurienne et le Graal,* 1952.

Gracq, Julien (pseud of **Louis Poirier**): (1910-) Although this professor of history is not a prolific writer, having written only three novels, one play and two essays, has achieved a certain desirable literary notoriety by having spurned the *Prix Goncourt* (q.v.) offered him for his *Le Rivage des Syrtes* (1951). This work, as well as his first two novels, *Au Château d'Argol* (1938) and *Un Beau Ténébreux* (1945), are written in a surrealistic (see *Surrealism*) vein—exploring as they do the strangely mysterious. They make use of symbolical stories with enchanted castles and secret passages. Nevertheless, they are free of any "automatic" writing. Gracq's style, not simple, consists of long, involved sentences, with frequent epithets and italics. A ready disciple of André Breton (q.v.), to whom he devoted a study, he is preoccupied, more than are the Surrealists, with a meditation on destiny and an obsession with death that frequently call to mind the catastrophes of classical tragedy. For similar reasons, his main protagonists are "marked" creatures and bring in their wake inevitable misfortune.

Grail (or Holy Grail): See *Graal*.

Grandes Familles, Les (1948): See *Druon, Maurice*.

Grand Guignol: This Parisian theater was founded by Oscar Métenier (q.v.) in 1897 and has endured until the present day. Although its plays are basically melodramatic and full of breath-taking terror, it alternates drama with comedy, a policy adopted by the management. Those whose plays or adaptations of whose plays have been presented here include Maupassant (q.v.), Courteline (q.v.), André de Lorde (1871-   ), Mirbeau (q.v.), Lenormand (q.v.), Savoir, and Henri Duvernois (q.v.). In 1923 the Selwyns brought the Grand Guignol Players to New York. For seven weeks they presented both horror melodramas and comedies.

Grand Meaulnes, Le (1913): See *Fournier, Alain*.

Graziella (1852): See *Lamartine*.

Greban, Arnoul: (1410?-1471?) Native of Le Mans, he studied in Paris and became organist and master of the choir boys of Notre Dame. Author of an important *Mystère de la Passion* (*c.* 1450; q.v.), he wrote, with the collaboration of his brother Simon, the *Actes des Apôtres*, performed at Bourges in 1536, and various *élégies* and *complaintes*. His version of the *Passion*, very popular, was imitated four times, the most celebrated reworking of which was that by Jean Michel (*c.* 1486; q.v.).

Grécourt, Joseph de: (1683-1743) Born in Tours, this poet published a number of *épîtres* and *épigrammes*, which are often licentious in tone, light, amusing, and little more.

Green, Julien: (1900-   ) This French novelist, born in Paris of American parents, sees, in his obsession with the supernatural forces of evil and of death, evidences of his Irish, Scottish, and American heritage. The themes of his novels, treated at times melodramatically, relate to fears, guilty desires, crimes and haunting remorse. His characters, frequently pathological or abnormal, are visionaries or dreamers, full of frustration, lonely tragic souls incapable of communication with other human beings. In this respect, they reflect a metaphysical anxiety characteristic of much of contemporary French literature. The action of his novels *Mont-Cinère* (1926) and *Moïra* (1950) is set in the United States; the events of *Adrienne Mesurat* (1927) and *Léviathan* (1926) take place in the French provinces. With his return in 1940 to Catholicism, however, Green has lost some of his despair, which he has replaced with ideals of serenity and faith, as can be seen in *Varouna* (1940) and *Si j'étais vous* (1947).

Marc Eigeldinger, *Julien Green et la tentation de l'irréel*, 1947; Pierre Brodin, *Julien Green*, 1957.

Gresset, Jean-Baptiste Louis: (1709-1777) Poet and dramatist, he is especially remembered for *Vert-Vert* (1734). This poem, written in the spirit of badinage of a Marot (q.v.), relates what happens to a parrot, reared in decency in one nunnery, when it falls into bad company before reaching another nunnery to which it is sent. For the malice of this poem, Gresset was expelled from the Jesuit order of which he was a member. In 1745 he wrote *Sidney*, a play containing elements of the *comédie larmoyante* (q.v.), in which the hero is intent on committing suicide. *Le Méchant* (1747), his masterpiece, recalls Molière's (q.v.) *Tartuffe,* and is based on the depravity of manners and characters he observed in Parisian society. Included among his other works are: *Le Carême impromptu* (1734) and *Le Lutrin vivant* (1743)—both in verse—and *Édouard III* (1740), a tragedy. J. Wogue, *Essai sur la vie et les œuvres de Gresset,* 1894.

Grévin, Jacques: (1538-1570) Characteristically turning to the favorite subjects of the Renaissance, he wrote *César* (1561), a tragedy on Caesar. His comedies, of Italian inspiration, include *La Trésorière* (1559) and *Les Ébahis* (1561). Grévin's early association with Ronsard (q.v.) came to an end after he had been converted to Protestantism. L. Pinvert, *Jacques Grévin,* 1899.

Grimm, Friedrich-Melchior, Baron von: (1723-1807) Intimate friend of Diderot (q.v.), Mme. d'Épinay, and, for a while, of Rousseau (q.v.), this writer, a native German, spent the greatest part of his life in France. A literary critic, he is especially known for his editorship of *Correspondance littéraire* (1753-1773), a kind of political, social and artistic journal sent to various courts of Europe.

Gringoire (or Gringore), Pierre: (*c.* 1475-1538?) A Norman dramatic and satiric poet, he wrote *Le Mystère de saint Louis* (1513), and *Le Jeu du Prince des Sots,* produced at the Halles in Paris in 1512. The latter consists of four parts: a *cry* (q.v.) to summon the people, a *sottie* (q.v.) to provoke them against the Pope, a *moralité* (q.v.) to win them to the policy of Louis XII—whom Julius II had shamefully betrayed—and a *farce* (q.v.) to satisfy their thirst for ribaldry and fun. This play is typical of medieval comedy as a whole.

Guéhenno, Jean: (1890-) This scholar, born to the working class, to which he has always remained loyal and which he undertook to im-

prove and cultivate as an act of faith, has expressed his fraternity with it in such works as *Conversion à l'humain* (1931), *Journal d'un homme de quarante ans* (1934) and *Journal des années noires* (1947), a part of which—*Dans la prison*—appeared clandestinely during the German occupation. The same ideal, a kind of social romanticism, is seen in his *Rousseau* (1948).

Guérin, Raymond: (1905-) In *L'Apprenti* (1946), the first volume of his *Ébauche d'une Mythologie de la Réalité,* he describes, using the device of the internal monologue, the perversions of childhood. The long sordid confession is related in a lucid, detached and realistic style. Included among his other novels are *La Confession de Diogène* (1947), which betrays a spirit of skepticism, and *Parmi tant d'autres Feux* (1950) which is reminiscent of Sade (q.v.) and Henry Miller.

Guerre de Troie n'aura pas lieu, La (1935): See *Giraudoux.*

Guillaume de Machaut: (*c.* 1300-1377) This poet, who was in the service of Jean de Luxembourg, cultivated particularly the *rondeau, ballade* (qq.v.), and the *lai* [a lyrical form of poetry not to be confused with the narrative *lai* (q.v.)]. The *Voir dit* (*c.* 1363) is the story of his love of a young girl. Guillaume de Machaut was, in addition, the most celebrated of the French composers of the fourteenth century and one of the founders of classical polyphony.

Guillevic: (1907-) Much like Ponge (q.v.), this poet from Brittany evokes, in his short, precise, but elliptical poems, the world of natural objects, especially rocks and stones. Like Ponge, too, he has the realistic existence of these things depend upon man, their source and end. Unlike Ponge, however, the poet's identification with the object he describes carries with it more love and magic than logic. Through the images that he weaves, various *rap-*

prochements are established, together with a universe of memories, visions, and sensations. Such is the spirit and such are the themes of his collections *Terraqué* (1942) and *Exécutoire* (1947), as well as others. In *Fractures*, poems of the *Résistance* (q.v.), the bloody story of the war is related through the description of objects and things.

Guilloux, Louis: (1899-   ) Early memories of working-class life together with his love for humanity dominate the early proletarian writings of this novelist from Brittany. Among these novels are *La Maison du Peuple* (1927), *Compagnons* (1931), and *Hyménée* (1932)—all written in a simple style. His masterpiece, however, and perhaps one of the best novels written in the last thirty years, is *Le Sang noir* (1935), the scene of which is laid in a small town in Brittany during the War. The action in this novel, which takes place in twenty-four hours, revolves around an old philosophy teacher who, lost between conflicting ideals—that which attacks the bourgeoisie and the passion for money which he stores away in securities and real estate—finally commits suicide. *Le Jeu de patience* (1949) describes a city in Brittany under the Occupation.

Guirlande de Julie, La: Composed for Julie d'Angennes, the eldest daughter of Mme. de Rambouillet, this celebrated series of poems (1641) represents the collaboration of most of those who frequented the Hôtel de Rambouillet (q.v.). The "garland," a collection of 62 poems, had 29 flowers, each one of which was accompanied by a madrigal—that is, a short poem usually expressing a tender sentiment—and by one or several sonnets. It is a fine example of the *précieux* spirit (see *Préciosité*).

Guitry, Sacha: (1885-1957) An actor, like his father Lucien, Sacha was born in Saint Petersburg (Leningrad). In addition to his very successful acting and directing, more recently at work in such films as *Les Perles de la Couronne* and *Le Roman d'un tricheur*, he has written more than a hundred plays, fantastic ones, with good, witty dialogue, the purpose of which is to entertain. The *boulevard* spirit of these plays, which bring on the boards amoral characters, does not aid in their delineation; in truth, beneath the mask of the different rôles created in these numerous pieces, the real hero is Sacha himself, who, moreover, has a frank and realistic view of his fellow men and life. Among his gay comedies are: *La Jalousie* (1915), *Faisons un rêve* (1916), *Mon père avait raison* (1919), *Désiré* (1927), and *Quadrille* (1937). Among his more serious subjects, to which he later turned, are the biographical *Jean de La Fontaine* (1916), *Deburau* (1918), *Pasteur* (1919), and *Mozart* (1925).

Gyp (pseud. of **Marie Antoinette de Riquette de Mirabeau, comtesse de Martel de Janville**): (1850-1932) Her novels, many in dialogue form, are written with wit and show a knowledge of Parisian life. Although they appear frivolous, in reality they are amusing satires of the society of her times. Included among them are: *Autour du mariage* (1883), *Autour du divorce* (1886), *Le mariage de chiffon* (1894), and *Un Ménage dernier cri* (1903).

H

Halévy, Ludovic: (1834-1908) See under *Meilhac, Henri.*

Hardy, Alexandre: (1570-1631) Of the seven hundred-odd plays which this prolific dramatist, employed by the Hôtel de Bourgogne (q.v.), is said to have written, only five *pastorales* (q.v.), eleven tragedies (including *Didon se sacrifiant,* 1603; *Marianne,* 1610; and *La Mort d'Alexandre,* 1621), and twenty-five *tragi-comedies* (q.v.) were published. Through an emphasis on dramatic action and the elimination of the lamentations and the choruses, his popular *tragi-comedy,* which he firmly established as a dramatic type and which was largely based on Greek and Roman histories and romances, contributed to the development of Cornelian tragedy (see *Corneille* and *Tragedy*). Included among the *tragi-comedies* are *Cornélie* (1609) and *La Force du sang* (1612). With the subsequent introduction of the unities (q.v.), this type of drama disappeared.

E. Rigal, *A. Hardy et le théâtre français,* 1889.

Harmonies poétiques et religieuses (1830): See *Lamartine.*

Harry, Miriam (pseud. of **Madame Perrault Harry**): (1875-1958) Born in Jerusalem, this writer is author of exotic and erotic novels. Included among them are: *La divine chanson* (1912), *La petite fille de Jérusalem* (1914), and *Les Amants de Sion* (1924).

Hazard, Paul: (1878-1944) Professor at the Sorbonne and a member of the faculty of the Collège de France,

this scholar and critic devoted himself especially to the study of comparative literature. Editor of the *Revue de littérature comparée,* which he founded with Fernand Baldensperger, he also reveals his varied interests in such studies as *Leopardi* (1913), *Stendhal* (1927), and *Don Quichotte* (1931). His *Histoire de la Littérature française* (1923-1924), written in collaboration with Joseph Bédier (q.v.), is a standard reference work.

Hector (1809): See *Luce de Lancival.*

Helvétius, Claude-Adrien: (1715-1771) This wealthy Parisian-born *philosophe* (q.v.), who contributed articles to the *Encyclopédie,* is the author of *De l'Esprit* (1758)—which involved the *Encyclopédie* in censorship difficulties—and *De l'Homme, de ses facultés intellectuelles et de son éducation* (1772), philosophical works that apply the sensationalist theories of Locke. Seeing self-interest as the basis of society, he points to the importance of environmental factors, while denying the role of heredity or of innate faculties.

A. Keim, *Helvétius, sa vie et son œuvre,* 1907.

Hémon, Louis: (1880-1913) This novelist, born in Brest, is especially known for his *Maria Chapdelaine* (1916), a portrait of Canada, where, as a result of a tragic accident, he died.

Hennique, Léon: (1851-1935) One of the authors of the *Soirées de Médan* (q.v.), and an exponent of naturalism (q.v.), this novelist and dramatist wrote for the Théâtre-Libre (q.v.) *Esther Brandès* (1887), *Jacques Damour* (1887), and *La Mort du duc d'Enghien* (1888).

Henriade, La (1728): See *Voltaire*.

Henri III et sa cour (1829): See *Dumas* PÈRE.

Heptaméron (1558): See *Marguerite d'Angoulême*.

Hérédia, José Maria de: (1842-1905) Born in Cuba to a Spanish father and French mother, this Parnassian (q.v.) poet received most of his education in France. Friend and disciple of Leconte de Lisle (q.v.), he was one of the first to contribute to the *Parnasse Contemporain* of 1866. The author of a single volume of poems, *Les Trophées* (1893), on which he patiently labored for some 30 years, he best exemplifies the Parnassian ideal. This collection, consisting of 118 sonnets, draws its material from history and archeology, especially from Greece, Rome, and the Renaissance. Treating of great men, as well as of aspects of nature and works of art, Hérédia depicts in these poems, with a rigorous impersonality, scenes of the past. Combining erudition with the cult of beauty, he achieves in his poetry technical perfection of form; his precise pictorial and sculptural effects, his use of descriptive metaphors, of rare and technical vocabulary, his sonority of rhythm and richness of rhyme, personify Art for Art's sake. The success of *Les Trophées* becomes all the more notable when it is realized that its publication came at a time when Symbolism (q.v.) had already firmly entrenched itself.
Miodrag Ibrovac, *José-Maria de Hérédia*, 1923.

Hermant, Abel: (1862-1950) This novelist and dramatist, removed as a member of the French Academy because of his sympathies for the Pétain regime during the Second World War, manifests in his prolific writings strong naturalistic influences (see *Naturalism*), with an eye

that is cruel in its observation of his contemporary society. *Le Cavalier Miserey* (1887) is a realistic novel of military life. The huge series of his *Mémoires pour servir à l'histoire de la société* (1901-1937) reveal the wit and sarcasm of the author. Unlike the indulgent Capus (q.v.), the plays of Hermant are serious and, as in *La Meute* (1896) and *Monsieur de Courpière* (1907)—based on his novel—portray the wicked and the repugnant. At times he advocates reform; at times, as in *Transatlantiques* (1898), he pictures cosmopolitan society. In general, he reports, without moralizing and without illusion, the folly, vice, and heartlessness of a decadent aristocracy.
A. Thérive, *Essai sur Abel Hermant*, 1926.

Hernani: The *première* of this *drame* (q.v.) in verse by Hugo (q.v.), produced at the Théâtre-Français February 25, 1830, was marked by a "battle" between the Classicists and Romanticists, resulting in the triumph of the new Romantic School. Set in sixteenth-century Spain, this play, which applies, however imperfectly, the principles of the *Préface de Cromwell* (q.v.), deals with the themes of love and honor. The dénouement is effected by a transformation of characters, typical of Hugo's principles of antithesis, who in the end suffer a reversal of their former positions. Don Carlos, King of Spain, though previously in pursuit of Hernani, the outlaw who conspires against him, exercises magnanimity upon becoming emperor (Charles V) of the Holy Roman Empire, restores to him his title and lands, and bestows Doña Sol, the heroine, upon him. Don Ruy Gomez, on the other hand, the jealous old guardian of Doña Sol, the girl he intends to marry, who had previously spared Hernani, his rival, from the King's wrath, sounds the horn, the call of death, to whose signal Hernani had sworn in gratitude to obey, as the latter is about to marry Doña Sol. The final death of the lovers, and that of Don Gomez, who stabs himself, is melodramatic. Based on this play is the opera *Ernani* (1844), by Verdi.

Hernani (battle of): See *Hernani*.

Hérodiade (1869): See *Mallarmé*.

Héroët, Antoine: (*c.* 1492-1568) A protégé of Marguerite d'Angoulême (q.v.), this poet from Lyons, like his friend Maurice Scève (q.v.), did much to popularize the doctrine of neoplatonic love to idealize woman. In the three cantos of his *La Parfaite Amie* (1542), the ideal lover strives for a spiritual love with his lady.
J. Arnoux, *Un précurseur de Ronsard, Antoine Héroët, néoplatonicien et poète,* 1913.

Hervieu, Paul: (1875-1915) In his attempt to restore, through the simple and logically devised plots, the spirit and intensity of the classical tragedy, and through his essentially literary and unrealistic language, this dramatist represents a reaction against the "slices of life" of the Naturalistic theater (see *Naturalism* and *Théâtre Libre*). Making use of the *raisonneur,* and following in the footsteps of Dumas *fils* (q.v.), he demonstrates or proves, in a rather mathematical manner, his theses. We are thus shown in *Les Paroles restent* (1892) how scandal has the power to destroy, in *Les Tenailles* (1895) the tyranny of the marriage law, in *La Loi de l'homme* (1897) that woman is unjustly subjected to the man-made double standard. Not only does Hervieu attack social iniquities, but also the cruelties wrought by human nature. In the psychological crises in *La Course du flambeau* (1901), he illustrates the natural inclination of parents to sacrifice themselves for their children with the concomitant ingratitude of children toward their parents. Further illustrations reveal, in *Connais-toi* (1909), the inconsis-

tency with which one applies principles to oneself and to others, in *Le Destin est maître* (1914), the tragedy of honor. The pessimistic and generally fatalistic view of human nature in his theater is also seen in his novels, *Peints par eux-mêmes* (1893) and *L'Armature* (1895), which, however, have a more realistic style.
Edmond Estève, *Paul Hervieu, conteur, moraliste et dramaturge,* 1917.

Histoire de Charles XII (1730): See *Voltaire*.

Histoire de France (1843-1867): See *Michelet*.

Histoire de l'Académie française (1652): See *Pellisson-Fontanier*.

Histoire de la littérature anglaise (1863): See *Taine*.

Histoire de la littérature française (1844-1849): See *Nisard, Désiré*.

Histoire des Girondins, L' (1847): See *Lamartine*.

Histoire des oracles (1687): See *Fontenelle*.

Histoire des origines du Christianisme (1863-1883): See *Renan*.

Histoire des variations des églises protestantes (1688): See *Bossuet*.

Histoire du Jansénisme (1861): See *Rapin, René*.

Histoire du peuple d'Israël (1887-1895): See *Renan*.

Histoire d'un crime (1852-1877): See *Hugo*.

Histoire d'un fait divers (1946): See *Gautier, Jean-Jacques*.

Histoire naturelle (1749-1804): See *Buffon*.

Holbach, Paul Heinrich Dietrich, Baron d': (1732-1789) A German who settled at a very early age in Paris, he encouraged, through his *salon* and through his generosity, the Encyclopedists. In addition to his articles on chemistry and mineralogy, which he wrote for the *Encyclopédie* (q.v.), he published *Le Christianisme dévoilé* (1767), in which he attacks Christian dogma, and *Le Système de la nature* (1770). The latter work, written in collaboration with Diderot (q.v.), advocates an atheistic and materialistic view of the universe, according to which sensibility and intellect are functions of matter. R. Hubert, *D'Holbach et ses amis*, 1928; P. Naville, *D'Holbach et la philosophie scientifique du 18ᵉ siècle*, 1943.

Homme et ses fantômes, L' (1924): See *Lenormand*.

Homme machine, L' (1747): See *La Mettrie*.

Homme qui assassina, L' (1907): See *Farrère, Claude*.

Hommes de bonne volonté, Les (1932-1946): See *Romains, Jules*.

honnête homme: Created as a type in seventeenth-century literature, partly as a result of the influence exerted by the Hôtel de Rambouillet (q.v.) and other *salons*, he possesses the qualities of respect, refinement, elegance, wit and talent, the ability to converse, without pedantry, on all matters and, in general, observes the social code of the time. M. Magendie, *La politesse mondaine et la théorie de l'honnêteté en France de 1600-1660*, 1925.

Horace: This play (1640) by Corneille (q.v.), sometimes described as a tragic, sometimes as a heroic, masterpiece, is based on the Roman historian Livy's account of the war between Alba and Rome. To put an end to this war, a combat between three champions of each army is decided upon. By a cruel trick of destiny, these champions are chosen from two families—the Horatii (*Horaces*) and the Curiatii (*Curiaces*)—bound to each other by ties of marriage and love; Sabine, sister of the Curiaces, is married to the eldest of the young Horaces, and Camille, Horace's sister, is engaged to the eldest of the Curiaces. The ensuing struggle in the hearts of the four-named characters, who, in effect, do not deliberate, but who merely rationalize decisions they have instinctively made—decisions

that are motivated by a sense of *gloire*—constitutes the interest of this Cornelian drama. In the battle that follows, two of the Horaces, according to the report delivered by the messenger, are killed, and the third, the eldest, has fled; the action of the eldest Horace, as it turns out, is but a ruse to divide the Curiaces. When the combat is finally over, Rome is triumphant; Horace returns with the traditional and symbolic spoils of his vanquished enemies. At the sight of these symbolic spoils Camille curses Rome; in a fit of patriotic zeal, Horace kills his sister. The King, who does not minimize the seriousness of the act, nevertheless absolves Horace of his crime.

Hôtel de Bourgogne: Owned by the *Confrérie de la Passion* (q.v.), this theater, the only regular one in Paris until 1599, was leased that year to the troupe of Valleran-Lecomte. After finally establishing itself here in 1628, this troupe, authorized by Louis XIII to assume the name of "Troupe Royale," produced farces at first and then specialized in tragedies. As a result of a royal order in 1680, it amalgamated with the *Théâtre du Marais* (q.v.) and with Molière's (q.v.) troupe—which, following the latter's death in 1673, left the Palais-Royal to install itself at the Hôtel Guénégaud—thus forming the Théâtre-Français or the *Comédie Française* (q.v.). The year of the merger, the Italian troupe took possession of the Hôtel de Bourgogne, remaining there until 1783, when the Opéra-Comique (q.v.) theater was constructed.

Hôtel de Rambouillet: Shocked at the libertarianism of the court of Henry IV, Catherine de Vivonne, later the Marquise de Rambouillet, attracted to her home, which she transformed into the first and most famous of the *salons* of the seventeenth century, men and women, members of fashionable society, and the greatest writers of the period who, in their conversations, excluded all vulgarity and maintained an atmosphere of respect and good taste. Though not the sole preoccupation of these weekly meetings—parlor games, dancing and music figured prominently—these conversations dealt with every possible question of taste and art, with literature, and with grammar and vocabulary. Despite the inevitable affectation or preciosity (q.v.) that resulted from this search for elegance, wit and refinement and that entered into the literature of the day, these discussions enriched the French language with many new words and expressions. This *salon*, which flourished from 1618 until about 1645, went into decline after the marriage of Julie d'Angennes, Mme. de Rambouillet's daughter, and the deaths of Voiture (q.v.) and the Marquis de Rambouillet (1652). After the death of Mme. de Rambouillet (1665), another *salon*, somewhat different, was set up by Mlle. de Scudéry (q.v.).

V. Du Bled, *La société française du XVIᵉ au XIXᵉ siècles*, Tomes I—IV, 1900-1909; E. Magne, *Voiture et les années de gloire de l'Hôtel de Rambouillet*, 1912.

Houdar de la Motte, Antoine: (1672-1731) Also known as Lamotte-Houdar, this writer's chief claim to fame is based on his verse rendering of the *Iliad* (1713) and on his preface to it; both represent a serious attempt to discredit Mme. Dacier's prose translation of the *Iliad* (1699) and brought about a resumption of the *Querelle des Anciens et des Modernes* (q.v.). His tragedy *Inès de Castro* (1723) enjoyed much success.

P. Dupont, *Houdar de la Motte*, 1898.

Houville, Gerard d', Madame: (1875-) This poetess and novelist is the daughter of José-Maria de Hérédia (q.v.) and wife of H. de Régnier (q.v.). In *Poésies* (1931), a collection of poetry written in a pure, classical form, she expresses the sadness of human existence as well as her love of nature and revery. Her novels—*L'Inconstante* (1903), *Esclave* (1905), *Le Séducteur* (1914), and *Jeune Fille* (1916)—are filled with charming but egoistical men and women who trifle with each other's hearts, much in the manner of Musset's (q.v.) characters, and even with life and death, as if they were but adolescents. Though she loves flowers, voluptuousness, and youth, she is capable of understanding the tragedy of complex beings, of pitying and excusing them.

Hugo, Victor: (1802-1885) This poet, dramatist, and novelist, leader of the Romantic School in France, and "echo" of man's sufferings and joys as well as of the social and political currents of his lifetime, was born in Besançon, the son of a general in Napoleon's army and of a royalist mother. A perspicacious youth who wanted to be "Chateaubriand (q.v.) or nothing," he won many poetry prizes, including that of the *Jeux Floraux de Toulouse* (1819), and received for his neo-classical *Odes et poésies diverses* (1822), his first collection, a pension from Louis XVIII. With his brother he had also established *Le Conservateur littéraire* (1819-21), a journal whose tendencies, like those of the previously cited *Odes*, were royalist and Catholic. His *Odes et Ballades* (1828), containing additional odes, were more personal and drew their inspiration from medieval sources; the preface to this collection was a profession of romantic faith. The *Préface de Cromwell* (1827; q.v.) epitomizes Hugo's conversion to Romanticism. This manifesto sets forth the dramatic theories contained in the *drame* (q.v.), rejecting the Classical separation of Tragedy (q.v.) and Comedy (q.v.). For French romantic poetry, it represented an *Ars Poetica*. It was as a dramatist, however, that Hugo, after the triumph in 1830 of his *Hernani* (q.v.), a play whose *première* was to be marked by a "battle" between the partisans of Classicism and those who embraced his innovations, was to become the uncontested leader of the Romantic School; this play not only incorporated the dramatic theories of the *Préface de Cromwell*, but also represented, by the use of such poetic devices as *enjambement* (q.v.) and the displacement of the *cæsura*, a break with traditional versification. Although, in the wake of previously published novels, Hugo had added to his reputation as a novelist his successful *Notre Dame de Paris* (1830; q.v.), which revived the Paris of the fifteenth century, his work until 1843—in 1841 he had already been admitted to the *Académie française*—consisted mainly of poetry and drama.

Among his poetic collections of this period are: *Les Orientales* /1829), flamboyant descriptions, much like those of Chateaubriand (q.v.) and based largely on imagination, of the Orient, containing many acrobatic rhythms; *Les Feuilles d'automne* (1831), lyrical and sonorous meditations upon man's aspirations and destiny; *Les Chants du crépuscule* (1835), melancholy songs expressing Hugo's disillusionment with the Restoration and the Revolution of 1830 and showing more clearly the Bonapartist rapprochement, that was already evident in 1827, as well as the beginnings of humanitarian sentiment; *Les Voix intérieures* (1837), asserting the poet's mission to free men from doubt by placing faith and confidence, not in God, but in a beneficent nature; and *Les Rayons et les Ombres* (1840), a foreshadowing of

Hugo's compassion for the unfortunate and of his social role. These collections, when viewed together, reveal a romantic chronicle or confession. The central themes relate to nature, love, and death, to Hugo's preoccupation with children and family, with memories and happiness, with his fading religious beliefs. In their "orchestration" Hugo betrays a wealth of imagination, a prodigious vocabulary, mastery of verse forms and rhythm, much visual and verbal imagery, and, in general, rhetorical brilliance. These poetic qualities also help explain the relative success of his otherwise poorly contrived plays, like *Hernani* (1830), *Marion Delorme* (1831), *Le Roi s'amuse* (1832), and *Ruy Blas* (1838), written in verse, as compared with *Lucrèce Borgia* (1833), *Marie Tudor* (1833), and *Angelo* (1835), which were written in prose. All these plays are historical and betray Hugo's love of antithesis, as seen, for example, in contrasting scenes and in the antithetical qualities possessed by the same characters—characteristics which reflect, at the same time, his conception of life as a struggle between good and evil.

The failure of *Les Burgraves* (1843), an epic play written in verse, added to the grief brought him by the accidental death the same year of his daughter Léopoldine, caused Hugo to do very little writing during the next ten years. He devoted himself almost entirely to politics. Named a peer in 1845, and distinguished as an orator, he espoused the cause of the less fortunate and advocated generally liberal ideas, thus setting aside his earlier legitimist principles. Believing that Prince Louis-Napoleon would realize his program of order and progress, Hugo led the campaign which resulted in the Prince's election to the Presidency (1848) of the Second Republic. Disillusioned, however, by Louis-Napoleon's *coup d'état* of December 2, 1851, Hugo denounced him and found refuge, first in Belgium, then on the islands of Jersey and Guernsey.

During this period of exile, which lasted from 1851 until 1870, his renewed literary inspiration was more satiric and epic than lyric, although *Les Contemplations* (1856), which includes poems that sing of love and sorrow, is a lyrical masterpiece. Denouncing Napoleon III in the political *Histoire d'un crime* (1852-1877) and in *Les Châtiments* (1853), poems that reach lyrical heights in their indignation, Hugo's chastisement becomes grandiloquent satire. Hugo's basic belief, moreover, in the poet's mission, as philosopher, politician, and sociologist, to enlighten and lead humanity is further illustrated in the very successful epic novel *Les Misérables* (1862; q.v.), in which he depicts the victims of a social order that he condemns, and in *La Légende des Siècles* (1859, 1877, 1883), epic poems that trace the history of humanity as it marches on toward knowledge and happiness. In this collection, man becomes the artisan of his own liberation. Encouraged by the public reception of *Les Misérables,* Hugo wrote other novels, including *Les Travailleurs de la Mer* (1866), *L'Homme qui rit* (1869), and *Quatre-vingt-treize* (1874), the last depicting the Reign of Terror in Paris.

With the fall of the Empire, Hugo returned to Paris amid acclamation; he was also to see the horrors of the siege. His last years were marked by political activity as Senator and by a continuing literary productivity, including the collections of *L'Art d'être grand-père* (1877), inspired by his grandchildren, and *Religions et Religion* (1880), a deistic poem. His eightieth birthday was celebrated by all Paris and, after his death, his remains were taken to the Panthéon.

Hugo is the grand literary figure dominating the entire nineteenth century. The theories expressed in his *Préface de Cromwell* and applied—though somewhat artificially—in *Hernani* and other plays, together with the lyrical qualities of his poetry, a veritable musical orchestration, make of him the chief exemplar of French Romanticism. Many of these qualities served as main sources for the Parnassians (q.v.) and, to a certain degree, for the Symbolists. His humanitarian ideals and liberalism reveal not only a conversion from his earlier royalist and Catholic tendencies, but also a personal identification with the collective sentiments of humanity.

Paul Berret, *Victor Hugo,* 1927; André Bellessort, *Victor Hugo, Essai sur son œuvre,* 1930; Matthew Josephson, *Victor Hugo,* 1942; André Maurois, *Olympio,* 1954.

HUMANISM: The name given to the rediscovery, translation, and interpretation of ancient texts (mainly Greek, Roman, and Alexandrian) between Petrarch and Erasmus is Humanism, or the Revival of Learning. Since the works being revived were not Christian in character, a distinction evolved between humane and divine letters. The dedication of Hellenic literature after Socrates to the study of man the individual or microcosm gave impetus to the choice of the term Humanism. Indeed, the scholars, and writers of this movement borrowed the Latin claim, "Nothing concerning man do I deem alien to myself." Michelet (q.v.) defined Humanism as "la découverte de l'homme par l'homme." A renewal of interest in the classics was due. Greek had been almost forgotten during the Middle Ages and many of the writers of Latinity were inadequately remembered as pagan authors. By the twelfth century a limited number of Latin authors were known (Livy, Ovid, Martial, Terence, Vergil) and a search was instituted for ancient manuscripts in monasteries, libraries, archives, and elsewhere. Indeed, the search extended to coins, maps, inscriptions, and any *antiquaille* which might "wake the dead." The Greek works being resurrected increased notably with the westward tide of refugee scholars after the fall of Constantinople (1453). By the time that printing had been established in Mainz, Paris, Lyon, Amsterdam, Venice, and elsewhere, Greek and Latin writings received wide circulation by letterpress, in the original versions as well as the vernacular. The enthusiasm for Greek letters by the sixteenth century is epitomized in Pierre de Ronsard's (q.v.) "Je veulx lire en trois jours *l'Iliade* d'Homère." Needless to add, the edition of Homer which Ronsard intended to read in three days was in the original Greek. So great was the tergiversation of the literary humanists upon the Scholastic period and all it stood for that Joachim du Bellay (q.v.) was able to dismiss all French literature preceding the Humanistic revival as *épiceries*. So thoroughly did the French Humanists disregard mediaeval literature in both Latin and the vernacular that it fell into an ignominy from which it did not recover until the early nineteenth century. The aim of the Humanists —in literature and other disciplines —was to imitate the ancients. Ronsard cried in humility, "A genoulx, *Franciade,* adore *l'Iliade.*" The French writers took seriously the Horatian counsel to set up as their goals the Hellenic models. They introduced literary forms and genres which were part of the Hellenic legacy (odes, satires, elegies, epigrams, eclogues, regular comedy and tragedy, epic) and their pride in finding Greek archetypes for their efforts led them to address one another as the new Pindar (Ronsard; q.v.), the new Aristophanes (Rabelais; q.v.), the new Sappho (Louise Labé, Pernette du Guillet, or almost any female poet), and so on. This attitude on the part of the French literary humanists led to the error of failing to distinguish between plagiarism and emulation. Indeed, the doctrine of imitation (mimesis) which dominated Italy and France in the sixteenth century and was affirmed by Vida and Du Bellay was essentially plagiaristic. At the basis of this tremendous veneration for Greek thought (rhetorical and philosophic as well as literary) there lurked a conviction that these primitive people were endowed with a genius bestowed upon them by their greater proximity to nature and to God. This clue to the veneration of the Greek was found in Ronsard's "Ode à Michel de l'Hospital": "Divins, d'autant que la nature/Sans art librement exprimoyent," *etc.*

In recent times historians of the Renaissance have stressed the compatibility of Humanist and the Roman Church. It is true that many Churchmen like Bembo espoused pre-Christian learning with curiosity and enthusiasm. Indeed, this prelate was able to advise another cardinal, Sadoletus, to "avoid the Epistles of Saint Paul, lest his barbarous style spoil your taste." Many a learned cleric attempted to reconcile Catholic theology with Plato, Pythagoras, Lucretius, and other ancient thinkers or systems. However, even when Humanism embraced no other areas than philology or philosophy, it often came into conflict with the Inquisition, the *Index Expurgatorius,* the *obstat,* or at least with censorship of some sort. The burning of Estienne Dolet in the Place Maubert, as well as the martyrdoms

157

of Berquin and Aneau, show that in France as elsewhere Humanism had its brief Golden Legend. The revival of ancient science, as part of the parallel Humanistic study of the macrocosm, again showed the incompatibility between the *savant* and the *clerc*. As astrology gave way to astronomy, alchemy to chemistry, as physiology was founded on anatomical dissections, scientists like Servetus found themselves in grave personal peril. If France does not furnish a trial so celebrated as that of Galileo, it does not mean that the Sorbonne approved the enlarging concepts of the physical sciences in that nation. In the area of the fine arts, Michelangelo's pagan *Leda* shocked contemporary sensitivities to such an extent that the original disappeared.

Typical of Humanism in France and elsewhere was the widespread cult of the Universal Mind, the goal of erudition which might make of every man and woman, in Rabelais's words, an "abyss of knowledge." Everyone aspired to "cette louange et manne céleste de bonne doctrine" (*Pantagruel,* viii). The wisdom of the Scaligers (q.v.) or of Pontus de Tyard (q.v.) which embraced both arts and sciences won for them the same esteem which Leonardo won in Italy and later in France. A simple but memorable motto for what we have come to call the Renaissance mind is found in the sixteenth-century *Tableau de Cebes de Thèbes et Emblèmes* where a stanza dedicated to the "homme sçavant" enters a plea for the learning of as many arts and sciences as possible:

Le beau bouquet est de très bonne grace
Quand il y a diversité de fleurs.

As early as Montaigne (q.v.) Humanistic dispassion, objectivity, and even skepticism prepared the way for the cult of reason which the

Humanistic period bequeathed to the generation of Descartes (q.v.) and, indeed, to the generation of the Encyclopedists (q.v.).

Henry O. Taylor, *Thought and Expression in the Sixteenth Century,* 1920; Jean Plattard, *La Renaissance des Lettres en France de Louis XII à Henri IV,* 1925; Abraham Wolf, *A History of Science, Technology, and Philosophy in the Sixteenth and Seventeenth Centuries,* 1935; G. Toffanin, *Storia dell'umanesimo,* 1950; P. O. Kristeller, *The Classics and Renaissance Thought,* 1955.

ROBERT J. CLEMENTS

Huysmans, Joris Karl (pseud. of **Charles Marie Georges Huysmans**): (1848-1907) This novelist, of Dutch ancestry on his father's side, was born in Paris. At first a naturalist like Zola (q.v.), he wrote *Sac au dos,* a short story, which re-appeared in the *Soirées de Médan* (1880; q.v.), as well as such novels as *Les Sœurs Vatard* (1879), *En ménage* (1881), and *A vau l'eau* (1882). These novels, dealing with proletarian subjects, depict life as petty and sordid; unlike those of Zola, however, they do not follow the scientific theories of determinism. Grown more introspective in the second stage of his development, and drawn to the aesthetics of Symbolism (q.v.) as well as to impressionist painting, he wrote *A rebours* (1884), a novel in which his hero, like himself, is in search of rare and perverse sensations that derive from decadent literature and art. For his betrayal of naturalism as seen in this book, he was upbraided by Zola. Soon, however, like Des Esseintes, the hero of *A rebours,* who sees a solution not in this artificial universe but rather in faith and religion, Huysmans, now openly converted to Catholicism, expresses his spiritual adventure in *Là-bas* (1891), a diversion into black magic, and then, more positively, in *En route* (1895),

in which the virtues of monastic life are discovered, and in *La Cathédrale* (1898) and *L'Oblat* (1903), kinds of aesthetic meditation on the ceremonies of Christianity and on the beauty of its cathedrals. Although in his documentation Huysmans is naturalistic, his preoccupation with literary form relates him more closely to Flaubert and the Goncourt brothers (qq.v.).
A. Thérive, *J.-K. Huysmans, son œuvre*, 1924; H. Bachelin, *J.-K. Huysmans*, 1926.

I

Idées de Mme Aubray, Les (1867): See *Dumas* FILS.

Idéologues: Deriving their philosophy from Condillac (q.v.), this group of mechanistic psychologists, including Condorcet (q.v.), Cabanis, Destutt de Tracy and Volney, made their influence felt toward the end of the eighteenth and the beginning of the nineteenth centuries. Among those of the latter period who reflect this influence are Benjamin Constant and Stendhal (qq.v.). Studying the formation of ideas, these *Idéologues* analyse the sensations from which, according to them, ideas emanate.
F. Picavet, *Les Idéologues*, 1891.

Ile des pingouins (1908): See *France, Anatole*.

Illustrations de Gaule et Singularités de Troie (1510-1513): See *Lemaire de Belges, Jean*.

Illustre Théâtre: See *Molière*.

Immoraliste, L' (1902): See *Gide*.

IMPRESSIONISM: As applied to the open air painting of Edouard Manet (1832-1883), Camille Pissarro (1830-1903), Paul Cézanne (1839-1906), Alfred Sisley (1839-1899), Claude Monet (1840-1926), *etc.*, or to the music of Claude Debussy (1862-1918), *impressionism* was a well-chosen word. With respect to literature, however, it has been widely misused. Impressionism is only an incidental factor in modern French literature (*c.* 1870 to date).

It is clear to-day, for instance, that free choice of subject-matter, free judgment and free treatment are not in themselves sufficient to define literary impressionism. Thus, when affixed to the charming, lackadaisical criticism of Anatole France (1844-1924; q.v.) and Jules Lemaitre (1853-1914; q.v.), such a label is little better than a misnomer. Neither they, nor the novelist, Pierre Loti (1850-1923; q.v.), despite a certain fugitive quality in his style and notations, ever understood, or cared to understand, what the true impressionists were fighting for.

Likewise, it is impossible to say that sympathy for their purposes automatically made impressionists out of their defenders. The naturalist writers are a case in point. Emile Zola (1840-1902; q.v.) befriended them, supported them, only to end with grave doubts about the potentialities of the movement. The Goncourt brothers (Edmond, 1822-1896, and Jules, 1830-1870; qq.v.) came closer to the mark in that they "invented" a modernistic style—nervous, affected, arhythmic—called *l'écriture artiste*. Yet, the Goncourts and their nearest imitators (*e.g.*, Alphonse Daudet, 1840-1897, and Joris-Karl Huysmans, 1848-1907; qq.v.) remained well within the bounds of tradition, and outside those of impressionism, through their insistence on a well-rounded subject and rigid rules of composition. The doctrine of "sense transference," as preached by Charles Baudelaire (1821-1867; q.v.) led his successors, the symbolist poets (Paul Verlaine, 1844-1896; Stéphane Mallarmé, 1842-1898; Arthur Rimbaud, 1854-1891; Jules Laforgue, 1860-1887; qq.v., *etc.*), to cultivating a contempt of rhetorics, of perspective, of anthropomorphous reality, which was indeed akin to impressionistic technique. Most of them, however, including their spokesman and interpreter, Remy de Gourmont (1859-1915; q.v.), made a philosophical fetish of the dissociation of images and ideas. Such propensities, whether esoteric or pseudo-scientific, went far beyond the tenets of impressionism proper.

Impressionism, in the last analysis, spells out the artist's freedom much less than it does his subservience to the whims of nature and the tyranny of the fleeting moment. Pictorially, musically, poetically, a ray of sun, a drop of rain, a melodic line of color or sound, a flash of subconscious memory, an ecstasy, an illumination (Rimbaud's word) must be instantaneously captured or irretrievably lost. Anything that interferes with the privileged impression, be it a preconception or an ideological follow-up, deals it a fatal blow. Thus, cubism and surrealism (qq.v.) turned out to be human devices after all and re-designed sense data in a manner no longer consonant with impressionistic candor. The paradox of it is that, when painting and music began to be estranged from impressionism at its purest, literature made a belated effort to espouse its principles. So

did Marcel Proust (1871-1922; q.v.) in his huge novel, *A la recherche du Temps perdu*, at least in so far as it purports to be a record of *les intermittences* of heart and memory. So did Valery Larbaud (1881-1957; q.v.), an exquisite poet, novelist, and critic, whose "fugal developments," in the words of one commentator, "fed upon cosmopolitan culture." Feminine intuition and sensual receptivity make, in principle, ideal preconditions for impressionistic writing; and while Anna de Noailles (1876-1933; q.v.) diluted those qualities in her somewhat verbose poetry, Colette's (*i.e.*, Sidonie Colette, 1873-1954; q.v.) impeccable prose was truly the Baudelairian "vial" which encloses and preserves the transient aroma of things. Francis Jammes (1868-1938; q.v.) as a poet of the humble countryside and Léon-Paul Fargue (1878-1948; q.v.) as a poet of Paris were probably more faithful to the spirit of impressionism than, say, Guillaume Apollinaire (1880-1918; q.v.) or Jean Cocteau (1891- ; q.v.) whose main allegiance lay with Pablo Picasso (1881-   ). There are definite signs of impressionistic, but also cinematic, influence in the vivid stories and travelogues of Paul Morand (1888-   ; q.v.); aggressive and almost caricatural splurges of it in the writings of Joseph Delteil (1894-   ). The best exemplar, however, remains Jean Giraudoux (1882-1944; q.v.), especially in his early novels. He may well have been, from the literary standpoint, the only genuine counterpart of Monet and Debussy. A master of pointillistic technique, he, far more accurately than Mallarmé, was able to describe his work as a "poetical divagation"—without subject, without order, without center, just a sensuous venture of intelligence into the realm of harmony and light.

André Lamandé, *L'Impressionnisme dans l'art et la littérature*, 1925;

Ruth Moser, *L'Impressionnisme français: Peinture—Musique—Littérature*, 1952. Also: Charles Lalo, *Introduction à l'esthétique*, 1912; Pierre Sabatier, *L'Esthétique des Goncourt*, 1920; Marcel Raymond, *De Baudelaire au Surréalisme*, 1933; John Rewald, *Cézanne et Zola*, 1936.

JEAN-ALBERT BÉDÉ

Inconnue d'Arras, L' (1935): See *Salacrou, Armand.*

Institution de la religion chrétienne (1541): See *Calvin, Jean.*

Intimité (1922): See *Pellerin, Jean-Victor.*

Introduction à la vie dévote (1608): See *François de Sales.*

Invitée, L' (1943): See *Beauvoir, Simone de.*

Iphigénie (1674): See *Racine.*

Irène (1778): See *Voltaire.*

Irrésolu, L' (1713): See *Destouches.*

Israël (1908): See *Bernstein, Henry.*

Itinéraire de Paris à Jérusalem: This work, published by Chateaubriand (q.v.) in 1811, contains his impressions of a voyage he had undertaken in 1806 to Greece, Constantinople, and Palestine in order to assemble material in preparation for his *Les Martyrs* (q.v.). Many of the pages contain powerful descriptions of Sparta, Athens, and other places in his itinerary.

J

Jacob, Max: (1876-1944) Versatility characterizes the talents and interests of this poet, novelist, illustrator, and painter, born in Brittany. His poetry, a kind of jugglery that at once associates and dissociates words, is a mixture of parody or humor with lyricism. *Le Cornet à dés* (1917), his first collection of poems in prose, made him famous. In 1919 he was converted to Catholicism. *La Défense de Tartuffe* (1919) are poems in prose that touch on this conversion. In later collections he does not completely renounce, however, the eccentricity that blends mysticism with burlesque. His novels —*Le Terrain Bouchabelle* (1923), *Filibuth* (1924), *L'Homme de chair et l'homme reflet* (1924)—give evidence of the same basic technique used in his poetry: through verbal fun and parody, characters are illusions, personalities are words; as a humorist, he is thus able to reveal people's stupidities, foibles, and absurdities. Max Jacob also wrote art criticism, biographies, a children's book, plays, and an operetta. He died at the Drancy concentration camp.

André Salmon, *Max Jacob, poète, peintre mystique et homme de qualité*, 1927; André Billy, *Max Jacob*, 1945.

Jammes, Francis: (1868-1938) This poet, born in the Hautes Pyrénées, does not, strictly speaking, belong to any "School," despite the fact that he is generally associated with the Symbolistic movement (see *Symbolism*). In his first important collection of poetry, *De L'Angelus de l'aube à l'Angelus du soir* (1888-1897), he is attentive to the most minute aspects of rustic life; his observation of detail is lucid and meticulous; his attitude in the presence of Nature—fields, flowers, vegetables or animals—is "primitive," simple, naïve, spontaneous and romantic; the forms he uses are the distich and the classical alexandrine (q.v.) line. After his conversion to Catholicism, he published such volumes as *Les Géorgiques chrétiennes* (1912), of Christian as well as bucolic inspiration, which describe the life of the good peasants who cultivate their fields with a spirit aware of the presence of Divine creation. Jammes also wrote several novels. A. de Bersancourt, *Francis Jammes, poète chrétien*, 1910.

Jamyn, Amadis: (*c.* 1540-1593) Ronsard's (q.v.) secretary and favorite disciple. In 1575 he published a first collection of *Œuvres poétiques,* and in 1584 a second collection. A translation of Homer, containing the entire *Iliad* and the first three cantos of the *Odyssey* appeared in 1584.

Jansenism: Based on a book called *Augustinus* (1640) by Cornelius Jansen, archbishop of Ypres (*d.* 1638), this religious doctrine, advocating a return to the religion of Saint Augustine, asserts that, because of the depravity of human nature, redemption can come only through divine grace and predestination. Introduced through Saint-Cyran (1581-1643), a friend of Jansen, into Port-Royal (q.v.), where the former was spiritual adviser, it soon gained as adherents the "Solitaires" (q.v.) at Port-Royal. As the Jansenists grew in numbers, the Jesuits, realizing that their attempt to make religion attractive was meeting with difficulty because of the religious austerity of the former, launched a campaign against them. Declaring five of the propositions found in the *Augustinus* heretical, they succeeded in having the work condemned first by the Sorbonne, then by the Pope (1653). When, moreover, Antoine Arnauld (q.v.), a Jansenist professor, was expelled from the Sorbonne because of here-

sy, Pascal (q.v.), in defense of Port-Royal and its Jansenist principles, composed *Les Lettres provinciales* (1656-1657). Other developments in this religious dispute include the final dissolution, ordered by Pope Clement XI in 1705, of the Port-Royal convent, and the destruction, in 1710, of its other buildings. Jansenist influence and doctrine, however, persisted, right up to the nineteenth century. L. Séché, *Les derniers Jansénistes,* 1891; J. Paquier, *Le Jansénisme,* 1909; A. Gazier, *Histoire générale du mouvement janséniste,* 1922; J. M. Laporte, *La Doctrine de Port-Royal,* 1923; J. Orcibal, *La Correspondance de Jansenius,* 1947; *Jean Duvergier de Hauranne, abbé de Saint Cyran et son temps* (1581-1638), 1947-48.

Jardins, Les (1782): See *Delille*.

Jarry, Alfred: (1873-1907) Notoriety in the form of a new "bataille d'*Hernani*" came to this dramatist on December 10, 1896, when *Ubu roi,* a satirical drama which he had written at the age of 15 in collaboration with a classmate, was presented in expanded form at the Théâtre de l'Œuvre. Originally produced in 1888 at a marionnette theater with the intention of ridiculing a pompous teacher, in its recast version it depicted Père Ubu, the incarnation of bourgeois cupidity and vanity who, in language that is at once derisive, pretentious, deformed (as an example, the word *oveilles* was used instead of *oreilles*), and vulgar —a language that outraged the audience—expresses his stupidity and cruelty as he abuses his authority in the name of questionable principles. Humor, as in this instance a parody of tragedy, is metaphysical and social; it demonstrates the impossibility of resolving the enigma of human nature and destiny. The hidden propensities for evil in each human being as seen in this play caused the surrealists (see *Surrealism*) to see in the author a precursor of their movement. In addition to *Ubu enchaîné* (1900), a sequel to the previous play, Jarry published some novels, including the well-constructed surrealist *Le Surmâle* (1902). Fernand Lot, *Alfred Jarry*, 1934.

Jaucourt, Louis Chevalier de: (1704-1779) Devoted friend of Diderot (q.v.), for whose *Encyclopédie* (q.v.) he did much of the hack work, he wrote many of its articles dealing with science, politics and history.

Jaurès, Jean: (1859-1914) This brilliant orator and leader of French socialism was assassinated on the eve of the declaration of war. During the Dreyfus affair he played a significant role. He was also the founder of *L'Humanité* and *Le Parti socialiste unifié* (1905), in which he tried to reconcile his idealistic tendencies with Marxism.

Jean Barois (1913): See *Martin du Gard.*

Jean-Christophe (1903-1912): See *Rolland, Romain.*

Jean de la Lune (1929): See *Achard, Marcel.*

Jean Renart: (13th century) In *L'Escoufle* (c. 1200) and *Guillaume de Dôle* (c. 1212), *romans d'aventures* (q.v.) that are early examples, by their realistic setting, of the novel of manners, this poet offers love romances that contain pictures of chivalrous and bourgeois society. His refined analysis of love is to be seen in *Lai de l'Ombre* (c. 1221). R. Lejeune-Dehousse, *L'Œuvre de Jean Renart*, 1935.

Jean Santeuil (1952): See *Proust.*

Jettatura (1856): See *Gautier.*

jeu: This word is, until the sixteenth century, synonymous with *comedy* or *drama*. This meaning is still to be found in the title of one of Marivaux's (q.v.) plays, *Le Jeu de l'amour et du hasard*. Note that it also has been applied to a sacred play (see *Jeu d'Adam*).

Jeu d'Adam (or Représentation d'Adam): This oldest of plays written entirely in the French vernacular (the directions of which were in Latin) of unknown authorship was written in the middle of the twelfth century, in the Anglo-Norman dialect. Its action is divided into three consecutive parts: Man's fall from Paradise into Hell, Cain's murder of Abel, and the announcement by the prophets of the Redemption. In the first part, the most interesting from a dramatic point of view, "God" appears as an actor, moving into and coming out of the church. After the downfall, the demons invade the stage to throw Adam and Eve into chains and drag them to hell. The play was performed in front of the church door, not inside the church. This practice gradually became a set rule. Paradise was placed on an elevated height and adorned with flowers, foliage and cloth goods. G. Frank, *The Medieval French Drama*, 1954.

Jeu de la Feuillée (c. 1276): See *Adam de la Hale.*

Jeu de l'amour et du hasard, Le (1730): See *Marivaux.*

Jeu de Robin et Marion (c. 1285): See *Adam de la Hale.*

Jeu de Saint Nicolas: The first example of a *miracle* (c. 1201; q.v.), written by Jean Bodel (q.v.) of Arras, and celebrating the feast day of St. Nicholas. An old Christian, sole survivor of a battle between the Saracens and Christians, is found praying to a statue of Saint Nicholas and is brought before the Saracen King. The King, mocking the old man's faith and piety, declares he is going to put the Saint to the test by leaving the royal treasury guarded only by the statue. Later, when thieves return to their tavern with the royal treasury they have stolen, the King, who is furious, orders the death of the old man. The latter's life is spared, however, through the miraculous appearance of St. Nicholas, who orders the stolen money restored.

Jeu du Prince des Sots: See *Gringoire, Pierre.*

Jeune-France, Les (1833): See *Gautier.*

Jocelyn (1836): See *Lamartine.*

Jodelle, Etienne: (1532-1573) Despite his numerous lyrical poems in every genre typical of the sixteenth century—*sonnets, odes, épîtres, élégies* (qq.v.), and so forth—this member of the *Pléiade* (q.v.) is especially known for his dramatic works in verse. His *Cléopâtre* (1552) is the first French tragedy (q.v.) written according to the precepts set down by the humanists; the first French modern comedy (q.v.) is his *Eugène* (1552). These plays represent the beginnings of the French classical theater.

Joinville, Jean de: (1224-1317): Knight of Champagne, he accompanied Louis IX, or Saint Louis, as he was called, on the Seventh *Crusade* (q.v.), and was taken captive by the Saracens. Years later, at the age of eighty, he composed, at the request of Queen Jeanne, wife of Philip the Fair, the *Livre des saintes paroles et des bonnes actions de Saint Louis,* more usually referred to as the *Vie de Saint Louis* (1309). In this book, Joinville narrates, in the tone of familiar conversation, his reminiscences of his relations with the King, whose memory he held in adoration. In contrast with Villehardouin (q.v.), Joinville always speaks of himself, and he has a bent for the picturesque and the trivial. As to the political side of the campaign, however, he leaves us in the dark.

G. Paris and A. Jeanroy, *Extraits des Chroniqueurs français, 16ᵉ ed.,* 1932.

jongleur: A minstrel in the Middle Ages who would sing an epic (see *chanson de geste*) or lyric poem while accompanying himself with the *vielle,* generally a three-string musical instrument. In many instances, the *jongleur* also composed his own poems, which he later recited.

Joueur, Le (1696): See *Regnard.*

Jouhandeau, Marcel (pseud. of Marcel Provence): (1888-   ) In his faithful picturing of man's perversity—his foibles, hidden vices and obsessions —Jouhandeau's mirror is one of pessimistic lucidity. His novel *Chaminadour* (1934, 1936, 1941), made up of three different volumes dealing with a provincial town that resembles his native Guéret, evokes the life of its inhabitants, with their sordid rivalries, gossip and general goings-on. Despite the cruel reality of his observations, however, the world he paints is bathed in an atmosphere of the supernatural; in their struggles against sin, the characters whom he has created confirm the presence of Satan and the anguish caused by his influence. The absence of any positive philosophy, however, explains no doubt why Jouhandeau in 1940 was an easy prey to German propaganda.

Claude Mauriac, *Introduction à une mystique de l'enfer,* 1938.

Journal de Barnabooth (1913): See *Larbaud, Valery.*

Journal d'un Curé de campagne (1936): See *Bernanos.*

Jours de notre mort, Les (1947): See *Rousset, David.*

Jouve, Pierre Jean: (1887-   ) In 1924, after an earlier affiliation with Unanimism (q.v.), and pacifism—in Switzerland during the First World War his views were considerably fortified by Rolland (q.v.) whom he met and to whom he was later to devote a study—this poet, novelist, and critic was influenced by Freudian psychoanalysis. The discovery of the sexual impulse as a basic force in human conduct, which revealed to him the drama of the human being torn between the tyranny of instinct and his spiritual needs, led him at the same time to a return to the Catholic faith. The subconscious ambivalence of feeling in the exaltation of the erotic, and the consequent exorcism of man's deepest nature, is the critical theme in such collections as *Les Noces* (1928), *Le Paradis Perdu* (1929), and *Matière céleste* (1932), and in such novels as *Paulina 1880* (1925), *Le Monde désert* (1926), and *Histoires sanglantes* (1932). In *Sueur de sang* (1935), moreover, he not only expresses, as in the previous collections, the contradictory forces of passion and spirituality, but, in its preface, is the prophet of catastrophe and cataclysm. In 1940 his sex obsession is superseded by patriotic feeling and expression, as can be seen in *Porche à la nuit des saints* (1941), a collection that reflects the tragic destiny of our time and which at the same time is an act of faith. *La Vierge de Paris* (1945) is a collection of his poetry written during the *Résistance* (q.v.).

Alexandre Starobinski, *Pierre-Jean Jouve*, 1946.

Jouvet, Louis: (1887-1951) After two failures at the *Conservatoire*, and an invaluable dramatic association with Copeau (q.v.)—who had also molded Dullin (q.v.)—over a period of about ten years (1913-1922), this actor, theatrical *directeur, metteur-en-scène*, even stage director of the Comédie Française (q.v.), became director in 1924 of the *Comédie des Champs-Elysées*. Here he selected for his repertoire modern plays, the comedies of Jules Romains (q.v.), Marcel Achard (q.v.), and Giraudoux (q.v.). These plays—and this is a vital point—appealed to the intellect rather than to the imagination, and therefore Jouvet gave them a perspicacious interpretation that combined both intelligence and fancy. His vigorous spirit—and it should not be forgotten that Jouvet was an extraordinary actor—made it possible for him later, when he moved his company in 1934 to the *Athénée*, to give dynamic interpretations to Giraudoux's plays and, especially, to Molière's (q.v.) *L'École des femmes*. In the simplified settings of these plays, light, which caught the expression of intelligence, was used abundantly. The staging and acting, highly stylized, won the enthusiasm of the fashionable world. Jouvet was also seen in several films, including *Knock, La Kermesse héroïque, La Fin des jours,* and *Carnet du bal*.

C. Cézan, *Louis Jouvet et le théâtre d'aujourd'hui*, 1938.

Judith (1573): See *Du Bartas*.

Jullien, Jean: (1854-1919) A follower of Antoine (q.v.), he produced at the *Théâtre-Libre* (q.v.) three plays —*La Sérénade* (1887), *L'Échéance* (1889), and *Le Maître* (1890)—two of which were of the *comédie rosse* (q.v.) type. His claim to fame, however, is due to his having coined the phrase, *tranche de vie* (q.v.), which he defined in his *Le Théâtre vivant* (1892) and which became one of the important theories incorporated into the plays produced by the Théâtre-Libre.

Jument verte, La (1933): See *Aymé, Marcel*.

K

Kahn, Gustave: (1856-1936) This poet, identified with Symbolism (q.v.), "invented," together with Laforgue (q.v.), the *vers libre* (q.v.), of which he is the theoretician. His poetic collections include *Les Palais nomades* (1887), *Chansons d'amant* (1891), and *Le Livre d'images* (1897). He also wrote *Symbolistes et décadents* (1902) and other works of criticism.

L

Labé (or **Labbé**), **Louise:** (*c.* 1524-1565) This wife of a wealthy ropemaker—hence the name *La Belle Cordière* by which she was known—was one of the principal Lyonese poets. In addition to three elegies, she wrote 24 sonnets in the Italian form in which she expressed her own feelings with passion, melancholy, and conviction. In contrast to her contemporary, Maurice Scève (q.v.), she employed in her poetry less artifice and more directness and simplicity. Her work, published in 1555, also includes *Débat de Folie et d'Amour*, written in prose.

J. Larnac, *Louise Labé*, 1934.

Labiche, Eugène: (1815-1888) Along with his many farces and vaudevilles (qq.v.), this Parisian-born dramatist wrote some worthwhile comedy. Most of his plays are only intended to amuse, without any serious application to life. These include *Le Chapeau de Paille d'Italie* (1851) and *La Cagnotte* (1864). Some of the devices used by Labiche to create laughter are misunderstandings, mistaken identity, caricature, the portrayal of ridiculous personages, and generally amusing situations. In many other plays he depicts, with good-humored irony, the vices of the petty French bourgeois of the Second Empire. *Le Voyage de M. Perrichon* (1860) is a caricature of a merchant seeking self-improvement in travel; in *La Poudre aux yeux* (1862), the characters try to appear richer and more important than they really are. Other plays worthy of note are: *Le Misanthrope et l'auvergnat* (1852), *Célimare le bien-aimé* (1863), and *La grammaire* (1867).

Philippe Soupault, *Eugène Labiche, sa vie, son œuvre*, 1945.

La Boétie, Étienne de: (1530-1563) He is perhaps remembered as much for his friendship with Montaigne (q.v.), whom he had met around 1557 in Bordeaux where he was a *conseiller au Parlement*, as for his famous *Discours sur la servitude volontaire* (*c.* 1553), a treatise against tyranny. In addition to his translations from Xenophon and Plutarch, he wrote several Petrarchan sonnets, first published in Montaigne's *Essais* (1580), and *Mémoire sur l'édit de janvier 1562.* L. Feugère, *Étienne de le Boétie, sa vie et ses ouvrages*, 1845; P. Bonnefon, Introduction to La Boétie, *Œuvres complètes*, 1892.

La Bruyère, Jean de: (1645-1696) Among the greatest of the prose writers, this moralist and satirist was born of a bourgeois family in Paris. In 1684 he became, thanks to his friend Bossuet (q.v.), tutor (1684-1686) to the duc de Bourbon, grandson of the Prince de Condé. Residing thus at Chantilly, he had every opportunity to observe and study, as he had previously studied other milieux, the society of the courtiers and of the King himself. Keenly aware of his subordinate position and sensitive to the existing social inequalities, he satirized in his *Les Caractères ou les Mœurs de ce siècle* (1688) many of his contemporaries and depicted many of the social evils and abuses—those especially resulting from the corrupting influence of money—of his time. Though not a revolutionary, La Bruyère already foreshadows in this single work of his the spirit of the eighteenth century; as a document, it is an unflattering and critical portrait of French society during the declining years of Louis XIV's reign. But this book is not only a work of social and political criticism; it also portrays—following the classical principle (cf. *Classicism*)—universal man, and includes, besides the character sketches, reflections and maxims, many of which, though less pessimistic, resemble those of La Rochefoucauld (q.v.). La Bruyère's

classical leanings, moreover, are reflected in the first part of the title— *Les Caractères de Théophraste traduits du grec*—given to the first edition of this work, and in the cause of the ancients, which he championed in the *Querelle des Anciens et des Modernes* (q.v.). Combining these classical traits with an attitude more characteristic of the eighteenth century and with a style that is more picturesque, ironical, and concrete than that of his contemporaries, La Bruyère serves as an author of transition.
E. Magne, *La Bruyère*, 1914; E. Gosse, *Three French Moralists*, 1918; G. Michaut, *La Bruyère*, 1936.

La Calprenède, Gautier de: (1614-1663) Following *Essex* (1638), a tragedy, he wrote novels of adventure, pseudo-historical in character, that mark the end of the pastoral novel (cf. *Honoré d'Urfe*) in France. The subject of the ten-volume *Cassandre* (1642-1645) is the destruction of the Persian Empire; *Faramond*, in twelve volumes, completed by Vaumorière in 1670, retraces the history of Merovingian times. He also wrote *Cléopâtre* (1647-1658), in twelve volumes. These novels mix gallantry with heroism and were the delight of the *précieuses* (q.v.).
E. Seillière, *Le Romancier du Grand Condé, La Calprenède*, 1921.

La Ceppède, Jean de: (*c.* 1550-1622) This baroque poet, esteemed by Malherbe (q.v.), expresses a religious symbolism that is marked by a poignant realism in the sonnets making up his *Théorèmes spirituels* (1613-1622).
D. Aury, *Anthologie de la poésie religieuse française*, 1943; F. Ruchon, *Essai sur la vie et l'œuvre de Jean de La Ceppède, poète chrétien et magistrat (1548-1623)*, 1953.

La Chaussée, Pierre-Claude Nivelle de: (1692-1754) Despite a late beginning in his dramatic career, he is credited with having developed, as no one had done before him, the *comédie* *larmoyante* (q.v.) into an independent dramatic genre. In many of his plays, including *La fausse antipathie* (1733), *Le Préjugé à la mode* (1735), *Mélanide* (1741) and *La Gouvernante* (1747), audiences wept; for in them virtuous women had to undergo countless misfortunes. La Chaussée was to have an influence on the social theater of Augier and Dumas *fils* (qq.v.).

G. Lanson, *Nivelle de La Chaussée et la Comédie larmoyante*, 2ᵉ ed., 1903.

Lacretelle, Jacques de: (1888-) This member of the French Academy, son of an illustrious literary family, is a writer of novels, short stories, and essays. His novels, psychological analyses of the human soul and especially of those who because of their sensitivity are unjustly persecuted or misunderstood, include *Silbermann* (1922) and its sequel, *Le Retour de Silbermann* (1930), a tale that unfolds the tragic loneliness and misery of a Jewish person. *Les Hauts-Ponts* (4 volumes consisting of *Sabine*, 1932; *Les Fiançailles*, 1933; *Années d'espérance*, 1934; *La Monnaie de plomb*, 1935), is the story of family misunderstandings, of a son who ill-judges his mother, and of a complex and not too scrupulous woman who succeeds in reorganizing the family property.

La Fayette, Marie-Madeleine Pioche de la Vergne, Comtesse de: (1634-1693) This Parisian-born writer, probably the most important novelist of the seventeenth century, enjoyed the close friendship of such illustrious figures as Madame de Sévigné (q.v.), Henriette d'Angleterre and La Rochefoucauld (q.v.); in their company she found consolation for her unhappy marriage. After publishing, under the name of Segrais (q.v.), a number of works, including *Mlle de Montpensier* (1662), a short story (q.v.), and *Zaïde* (1670), a novel of sentiment and adventure in the *précieux* (q.v.) tradition, she wrote *La*

Princesse de Clèves (1678; q.v.). This book, her masterpiece, is the first novel in the modern sense of the word. Unlike the unreal and interminable stories produced by the *précieux* society, this novel is brief and psychological; written in a simple and precise style, it depicts, in its analysis of a passionate crisis —an analysis that often calls to mind Corneille, Racine and La Rochefoucauld (qq.v.)—the true feelings and motivations of the characters which determine their actions. Fulfilling a classical ideal, this novel (q.v.) is also the ancestor of all the important French psychological novels, from l'abbé Prévost to Proust (qq.v.).

H. Ashton, *Madame de La Fayette, sa vie et ses œuvres*, 1922; M. Turnell, *The Novel in France*, 1950.

La Fontaine, Jean de: (1621-1695) In spite of what his name suggests, this classical writer, famous for his fables, was not of noble birth. Born at Château-Thierry, the son of bourgeois parents, he led a generally idle existence, being interested neither in performing his duties as *maître des eaux et forêts*, a post he had inherited from his father, nor even in fulfilling his obligations as a husband and father. His talents as a poet, however, together with his personal charm, earned him sponsors who maintained him throughout his life. Not long after his first publication—a verse translation of Terence's *The Eunuch* (1654)—La Fontaine came under the protection of Fouquet, for whom, in return for a pension, he wrote *Le Songe de Vaux* (1658), an unfinished poem describing the latter's magnificent palace. When, incidentally, Fouquet was disgraced by Louis XIV, La Fontaine, in his *Élégie aux Nymphes du Vaux* (1661), showed his loyalty to his patron by asking for royal clemency. In 1664, after Fouquet's downfall, La Fontaine found other patrons—including the

Duchesse d'Orléans (1664-1672), Madame de la Sablière (1672-1693) and the Marquis d'Hervart (1693-1695). In these circles, moreover, he met and befriended such illustrious contemporaries as Mme. de La Fayette, Mme. de Sévigné, La Rochefoucauld, Racine, Molière and Boileau (qq.v.), and had the opportunity to observe contemporary society, to reflect on life, and to engage in intelligent discourse. The publication of his *Fables* (Books I-VI, 1668; VII-XI, 1678-79; XII, 1692-1694) revealed La Fontaine's true genius. These, classical in source, are based especially on the fables of Aesop, Phaedrus, Horace and the Indian collection by Pilpay. Their originality, however, is to be found in their form. Containing all the elements of a comedy —*"une ample comédie à cent actes divers"*—their essential purpose is not to moralize—although the moral element is included—but rather to relate a charming tale which, dramatically told, holds the reader's interest; at the same time they serve as vehicles for psychological observation. In a background of natural scenery, the actors—mainly animals —behave, in different situations, like human beings and, in addition to their own characteristics, represent those of certain classes of society. Composed with artistic perfection in a variety of verse forms, from which the one that best expresses the action and the sense of the story is chosen, their language is simple and concise. Classical in form, they portray, in the final analysis, much like the Molièresque comedy, the inherent vices of all ages, and suggest our following the laws of nature in order to attain happiness.

Included among his other works are: his licentious *Contes* (1665-1674), whose themes are often borrowed from Boccaccio; *Les Amours de Psyché et de Cupidon* (1669),

written in prose; and libretti that he wrote for three operas, of which only *Astrée* (1691) was produced.
H. Taine, *La Fontaine et ses Fables*, 3rd ed., 1861; G. Michaut, *La Fontaine*, 1912-1914; F. Gohin, *La Fontaine, études et recherches*, 1937; P. Clarac, *La Fontaine*, 1943; P. A. Wadsworth, *Young La Fontaine*, 1952; a notable English translation: Marianne Moore, *The Fables of La Fontaine*, 1954.
La Fontaine et ses Fables (1853): See *Taine.*

Laforgue, Jules: (1860-1887) This symbolist (See *Symbolism*) poet, who died prematurely of tuberculosis, was born in Montevideo, Uruguay, of French parentage. After completing his studies in Paris, he was secretary to the director of the *Gazette des beaux-arts*, then reader (1881-1886) to Empress Augusta of Germany. There, under the influence of the philosophy of Schopenhauer and Hartmann, his own sadness became a systematic pessimism. Three of his collections, *Complaintes* (1885)—written while in Germany and which won him a certain fame—*L'Imitation de Notre-Dame la Lune* (1886), and *Le Concile féerique* (1886) were published during his lifetime. *Le Sanglot de la terre* (1901), a philosophical poem, and *Moralités légendaires* (1887), a collection of tales in prose about Hamlet, Lohengrin, and Salome, appeared posthumously. As a form of self-defense against the cruelties of existence and his own melancholy, the poet uses irony and humor, and juxtaposes trivial phrases of popular speech with semi-philosophical jargon. Like Verlaine (q.v.), he, too, renounced the principles of classical French verse, and made use of internal rhyme and assonance (q.v.). Even more important, together with Gustave Kahn (q.v.), he is considered to have "invented" free verse (see *vers libre*). His influence is evident in the

poetry of Apollinaire (q.v.), and generally in that of the surrealists (see *Surréalism*); it also manifests itself in T. S. Eliot's "The Love Song of J. Alfred Prufrock."
F. Ruchon, *Jules Laforgue*, 1924; P. Guichard, *Jules Laforgue*, 1950; W. Ramsey, *Jules Laforgue and the Ironic Inheritance*, 1953.

La Harpe, Jean-François de: (1739-1803) Dramatist and critic, he is especially known for *Lycée* (1799), a collection of his studies on French literature. In this volume he gives evidence of being perhaps the first to view literature in its entire historical development. As a dramatist, he obtained his first success with *Warwick* (1763), a tragedy, which was later followed by such plays as *Philoctète* (1783) and *Coriolan* (1784), modern adaptations of historical subjects.

lai: Of Celtic origin, this word designates a "short-story," almost always in octosyllabic verse, which was originally sung by the Welsh bards to the accompaniment of the "rote," a kind of harp. Much like the *roman breton* (q.v.), it deals with love and the supernatural and reflects the courtly spirit. Among the better known of the *lais* are *Le Chèvrefeuille, Le Rossignol* and *Eliduc*. The most celebrated author in this genre is Marie de France (q.v.), who left a collection of French *lais* (begun *c.* 1165).
E. Hoeffner, *Les Lais de Marie de France*, 1935.

Lamartine, Alphonse de: (1790-1869) This poet, later statesman, was born of a wealthy noble family in Mâcon, where he spent a happy childhood. As a young man of twenty-one, he went to Italy, where he met a Neopolitan girl whom he was later to evoke under the name of Graziella. But it was Madame Charles, whom he had met in 1816 while vacationing at Aix-les-Bains, who inspired a love in him that was to be immortalized, after her sudden death in 1817, in his *Méditations poétiques*

(1820). These poems, which retrace the various stages of his love for Elvire, the name given Madame Charles, and which mourn her passing in a setting of nature, where the poet finds comfort and sympathy, were eagerly hailed, because of their sincerity of sentiment and expression, by a generation already accustomed to the melancholy outpourings of such writers as Rousseau and Chateaubriand (qq.v.), and can be considered as the first examples of French romantic poetry.

The collection which followed, *Nouvelles Méditations poétiques* (1823), although containing some fine poems, did not meet with the same success. But a growing interest in, and preoccupation with, spirituality, faith, God, and immortality —reflecting his own religious belief —was to be revealed as a new poetic theme in such collections as *La Mort de Socrate* (1824), *Le Dernier Chant du pèlerinage de Childe Harold* (1825) and, especially, *Harmonies poétiques et religieuses* (1830).

In 1833, after serving several years as secretary to the French embassy at Naples and Florence, and following a trip he took with his family to the Orient, he was elected to the Chamber of Deputies, where he was to play, thanks in part to his fine voice and oratorical ability, an important role for almost twenty years. His political life, during 1847-1848, was especially active. He participated in the electoral campaign which led to the downfall of Louis-Philippe, was instrumental in forestalling a Regency, became a member (in 1848) of the Provisional government and, in February of the same year, Minister of Foreign Affairs. Lamartine, as a statesman, was indeed immensely popular; he even opposed Louis-Napoleon for the Presidency of the Second Republic. It was only in 1851, with the coup d'état of Napoleon III, that his political career, inspired by a generally humanitarian, liberal, and pacifist ideal, came to an end.

All during his political career Lamartine continued to write. Following the tradition of many of his contemporaries, who were concerned with the problems of human destiny, he wrote *Jocelyn* (1836), a huge epic poem the real hero of which is all humanity as it marches, through suffering and sacrifice, toward moral progress and happiness. Full of personal memories—the poet identifies Jocelyn, the self-sacrificing country priest, with himself—this poem contains marvelous descriptions of nature and psychological analyses, and was accepted by the public with much the same success as his *Premières Méditations;* some members of the Church, however, because of certain unorthodox aspects, received it with some reservation. *La Chute d'un ange* (1838), though written two years later, was intended to be the first episode of this same epic poem, and relates the tribulations, during the beginnings of the world, of a fallen angel in love with a mortal. This poem, however, is much inferior to *Jocelyn.* Other poetic collections include *Recueillements poétiques* (1839) and *La Vigne et la Maison* (1857), a lyrical masterpiece he wrote during a period of financial distress following his retirement from politics. His prose writings relate either to his sentimental experiences or to his political life. *Raphaël* (1849) is a novel of his love for Mme. Charles; *Graziella* (1852) concerns his earlier romantic affair; *Les Confidences* (1845) is a biographical account of the author and his family. His *Voyage en Orient* (1835), the result of his trip with his family to the Orient, follows pretty closely the itinerary of his illustrious predecessor Chateaubriand (q.v.). *L'Histoire des Girondins* (1847), well-documented despite occasional errors, reveals political affinities between the Girondins, eloquent and idealistic reformers, and the author.

Lamartine is essentially a lyricist. Even when concerned with problems relating to man's destiny and the future of society, his meditations become poetic and sentimental. His main themes are love, nature, and death. Although a gentle melancholy pervades his work, his deep religious faith and belief in the goodness of nature bring to his troubled soul a sense of tranquillity. The personal element that characterizes his entire work, the sincerity and spontaneity of his expression, and the melodious charm of his verses brought back qualities absent for more than two centuries from French poetry. These innovations mark Lamartine as the first great Romantic poet. He did for French poetry what Chateaubriand (q.v.) did for its prose. What is more, he achieved, perhaps more closely than any other writer in France did, the Romantic ideal of the "poet-statesman."

Paul Hazard, *Lamartine,* 1925; Henri Guillemin, *Lamartine, l'homme et l'œuvre,* 1940.

Lamennais (or La Mennais), Félicité Robert de: (1782-1854) Ordained a priest in 1816, he denounced in his *Essai sur l'Indifférence en matière de religion* (1817-1823) the spiritual inertia of his contemporaries and defended the Church as a depositary of Truth. Exponent, after the Revolution of 1830, of a Liberal-Catholic movement, he espoused, together with many other Romantics, including Lamartine (q.v.) and Hugo (q.v.), the cause of social justice. He saw in the humanitarian movement an application of Christianity to human problems. In 1834 he wrote his revolutionary *Paroles d'un croyant.* This work, consisting of parables and visions, and written in a Biblical style that alternates tenderness and violent ardor, represents an attempt to make democratic liberalism an integral part of Catho-

lic orthodoxy. When the Pope condemned this work, Lamennais broke with the Church. Many writers, including Lamartine and G. Sand (qq.v.), were influenced by Lamennais.
Ch. Maréchal, *La Mennais*, 1925.

La Mettrie, Julien Offroy de: (1709-1751) Physician and philosopher, he expressed, in such books as *Histoire naturelle de l'âme* (1745) and *L'Homme machine* (1747), his best-known work, materialistic views that defied all religious beliefs. Not only, according to these views, is the soul a product of bodily growth, but the brain, too, consists of growing matter or bodily change. For disproving the theory, moreover, in the previously-mentioned *L'Homme machine,* that animals were like machines, without feeling or thought, La Mettrie won the friendship and esteem of Frederick the Great of Prussia and membership in the Academy of Sciences at Berlin.

La Mothe le Vayer, Jean-François de: (1588-1672) A scholar and grammarian, he opposed, in his *Considérations sur l'éloquence française de ce temps* (1637) and *Quatre lettres touchant les nouvelles Remarques sur la langue française* (1647), the linguistic theories of Vaugelas (q.v.). One of the chief *libertins* (q.v.) or skeptics of the seventeenth century, he wrote, while the tutor of Louis XIV (1652-1657), several pedagogical works.
R. Pintard, *Le Libertinage érudit,* 1943.

Lancelot (or **Le Chevalier de la Charette**): Written some time after 1164 by Chrétien de Troyes (q.v.), at the behest of Marie de Champagne, this is perhaps the first French Arthurian romance to make use of the theory of courtly love. It relates the adventures of Lancelot, a Knight at the court of King Arthur, who sets out in search of Queen Genièvre, taken captive by the mysterious Méléagant. On the way, Lancelot loses his horse and, in order to continue his search, rides in a peasant's cart. He gladly suffers this disgrace as a duty towards his lady. He does even more for her; he passes over a sword bridge in order to enter the land of Méléagant and fight for the Queen's freedom. After many episodes, he sees the Queen, but the latter receives him in a cold and imperious manner in order to better test his love. After acceding to her request that he be a coward in battle with Méléagant, he is walled up by the latter in a tower. In the continuation of this narrative by Godefroi de Laigny, Lancelot is permitted to have his revenge; at Arthur's court, he fights with Méléagant in a tournament and slays him.

LANGUAGE: In the year 813, approximately one year before his death, the Emperor Charles the Great solemnly presided over the ecclesiastical Council of Tours. In the course of their deliberations on church affairs the assembled prelates took official note of the fact that the people of his Empire no longer understood the Latin language of the clergy. They consequently decreed that although the liturgical services were to continue to be celebrated in Latin as usual, the sermons or instructions addressed to the people should be given in the *rustica romana lingua aut theotisca,* that is, in the vernacular of his French and Germanic subjects, so that they might be more easily understood. This decree makes it clear that the people of France spoke a language derived from the Latin but differing so markedly from the parent tongue that those who spoke it no longer understood the Latin of the church services with ease. At this point, then, it must be considered as a new and distinct language, no longer identical with the old *lingua latina,* but a new *lingua romana rustica,* an uncultivated Romance tongue, as the Council of Tours called it. This decree of 813 is therefore rightly considered to be the birth certificate of the French language.

The vernacular speech referred to by the Council did not grow directly out of the classical Latin language which is taught in our schools today, based as it is on the usage of the best writers of the time of Caesar and Augustus. Their language was distinctly literary in character, and it was in many ways far removed from the language spoken by the uncultivated and largely illiterate Roman masses of their day.

As the general level of culture sank during the later Empire when Rome became more and more a cosmopolitan city rather than the center of a purely Latin people, the speech of the city and of the rest of the Empire admitted more and more vulgarisms, some of which would have been considered "plebeian" or "rustic" by Cicero, and others which were new and more recent developments. Toward the fourth or fifth century the spoken language of the vast majority of the Roman citizens would very probably have been at least in part unintelligible to Cicero who would undoubtedly have considered it barbaric.

For one thing, the whole vowel system of classical Latin had been based on the distinction between long and short vowels. The difference between *rosă* (nominative) and *rosā* (ablative) was unmistakable to Cicero's contemporaries because of the difference in the quantity of the final vowel, but that distinction was lost in the popular speech of the fourth and subsequent centuries. Since the final *m* of *rosam* (accusative) had not been clearly pronounced for centuries, the distinction between the nominative, accusative, and ablative singular of the first declension was no longer audible in ordinary speech. The

situation was similar in the other declensions, and would have led to great confusion had there not been another concurrent phenomenon which compensated for it. In common with many other "popular" languages, the later Latin popular speech made much more frequent use of prepositions and combinations of prepositions, and sometimes of adverbs, than the classical language would have allowed. It had always been possible to use the preposition *ad* followed by the accusative instead of the dative without a preposition, *ad aliquem* instead of *alicui*, or *ex* or *de* followed by the *ablative* instead of the genitive without any preposition, *unus ex eis* instead of *unus eorum*. But it had never been "correct" to say *de de intus* for "within," and still that construction must be posited to explain the modern French word *dedans*.

There was also a radical change in the very nature of the accent given to the main syllable of a word. In the literary Latin of the classical period, the accent was apparently a musical one, with the accented syllable pronounced on a higher "note" than the others. In the vulgar speech, possibly already in Caesar's time, it was replaced by the accent of stress which is characteristic of the modern Romance languages, as it is of English. Even today in our own spoken language it is distinctly noticeable that people of little culture or education tend to use a much stronger stress on accented syllables than is usual in the more carefully modulated speech of cultivated speakers.

The very strong stress accent of vulgar Latin was continued into the early centuries of the French language and resulted in the weakening of the unstressed syllables, many of which were completely dropped. Thus it is that words like Latin *tepidum* and *dubitare* finally lost their weak second syllables altogether and became the modern French *tiède* and *douter*.

There were similar new developments in the grammatical forms, the vocabulary, and the syntax in the late popular spoken Latin. The whole passive voice disappeared virtually completely, leaving only the barest vestiges in the Romance languages. It is replaced by a new construction using the infinitive of the verb *to be* plus the past participle of the principal verb, *est amatus* instead of *amatur*.

On the other hand, entirely new forms were created: a new future tense formed with the present infinitive of the main verb followed by the endings of the present indicative of the verb meaning "to have"; *cantabo*, I shall sing, is replaced by *cantare habeo*, pronounced *cantáraio*, which eventually becomes *chanterai*.

In vocabulary, as in modern English usage, many words originally vulgar or slangy became so widely used as to be finally accepted as "correct." *Testa* (tile, pot) and *caballus* (nag) came to be used so frequently instead of *caput* (head) and *equus* (horse) that they eventually replaced those words in common usage as the ordinary word without any comic or derogatory significance. It is as if "noodle" or "bean" and "pooch" or "mutt" should completely replace the words "head" and "dog" in ordinary usage.

It was this sort of uncultivated, radically changed "Latin" which came to be widely spoken in Roman Gaul after the conquest, as the original Celtic language spoken by the Gauls gradually died out. With the progressive weakening of the central authority in the Italian peninsula, the far-flung provinces of the Empire were no longer restrained by a disciplined political and cultural authority emanating from Rome. Before its complete disappearance, the old Gaulish tongue bequeathed to the vulgar Latin which replaced it a certain number of words and place-names, and perhaps, according to some scholars, certain peculiarities of pronunciation and of grammar. Just as the English- (and Spanish-) speaking colonists of this hemisphere took over words and place-names from the previous inhabitants of the territory, such as "potato," "squaw," "tobacco," "tomahawk," "tomato," "Manhattan," "Mississippi," etc., so the Latin-speaking inhabitants of Gaul borrowed from the Celtic language of the Gauls words and names which have often survived in the modern French language, such as *chemin, changer, druide, vassal, arpent, bruyère, charrue, Lyon, Rouen, Verdun*, etc.

During the period of anarchy during the successive waves of Germanic invasions, the fall of the Roman Empire in the West, and the ensuing reign of the Merovingian dynasty in France (486-752), the central political authority became increasingly weaker, and the state of learning also declined to its lowest ebb. At the same time the vernacular speech of virtually the entire population, both clerical and lay, of the country, deviated so widely from the original parent tongue of classical Latin that it was scarcely recognizable as a form of the same language. Its grammar was further simplified; the case system, for instance, was further reduced until there remained two cases only, one for the subject, and the other for all the former object cases. To the relatively small number of Celtic words incorporated into the impoverished Latin vocabulary of the populace was added a very considerable number of words drawn from the Germanic tongues of the reigning conquerors. Many, but not all, of these words have survived in modern French, such as for example, *auberge, baron, blesser, bleu, fief, gagner, garant, guérir, guerre, haïr, navrer, orgueil,* and a host of others. The great majority of men's names which are considered typically French are in reality of Germanic origin, as, for example, *Charles, Gautier, Gui, Guillaume, Henri, Louis, Raoul, Roland,* etc. The pronunciation of the Germanic rulers no doubt also influenced that of the vulgar Latin spoken in their domains.

When this highly transformed variety of the Latin language came to differ so radically from the more or less classical language of the Fathers of the Church, the Vulgate, and the liturgy, that the people no longer understood the Latin of the Church, the Council of Tours finally was obliged to recognize the situation and so to decree that the instructions and exhortations addressed directly to the people be delivered in their own vernacular tongue, the *lingua romana rustica,* and not in the church Latin which had become virtually incomprehensible to them.

The earliest extant text written in this language, now officially recognized as separate and distinct from Latin, dates from the year 842, when the grandsons of Charlemagne, Charles the Bald of France and Louis the German made an alliance against their brother Lothar. The King of France swore his oath before the assembled armies in German so that the German King's army might hear and understand his promises to their lord, and conversely, Louis of Germany pronounced his oath in the language of the men of the army of Charles of France. Its sounds, grammatical forms, and choice of words are those of the popular tongue, but its composition is couched in the sonorous Latin rhythms and word order of contemporary diplomatic documents. The German King solemnly pronounced his oath in the following words:

Pro Deo amur et pro christian poblo et nostro commun salvament (For the love of God and for the welfare [salvation] of the Christian people and our common welfare), *d'ist di in avant* (from this day forward), *in quant Deus savir et podir me dunat* (in so far as God grants me the knowledge and power), *si salvarai eo cist meon fradre Karlo* (I shall aid this my brother Charles) . . .

This most ancient of all French texts already shows clearly the most distinctive traits of the French language as opposed to Latin: the dropping of virtually all unaccented vowels and syllables (*amur* [<*amore*], *christian* [<*christiani*], *poblo* [<*populi*], etc.), the indistinct articulation of all remaining unaccented vowels, making them all sound very much alike, perhaps something like the unstressed *a* when we say "a house." The word *fradre* above, for instance, is written *fradra* further on in the text, showing that the final unaccented vowel was not pronounced with a clear vowel value. And in the Strasbourg Oaths we already find the two-case declensional system characteristic of the French language of the early centuries.

This young French language and its sister tongue in Southern France (Provençal; q.v.) are distinguished from all other Romance languages precisely in that this two-case declensional system was observed in the noun and the adjective until about the fourteenth century. In the earliest extant texts in the other languages (Italian, Spanish, Portuguese, Rhaeto-Romance, Roumanian, etc.) there is no trace of such a declensional system, and there is only one form for the singular and one for the plural of every noun and adjective, as in the modern Romance languages. Gradually from the thirteenth century on the form of the object case came to be more and more frequently used in popular speech instead of the subject case. When the form of a noun no longer indicated whether it was the subject or the object of the verb that distinction came to be shown by its position in the sentence. Consequently, in the modern languages, when the noun is the subject it precedes the verb, and when it is the object it follows it, and we have now a fixed word order in place of the free word order made possible in the early language by the case system.

In the first stages of the language, also, most of the vowels in the stressed syllable underwent a series of profound transformations—far more in French than in any other Romance language—with the result that the vowels in most French words are very much further removed from those in their Latin etyma than is the case with Italian or Spanish. Compare, for example, the French word *mer* (<*mare*) with the Italian *mare*, and Spanish, Portuguese *mar;* French *fleur* (<*florem*) with Italian *fiore* and Spanish, Portuguese *flor.*

Similarly, French has gradually weakened unstressed vowels and syllables and most often lost them completely, as for instance in the words *mur* (<*murum*), *âne* (<*asinum*), *dortoir* (<*dormitorium*), etc.

Since the stress accent in the early language was very much stronger than in modern French, probably quite similar in its effect to that of modern uncultivated English and American speech, the unstressed syllables after the stressed syllable, in particular, dropped out completely, or at best remained with a mute *e.* The typical French rhythm pattern accordingly came to place the stress accent on the last syllable of all words, since all syllables which

had originally come after it had been dropped. The result is one of the most striking features of what is called a French "accent," the placing of the accent on the last syllable of all words, even of foreign words in which the accent was originally on another syllable. That is why, for instance, the French word *opéra* is accented on the last syllable, although it is taken from the Italian word *opera* which is accented on the first syllable, and similarly *revolver* in French is accented on the last syllable, although it is borrowed from the English "revolver," which is accented on the second syllable.

Since there was no strong central political power or predominant cultural center under the late Carolingians (751-987) and the early Capetians (987-), the popular speech developed independently and differently in the different regions of France, and these local varieties of speech were used in literary texts as well as in the everyday business of life. But as the cultural and political pre-eminence of the royal domain with Paris as its center became more and more pronounced, and as the great lords became increasingly attracted to, and subordinated to the royal power under the later Capetian (-1328) and the Valois dynasties (1328-1589), a more or less standardized national language, based essentially on the dialect of the Ile de France and the royal court came to be used, at least in aristocratic and literary circles throughout the North of France, and eventually throughout the entire country.

Conon de Béthune (a great baron and a poet of the end of the twelfth and beginning of the thirteenth centuries) complains that the Queen and her son King Philip Augustus made fun of his French because of his provincial accent, and he claims that despite it, he is perfectly well understood *"en franchois."*

Plate 9. Victor Hugo

Plate 10. Molière

Plate 11. Michel Eyquem de Montaigne

Plate 12. Marcel Proust

In the succeeding two centuries France traversed a sad period of foreign invasions and internal convulsions during which at times the English occupied the greater part of the land and came very close to annexing the entire kingdom. And still, during these tragic centuries of the Hundred Years' War and the ensuing struggles with Burgundy, the monarchs of the Valois dynasty continued to battle for control of their kingdom against the English invaders and the rebellious nobles alike, and at the end of the fifteenth century the royal power was more firmly established and more effective throughout the entire land than it had ever been before. At the same time the language of the court and of the king's government came to be written throughout all of northern France in literary as well as in legal texts. It is often said that Froissart (1337-1410/1414; q.v.) was the last important French writer to compose his works in a dialect, but although Froissart's language always bore traces of his native Valenciennes, it would be more accurate to describe it as a mixture of standard literary French and forms derived from his native dialect, rather than as a true representative of the latter.

In the fourteenth, fifteenth, and sixteenth centuries literature written in prose becomes increasingly important, and the forms, syntax, and vocabulary of that prose reflect the influence of the developing royal bureaucracy, composed of secretaries, ambassadors, and magistrates, many of whom are also important literary figures as well. The old two-case declensional system gradually disappears as the object case comes to be used more and more frequently for the subject. That is why, in the great majority of cases, the modern French form of nouns and adjectives is derived from the object case and not the subject case of the early language. A certain number of the former subject case forms have been retained, however, for a few nouns designating persons, such as *fils, maire, peintre, sire,* etc.

As the declensional system was simplified, sentence structure, on the other hand, became more complex, and frequently reflected the highflown rhetorical style which was developed in imitation of the Latin writers whose works were increasingly studied and translated. The spelling of the period also reflects this latinizing tendency, and begins to introduce unpronounced letters for purely etymological reasons. It was at this period that we find more and more frequently such spellings as *aultre, faict, nopces, recepvoir, sçavoir* (erroneously thought to be derived from Latin *scire*), etc. Most of these letters were eliminated by the end of the seventeenth century, but some of them have persisted to this day, in such words as *corps* (O.F. *cors*), *doigt* (O.F. *doit*), *poids* (O.F. *pois* < *pensum*, erroneously thought to come from Latin *pondus*), *temps* (O.F. *tens*), *vingt* (O.F. *vint*), etc

The vocabulary was also enormously enriched by borrowings from learned Latin words which were either first used at this time, or at least first popularized in general usage then, a host of words such as *adhérer, estimer, fragile, hospitalité, monarchie,* and innumerable others which are now an integral part of the French vocabulary.

These tendencies toward the enrichment of the French vocabulary and the humanistic embellishment of the language were greatly intensified during the sixteenth century due to the combined influence of the new humanism and of the developing spirit of nationalism. The *Defense et illustration de la langue française* published by Joachim du Bellay (q.v.) in 1549 is the most striking and most explicit statement of this general movement.

Long before du Bellay, the so-called *Grands Rhétoriqueurs*, the poets Maurice Scève and Antoine Héroet (qq.v.), as well as prose writers, Rabelais (q.v.) in particular, abound in imitations of Latin style and vocabulary. Rabelais, in this respect at least, anticipated the precept of the Pléiade (q.v.) poets and enriched the French language with words derived from any and every available source: Latin, Greek, Italian, French and Provençal dialects, slang, technical jargons, as well as numbers of serious and nonsensical word-formations of his own concocted and piled up with a supreme frenzy of creative verbal intoxication.

In the seventeenth and eighteenth centuries, pronunciation and spelling gradually approached that of the modern language. In the preceding period, for instance, the diphthong *au* was still generally pronounced as a diphthong, something like *ow*, but by the seventeenth century it had been reduced to the vowel *o*, as it is pronounced today. Most final consonants also became silent by this time. The diphthong *oi* (as in *foi, moi,* etc.) was pronounced *ouè* (to rhyme with *fouet*) in the elegant language of the court, but in the popular language of the streets of Paris it was pronounced *oua*, as it is today, although in some other words (such as *craie, harnais, monnaie,* etc.) and in the endings of the imperfect and conditional tenses, the final pronunciation came to be *ai*.

The grammarians of the period, aided by the ladies and gentlemen of the court, worked diligently and on the whole effectively to discipline and purify the somewhat over-luxuriant and undisciplined language bequeathed to them by the Middle Ages and the Renaissance. For the first time both worldly and learned groups interested themselves in a systematic study of the French language, and in an attempt to bring order into the pronunciation, grammar, vocabulary, spelling, and syntax of the language. Probably at no other time since has there been so strong and so widespread an interest in the niceties of correct and elegant speech and writing.

It was during this period that the language we read in the literary works becomes recognizable as substantially that of our own modern usage. The first task confronting the grammarians, lexicographers, and academicians of the day was to purify the language by eliminating much of the luxuriant overgrowth in vocabulary, spelling, and the florid rhetorical style developed by the writers of the sixteenth century. They proscribed words considered *"sales,"* archaic, dialectal, pedantic, or eccentric. The qualities sought for by all critics were above all: order, clarity, precision, and purity.

In poetry everything brusque or undisciplined was prohibited: hiatus and *enjambement* were strictly forbidden by Malherbe (1555-1628; q.v.). In everything—language, literary style, costume—the ideal sought for was a decorous elegance, carefully studied but unencumbered by any heavy display of wealth and ornament.

For Vaugelas (1585-1650; q.v.), thirty years younger than Malherbe, the true criterion of good usage is no longer the practice of the ordinary people of Paris, as it was for his predecessor. On the contrary, he says that "il sera toujours vrai qu'il y a un bon et un mauvais usage, que le mauvais usage sera composé de la pluralité des voix, et le bon de la plus saine partie de la cour, et des écrivains du temps, qu'il faudra toujours parler et écrire selon l'usage qui se forme de la cour et des auteurs . . ."

The eighteenth century was not a period of profound changes in linguistic usage or theory. Many French grammars were written, it is true, but they are more concerned with logic than with language, and although many dictionaries were published, they are mostly re-editions of those of the seventeenth century, those of the Académie (q.v.), of Furetière (q.v.), Richelet, *etc.* Even the great social upheaval of the Revolution, while it was decisive in the triumph of the popular pronunciation of the diphthong *oi* as *oua* (or *wa*), as against the Court's pronunciation *wè*, was not the cause of any abrupt or profound change in habits of speech or writing.

Although a living language is always in a state of development, there has been relatively little change, on the whole, in the structure of the French language since the early nineteenth century. The combined effects of universal education, military service, ever more centralized government, and today of the press, the radio and television, tend to impose and maintain a standard and stable form of language. The chief development in pronunciation during the nineteenth century was the gradual disappearance of the so-called *l mouillé*, which was originally pronounced like *gl* in Italian *figlia* and like *ll* in Castilian Spanish *llamar*. It has come to be pronounced as a "yod" (semi-consonantal *y*), just as the *ll* has in American Spanish, although we still call the sound by its old name, *l mouillé*. Perhaps the other most significant sound change in modern times has been the progressive elimination of many cases of *liaison*. While there is still a solid core of situations in which *liaison* is obligatory, it is certain that in current speech there is a marked tendency in rapid speech to omit it where it would have been habitually made a generation or two ago, as, for instance, in phrases like *venez] avec moi; ils vont] en France; elles ont] acheté . . . ,* etc.

In our own times, perhaps the most striking development in pronunciation is the increasing frequency with which we hear the nasal *un* pronounced as *in*. This probably took place first when the nasal was not in the accented position, as in *lundi* (pronounced *lindi*), and then spread to the accented position.

There is also a less marked tendency to confuse the sounds of the other two nasals, *an* and *on*, in some cases the *an* being pronounced so close to *on* as to be virtually indistinguishable from it. Though this development is somewhat less widespread than the preceding one, nonetheless, if present tendencies continue, the end of this century may find the French language with only two vowel sounds, *on* and *in*.

The passage of *un* to *in* was at first a vulgar Parisian pronunciation, and then it spread gradually to other regions. This is only one illustration among many of the progressive influence exercised by the language of the capital over all the local variations of language. The non-French speaking pockets seem to be receding under this pressure, slowly but steadily in Brittany, in the Basque country, and throughout the Provençal speaking area generally. Similarly, local dialects and patois in the North are gradually yielding to the national tongue, ever more powerfully aided as it is by the school system, the press, the army, the radio, and television.

In French-speaking regions outside of continental France, the language is for the most part holding its own very well, as in the Caribbean area, in Northern Africa and the Near East (despite current political upheavals which may eventually, but not necessarily, challenge its influence), in Switzerland and Belgium, and in French Canada. On the other hand, the supremacy of French as the international lan-

179

guage of diplomacy, of culture and learning, is being increasingly challenged by English, although the process is by no means as yet terminated.

With the growing frequency of international political, military, scientific, and cultural exchanges, the French language of today is itself being increasingly permeated by words of foreign origin, particularly by those taken from English and American words in the fields of sports, entertainment, politics, economics, and many others. In reading the pages of such a lively current weekly as *Paris-Match*, for instance, one is constantly struck by the very great number of new English words which seem to have become current in French, and sometimes even of an anglicized use of French words, such as *réaliser* instead of *se rendre compte de*, and *investir* in the sense of "to invest funds," usages which would have been considered entirely incorrect only a short time ago.

The future development of the language will depend primarily on social and political developments. If, as it seems likely, the working class becomes increasingly influential economically and politically, there is no doubt that its speech habits will likewise exercise an increasing influence on those of the entire nation. Similarly, as international contacts become more and more frequent, the language of continental France will at once feel the effects of the influence of other languages, particularly in the realm of vocabulary, and to some extent in idiom and usage, and at the same time it will itself influence the speech of others beyond the borders of France, not only in Europe, but also in the Western hemisphere. The French spoken in Canada today, for instance, has changed markedly from what it was a quarter of a century ago, under the in-fluence of "le français de Paris," as they say in Quebec. And French words and idioms are becoming familiar to more and more people in non-French speaking lands because of the enormous contemporary development of international exchanges of all kinds and the inevitable growth of foreign language study, as its value and necessity are increasingly appreciated in our contemporary world.

History of the Language: Kristoffer Nyrop, *Grammaire Historique de la Langue Française*, 1914 et ss. (3rd ed.); Ferdinand Brunot, *Histoire de la Langue Française des Origines à 1900*, 1924 et ss; Alfred Ewert, *The French Language*, 1933; Albert Dauzat, *Les Étapes de la Langue Française*, 1944; Marcel Cohen, *Histoire d'une Langue: le Français*, 1947; Ferdinand Brunot and Charles Bruneau, *Précis de Grammaire Historique de la Langue Française*, 1949 (3rd ed.); Charles Bruneau, *Petite Histoire de la Langue Française*, Vol. 1 (Des Origines à la Révolution), 1955.

Etymological Dictionaries: Bloch-Wartburg, *Dictionnaire Etymologique de la Lanque Française*, 1932; Albert Dauzat, *Dictionnaire Etymologique de la Langue Française*, 1938.

JEAN MISRAHI

langue d'oc: was the dialect spoken in the South of France during the Middle Ages. The *troubadour* (q.v.) wrote in this dialect. See under *Language* and *Provençal.*

langue d'oïl: was the dialect spoken in the North of France during the Middle Ages. The *trouvère* (q.v.) wrote in this dialect. See under *Language.*

LANGUES ROMANES: The *langues romanes* are those languages which developed from the regional varieties of Latin spoken in the European areas of the Roman Empire which had accepted Latin as the popular tongue to a sufficient degree that it persisted after the dissolution of the Empire. The inhabitants of the conquered areas were called *Romani,* and from this term came the word *Romania* used to designate the Empire of the West after it had been detached from Constantinople until the term disappeared about the ninth century from all regions save modern Roumania.

The modern Romance Languages comprise French, Italian, Portuguese, Roumanian, Romansch (recently made one of the four national languages of Switzerland), and Spanish, plus the non-national languages Catalan, Provençal, and Sardinian. The extension or contraction of this list depends upon the unresolved problem of the distinction between "language" and "dialect."

Just as the earliest stages of the Romance Languages stemmed in an uninterrupted development from Popular Latin after the break-up of the Empire, so the regional varieties extended by continuous dialectal transitions from one end of *Romania* to another, save for Roumania which was isolated from the rest of the Latin-speaking regions prior to the end of the Empire in the West.

Due to the fact that our knowledge of the early development of the Romance Languages must be derived from scanty written materials, which probably reflect imperfectly the contemporary spoken language, we do not have a continuous picture of their progressive evolution from Popular Latin. Among the principal written sources of knowledge for the beginnings of the Romance Languages, as distinguished from Popular Latin, are legal documents, writings of Latin grammarians who reveal popular forms by citing them as "incorrect," inscriptions primarily on tombstones by stone-cutters who knew little or no classical Latin. The Reichnau glos-

sary (8th century) is extremely important, for it explains Classical Latin words in vernacular equivalents. The Cassel glossary (8th to 9th century) gives Latin, Romance and Old High German forms.

Early information for the beginnings of French (see *Language*) is found in the earliest extant connected piece of writing in the Romance languages: the *Serments de Strasbourg* (842; q.v.). However, the Church Council of Tours in 813 had already recognized the existence of a new language in prescribing that the priests should use *rusticam romanam linguam* in their sermons. Further early specimens are the earliest literary compositions: *Cantilène de Sainte Eulalie* (about 881; q.v.) adapted from a Latin original, *Sermon de Jonas* (a mixture of Latin and Romance), *Passion de Christ, Vie de Saint Leger* (based on a Latin work; q.v.). From the eleventh century we have our earliest extant epic in a Romance language, *Gormont et Isembart;* also a Saint's life, *Vie de Saint Alexis* (about 1040; q.v.). There were translations and adaptations of the Bible: *Song of Solomon* (about 1100) in verse, the *Psalter de Montebourg* (about 1100) in prose.

In the early stages of Spanish some divergences from Classical Latin are contained in the writings of Isidore of Seville (6th century) who lists, for example, *thius* (> Span., Port. *tío*), *capanna* (> Span. *cabaña*), *cattus* (> Span. *gato*). Saint Eulogius and Saint Alvarus (9th century) attempted to bring about corrections in the contemporary Latin. The legal documents of the region of León in the tenth century reveal many compromises between Latin and the vernacular. We have to wait until the time of Alfonso el Sabio (13th century) for the first examples of Spanish (Castilian) prose.

The first extant texts in Provençal

181

(*langue d'oc*) consist of fragments of lyric poetry from the eleventh century. In Catalonia the vernacular first appears in the *Glosas de Silos* which belong to the second half of the tenth century. The oldest examples of the Italian language belong to the second half of the tenth century and consist of phrases in a southern dialect found in Latin documents. The earliest literary documents are Tuscan from the middle of the twelfth century.

Before considering the early development of the Romance Languages individually, it will be well to note the more important characteristics common to all, with the major exceptions, at the period of transition from Vulgar Latin. In the Western Romance Languages (French, Northern Italian, Portuguese, Spanish, Catalan, Provençal (q.v.)), the Classical Latin declensional system of nouns and adjectives had been reduced predominantly to a single case—the accusative—which, besides being used as the nominative, had, through the use of prepositions, acquired the functions of the other cases. This process was hastened by phonological developments which included the disappearance or lack of differentiation of so many vowels in final syllables as to make the case functions indistinguishable through case endings. (But see below a qualification of this development in French.) Under this system, -*s* became the general sign of the plural. But in Italian and Roumanian the plural is based on the Classical Latin *nominative* plural. The following schematic arrangement illustrates the developments in the plural:

	Latin	French	Catal.
nom. case	*muri*	*mur*	—
obl. case	*muros*	*murs*	*murs*

	Port.	Span.	Ital.
nom. case	—	—	*muri, mura*
obl. case	*muros*	*muros*	—

	Roum.	
nom. case	*muri*	
obl. case	—	

Just as for the inflection of nouns, adjectives, and the regular comparison of adjectives and adverbs, the synthetic system of verbal inflection was replaced by an analytic system. In this process, the whole classical Latin passive voice was lost, and to serve in this function a paraphrastic combination of *esse* (V.L. *essere,* Fr. *estre,* Span. *ser*) with the past participle developed. The past participle in this context was an adjective. However, Roumanian used *fieri,* instead of *esse,* for this purpose. A new future tense was created by using *habeo* enclitically with the infinitive (Fr. *chanterai,* Prov. *cantarai,* Catal., Span. *cantaré,* Port. *cantarei,* Ital. *cantarò*). But Roumanian constructed its future with *velle* instead of *habeo.* On the analogy of the new analytical future tense, a conditional tense was formed with the imperfect of *habére* and the infinitive, except in Italy where the perfect tense of *habére* was used (*canterei* < *cantar(e)* plus *abui*). The earliest texts in French and Italian show the composition already constituted, but in Portuguese and Spanish the component parts, at the same period, were frequently separated.

Through frequent use, the Classical Latin forms of the demonstrative *ille, illa* with nouns lost force and had assumed the unstressed function of an article in lieu of the declensional endings which had disappeared. In the Western Romance languages (including Italian) the article stood before the noun; in Roumanian it was appended to the end of the noun (*fratele*).

From the demonstrative pronouns *ille, illa* and the personal pronouns of Classical Latin, the Romance Languages obtained two very rich series of pronouns: the one, unstressed, inflectional conjunctives to denote the subjects and objects of verbs (*je, me, le, lo, la,* etc.); the other stronger in form and frequently more emphatic and which are frequently also disjunctive (*moi, ellos, egli,* etc.).

By the end of the Vulgar Latin period, due to an earlier tendency to push the phrase stress towards the end, unaccented syllables, save the initial syllable of words, tended to disappear or to be strongly modified. The cases of retention of unstressed vowels are most numerous in Italian. Classical Latin vowel quantity had been replaced by quality; that is, long vowels generally became closed in pronunciation, and short vowels became open. Under the new system and with a slowing down of pronunciation, the stressed vowels tended to diphthongize unless checked by a following consonant in the same syllable, in which case the vowel tended to remain unchanged. The degree to which diphthongization took place varied widely among the Romance Languages; French developed the most complex series, and Portuguese presented the most conservative behavior in this respect.

The phenomenon of palatalization and its consequences in the Romance Languages is too complex and diversified to receive more than a brief, introductory treatment here. It concerned primarily the effect upon sounds, such as *c* (*k*) and *g* (though palatalization could and did happen to other sounds) produced in the region of the soft palate, as their point of articulation moved to, or through, the region of the hard palate under the influence of contiguous sounds as, for example, one of the front vowels *e, i,* and additionally in France, the intermediate vowel *a*. A mere indication of this phenomenon can be seen in the following table:

Latin	French	Prov.	Catal.
lactem	lait	lach	llet
clamare	clamer	clamar	clamar

Span.	Port.	Ital.	Roum.
leche	leite	latte	lapte
llamar	chamar	chiamare	chema

The consonant *l* frequently vocalized before another consonant: *alterum* > Fr. *autre,* Span. *otro,* Port. *outro,* but Italian *altro,* Roum. *alt.*

In France and Portugal, the nasal consonants *m, n* influenced the enunciation of a preceding vowel sufficiently to produce the nasalization of the vowel, the nasal consonant still being pronounced. In France, a second stage took place: denasalization of the nasal consonant which disappeared from pronunciation, but the nasalized vowel remained.

On the basis of these general developments, we find that the Romance Languages may be divided into Western and Eastern groups with Italian belonging preponderantly with the Western group. However, at the same time, many Italian dialectal developments constituted with Roumanian the Eastern group. Italian, therefore, occupied the position of Janus between the two groups, but, in general terms, it may be said that Northern Italian belonged with the Western group and Southern Italian with the Eastern group, while Central Italian (Tuscan), which has become in modern times the basis of standard Italian, belonged to both.

French—Of all the Romance Languages, French departed to the greatest extent from the mother tongue, Latin. It is, as yet, an undetermined question to what extent the sub-stratum influences of the Celtic inhabitants of Gaul may have been responsible for this greater degree of change. Certainly, the French vocabulary received a number of Celtic words in the same fashion as other Romance Language areas gained indigenous words. Whether the exclusively French step of fronting *u* to the phonetic value of [y] was due to Celtic influence is a debatable point. There is no testimony that the sub-stratum had any influence upon French morphology or syntax.

In addition to the traits of early medieval French already indicated in connection with those common to the Western Romance Languages, the *langue d'oïl* (Northern French as distinguished from Provençal) had the following individual developments among many: 1) the loss of all final unaccented syllables; 2) of all the vowels in final syllables only *a* remained as a mute *e*, and a final *e* remained as a supporting vowel where demanded for the pronunciation of a preceding consonant or a group of consonants (*faba* > *fève*, *matrem* > *mère, cinerem* > *cendre*); 3) tonic free *a* changed to *e* (*salem* > *sel, pratu* > *pré*).

Catalan—In the northeast corner of Spain, with Barcelona as its capital since the tenth century, Catalan formed a linguistic transition from Provençal to the northern dialects of Spain. It had close literary ties with Provençal, due largely to the cultural and linguistic divisions in the rest of the Iberian peninsula. Catalan was closer to Provençal linguistically than to Castilian and enjoyed the status of an independent language to about the same degree as Provençal.

In the elimination of unaccented syllables, Catalan has gone farther than Castilian and, in this respect, is closer to French and Provençal. While Spanish is predominantly trochaic in accent, and French, due

to the elimination of final unaccented syllables, is iambic, Catalan has both systems of accent through its retention of final -*a* (like Spanish) and -*e* in a supporting position (like French). But unlike Spanish or Provençal, Catalan forms the plural of nouns ending in -*a* by -*es* (*casa, cases*). Unlike French and Provençal, it does not front *u* to [y].

Catalan, in agreement with French and Provençal, kept the third Latin conjugation in -*ēre* which did not remain in Portuguese or Spanish. In declension, Catalan departs from French and Provençal, however, and follows Portuguese and Spanish in developing a single case (oblique) system.

In vocabulary, the similarity between Catalan and Provençal was very close and can best be seen in the medieval Provençal rhyming dictionaries for the aid of Catalan poets. The first literary language of Catalonia was the *langue d'oc* based on the dialect called *lemosi* (Limousin) supported by Provençal grammars by Ramón Vidal and Jofre Foixa.

Spanish and Portuguese—In the Iberian peninsula following the break-up of the Roman Empire, the Visigothic invaders (6th century) and the Franks adopted the *lingua romana* and continued many aspects of Roman rule, the language and culture, until the Arabs occupied Spain early in the eighth century with resultant divisions culturally and linguistically.

The early entrenchment of Christianity was responsible for the gradual expulsion of the Arabs. The campaigns of reconquest during the medieval period followed three main paths from north to south which gave rise to three accompanying linguistic bands across the Iberian peninsula: Catalan, Castilian, and Portuguese. The Castilian dialect, which had been on a par with Leonese and Aragonese, im-

184

posed itself through its military and political leadership as the literary and official language of Spain after the eleventh century. It was an innovating speech which developed some differences from the other Iberian dialects. For example, the Vulgar Latin initial *f* became an aspirated *h* and then disappeared from pronunciation (*facere* > *hacer*). Spanish, and especially Portuguese, remained closer to Latin than French and Provençal, with Catalan representing a middle position. Portuguese was so conservative that it came to resemble an archaic type of Spanish. Yet Portuguese had some independent developments, among which were the nasalization of vowels and the use of *tenere* (*ter*) principally to form compound tenses.

Portuguese and Spanish kept the final vowels *a, e, o*.

In the verbal system, nearly all the irregular past participles disappeared and the irregular preterite forms were much reduced. In addition to the analytical passive voice formed with *essere*, the reflexive construction with the reflexive pronoun *se* was used largely for the same purpose. The richness of the verbal system is indicated by the existence of two auxiliaries "to have" (*haber, tener*) and two meaning "to be" (*ser, estar*).

Vestiges of Gothic military customs are to be found in the epic *Poema del Cid* (1140). The Germanic (Frankish) influence is restricted to place names and other elements of vocabulary, largely warfare. The Arabic influence, which reached its height in the tenth century, contributed importantly in many categories of vocabulary which represent cultural contact between the Arabs and Spaniards: names of objects, institutions, administration, place names, commerce and business, trades, agriculture, and sciences. In addition, the article *al-* which was

so frequently incorporated into Spanish words (*alcázar, aldea*).

In the second half of the eleventh century, influences in the direction of linguistic standardization began to operate. Among these was the recapture from the Arabs in 1085 of Toledo, which had been the Visigothic capital and the symbol of Spanish unity. Also the replacement in official documents of Visigothic writing by the French Caroline system; thus encouragement was given for French influence at the very beginning of Spanish literature. At the same time came the monks of Cluny, and the development of Christian pilgrimage routes in Spain with the accompanying spread of epic poetry.

Italian—As has already been noted above, Italian developed a large variety of sharp regional differences which, for purposes of a very brief analysis, may be treated in three groups: 1) Southern, which had been influenced somewhat by the Arabs and later by the Normans in the eleventh century. Of chief literary importance was the "Sicilian school" of lyric poetry. 2) Northern, which underwent the early influence of the Ostrogoths and later of the Lombards in the eighth century. 3) Tuscan, lying between the Northern and Southern groups and much influenced by the "Sicilian school" towards conservatism with respect to Latin with the result that standard Italian, based principally on Tuscan, remained closer to Latin than has any of the other Romance Languages.

Though the transformation of Vulgar Latin was continuous and gradual in Italy, it seems to have been accelerated in the sixth and seventh centuries, so that this period can be considered as the beginning of the Italian language.

In line with its conservative treatment of Vulgar Latin, word stress generally remained on the same syllable (V.L. *bonitáte* > Ital. *bontáde, cómputu* > *cónto*). The stressed open vowels *e, o* in free position tended to be pronounced long and to diphthongize (*venis* > *vieni, tonat* > *tuona*). Unaccented vowels in initial syllables generally remain unchanged, except when lost by elision with an article or some other word. Unlike the other Romance Languages, Italian kept all the Vulgar Latin vowels in final syllables, except in Sicily where final *e* > *i, o* > *u*. In early Italian when two vowels came together in hiatus, the weaker vowel dropped: *la istória* > *lá 'storia, ló impéro* > *lo 'mpero, la árte* > *l'arte*. In Tuscan, the syllables standing between stresses tended to drop in popular pronunciation (*civitáte* > *città*); the cultivated tendency was to keep such syllables. The former won out in the common words. Consonants that were double in Latin remained in Italian, except in the North.

Roumanian—The Latin basis of Roumanian seems relatively less impregnated with literary elements. The Latin vocabulary conserved in Roumania is rustic and denotes especially country life, perhaps due to the fact that Roumania was abandoned by the Romans during the third century A.D., leading to the disorganization of the cities. The language did not participate in the later changes in Vulgar Latin throughout the Empire, with the result that Roumanian represents an older stage of Latin than the Western Romance Languages.

Among the dissimilarities of Roumanian with the Western Romance Languages are: 1) Latin *ŭ* did not coincide with close *o*. 2) Tonic open *o* remains (as in Sardinia, Sicily, Portugal) instead of diphthongizing to *uo*. 3) Prosthetic *e* or *i* (*espíritum*) did not develop before *sc-, sp-, st-*. 4) Final *-s* was not kept. 5) There is no ancient Germanic element, for Roumania was cut off from Italy

before the latter region underwent the Germanic influence. 6) Slavic influence since the middle of the sixth century affected Roumanian morphology slightly and the vocabulary greatly, especially during the sixth and seventh centuries, and continued to a lesser degree in the following centuries in nearly all kinds of words. This resulted in many doublets with words of Latin origin.

Since, apparently, that part of Roumania known as Dacia (north of the Danube) received its Vulgar Latin from Italy as it spread eastward through Dalmatia and Illyria, Roumanian resembles Italian more than any other Romance Language. Among these similarities are: 1) *C* and *g* before *e, i*, pronounced as in Italian. 2) Final *-s* and *-t* dropped. 3) Final *-i* of Latin second declension nominative plural remained (*cinti*). There are additional similarities with Southern Italian dialects; likewise a few isolated resemblances with Northern Italian dialects, among the most important being the use of *fir* (*fieri*), instead of *esse*, to form the passive voice.

As in the other Romance Languages, phenomena to be attributed to sub-stratum influences are not agreed upon. Possibly to be explained on this basis are: 1) The development of the vowels *ă, î*. 2) Identity of the genitive case with the dative. 3) Formation of numerals with the preposition *spre*. 4) The post-position of the article after the substantive. 5) A few words such as *copac* (tree), *mos* (old).

Due to the control of Roumania and the region south of the Danube by the Bulgars, beginning possibly as early as the middle of the seventh century, Roumania owed its political and ecclesiastical organization and its civilization of the Middle Ages to them, and it was from the Bulgars that the Roumanians received their earliest literature. However, the earliest preserved written material in the Roumanian language is relatively late—sixteenth century—though it probably represents the language of the thirteenth century. Ovide Densusianu, *Histoire de la langue roumaine*, Vol. I, 1901; Joseph Anglade, *Grammaire de l'ancien Provençal ou ancienne langue d'oc*, 1921; Charles H. Grandgent, *An Introduction to Vulgar Latin*, 1907; *From Latin to Italian*, 1927; Kr. Nyrop, *Grammaire historique de la langue française*, vol. I, 4th edition, 1935; W. J. Entwistle, *The Spanish Language together with Portuguese, Catalan, and Basque*, 1936; Alfred Ewert, *The French Language*, 1938; Pierre Groult, *La Formation des langues romanes*, 1947; Sever Pop, *Grammaire roumaine*, 1948.

MILAN S. LA DU

La Noue, François de: (1531-1591) A valiant captain on the side of the Protestants during the time of the religious wars in France, he tried to bring about a reconciliation between the opposing factions. *Discours politiques et militaires* (1585), an account of this warfare, is interspersed with moral and religious reflections. H. Hauser, *François de la Noue*, 1892.

Lanson, Gustave: (1857-1934) Appointed in 1900 professor at the Sorbonne and in 1919 director of the *École Normale Supérieure*, this scholar, literary historian, and critic was to have a lasting influence on many university scholars and disciples who adopted his methodical and scientific approach to literary history. This method involves a scrupulous and disciplined study of sources, chronology and bibliography. In addition to his standard reference works—*Historie de la Littérature française* (1894; 17th ed., 1922) and *Manuel bibliographique de la Littérature française* (1909 and 1912)—his major publications

include individual studies of *Bossuet* (1890), *Boileau* (1892), and *Corneille* (1895), and *Esquisse d'une Histoire de la Tragédie française* (1925).

lapidaire: A didactic poem of the Middle Ages in which the characteristics and properties of precious or exotic stones are enumerated and then interpreted in the light of Christian morality. The most celebrated example is the *Lapidaire* (*Lapidarium*) by Marbodius, a Latin poem translated several times into French during the 12th and 13th centuries.

Laporte, René: (1905-   ) This journalist, poet, novelist, and dramatist, born in Toulouse, shows much brilliance and versatility. *L'An Quarante* (1943) contains all his poems from 1930 to the German occupation. In *Les Membres de la Famille* (1948), he depicts the history of the French bourgeoisie during the period between the two World Wars.

Larbaud, Valery: (1881-1957) The cosmopolitanism that characterizes the literary tastes of this poet, novelist, and essayist, born in Vichy, is also characteristic of the French school described in the novelette *Fermina Marquez* (1911). The student body of this school is South American, and the school itself similar to the one Larbaud attended as a boy; the novelette also reflects his experiences and travels through various countries. Sometimes this cosmopolitanism seems to weigh heavily, as in the *Journal d'A. O. Barnabooth* (1913), where the main protagonist, a young, blasé South American multi-millionaire, in his round of varied experiences, is bored and unhappy because, with his wealth, he can without any difficulty or frustration buy, see, or do anything he pleases. The same cosmopolitanism explains Larbaud's enthusiasm for Whitman, Joyce, Butler, and Conrad—American and English authors whose works he introduced to France—and the part he played in making contemporary French literature known in England and South America. Other creative works by this scholar, linguist, and translator include two collections of stories, *Enfantines* (1918) and *Amants, heureux amants* (1924)— the latter written with that Joycean stream-of-consciousness technique— which deal with love in children and young men. There is a subtle, ominous atmosphere surrounding the love relationships in these stories.

G. Jean Aubry, *Valery Larbaud,* 1949.

Larivey, Pierre de: (*c.* 1540-1619) The most remarkable writer of comedies during the Renaissance, his sources of inspiration and his own origins were Italian. His plays, adaptations from various Italian dramatists, include *Le Laquais, La Veuve, Les Esprits, Les Écoliers,* which were published in 1579, and *Constance* and *Les Trompeurs,* published in 1611. Of these, the most celebrated is *Les Esprits;* from it Molière (q.v.) borrowed the scenes of the stolen cash-box in *L'Avare* and conceived the character of Sganarelle in *L'École des Maris.* All of his plays, in imitation of the Italian, are written in prose, and depend for their effect on the surprise of the situation and the plot.

M. Amato, *La Comédie italienne dans le théâtre de Larivey,* 1909; E. Rigal, *De Jodelle à Molière,* 1911.

La Rochefoucauld, François VI, Duce de: (1613-1680) A moralist who distinguished himself as one of the greatest writers of maxims, he spent the first part of his life in intrigues against Richelieu and Mazarin, both of whom sought to reduce the privileges of the nobility. His active participation in the Fronde (1649-1653), which almost cost him his sight, resulted in disgrace and exile. Partly to justify himself, he wrote his *Mémoires* (1662), an account of his political career. When he returned, in 1656, to Paris, he frequented several salons, particularly that of Mme. de Sablé, where the maxim was cultivated; his special talent in expressing epigrammatically a psychological or moral observation led to the publication of the *Maximes* (1665). Ascribing a basic selfishness and self-interest to all human activity, they are pessimistic in tone and philosophy. Their principal merit, however, is their style; clear, precise, incisive and polished, they are a model of prose writing, and represent one of the important features of Classicism (q.v.).

J. Bourdeau, *La Rochefoucauld,* 1895; E. Magne, *Le vrai visage de La Rochefoucauld,* 1923; H. A. Grubbs, *The Originality of La Rochefoucauld's Maxims,* 1927.

La Taille, Jean de: (*c.* 1535— *c.* 1617) In the preface to *Saül furieux* (written in 1562), a tragedy depicting King Saul's madness and one of the two finest biblical plays of the sixteenth century—the other one being Garnier's (q.v.) *Les Juives* —he prescribed for the first time the unities (q.v.) of time and place, and condemned scenes of physical horror on the stage. His comedies, of Italian inspiration, include *Le Négromant* (*c.* 1560), a translation from Ariosto, and *Les Corrivaux,* a play written in 1562.

T. A. Daley, *Jean de la Taille,* 1934.

La Tour du Pin, Patrice de: (1911-   ) Not too unlike Pierre Emmanuel (q.v.) is this Parisian-born poet who bears the mark of his aristocratic origins and Christian upbringing. In his poetry—removed from the currents and the trends of contemporary life—he has evoked, in a partially restored classical prosody and with clarity in expression, the spiritual atmosphere of legendary lands and myths. For his *Quête de Joie* (1933) he was hailed as the greatest poet of his generation. During the War he was wounded and taken prisoner. After a silence of about nine years—his *Psaumes, la Vie recluse en poésie* appeared in 1938—he emerged in 1947 with *Une Somme de Poésie,* a poetic monument of some six hundred pages, which is a spiritual epic and a didactic treatise.

Latude (1834): See *Pixerécourt.*

Lautréamont, comte de (pseud. of **Isidore Ducasse**): (1846-1870) Born in Montevideo, of French parents, this poet came to Paris to prepare for the École Polytechnique. Living in complete poverty, he composed a poem in prose, *Les Chants de Maldoror* (1890), one canto of which appeared in 1869. In the beginning of this fantastic epic, which reflects influences of Byron, Milton, and Poe, Maldoror, a symbolic hero, incarnates, in his hallucinatory visions, the miseries, calamities and sufferings heaped on humanity. As a consequence, he gives himself up to despair and revolts against God. From then on, as an infernal symbol he becomes metamorphosed into a kind of Minotaur. The originality of the ghastly and gruesome poetic visions of this poem, with their lofty imagery, could not help but leave a strong impression on the early surrealists (see *Surrealism*), who saw in Lautréamont a precursor of their movement. For his unfinished *Poésies* Lautréamont wrote a preface in which he expressed his intention to follow, paradoxically enough, the classical literary tradition.

G. Bachelard, *Lautréamont,* 1940.

Lavedan, Henri: (1859-1940) The tone in the plays of this dramatist ranges from the trifling to the grave, from the satiric to the stern. He draws with wit and understanding his contemporaries, who include descendants of the old nobility as well as those from the middle and lower middle classes; he shows a catho-licity of interests, as he depicts their various foibles and vices. Included among his comedies are *Les deux Noblesses* (1894), *Le vieux Marcheur* (1899), *Le Marquis de Priola* (1902), and *Le Goût du vice* (1911). *Le Prince d'Aurec* (1892), more serious, depicts the conflict between a dissipated nobleman and a Jewish banker. *Le Duel* (1905), his best play, portrays the conflict between science and religion.

Laya, Jean-Louis: (1761-1833) His chief claim to fame is his *L'Ami des lois* (1793), the most famous of all Revolutionary plays. This comedy, performed during the trial of Louis XVI—nineteen days before his execution (Jan. 21, 1793)—represented, in its protest against the extremists among the revolutionists, a political event. Included among his other plays are *Les Dangers de l'opinion* (1790), a comedy, and *Jean Calas* (1790), a tragedy inspired by M.-J. Chénier's (q.v.) *Charles IX* (1789).

H. Welshinger, *Le Théâtre de la Révolution,* 1881.

Lebrun, Ponce-Denis Ecouchard: (1729-1807) Called by his contemporaries, because of his declamatory and pompous *Odes,* Lebrun-Pindare, this poet also wrote *Élégies, Épitres* and highly satirical *Epigrammes.*

Leconte de Lisle, Charles: (1818-1894) After twice returning to the island of Bourbon (now Réunion) in the Indian Ocean east of Africa, where he was born, this poet, who was to become the head of the Parnassians (q.v.), remained the rest of his life in Paris. Disillusioned by the results of the Revolution of 1848—his unconservative ideas were influenced by the Fourierists—he took refuge by devoting himself thenceforth to literature. His collections of verse— *Poèmes antiques* (1852), *Poèmes barbares* (1862), *Poèmes tragiques* (1884) and *Derniers poèmes* (1895) —reflect the inspiration he found in the civilizations of antiquity, notably those of Greece, India, and Scandinavia; at the same time they reveal his preoccupation with history, archeology, philology, philosophy, religion, and nature. In his reconstitution of ancient religions and myths, he manifests much objectivity and an impassive attitude; he excels in accurate and beautiful descriptions of animals and nature. Combining the cult of form and beauty with his impersonality and erudition, Leconte de Lisle's artistic ideal approaches that of Flaubert (q.v.). His aesthetics represents a condemnation —expressed in the preface to the previously mentioned *Poèmes antiques* and in his poem "Les Montreurs"—of romantic effusion and lyricism. Restraint of language and precision characterize even those poems in which his pessimistic and pantheistic views come forward; his lofty impersonality, however, did not leave him indifferent to human suffering. Leconte de Lisle also translated Homer and the Greek tragedies.

E. Estève, *Leconte de Lisle, l'homme et l'œuvre,* 1923; P. Flottes, *Le Poète Leconte de Lisle,* 1929.

Lefèvre d'Etaples, Jacques: (1455-1536) For his translation into French of the entire Bible (1528-30)—the first such translation—this humanist and Hellenist was accused of heresy; he was protected, however, by King François I. His commentaries on the Gospels are said to have paved the way for the Reformation.

E. Petravel, *La Bible en France ou Les traductions françaises des Saintes Écritures,* 1864; A. Renaudet, *Préréforme et Humanisme à Paris pendant les premières guerres d'Italie (1494-1517),* 1916; J. Barnaud, *Lefèvre d'Etaples,* 1936.

Lefranc, Jean-Jacques, Marquis de Pompignan: (1709-1784) Friend and disciple of Jean-Baptiste Rousseau (q.v.), on whose death he wrote his celebrated *Ode* (1742), he is known as an anti-rationalist and as a religious poet. In addition to his

Poèmes sacrés (1755)—railed at by Voltaire (q.v.)—and *Odes chrétiennes et philosophiques* (1771), he wrote the tragedy *Didon* (1743).

Légataire universel, Le (1708): See *Regnard.*

Légende des Siècles, La (1859-1883): See *Hugo.*

Légende dorée, La: This name designates the vast collection of lives of the saints, written in Latin in the thirteenth century, by an Italian Dominican known (in Latin) as Jacobus de Voragine (*c.* 1230-1298). These tales about the saints were often translated into French and often inspired religious painting.

Légendes épiques, Les (1908-1913): See *Bédier, Joseph.*

Leiris, Michel: (1901-   ) Known especially, after his flirtations with Surrealism (q.v.), as the author of *Aurora* (written in 1928, published in 1946), a story with a strange sacrificial concept of man, and of *L'Age d'Homme* (1939), a love story the confession of which is an act of heroism, he represents a literature that can be characterized as a "metaphysical naturalism." *Biffures,* the first volume of *La Règle du Jeu* (1948), is a collection of his dreams and memories from 1940 to 1947.

Lélia (1833): See *Sand, George.*

Lemaire de Belges, Jean: (1473-1524) Born in Bavay, the old capital of Belgium, this poet belongs, as does his uncle, Jean Molinet, to the group of poets known as the *rhétoriqueurs* (q.v.). Author of *Le Temple d'honneur et de vertu* (1503), *Épitres de l'Amant vert* (1505), and of *La Plainte du Désiré* (1509), poetic works which reflect the influence of the *Roman de la Rose* (q.v.) and its use of allegory, he is especially noted for his *Illustrations de Gaule et Singularités de Troie* (1510-1513), a work in prose in which he develops a legend, current in the Middle Ages, and soon to be used again by Ronsard (q.v.) in his *Franciade,* which makes of the

French the descendants of Francus (Astyanax), son of Hector and Andromache. Other important works in prose include *Traité de la Différence des Schismes* (1511), a diatribe against the temporal power of the Holy See, and *Concorde des deux langages* (*c.* 1510), a work on the relative values of Italian and French. In his prose, Lemaire reveals an affinity to classical culture. His poetry is occasionally enlivened by a wit that foreshadows Marot (q.v.).

Kathleen M. Munn, *A Contribution to the Study of Jean Lemaire de Belges*, 1936.

Lemaître, Jules: (1853-1914) The same qualities of wit and literary charm found in his several works of impressionistic criticism (see, for example, his *Impressions de théâtre*, 1888-1898) characterize his plays. With subtle psychology and with moral overtones, he traces the conflict between democratic and autocratic ideals, and discusses politics, family relations, love and jealousy. His better plays include *Le Député Leveau* (1890), *Mariage blanc* (1891), *Le Pardon* (1895), *L'Aînée* (1898), and *La Massière* (1905).

H. Morice, *Jules Lemaître*, 1924; G. Durrière, *Jules Lemaître et le théâtre*, 1934.

Lemercier, Népomucène (1771-1840) After writing his successful *Agamemnon* (1797)—typical of the still-popular tragedy (q.v.) during the Revolutionary period—he felt the need of innovations in the theater in order to save it. In *Pinto* (1800), an historical comedy written in prose, he mingled, long before Hugo (q.v.), tragic with comic elements. Also he drew on medieval subjects in such plays as *Christophe Colomb* (1809)—where he disregarded the unities (q.v.)—*La démence de Charles VI* (1820), and *Frédégonde et Brunehaut* (1821). He also wrote epic poetry of a bizarre kind.

G. Vauthier, *Essai sur la vie et sur les œuvres de Népomucène Lemercier*, 1886.

Lenormand, Henri René: (1882-1951) This Parisian-born dramatist, son of the composer René Lenormand, bridges the gap between the psychological and the psychoanalytical drama. Interested in man's subconscious motivations, he depicts the tragedy of human destiny, as he dissects the tortures of the heart and mind. The forces of evil, those of instinct and nature, victimize man, who struggles against them. As these forces are within man himself, the dramatic conflict becomes a dialogue between the conscious and the subconscious. Other dramatic struggles portrayed, basically the same, are those of the subconscious against the forces of climate, of society and its morality, and of fate. To reveal these struggles with the emotional and spiritual upheavals caused by them, Lenormand chooses most frequently abnormal or pathological cases, and makes use of the technique of a series of changing "tableaux" (instead of logically developed acts and scenes) which show the various facets that go to make up the inner personality of the characters. The inner enigma of these characters is ultimately revealed; in the final analysis, they are in flight or in search of themselves. Stage setting and scenic effects, important for their symbolistic or expressionistic value, are an essential part in these plays, as can be seen in the excellent productions by Georges Pitoëff and Firmin Gémier (qq.v.).

Le Temps est un songe (1919) is the first of his plays that portray the tragedy of human destiny (cf. *Georges Pitoëff*). In *Les Ratés* (1920) he depicts the physical and moral disintegration of a playwright and his actress wife, whose lives, under the pressure of adversity, end in murder and suicide. *Le Simoun*

(1920), probably the simplest of his plays, shows the influence of climate and of life in the tropics on the subconscious incestuous passion of a father for his grown daughter, who is the image of his dead wife (cf. *Gaston Baty*). The title of the play, which refers to the soul-sapping desert simoon, represents the elemental forces of nature that undermine the morale and sanity of its victims. *Le Lâche* (1925) is a study of fear as it affects one about to go to war. The truly psychoanalytical plays include *Le Mangeur de rêves* (1922) and *L'Homme et ses fantômes* (1924), in both of which are to be found Freudian elucidations of the Œdipus complex, an insight gained, according to the author, without the influence of Freud. Other plays include *Les Possédés* (1909), *A l'Ombre du mal* (1924), *Une Vie secrète* (1929), and *Asie* (1931), another example of the climatic theme. In all his plays, moreover, Lenormand reflects the mental unrest and feeling of insecurity that are characteristic of modern times.

Daniel-Rops, *Sur le théâtre de H.-R. Lenormand,* 1926.

Léonard, Nicolas-Germain: (1744-1793) Born on the island of Guadeloupe, off the coast of South America, this poet foreshadows Lamartine (q.v.) by his sentiment and feeling for nature as expressed in *Idylles et poésies champêtres* (1775-1782).

Léon Morin, prêtre (1952): See *Beck, Béatrix.*

Lesage, Alain René: (1668-1747) Known especially as a novelist, this writer also distinguished himself as a dramatist in the Molièresque tradition. Writing and collaborating in some hundred plays, he is remembered for two important comedies— *Crispin rival de son maître* (1707) and *Turcaret* (1709). The last-named play, one of the dramatic masterpieces of the eighteenth century, depicts the contemporary *traitant*—the tax-gatherer—as Lesage mirrors the social abuses during the Regency. Even more than a comedy of character, it is a caustic comedy of manners, the forerunner of the nineteenth-century French plays treating the money question. As a novelist, he reflects his interest in Spanish literature and in the picaresque novel in particular. *Le Diable boiteux* (1707), an adaptation of Guevara's *El diablo cojuelo* (1641), takes place in Madrid. But as the devil, removing the roofs, reveals what goes on inside the houses, it becomes apparent that, in reality, this is a portrait of French bourgeois life at the beginning of the eighteenth century. In *Gil Blas* (1715-1735; q.v.)—his masterpiece and the first veritable French novel (q.v.) of manners—the action again takes place in Spain; in the guise of a Spanish picaresque novel, it is a portrait of all French society during the early part of the eighteenth century.

L. Clarétie, *Lesage romancier,* 1883; E. Lintilhac, *Lesage,* 1893.

Lettre à d'Alembert sur les spectacles (1758): See *Rousseau, J. J.*

Lettres de Dupuis et Cotonet (1836-1837): See *Musset.*

Lettres de mon moulin, Les (1866): See *Daudet.*

Lettres Persanes, Les (1721): See *Montesquieu.*

Lettres philosophiques: These twenty-five letters, also known as *Lettres Anglaises* and *Lettres sur les Anglais,* are the result of Voltaire's (q.v.) stay in England (1726-1729), where, following his second imprisonment (1725), he was exiled. Embodying his discoveries of English civilization, they condemn, by implication, French institutions, thus contributing to the spirit critical of the established order that prevailed in eighteenth-century France. Idealizing England as the country of liberty in all its forms, Voltaire deals in these letters with religion, politics, philosophy and literature. In contrast to France, Voltaire finds that in England numerous religious sects co-exist in peace and that government is more democratic. Moreover, he is impressed by the progress made in scientific thinking and especially by the importance given to the experimental method; in this connection, he singles out most enthusiastically the contributions of Bacon, Locke and Newton. Dealing a severe blow to the forces of oppression in France, these letters, when published in 1734, were attacked, and Voltaire was forced to leave Paris and seek refuge elsewhere.

Lettres provinciales (1656-1657): See *Pascal*.

Lettre sur les aveugles (1749): See *Diderot*.

L'Hospital, Michel de: (1505-1573) Under the Regency of Catherine de Médicis he was chancellor of France. A devout Catholic, he sought to prevent fanaticism and religious intolerance. His conciliatory ideas, expressed with eloquence on several different occasions, are contained in *Harangues, Mercuriales, Remonstrances* as well as in *Mémoire au roi sur le but de la paix* (1568). A. Buisson, *Michel de L'Hospital*, 1950.

Liaisons dangereuses, Les: Published in 1782 by Choderlos de Laclos (q.v.), this novel, written in the form of letters and composed in a clear and precise style, is, despite its rather intricate plot, essentially a psychological analysis of depraved aristocratic characters who seek to use love as a means of satisfying a desire for revenge. The cynical Marquise de Merteuil, wanting revenge against the Comte de Gercourt, a former lover who now seeks to marry the young and innocent Cécile de Volanges, plans to destroy this marriage by having the Vicomte de Valmont, who also has been her lover—and who is a professional Don Juan—seduce the naïve girl. Since Cécile, moreover, is really in love with the young Chevalier Danceny, the Marquise takes the latter unto herself as a lover. The carefully laid plans of the two diabolical characters prove to be successful, and the lives of the innocent characters are destroyed. The Don Juanesque Valmont, moreover, also succeeds in seducing Mme. de Tourvel, a married woman of high principles. As a psychological study in libertinism, this novel is a masterpiece; in many respects, too, it foreshadows the novels of Stendhal (q.v.).

libertins: Those who, from Montaigne (q.v.) on, were champions of free thought or opposed religious doctrine and tradition. During the seventeenth century, in a predominantly conformist society, they rebelled against the idealism and dogmatism of the Church and State, advocating tolerance, liberalism, and an epicurean view of life. The most important of the *libertins* during this century include Saint-Evremond, La Mothe le Vayer, Théophile de Viau and Cyrano de Bergerac (qq.v.). Molière (q.v.), in *Don Juan* (1665), portrayed the libertin of his time. Gassendi (q.v.), a philosophical foe of Descartes (q.v.), not only held that "nature" is the safest guide in life, but also substituted his empiricism for the latter's "innate ideas." Opposition to the unerring validity of Descarte's "reason" was continued by Bayle and Fontenelle (qq.v.). Representative of the *libertins* during the eighteenth century are Voltaire (q.v.) and the Encyclopedists (q.v.). During the nineteenth century the term *libertin* is generally used to designate one who is guilty of moral license or corruption (cf. *libertinage*).

F. Perrens, *Les Libertins en France au XVII⁰ siècle*, 1896; R. Pintard, *Le Libertinage érudit dans la première moitié du 17⁰ siècle*, 1943.

libertinage: A current which forms the link between the pagan naturalism of the Renaissance (q.v.) and the atheism of the Encyclopedists (q.v.). The religious or philosophical connotations of this term from the sixteenth through the eighteenth centuries are replaced, in the nineteenth, by those of moral license or corruption.

Littré, Emile: (1801-1881) Philologist and philosopher, he is especially known for his remarkable *Dictionnaire de la langue française* (1863-1872). A disciple of Auguste Comte (q.v.), he is the author also of *Auguste Comte et la philosophie positive* (1863).

liturgical drama: See *drama, liturgical.*

Livre des quatre dames: See *Chartier, Alain.*

Loti, Pierre (pseud. of **Julien Viaud**): (1850-1923) Out of his many voyages to distant lands across the seas, Loti created an exotic literature. *Aziyadé* (1879) is set in Turkey, *Le Mariage de Loti* (1880) in Tahiti, *Le Roman d'un Spahi* (1881) in Africa, *Madame Chrysanthème* (1887) in Japan, *L'Exilée* (1893) in Roumania, *Jérusalem* (1898) in the Holy Land, *Les Derniers Jours de Pékin* (1901) in China, and *Vers Ispahan* (1904) in Persia. *Mon frère Yves* (1883), a sea tale laid in Brittany, and *Pêcheur d'Islande* (1886), set in Brittany and Iceland, are without doubt his best works. The works of this officer of the French navy can scarcely be called novels—they are hardly more than detached incidents and contain no psychological development; his preferences indeed lie with simple, primitive people as can also be seen in his *Ramuntcho* (1897), which deals with the Basque peasants. His descriptions of exotic civilizations in the remote corners of the globe are filled with the anguish of a melancholy soul constantly haunted by death. His vague, dreamy, personal, unconsciously impressionistic style enjoyed much popularity at a time when French literature was passing through a phase of reaction to Naturalism (q.v.). In 1891 Loti was admitted to the French Academy.

N. Servan, *Pierre Loti; sa vie et son œuvre,* 1920; R. de Traz, *Pierre Loti,* 1949.

Louis Lambert (1832): See *Balzac.*

Louis XI (1832): See *Delavigne, Casimir.*

Louÿs, Pierre (pseud. of **Pierre Louis**): (1875-1925) Disciple of Heredia (q.v.), whose youngest daughter he married, this poet and novelist founded, with the help of such collaborators and friends as Gide, Valéry, and Henri de Régnier (qq.v.), two reviews, first *La Conque* (1891) and then *Le Centaure* (1896). His devotion to the Parnassian (q.v.) cult of beauty of form, to Hellenistic scholarship and to sensuality can be seen in *Les Chansons de Bilitis, traduites du grec par Pierre Louÿs* (1894), licentious poems in prose that for a time were taken to be the authentic, original work by a contemporary of Sappho, and *Aphrodite* (1896), an historical novel depicting the life of a courtesan at Alexandria. François Coppée (q.v.) called the latter work a masterpiece because of its literary and stylistic merit. *Aphrodite* represented a reaction to Naturalism (q.v.) and, in many of its aspects, calls to mind Anatole France (q.v.).

E. Gaubert, *Le Tombeau de Pierre Louÿs,* 1925.

Luce de Lancival: (1764-1810) A disciple of Voltaire (q.v.), he is the author of *Hector* (1809), one of the best pseudo-classic tragedies written during the First Empire.

Lucien Leuwen (*p.* 1894): See *Stendhal.*

Lucrèce (1843): See *Ponsard.*

Lucrèce Borgia (1833): See *Hugo.*

Lugné-Poe, Aurélien François: (1869-1940) This Parisian-born theatrical producer and director, who studied at the *Conservatoire* (1888-1892), and acted at the *Théâtre-Libre* (q.v.)

from 1888 to 1890, and from 1891 to 1892 at Paul Fort's (q.v.) *Théâtre d'Art*—where symbolist plays (see *Symbolism*) consisting of scenic adaptations of the poetry of Rimbaud, Mallarmé, and Jules Laforgue (qq.v.) and of pieces by Verlaine, and Maeterlinck (qq.v.) were produced—converted the *Théâtre d'Art* into the *Théâtre de L'Œuvre*, which he founded in 1893. This theater, whose first dramatic success was Maeterlinck's *Pelléas et Mélisande* (1893), represented a reaction to the aesthetics of the Théâtre-Libre. Of an essentially symbolist character, especially until 1897, the plays in its répertoire included Scandinavian and other foreign masterpieces as well as pieces by such French dramatists as Crommelynck, Sarment, Achard, Romain Rolland, and Paul Claudel (qq.v.). On the stage of this *avant-garde* theater, moreover, the actors and *metteur-en-scène* created the atmosphere of poetry and mystery that properly belonged to the text of the plays. The *Théâtre de L'Œuvre* has endured until the present day.

Lutrin, Le (1674): See *Boileau.*

LYRIC POETRY, ORIGINS OF: The approximately fifty important collections (*Chansonniers*) of early French lyric poetry which are extant today attest the existence in the twelfth and thirteenth centuries of a very large body of lyric poetry in Northern French as distinguished from Provençal (q.v.). However, the origins of this poetry remain obscure and problematical because the antecedent, truly popular poetry has not been preserved, the extant versions having been subjected to "learned" modifications in form and content.

Among the many significant studies of the question of the origins of French lyric poetry, probably the most comprehensive, and perhaps the most significant, is that of Alfred Jeanroy (*Les Origines de la poésie lyrique en France au moyen âge,*

3rd edition, Paris, 1925). Several of Jeanroy's conclusions have been subjected to modifications and disagreements by other prominent investigators of the subject, among whom may be mentioned Joseph Bédier and Gaston Paris.

On the basis of the best analyses of the extant materials and the hypotheses carefully developed therefrom, it seems justifiable to assume that there were popular lyrics of a very rudimentary nature, developed in connection with the dances celebrating the arrival of the spring season, perhaps descending in unbroken line from Roman and Gallo-Roman festivities. The original forms, of course, have not come down to us, but it is possible that they existed in all regions of France, with certain differentiation as to varieties. Jeanroy believes, however, that the origin of these spring-time or May-day lyrics was localized in a border region—Poitou and Limousin—between the French and Provençal territories, and spread thence in both directions. An important objection to this explanation of the origins lies in the fact that Limousin was identified with Provençal, being the standard dialect for Provençal poetry, together with the further difficulty that no trace has been found of early lyric poetry originating in Poitou. In this connection, it is important to note that Guillaume VII of Poitiers (also known as Guillaume IX of Aquitaine, 1071-1127), the earliest lyric poet whose compositions have been preserved, wrote in Limousin, not in Poitevin. At the same time, there is much evidence that popular lyric poetry was abundant in the North and East of France.

This body of early popular lyric matter was adapted and reworked by professional poets (*trouvères* (q.v.)—the northern counterparts of the southern *troubadours* (q.v.)) early in the twelfth century. Among

195

these poets were Jean de Brienne, Jaufré Rudel, Blondel de Nesles, and Gautier de Dargies. From their extant works a considerable amount of information can be gained as to the character of the antecedent popular poetry. It would appear that the following types of truly popular lyric poetry had existed in Northern France—whether or not they had come from the Limousin-Poitevin border region remaining an unresolved problem: *chansons d'histoire, reverdies, rotrouenges, mal mariée* songs, *pastourelles, estrabots, serventois, débats,* and crusade songs.

Before describing these lyric types, a word must be said about the *refrains* which are one of the most abundant and important popular elements and which constitute one of our important sources of information concerning the lyrics. It is thought that these *refrains* are fragmentary remnants of early dancing songs in which the *refrain* was an addition after one or more narrative lines of the song. It is probable that the narrative lines were sung in turn by individuals while the *refrain* was sung as a chorus by the group. They are sometimes called *rondets* and developed into the later typical form of the *rondel* of the fourteenth and fifteenth centuries by Deschamps and Christine de Pisan. In extant form, they consist of from one to four verses, sometimes standing alone and sometimes interpolated into other works. It is likely that the single verse represents the earliest stage, being possibly merely a lyrical exclamation belonging to old dancing songs. As the compositions were later less used for dancing, the place of the *refrain* was reduced. The earliest examples of *refrains* interpolated into other lyric works occur in the poems of Jaufré Rudel and Jocelin de Bruges. Since at least through the early part of the medieval period, danc-

ing was restricted to women, the *chanson à danser* contained several themes developed by and for women which reflect their sentiments and attitudes. Among these are the following:

1) *Chansons d'histoire* (or *chansons de toile*) which were working songs in which the girl has the leading rôle and sings of her lover who is absent or who is inattentive to her. This is a very old popular lyric type, for the girl in love plays the active courting rôle.

2) *Chansons de mal mariée* in which the primitive form is a monologue by the wife who complains of her husband and presents the marriage situation from the point of view of the oppressed, unhappy wife. The tone is frequently both libertine and cynical, but not to be interpreted literally in terms of behavior; rather they probably represent vestiges of early religious rites. Later adaptations expanded the monologue to a dialogue between wife and husband, with sometimes the poet present as a listener. This type was treated in a great variety of rhyme schemes.

3) *Rotrouenges* were dance lyrics whose exact form and origin are not known.

4) *Reverdies* were songs in celebration of the arrival of the spring season.

One of the most abundant lyric forms is the *pastourelle* (q.v.) which in both form and content developed greater complexity than the foregoing categories. This complexity arose at least partially from the dramatic situation. The central figure is the shepherdess who is entreated by a chevalier, usually the poet, who is also usually unsuccessful in his quest, either by virtue of the girl's rejection—sometimes quite abusive—or by appeal to her rustic sweetheart or relatives. Sometimes the chevalier is subjected to a beating. Thus there are always two central personages and frequently several secondary characters. In some cases, the rustic lyricism brings to mind scenes from Watteau and Boucher. This *genre* was over-coated, beginning in the fourteenth century, with political and moral themes. The *pastourelle* cannot, with any assurance, be derived from the songs of women or from May songs.

The *estrabot* and *serventois* were additional lyric types of less importance: the *estrabot* being generally a satire and the *serventois* usually personal praise or criticism, both becoming largely political in application.

The *débat* (an imaginary dialogue) possibly was indigenous to the North or it may have been introduced from the South prior to courtly influence.

Our earliest surviving lyric poem in French is a Crusade poem written for the Second Crusade (1147).

The third stage in the evolution of the early northern French lyric is that of the conscious development of the courtly lyric under the influence of southern poetry. This adaptation began predominantly in the second half of the twelfth century, primarily in the Parisian region and in the North and Northeast of France through the influence of Eleanor of Aquitaine (grand-daughter of Guillaume IX of Aquitaine), first wife of Henri VII, and her daughters, Marie de Champagne and Aélis de Blois. Among the principal poets attached to their courts were Ricaut de Barbezieux, Gace Brulé, the Châtelain de Couci, and Gautier d'Arras. The courtly poetry was essentially characterized by the intellectual element in contrast to sentiment in the earlier lyrics.

Gaston Raynaud, *Bibliographie des chansonniers français des XIII* *et XIV* *siècles,* 1884; F. M. Warren, "The Romance Lyric from the standpoint of antecedent Latin documents," *Publications of the Modern Language Association of America,* vol. 26 (1911), 280-314; Alfred Jeanroy, *Les Origines de la poésie lyrique en France au moyen âge,* 3rd edition, 1925; Karl Voretzsch, *Introduction to the Study of Old French Literature,* 1931; Urban T. Holmes, Jr., *A History of Old French Literature from the origins to 1300,* 1948.

MILAN S. LA DU

M

Mabillon, Jean: (1632-1707) One of the most famous Benedictine scholars in France, he studied, in his *Annales* (1703-1739), the lives of Benedictine saints. In addition to this monument to the Order of Saint-Benoît, he inaugurated, in his *De Re Diplomatica* (1681-1704)—his masterpiece —the science of paleography, which he used in the study of medieval documents.

H. Jadart, *Dom Jean Mabillon,* 1877-1878; E. de Broglie, *Mabillon et la société de l'abbaye de Saint-Germain,* 1888.

Mably, Gabriel Bonnot, Abbé de: (1709-1785) Brother of Condillac (q.v.), he too gave impetus to the philosophical movement of the eighteenth century by his attacks on despotism and by his advocacy of liberty, equality and separation of powers. His principal works include: *Droit public de l'Europe fondé sur les traités* (1748), *Entretiens de Phocion sur le rapport de la morale avec la politique* (1763) and *De la législation ou principe des lois* (1776).

Mac-Orlan, Pierre (pseud. of Pierre Dumarchais): (1883-   ) As a Montmartre bohemian and cartoonist, this novelist, in his youth, adopted his Scottish pseudonym. Influenced, too, by the stories of pirates and buccaneers which he had read, this writer discovered that adventure, as a means of escape from reality, could be found in imagination, and that to satisfy this need travel—as can be seen in his *Petit Manuel du parfait Aventurier* (1920)—was completely unnecessary. The realities of war and post-war materialism seen, moreover, as permitting few illusions, this novelist chose, in order to free the mind of these ugly realities, to write fantastic adventure stories and stories concerned with superstitions and legends. Included among them are: *Le Chant de l'Équipage* (1918), *Le Nègre Léonard et Maître Jean Mullin* (1920), and *La Vénus internationale* (1923).

Madame Bovary: Published in 1857, this book by Flaubert (q.v.), considered the realistic novel *par excellence,* portrays, in an impersonal style and impeccable form, contemporary bourgeois society in France. Inspired by a news-item that was called to Flaubert's attention, it is the touching story of a provincial doctor's wife whose romantic desires lead to despair and then to suicide. Not long after her marriage to Charles Bovary, contracted in part by her wish to escape the monotony of country life, Emma finds disillusionment in her husband's prosaic, mediocre, and bourgeois mentality. Dreaming of romantic love,

she becomes involved in illicit love-affairs with Rodolphe and Léon. When the latter do not help her repay her debts, the result of reckless spending on jewelry and clothes, she is faced with the reality of no longer being able to deceive Charles, from whom she has until now successfully kept the source of her debts a secret. Resolved to kill herself, she swallows arsenic, which she has been able to obtain at Homais' shop. The final revelation, following Emma's death, of her infidelity causes the death of Charles.

Mademoiselle de Maupin (1836): See *Gautier.*

Maeterlinck, Maurice: (1862-1949) In 1889, with the publication of his collection *Serres chaudes,* this Belgian-born writer from the city of Ghent revealed himself a follower of the Symbolist (see *Symbolism*) poets. His theater, however, proved a more suitable vehicle for his Symbolism, and represented thereby a reaction against Naturalism (q.v.). The themes of his plays are drawn either from the Middle Ages or from pure fantasy. *La Princesse Maleine* (1890), *Pelléas et Mélisande* (1892)—which inspired Debussy—and *Intérieur* (1894) are a few examples in which are found weak, trembling, ethereal characters who are prisoners of a tragic destiny they do not understand but who have an intuitive presentment of the secrets of life and death. The fatality and mystery of love and death are evoked through the endless half-utterances, stammerings, repetitive dialogues, and silences of the characters. *Monna Vanna* (1902) is less pessimistic, and in *L'Oiseau bleu* (1909) the secret of happiness is discovered.

Maeterlinck's philosophy, expressed in his prose work, reveals an evolution in three stages. First, under the influence of Novalis and Emerson, he is convinced, in *Le trésor des humbles* (1896), that man is incapable of either understanding the mystery of his destiny or of controlling the obscure forces that govern his life. Later, in *Sagesse et destinée* (1898), a kind of manual on stoicism, he exalts energy and goodness as the surest way to happiness. Finally, almost as a corollary to this book, *La Vie des abeilles* (1901), *L'Intelligence des fleurs* (1907), and *La Vie des termites* (1927) display his newly-found faith in science, human intelligence, and fraternal tenderness as means of reaching the unknown in nature and the soul. In the end, although his faith in the spiritual nature of life was confirmed, in the presence of destiny his ultimate attitude was one of melancholy agnosticism. Maeterlinck won the Nobel prize for literature in 1911.

Gérard Harry, *La Vie et l'œuvre de Maurice Maeterlinck*, 1932; Adela Guardino, *Le Théâtre de Maeterlinck*, 1934.

Maintenon, Madame de: (1635-1719) *Née* Françoise d'Aubigné, granddaughter of the Protestant poet Agrippa d'Aubigné (q.v.), this epistolary writer was the wife of the novelist Paul Scarron (q.v.). After the latter's death, she became governess to the children of Mme. de Montespan and Louis XIV. Becoming eventually the King's confidante, after the death of Queen Marie-Thérèse she was secretly married to him (1684). Her conversion (1648) from Protestantism to Catholicism helps explain the role she played in the King's decision to revoke the Edict of Nantes (1685). Her preoccupation with education and with the school of Saint Cyr, a school for the daughters of poor but noble parents which she founded in 1686, are reflected in her *Lettres*. Written from 1655 to 1719, they deal with politics, religion and personal matters. Although they reveal clarity of expression, logical development of thought, and a passion for reason, they do not, however, have the wit characterizing the letters of Mme. de Sévigné (q.v.).

M. Cruttwell, *Madame de Maintenon*, 1930; M. Langlois, *Madame de Maintenon*, 1932; C. Aragonnès, *Madame Louis XIV*, 1938.

Mairet, Jean: (1604-1686) After advocating, in the preface to *Silvanire* (1631), a *tragi-comédie pastorale* (q.v.), the doctrine of the three unities (q.v.), which he justifies on the basis of logic and reason, this dramatist applied it, more or less scrupulously, to *Sophonisbe* (1634). With its historical basis and psychological portrayal of human conduct, this tragedy, the first one to observe the unities, represents an important influence on Corneille (q.v.).

G. Bizos, *Étude sur la vie et les œuvres de Jean de Mairet*, 1877; H. C. Lancaster, *History of French Dramatic Literature in the 17th Century*, I, 1929.

Maistre, Joseph de: (1754-1821) This royalist and Catholic writer reacted against the irreligious and materialistic tendencies of the eighteenth century. His principal works include *Considérations sur la France* (1796), *Du Pape* (1819), and *Soirées de Saint-Pétersbourg* (1821), his posthumous masterpiece. The last-named work—the sub-title of which, *Entretiens sur le gouvernement temporel de la Providence,* reflects his belief that the Monarch is God's representative on earth—consists of a series of eleven conversations between an émigré Frenchman and a Russian senator. The writer, who spent some fourteen years in Russia as Minister Plenipotentiary for King Victor-Emmanuel, also takes part in these conversations, which are written at times with much naturalness, and at others, with eloquence and wit that recall Pascal and Bossuet (qq.v.). In his letters to his wife and children he shows the romantic characteristic of a spontaneous outpouring of sentiments. A curious streak of illuminism also accounts for his influence on Baudelaire (q.v.).

E. Grasset, *Joseph de Maistre,* 1901; E. Dermenghem, *J. de Maistre mystique,* 1923.

Malade imaginaire, Le (1673): See *Molière.*

Mal court, Le (1947): See *Audiberti.*

mal du siècle: Characterizing the romantic generation, this term represents a state of mind that suffers from purposelessness, *ennui,* lassitude, vague passions, repressed energy, melancholy, excessive imagination, moral apathy, and disenchantment. It is delineated in Chateaubriand's *René* (q.v.) and Senancour's (q.v.) *Obermann,* and outlined in Musset's (q.v.) *La Confession d'un Enfant du siècle* and Vigny's (q.v.) preface to his *Grandeur et Servitude militaires.*

Malebranche, Nicolas: (1638-1715) A priest and member of the *Congrégation de l'Oratoire,* he reconciled Church dogma with Descarte's (q.v.) philosophy. In the search for truth, the use of reason, which characterized much of the seventeenth century in France, thus becomes identified with the will of God. His principal works include *La Recherche de la vérité* (1674) and *Entretiens sur la métaphysique et la religion* (1688).

H. Joly, *Malebranche,* 1901; H. Gouhier, *La Philosophie de Malebranche,* 1926.

Malherbe, François de: (1555-1628) Recognition came to this writer, born in Caen, Normandy, when he was presented in 1605 at the court of Henry IV; the rest of his life he was poet-laureate of the court. His poetry, comparatively small in volume, consisting of odes—of which *Consolation à M. du Périer* (1600) is considered his best—*stances, sonnets,* and *chansons,* was most often dedicated to members of the royal family or to some of the nobility.

These poems, including *Ode à Marie de Médicis* (1600), *Prière pour le Roi allant en Limousin* (1605), *Sonnets à Caliste* (1609), and *Ode au roi Louis XIII allant châtier la rébellion des Rochelois* (1628), are technically perfect even when uninspired; the preciseness and simplicity of their imagery and vocabulary, offering a striking contrast to his earlier *Les Larmes de Saint Pierre* (1587), reflect an evolution away from the poetic precepts of Ronsard and the *Pléiade* (qq.v.) which he had, in a general way, previously followed, as well as from his fanciful and baroque (q.v.) poetry. The impersonality and rhetorical aspects of Malherbe's poetry, as well as his tendency to demonstrate general truths, were characteristics, moreover, that were to become common to the seventeenth century. His opposition to the *Pléiade* and his new aesthetics—for which he was hailed by Boileau (q.v.)—represent principles, for the first time expressed, that determined the course of Classicism in France; his rôle in its development makes him an important theorist. The reforms he advocated for the French language and versification, as seen in his *Commentaire sur Desportes* (ed. F. Brunot, 1891) and in the *Mémoires pour la vie de Malherbe* (1672) by Racan (q.v.), stress the elimination of foreign words—especially Latin, Greek, and Italian—and the development of a purity of language and of an exclusively French vocabulary whose standard of good usage was to be based on that of the working people in Paris (cf. *Vaugelas*). For the first time, too, he formulated categorically the fundamental rules for the "classic" alexandrine (q.v.) line, insisting on the caesura after the sixth syllable and on rich rhymes that would satisfy the eye as well as the ear, and forbidding hiatus and *enjambement* (q.v.). These poetic reforms, representing a movement towards uniformity, order, reason and clarity, affected French literature as a whole and, more particularly, the literature of the seventeenth century. J. de Celles, *Malherbe*, 1937; R. Fromilhague, *La Vie de Malherbe; Apprentissage et luttes (1555-1610)*, 1954; *Malherbe, Technique et création poétique*, 1954.

Malheur d'Henriette Gérard, Le (1860): See *Duranty*.

Mallarmé, Stéphane: (1842-1898) Following his early education in Paris and two years (1862-1864) spent in England, he taught English in several cities in France, including Paris, for a livelihood. His poetry, to which he was completely dedicated, first appeared in several magazines and collections, including the *Parnasse contemporain* (1866, 1869), put out by the *Parnassians* (q.v.) with whom he was at first associated. Although by 1876 he had already written two great works, *Hérodiade* (1869), a drama in verse, and *Igitur* (pub. in 1925), a drama in prose—not to mention the poem that later inspired Débussy, *L'Après-midi d'un faune* (1876)—it was only in 1884, when Huysmans (q.v.) paid him homage in *À rebours* that he became known. From that time on, the principal poets and artists, French and foreign, would gather regularly at the celebrated Tuesdays in his home. His writings include *Poésies complètes* (1887, 1889), *Vers et Prose* (1893), his translations of the poems of Edgar A. Poe (1888), and his articles on the aesthetics of poetry and style collected in *Divagations* (1897). In 1896 he succeeded Verlaine (q.v.) as the "Prince of Poets."

Mallarmé has been considered the head of the Symbolistic School (see *Symbolism*) not only because he explores in his poetry the subconscious secrets of the soul, but because of his style, which is at once suggestive, musical and condensed. He builds each poem around a central symbol or idea which becomes vivified by his frequent use of analogy and by the subtle and mysterious meanings he gives to his words. However, the elliptical phrases and complicated syntax he often uses in the attempt to express the dream, the inexpressible and the mysterious in life, result in occasional obscurity. But this was "pure poetry" as visualized by Mallarmé.

E. Noulet, *La Poésie de Stéphane Mallarmé*, 1940; H. Mondor, *Vie de Mallarmé*, 1942.

Malraux, André: (1901-) An adventurous career has been the main and direct source of inspiration in the literary output of this writer. His archeological expedition in Indo-China (1923), his part in the "Young Annam" movement, and the legend—true or false—of his subsequent militant political participation in the Chinese Civil War (1926-27) were experiences that he utilized in his early books, *Tentation de l'Occident* (1926), *Les Conquérants* (1928), *La Voie royale* (1930), *La Condition humaine* (1933), the background of which is laid in the Far East. Back in Europe, he devoted himself entirely to fighting Nazism and Fascism. *Le Temps du mépris* (1935), whose action unfolds in the Nazi prisons, deals with the escape of a German underground leader, while *L'Espoir* (1938) evokes the battles of the Spanish Loyalists whose cause against Franco Malraux had espoused in 1936.

In all his novels, Malraux has established man's historicity, linking him with the temporal, with the specific event; wars and revolutions, murder and death are the order of the day. To these vast frescoes, however, of man's torture, suffering and humiliation, so realistically and dramatically drawn, Malraux has brought a philosophical speculation, expressed simply and without rhetoric, that gives meaning to life and death and also hope to man. In *La Condition humaine*, the novel for which he was given the Goncourt prize, Malraux poses a philosophy of action, of "involvement," which, in erasing man's humiliating servitude and despair, would raise him to his "dignity." Risking his life, thus, man is no longer its slave; accomplishing an act of liberty, he is master of his own destiny. Exalting the tragic, Malraux, in the previously cited *L'Espoir,* brings the further message of human betterment, of fraternal devotion, of a united cause.

The Second World War occasioned further instances of heroism on the part of Malraux, and further reflections, as can be seen in his *Les Noyers de l'Altenburg* (1945), which was to have been the first volume of his unfinished *La Lutte avec l'ange.* A certain Nietzchean attitude no doubt explains his turnabout from his past Communistic leanings to his present De Gaullist espousals. His most recent achievement is not as novelist but as historian of art, as attested in his four-volume monumental *Psychologie de l'art* (1948-1952).

Gaëtan Picon, *André Malraux,* 1946; Wilbur M. Frohock, *André Malraux and the tragic imagination,* 1952.

Mamelles de Tirésias, Les (1917): See *Apollinaire, Guillaume.*

Mandarins, Les (1954): See *Beauvoir, Simone de.*

Manon Lescaut: Written in 1731 by L'Abbé Prévost (q.v.), this book is the first great modern novel of passion. It depicts, in a style at once simple and natural, a romantic type —the first in French literature—not too different from Rousseau's (q.v.) Saint Preux or Chateaubriand's (q.v.) René, who suffers the agonies of a fatal passion. The Chevalier des Grieux, a lad of seventeen, gives up his studies after meeting Manon Lescaut, a young girl with whom he falls madly in love. He takes her to Paris, where he hopes to marry her. Although Manon gives every evidence of loving Des Grieux, she cannot live in poverty; she accepts, as any courtesan would, the luxuries provided her by her lovers. In despair because of her infidelity, Des Grieux decides to enroll as a student of theology at the Seminary of Saint-Sulpice. Visited, however, by Manon, he is easily persuaded that she loves him, and he returns to live with her. The rest of the story amounts to a repetition of Manon's infidelities and of Des Grieux's inability to give her up. Even when Manon is deported, as a result of his father's influence, to the colony of Louisiana, Des Grieux follows her. His pathetic adventure in love comes to an end when Manon, ill and exhausted, dies in a lonely field after fleeing with him from the governor's nephew, whom Des Grieux believes he has killed.

Marcel, Gabriel: (1888-) This leader of Christian Existentialism (q.v.), who, as early as 1925, introduced into France the philosophy of Kierkegaard, is also a literary critic and a psychological dramatist. His plays continue, on the one hand, the *théâtre d'amour* of Porto-Riche (q.v.), and, on the other, the ideological conflicts dramatized by Curel (q.v.). The problem of marriage in a Christian context becomes the subject of *Un homme de Dieu* (1925); *Le Monde cassé* (1932) and *Le Dard* (1937) revolve around the moral and political conflicts of our times. The tragic effects of memories are seen in *Le Fanal* (1938), while *Le Mort de demain* (1931) deals with a scabrous subject. His philosophical work includes *Journal métaphysique* (1927), *Être et avoir* (1935), and *Du refus à l'invocation* (1940).

Joseph Chénu, *Le théâtre de Gabriel Marcel et sa signification métaphysique*, 1948.

Marchands de gloire, Les (1925): See *Pagnol, Marcel.*

Mare au Diable, La (1846): See *Sand, George.*

Marguerite d'Angoulême (or de Navarre): (1492-1549) Sister of Francis I, upon whom she exercised a happy influence, she often identified herself with the Reform movement and its ideas, protecting those like Marot, Calvin (qq.v.) and others, whose religious opinions brought persecution upon them. She was the author of *Le Miroir de l'âme pécheresse* (1531), theological discussions in verse inspired by her religious mysticism, of a number of comedies, of *Les Marguerites de la Marguerite des Princesses* (1547), a miscellaneous collection of light verse, and of the incomplete *Heptaméron* (1558) —modeled after the *Decameron*— which mingled licentiousness with idealism both in the 67 stories (out of 100 planned) and in the generally more interesting discussions that follow each story.

Abel Lefranc, *Les idées religieuses de Marguerite de Navarre*, 1898; P. Jourda, *Une princesse de la Renaissance, Marguerite d'Angoulême*, 1932.

Maria Chapdelaine (1916): See *Hémon, Louis.*

Mariage de Figaro, Le (1784): See *Beaumarchais.*

Mariage d'Olympe, Le (1855): See *Augier.*

Mariane (1636?): See *Tristan L'Hermite.*

Marie de France: (second half of the 12th century) The first poetess in France, she lived in England and frequented the court of Henry II. Noted especially for her collection of *Lais* (begun *c*. 1165; q.v.), in which love and the role of woman are emphasized, she is also the author of the first *Ysopet*, or collection of fables (derived from the word *Æsop*), in French verse.

E. Hoepffner, *Les Lais de Marie de France*, 1935.

Marino Faliero (1829): See *Delavigne, Casimir.*

Marion Delorme (1831): See *Hugo.*

Maritain, Jacques: (1882-) This Parisian-born philosopher and theologian, though brought up in Protestant surroundings, is today one of the foremost exponents of Catholic doctrine. At first he championed, in *Le Bergsonisme* (1913), the philosophy of one of his masters. Later, he replaced Bergson's metaphysics by that of neo-Thomism, as can be seen in his *Saint-Thomas d'Aquin* (1925). His influence has also been felt in aesthetics, ethics, and politics. His aesthetics, based on a Scholastic philosophy, are expressed in *Art et scolastique* (1920). *Situations de la poésie* (1938) deals with philosophical criticism of modern poetry.

Gerald Phelan, *Jacques Maritain*, 1937.

Marivaudage: Derived from Marivaux (q.v.), although applied in a disparaging sense to inferior imitations of his style, the term is used to suggest the shy, sincere and tender sentiment, seen in his plays, that is expressed in refined, subtle, though not affected, language. More precisely, it refers to the penetrating analyses and careful observations exercised by lovers in search of happiness through true love. *Marivaudage*, characterized by sincerity in love, should not be confused with the affectation of the *précieux* (q.v.), to whom love is but a game.

Marivaux, Pierre Carlet de Chamblain de: (1688-1763) Known especially as a dramatist, this Parisian-born writer also distinguished himself as a novelist. The two novels for which he is remembered—*La Vie de Marianne* (1731-1741; q.v.) and *Le Paysan parvenu* (1735-1736)—are essentially psychological studies, autobiographical in form, of middle class characters who end up by finding success and happiness; at the same time they reflect the manners of French contemporary society, especially of the bourgeoisie, whose primary concern is with money matters. Marivaux's personal financial reverses, incidentally, suffered as a result of speculations under John Law's system in 1722, obliged him to earn his living by writing. The numerous comedies produced after 1722 are a case in point. Identified with what has been called *marivaudage* (q.v.), his plays, full of wit, fancy and sentimentality—characteristics that explain, in part, why he was welcomed in the salons (q.v.) of Mme. de Lambert and Mme. de Tencin—are written in a style different from that generally found in his novels. These comedies, to which he owes his fame, deal, for the most part, with love and female psychology. *Le Jeu de l'amour et du hasard* (1730), considered his masterpiece, centers around two lovers, Silvia and Dorante, who disguise themselves in order to better test their love. Depicting, in the end, the dawn of love and its concomitant rewards, this piece is typical of the subtle analysis Marivaux applies to delicate sentiments involved in the stirrings of love and happiness. Exploring hidden emotions and sensibilities, picturing the growth of a shy and timid love in a refined social setting, Marivaux, a "miniature Racine (q.v.)," occupies a unique position in eighteenth-century comedy. His originality owes little, if anything, to Molière (q.v.). Representative of his other plays are: *Arlequin poli par l'amour* (1720), *La Surprise de l'amour* (1722), *La Double inconstance* (1723), *La Seconde surprise de l'amour* (1727), *La Mère confidente* (1735), *Les Legs* (1736), *Les Fausses confidences* (1737) and *L'Epreuve* (1740).

G. Larroumet, *Marivaux, sa vie et ses œuvres*, 1882; G. Deschamps, *Marivaux*, 1897; M. Arland, *Marivaux*, 1950.

Marmontel, Jean-François: (1723-1799) Gifted with versatility, this writer is the author of *Denys le Tyran* (1748), a tragedy, of two "philosophical" novels—*Bélisaire* (1766), a plea for tolerance, and *Les Incas ou La Destruction de l'Empire du Pérou* (1777), an indictment against slavery—of *Contes Moraux* (1761), in which he preached virtue, and of *Éléments de littérature* (1787), a work of literary criticism. His *Mémoires d'un père*, however, composed in the latter part of his life, remains the most interesting part of his work; it offers valuable information pertaining to French society of the eighteenth century.

S. Lenel, *Un homme de lettres au XVIIIᵉ siècle: Marmontel*, 1902.

Marot, Clément: (1496-1544) Valet de chambre to King Francis I, and then secretary to Marguerite d'Angoulême (q.v.), the King's sister, this court poet uses both the old poetic forms of the Middle Ages and the new forms of the Renaissance. The medieval aspect is seen in his editions of the *Roman de la Rose* (1527; q.v.) and the poetry of Villon (1532; q.v.), and in the influence on his early work of the *rhétoriqueurs* (q.v.), of whom his father, Jean Marot, was one. Like them, he cultivated the traditional genres of the *rondeaux, ballades,* and *chansons* (qq.v.) and employed many of their complicated and artificial poetic devices.

While long retaining the complexities of the *rhétoriqueurs*, Marot also betrays the humanistic influences of the Renaissance: in addition to introducing the Petrarchan *sonnet* (q.v.) into France, he brought from Italy the poetic forms it had borrowed from antiquity—the *épigramme*, the *épître*, and the *églogue* (qq.v.). Marot excelled in the *épigramme* and was even more successful in his use of the *épître*, which he employed whenever he wished to refer to his personal misadventures or to solicit favors needed because of his numerous persecutions. He gave to both forms perfect intelligibility, naturalness, and sobriety. Marot also translated the ancients, especially Ovid and Vergil, and borrowed from mythology.

His Protestant sympathies, which put him under suspicion of heresy and caused him persecution, imprisonment and exile, inspired his translation of the Psalms (the first thirty *Psaumes* appeared in 1541); the translation, considered a profanation of the Bible, was condemned by the Sorbonne and Marot fled to Geneva (1542). In this connection, it should be noted that Marot's "élégant badinage," for which he is renowned, and his humor, often reminiscent of Rabelais (q.v.), never left him even in his most trying moments; as a matter of fact, his imprisonments prompted some of his best humorous, light verse. Included among his other works is *Adolescence Clémentine* (1532), his first poetic collection.

P. Villey, *Marot et Rabelais*, 1923; H. Guy, *Histoire de la poésie française au XVI⁰ siècle*, Vol. II, 1926; J. Plattard, *Marot, sa carrière poétique, son œuvre*, 1938.

Marseillaise, La (1792): See *Rouget de Lisle*.

Martin du Gard, Roger: (1881-   ) This Parisian-born novelist, winner of the Nobel Prize in 1937, has led a rather uneventful life. Author of *Le Testament du Père Leleu* (1920) and *La Gonfle* (1928), two peasant farces, and of *Un Taciturne* (1931), a drama which deals with a brother's pathological passion for his sister, his reputation stems, however, essentially from two prose works written in the naturalistic tradition. *Jean Barois* (1913), written before

the war, describes in dialogue form the evolution of an intellectual who, as a result of the *Dreyfus* Affair, adopts the materialistic and scientific doctrines of his age, but then, with sickness and old age, returns to religion. This novel, hailed as the "témoignage" of a generation, was the sum of the social and philosophical systems of the period it described. *Les Thibault* (1922-1940) was the first great post-War *roman-fleuve* (q.v.); in ten volumes, it portrays the life of two bourgeois families, the Thibaults and Fontanins, during the years preceding the First World War, and thus becomes a history of the pre-War period. Antoine and Jacques Thibault, two brothers, revolt against a tyrannical father with antiquated, bourgeois ideas. Jacques, aided by his older brother, an intern, to escape from his father's strict vigilance, later disappears, going off to Switzerland, where he becomes an international socialist. Only when informed by Antoine that his father is dying does Jacques come back; he can hardly wait, however, to return to Geneva to resume his pacifist activities. His desperate attempts to end the war result in his own death. Antoine, who has become a successful physician, is also a casualty of the war, dying disenchanted, after much physical suffering. Daniel de Fontanin, whose early friendship for Jacques caused the latter to be put by his father in a reformatory, returns from the war terribly mutilated.

In that section of the novel called *Été 1914* (1936), the author not only relates the personal dramas of Jacques and Antoine, but also analyzes the causes and responsibilities of the war. In *Épilogue* (1940), the last section, one witnesses the almost complete disappearance of the Thibault and Fontanin families and, more specifically, those moments during which Antoine, perhaps the most sympathetic character, slowly wastes away. This novel is for the twentieth century, somewhat like Flaubert's (q.v.) work, the impersonal and objective novel *par excellence*. Because of his impersonality, Martin du Gard has been accused by the "engagés" writers of the Existentialist period of lacking an ethic.

René Lalou, *Roger Martin du Gard*, 1937; H. C. Rice, *Roger Martin du Gard and the World of the Thibaults*, 1941.

Martine (1922): See *Bernard, Jean Jacques*.

Martyrs, Les: Published by Chateaubriand (q.v.) in 1809, this prose epic, inspired by his religious faith, sets out to prove that Christianity lends itself more than does paganism to the use of the *marvelous* in literature. To prove his thesis, Chateaubriand involves Heaven and Hell, angels and demons, much in the manner of Milton, in the plot of his epic. Many of the pages in this work contain admirable historical reconstructions and poetic descriptions of nature, a feeling for which he renewed in French literature.

Mascaron, Jean: (1634-1703) Bishop of Agen, he was a rival of Bourdaloue (q.v.), whose reputation as orator, however, he never attained. His funeral orations, the best known of which are those on *Anne d'Autriche, Henriette d'Angleterre* and *Turenne*, have often been compared to those of Bossuet (q.v.).

Lehanneur, *Mascaron, d'après des documents inédits*, 1878.

Massillon, Jean-Baptiste: (1663-1742) Bishop of Clermont-Ferrand, this orator, unlike Bossuet (q.v.), was preoccupied—to a greater extent even than Bourdaloue (q.v.)—with moral teachings more than with dogma. He is especially known for his sermons and funeral orations. Noteworthy among the latter is the one on *Louis XIV* (1715), at whose court he had enjoyed great popularity.

A Chérel, *Massillon*, 1944.

Mas Théotime, Le (1944): See *Bosco, Henri*.

Mateo Falcone (1829): See *Mérimée*.

Mathurins, Les: See *Pitoëff, Georges*.

Matière et mémoire (1896): See *Bergson*.

Maupassant, Guy de: (1850-1893) This incomparable master of the short story (q.v.) and novelist was born in Normandy, the birthplace, too, of Flaubert, who taught him the value of the "mot juste" and of accurate detail. His close observation of the Norman peasant and fisherman, of the provincial bourgeois, and later, of the Parisian government functionaries whom he had met while employed in the Ministry of the Navy and in the Ministry of Education, not to mention the other classes of Parisian society, explains the photographic and impersonal nature of his work. His first success as a short-story writer came in 1880, when his *Boule de Suif* appeared in the collective work known as the *Soirées de Médan* (q.v.). Thereafter, within a period of ten years (*c.* 1880-*c.* 1890), he wrote some three hundred short stories, six novels, several plays, and travel books. The collections of his short stories, published in some twenty volumes, include *La Maison Tellier* (1881), *Contes de la bécasse* (1883), *Clair de lune* (1884), *Les Sœurs Rondoli* (1884), *Toine, Contes du jour et de la nuit* (1885), *Le Horla* (1887), and *L'inutile Beauté* (1890). The technical perfection of form, lucidity of style, economy of words, precision of detail, and holding of interest in these stories relate them, despite their general pessimism, closer to Flaubert (q.v.) and Realism (q.v.) than to Naturalism (q.v.). Even in the novel—in which he was less successful—he did not champion the theories of scientific determinism so dear to Zola (q.v.) and the naturalists. Passions, vanities, and material interests do, however, dominate the unhappy lives of the society he depicts in his novels. *Une vie* (1883) is the sad story of a suffering wife and mother, victim of her own weakness; *Bel Ami* (1885) is the portrait of unscrupulousness in the world of politics and journalism; *Pierre et Jean* (1885)—his best novel, in the preface of which he defines his aesthetic ideas—is the dramatic story of suffering that results when the secret of a mother's past sin is uncovered by her son.

The uncanny stories of the previously cited *Le Horla* (1887) reflect Maupassant's fears and morbidity, which were to lead, toward the end of his life, to a complete mental breakdown.

E. Maynial, *La Vie et l'œuvre de Guy de Maupassant*, 1907; R. Dumesnil, *Guy de Maupassant*, 1933; A. Artinian, *Maupassant Criticism in France*, 1941; E. D. Sullivan, *Maupassant the Novelist*, 1954.

Mauprat (1836): See *Sand, George*.

Mauriac, François: (1885-) Bordeaux, where he was born and educated, is the setting in most of his novels—especially the most interesting. The characters depicted in his novels—bourgeois, peasants, servants, simple as well as complex people—evolve out of the provincial families and provincial life he knew so well. Also influential for his work were his early Catholic upbringing and training, which help explain why he was drawn to such authors as Pascal, Francis Jammes, and Paul Claudel (qq.v.), and why his characters reflect the view that life is filled with tragic, limitless consequences and that it is a conflict between the temptations of the flesh and love of religion. Remorse and a consciousness of sin torture these characters, who indulge in the vices and passions of avarice, pride, hatred, revenge, possession of material property, and, above all, sensual love. The simultaneous attraction of religion and voluptuousness, the central theme of his entire work, gives play to the subtle psychology of a Racinian tragedy. Various facets of this theme can be seen in such novels as *Le Baiser au Lépreux* (1922), *Génitrix* (1923), *Le Désert de l'Amour* (1925), *Thérèse Desqueyroux* (1927), and *Le Nœud de vipères* (1932)—probably his best. It is interesting to note, incidentally, that Sartre (q.v.) accuses Mauriac of bad faith, of refusing liberty to his "monstrous" characters whose sins reflect a Jansenist conception of nature.

As a dramatist, Mauriac has made use of the themes found in his novels. His plays include *Asmodée* (1938), *Les Mal-Aimés* (1941) and *Passage du Malin* (1947). In addition to his biographical studies on Racine, Proust, and others, he has written several volumes of essays, not to mention his *Journal* (1932-1947), collections of articles that include some of his finest prose. During the Second World War he adopted an attitude of noteworthy resistance to the German occupation. Mauriac is a member of the French Academy.

Charles Du Bos, *François Mauriac ou le problème du romancier catholique*, 1933; Alain Palante, *Mauriac, le roman et la vie*, 1946.

Maurois, André (pseud. of Émile Herzog): (1885-) Prolific and versatile, this writer—essayist, historian, biographer, novelist—in his life as well as in his works has been an ambassador of good will between the English-speaking countries and France. He turned to writing, his great love, after having served, reluctantly but out of a sense of duty, in the cloth factory founded by his family in Elbeuf, Normandy. After the First World War he launched his literary career. *Les Silences du*

Colonel Bramble (1918) and *Les Discours du Docteur O'Grady* (1921) are humorous recollections of his British comrades whom he got to know while a liaison officer and interpreter with the British army. His numerous biographical studies—on Shelley, Byron, Disraeli, Dickens—and histories of England and the United States (*Histoire d'Angleterre*, 1937; *Histoire des États-Unis*, 1943) testify to his knowledge of, and interest in, the Anglo-American community. Other biographies are of illustrious French authors and statesmen—Voltaire. Chateaubriand, Hugo, Proust, George Sand, Lyautey. Finally, philosophical tales —*Le Peseur d'âmes* (1931), *La Machine à lire les pensées* (1937)—and novels, such as the partly autobiographical *Climats* (1928) and *Le Cercle de famille* (1932), both of which represent a sentimental or moral crisis—all show a facile pen and a lucid style with the qualities of the moralist. His style renders his erudition accessible to the general reading public. In 1938 Maurois was elected to the French Academy; after the military collapse of France, during the Second World War, he was in the United States, where he lectured and taught.

G. Lemaitre, *André Maurois*, 1939.

Maurras, Charles: (1868-1952) This journalist, essayist, and political critic, was one of the founders of the *École Romane* (1891; q.v.) and of the *École Parisienne du Félibrige* (1892). In 1899 he joined the *Action Française*, a political group whose aim was to overthrow the Republic. His articles in *L'Action Française* continued to exercise an important influence after the First World War on reactionary groups. After the defeat of France in 1940, his program was implemented by the Vichy government. In 1945, however, when brought to trial as an enemy of the republic, he was con-demned to life imprisonment. His ideas on a variety of subjects are expressed in the five volume *Dictionnaire politique et critique* (1932-1934).

A. Thibaudet, *Les idées de Charles Maurras*, 1920.

Maximes (1665): See *La Rochefoucauld.*

Maya (1924): See *Gantillon, Simon.*

Maynard, François: (1582-1646) A disciple, though somewhat independent, of Malherbe (q.v.), whom he had met when he was secretary to Marguerite de Valois, the first wife of Henry IV, this poet frequented the *libertins* (q.v.) and was one of the earliest members of the *Académie Française* (q.v.). His poetry, not voluminous, consists of *odes*—the best-known of which is *La Belle Vieille*—*stances, chansons, sonnets* and *épigrammes* (qq.v.). Although, like Malherbe, he sought perfection of form, purity of language and precision in vocabulary, his inspiration is more varied, as can be seen from the diversity of his themes and verse forms.

Ch. Drouet, *François Maynard, étude critique d'histoire littéraire,* 1909.

Méchant, Le (1747): See *Gresset.*

Médan (group of): A group consisting of Paul Alexis, Henri Céard, Huysmans, Léon Hennique, and Maupassant (qq.v.) who, after the publication of Zola's (q.v.) *L'Assommoir* (1877)—which established the latter's reputation as the head of the naturalistic School (see *Naturalism*) —attended the Thursday reunions held at Zola's home in Paris, and later, at his villa in Médan, near Paris. Constituting a nucleus of the Naturalistic school, they published, in 1880, *Soirées de Médan* (q.v.), a collection of short stories inspired by the War of 1870.

L. Deffoux et E. Zavie, *Le Groupe de Médan,* 1924.

Médecin de campagne, Le (1833): See *Balzac.*

Plate 13. François Rabelais

Plate 14. Jean Racine

Médée (1635): See *Corneille, Pierre*.
Méditations poétiques (1820): See *Lamartine*.

Meilhac, Henri (1831-1897) and **Halévy, Ludovic** (1834-1908): The collaboration of this dramatic team, which lasted for more than twenty years, was to be followed, some years later, by that of Flers and Caillavet (qq.v.). Unlike the latter, whose theater portrayed the society of the Third Republic, they depicted especially that of the Second Empire. The combination of Meilhac's ability to contrive a plot and Halévy's wit and intelligence resulted in numerous light comedies (*Frou-Frou*, 1869; *La petite Marquise*, 1874) and in operettas, written for Offenbach's music (*La Belle Hélène*, 1865; *La Vie parisienne*, 1866; *Mam'zelle Nitouche*, 1886), that contain buffoonery and irony. Halévy is also the author of the well-known novel *L'abbé Constantin* (1882).

Mélite (1629): See *Corneille, Pierre*.

MELODRAMA: Originally, melodrama was a drama with musical accompaniment or, more precisely, a drama accompanied by musical leitmotifs emphasizing the entrance of major characters and important situations. However, since its appearance in France around 1760, melodrama might be defined as a sensational play abounding in suspense and in terrifying incidents in which the characters are thrust into perilous situations by a chance conjunction of circumstances. During the 19th century, the writers who attracted popular favor were those who tried to provoke strong emotions in the naive spectator as well as a frightened sympathy for the particularly innocent and dangerously threatened hero or heroine.

Mysteries, ghosts, fires, villains, and last minute rescues are the principal attractions of the works of Loaisel de Tréogate (*Le Château du Diable*, 1792) and Pixérécourt (*Cœlina ou l'Enfant du Mys-*

tère, 1799; q.v.). Later on, the public was to cry over the misfortunes of Dennery's (1811-1899) *Deux Orphelines* (1874) or to shiver through the lessons in heroism of Paul Féval's (1817-1847) *Bossu* (1862).

The melodrama had considerable influence on the romantic drama (q.v.). Today, the term "melodramatic" is used to describe any dramatic situation in which the pathos is overstated by means of facile methods or in which the tension is artificially provoked by an element of chance.

One of the contemporary forms of melodrama is the "horror play," given almost exclusively at the Théâtre du Grand Guignol (see *Grand Guignol*).

P. Ginisty, *Le mélodrame*, 1910; J. F. Mason, *The Melodrama in France from the Revolution to the Beginning of the Romantic Drama*, 1912.

JACQUES GUICHARNAUD

Mémoires (1773-1774): See *Beaumarchais*.
Mémoires (1488-1498): See *Commines*.
Mémoires (1662): See *La Rochefoucauld*.
Mémoires (1671-1675): See *Retz, Cardinal de*.
Mémoires (pub. 1830): See *Saint-Simon, Duc de*.
Mémoires de M. Joseph Prudhomme (1857): See *Monnier, Henri*.
Mémoires d'Outre-Tombe: This posthumous monumental work by Chateaubriand (q.v.), nurtured for nearly forty years (1811-1848), and published in 1849-1850, draws a portrait of his childhood as well as of his maturity. More than merely a confession of himself, a confession, incidentally, that is more discreet than that of J. J. Rousseau (q.v.), it is a sumptuous fresco of the times. As a re-creation of time past, beginning with the *Ancien Régime*, it heralds not only Proust's (q.v.) work (both as a fresco and a con-

fession), but, more generally, the Symbolists' insistence on the poetical or creative value of the metaphor.

Mémoires d'un homme de qualité (1728-1731): See *Prévost, L'Abbé*.

Mémoires pour servir à l'histoire d'Anne d'Autriche (1643-1666): See *Motteville, Mme. de*.

Ménage, Gilles: (1613-1692) Ridiculed as a pedant by Molière (q.v.) in *Les Femmes savantes*, under the name of Vadius, this writer was a scholar, grammarian and etymologist. His principal works are *Origines de la langue française* (1650) and *Observations sur la langue française* (1672). The verses he wrote were generally *précieux* (cf. *Préciosité*). His reputation, second to that of Vaugelas (q.v.), is also based on the fact that he was Mme. de Sévigné's (q.v.) tutor.

E. Samfiresco, *Ménage polémiste, philologue, poète*, 1902; H. Ashton, *Ménage et ses élèves*, 1920.

Mendès, Catulle: (1843-1909) In 1861, one year after he settled in Paris, this poet launched *La Revue fantaisiste*, a journal that reacted against romantic declamation. Together with Louis Xavier de Ricard and other young poets, he published the first installment of *Le Parnasse contemporain* (1866), the Parnassian (q.v.) collection that was later printed serially by Lemerre. A virtuoso in almost every form of poetry, Mendès showed a special preference for light poetry and a dislike for any literature that was "utilitarian." Mendès also wrote novels and plays. Included among the latter are *La Reine Fiamette* (1898), and *Médée* (1898).

M. Souriau, *Histoire du Parnasse*, 1929; A. Schaffer, *The Genres of Parnassian Poetry*, 1944.

Ménechmes, Les (1632): See *Rotrou*.

Menteur, Le (1643): See *Corneille, Pierre*.

Mercier, Louis-Sébastien: (1740-1814) In such plays as *Le Juge* and *La Brou-*

ette du vinaigrier (1784), this dramatist offers successful examples of Diderot's *drame bourgeois* (q.v.). Other plays, including *La Destruction de la Ligue* (1782) and *La Mort de Louis XI* (1783), are historical.

L. Béchard, *Sébastien Mercier, sa vie, son œuvre, son temps*, 1903.

Mérimée, Prosper: (1803-1870) Beginning his literary career with the so-called *Théâtre de Clara Gazul* (1825), plays he claimed were written by a Spanish actress and translated by himself, and the equally mystifying *La Guzla* (1827), a collection of spurious Illyrian ballads, this Parisian-born writer early showed his disinclination to take the romanticism of his contemporaries seriously. Again, in his *La Chronique du règne de Charles IX* (1829), an historical novel dealing with the Wars of Religion in the sixteenth century, he showed the un-romantic qualities of brevity and objectivity, holding a brief neither for the Catholics nor for the Protestants. A linguist, and very erudite, Mérimée was appointed in 1831 Inspector-general—thanks to his knowledge of archeology—of historical monuments. In this capacity, he traveled to England, Spain— where he was to meet the Countess of Montijo, whose daughter was to become Empress Eugénie—Corsica, Italy, Greece, and Asia Minor. His travels and archeological preoccupations were to overflow into his *nouvelles* (q.v.), the short and long-short stories for which he is mainly known and which he wrote from 1829 until about 1848. Typical of these *nouvelles* are *Mateo Falcone* (1829), *Colomba* (1841; q.v.) and *Carmen* (1845), with their settings in Corsica and Spain; in addition to their exoticism, they are noted for the importance they give to violent and primitive passions. In the delineation of these romantic passions and characters, however, Mérimée shows much restraint; precise in his use of detail, often defining his characters by a gesture, his descriptions are reduced to a minimum. His style, moreover, is simple, clear and concise. Other important *nouvelles* include *L'Enlèvement de la redoute* (1830), *Tamango* (1830), *Le Vase étrusque* (1830), and *La Venus d'Ille* (1837). Like his friend Stendhal (q.v.), with whom he has many traits in common, Mérimée serves as a transitional author between romanticism and realism (q.v.). Mérimée was one of the first in France to translate such Russian authors as Pushkin, Turgenev, and Gogol.

A. Filon, *Mérimée*, 1894; P. Trahard, *Prosper Mérimée*, 1925-31; R. de Luppé, *Mérimée*, 1945.

Merleau-Ponty, Maurice: (1908-) Professor at the Collège de France, director—together with his friend Sartre (q.v.)—of the *Bibliothèque de Philosophie,* he is the chief political thinker of the Existentialists. A Phenomenologist, he attempts to substitute existentialism for Marxism as a philosophy for the proletariat. His principal works include *La Structure du comportement* (1942), a study of the relations between consciousness and nature, *Phénoménologie de la Perception* (1945), and *Sens et non-sens* (1948), which contains an excellent essay on Sartre.

Merrill, Stuart (1863-1915) Born in Hempstead, Long Island, this Symbolist poet (see *Symbolism*) came with his family to Paris in his early youth. Later, he returned to America to study law at Columbia University (1884-1888) while actively taking part in the socialist movement. During his stay in New York, he published *Pastels in Prose* (1890), a translation of the poetry of Banville, Baudelaire, Mallarmé, Régnier (qq.v.), and others; at the same time there appeared in France *Les Gammes* (1887), his first collection of poems. Returning to France in 1891—this time for good—he de-voted himself entirely to literature and, under the spell of Wagner, to music. In *Les Fastes* (1891) and *Poèmes* (1887-1897) he obtains his musical orchestration more by making use of assonance (q.v.) and alliteration than by employing the *vers libre* (q.v.). *Les Quatre Saisons* (1900) is a revery and a confession of a soul.

Marjorie L. Henry, *La Contribution d'un Américain au Symbolisme français, Stuart Merrill,* 1927.

Métromanie, La (1738): See *Piron, Alexis.*

Michaux, Henri: (1899-) This Belgian-born poet and painter, a major figure among present-day writers, shows, to a certain degree, the influence of Lautréamont (q.v.) and, more particularly, of the Surrealists. His writings before the Second World War include *Ecuador* (1929) and *Un Barbare en Asie* (1932)—poems which serve as a document of his voyages to the Far East and South America—as well as *Voyage en Grande Carabagne* (1936), typical of his works dealing with imaginary trips. His fantasies, in effect, are not so much a refuge from reality as they are a weapon against it. Obsessed by the hostile forces that surround modern man, in *Plume* (1937), the name of the main protagonist, he symbolically suggests that man, tossed about by daily circumstances, is like a fragile feather in the wind. The cruelties of life and of the present world Michaux refuses to accept, and in *Épreuves, Exorcismes* (1945), written during the War, he protests against them in his soberly humorous exorcisms. These prose poems, like most of his others, mark him as a remarkable poet and reveal a new poetic style. His words take on the value of "exorcism," while expressing the chaos of his inner world. Other collections in the same vein written during this latter period include *L'Espace du Dedans* (1944), *Liberté* *d'action* (1947), and *Face aux Verrous* (1954).

Rene Bertelé, *Henri Michaux*, 1946.

Michel, Jean: (? -1502) His version of the *Passion* (*c.* 1486), a re-working of that of Greban (q.v.), with its tendency to secularize, became the most celebrated, and was officially adopted by the *Confrérie de la Passion* (q.v.).

Petit de Julleville, *Les Mystères*, 1880.

Michel Auclair (1922): See *Vildrac, Charles*.

Michelet, Jules: (1798-1874) Greatest of all French romantic historians, this scholar began his career as a professor of history, first at the *Collège* Sainte-Barbe, then at the *École Normale Supérieure*, and finally, at the *Collège de France* (q.v.), where he attracted to his lectures large audiences. In 1830, he was put in charge of the historical section at the *Archives Nationales,* and a few years later he began his *Histoire de France* (1843-1867), which was to be his *magnum opus,* but which he was never to complete. This work, the composition of which consists of three parts, includes 6 volumes on the Middle Ages (1833-1843), followed by *L'Histoire de la Révolution française* (1847-1853), and terminated in 11 volumes by the intervening period of the *Renaissance et Temps modernes* (1855-67). Much like Hugo (q.v.), Michelet aims to resurrect, rather than simply describe, the past. To achieve this end, he is aided by qualities of erudition and imagination which he applies to events, personalities, and institutions. Leaning on scrupulous documentation, he lends life and movement to the facts by the use of an imaginative and poetic style. Showing the influence of geography upon history, he reconstructs the history of France as though it were a living human being, as he traces the various stages and multiple factors in its development. His chapter on *Jeanne d'Arc,* a veritable monograph, is a case in point; she becomes the symbol and soul of medieval France. His final idealization of the *people,* whom he championed against the Monarchy and the Church, and his passionate enthusiasm for the Revolution reveal, in the last stages of the work, a conception of history that is at once a lyrical evocation, a vision, and, at times, an hallucination. Other works of his, dealing with non-historical subjects, include *L'Oiseau* (1856), *L'Insecte* (1857), *La Mer* (1861) and *La Montagne* (1868).

G. Monod, *La Vie et la Pensée de J. Michelet*, 1924; D. Halévy, *J. Michelet*, 1928.

Michel Pauper (1870): See *Becque*.

Micromegas (1752): See *Voltaire*.

miracle: A medieval play which portrays the miraculous intervention of the Virgin Mary in human events, usually to save the repentant sinners. Often, too, it is based on the life of a saint. The two prominent examples of the thirteenth century are the *Miracle* or *Jeu de saint Nicolas* (q.v.) by Jean Bodel (q.v.) and the *Miracle de Théophile* (q.v.) by Rutebeuf (q.v.). [It is important to note that, although in English literary scholarship a distinction is not often made between the *miracle* and *mystère* (q.v.), in French scholarship the two types are clearly distinguished.] Cf. *Miracles de Notre Dame.*

Miracles de Notre Dame: Forming a kind of cycle consisting of some forty plays of the fourteenth century, the authorship of which is unknown, these *miracles* (q.v.) were all composed in octosyllabic lines rhyming in pairs. Written for a *puy* (q.v.), probably located in Paris, which organized dramatic productions for the feast-day celebrations of saints or in honor of the Virgin, they brought to the public subjects it already had been familiar with.

The denoument of each of these miracles was the intervention of the Virgin, who appeared carried by angels, and who returned to Heaven. The chief value of these plays is sociological rather than literary; they throw light on the manners and customs of the age, reflecting as they do all the social classes and milieux. Some of the better-known ones are *Berthe, femme du roi Pepin, Robert le Diable* and *la Conversion de Clovis.* In the fifteenth century the miracles gave way to the *mystères* (q.v.).

G. Paris and Ulysse Robert, *Les Miracles de Nostre Dame,* 1876-1893.
Miracle de Théophile: Written by Rutebeuf (q.v.) toward the latter part of the thirteenth century, this short Faustian *miracle* (q.v.) of some 700 lines relates how Théophile, despoiled of his wealth by a bishop, renounces God and makes a pact with the Devil in order to have his possessions restored to him. Seven years later, however, having grown repentant, Théophile recovers his soul through the intercession of the Virgin.
Mirbeau, Octave: (1850-1917) This writer continues in his novels and plays the naturalistic tradition. In addition to his biographical novels, his fiction includes *Le Jardin des supplices* (1899), terrifying in its sadism, and the naturalistic *Le Journal d'une femme de chambre* (1900). His plays, directed against the exploitation of the laborer by dishonest politicians, as in *Les Mauvais Bergers* (1897), or against the business ethics of financiers, as in *Les Affaires sont les affaires* (1903), are bitter in tone and protest.

M. Revon, *Octave Mirbeau; son œuvre,* 1934.
Misanthrope, Le: Written in 1666 by Molière (q.v.), this play, a *comédie de caractère* (q.v.) and regarded as the most perfect example of "high comedy," is essentially a psychological study of human nature. Alceste,

the main protagonist, is obsessed with the ideal of honesty and truth, hating insincerity and hypocrisy. He always expresses himself with candor, thus alienating whomever he meets. Uncompromising, and refusing to adopt the easy-going diplomacy of his friend Philinte, he finds life in society unbearable. Yet, ironically enough, he is helplessly in love with Célimène, a coquettish woman whose character and principles represent the antithesis of what he stands for. When, at last, Célimène's flirtatious relationships with three young noblemen become known to him, Alceste, though overcome with grief and jealousy, makes Célimène a final offer of marriage provided she consent to give up society and follow him into his "desert." When she refuses, he decides to leave the city and spend the rest of his life in solitude.
Misérable, Les: Except for the long historical digressions dealing with the Battle of Waterloo and the Revolution of July 30, this massive novel, part of which was begun in the early 'Forties and which was finally published by Victor Hugo (q.v.) in 1862, is replete with social and humanitarian theses. Set in France, the action, which takes place from about 1815 to 1835, centers around the sufferings and struggles of Jean Valjean, a victim of the injustices of society. For having stolen a piece of bread out of pity for his sister's starving children, he is thrown into prison. Because he makes several attempts to escape, his sentence is lengthened to nineteen years. When finally free, he steals the silverware of Bishop Myriel, whom he has befriended and who now charitably declares to the police that he had presented the ware to Valjean as a gift. The Bishop adds to this gift his silver candlesticks. This act changes the whole life of Jean Valjean who, under the name of M. Madeleine,

213

henceforth prospers. Later, as mayor of his city, he sets free the unfortunate Fantine, forced into a life of degradation to support her child Cosette. Although Valjean at first manages to evade the detective Javert, who has recognized him, he is returned to prison when, to save an innocent man, he admits his true identity. Escaping again, he rescues little Cosette who, since the death of her mother, has been living with the cruel Thenardiers. When, years later, Cosette falls in love with Marius, Valjean arranges the marriage and provides for her future. Being misjudged, however, by Marius, Valjean leaves Cosette. When Marius discovers that he owes his life to Valjean, he rushes, together with Cosette, to the dying Valjean. Into the loosely woven plot of this novel, Hugo injects the idea of pity for the social outcasts, the weak and the suffering.

Mistral, Frédéric: (1830-1914) See *Provencal* (literature).

Mithridate (1673): See *Racine*.

Mois, Les (1779): See *Roucher*.

Molière (pseud. of **Jean-Baptiste Poquelin**): (1622-1673) The greatest writer of comedies in France, he was drawn to the theater from his early childhood, when he would go to the Hôtel de Bourgogne (q.v.) or to the Pont Neuf in Paris in order to see the farces presented by traveling players. Instead of becoming, like his father, bedmaker, upholsterer and furnisher (*tapissier et valet de chambre*) at court, in 1643 he decided to form, with Madeleine Béjart, his mistress and business partner, the *Illustre Théâtre* (1643-1645). Not discouraged by the failure of this venture, he left Paris with his troupe and toured the provinces for more than twelve years (1645-1658). During this period he not only profited as an astute observer of the laboratory of life, studying the different types of society—nobles, bourgeois and peasants—which he en-

countered, but also launched his own dramatic career, after first producing adaptations of the Italian farces, with two comedies, *L'Étourdi* (1655) and *Le Dépit amoureux* (1656), characterized by intrigue and complicated situations. Upon his return to Paris in 1658, he presented at the Louvre, in the presence of Louis XIV, his farce *Le Docteur amoureux*. As a result, he was given permission to use, jointly with the Italian players, the Petit-Bourbon stage, and his company was given the privilege of being called the "troupe de Monsieur." On this stage he produced the following year *Les Précieuses ridicules* (1659). Essentially a satire on preciosity (q.v.), this play inaugurated in France the *comédie de mœurs* (q.v.) while invoking the rule of *le bon sens* and of naturalness. More than thirty plays—some in prose, some in verse—were to follow this dramatic triumph before Molière was to breathe his last; most were produced at the Palais Royal theater, where in 1661 he permanently established himself after the Petit-Bourbon had been demolished. Molière's rising fame, following the success of *Les Précieuses ridicules,* kindled the flame of jealousy among his rivals, resulting in an attack against *L'École des Femmes* (1622; q.v.). This play, the first example of "high comedy," is based on observation of reality and depicts a psychological study; followed by *La Critique de l'École des Femmes* (1663), written as a reply to his adversaries, it represents the essence of his art and his conception of comedy. Molière afforded his enemies further opportunities for attack against him when, in 1662, he married Armande Béjart—believed to be either the sister or the daughter of his former mistress—and, later, when he wrote *Tartuffe* (1664; q.v.). This play, and *Don Juan* (1665), to a lesser extent, offended the Church. Dramatically speaking, however, *Tartuffe* ushered in the *comédie de caractère* (q.v.); it was to be followed by such other masterpieces as *Le Misanthrope* (1666; q.v.), *L'Avare* (1668) and *Les Femmes savantes* (1672). Molière's health, now undermined by overwork—he combined the functions of author, director and actor—and affected by his personal chagrins and struggles, had deteriorated. His dramatic career came to an end while acting the leading role in the fourth performance of *Le Malade imaginaire* (1673); he was stricken with a hemorrhage of the lungs, and a few hours later died in his home. Notable among his other plays are *L'École des maris* (1661), *Le Médecin malgré lui* (1666), *Amphitryon* (1668), *Georges Dandin* (1668) and *Le Bourgeois gentilhomme* (1670; q.v.)—a combination of comedy of character, comedy of manners, farce and ballet. The last-named play is one of his most popular.

Strictly speaking, there is no evolution in Molière's theater; in such a late play as *Les Fourberies de Scapin* (1671) he still turns to farce, in which, incidentally, he excelled. Moreover, while his plays can be classified, somewhat arbitrarily, according to their predominant characteristics, they represent a combination of different types ranging from ballet-comedy to high comedy. His originality, however, is in the creation of the comedy of manners and character. In the latter two *genres* he reveals his genius. A careful observer of the different classes of his contemporary society, and one of the keenest students of human nature, he depicts, in their complexities, universal characters and types. When this study reveals man's foibles and obsessions deforming nature, it results in satire; the spectacle of human ugliness becomes transfigured, however, by the playwright's laughter and verve of style. Molière's philosophy, in the end, is that of *le bon sens*, of reason, moderation and proportion. His influence is evident not only in later French comedy, but indeed in subsequent European drama generally. It is a fitting tribute to this master that the Comédie-Française (q.v.) theater is often called today the "House of Molière."

E. Rigal, *Molière*, 1908; G. Michaut, *La Jeunesse de Molière* (1922), *Les Débuts de Molière à Paris* (1923), *Les Luttes de Molière* (1925); J. Palmer, *Molière*, 1930; A. Tilley, *Molière*, 1936; D. Mornet, *Molière, l'homme et l'œuvre*, 1943; W. G. Moore, *Molière: A New Criticism*, 1949; R. Jasinski, *Le Misanthrope de Molière*, 1951.

Monde où l'on s'ennuie, Le (1881): See *Pailleron*.

Monluc, Blaise de: (1502-1577) Much like Caesar, in his *Commentaires* which were published posthumously in 1592, he relates with sincerity and veracity the campaigns he waged over a period of fifty years under Francis I, Henry II and Charles IX. His defense of Sienna (1555) and the part he played in the war against the Huguenots are noteworthy as examples of patriotic zeal and religious devotion.

P. Courteault, *Blaise de Monluc, historien*, 1907.

Monnier, Henri: (1805-1877) This Parisian-born novelist and actor launched his career as a clever illustrator. His drawings and book illustrations brought him immediate attention. His talent as a caricaturist, inspired by the types he encountered as an employee in the ministry, attained its zenith in his creation of Joseph Prudhomme, a smug bourgeois, first seen in his *Scènes populaires dessinées à la plume* (1830)—written the same year as Hugo's (q.v.) *Hernani*—who reappears in two other series of "scènes populaires" (1835-1852) and, more fully developed, in *Mémoires* *de M. Joseph Prudhomme* (1857). The impersonality of Monnier's descriptive sketches of bourgeois character and of social classes, his capacity for observation and his gift for humor and irony, make of him one of the most authentic precursors of realism (q.v.). His influence is especially felt in such writers as Murger and Champfleury (qq.v.).

P. Martino, *Le Roman Réaliste sous le Second Empire*, 1913; E. Melcher, *Life and Times of Henri Monnier*, 1951.

Monsieur Bergeret à Paris (1901): See *France, Anatole.*

Monsieur Ouine (1946): See *Bernanos.*

Montaigne, Michel Eyquem de: (1533-1592) Born at the château Montaigne, he was taught to speak Latin even before French, and later was trained in law. He became counsellor of the *Cour des aides* at Périgueux in 1554, succeeding his father, and three years later was attached to the Parlement of Bordeaux. In 1571, two years after the death of his father, whom he cherished, he retired to private life, to devote himself, in his "librairie," to study and reading, jotting down his commentaries which were to serve as the groundwork of his *Essais* (q.v.), the first two books of which were to appear in 1580. The period, one of civil and religious war in France between the Catholics and Protestants, was hardly favorable for meditation, although it nurtured his philosophy of conservative skepticism. While travelling through Germany, Switzerland and Italy (1580-1581), Montaigne received news of his election as Mayor of Bordeaux; he performed the duties of this position until 1585, when he once again retired to private seclusion, to resume his *Essais*. In 1588, in a revised edition of his *Essais*, Montaigne included a third book, which gave further evidence of his intentions to make himself the object of his study. The posthumous edition of 1595 was supervised by Marie de Gournay, called, because of her devotion to him, his *fille d'alliance*.

In portraying himself in the *Essais*, Montaigne wished to portray all humanity, a preoccupation, moreover, that was to influence classicism. He also wished to show man's contradictions and incapability of arriving at metaphysical truth. Although an epicurean and skeptic—the spiritual ancestor of such French writers as Voltaire, Renan, and Anatole France (qq.v.) —Montaigne believed that life is good. His motto "Que sais-je?" reflected his doubting spirit, his distaste for fanaticism of any kind and his ideal of absolute toleration. His final faith in man, despite man's limitations, is characteristic of the Renaissance (q.v.).

Contributing by the charm, spontaneous wit and conversational tone of his style, to the development of the French language, Montaigne, in his *Essais*, also created in France a literary genre in which writers of other lands, Bacon in England, Emerson in America, were later to distinguish themselves. Other writings of his are his translation of Raymond Sébond's *Theologia naturalis* (1569) and the *Journal de voyage*, first published in 1774 by Meusnier de Querlon.

F. Strowski, *Montaigne*, 1906; J. Plattard, *Montaigne et son temps*, 1933; D. Frame, *Montaigne's Discovery of Man*, 1955.

Montchrétien, Antoine de: (1575-1621) His sententious writings serve as a marked contrast to his life, which was full of adventure and which included a series of duels forcing him subsequently to flee to England. *L'Ecossaise ou Marie Stuart* (1605), a tragedy based on the life of Mary Stuart, so pleased James I that he effected Montchrétien's return to France. Dealing with a modern subject and therefore not conforming to the humanistic precepts of the

Pléiade (q.v.), it nevertheless foreshadows Racine (q.v.) by its lyrical qualities, elegant diction and harmonious imagery. His second best play is *Aman ou la vanité* (1601), whose biblical subject is once again seen in Racine's (q.v.) *Esther.* Besides *David* (1601), also of biblical inspiration, he wrote *Sophonisbe* (1596), *Hector* (1603) and *Les Lacènes* (1601), tragedies that draw their inspiration from Italy and antiquity.

R. Lebègue, *La Tragedie française de la Renaissance,* 1944.

Montesquieu, Charles-Louis de Secondat, Baron de la Brède et de: (1689-1775) The first of the great "philosophes" (q.v.) of the eighteenth century, this writer, born near Bordeaux, was of a family of ancient nobility. Magistrate, at the age of twenty-five, in the Bordeaux *Parlement,* two years later he was its president. His first great work, *Les Lettres Persanes* (1721), reflects, however, interests other than legal. Catching the public's interest and curiosity by their exotic setting, these letters, presumably written by Rica and Usbek, two Persians travelling through Europe and more particularly France, to their friends in Persia, contain a satirical portrait of French life and of its social, religious and political conditions under the Regency. To satisfy his scientific bent of mind, and to get a first-hand knowledge of political institutions, in which he was particularly interested, Montesquieu later embarked on a trip (1728-1731) through Europe, spending the last two years in England. His admiration for England's institutions and political system led to the publication of *Considérations sur les causes de la grandeur des Romains et de leur décadence* (1734). This study of Roman history, viewed generally as a preparation for his *L'Esprit des Lois* (1748), reflects his wish to illustrate his theories born of his recent experiences and his attempt to demonstrate how a democracy perishes as a result of tyranny. Unlike Bossuet (q.v.), moreover, who explains history as the result of Divine Providence, he approaches history here as a scientist, seeking out its moral and physical causes. The same method and approach appear even more evident in *L'Esprit des Lois* (1748), his major work. From an investigation into the varieties of laws and customs, Montesquieu derives the important principle of relativity; governments and laws, he shows, differ as a result of a kind of historical determinism—varying geographical, climatic, racial, economic and moral conditions. His preference, however, is, as has already been indicated, for the English constitutional monarchy, which, according to him, guarantees freedom and liberty; in the same spirit, he recommends a separation of powers that was later to be embodied as part of the American Constitution.

Pointing the way to justice, expressing ideas of tolerance and political liberty, Montesquieu represents one of the most important contributions to eighteenth-century thought. As a political scientist, he exercised an influence that was to inspire, if not the French Revolution itself, at least the French Constitution during its first period. Included among his later works are: *Défense de L'Esprit des Lois* (1751) and *Arsace et Isménie* (1754), which is reminiscent of Fénelon's (q.v.) *Télémaque.*

H. Barckhausen, *Montesquieu, ses idées et ses œuvres,* 1907; J. Dedieu, *Montesquieu, l'homme et l'œuvre,* 1943; P. Barrière, *Montesquieu,* 1946.

Montherlant, Henri de: (1893-   ) This gifted writer, a determined individualist devoted to the ideal of personal achievement—an ideal so aristocratic and egotistic in its point of view that it regards with contempt the coddling of the inept—personifies the cynicism of the post-War generation. His works reflect a romantic hedonism: Such novels as *Le Songe* (1922), *Les Olympiques* (1924), *Chant funèbre pour les morts de Verdun* (1924) and *Les Bestiaires* (1926), exalt physical pleasures, sports—bullfighting in particular (together with the personal risks and dangers involved)—violence and war. In other novels—*Les Célibataires* (1934) and *Les Jeunes Filles* (1936)—Montherlant manifests an attitude of cynicism or brutality toward relationships between the sexes. More recently, his characteristic philosophy has been incorporated in such plays as *Le Maître de Santiago* (1946) and *Malatesta* (1948), which reflect at the same time strong Spanish influences, and in *Port-Royal* (1954).

E. Nériel, *Henry de Montherlant: son œuvre*, 1936.

Montpensier, Anne-Marie-Louise d'Orléans, Mlle. de: (1627-1693) This writer of memoirs, also called *"la Grande Mademoiselle"* because of her height, took an active part in the Fronde. In her salon (q.v.), the *portrait,* much like the *maxim,* was cultivated as a genre; many of these are to be found in her *Mémoires* (1652; 1688-1693).

moralité: A dramatic work of the Middle Ages, the characters of which were allegorical, and the purpose of which was to present, in a constructively moralizing though not necessarily religious tone, rules of conduct. Most of the 65 extant *moralités* were written in the second half of the fifteenth and the first half of the sixteenth centuries. *La Condamnation de Banquet* by Nicolas de la Chesnaye serves as an example of a *moralité* that attacks a vice, that of gluttony. Another representative example—this one, more edifying—is *Bien avisé, Mal avisé.*

Morand, Paul: (1898-   ) Cosmopoli-tanism distinguishes all the novels and travel books—a veritable documentary of the Post-War era—of this diplomat and globe-trotter. An English setting, with portraits of three young women, marks *Tendre Stocks* (1921). The "Jazz Age" and the travelling frenzy following the First World War are evident in *Ouvert la nuit* (1921), *Fermé la nuit* (1923) and *L'Europe galante* (1925) —collections of short stories dealing with the large hotels and night clubs of various cities. Among the cities and countries written about are Barcelona, Constantinople, Rome, Paris, London, Budapest, Berlin and Scandinavia. *Champions du Monde* (1930) is a novel dealing with America; *New York* (1929) is an account of his sojourn there.

Moréas, Jean (pseud. of Iannis Papadiamantopoulos): (1856-1910) Born in Athens, this poet, who had transplanted himself to Paris, came first under the influence of Baudelaire and Verlaine (qq.v.). His publication in 1886 of a manifesto and of a collection of verse, *Les Cantilènes,* established him as one of the leaders of Symbolism (q.v.). The excesses of the Symbolistic School, however, with its obscurity, together with Moréas' nostalgia for his native country and his predilection for ancient forms, caused him to renew the Greco-Latin tradition and to break with Symbolism. In 1891 he founded, together with others, the *École Romane* (q.v.), which restored the classical traditional forms, the use of mythological references and even archaic words. In his last collections, notably *Les Stances* (1899-1920), in several volumes, a sobriety of emotion with a clear, disciplined, classical form are evident.

E. Raynaud, *Jean Moréas et les Stances,* 1929; R. Niklaus, *Jean Moréas, poète lyrique,* 1936.

Morellet, André, Abbé: (1727-1819) Serving the cause of the philosophical movement during the eighteenth century, he wrote for the *Encyclopédie* (q.v.) articles on theology and metaphysics. In addition, he is the author of several polemical and witty works, including *Petit Écrit sur une matière intéressante: la Tolérance* (1756) and *Les Manuels des Inquisiteurs* (1762). His interesting *Mémoires sur le XVIIIe siècle et la Révolution* appeared posthumously in 1822.

A. Mazure, *Les Idées de l'abbé Morellet*, 1910.

Mort d'Agrippine, La (1653): See *Cyrano de Bergerac, Savinien.*

Mort de César, La (1635): See *Scudéry, Georges de.*

Motteville, Françoise Bertaut, Mme. de: (1621-1689) In her *Mémoires pour servir à l'histoire d'Anne d'Autriche* (1643-1666), which were published in 1723, she offers valuable historical and biographical information. In them she deals with the period of the Fronde during the Regency of Anne of Austria, whose *confidante* and *femme de chambre* she was (1643-1666). Written with wit, they reveal a sense of impartiality and exactitude.

Mouches, Les (1943): See *Sartre.*

Mur, Le (1939): See *Sartre.*

Murger, Henri: (1822-1861) Son of a *concierge*, this Parisian-born writer, together with Champfleury (q.v.) and Courbet, was a member of the "Bohème" (q.v.) group he was to make famous in his *Scènes de la Vie de Bohème* (1851). The latter novel, depicting the poverty that added pathos to the loves of a group living in the Latin Quarter, appeared first as a serial in "Le Corsaire," and then as a play, prepared in collaboration with Barrière (q.v.), under the title of *La Vie de Bohème* (1849); later still, Puccini made it famous as the opera *La Bohème*. The novel, based on the author's own personal life, and embodying his own emotions as well as reflecting his sympathy with his char-

acters, contains many romantic qualities. These qualities, however, are blended with descriptions of sordid detail in Bohemian life and in contemporary society. An additional realistic feature is the simple style that characterizes the entire work. However, although Murger tried to be a realist, he is essentially a lyrical poet, as can be seen especially in his romantic poetry. Other works of his include *Scènes de la Vie de Jeunesse* (1851) and *Le Pays latin* (1852).

Georges Montorgueil, *Henri Murger, romancier de la bohème,* 1928.

Musset, Alfred de: (1810-1857) Endowed with a generous amount of common sense and humor, this Parisian-born poet, dramatist, and prose writer, became the "enfant terrible" of the Romantics. Having inherited the traditions of a noble family, and having obtained a good classical education, he could not adopt slavishly the doctrines of the romantic movement even though he was favored by acceptance, as its youngest member, into the *Cénacle* headed by Victor Hugo (q.v.), and even though his first collection, *Contes d'Espagne et d'Italie* (1830), seemed to emulate the metrical virtuosity and local color of Hugo's *Orientales*. As a matter of fact, in *Un Spectacle dans un fauteuil* (1832), written after the unsuccessful performance of *La Nuit vénitienne* (1830), Musset rails at the cult of exoticism. He soon broke with the dogmatic tenets of Romanticism, claiming his independence, and condemning, moreover, the social mission claimed for the romantic writer. In *Rolla* (1833), however, a poem in which he transcribes, as one gone astray because of lost faith, his own disquietude, and in *Les Caprices de Marianne* (1833) and *Fantasio* (1833), published in the *Revue des deux mondes* as a result of his decision following his initial dramatic failure never again to write plays for the stage, he reflects different facets of his own character. In his plays he reveals these facets through the depiction of the male characters. The romantic element becomes most evident in his "Nuits" (1835-1837), consisting of "La Nuit de Mai," "La Nuit de Décembre," "La Nuit d'Août," and "La Nuit d'Octobre," as well as in other poems of love, including "Souvenir" (1841), inspired by his disastrous love affair with George Sand (q.v.), which had come to an end in 1835. Suffering (as suggested by the metaphor in "La Nuit de Mai" of the pelican's rending his breast to feed the young) here becomes the main source of that which ennobles; poetry, as conceived by Musset, is a means of expressing sincerely and spontaneously, without the Hugolian artifices or perfection of technique, those emotions that are inspired by love. As the poet of love, moreover, Musset was the poet of youth, to which he appealed. Despite, however, the subjective, lyrical, and melancholy note of his poems, and in spite of his *La Confession d'un enfant du siècle* (1836), a semi-autobiographical novel covering his relationship with George Sand and analyzing the *mal du siècle* (q.v.) of the generation born in the beginning of the nineteenth century, he was able to satirize, in the series of letters called *Lettres de Dupuis et Cotonet* (1836-1837), the sentimental extravagances of the romantics. He could also write with verve and wit, or with restrained emotion, a number of *Contes et Nouvelles* (see *Short Story*), including *L'Histoire d'un merle blanc* (1842), *Mimi Pinson* (1843), and the historical *La Mouche* (1853). His plays, too, which were written, after the failure of *La Nuit vénitienne*, to be read and not staged, were sad (*Les Caprices de Marianne*, 1833), gay (*Le Chandelier*, 1835), and comical (*Il ne faut*

jurer de rien, 1836), in turn. These plays, most of which were written in prose, and some of which, like *On ne badine pas avec l'amour* (1834) and *On ne saurait penser à tout* (1849), were representative of his dramatized "proverbes," were, unlike those of Hugo, lacking in *couleur locale*, grandiloquent speeches, melodrama, and antithesis. On the other hand, they contain vagueness of locality and characterization, elements of Shakespearean fantasy, unrestricted freedom in their shifting of scenes as they unfold, much like a classical play, the inner drama of the characters. The central theme, in all these plays, is, in any event, that of love, and the principal hero is Musset himself as the young male protagonists reveal his inner emotions and traits.

Despite the comparatively early deterioration of his precocious youth and the late recognition of his dramatic talents, brought about by Mme. Allan-Despréaux, a French actress who happened to discover unusual qualities in his *Un caprice* (1847), played at St. Petersburg in Russian, Musset was, of all the Romantic writers, the most gifted dramatist. His theater, insubordinate to Romantic doctrine, possessed the same kind of lyrical quality that made his poetry the most sincere expression of love. Musset's theater is much alive today and, next to Molière and Racine (qq.v.), the foremost item in the repertoire of the Comédie-Française (q.v.).

P. Gastinel, *Le Lyrisme de Musset,* 1933; Ph. Van Tieghem, *Musset, l'homme et l'œuvre,* 1945.

mystère: Flourishing in the fifteenth century, this type of play, presented in celebration of some great event, was based, unlike the *miracle* (q.v.), almost always on the Old Testament, the New Testament and the Acts of the Apostles. Of the sixty extant *mystères,* all of which were written between 1400-1548, the best known, popularly referred to as *mystères de la Passion* (q.v.), are those which recount the entire life of Christ. They are tremendous in length, and their performances, which lasted several days, took place in the public square. A kind of pageant, appealing to the eye as well as to the mind, with elaborate costuming and complicated mechanical devices, the stage setting consisted of juxtaposed booths or *mansions* representing the chief places of the action, which was completely lacking in unity of time or place. The use of simultaneous scenes allowed for and often required hundreds of actors, who were recruited from the guilds and particularly from the *Confrérie de la Passion* (q.v.). The unrelated comic interludes, given for relief, which were often sacrilegious, resulted in the decree of Parliament, Nov. 17, 1548, which suppressed further performance of the *mystère*. The classical French theater, developing in this period, no doubt also played an important role in the almost total disappearance of this genre. (See *Tragedy*).

Petit de Julleville, *Les Mystères,* 1880; G. Cohen, *Histoire de la mise en scène dans le théâtre religieux français du moyen âge,* 1906; *Le Théâtre en France au moyen âge,* I, 1928.

Mystère de la charité de Jeanne d'Arc (1910): See *Péguy*.

Mystère de la Passion: A dramatic representation of the sufferings of Christ. The most notable versions are those by Arnould Greban (*c.* 1450) and Jean Michel (*c.* 1486; qq.v.).

Mystères de Paris, Les (1842-1843): See *Sue, Eugène.*

N

Nadja (1928): See *Breton, André.*
Nana (1880): See *Zola.*
Nanine (1749): See *Voltaire.*
Natchez, Les: The manuscript volume of this long epic narrative, although written by Chateaubriand (q.v.) in 1796 when he was still in England, was first published in 1826. Interwoven with the subject of the massacre of the French colony of the Natchez in 1727 is the story of René's love (cf. *Atala* and *René*) for Celuta, niece of Chactas, whom he weds through gratitude. Celuta undergoes a conflict between her love for René and her duty to her tribe when René is suspected of having betrayed her tribe. This romance is based in part on the author's experiences in America.

NATURALISM: This term designates a literary movement in France which continues and exaggerates the characteristics of realism (q.v.). Often confused with realism, with which it has much in common, it nevertheless represents a different artistic doctrine.

This doctrine, as formulated by Zola, is essentially scientific. It reflects many of the theories that the nineteenth century—which made of science a fetish—had absorbed. Essentially, these theories were mechanistic, materialistic and deterministic; they shed light on the laws that govern the world and on man's relationship to society. Some of these theories, adopted by Balzac (q.v.) and applied in the composition of his *Comédie Humaine* (1830-1850), made man dependent on and the product of his environment. Taine (q.v.), the first perhaps to see naturalistic features in Balzac, himself added to the naturalistic formula the theory of *race, milieu,* and *moment,* which he developed in *La Fontaine et ses Fables* (1860) and in *Histoire de la littérature anglaise* (1864) and which he applied to literature itself. If, moreover, Comte's (q.v.) positivism and Lamarck's theory of transmission of acquired characteristics took firm root in Balzac's mind, Taine's hereditary determinism—not to mention Claude Bernard's ideas of experimental medicine, expressed in his *Introduction à l'étude de la médecine expérimentale* (1865)—were to exert an equally important influence on Zola (q.v.), the leader of naturalism.

Zola's scientific pretensions are already seen in *Thérèse Raquin* (1867), his first "naturalistic" novel, a study of remorse as an organic disorder; he defines in the preface to the second edition to this book, moreover, his conception of the scientific novel as a surgical autopsy. A doctrinaire of naturalism, he further formulated his theories in such works as *Le Roman Expérimental* (1880) and *Les Romanciers naturalistes* (1881). In his zeal to show, however, that the naturalistic movement did not originate with himself, but with such literary forebears as Diderot, Balzac, Stendhal, Flaubert and the Goncourt brothers (qq.v.), Zola overlooked important differences that separated him from the novelists he pointed to. These writers, apart from their individual differences, did not have an aesthetics consonant with Zola's scientific criteria or views applied to literature. Flaubert's *Madame Bovary* (1857), the "realistic" novel *par excellence,* and considered the Bible of naturalism, aims primarily at artistic perfection and an impassive attitude in its depiction of truth. This attitude, "scientific" only in its impersonality, observation and method of precise documentation, is not, however, based on any scientific theory; not seeking to prove anything, it does not consciously seek out types or examples that deviate from the normal. Flaubert's interest, unlike that of Zola, whose theories inevitably led him to depict especially the lower classes and their abnormalities, was in the average middle class, the *bourgeois.*

The Goncourts, on the other hand, despite their "impressionistic" style that suggests an emphasis on artistic form which is absent in Zola, and in spite of their wish to be disassociated from any literary school, do have closer affinities with naturalism. *Germinie Lacerteux* (1864)—the *Hernani* (q.v.) of naturalism—reveals a clinical approach that led directly to the previously mentioned *Thérèse Raquin,* in the preface of which, incidentally, Zola referred to himself as a naturalist. This novel, moreover, is a good example of the Goncourts' predilection for the pathological which they sought in quest of the "document humain." Their interest in the lower classes and use of documentation reflect a "scientific" conception of the world which does not, however, lean on a specific or dogmatic theory.

The scientific experimentation that Zola, applying his theories to literature, was to conduct in *Les Rougon-Macquart* (1871-1893), and that continues a tradition perhaps first anticipated in Diderot's (q.v.) *Le Neveu de Rameau* (written in 1762; pub. in 1821), was to be the crowning achievement of the naturalistic novel. Under the erroneous illusion that he could reconstruct human existence just as a scientist does a chemical substance, Zola attempted to perform in this huge series of 20 volumes a controlled experiment in which the effects of heredity and environment on five successive generations were to be carefully traced. Although he failed to win any new adherents to the scientific theories exemplified in this work, his scientific approach inspired others to concern themselves with proletarian subjects, with the sordid and the morbid, and to base their works on observation and careful documentation. Several of the novels by the Goncourts, Daudet and Huysmans are good examples.

Although, moreover, the naturalistic movement never represented a completely unified or inflexible doctrine, it gained greater cohesion with Zola's successful *L'Assommoir* (1877). His reputation as a novelist now established, Zola attracted a number of followers—including Paul Alexis, Henri Céard, Huysmans, Léon Hennique and Maupassant (qq.v.)—to his house at Médan, near Paris. Three years later, in 1880, this group published, as a joint enterprise, *Soirées de Médan,* a collection of short stories inspired by the War of 1870 of which it gave a very depressing picture. But the differences existing among these writers, and the lack of a common philosophy, made their disintegration as a group—under the aegis of Zola—inevitable.

In *A Rebours* (1884) Huysmans entered upon a new stage of development that betrayed the principles of naturalism as conceived by Zola. Maupassant, whose literary career was really launched in *Soirées de Médan,* possessed an aesthetics that was more closely related to Flaubert. Daudet (q.v.), naturalistic in such novels as *Jack* (1876), *Le Nabab* (1877) and *Sapho* (1884), had too poetic a soul not to wish to escape from its doctrine. Not guided by a deterministic philosophy and, what is more, confusing their own cynicism and pessimism with the scabrous situations investigated by Zola, these and other novelists failed to understand the latter's basic motivation—which was optimistic in its wish to morally regenerate society and cure its ills. It was not long before they deserted Zola; in 1885 they joined other dissident naturalists at Edmond de Goncourt's studio at Auteuil. The *coup de grace* was given the naturalistic novel when, two years later, five of this group— J. H. Rosny *aîné,* Lucien Descaves, Paul Bonnetain, Paul Margueritte and Gustave Guiches—issued, probably at the instigation of E. de Goncourt and Daudet, a protest against the scandalous nature of Zola's *La Terre* (1887).

In the theater, too, the naturalistic doctrine was to be formulated by Zola in such works as *Le Naturalisme au théâtre* (1881) and *Nos Auteurs dramatiques* (1880). Despite the successful dramatic adaptation of his *L'Assommoir* (1879), the high priest of naturalism, convinced that the theater was lagging behind the novel, urged—again in the name of scientific truth—that the dramatist seek out the social causes and hereditary aspects that explain the life of each individual. The plays at the Théâtre-Libre (1887-1896; q.v.), which assured the triumph of naturalism on the stage, were to incorporate many of Zola's theories, while profiting at the same time from the new dramatic technique seen in Becque's (q.v.) *Les Corbeaux* (1882) as well as from the naturalistic novel.

Although, around 1890, the "bankruptcy of science" was declared and naturalism as a movement had disintegrated, many of its aspects and traditions still survive. Replaced by such tendencies as *Naturisme* (q.v.)

and *Populism* (q.v.), many of its features are still alive today as is evident in the plays, novels and short stories by the existentialist Sartre (q.v.).

P. Martino, *Le Naturalisme français*, 4° ed., 1945; Ph. Van Tieghem, *Petite Histoire des grandes Doctrines Littéraires en France*, 1950; P. Cogny, *Le Naturalisme*, 1953; F. W. J. Hemmings, "Origin of the terms *naturalisme*, *naturaliste*," *French Studies*, VIII (1954), 109-121; E. Henriot, *Réalistes et Naturalistes*, 1954; R. Dumesnil, *Le Réalisme et le Naturalisme*, 1955.

Naturisme: Advocated by Saint-Georges de Bouhélier, who in 1897 created the term, its aim was to interpret life on the stage in such a way that the humble and drab would become spiritualized in a poetic manner. In *Le Carnaval des enfants* (1910), Saint-Georges de Bouhélier has love triumph in a sordid incident which takes place in a laundry shop. The ideal that he set for his theater, though never fully realized, attempted to reconcile the naturalistic with the poetic; it suggests an analogous movement, that of the *Théâtre du Peuple* (q.v.). In poetry, it manifested itself by a reaction against both the impassivity of the Parnassians and the subtleties of Symbolism. Seeking inspiration in the wholesome aspects of life, its principal themes are love, life, nature, work and heroism. Although not exponents of this doctrine, Anna de Noailles and Francis Jammes (qq.v.) show its effects.

Nausée, La (1938): See *Sartre*.

Nerval, Gérard de (pseud. of **Gérard Labrunie**): (1808-1855) This Parisian-born writer, whose life ended in madness and suicide, began his career as one of the young Romanticists who gathered around Hugo (q.v.). Especially influenced by German culture, he translated *Faust* (1828). He was also attracted, as can be seen by his story *La Main de Gloire* (1832), to the fantastic in Hoffmann. The violent passion he conceived for the actress Jennie Colon, together with the news of her death in 1842, left him in a state of mind from which he never fully recovered. The travel sketches in *Le Voyage en Orient* (1843-1851), written after a visit to the Orient, contain much sentimental revery and an intense interest in the different esoteric religions he encountered during the course of this journey. His obsessions, following a third attack of insanity, become more evident in *Les Illuminés* (1852), studies on various "seers." The mysterious incantations evoked in his collection of sonnets entitled *Les Chimères* (1853) are followed by the fantastic short stories in *Les Filles du feu* (1854), which include the semi-autobiographical masterpiece *Sylvie* (1853) and which blend reality with the happy memories of his past. The tortured moments of his lucidity are also reflected in *Aurélia* (1853), a kind of fantastic spiritual autobiography. The mirage of ideal Woman, personified in Adrienne, Sylvie, and Aurélia, as seen in his previous works, is dispelled in *Pandora* (1853-54), his last prose work, in which she becomes the instrument of all human misfortune. Previously identifying himself with Faust, here Nerval compares himself to the most pitiable of men. It is noteworthy that to all his imaginative creations he gives an air of naturalness through a simple and unaffected style; the dream-like play of his fancy makes him a precursor of the Symbolists (see *Symbolism*), and, to a certain degree, of the Surrealists.

A. Marie, *Gérard de Nerval, le poète et l'homme*, 1914; A. Béguin, *Gérard de Nerval*, 1945; J. Richer, *G. de Nerval et les doctrines ésotériques*, 1947; S. A. Rhodes, *Gérard de Nerval, poet, traveler, dreamer*, 1951.

Neveu de Rameau, Le (wr. 1762): See *Diderot*.

Nicomède (1651): See *Corneille, Pierre*.

Nisard, Désiré: (1806-1888) Professor at the *École Normale Supérieure* and literary critic, he condemns romanticism in his *Manifeste contre la Littérature facile* (1833). Setting up dogmatic criteria, he judges French literature, in his *Histoire de la Littérature française* (1844-1849), in accordance to the degree that it conforms to the "esprit français," which he defines as the expression of general verities in language that is perfect. According to him, only Classicism (q.v.) marks the triumph of the French national genius.

Nizan, Paul: (1905-1940) This Marxist philosopher and novelist was killed during the Second World War. In his novel *Antoine Bloyé* (1933) he wanted to show the disintegration of his protaganist at the hands of a bourgeois society. In addition to *Le Cheval de Troie* (1935), he wrote *La Conspiration* (1938), which was to have been the first volume of a series in which the formation of young intellectuals in a bourgeois society was to be studied. He was a good friend of Sartre (q.v.), who, in his *Situations* I, 1947, wrote an article about him.

Noailles, Anna, comtesse de: (1876-1933) Daughter of a Rumanian Prince and of a Greek mother, wife of a French nobleman, this poet spent most of her life in Paris, where she was born. Her early collections, *Le Cœur innombrable* (1901) and *L'Ombre des jours* (1902), are lyrical in tone and express sensuous love of love, beauty, youth and nature. In later volumes of verse, such as *Les Vivants et les Morts* (1913), *Les Forces éternelles* (1920), and *L'Honneur de souffrir* (1927), this self-declared pagan reveals a disillusionment with life and an awareness of death. Melancholy replaces her former *élans* of joy and passion.

Her poetry, autobiographical in inspiration, continues, in the treatment of the above themes, the traditions of *Romanticism* (q.v.); her technique is traditional, but the form of her verse is classical; the use of intuitive imagery she learned from Baudelaire (q.v.). In 1921 she was awarded the *Grand Prix de Littérature*.

Jean Larnac, *Comtesse de Noailles; sa vie, son œuvre*, 1931.

Noces d'argent, Les (1917): See *Géraldy, Paul*.

Nodier, Charles: (1780-1844) Known especially for his short stories (see *Short Story*), this writer, born in Besançon, also wrote poems, novels, and criticism. In his early novels, including *Les Proscrits* (1802) and *Le Peintre de Salzbourg* (1803), he expresses a *Wertherean* melancholy. Somewhat later, he emphasizes, as in *Jean Sbogar* (1818) and *Smarra* (1820), the "frantic" in his presentation of mysterious bandits and of the macabre. His masterpiece, however, is *Trilby* (1822), a fantastic tale concerning a Scottish maiden haunted by a goblin. In other stories, including *La Fée aux miettes* (1832) and *Le Chien de Brisquet* (1844), he indulges in an escape from reality into the world of imagination and revery. Thus he enlarged the literary horizon of the Romantic writers; in addition, through his *salon* at the Arsenal, to which he had been named librarian in 1824, and where several writers, including Hugo (q.v.), met regularly, he served as a leader of the first romantic *cenacle*.

M. Salomon, *Ch. Nodier et le groupe romantique*, 1908.

Nœud de vipères, Le (1932): See *Mauriac*.

Notre-Dame de Paris: This historical novel, which combines many of the features of Romanticism, was published by Victor Hugo (q.v.) in 1831. It is epic in its evocation of fifteenth-century Paris, where the scene of action is laid, with its bourgeois, students, bohemians, and beggars. Thanks to Hugo's powers of imagination, the gothic cathedral of Paris, the real heroine of the book, is vividly described in extraordinary vocabulary and magnificent images. The story itself, full of violence, deals with the archdeacon Claude Frollo's passion for the beautiful Esmeralda, whom he attempts to kidnap with the aid of his devoted Quasimodo, the hunchback bell ringer of Notre Dame. Esmeralda is rescued, however, by Captain Phébus, and Quasimodo is punished. Frollo later stabs Phébus, but Esmeralda is accused of his murder and condemned to death. Before being led to the scaffold, however, she is sentenced to do penance on the great porch of Notre Dame. But when Quasimodo sees her on the porch, he carries her to sanctuary within the church. When the mob in fury begins to sack the Cathedral, he defends it by hurling stones upon them. Frollo, in the meantime, succeeds in making off with Esmeralda. Since she refuses, however, to yield to him, he turns her over to the authorities. When Quasimodo sees Frollo laughing as Esmeralda is being put to death, he throws him from the heights of Notre Dame to his death. Quasimodo himself will die near the dead body of Esmeralda. This novel, like the plays of Hugo, makes use of antithesis in the physically hideous but beautiful soul of Quasimodo and in the contrast to him that Frollo offers.

Nourritures terrestres (1897): See *Gide.*

nouvelle: See *Short Story.*

Nouvelle Héloïse, La: Written in 1761 by Rousseau (q.v.), this epistolary novel, one of the most important of the eighteenth century, is the forerunner, by its emphasis for the first time on individualism, lyricism, excessive sentimentality and descriptions of nature, of the Romantic novel. It relates, amid the idyllic setting of the Swiss Alps, the difficulties and sufferings experienced, because of class distinctions, by two young lovers. Julie, the daughter of an aristocratic family, and Saint-Preux, her young but poor tutor, are in love with each other, but cannot marry because of the opposition of Julie's family. Acceding, though reluctantly, to the wishes of her father, the Baron d'Etanges, Julie weds the much older, but wealthy, M. de Wolmar. Though accepting her obligations as a dutiful wife, after several years of marriage she confesses her feelings for Saint-Preux to her husband. By an act of generosity, M. de Wolmar invites Saint-Preux, who all the while has been travelling in the hope of forgetting Julie, to live with them, as a proof of his confidence in them both. This confidence is justified. The moral impasse of the relationship is resolved, however, when Julie, after saving one of her children from drowning, contracts pleurisy and dies. This novel, it may be added, is a transposition of Rousseau's own frustrated love for Mme. d'Houdetot; moreover, it contains Rousseau's social, political, religious and pedagogical ideas.

Nouvelle Idole, La (1899): See *Curel.*

Nouvelles Méditations poétiques (1823): See *Lamartine.*

NOVEL: Unlike the English word *novel* which acquired its modern meaning only at the end of the eighteenth century, the equivalent French word *roman* has a much longer history and originally meant a long narrative poem in the vernacular, the *lingua romana.* The *roman* differed from the older epic (*chanson de geste;* q.v.) in the fact that it was written to be read rather than recited by a minstrel, and it seems to have been the result both of the classical revival of the twelfth century and of a hoax which the Englishman Gaufrei de Monmouth perpetrated in his *Historia Regum Bri-*

tanniæ where he apparently invented the essential themes of the Arthurian romance. (This is Bédier's stand in the matter, but the earlier belief was that the Arthurian romances sprang from the lays of wandering Breton minstrels.) In a broad sense, this new genre of the *roman*, which soon contaminated the *chanson de geste* itself, represented the triumph of fiction over history in the narrative. The best writer in the new genre was Chrétien de Troyes (q.v.). His romances are plotless and episodic, but, in the other narrative poems of the same period like Thomas' *Tristan et Iseut* (q.v.), of which only fragments have survived, the central theme of love was producing a semblance of plot. From its inception, the *roman* tended to be a long narrative of love and adventure.

Beginning in the thirteenth century, as medieval civilization declined and as bourgeois society began to emerge in the cities, a process of de-rhyming commenced in the *chanson de geste* and in the *roman*. By the time of the French renaissance, the *roman*, which had meanwhile absorbed the *chanson de geste*, had definitely become a prose rather than a poetic genre. The *chantefable* of *Aucassin et Nicolette* (13th cent.; q.v.), written partly in verse and partly in prose, may be considered a dividing line between poetry and prose and between originality and imitation. In the two centuries which followed, prose versions of the poetic narrative proliferated but practically no original prose *romans* were composed. However, the French can be said to have rediscovered the genre of the long prose fictional narrative, apparently unknown to classical literature but already practiced in Greek by the Sophists of Alexandria during the first centuries of our era. There are only tenuous connections between the Greek novel and the French

novel: the *roman* of *Jourdain de Blaives* (13th cent.) is the story of *Apollonius of Tyre*, known throughout medieval Europe and presumably of Alexandrian origin, and Gautier d'Arras' *Éracle* (12th cent.) and the anonymous *Floire et Blancheflor* (13th cent.) are thought to have a similar source; but the only Alexandrian novels extant today did not enter French literature until the sixteenth century when Amyot (q.v.) translated *Theagenes and Chariclea* and *Daphnis and Chloe*.

Despite the degeneration of the *roman* in the late Middle Ages, the art of fiction made great progress in the specialized area of the short story when the French, in the *Cent Nouvelles Nouvelles* (1462) and in Marguerite de Navarre's *Heptaméron* (1559; q.v.), set about imitating Boccaccio who, in turn, owed a debt to the French *fabliaux* (q.v.) of the Middle Ages. In the *nouvelle* (q.v.) the narrative form was perfected, even to the point of stereotype, and a spirit of realism entered prose fiction; but the new spirit did not permeate the novel, and Antoine de la Sale's (q.v.) *Le Petit Jehan de Saintré* (about 1456), often called the first modern novel, remained an isolated example of this new realism in the novel proper.

In the sixteenth century, Spain, rather than France, became the center of novelistic development. At the moment when Spanish chivalry was going out in one final burst of glory, Montalvo wrote his *Amadís de Gaula* (1508), reviving on a lavish scale the Arthurian romance with what were ostensibly a new set of characters (actually the Portuguese seem to have invented them somewhat earlier) and a mild approximation of a central plot. Francis I so admired this novel during his captivity in Spain that he caused it to be translated into French in 1540. Spain produced many other new novels in the same vein, and with Montemayor's *Diana* (1559), rediscovered the pastoral novel which had already had a sporadic existence among the Italian humanists, culminating in Sannazaro's *Arcadia* in 1504. For modern palates, Spain's greatest discovery was the *picaresco* novel whose rogue heroes swung the novel back to realism, as Spain of the golden age began to decline. In France of the same period there were only faint echoes of all this. The greatest novelist of the French sixteenth century was undoubtedly Rabelais (q.v.) who, despite his gift for vigorous narration, really subverted the novel for philosophical purposes. His choice of the genre as a vehicle attests to the popularity of the *roman* at this time.

Most historians of the French novel begin by saying, "First came *L'Astrée* (q.v.)." For the French, Honoré d'Urfé's (q.v.) interminable 5500-page pastoral, published from 1610 to 1627, is truly a beginning, but the originality of its author pales somewhat if we consider his debt to Sannazaro and to Montemayor. One of the most widely read and appreciated works of literature for nearly two centuries (even Boileau liked it), *L'Astrée* interests us today only as a very illuminating document on the special mentality of the *précieuses* (q.v.) of the Hôtel de Rambouillet (q.v.) whom Molière (q.v.) tried to laugh out of existence. The other interminable novels of this century, Georges and Madeleine de Scudéry's (qq.v.) *Artamène ou le Grand Cyrus* (1649) and their *Clélie* (1654), Gomberville's (q.v.) *Polexandre* (1632), and La Calprenède's (q.v.) *Cléopâtre* (1647) and his *Pharamond* (1661), to mention only a few titles, purport to take their subjects from classical antiquity (*Pharamond* is an exception since it is Merovingian), but in no other respect, except in their futile attempts to present a "hero" in the

Plutarchian sense, do they show any affinity to the reigning classical literature over which Boileau (q.v.) presides. It is little wonder that Boileau and the classical school of writers condemned the novel as a genre, as they were authorized, moreover, to do by the lack of a precedent for the novel in classical antiquity. Nevertheless, the novel has made great progress since the Middle Ages: the leisurely, episodic plots are beginning to acquire more shape and, although characters do not exist as individuals, there are rudiments of psychological analysis of which the notorious example is the Carte de Tendre (q.v.) in *Clélie*. Parallel to this aristocratic literature and in derision of it, there sprang up a new bourgeois realistic novel inspired by the Spanish picaresque novel: Sorel's (q.v.) *Francion* (1622), Scarron's (q.v.) *Roman comique* (1651), and Furetière's (q.v.) *Roman bourgeois* (1666). In his realistic parody, *Le Berger extravagant* (1627), Sorel tried to demolish the pastoral novel as Cervantes in Spain had demolished the romance of chivalry. For the first time, in these bourgeois novels, strong type characters appear in recognizably real settings, but the modern reader still finds considerable arbitrariness in plot and a coarse kind of humor which prevents the novelist from taking his function seriously.

A modern statistician tells us that the French wrote 1250 novels between 1600 and 1699; among these only one is today counted as a great novel, Madame de la Fayette's (q.v.) *La Princesse de Clèves* (1678). Its uniqueness is explained by the fact that its author was the one writer of real talent imbued with the classical spirit of the age who did not disdain the novel. Its originality consists in putting reality inside rather than outside the characters whose fate is determined not by some fortuitous combination of adventures but by their own nature, just as in the tragedies of Racine (q.v.). Madame de la Fayette was the first novelist to arrive at this fundamental principle of the French novel. By reading her earlier novel *Zayde* (1670), situated in a conventionalized Spain and replete with shipwrecks, battles, assumed identities and an elementary love triangle, we realize the sudden spurt which the novel has taken with *La Princesse de Clèves*.

Madame de la Fayette did not succeed in removing the stigma which the classicists had attached to novel-writing, and her immediate influence on the destinies of the novel was quite unexpected: by inaugurating the convention of pretending that her novel was authentic memoirs, she precipitated an avalanche of *annales, histoires secrètes* and *mémoires* which momentarily replaced the *roman* in popular favor. Although some of these writings were authentic, most of them were spurious, as was the case with the innumerable tomes of memoirs which the Sieur de Sandras, the author of the *Mémoires de M. d'Artagnan* (1700), transposed from his own picaresque existence. In reality, these memorialists were advancing the art of the novel by bringing it closer to real life. Even in classical literature, there was a great curiosity about contemporary people culminating in the *Caractères* of La Bruyère (q.v.) whose vignettes are really incipient novels.

Any reader of the novels of the eighteenth century is impressed with the effort which novelists make to authenticate their novels and to set up what, in modern terminology, we would call the illusion of reality: the Abbé Prévost (q.v.) writes memoirs, Marivaux (q.v.) pretends to find his allegedly autobiographical manuscript in a closet, and, imitating Richardson, who invented the English novel at this time, Rousseau (q.v.) composes a correspondence.

Two novelists in this century fall outside this trend and make no real contribution to the technique of the novel. The first is Lesage (q.v.) whose *Diable boiteux* (1707) and whose *Gil Blas* (1715; q.v.) resurrect the Spanish picaresque novel, complete with an artificial Spanish setting which hides his didactic purpose. The second is Voltaire (q.v.) who, as a practicing classicist, disdains the novel and yet, like Fénelon and Montesquieu (qq.v.), uses it to his own purposes with extraordinary effectiveness but also to the detriment of the novel as a work of the imagination. It is significant that these authors look upon the novel as a disconnected series of adventures, frequently incredible, all interwoven according to the system of *romans à tiroirs* whereby each new character interrupts the action to tell his own story. The method is as old as the novel itself; in spite of Madame de la Fayette's shining example, the novelist of the eighteenth century has little notion of structural unity. The interminable novels of the Abbé Prévost, *Mémoires d'un homme de qualité* (1728), *Cléveland* (1731), *Le Doyen de Killerine* (1735), are just as episodic but they are radically different in the seriousness with which their author attempts to express himself and his way of life. One chapter of the *Mémoires d'un homme de qualité* survives, the story of *Manon Lescaut* (published in volume 7 in 1731; q.v.) whose simplicity of form is both an accident and a crowning achievement; the most powerful novel of the century, it is full of the strongest elementary human emotions; in short, it is *the* novel of passion, which has never been surpassed. If the sudden progress in form was accidental, the novel is now concentrating on character in a realistic setting; even where form is lacking, as in Marivaux's unfinished *Vie de Marianne*

(1731) and *Paysan parvenu* (1735), there is progress towards plot simplification and great advance in psychological analysis.

The ultimate mistake of the eighteenth century was to try to improve on *Manon Lescaut*. Rousseau attempted to do so in his epistolary novel, *Julie ou la Nouvelle Héloïse* (1761; q.v.), which is so lyrically passionate that it is insipid for modern tastes. Pretending to describe real life in the manner of his contemporaries, Rousseau puts his uncritical characters in such incongruous situations to motivate his philosophy that he deflects the novel from its realistic course and opens up the dikes to romanticism (q.v.). It was he who spawned Bernardin de Saint-Pierre's (q.v.) idyllic *Paul et Virginie* (1787) and Chateaubriand's (q.v.) sentimental *Atala* (1801) with its Rousseauistic Indians, not to mention George Sand's (q.v.) novels in the next century. In this waning eighteenth century, we moderns prefer another much more subtle novel, full of perversions and cynicism, written in an anti-Rousseau spirit although mimicking him in the epistolary structure: Choderlos de Laclos' (q.v.) *Liaisons dangereuses* (1782), a carefully constructed novel which makes us regret that the eighteenth century, so close to us in spirit, did not perfect the form of the novel much sooner. To complete the catalogue of eighteenth-century novels, the realistic character-study novel *Le Neveu de Rameau* by Diderot (q.v.) must be mentioned although it is outside the developmental history of the novel since it remained in manuscript until 1823.

The period which extends from the fall of the Bastille to the publication of Lamartine's (q.v.) poems in 1820 is a literary doldrum. Although such a statement would cause the average Frenchman to wince because of Chateaubriand,

the fact remains that this incomparable master of French rhetoric concentrated on prose epics like *Les Martyrs* and *Les Natchez* (qq.v.) which are unreadable today. His lyrical defense of Catholicism, the *Génie du Christianisme* (q.v.), imitating Bernardin de Saint-Pierre's *Études de la nature,* is as puerile as its model. Like Bernardin, who was only once a novelist when he detached his *Paul et Virginie* from the *Études,* Chateaubriand was only once a novelist when he detached his *Atala* and his *René* (1805; q.v.) from his *Génie du Christianisme.* These short novels of Bernardin and Chateaubriand satisfy modern taste only because of the succinctness of the narration; otherwise their lack of psychological pentration causes the novel to retrogress. The practicing, but mediocre novelists of this period, Mesdames de Charrière, de Souza, de Duras, de Krüdner and Madame Cottin, imitating Rousseau, keep the novel, however feebly, in the tradition of eighteenth-century psychological analysis. Among these sentimental females, the greatest feminist of them all, Madame de Staël (q.v.), deserves mention for her *Delphine* (1803) and her *Corinne* (1807), although they are very boring novels; like her contemporaries, she knew only one novelistic theme, unrequited love. In defense of Chateaubriand's short confessional *René* or Senancour's (q.v.) much longer *Obermann* (1804) there is little to say, for it is questionable whether this lyrical attitude towards oneself did anything but retard the development of the novel. In this introverted literature, one little masterpiece, neglected in its day, stands out: *Adolphe* (1816) by Constant (q.v.), another story of unrequited love, in which the autobiographical confession is transmuted into real novelistic coin, that is to say objective psychological analysis.

The French romantics themselves never wrote any great novels and yet they made three major contributions to the development of the modern French novel. In spite of high-lighting adventure once more, as practicing dramatists they had a sense of plot which, although it left much to be desired, at least established the principle that a novel must go somewhere and that episodes must lead to other episodes; until their arrival on the scene, unity in the novel, as we have noted, had been largely accidental. Secondly, the romantics, escaping imaginatively into other countries or into other centuries, developed techniques of description which had hitherto been a neglected art in the novel. The third contribution of the romantics, a necessary corollary of the second, was a renewal of the French language by giving it a verbal density and a rhythm which it had seldom known before, even in the hands of Rousseau, Bernardin de Saint-Pierre and Chateaubriand, who had already begun to forge a new language. However, it must be pointed out that, in the novel, the French romantics were largely imitators of Walter Scott, who had already shaped the English historical novel and that, furthermore, they confused the true spirit of Scott with the degenerate Gothic novels of Hugh Walpole and Ann Radcliffe, specializing in the supernatural. Nothing is more crudely fantastic, for example, than young Hugo's (q.v.) *Han d'Islande* (1823), and something of the same spirit of exaggeration distorts his later *Notre-Dame de Paris* (1831; q.v.) which is one of the finest examples of romantic prose even though an unsatisfactory novel. Even when Hugo attempts a social novel years later in *Les Misérables* (1862; q.v.), there is no technical progress. For want of a great romantic historical novel, critics fall back on Vigny's (q.v.)

Cinq-Mars (1826), which is a colorless but a more faithful imitation of Scott, and on Mérimée's (q.v.) cynical *Chronique de Charles IX* (1829), which marks the beginnings of a good short story (q.v.) writer but not of a true novelist. His *Colomba* (1840; q.v.) and his *Carmen* (1847), really post-romantic in date, are superior to the *Chronique* and should be counted among the best romantic novels. Another, but irregular, romantic was the feminist George Sand (q.v.) who inaugurated a romantic novel of manners in *Indiana* (1832) and *Valentine* (1832) which would be more significant if she had been more definitely a predecessor of Balzac. In 1844, with *Les Trois Mousquetaires,* Dumas (q.v.) opened his novel factory which turned out reams of historical novels for bourgeois newspaper readers.

It is noteworthy that Hugo did not sign his early novels and that the romantic school did not include the novel in its various manifestoes. After 1830, a critical year of social revolution, the situation changed abruptly and the novel became the principal literary genre. In keeping with the bourgeois spirit of the age, the new novel was realistic and its inventor was the bourgeois Balzac (q.v.). Trained in the romantic historical novel in its worst forms and in its best (after doing romantic pot-boilers he managed one of the best historical novels in *Les Chouans* [1829]), he knew the value of plot and description but, unlike the romantics, he also knew the value of character; he struck upon the original device of making description reveal character and he returned to the primordial principle of French classical tragedy by making the characters responsible for the plot. Balzac differed radically from his contemporaries in his ability to project himself outward and to imagine a "human comedy" acted by characters very different from himself. In his enormous fictional cosmos, of which the high spots are *Eugénie Grandet* (1833; q.v.), *Le Père Goriot* (1834; q.v.), *La Cousine Bette* (1846), but in which there are few low spots, he has revealed himself to be the most prodigious creator of all French literature.

Stendhal (q.v.), another realist with his roots deep in the romantic period, worked independently of Balzac but parallel to him, and so disdained the reading public of his day that about his only admirer was Balzac himself. Taine (q.v.) and his generation discovered him, and the twentieth century, with some injustice to Balzac, has acclaimed him as the greatest French novelist. He was not a creator like Balzac and a large part of his work aborted, but he still produced two masterpieces, *Le Rouge et le noir* (1830; q.v.) and *La Chartreuse de Parme* (1839; q.v.). Introspective and therefore essentially romantic in his technique, he was nevertheless lucid in his romantic revolt, being steeped in the materialistic philosophy of the eighteenth century. There is a realistic cosmos in Stendhal as well as in Balzac, complete with décor and strongly drawn minor characters, but he goes further than Balzac by concentrating on a few major introspective characters whom he probes more deeply than any author had ever done before him.

Despite a very conscious novelistic technique, there was always something slightly arbitrary in Stendhal and Balzac, and the latter, in particular, did not hesitate before a romantic *coup de théâtre;* in the next literary generation, Flaubert (q.v.) with his *Madame Bovary* (1857; q.v.) carried the novel to a pinnacle of artistic perfection, constructing his novel according to a subtly articulated system of cause and effect which is the literary representation of the philosophy of determinism. Flaubert's novel is a modern tragedy which inspires pity but which does not grip the reader, for the novelist is aloof from his creation according to the principle of objectivity which his disciple, Maupassant (q.v.), defined a few years later in the preface to *Pierre et Jean* (1888). Beneath the surface of *Madame Bovary* there was a lot of experimentation with the technique of the novel in an attempt to transcend the visual limitations of realism; in his one other great novel, *L'Éducation sentimentale* (1869), Flaubert thought he had solved the ultimate problem of psychological realism by writing about an ordinary person to whom nothing happened. This novel, rated a failure in its day, leads straight to Proust.

The immediate successors of Flaubert saw nothing in him but his determinism; with assistance from Taine, the school of the naturalists exaggerated this principle to demonstrate some of the poorly digested scientific principles of the age. Zola (q.v.) was the leader. Like his contemporaries, the Goncourt (q.v.) brothers, he described with documented precision the various social groups which make up a modern industrial society. He was a pioneer in what modern psychologists term "group psychology" and, as a writer, he had certain gifts for epic description which relate him to Hugo, whom he admired; but his characters, taken individually, are rudimentary and he is not above enlivening his plots with distinctly romantic situations, such as the final chapters of his masterpiece, *Germinal* (1885; q.v.). In point of view of technique, the novel retrogressed in Zola's hands. Nevertheless, he was a prolific writer and, in sheer weight of printed pages, dominated the last half of the century. Zola and his contemporaries, especially Maupassant and Daudet (q.v.), practiced their novelistic trade so methodically that it was evident that the realistic-psychological novel, which had taken seven hundred years to reach this stage, had become a kind of stereotype. The subsequent history of the novel in France is an attempt to break this stalemate.

In the first place, although Zola was and is anathema to many, there were post-naturalists like Hermant and Mirbeau (qq.v.) and even today there is a minor school of populists (see *Populism*), with Thérive, Dabit, Jean Prévost, who continue the fundamental Zola. Jules Romains (q.v.), though an innovator in novelistic technique, owes to Zola both his realism and his personal system of unanimism (q.v.), an original approach to the problems of group psychology. Zola has also had a curious effect on the destinies of the French novel because, imitating the *Comédie humaine* (q.v.) of Balzac, he linked all his novels together in the series of *Les Rougon-Macquart* (q.v.). Since then, no major novelist has felt that he has fulfilled his promise unless he has written a *roman-fleuve* (q.v.), which ironically takes the French novel back to its very beginnings in *L'Astrée*. While some of these, like Proust's (q.v.) work or Romain Rolland's (q.v.) *Jean-Christophe* (1904), are very different in spirit from Zola, others, like Duhamel's (q.v.) *Chronique des Pasquier* (1933) or Jules Romains' *Les Hommes de bonne volonté* (1932), are firmly in the tradition of the realistic-naturalistic novel, while Martin du Gard's (q.v.) *Les Thibault* (1922) is both in and out of it, depending on which half one considers. In a broader sense, the tradition of the realistic-psychological novel with clear-cut dramatic action is far from dead and still dominates the scene because it is so distinctly in keeping with the spirit of the French nation. With due reservation for some specific novels, one may say that Duhamel, Romains, Estaunié, Arland, Mauriac, Maurois, Radiguet, Lacretelle, Schlumberger (qq.v.), Chateaubriant, Boylesve (q.v.), Montherlant, Aragon (qq.v.), Troyat write traditional novels from a structural point of view, although, otherwise, they may make strange bedfellows.

The immediate successors of Zola denounced naturalism (q.v.) without attempting to invent a new kind of novel. In his attack on Taine in *Le Disciple* (1889) and in his other thesis novels aimed at the positivistic way of life, Bourget (q.v.) claimed to renew the tradition of the "psychological" novel. In a chastened classical style, Anatole France (q.v.) revived the philosophical novel of the eighteenth century in *Thaïs* (1890) and the *Ile des Pingouins* (1908). More recently André Gide (q.v.), in his search for *authenticité*, resurrected the epistolary novel, the diary-novel and the first-person narrative, so distinctly eighteenth century in flavor. Soon new schools of novelists sprang up with the avowed purpose of breaking the grip of the Paris-dominated bourgeois realistic novel; the result was exoticism (Loti, Morand, Larbaud [qq.v.], later Saint-Exupéry [q.v.] in a new form) and regionalism (Chamson, q.v., Genevoix, Pourrat), frequently, though not always, expressed in traditional forms. But the real assault on the realistic novel came from the symbolists who, in their disdain for commercial literature, appropriated the novel as a vehicle for their ideas with utter disregard for the prescribed formulas. The result was esoteric novels like Huysmans' (q.v.) *A Rebours* (1884), Gourmont's (q.v.) *Sixtine* (1890), Barrès' (q.v.) *Le Jardin de Bérénice* (1891). The most significant manifestation was Proust whose *A la Recherche du temps perdu* (1913), despite its grandiose esoteric structure, is essentially a plotless, static novel, negating the traditional French novel. Proust was such a powerful innovator that he was both a beginning and an end. A great poet, who forged a new metaphorical style, and a subtle aesthetician, who invented a whole subjective theory of the novel to validate his work, Proust is also a great French novelist in the classical tradition because he consciously brought to their logical conclusion the psychological investigations of Stendhal and Flaubert by probing into the subconscious.

With his doctrine of the uniqueness of the work of art, Proust crystallized an aesthetic principle which dominated the French novel until the Second World War. If the novel is to be the expression of the novelist's unique genius, there are no rules and the more spontaneous the work is, the greater it is. From this principle come the ungoverned novels of Green (q.v.) or that masterpiece of subconscious subtlety, Bernanos' (q.v.) *Monsieur Ouine* (1943), acclaimed by the initiate as the greatest novel since Proust. From this principle come the *précieux* novels of Giraudoux (q.v.), Alain-Fournier's (q.v.) adolescent dream in *Le Grand Meaulnes* (1913), the sensual world of Colette (q.v.), the poetic peasant world of Giono (q.v.), the supernatural peasant world of Bosco (q.v.). From it stem the innumerable experiments in the technique of the novel, one of the most interesting of which is Gide's *Les Faux-Monnayeurs* (1926; q.v.). Not from it but parallel to it comes the philosophy of André Gide, who preached the supremacy of the individual. French literature between the two world wars, dominated by the novel, is the literature of the individual.

This variegated pattern of individuality and introspection, of deep psychological subtlety, became so general that it too developed into a manner of stereotype. When that happens in literature there is inevitably a reaction. The reaction began in the 1930's when André Malraux (q.v.) invented the French novel of violence. The characters of his novels like *La Condition humaine* (1933) live and act only in the present and achieve themselves only through violent action. After the Second World War, the French welcomed the American novel of violence of Hemingway and Faulkner partly because the American characters were more primitive and hence more violent and partly because the Americans were experimenting with a technique of spontaneous writing which showed great artistry. This influence is apparent in the amorphous hero of Camus' (q.v.) *L'Étranger* (1942) or in the somewhat artificial imitation of the simultaneous technique in the second volume of Sartre's (q.v.) *Les Chemins de la liberté* (1945). In a broader sense this reaction to the literature of the individual resulted in the philosophy of existentialism (q.v.) and in the doctrine of *engaged* literature according to which the writer must have a social or a philosophical mission. The best artistic realization of this doctrine so far has been Camus' *La Peste* (1947), a symbolical novel which remains on the human level but which fails to move the reader as much as a great novel should. If there is any constant in the history of the novel it is the rule that the novelist must first of all create living characters who appeal to the imagination of the solitary reader as he settles down with his book. A novel written for any other purpose may be geared to a passing fashion and will perish with it. There is no telling where the French novel will go next; but its fecundity and attempts at renewal in the last hundred years augur a continued development just as, in the deviation from the fundamental principle of character analysis, it contains the seeds of its own destruction. André Le Breton, *Le Roman au dix-septième siècle*, 1890; . . . *au dix-huitième siècle*, 1898; . . . *au dix-neuvième siècle (avant Balzac)*, 1901; F. M. Warren, *A History of the Novel Previous to the Seventeenth Century*, 1895; George Saintsbury, *A History of the French Novel*, 2 vol., 1917-1919; F. C. Green, *French Novelists, Manners and Ideas*, 1929, and *French Novelists from the Revolution to Proust*, 1931; Maurice Magendie, *Le Roman français au dix-septième siècle*, 1932; Anon., *Problèmes du roman*, 1943; Georges Poulet, *Études sur le temps humain*, 2 vol., 1949-1952; Claude-Edmonde Magny, *Histoire du roman français depuis 1918*, 1950; Martin Turnell, *The Novel in France*, 1950; Janet M. Ferrier, *Forerunners of the French Novel*, 1954; Germaine Brée and Margaret Guiton, *An Age of Fiction*, 1957.

DOUGLAS W. ALDEN

Nuits, Les (1835-1837): See *Musset*.
Nuit vénitienne, La (1830): See *Musset*.

O

Obermann (1804): See *Sénancour*.
Observations sur la langue française (1672): See *Ménage, Gilles*.
Observations sur le Cid (1637): See *Scudéry, Georges de*.
Ode: A lyrical poem, whose main characteristic, despite its many different themes, was that it was to be sung or accompanied by some musical instrument as in the Greek tradition. In France it was introduced by the *Pléiade* (q.v.). Ronsard (q.v.), chief of the *Pléiade*, imitated especially the Pindaric and Horatian odes, and devised a variety of rhythms with a scholarly and studied arrangement of the strophes. Its rhymes were reduced in the seventeenth century by Malherbe (q.v.), who gave it a rather harsh and oratorical force. The *heroic* ode, whose theme and style are noble and elevated, had a somewhat checkered career: Boileau (q.v.) had no success with it, but in the 18th century J.-B. Rousseau (q.v.) wrote some fine religious and philosophical odes. The 19th century freed the ode from its classical conventions, and it was used greatly by Lamartine, C. Delavigne, and Hugo (qq.v.).
Odes et Ballades (1828): See *Hugo*.
Œdipe (1718): See *Voltaire*.
Olive L' (1549): See *Du Bellay*.
Ondine (1939): See *Giraudoux*.
On ne badine pas avec l'amour (1834): See *Musset*.
Opéra-Comique: Founded in the beginning of the eighteenth century, this theater produced at first *vaudevilles* (q.v.) and parodies—especially of plays presented at the *Opéra;* hence the name *Opéra-Comique*. Soon it presented the *opéra-comique*, a type of play with songs and music, derived from the *comédie à ariettes* (q.v.), that was being developed by the *théâtres de la foire* (q.v.). When, in 1762, the *Comédie Italienne* (q.v.) —which for a long time had been opposing the use of music by the

théâtres de la foire—merged with the *Opéra-Comique*, this genre, whose chief exponent was Charles-Simon Favart (1710-1792), was firmly established. The theater itself underwent many vicissitudes; today it is, like the *Comédie-Française*

(q.v.), subsidized by the government.

Orientales Les (1829): See *Hugo.*

Origines de la France contemporaine, Les (1875-1894): See *Taine.*

Origines de la langue française (1650): See *Ménage, Gilles.*

P

Pagnol, Marcel: (1895-   ) This dramatist, in *Les Marchands de gloire* (1925), satirizes those civilians who capitalized on the heroism of soldiers of the First World War. In *Topaze* (1928), the play that brought him especial renown, he draws, around the figure and career of a formerly honest and obscure professor, a social satire of political and financial customs dominated by venality. At about the same time he composed a trilogy containing the local color of Marseille, the city near which he was born, which includes *Marius* (1929), *Fanny* (1931), and *César* (1936), all of which were to become moving pictures, to which in the 'Thirties he turned his interest.

Other films which contributed to the enhancement of his reputation include *La Femme du boulanger, La Fille du puisatier, La Belle meunière,* and the trilogy based on Daudet's (q.v.) *Lettres de mon moulin.* His satires have wit and humor, and his characters, who express themselves in simple language, both amuse and move the spectator.

Louis Combaluzier, *Le Jardin de Pagnol,* 1937.

Pailleron, Édouard: (1834-1899) His reputation is based essentially on *Le*

Monde où l'on s'ennuie (1881), a play satirizing the salon society of the Third Republic. The affectation and snobbery of society women—calling to mind Molière's (q.v.) *Femmes Savantes*—of ambitious though talentless scholars, writers and politicians, are here berated and evoke well-bred laughter. Other plays include *L'Étincelle* (1879), *La Souris* (1887) and *Cabotins* (1894).

L. d'Almeida, *L'œuvre litt. de Pailleron,* 1888; A. Lelia-Paternostro, *Édouard Pailleron,* 1931.

Palais des Papes: See *Vilar, Jean.*

Palaprat, Jean: (1650-1721) See under *Brueys, David-Augustin de.*

Palissot, Charles: (1730-1814) An implacable enemy of the eighteenth century *philosophes* (q.v.) and of the general philosophic movement, this dramatist attacked Rousseau (q.v.) in his comedy *Le Cercle ou les Originaux* (1755). Diderot, especially, became the butt of his attacks in *Petites lettres sur de grands philosophes* (1757) and in *Les Philosophes* (1760). The last-named work —a satirical play containing elements of a Molièresque comedy of character and of social conditions as emphasized in Diderot's *drame bourgeois* (q.v.)—marks an important date in French dramatic history. Producing a literary storm reminiscent somewhat of the first performance of Hugo's (q.v.) *Hernani* (1830), it struck out against the ideas represented by the *philosophes.* D. Delafarge, *La vie et l'œuvre de Palissot,* 1912.

Pantagruel: A gigantic hero with an insatiable appetite who appears in the book (1532) of the same name (Book II), and whose birth, education and adventures Rabelais (q.v.) relates. Son of the equally gigantic Gargantua (q.v.), he is reduced to more human proportions in his adventures with Panurge (q.v.), his companion. His relationship with the latter, with whom he embarks on several journeys in order to consult the oracle of the *Dive Bouteille* (these journeys extend through Books III, IV and V), is a convivial one, and he becomes a genial sage.

Pantagruelism: A wholesome and serene cheerfulness, a Rabelaisian attitude reflected in *Pantagruel* (q.v.), whose humanistic philosophy stresses the enjoyment of those pleasures that life has to offer.

Panurge: One of the principal characters in Rabelais' (q.v.) *Pantagruel* (q.v.). Pantagruel is the friend to whom Panurge becomes attached as he undergoes his fantastic Odyssey to learn whether or not he should marry. "Valiant in speech and cowardly in action," he is cynicism personified. Although subject to the disease of "lack of money," he manages somehow, mostly through larceny, to obtain it when he needs it, which is often. The episode dealing with his sheep, in the course of which he succeeds in wreaking revenge on Dindenault, who insulted him, is especially popular and hilarious.

Paquebot Tenacity, Le (1920): See *Vildrac, Charles.*

Parallèles des Anciens et des Modernes (1688-1696): See *Perrault, Charles.*

Parents terribles, Les (1938): See *Cocteau.*

Parfaite Amie, La (1542): See *Héroët, Antoine.*

Paris, Gaston: (1839-1903) Professor at the *Collège de France* (q.v.), teacher of many eminent scholars, including Joseph Bédier (q.v.), he devoted himself especially to the study of philology. He founded *Romania,* a philological journal, and published etymological and other studies, including *Manuel d'ancien français* (1888), *La Poésie du Moyen Age* (1885) and *Poèmes et Légendes du Moyen Age* (1900).
J. Bédier, *Hommage à Gaston Paris,* 1904.

Parisienne, La (1885): See *Becque.*

Parnasse Contemporain, Le (1866; 1869; 1877): See *Parnassians.*

Parnassianism: See *Parnassians.*

Parnassians: Those poets represented in *Le Parnasse Contemporain* (1866, 1869, 1877), an anthology of poems published serially by Lemerre, were called Parnassians. Included among them are Leconte de Lisle (q.v.), recognized as the head of their "school," Hérédia (q.v.), who best personifies their ideal, Coppée, Sully-Prudhomme, Banville, Mendès (qq.v.), and such future dissidents as Verlaine and Mallarmé (qq.v.). Other poets, principally Gautier and Baudelaire (qq.v.), may be regarded as the main precursors of this "school."

Corresponding to Realism in the novel as propounded by Flaubert and the Goncourts (qq.v.), the Parnassian doctrine represents essentially—despite the individual differences among the poets listed—the cult of artistic perfection, emphasis on the plastic, erudition that evokes the different periods of history, and an aloofness or pseudo-impersonality that shows impatience with romantic egotism and imagination. Inspired by the objective and scientific attitude of precision that was

237

common to the Age, much of this poetry is descriptive as well as colorful. The Parnassian ideal was given orientation by several journals, including *La Revue fantaisiste* (1861), founded by Catulle Mendès, which reacted against romantic declamation, *La Revue du Progrès* (1863-64), which vaunted scientific poetry, and *L'Art* (1865-66), influenced by Leconte de Lisle.

P. Martino, *Parnasse et Symbolisme*, 1925; M. Souriau, *Histoire du Parnasse*, 1929; A. Thérive, *Le Parnasse*, 1929; A. Schaffer, *Parnassus in France*, 1929; *The Genres of Parnassian Poetry*, 1944.

Parny, Évariste-Désiré de: (1753-1814) Born at Reunion Island, off Africa, this poet foreshadows Lamartine (q.v.) by the sincerity of feeling expressed in his *Poésies érotiques* (1778-1784). After the Revolution, he wrote *La Guerre des Dieux* (1799), anti-religious poems that are licentious in tone.

R. Barquissau, *Les poètes créoles du 18ᵉ siècle*, 1949.

Paroles d'un croyant (1834): See *Lamennais*.

Pascal, Blaise: (1623-1662) Mathematician, physicist, philosopher, mystic and great prose writer, he showed from his early youth signs of precocity. At Clermont-Ferrand, where he was born, and later, in Paris, he was taught by his father, an Auvergnat magistrate who was very much interested in the sciences and who recognized his son's genius. At the age of twelve, Blaise discovered for himself the thirty-two geometrical principles; at sixteen he composed a treatise on conic sections; at eighteen he invented a calculating machine. His first introduction to Jansenism (q.v.), in 1646, came as a result of his father's having dislocated his hip; the Jansenist bonesetters, who spent much time in the Pascal home converted the whole household to their religion. Blaise, however, more interested still in his experiments in physics, proved (1648) Torricelli's theories of atmospheric pressure and wrote several treatises, including *Traité du vide* (*c.* 1651), *Traité de l'équilibre des liqueurs* and *Traité de la pesanteur de la masse de l'air*, the latter two being published in 1663. In 1654, after a spiritual crisis following a very close escape he had had in an accident on the Pont de Neuilly, he renounced science and turned to Port-Royal (q.v.), where his sister Jacqueline had become a nun, for religious guidance. Two years later, when urged to defend Antoine Arnauld (q.v.), accused by the Sorbonne of heresy, and Port-Royal, attacked by the Jesuits for its Jansenist views, he composed the *Lettres provinciales* (1656-1657). These eighteen letters, which range in tone from subtle to bitter irony, and then to vehement protest and indignation, have been compared by Voltaire (q.v.) to the best of Molière's (q.v.) comedies, and, as examples of prose, are regarded, because of their classical style, as the first work of genius. Bringing the religious controversy between the Jesuits and the Jansenists directly into the open, they defend, against the attacks of the former, the Jansenist conception of divine grace and pre-destination and criticize the Jesuits for their casuistry (q.v.) and for their over-indulgent conception of morality. The success of these letters, incidentally, has often been explained by the fact that at the time they were being written, Pascal's niece, who had been suffering from a fistula on the eye, had been miraculously cured at Port-Royal and that this miracle had become widely known. In any case, the rest of Pascal's short life was devoted to preparing an apology for the Christian religion that would, by its appeal to reason, convince the atheist and the unbeliever. Not completed during his lifetime, however, this work in prose, known as *Les Pensées*, consists of disjointed notes that have been assembled and arranged by different editors and scholars. After the first fragmentary publication in 1670 by the "Messieurs de Port-Royal" (see *"Solitaires"*), a fully revised edition appeared in 1844, prepared by Prosper Faugère; noteworthy among the more modern editions are those by L. Brunschvicg (1904), F. Strowski (1930), Z. Tourneur (1942) and L. Lafuma (1948).

Exerting an influence, because of its clarity and precision of style and its logical method of thinking, on French literature of the seventeenth century, *Les Pensées* also foreshadowed, by its emphasis on man's eternal misery, nineteenth century romanticism (q.v.).

V. Giraud, *Pascal, l'homme, l'œuvre, l'influence*, 1922; J. Chevalier, *Pascal*, 1922; M. Bishop, *Pascal, The Life of Genius*, 1936; G. Chinard, *En lisant Pascal*, 1948; J. Mesnard, *Pascal, l'homme et l'œuvre*, 1950.

Pasquier, Etienne: (1529-1615) A jurist, humanist, and historian, he did not confine his erudition to the world of antiquity. His major work, *Recherches de la France* (1560-1621), consisting of nine books, touches on the history, politics, culture and literature of France, and constitutes an important body of documents. Noteworthy are his observations relating to the history of the French language (q.v.), to the writers of the *Pléiade* (q.v.), to Montaigne (q.v.), and especially, to his defense of French against Latin. This work makes Pasquier France's first literary historian.

M. J. Moore, *Etienne Pasquier, historien de la poésie et de la langue française*, 1934.

Passerat, Jean: (1534-1602) Professor at the Collège du Plessis and in 1572 at the *Collège de France* (q.v.). In addition to having collaborated on the *Satire Ménipée* (q.v.), he published in 1597 *Vers de Chasse et d'Amour*. He blends in his poetry erudite forms that are dear to the *Pléiade* (q.v.) group with a certain *esprit gaulois* (q.v.). See in this connection his *Sur la mort de Thulène*.

Passeur, Stève: (1889-   ) The combination of the psychological drama with the comedy of manners is seen in this dramatist's portraits of lustful dowagers and social parasites. His characters, straining under moral, social, and conventional pressures, break down in unusual situations and reveal, in violent language, their most secret instincts, lusts and hates. The women, in particular, are intent upon satisfying their needs of love at any cost. When, as in *L'Acheteuse* (1930), his masterpiece, the love Elisabeth "bought" with money cannot give her the affection she seeks, she indulges in sadistic perversions and, in the end, kills herself. Included among his other dramas of passion and sentiment are *La Chaîne* (1931), *Les Tricheurs* (1932), and *Je vivrai un grand amour* (1935).

pastorale: Drawing its inspiration from Spanish and Italian works, mainly Montemayor's *Diana Enamorada* (1542), Tasso's pastoral *Aminta* (1581) and Guarini's *Pastor Fido* (1585), and flourishing at the beginning of the seventeeth century, this type of play is linked to the tradition of the medieval *Jeu de Robin et Marion* (q.v.) and to that of the pastoral novel, *L'Astrée*, by Honoré d'Urfé (q.v.). Placed in a bucolic setting, its characters, whose chief preoccupation is love, are shepherds and shepherdesses. Representative of the *pastorale* are Racan's (q.v.) *Les Bergeries* (1618) and some of the dramatic pieces by A. Hardy (q.v.). The *pastorale* was generally more lyrical and sentimental than the *tragi-comedy* (q.v.). It was displaced (*c.* 1630), as was the *tragi-comedy*, by tragedy (q.v.).

J. Marsan, *La Pastorale drama-*

tique à la fin du XVI et au commencement du XVII* siècle,* 1905.

pastourelle: A poetic genre of the twelfth and thirteenth centuries, the theme of which, developed in the celebrated piece of Adam de la Hale (q.v.), *Robin et Marion* (q.v.), is the meeting in the country of a Knight with a shepherdess, whose love he implores. See *Lyric Poetry.*

Patelin (or **Pathelin**): Of anonymous authorship, this most celebrated farce (*c.* 1470; q.v.) deals with roguery. In one of the most witty scenes of the play, which takes place in court, Guillaume, a draper, who accuses his shepherd of having stolen his sheep, manifests complete bewilderment and confusion upon seeing Pathelin, the shepherd's defense attorney, who had just cheated him out of a piece of cloth by feigning illness. Trying to bring order out of confusion, the judge hastens to recall to the draper the subject of his original complaint, the stolen sheep, in the famous line: *"Mais revenons à ces moutons"* (hence the proverb used today to indicate the wish to get back to the original subject). After winning the case for his client, however, Pathelin is outwitted by the wily shepherd, who now refuses to pay him his fee by continuing the assumed stupidity which he had adopted in court in self-defense at the advice of his attorney.

Petit de Julleville, *Répertoire du théâtre comique en France au moyen age,* 1885; *La Comédie et les mœurs en France au moyen age,* 1886; Grace Frank, *The Medieval French Drama,* 1954.

Patrie, La (1869): See *Sardou.*

Pattes de mouche, Les (1860): See *Sardou.*

Paul et Virginie (1787): See *Saint-Pierre, Bernardin de.*

Paulhan, Jean: (1884-   ) Former surrealist (see *Surrealism*), this essayist, for many years editor of the *Nouvelle Revue Française* (1925-1945), is preoccupied with problems of language and poetic technique. After having denounced, in *Jacob Cow le pirate* (1922), a philosophical tale, the abuse of words in all genres, and having advocated for poets extreme compression of statement, he made a complete turnabout in *Les Fleurs de Tarbes* (1941). In this work he writes on the usage of rhetoric. He has a special predilection for paradox.

M. J. Lefebvre, *Jean Paulhan,* 1949.

Paysan parvenu, Le (1735-1736): See *Marivaux.*

Paysan perverti, Le (1775): See *Restif de la Bretonne.*

Peau de chagrin, La (1831): See *Balzac.*

Pêcheur d'Islande (1886): See *Loti.*

Pêcheur d'ombres, Le (1921): See *Sarment, Jean.*

Pédant Joué, Le (1654): See *Cyrano de Bergerac, Savinien.*

Péguy, Charles: (1873-1914) Essentially a poet, although the author of several works in prose, his entire literary output can best be understood in the light of his life and his ideas. Born of humble conditions in Orléans, only by dint of hard work did he manage to be admitted to the École Normale Supérieure (1894), which he soon left out of genuine conviction because of the *Dreyfus Affair.* Since his childhood days, never once did he renounce his passion for justice; he was therefore bent on putting his ideas into practice, especially when he became aware of the fact that former friends had betrayed truth and justice. His dissident socialism, which repudiated what he considered a *politique* in favor of a *mystique,* was given further expression by the publication of the *Cahiers de la Quinzaine* (1900), which he founded alone and to which he devoted the rest of his life. In these "Cahiers" appeared works of diverse tendencies—works by Romain Rolland, André Suarès, the Tharauds (qq.v.), Daniel Halévy, André Spire (q.v.), and Péguy himself—whose spirit was one of loyalty to truth. Faithful to his ideas, Péguy struck out against the Church and those forces—the Universities and the Socialist Party—that had degenerated into a *politique*. Other polemics in prose include *Notre Patrie* (1905), a warning of the German danger, *Notre Jeunesse* (1910), a justification of the *dreyfusist* idealism, and *L'Argent* (1912), an attack against his former socialist friends. Many of his ideas, incidentally, are contradictory, since as a socialist he was nationalistic; as a *dreyfusist* he loved the French army; as an anticlerical, he was a devout, if unorthodox, Catholic. But that is because he could only be true to his own *mystique*.

His poetic works are devoted to religious themes. Included among them are his *Tapisseries* (*Tapisserie de Sainte-Geneviève*, 1912; *Tapisserie de Notre Dame*, 1913) —written in *quatrains* with the same rhymes and assonances. As a matter of fact, Péguy, who in his poetry most always uses the classical alexandrine (q.v.) line with the hemistich in the middle, applies even to his prose the same repetitive, monotonous rhythm, together with the same key words and phrases. His masterpiece, *Mystère de la charité de Jeanne d'Arc* (1910), a reworking of his earlier *Jeanne d'Arc*, is a drama in prose mixed with verse, whose action is almost nil, and whose lyrical monologues alternate with pious meditations, *Ève* (1913) is a long poem which evokes the destiny of Christian humanity and which exalts the mission of women.

Péguy died in the Battle of the Marne in the First World War—a fitting end for one who never betrayed his ideal.

Daniel Halévy, *Péguy et les Cahiers de la Quinzaine,* 1918; Roger Secrétain, *Péguy, soldat de la vé-*

rité, 1941; Romain Rolland, *Péguy,* 1946; Alexander Dru, *Péguy: His Prose and Poetry,* 1957.

Peints par eux-mêmes (1893): See *Hervieu.*

Peletier, Jacques: (1517-1582) Like Pontus de Tyard (q.v.), he, too, was a member of the *Pléiade* (q.v.). In his *Art poétique départi en deux livres* (1555), he formulated, even more cogently than the *Pléiade,* the principal ideas relating to poetic art and inspiration. He published his *Œuvres poétiques* in 1547.

C. Jugé, *Jacques Peletier du Mans,* 1907; H. Chamard, *Histoire de la Pléiade,* 1939-1940.

Pelléas et Mélisande (1892): See *Maeterlinck.*

Pellerin, Jean-Victor: (1899-) Freudian and Pirandellian influences are seen in the theater of this dramatist; he probes the secret thoughts of his characters, which he "externalizes" by making use of new scenic effects. These secret thoughts, moreover, reveal the characteristic restlessness of the post-war era and the spiritual urge to escape from the frustrating atmosphere of daily existence. In *Intimité* (1922), his first play, husband and wife are seen spending an evening at home together; but their secret thoughts are personified by the presence of other characters, who are at the rear of the stage. Not personification, but dramatization that reveals a dozen ghosts at a dinner table represents the daydreams of the hero in *Têtes de rechange* (1926). The title is symbolic of the different characters with which the young man, seated with his uncle who has come to discuss business matters with him, identifies himself in his imagination (cf. *Gaston Baty*) during the conversation to which he does not really listen. Of course this was but an interlude in the play; in the course of the drama, ideas reflecting the dramatist's point of view, ideas that are bitter and full of disillusionment, are expressed on contemporary bourgeois society as it is contrasted with the old respectable generation. Included among his other plays are: *Le plus bel homme de France* (1925), *Cri des cœurs* (1928), and *Terrain Vague* (1931).

Pellisson-Fontanier, Paul: (1624-1693) This historian is known especially for his *Histoire de l'Académie française* (1652), a critical edition of which was prepared in 1858 by C. L. Olivet. After abjuring Protestantism, he was appointed by Louis XIV royal historiographer.
F. L. Marcou, *Pellison*, 1859.

Pensées, Les (1670): See *Pascal.*

Pensées sur la comète (1682): See *Bayle, Pierre.*

Perceval (or **le Conte del Graal**): A *roman breton* (q.v.) written by Chrétien de Troyes (*c.* 1175; q.v.), but which he never completed. This romance, which combines the tale of one of King Arthur's Knights with the legend of the Holy Grail, relates how this fatherless boy, Perceval, after having met in the forest some knights with whom he has engaged in conversation, escapes from his too vigilant mother to make his way to Arthur's court and to the King's castle. There he catches a glimpse of the Holy Grail, but instead of venturing to ask the meaning of this wonder, he remains silent. The sequel to this romance can be found in *Parzival,* by the German poet, Wolfram d'Eschenbach (*d.* 1230), which inspired Wagner's *Parsifal.*
M. Wilmotte, *Le Poème du Graal et ses auteurs,* 1930; A. Hilka, *Christian von Troyes, Percevalroman (Li Contes del Graal),* 1932; J. Marx, *La Légende Arthurienne et le Graal,* 1952.

Père de famille, Le (1758): See *Diderot.*

Père Goriot, Le: This book, written by Balzac (q.v.) in 1834, is a good illustration, through the relationship he establishes between the charac-

ters and society in which money plays a most significant rôle, of his conception of the novel. It depicts the tragedy of a father whose sacrifices and devotion for his daughters are repaid by their ingratitude. Goriot is practically penniless and lives in shabby circumstances at Mme. Vauquer's boarding house in Paris, as a result of his depriving himself in order to provide his daughters (now Anastasie de Restaud and Delphine de Nucingen) with sizeable dowries and also to pay off their other debts. They do not come to see him when he is on his death-bed, finding it more important to attend a ball given by Mme. de Beauséant. Eugène de Rastignac, an impoverished law student and cousin of the latter, has been able to make the acquaintance of Goriot's daughters—and indeed becomes Delphine's lover—while living at the *Pension* Vauquer, where he meets Goriot. When Goriot dies, he and a poor medical student are the only mourners at the funeral; Anastasie and Delphine send their empty carriages to follow the coffin.

Perrault, Charles: (1628-1703) The youngest of four distinguished brothers (Claude, 1613-1688; Nicolas, 1611-1661; Pierre, 1608-1680), this writer, famous for his *Contes de ma mère l'Oye* (1697), immortal fairy-tales, in his poem *La Siècle de Louis le Grand* (1687), which he read before the *Académie Française* (q.v.), began the main phase of the *Querelle des Anciens et des Modernes* (q.v.); comparing in this poem his Age with that of Augustus, he clearly stated his belief that the moderns were superior to the ancients. He further developed this thesis in a prose work entitled *Parallèles des Anciens et des Modernes* (1688-1696). Boileau (q.v.), his chief target, countered these attacks with his *Réflexions critiques sur quelques passages du rhéteur Longin*

(1693). Perrault and Boileau were reconciled in 1694, although the dispute itself continued until 1715. H. Gillot, *La Querelle des Anciens et des Modernes*, 1914; A. Hallays, *Les Perrault*, 1926; E. Storer, *La mode des contes de fées*, 1928.

Perse, Saint-John (pseud. of **Alexis Léger**): (1887-) This poet, born on an island of Guadeloupe, came with his family to France, where, in 1914, he was to enter the Diplomatic Service. In 1933 he rose to the position of *Secrétaire Général*. His life as a diplomat, which carried him to the four corners of the earth, ended in 1940 when he fled to the United States. Here he has held an important post at the Library of Congress, and has served as advisor to the late President Roosevelt. Five short collections, two of which—*Éloges* (1911) and *Anabase* (1924) —were written before his stay in America, constitute his poetic output. *Exil* (1942)—an appropriate title for his own experience and a collection for which he received much celebrity—*Vents* (1947), and *Amers* (1953), make up the rest of his poetry. The cosmic theme of the last two collections, eloquently sustained in the exaltation of the natural forces of rain, snow, wind, and sea, is frequently expressed through the Claudelian (see *Claudel*) verset. Using majestic images, with a vocabulary that is at once precise, technical, scientific, frequently exotic, at times rare, he describes his dreamlands of the East and the West. His poetic vision sees in the ruins of buried civilizations vestiges of the past and, in these durable traces, an eternal profile of man. The area in which his imagination works is the entire world, reflecting a man of vast culture and good taste.

Maurice Saillet, *Saint-John Perse, poète de gloire*, 1952; Roger Caillois, *Poétique de St.-John Perse*, 1954.

Personnalisme: This doctrine, anti-rationalist and anti-totalitarian, hostile to Marx as well as to Descartes (q.v.), seeks to reestablish the primacy of the human spirit. In 1930, under the leadership of Emmanuel Mounier (q.v.), a disciple of Péguy (q.v.), and his journal *Esprit*, it established itself among the young Catholic students with rather advanced tendencies. After 1944, intellectuals of different camps—poets of the Résistance (q.v.) like Pierre Emmanuel and Jean Cayrol (qq.v.), as well as students and Christian workers, were attracted to it. It represented a union that symbolized the intellectual atmosphere in France at the moment of its liberation. Today, however, events have forced the separation of the Catholic from the Communist adherents. *Esprit*, however, refuses to let itself be identified with any political group. Thinkers who have, in one way or another, identified themselves with this doctrine include Jacques Maritain (q.v.), Denis de Rougemont, and Arnaud Dandieu (1898-1933). In the final analysis, *Personnalisme* bears resemblance to the Christian existentialism of Gabriel Marcel (q.v.).

Pertharite (1652): See *Corneille, Pierre.*

Peste, La (1947): See *Camus, Albert.*

Petit Café, Le (1911): See *Bernard, Tristan.*

Petit Chose, Le (1868): See *Daudet.*

Petit Jehan de Saintré (1456): See *Antoine de la Sale.*

Petit Testament, Le (1456): See *Villon, François.*

Petit Traité de Versification française (1872): See *Banville.*

Petrarchism (Influence of): Affecting profoundly French poetry during the Renaissance, this idea of love is based on Petrarch's love for Laura. Containing elements of neo-Platonism, it nevertheless stands out as distinct from the latter doctrine by its emphasis on the conflict existing between the spirit and the flesh. Its commonest literary form is the sonnet sequence that expresses the poet's love for the same woman. The notion, moreover, of a despairing and worshipful lover, who is in tears and joy in turn, is a continuation of the medieval courtly love tradition. Petrarchism is especially seen in the poetry of Maurice Scève, Pontus de Tyard, Joachim du Bellay and Ronsard (qq.v.).

J. Vianey, *Le Pétrarquisme en France au XVI° siécle*, 1909.

Peyrefitte, Roger: (1907-) This writer established his reputation with *Amitiés particulières* (1945), a psychological novel dealing with the theme of pederasty. Semi-autobiographical, this work betrays an elegant style and a lucid analysis. Other novels include *Mademoiselle de Murville* (1947), *L'Oracle* (1948) and *La Fin des ambassades* (1953).

Phèdre: This classical tragedy (1677), one of the best by Racine (q.v.), is based on Euripides' *Hippolytus*. A psychological play, it depicts the fatal passion of Phèdre, the wife of Thésée (Theseus), for Hippolyte (Hippolytus), her stepson, and her obsessive remorse. Believing her husband dead, Phèdre, no longer feeling a sense of guilt, declares, after being urged by Oenone, her nurse, her love for Hippolyte. At this very moment, however, Thésée returns very much alive, finding everyone in a state of consternation. As a result of Oenone's insinuations, leading him to believe that Hippolyte attempted to seduce his wife, Thésée curses his son and calls down the wrath of Neptune upon him. Seized with remorse, Phèdre is about to confess her guilt when she suddenly learns that Hippolyte is secretly in love with the princess Aricie. Overcome by jealousy, she allows the deceit to continue. When Thésée's prayer has been answered, causing the death of Hippolyte, Phèdre, suffering because of the catastrophe she has provoked, confesses her crime and kills herself by taking poison.

Phèdre et Hippolyte (1677): See *Pradon, Jacques.*

Philippe, Charles Louis: (1874-1909) The poverty from which he suffered, and which undoubtedly contributed to his illnesses, is reflected in his novels, the main theme of which is the suffering of the poor. The compassion he shows for the indigent relates him, at least spiritually, to Dostoyevsky and Nietzsche. His most impressive books include *Bubu de Montparnasse* (1901) —later produced as a play and as a film—*Père Perdrix* (1903), and the incomplete *Charles Blanchard,* an autobiographical portrait of himself and of his father's struggles against hunger.

H. Bachelin, *Charles Louis Philippe,* 1929; Emile Guillaumin, *Charles-Louis Philippe, mon ami,* 1943.

philosophes: As used in the eighteenth century, this term refers to a group of religious, social and political reformers—all enlightened thinkers (cf. *Enlightenment, Age of*)—who re-evaluated, in the light of reason and in accordance with the methods of natural science, long-established customs and institutions. Finding conditions in France far from ideal, they strove toward furthering the good of humanity and man's happiness. In their aims, beliefs and purposes, they ascribed much importance to man's progress and were essentially optimistic; their ethic was utilitarian and sensationalistic.

Philosophes, Les (1760): See *Palissot.*

Philosophe sans le savoir, Le (1765): See *Sedaine.*

Physiocratie, La (1768): See *Quesnay.*

Picard, Louis-Benoit: (1769-1828) Writer of comedies, at a time when comedy was regarded somewhat contemptuously, he produced such plays as *Duhautcours* (1801)—which may have influenced Balzac's (q.v.) *Mercadet*

—*La Petite ville* (1801), an amusing study of manners, and *Les Ricochets* (1807), a demonstration of the idea that the smallest causes may have most important results (cf. *E. Scribe*). His theater is characterized by a study of manners with laughter as a component part.

pièce à thèse: This type of play makes use of the stage as a pulpit for social reform. Although, to a certain degree, some of Molière's (q.v.) pieces may be considered as thesis-plays, it was Dumas *fils* (q.v.) who inaugurated, with *Le Fils naturel* (1858), the modern thesis-drama, the central theme of which is the incongruity between public opinion and the dramatist's viewpoint. In such a play, the *raisonneur* (q.v.) has a large role, for, as the dramatist's spokesman, he preaches to the public.

pièce bien faite: or the "well-made play," of which Scribe (q.v.) is the greatest modern exponent. Such a play is marked by dramatic craftsmanship, by ingenious plot construction, whose interest can be suspended or complicated in turn.

Pierre et Jean (1885): See *Maupassant*.

Piron, Alexis: (1689-1773) Although he wrote witty epigrams and other light verse, this author, a life-long enemy of Voltaire (q.v.), is especially remembered for his *La Métromanie* (1738). This Molièresque comedy in verse—forming what is really a self-portrait—deals with the mania of writing poetry. Included among his other works are such tragedies as *Gustave Wasa* (1733) and *Fernand Cortès* (1744).
P. Chaponnière, *Piron, sa vie et son œuvre*, 1910.

Pitoëff, Georges: (1886-1939) Together with his wife, Ludmilla (1896-1951), who, too, was Russian, he organized his *Compagnie Pitoëff* in Geneva (1915), and came to Paris (1919) at the invitation of H. R. Lenormand (q.v.), with whose play *Le Temps est*

un songe (1919) he began his career. Having no playhouse of his own, he stayed at different times in one theater or another, until finally he settled in 1934 at *Les Mathurins*. Acting with his wife, who always created in her rendition of her various roles an unforgettable atmosphere of poetry and mystery, he stressed, under the influence of his Russian heritage, a simplicity of staging. The sets usually consisted of hardly more than large curtains for the background and a few pieces of furniture. He stressed bareness because he wanted to fasten the attention of the audience on the characters, to create an effect of sincerity. The importance of the characters was heightened even further by a judicious use of lighting focused on them. For similar reasons and because he wanted to express the troubled spirit of the present age, his repertoire showed a preference for the Russian and contemporary French plays, as well as for those by Shakespeare, Shaw, Pirandello, and O'Neill. In his later staging, though inspired by the same idealism, he evolved somewhat toward the reproduction of subtle but more realistic effects.
R. Brasillach, *Animateurs de théâtre*, 1936.

Pixérécourt, Guilbert de: (1773-1844) King of the boulevard melodrama (q.v.), this dramatist, author of some 120 plays, of which fifty-nine were melodramas, wrote tragedies, comedies, dramas, comic operas, vaudevilles, lyrical dramas, and pantomimes. His first important melodrama was *Cœlina ou l'enfant du mystère* (1800), based on a novel by Ducray-Duminil. *Latude ou trente-cinq ans de captivité* (1834) may be considered his last melodrama, the romantic *drame* (q.v.) having contributed to the decline of the melodrama by which, it should be pointed out, it was influenced.
J. F. Mason, *The Melodrama in*

France from the Revolution to the Beginning of the Romantic Drama, 1912; A. Lacey, *Pixerécourt and the French Romantic Drama,* 1928.

Flaideurs, Les (1668): See *Racine.*

Platonism (Influence of): Revived in 1483 by the Italian Marsilio Ficino's translations into Latin, this doctrine, based on Plato's *The Symposium,* was to affect profoundly French poetry *c.* 1530—*c.* 1560. According to this theory of love, which was adapted and Christianized, the longings created by the sight of physical beauty may lead to the contemplation of a higher form of beauty which ultimately leads to divine love. Viewed as a ladder of love, it consists of a series of steps the highest one of which merges Ideal Beauty with Ideal Love. This new conception of spiritual love which idealizes woman is expressed in Antoine Héroët's (q.v.) *La Parfaite Amie* (1542). In the poetry of Marguerite d'Angoulême (q.v.) whose protégé Héroët was, one finds a mixture of neoplatonism and Christian mysticism.

R. V. Merrill and R. J. Clements, *Platonism in French Renaissance Poetry,* 1957.

Pléiade: This name, indicating a constellation of seven stars, which had been used to identify the group of poets in Alexandria during the third century B.C., applies to those poets of the sixteenth century— Ronsard, J. du Bellay, Belleau, Antoine de Baïf, Jodelle, Pontus de Tyard, Peletier, Dorat (qq.v.)— whose aim was to enrich the French language, rehabilitate French poetry in particular, and put French on an equal footing with other great languages. In their manifesto, *La Défense et Illustration de la langue française* (1549), published by J. du Bellay, the following general principles are enunciated: 1) The French language, to be made *illustrious,* must turn to Greek, Latin and Italian, which will serve as models to be followed; 2) it should create—taking example from the ancient and modern languages— new words, either by adopting terms used in the technical language of trades or professions, or by borrowing words from old provincial dialects or ancient languages, or by utilizing already existing words from which new derivatives can be formed; 3) poetic forms used by the ancients and the Italians—the *épopée, épigramme, élégie, épître, ode, tragedy, comedy, satire,* and *sonnet* (qq.v.)—are to be introduced and the fixed poetic forms of the Middle Ages (cf. *ballade, rondeau,* etc.) are to be discarded; 4) the poet must consciously and zealously strive for perfection of form. Although this document of artistic reform held the same importance for its age that the *Préface de Cromwell* (q.v.) had for romanticism, Malherbe (q.v.) in the seventeenth century was to react violently against it, and the poetic work of this school remained practically in oblivion until the beginning of the nineteenth century.

A. Rosenbauer, *Die poetischen Theorien der Plejade nach Ronsard und Du Bellay,* 1895; P. Villey, *Les Sources italiennes de la Défense et Illustration,* 1908; H. Chamard, *Histoire de la Pléiade,* 1939-1940.

Plisnier, Charles: (1896-) Before becoming a novelist and poet, this Belgian-born writer was first a militant Communist and then a Trotzkyite. His novels, the best of which are *Mariages* (1936) and *Faux-Passeports* (for which he received the *Prix Goncourt,* q.v., in 1937), bear the fruit of his experiences as a militant and implicitly condemn bourgeois society.

Poèmes antiques (1852): See *Leconte de Lisle.*

Poèmes antiques et modernes (1837): See *Vigny.*

Poèmes barbares (1862): See *Leconte de Lisle.*

Poèmes de la nuit et du brouillard (1945): See *Cayrol, Jean.*

Poème sur le désastre de Lisbonne (1755): See *Voltaire.*

POETRY: One thousand years of French poetry cannot enter the scope of a brief article except in the form of summary notations indicating the main currents at a given period. The fact, however, that there *are* currents, that they should be fairly discernible, is of itself quite significant. It testifies to a care for order, on the intellectual plane, which emerged in medieval France, long before Descartes (q.v.) happened to codify it in his *Discours de la Méthode.* The well-known essayist, Julien Benda (q.v.), has written a history of the French in their *will* to become a nation. One might just as aptly write a history of the French in the will to fashion their own language: primarily in prose, needless to say, but also in poetry. To create a poetical idiom which, while giving expression to particularly noble or subtle feelings, would at the same time develop and exemplify the limitless capacities of the French tongue—such was the common ideal of poets who often entered into deadly quarrels over the choice of proper means. Indeed there were occasions when they nearly killed poetical sensitiveness through too much insistence on defining its laws: a fact which may explain, for instance, why French romantic lyricism seldom achieved the splendid, exuberant abandon of its British counterpart. Yet the effort of centuries bore fruit at long last. It gave birth to a poetical language *sui generis* which reached maturity with Baudelaire (q.v.) and his successors—and the gamut of which proved so rich, so supple, so variegated, that it radiates to-day and serves as a model for poetical languages in other countries, much in the same manner as French impressionistic painting supplied the norm for the evolution of pictorial art at home and abroad.

The IXth century, which bequeathed to us the first document written in French (*Serments de Strasbourg,* 842; q.v.) has also left us the first poetical text, a short narrative entitled *Cantilène de Sainte-Eulalie* (*c.* 880; q.v.). Other lives of saints and martyrs, told in epic style, followed in the Xth and XIth centuries. This religious inspiration was likewise a popular one, for the Catholic Church, then the fountainhead of all spiritual life, restricted its use of Latin and resorted to the vernacular in order to indoctrinate the lower classes. The same remark applies to the *chansons de geste* (q.v.) or epics (q.v.) of the great feudal period (XIth and XIIth centuries; among them the celebrated *Chanson de Roland, c.* 1090-1120; q.v.), all of which betray a militant religiosity and were sung by the *jongleurs* (q.v.) before an audience of pilgrims and warriors who did not know and hardly would have enjoyed the refinements of superior taste.

Another public was needed to induce genuine strivings toward more delicate shades of thought and expression. The tempered *mores* of the late XIIth century provided such a public. Hence the vogue of the *romans courtois,* or romances in verse, which were recited, and no longer sung, in the privacy of the drawing-room, before a choice gathering of gentlemen and gentlewomen. Some of these romances borrowed their subject from antiquity (*e.g., Roman de Thèbes, c.* 1150); an even greater number went to Provençal (q.v.) and Celtic (Arthurian) sources for their aristocratic and sentimental evocations. Those were the times when flourished the first French poetess, Marie de France (dates unknown; q.v.), and most conspicuously the clever Chrétien de Troyes (*c.* 1130—*c.* 1180;

q.v.), whose many imitators exploited after him the cycle of the Round Table, that of Tristan and Isolde (q.v.), and that of the Holy Grail (q.v.).

The XIIIth century witnessed the decisive strengthening of royal power. The regional autonomy prevalent under the feudal regime gave way to an ever increasing centralization, truly the initial step toward the establishment of the absolute monarchic State. Far from suppressing thought, however, these transformations developed the critical spirit. In that era of hard-headed political realism, some poets, to be sure, entertained a nostalgia of the past which they regretted as a kind of lost paradise: so did Rutebeuf (died 1280; q.v.), undeniably the first in line of great French lyricists. Many more brought cool delight to probing the vices and foibles of their contemporaries: from 1170 to 1270 or thereabouts, the huge cycle of the *Roman de Renart* (q.v.) deepened more and more its satirical though dispassionate intent. But with Jean de Meung (*c.* 1240-1305; q.v.), who added 18,000 lines of his own to the unfinished *Roman de la Rose* (q.v.) by Guillaume de Lorris (died *c.* 1260), what had begun as an old-fashioned allegory became a *summa* of the knowledge of the times wherein social criticism, however stinging it may be, is relieved, or buttressed, by a sincere faith in science and progress.

The Hundred-Year War (XIVth-XVth centuries), while it brought disaster to France, consolidated rather than weakened the allegiance of the people to their King, the only visible symbol of national integrity; but, to a large extent, it estranged the poets from the people. There is perceptible, in those days, the first attempt of its kind at artistic evasion. François Villon alone (1431—*c.* 1463; q.v.) injects into his *Grand Testament* (1461) a touching note of solidarity with his "human brothers." Still the emotional power which issues from his work is partly due to the fact that this outstanding poet, so close to humble folk, hardly disengaged from the naïve faith of the Middle Ages, was at the same time a lucid and learned man, already in the throes of modern restlessness. In more than one passage he shows himself under the guise of a lone itinerant, cruelly conscious that the world around him is insensitive to poetical values. By contrast, such courtly writers as Alain Chartier (*c.* 1390—*c.* 1435; q.v.) or Charles d'Orléans (1394-1465; q.v.) prove to be detached spectators whose hearts, in order to vibrate, need the impact of selfishly personal misfortunes. As will happen in such cases, their care for form, often exquisite, overshadows the substance of their verse. They take their place in a movement of structural innovation, of prosodic inventiveness, which, originated by Guillaume de Machault (*c.* 1300-1377; q.v.) and Eustache Deschamps (*c.* 1340-1410; q.v.), will culminate in the incongruous experiments of the *grands rhétoriqueurs* [q.v.] (Georges Chastellain, *c.* 1404-1475; Jean Molinet, 1435-1507; Guillaume Cretin, died 1525, etc.). These latter stylists, intolerably artificial in their writing, incurred a rapid and legitimate discredit. Yet they had the merit of believing in their mission as creators of a poetical language *per se*, itself a reflection of aristocratic Beauty. When all is said, their abortive efforts anticipated those of the *Pléiade* (q.v.) after them, of the romanticists, of the symbolists, and of the poets of our day.

The history of French poetry during the Renaissance bears out this fact. Jean Lemaire de Belges (*c.* 1473 —*c.* 1525), Mellin de Saint-Gelais (1487-1558), and Clément Marot (1496-1544; qq.v.), the last two being the sons of *rhétoriqueur* poets, owe much to the technical research of their elders; but they are, too, writers of transition who undergo the Mediterranean influences, both ancient and modern, spread about in the wake of the Italian wars. Marot, in particular, lived in the familiarity of Queen Marguerite de Navarre (1492-1549; q.v.), a poetess in her own right, won over to the first manifestations of humanism, and, in the image of her brother François Ier, a protectress of arts and letters. To the same circles belonged Jean Héroët (1492-1568; q.v.), author of *La Parfaite Amie* (Lyons, 1562), whose Platonic inspiration, modified more often than not through the addition of Petrarchism (q.v.), graces the rich poetry of the Lyons School (Maurice Scève, *c.* 1510—*c.* 1564; Louise Labé, *c.* 1525-1565, etc.; qq.v.). A member of that school, Pontus de Tyard (1511-1603; q.v.) will soon rally the ranks of the *Pléiade,* itself Petrarchist on occasion, although it is fond of denouncing the excesses of Petrarchism. It is true, therefore, that, curiously fostered by personal contacts, subject, on the other hand, to many uncertainties, and highlighted by doctrinal disputes, there goes on, throughout the XVIth century, an unrelenting effort to raise ever higher the dignity of French poetry.

It was in the year 1556 that, at the instigation of Pierre de Ronsard (1524-1585) and Joachim Du Bellay (1522-1560; qq.v.), the group of seven poets was finally constituted who revived the stellar name of *Pléiade* formerly adopted by seven poets of Alexandria. Their program, however, had been traced as early as 1549 in Du Bellay's *Défense et Illustration de la Langue française.* This famous manifesto made the greater glory of French poetry contingent upon the rejection of all medieval forms in favor of those cultivated by the ancients (ode, both Pindaric and Horatian; epic, epis-

tle, eclogue, elegy, epigram, satire, tragedy, comedy, etc.; qq.v.) and by the Italians (sonnet; q.v.). To succeed in this undertaking, future poets must enrich their language through the creation of new words and new phrases, thus giving the lie to the "Latin maniacs" in whose opinion Latin remained the only worthy instrument of learned and literary expression. It may readily be seen that the common denominator of this "illustration" and "defense" of the French language was meant to be the linguistic and poetical exploitation of ancient models in a spirit of free (not servile) imitation and with due respect paid to national characteristics: a mixture of revolutionary boldness and cautious conservatism which will, just as typically, distinguish the beginnings of the romantic era. Du Bellay, as a matter of fact, turned out to be, in his masterful sonnets, a paragon of soberness and delicacy. The ebullient genius of Ronsard, while more uneven, seldom gets out of hand. Strikingly at ease in almost any genre, from the majestic ode to the love sonnet, this poet, the greatest manipulator and inventor of rhythms to appear in France before Victor Hugo (q.v.), learned, in the course of a long and glorious career, how both to ride and curb his Pegasus.

The doctrine of the *Pléiade* had, to the very end of the XVIth century and beyond, hosts of more or less orthodox adepts. The bombast of Guillaume Du Bartas (1544-1590; q.v.) in his sacred poems or the mawkish preciosity of Philippe Desportes (1546-1606; q.v.) adduce sufficient proof of the fact that Ronsard's emulators and continuators did not avoid the pitfalls and extremes against which the profession of faith of 1549 purported to guard them. Indeed the vast poetical experiment of the Renaissance was to end in a kind of anarchy, parallel, in some ways, to that of the religious wars which brought forth the somber and grandiose invectives of the Protestant Agrippa d'Aubigné (1552-1630; *Les Tragiques*, not published until 1616; q.v.). Lesser though not inconsiderable talents sprouted here and there: the truculent Mathurin Régnier (1573-1613; q.v.), or those whom romanticists will call the *grotesques*—a designation which, far from being derogatory, was intended to extoll their realism mixed with fantasy, their feeling for nature, their melancholy; in brief, the free play of their imagination (Théophile de Viau, 1590-1625; Marc-Antoine de Saint-Amant, 1594-1661; qq.v.).

The stage was ready for François de Malherbe (1555-1628; q.v.) who, fairly late in his life (1605 and after), undertook to sweep away the vestiges of the *Pléiade* and begin anew, from vastly different premises, the eternal task of giving France a poetical treasure worthy of her. This bespectacled pedagogue, as he liked to call himself, already embodies the need for order and reason which will be the hallmark of the classical era. His own way of defending the language is to purify it, not to enrich it; and his conception of how to "illustrate" French poetry is to resort to painstaking labors, to a "scraping of syllables," rather than favor, or tolerate, the straying whims of inspiration. Thus was insinuated, even into lyrical outbursts, the discipline of the "rules" which Nicolas Boileau (1636-1711; q.v.), another literary regent, ultimately codified in his *Art Poétique* (1674) and made binding upon his contemporaries. It is no exaggeration to say that Boileau, a good judge of talent, but severe and oftentimes narrow-minded (though far less so than some of his would-be successors), reigned over literature in the same absolute way as Louis XIV on the throne or Bossuet (q.v.) in the

religious realm. Even Molière and Racine (qq.v.) bowed to him on occasion; only the elusive Jean de La Fontaine (1621-1695; q.v.) displayed enough detachment to cultivate in his fables a comparatively free and independent Muse, prone to season her basic wisdom with a dash of venturesomeness and day-dreaming.

There is, nonetheless, deep substance to XVIIth-century poetry. Tightly constrained but not smothered by the rules, it remains intensely alive to all human emotions and, in the case of Racine (1639-1699), feeds itself, sometimes secretly, sometimes openly, at the sources of religious feeling. As we enter the XVIIIth century, the indirect effect of rational speculation will be to deprive all that is verse of this inner vibration. The age of enlightenment (q.v.), as a matter of fact, led in the name of reason— and of prose, the more logical instrument of reason—a concerted assault against the *poeta mendax*. He was confined to the task of putting to meter the current philosophy or, more frequently still, of catering, in a "light" or "fugitive" vein, to the less exalted instincts of his readers. Thus the neo-classical poets, or the least unambitious among them, set their limited sights upon a factitious observance of the rules for their own sake. That the grandiloquent odes of Jean-Baptiste Rousseau (1671-1741; q.v.; not to be mistaken for Jean-Jacques) should be deemed, and justly so, the greatest lyrical monument of the period is enough of a commentary on this decline of inspiration. Voltaire it was (1694-1778; q.v.) who saved the day, less by virtue of his personal achievements as a poet than through a peculiar and outspoken admiration for the aesthetic standards of the previous century. He transmitted the torch to André Chénier (1762-1794; q.v.), a victim of the Revolution at the age of 32, whose strong penchant for philosophical poems stamps him as a man of his times, but who broke away from them in several other respects, whether he imbued his eclogues with a freshness directly borrowed from the Greek masters, or revelled in prosodic audacities which prompted romanticists to claim him as one of them.

Yet it behooved a prosaic century, such as was the XVIIIth, to launch upon its course the simple but fruitful idea that the essence of poetry does not necessarily reside in verse forms; that, in other terms, a bad rimester is no poet, whereas this title may attach to a prose writer who makes full and gifted use of the musical and affective resources of his medium. Already the bishop Fénelon (1651-1715; q.v.), in his novel, *Les Aventures de Télémaque* (1699), had propounded a kind of rhythmic prose, and in his doctrinal treatises (*e.g., Lettre à l'Académie*, 1714), shown himself extremely sensitive to the poetical imagery of the Bible. His lesson was to fructify in the theory and practice of both Jean-Jacques Rousseau (1712-1778) and Denis Diderot (1713-1784; qq.v.), the former a musician, the latter an art critic, who accredited the notion, later perfected by Baudelaire, (q.v.), that every art has its poets, all brothers under the skin, all identifiable through their creative power, not through the nature of their tools.

Pre-romanticism and romanticism (q.v.) grew out of these tendencies, long self-contained to be sure, but destined to ride, before and after the Revolution, on a tidal wave of "sensibility." While Madame de Staël (1766-1817; q.v.) restored, against the supremacy of cold reason, that of enthusiasm, Chateaubriand (1768-1848; q.v.), a mediocre artisan whenever he ventured into verse, gave a prefiguration of the symbolistic "alchemy of the verb"

by transmuting, in what may be the most enchanting French prose ever written, the stuff and substance that his dreams were made of. The generation of 1820 credited him with having founded, in his *Génie du Christianisme* (1802), not only the aesthetics of religion but the religion of aesthetics; and since Chateaubriand was no integral revolutionist, since he professed to rejoin, over and above the XVIIIth century, some literary ideals of the ancestral past, his disciples accepted, for a time at any rate, his admonition and guarantee that a dynamic traditionalism, vitalized by their own progressive genius, would prove more realistic and constructive than the procedure of the *tabula rasa*. Thus Alphonse de Lamartine (1790-1869; q.v.) owed the triumphal success of his *Méditations poétiques* (1820) to the fact that they revealed a new artist rather than new themes or a new form of art. Victor Hugo (1802-1885; q.v.), although in precocious possession of his craftsmanship, was content at first to revive the classical ode and medieval ballad in praise of God and the King. Alfred de Vigny (1797-1863; q.v.), relying mainly on Biblical sources, came closest, at this juncture, to fulfilling Chateaubriand's requirement for personal inventiveness on the part of his followers. Instead of resorting to direct discourse or lyric effusion he wrapped his idea in a symbol, generally pregnant and effective. There is ample justification for Vigny's claim that in so doing he set the pace, not only for his future masterpieces, but for the new poetry in general.

So far the romantic crusade had devoted itself to unmixed aesthetic aims, first of which was doing away with the stultifying tyranny of neoclassical rules. Indeed, when Hugo became the acknowledged head of the movement, his ringing prefaces to *Cromwell* (1827) and *Les Orien-*

tales (1829) proclaimed the self-sufficiency and self-justification of the individual artist, bound by no conventions but self-imposed ones: both a throwback to the creed of the *Pléiade* and a blueprint of the future doctrine of art for Art's sake. Things changed, however, after the dynastic upheaval of 1830 and the massive advent of the industrial revolution. Social and humanitarian considerations began weighing heavily on the minds of most romanticists, convinced by then that they were spiritual directors divinely endowed with the power of prophetic vision. Vigny shared in this belief but, mature as always, warned his fellow-Messiahs that the leader's only reward lies in his own sense of dedication, since his prophecies are likely to come true long after his works, perhaps his very name, have been forgotten (cf. *Les Destinées,* posthumous, 1864). Lamartine, on the other hand, wrote *Jocelyn* (1836), an incredibly successful epic of the people and for the people; and as a deputy for fifteen years, an opposition leader for the last five, the foremost orator of his times, the main impresario of the revolution of February, 1848, and, for three months thereafter, the outstanding personality of the provisional government, he fulfilled with unsurpassed brilliance the romantic ideal of the poet-statesman. Hugo, for his part, despite a prolific output, experienced strange intellectual and moral difficulties. Only under the double shock of his daughter's death (1843) and of political exile (1851) did a clearcut and forceful attitude crystallize in his mind. Then, on the rock of Guernsey, conscious of striking a more genuinely Napoleonic pose than the small emperor who "cowered" in the Tuileries, the poet at long last found the range of his Olympian genius. The satirical *Châtiments* (1853), the lyrical and metaphysical *Contemplations* (1856), the epic *Légende des Siècles* (first series, 1859)—and, of course, the novel, *Les Misérables* (1862)—are only part of a gigantic production which overflowed into the next period, namely, that of Hugo's return to France (1870), and went on posthumously. Of all these works the commanding theme is the social-romantic theme *par excellence*—that of mankind rising through the ages from darkness into light.

Meanwhile others had taken up from *Les Orientales* the doctrine of non-utilitarian art forsaken by Hugo himself. Art for Art's sake received a measure of support from Alfred de Musset (1810-1857; q.v.)—from the delightful playwright, at any rate, if not from the emotionally intemperate poet of the lyrical *Nuits* (1835-1837). More authentically devoted to the cult of pure Beauty were the bohemians: Théophile Gautier (1811-1872), Gérard de Nerval (1808-1855; qq.v.), *etc.*, who wrote in the shadow of their big romantic brothers until the authoritarian regime of the Second Empire made it logical that socially and politically neutral literature should come into its own. The largest gathering of escapists ever contrived may well have occurred in 1866, when the publisher Alphonse Lemerre put out a collection of verse, entitled *Le Parnasse Contemporain,* in which 64 poets—old and young, major and minor—had collaborated. Their very numbers, however, suggest many differences below and within their common purpose. Some of the *Parnassians* (q.v.) became past masters at verbal pyrotechnics: the charming Théodore de Banville (1823-1891; q.v.), for instance, hardly had his equal in French letters as a pure virtuoso. Others followed Leconte de Lisle (1818-1894; q.v.), the nominal head of the school, in his contention that poetry is akin to the plastic arts and must strive for marmorean perfection: a somewhat stilted article of faith which led José-Maria de Heredia (1842-1905; q.v.) to spend his entire existence carving one book of impeccable sonnets (*Les Trophées*, 1893). On the other hand, Charles Baudelaire (1821-1867), Paul Verlaine (1844-1896), and Stéphane Mallarmé (1842-1898; qq.v.), all three of them contributors to the Lemerre anthology of 1866, veered resolutely to the belief that, within the great family of arts, music is the true sister of poetry. The author of *Les Fleurs du Mal* (1857) and *Petits Poèmes en Prose* (1868), no gregarious man by any means, no self-styled school leader, yet had the signal though posthumous fortune of opening wide the path of modern poetical inspiration by stressing the suggestive rather than the descriptive value of words. Baudelaire's fame, in the last analysis, rests on the fact that he retained and transmitted the romantic trust in intuition and second sight while, at the same time, divesting it of its utilitarian implications; so that, through him and after him, with a scale of freedom never attained before, poetry sought refuge in a mysterious world of artificiality and sense-transference where colors, sounds, and perfumes become symbols of far-off things that are real.

The symbolist branch (see *Symbolism*) thus grafted on the Parnassian trunk detached itself in due time and grew in a climate of its own, giving forth strange, sometimes monstrous flowers unlike anything the average amateur was accustomed to or willing to accept. The melodic line of Verlaine's "songs without words" was deceptively simple and actually foreshadowed the limitless revolutions of the *vers-libre* (q.v.): here again is the case of a poet with few didactic dispositions who boasts an especially large, albeit eclectic, posterity (Maurice Maeterlinck,

1862-1949; Henri de Régnier, 1864-1936; Francis Vielé-Griffin, 1864-1937; Francis Jammes, 1868-1938; Paul Fort, 1872- ; Léon-Paul Fargue, 1878-1948, etc.; qq.v.). The resolutely withdrawn Stéphane Mallarmé lost himself in a forest of Wagnerian symbols and wandered in quest of the Absolute as if it were a magic talisman; while, closer to us, his foremost disciple, Paul Valéry (1871-1945; q.v.), renounced at least some of the Mallarmean trappings and endeavored to illustrate the drama of man's intelligence within the bounds of a strict, almost classical prosody. Still in the wake of Baudelaire there appeared, in the second half of the XIXth century, a bevy of literary anarchists and social outcasts whose meteoric career was not traced until years later (Isidore Ducasse, who called himself the comte de Lautréamont, 1846-1870; Tristan Corbière, 1845-1875; Charles Cros, 1842-1888; Jules Laforgue, 1860-1887, etc.; qq.v.). Strangely enough, Arthur Rimbaud (1856-1891; q.v.), the most daring of them all, the most "accursed" poet ever to sail on his "drunken boat" (cf. *"Le Bateau Ivre,"* 1871), had a disciple of his own, and an outstanding one, in the person of Paul Claudel (1868-1954; q.v.) who, to the unprecedented accompaniment of quasi-Biblical verse, exchanged the Faustian pact signed by his predecessor for the secure and catholic possession of a universe guaranteed by God.

The divided kingdom of Baudelaire was, to an extent, reunited by Guillaume Apollinaire (1880-1918; q.v.) in the early years of our century; or, to put it differently, this gifted poet gathered strands from Verlaine, Mallarmé, and Rimbaud which, in turn, diverged from him into the several directions discernible after the First World War. Often enough he personally, together with

Max Jacob (1876-1944), André Salmon (1881-   ), and the younger Jean Cocteau (1891-   ; qq.v.), is ranged among the literary "cubists," that is to say, with a group of writers who underwent the influence of Pablo Picasso. They transferred to poetry that painter's contempt for traditional rhetorics, for perspective, for anthropomorphic reality. Yet the dissociations and associations thus achieved, the result of which is a new and synthetic image flashed on the screen of the poet's consciousness, do not differ radically from those arrived at by the "dadaists" [see *Dadaism*] (*e.g.*, Tristan Tzara, 1896-   ; q.v.) and the "surrealists" who also claim Apollinaire at least as their precursor. André Breton (1896-   ; q.v.), fathered the latter movement, the most extensive to take place in the 1920's and the 1930's, with Paul Eluard (1895-1952), Philippe Soupault (1897-   ), and Louis Aragon (1897-   ) among its active recruits, and Jules Supervielle (1884-   ), Pierre Reverdy (1889-   ; qq.v.), etc., as more remote sympathizers.

Surrealism (q.v.), Breton has always insisted, implies a new philosophy of life, the introduction of a "non-Euclidian" dimension into the pattern of thinking. This "revolution" was bound to acquire political overtones, and did, despite the asocial attitude assumed by its proponents in the early phase. Thanks to this phenomenon there was apparent, even before World War II, a somewhat contradictory reintegration of literature into politics, and, in the face of imminent danger, an assumption on the part of hitherto detached or downright contemptuous poets that they could not "disengage" themselves from the problems of the day. The break-out of hostilities, the defeat of France, the German occupation, the Resistance, post-war international rivalries, gave this tendency an almost irresistible momentum. There is, to be sure, more variety, more of an individualistic turn than ever to the poetical efforts of the newest generation. Post-surrealists like René Char (1907-   ; q.v.) and Georges Schéhadé (1910-   ) rub elbows with Catholic authors such as Patrice de La Tour du Pin (1911-   ) or Pierre Emmanuel (1916-   ; qq.v.); the anti-intellectualism of Jacques Prévert (1900-   ; q.v.) is poles apart from the introspective forays of Henri Michaux (1899-   ; q.v.) or the so-called "scientific spirit" of Francis Ponge (1899-   ; q.v.). Yet all of these writers, including the least positive-minded among them, avow a determination to renounce their elders' systematic aversion to the "order of things" and, as a token of this renewed interest in common humanity, unless one should say humanism, to use once again a fairly intelligible idiom. In short, despite the fact that French poetry is as mature as it ever will be, the pendulum of change keeps swinging. The only immutable element in its kaleidoscopic history is the poet's pride in his mission, best exemplified nowadays in the noble work of Saint John Perse (pseud. of Alexis Léger, 1887-   ; q.v.) who, in accents reminiscent of Ronsard, Malherbe, and Victor Hugo, tells us that poetry is the true voice of mankind; that it is, aside from prayer, the only knowable means of seeking plenitude; that it conquers the eternal life through the apprehension of death. (See *Epic; Lyric Poetry*).

Anthologies—1) General: Fernand Mazade, ed., *Anthologie des poètes français des origines à nos jours*, Paris (hereafter the place of publication unless otherwise indicated), 4 vols., 1926-28; Thierry-Maulnier, ed., *Introduction à la poésie française*, 1939; Marcel Arland, ed., *Anthologie de la poésie française*, 1943; André Gide, ed.,

Anthologie de la poésie française, 1949.

2) Limited: André Mary, ed., *La Fleur de la poésie française depuis les origines jusqu'à la fin du XVe siècle,* 1951; Georges Duhamel, ed., *Anthologie de la poésie lyrique en France de la fin du XVe siècle à la fin du XIXe,* 1946; Maurice Chapelan, ed., *Anthologie du poème en prose,* 1946; Anon., ed., *Anthologie de la nouvelle poésie française* (generally called *Anthologie Kra* from the name of its publisher), new ed., 1928; Georges Hugnet, ed., *Petite anthologie poétique du Surréalisme,* 1934; Marcel Béalu, ed., *Anthologie de la poésie française depuis le Surréalisme,* 1952.

3) In textbook form (American): Arthur Graves Canfield and Warner Forrest Patterson, eds., *French Poems* [from the XIVth to the XXth century], New York, 1941; Elliott M. Grant, ed., *French Poetry of the XIXth Century,* New York, 1940; William Leonard Schwartz, ed., *French Romantic Poetry: An Anthology,* New York, 1932.

Critical Studies: René Lalou, *Les Étapes de la poésie française,* 1947; Gustave Cohen, *La Poésie française au Moyen-Age,* 1952; Warner Forrest Patterson, *Three Centuries of French Poetic Theory: A Critical History of the Chief Arts of Poetry in France (1328-1630),* 2 vols., Ann Arbor, Mich., 1935; Robert John Clements, *Critical Theory and Practice of the Pléiade,* Cambridge, Mass., 1942; Raymond Lebègue, *La Poésie française de 1560 à 1630,* 1951; André Bellessort, *Sur les grands chemins de la poésie classique,* 1914; Henri Tronchon, *Romantisme et Préromantisme,* 1930; Pierre Moreau, *Le Romantisme,* vol. VIII of *Histoire de la littérature française publiée sous la direction de Jean Calvet,* 1932; Herbert J. Hunt, *The Epic in Nineteenth-Century France,* Oxford, 1941; Aaron Schaffer, *Parnassus in France,* Austin, Texas, 1929; Pierre Martino, *Parnasse et Symbolisme, 1830-1900,* 1925; René Lalou, *Vers une alchimie lyrique,* 1927; Kenneth Cornell, *The Symbolist Movement,* 1951; Marcel Raymond, *De Baudelaire au Surréalisme,* 1933 (English transl., 1950); Anna Balakian, *Literary Origins of French Surrealism,* New York, 1947; Gaëtan Picon, *Panorama de la nouvelle littérature française,* 1949; Jean Rousselot, *Panorama critique des nouveaux poètes français,* 1952; Joseph Chiari, *Contemporary French Poetry,* Manchester, England, 1952; Germaine Brée, "Literature: Poetry and the Novel," in: *Culture of France in Our Time,* Ithaca, N. Y., 1954.

JEAN-ALBERT BÉDÉ

Polexandre (1629-1637): See *Gomberville.*

Polyeucte: Written by Corneille (1641-1642?; q.v.), this tragic masterpiece is based on the account given by Surius, the Roman historian of the sixteenth century, of the martyrdom of Saint Polyeucte which took place in the fourth century in Armenia. Polyeucte, an Armenian nobleman, has been able, with the consent of Félix, now governor of Armenia, to marry, though without her love, Pauline, Félix's daughter. Formerly, in Rome, Félix refused to give the hand of his daughter in marriage, despite her genuine feelings of love, to Sévère, a Roman suitor. Pauline, however, once again sees Sévère; now a favorite of the Roman emperor, he appears in Armenia at the head of a victorious army. When in his presence, she reveals her troubled feelings, admits her love for him, but, as a dutiful wife, refuses ever to see him again. In the meantime, however, Polyeucte, won over to Christianity, has been converted; having profaned the Roman gods in the temple, he is thrown into prison. When his father-in-law and Pauline, whom he sincerely loves, ask him to renounce

255

his new faith, he resists, ready for martyrdom. and even urges his wife to marry Sévère. Pauline, now moved by her husband's ideal, beseeches her father to save him. Afraid of Sévère, however, Félix sends Polyeucte to his death. Polyeucte's act of faith, at the expense of his life and of his love for Pauline, brings about the conversion of Pauline and of Félix. Sévère, leaving them unmolested, promises to do his best to put an end to persecution.

Ponge, Francis: (1899-   ) The *word* is the *thing*, would be one way of characterizing the philosophical essence of the poetry of this writer from Montpellier. Between the "thing" and the poet an identification is in the process of taking place, one so complete that in the course of describing the object or animal, the poet himself runs the risk of becoming "involved" or entangled. Such, at any rate, seems to be the general theory behind *Le Parti pris des choses* (1942) and *Dix-Courts sur la Méthode* (1947), short poetic collections in prose.

Ponsard, François: (1814-1867) With *Lucrèce* (1843), a tragedy in verse written the same year that Hugo's (q.v.) unsuccessful *Burgraves* put an end to the Romantic "drame" (q.v.), this dramatist tried to revive the Classical tragedy (q.v.). In this attempt he represents the so-called school of Common Sense. The public's interest in contemporary types and themes, however, foredoomed this attempt to failure. Ponsard thus turned to writing comedies in verse. Among them are: *L'Honneur et l'Argent* (1853), and *La Bourse* (1856).

C. Latreille, *La fin du théâtre romantique, François Ponsard*, 1899.

Populism: In two different manifestoes (Aug. 1929; Jan. 1930), André Thérive (1891-   ), together with Léon Lemonnier (1892-   ), protested against the aristocratic and *mondain* literature that was then fashionable. In addition to being the author of literary criticism and of a pessimistic novel, *Les Souffrances Perdues* (1927), André Thérive wrote *Sans âme* (1928) and *Le Charbon ardent* (1929), "populist" novels, couched in a learned and elegant form. This type of novel, engaged in by such novelists as Eugène Dabit (1898-1936), a Parisian laborer, Jean Prévost (q.v.), Tristan Rémy (1897-   ), and others, along with Léon Lemonnier, who had written *Femme sans péché* (1931), portrays the life of humble people. Dabit's *Hôtel du Nord* (1929)—probably the outstanding example of the populist novel—depicts the life of a small "hôtel de quartier"; *Sans âme* evokes sad and humble Parisian landscapes; *Femme sans péché* analyzes an admirable woman of the people. These novels, furthermore, are practically without any plot.

The "populist" writers, including those from Belgium, though without any artistic doctrine, represent, more than a "school," a tendency that may be characterized as neonaturalist. Their writings, moreover, do not fall into the excesses of which Naturalism (q.v.) was guilty; they are presented with more truth and equilibrium and with less exaggeration. To the "populist" writers, reputed to possess a "bourgeois" spirit, Henri Poulaille (1896-   ) opposed his "proletarian" literature, which claimed to be one written for the people and by the people, and not by professional writers. Poulaille's *Pain de Soldat* (1936) is a profitable illustration of his approach. Poulaille is also the spirit behind many journals that pretend to address themselves to the working class.

Each year the "prix populiste," originally created by Mme. Antonine Coulet-Tessier in 1931, is awarded for the best work embodying "populist" aims. Its tradition still persists.

Michel Ragon, *Les Écrivains du peuple,* 1947.

Porte étroite, La (1909): See *Gide.*

Porto-Riche, Georges de: (1849-1930) Born in Bordeaux of Italian Jewish parents, this dramatist, after having written verses and plays in the romantic tradition, was brought to public attention by Antoine (q.v.) who produced at the Théâtre-Libre (q.v.) his *La Chance de Françoise* (1888). In this and subsequent plays he shows, within the framework of a simple, compact plot, a penetrating analysis of the human heart and its passions. The title *Théâtre d'amour,* the general heading of his plays, which include *Amoureuse* (1891), *Le Passé* (1897) and *Le Vieil Homme* (1911), describes their theme. Not unlike those of Racine (q.v.), to whom he has been frequently compared, the characters delineated in the different love crises in the above plays yield fatalistically to the call of passion. However, what interests Porto-Riche—and in this lies part of his originality—is the search for happiness in love in a situation where the man is characteristically polygamous and the woman instinctively monogamous. Husband and wife, in *Amoureuse,* his best known and most successful play, because of the different values they establish for marriage, create a tense, dramatic situation, the result of which suggests that the dissolution of their union, however tragic that union be, would serve no good purpose, since they are linked together by their antagonisms as well as by their intimacies. Their loves are unequal, and of the two, the suffering of the woman gets a greater portion of the author's sympathy. This psychological pattern is characteristic of this writer, who uses throughout a restrained classical style, one, however, which evokes poetically the violence

of desire. Other plays include *Zubiri* (1912), *Le Marchand d'estampes* (1917) and *Les Vrais Dieux* (1929).

W. Müller, *G. de Porto-Riche,* 1934.

Portraits littéraires (1836-1839): See *Sainte-Beuve.*

Port-Royal: Founded in 1204, this convent for women, located near Paris, had fallen in the seventeenth century into a state of decadence. Through the efforts of Angélique Arnauld (1591-1661), its Mother Superior, it underwent a religious reform, and in 1626 it was transferred to Paris. In 1637, following the appointment of Saint-Cyran (1635) as spiritual adviser to Port-Royal, where Jansenism (q.v.) was introduced, the original convent—Port-Royal des Champs—became a retreat for the *Solitaires* (q.v.)—those lay scholars and theologians who came here for study and meditation; these scholars, incidentally, were to foster in their Jansenist schools the study of Latin and Greek. Becoming synonymous with Jansenism, Port-Royal, attacked by the Jesuits, was later defended (1656-1657) by Pascal (q.v.). From this point on, its history is essentially that of Jansenism.

Sainte-Beuve, *Port-Royal,* 3ᵉ édition, 1867; A. Hallays, *Le pélerinage de Port-Royal,* 1909; J. Orcibal, *Jean Duvergier de Hauranne, abbé de Saint-Cyran, et son temps (1581-1638),* 1947-1948.

Port-Royal (1840-1859): See *Sainte-Beuve.*

Positivism: A philosophical system founded by Auguste Comte (q.v.) and based on the study and evidence of perceptible facts.

Poudre aux yeux, La (1862): See *Labiche.*

Pour et le contre, Le (1733-1740): See *Prévost, L'Abbé.*

Pradon, Jacques: (1644-1698) Although he wrote a number of tragedies, including *Pyrame et Thisbé* (1674), *Regulus* (1688) and *Scipion l'Afri-*

cain (1697), he is especially remembered for his *Phèdre et Hippolyte* (1677), which he wrote to rival Racine's *Phèdre* (1677; q.v.) at the request of the Duchess of Bouillon, an enemy of Racine.
T. W. Bussom, *Pradon*, 1922.

Précellence du langage français (1579): See *Estienne, Henri [II]*.

précieuses: They and the *précieux* frequented the Hôtel de Rambouillet (q.v.) and other similar *salons* and helped develop the movement known as *préciosité* (q.v.).

Précieuses ridicules, Les (1659): See *Molière*.

précieux: At the Hôtel de Rambouillet (q.v.), which they together with the *précieuses* frequented, they helped develop the movement known as preciosity (q.v.). In conversation and manners they were over-refined, and tended in general to exaggerate.

préciosité: A social and literary movement, first developed at the *Hôtel de Rambouillet* (q.v.). Here politeness and refinement, in language and manners, represented a reaction against the coarseness that characterized the court of Henry IV. Soon, as cultivated at the *salons* of Mlle. de Scudéry and others, this movement took on exaggerated features, resulting in affectation of language and manners, over-refinement and elegance. Ordinary terms of conversation were replaced by fastidious words and paraphrases; love became an artificial convention, manifesting platonic aspects, and entered into literature—especially in the novels composed by Mlle. de Scudéry (q.v.) in collaboration with her brother—as a kind of game. The excesses of *préciosité*, which spread even to the provinces, were satirized in Molière's (q.v.) *Les Précieuses ridicules* (1659) and ridiculed by Boileau (q.v.). Despite its evil influences, *préciosité* encouraged social intercourse between the nobles and writers. The latter, who had

rid themselves of the academic pedantry inherited from the Renaissance (q.v.), expressed themselves with distinction and elegance, and directed their attention toward the psychological analysis of human beings, which was to become an integral part of French classical literature. Analogous to *préciosité* in France is euphuism in England, gongorism in Spain, and marinism in Italy.
Ch. Livet, *Précieux et Précieuses*, 1859; E. Magne, *Madame de la Suze et la société précieuse*, 1908; G. Mongrédien, *Les Précieux et Précieuses*, 1939; R. Bray, *La Préciosité et les Précieux*, 1948.

preciosity: See *préciosité*.

Préface de Cromwell: A literary manifesto, written by Victor Hugo (q.v.) in 1827, which includes the basic theories for Romanticism (q.v.) as they apply especially to the theater. Stressing man's duality since the advent of Christianity, the last of the three great ages in the history of humanity that it discusses, it wages war, in the name of truth, against the classical distinction drawn between tragedy (q.v.) and comedy (q.v.). Since life, urges Hugo, is a mixture of both tragedy and comedy, the theater should combine the antithetical aspects of the grotesque and of the sublime. For similar reasons, the *drame*, incorporating the dramatic theories advanced by Hugo, would abolish the classical unities (q.v.) of time and place, but would retain the unity of action. Rendering the traditional *alexandrine* (q.v.) line of the classical tragedy more flexible by the use of such devices as *enjambement* (q.v.) and the displacement of the caesura, it would also offer a *couleur locale* that would reproduce with exactitude the decor of the period and country in which the action, now taken from the Middle Ages or from modern history, is laid. A good example of the application of these theories can be seen in Hugo's *Ruy Blas* (q.v.), which is typical, too, of many of the melodramatic characteristics of the romantic theater in France.

M. Souriau, *La Préface de Cromwell* (critical ed. with introduction), 1897.

Préjugé à la mode, Le (1735): See *La Chaussée.*

Prévert, Jacques: (1900-   ) Popular with the present younger generation, partly because of the scenarios and dialogues he has written for such well-known films as *Drôle de Drame* and *Les Enfants du Paradis,* this poet, influenced in his youth by Surrealism (q.v.), first revealed himself in 1931 when he wrote *Tentative de Description d'un Dîner de Têtes à Paris-France,* a humorous fantasy. His poetry, characterized by a voluntary disorder of ideas and puns, but by simplicity in rhythm, rhyme and assonance, draws most of its themes from familiar objects and street scenes in daily life. *Paroles* (1946)—a collection of poems that had previously appeared in magazines or that had been left with friends but which had since been set to music—and *Histoires* (1948), another collection, are satirical, and ridicule all those who represent conformism—financiers, magistrates, statesmen, teachers, and churchmen—and who thus prevent others from enjoying such simple pleasures of life as revery, friendship, and love. More recent collections include *Spectacle* (1951) and *La Pluie et le beau temps* (1955).

Prévost, L'Abbé Antoine-François: (1697-1763) Novelist and man of letters, he led an extraordinary and adventurous life. A member of the Jesuit order, then a soldier, then a member of the Benedictine order—which he entered after an unhappy love affair—he fled again, after being ordained a priest (1726), and spent several years in England and Hol-

land. His interest in English literature resulted in translations into French of *Paméla* (1742), *Clarisse Harlowe* (1751) and *Grandisson* (1775), novels written by Richardson. Devoted to a literary career, he published voluminously—twenty volumes of *Le Pour et le contre* (1733-1740), a literary and critical periodical, seventeen volumes of *Histoire générale des voyages* (1745-1761), works of travel, not to mention his memoirs and novels. Of all these works, however, he is best remembered for *Manon Lescaut* (1731; q.v.), which makes up the seventh volume of his *Mémoires d'un homme de qualité* (1728-1731). Depicting love as a passion causing untold suffering and rendering the main protagonist a helpless victim to its powers, *Manon Lescaut* foreshadows the romantic novel. Included among his other novels are: *Le Philosophe anglais ou Histoire de M. Cleveland* (1731-1739) and *Le Doyen de Killerine* (1735-1740).

H. Harisse, *L'Abbé Prévost, histoire de sa vie et de ses œuvres,* 1896; V. Schroeder, *L'Abbé Prévost, sa vie, ses romans,* 1898.

Prévost, Jean: (1901-1944) Author of critical studies on Montaigne, Saint-Evremond, and Stendhal (qq.v.), he also wrote *Dix-huitième année* (1929), dealing with "his boyhood memories, and two "populist" (see *Populism*) novels, *Les Frères Bouquinquant* (1930) and *Le Sel sur la plaie* (1935). He died in the *maquis* of Vercors in 1944. *Baudelaire,* a critical study, was published posthumously in 1953.

Prévost, Marcel: (1862-1941) With much psychological insight, this novelist and minor dramatist studies woman almost exclusively. *L'Automne d'une femme* (1893) depicts a woman of forty. Other novels, such as *La Confession d'un amant* (1891) and the *Lettres de femmes* series (1892-1897), because of their somewhat libertine tone, assured him popularity. Social and moral criticism are contained in such novels as *Les Demi-Vierges* (1894)—later adapted for the stage—which is the name given to those young women whose moral education is lax, and *Les Vierges fortes* (1900). The latter novel is an attack on the then prevalent concept of feminism that disregarded family traditions. In *Lettres à Françoise* (1902-1912) he outlines a program of moral education for women that is both realistic and enlightened.

Prince charmant, Le (1914): See *Bernard, Tristan*.

Prince d'Aurec, Le (1892): See *Lavedan, Henri*.

Princesse de Clèves, La: Written in 1678 by Mme. de la Fayette (q.v.), this short novel, the first psychological novel in French and in modern literature, is the tragic story of frustrated love. Mlle. de Chartres, following the advice of her mother, has married M. de Clèves, for whom, however, she feels only esteem and admiration. A Cornelian kind of conflict soon arises, however, after she meets the gallant Duc de Nemours: her love for him struggles against her sense of conjugal duty and honor. Troubled, and fearful lest she fall prey to her guilty passion, she turns to her husband, beseeching him to protect her against herself. Although the Prince de Clèves fully appreciates the spirit that motivates his wife's confession, he is so grief-stricken and tortured by jealousy that he falls ill and dies. The Princesse de Clèves, now free to accept the lover of her choice, retires instead to a convent.

Prix Goncourt: An annual prize awarded by the *Académie Goncourt* (q.v.) for the best work in prose. The first prize, inaugurated in 1903, was given to John-Antoine Pau for his *Forces ennemies*. Marcel Proust's (q.v.) reputation, it may be noted, was first established in 1919 when he received the *Prix Goncourt* for

his *A l'Ombre des jeunes filles en fleur*. The recipients of this award since 1950 have been: Paul Colin, *Les Jeux Sauvages* (1950); Julien Gracq (q.v.), *Le Rivage des Syrtes* (1951); Béatrice Beck (q.v.), *Léon Morin, Prêtre* (1952); Pierre Gascar (q.v.), *Les Bêtes*, suivis de *Le Temps des Morts* (1953); Simone de Beauvoir (q.v.), *Les Mandarins* (1954); Roger Ikor, *Les Eaux Mêlées* (1955); Romain Gary (q.v.), *Les Racines du Ciel* (1956); Roger Vailland, *La Loi* (1957).

Proust, Marcel: (1871-1922) This novelist, one of the most famous literary figures of his generation, came of a Parisian bourgeois family. His father was Professor at the *Faculté de Médecine;* his mother, born Jeanne Weil, came of a Jewish family. His studies completed, he frequented for several years the Parisian world of society and made friends with the literary and the fashionable figures. The deaths in rapid succession of his father (1903) and mother (1905), added to a recurrence of his chronic asthmatic condition, caused him to withdraw to his cork-lined chamber, where, in constant fear that death would soon overtake him and in the solitude of his invalidism, he was to create his *A la Recherche du temps perdu* (1913-1928), which, as the title suggests, was his spiritual adventure or meditation on life, on his life, in quest of whose meaning this work was to be the artistic result.

Du Côté de chez Swann (1913), the first book of *A la Recherche du temps perdu*, after being refused by several publishers, appeared at the author's expense; *A l'Ombre des jeunes filles en fleur* (1918), however, received the *Prix Goncourt* (q.v.), arousing much controversy. The next four years were to see the publication of *Le Côté de Guermantes* (1920) and *Sodome et Gomorrhe* (4 vols., 1921-1922). The remaining volumes of this *roman-*

fleuve (q.v.), *La Prisonnière* (2 vols., 1923), *Albertine disparue* (2 vols., 1925), and *Le Temps retrouvé* (2 vols., 1927), were to appear posthumously. The last named title is the key to the entire work.

The lack of apparent plan or "plot" in this work, the minutiae of detail, the long descriptions, the accumulation of historical and artistic comparisons and metaphors, the frequently long sentences interspersed with parenthetical phrases —all this is enough to disconcert the reader who approaches Proust for the first time. An understanding of some basic notions, however, will reveal to the reader much clarity and organization in Proust's intellectual universe—"intellectual," precisely because it is seen through the subjective mind. Proust's approach is based on Schopenhauer's concept that the world is the *idea* that each individual has of it; therefore, life is lived through Memory, which fuses the past, a past which is not dead but dormant, with the present, giving to Time a Bergsonian (see *Bergson*) sense. Through an artistic process that may be likened to Baudelaire's (q.v.) "correspondences" or "associations," Proust is inspired by "involuntary" or subconscious memory (*e.g.* the sensation aroused by the taste of a cake) to resurrect and re-create, *via* a conscious, intellectual effort ("voluntary memory"), the emotions and experiences of the past, which he now tries to understand in relation to his present *self*. Hence the narrator in *Du Côté de chez Swann* re-creates for himself a total, durable reality by bringing to the conscious surface once more his childhood days, those people, like Swann, whom he knew or associated with, and his vacation in the country at Combray. Similarly, the narrator evokes his vacation at Balbec, the seashore, his love for Albertine, the *salons* he frequented, the vices and foibles of the bourgeois and

aristocratic society that Proust knew so well and whose class distinctions at the end of *A la Recherche du temps perdu* disappear. The subjective and inner image of the outer world is also seen in Proust's psychological explorations of love, friendship and jealousy. Proust's influence has been considerable, especially on English and American literature.

Other writings of Proust are *Les Plaisirs et les jours* (1896), a collection of portraits and sketches, *Pastiches et mélanges* (1919), journalistic essays, *Jean Santeuil* (1952), a recently discovered first-draft of a novel, which, though lacking the author's preoccupation with time and the theme of the tragic futility of all human relations, nevertheless represents an introduction to his artistic philosophy and serves as a springboard for his *A la Recherche du temps perdu*, and *Contre Sainte-Beuve* (1954), a volume of criticism.

Léon-Pierre Quint, *M. Proust, sa vie, son œuvre,* 1935; André Maurois, *A la Recherche de Marcel Proust,* 1949; G. Brée, *Du Temps Perdu au Temps Retrouvé,* 1950.

PROVENÇAL:

A. LANGUAGE

During the last twenty-five years an imposing number of French poets, literary critics and scholars have advised discrimination in the use of the term "provençal" and urged the adoption of that of "occitan" as a general name for the romance dialects of southern France. These are still often referred to as the "langue d'Oc" dialects because of their common way, in the Middle Ages, of expressing the affirmation by *Oc* (Lat. *hoc*). *Oïl* (Lat. *hoc ille*) served the same purpose in the romance dialects of northern France. *Oïl* became *Oui* in modern French and *Oc* became *O* or *Vo* in modern Provençal. The "Occitanians" claim that "provençal" should be used only with reference to the dialects of Provence proper. However, in spite of its alleged impropriety, "provençal" has so far remained the consecrated term, especially outside France where philologists continue referring to the language of the troubadours of the twelfth and thirteenth centuries as "Old Provençal," and to that of the nineteenth- and twentieth-century "langue d'Oc" poets as "Modern Provençal."

Like French and the other Romance languages, Provençal may be considered as "evolved Latin." It developed according to the same general rules which governed Vulgar Latin itself: unstressed syllables weakened further or disappeared completely, both vowels and consonant sounds were modified, declensions simplified, articles, prepositions and new verbs created. But the "langue d'Oc" dialects did not develop as fast as those of the "langue d'oïl" (q.v.) and remained closer to Latin. The principal reason for this difference was the influence of the substratum, as the survival of old traditions and speech habits lasted longer in the south. Another important factor was the nature of Greek and Roman influences, which were more intense and thorough as they extended over a longer period.

One of the most striking differences between the northern and southern dialects, as they evolved from Latin, concerned the evolution of stressed vowels (Lat. *mel* > OP *mel,* OF *miel*) and intervocalic consonants (Lat. *pacare* > OP *pagar,* OF *payer*). Most interesting is the fate of the stressed free *a* which changed into a variety of *e*'s in the north but remained unchanged in the south (Lat. *cantare* > OP *cantar,* OF *chanter*). Also to be noted is the case of *c* which in most of the "langue d'Oïl" dialects was palatized before *a,* while it remained unchanged in "langue d'Oc" (OP *cantar,* OF *chanter*).

Toward the end of the thirteenth century Provençal lost most of its prestige as a literary language, but its various dialects continued to develop according to general laws: *cantar, pagar, mèl* have become *canta, paga* (or *paca*) and *mèu* in the phonetic spelling given to Modern Provençal a century ago. However, both the pronunciation and spelling vary greatly from province to province and sometimes from town to town. Thus *mèu* is *mèl* in Languedoc and in some regions of Provence, *mial* in Limousin, *miau* in Auvergne, *mea* or *miè* in Dauphiné, *amè* at Menton, etc.; "skin" or "hide" is *pèu* in Provence, *pèl* in Languedoc, *pèt* in Gascony, *pèr* in Dauphiné, *pè* in Auvergne; "to want" is *voulé* in Provence, *boulé* or *boulgué* in Languedoc, *vourgué* in the Alps, *voulei* in Auvergne and Limousin. Provençal also has a number of words of different origins which are not found in French or other "langue d'Oïl" dialects.

Finally, through the centuries, but especially during the last two hundred years, Provençal has been more or less altered by its contact with French. Provençalization of French words is still in process. As an example, the term *go* (drinking glass), *oulo* (kettle) and *cadiero* (chair), which were still commonly used three or four generations ago have been replaced by *veire* (Fr. *verre*), *marmito* (Fr. *marmite*) and *cheso* (Fr. *chaise*).

The "langue d'Oc" dialects usually tend to stress their differences rather than their common traits and have degenerated into an indefinite number of sub-dialects or patois. The failure to unify them is due in the first place to the disdain that the sophisticated classes have shown for the mother tongue, and secondly to the particularist attitude of writers who cannot come to an agreement on the question of spelling. Yet even though the death sentence of Provençal has been pronounced many times during the last hundred years, there are still several millions of people who speak it and a rather important number of young poets who insist on using it as a means of literary expression.

B. LITERATURE

It is very likely that a kind of literary language already existed in the langue d'Oc country before the eleventh century. But the oldest text which has come to us—257 verses of a poem on Boethius's *De consolatione philosophiæ*—was probably written after the year 1000. We have other pieces which belong to the 11th century: a poem on "Sainte Foy d'Agen" and a fragment of a "Song of Alexander" whose authors were also unknown and must have been clerics.

The golden age of Provençal literature, which found its best expression in the lyric poetry of the troubadours, was the twelfth century. The language used by the troubadours had, like that of the Boethius poem, many common traits with the Limousin dialect and was referred to as the *lengua limousina*. It was not a purely artificial and composite language, and recent scholars believe it was based mainly on the dialect of the Toulouse region.

The works of about four hundred troubadours have come down to us in collections made between the 13th and 16th centuries. Some of them contain short biographical and critical sketches that give a fair amount of reliable and interesting information on both the authors and the society in which they lived. There are also seventy known names of troubadours (q.v.) whose works have been lost.

The troubadours were natives of the various *Oc* provinces and belonged to all classes of society. Among them were kings and princes, feudal lords, clergymen, merchants, artisans, courtiers, and valets. Many of them were supported or protected by the great, and they had *jongleurs* (q.v.) to recite or sing their poems, which were originally meant to be sung. Some *jongleurs* learned the art of fine poetry and became troubadours while, inversely, some of the latter turned *jongleurs* when pressed economically.

It is apparent from their works that the troubadours practised an art which required a great amount of knowledge and training. They employed many different poetic forms—*canso, sirventes, tenson, balada, alba,* etc.—which they endlessly refined. In this respect their works presented a certain uniformity, but they varied greatly in content. While courtly love (q.v.) was their main theme, they occasionally dealt with love and women in a far less idealistic fashion. They also related their personal experiences, satirized society, and sometimes fiercely attacked the powerful lords whom they opposed. Some of them produced a very symbolistic, at times mystical and extremely esoteric poetry.

William IX of Poitiers (1071-1127), the earliest known troubadour as well as one of the most famous, dealt with courtly love in only four of his eleven extant poems. Marcabru, who wrote in the years 1130-1150, was a misogynist who assumed a hostile attitude toward love. Quite different were his contemporaries Jauffré Rudel, whose legend of the far away princess has fascinated some of our modern poets, and Bernard de Ventadour, who has been regarded as the greatest lyric poet of his time.

Also of the same period were Bertran de Born, who sang of both love and war, Arnaud Daniel, whose difficult and abstruse poetry was highly praised by Dante and Petrarch, and Raimbaud d'Orange, who denied the existence of love and was loved by the most famous *trobairitz* of his time, the Countess de Die.

Troubadouresque literature influenced not only the *trouvères* or troubadours of northern France (both terms meant "poet," literally "finder"), but also Spanish, Portuguese, Italian, and even German and English poets. Yet, due to a combination of circumstances, on the relative importance of which scholars do not agree unanimously, it was destined to decline rapidly during the following century. Perhaps it was destined to die a natural death because of its "artificiality" and incapacity to renew itself—as it has been affirmed—but the fact remains that in the 13th century conditions were hardly propitious for the production and development of genius.

The Albigensian Crusade, which put the south to fire and sword, and the Inquisition, which systematically burned religious writings in the vernacular, played probably the most important role in the destruction, if not of the Provençal language and literature themselves, at least of the civilization in which they had developed. This civilization, called *paratge* (*par* = equal) was based on such principles as the respect for the dignity of man—which entailed the principle of equality among men and between the sexes—tolerance in all matters (including religion), and scorn for the use of force. The Midi has always believed in peace and the arts. After the Crusade, which began in 1209, a tyrannical centralizing regime replaced that aristocratic democracy in which talent had drawn together princes and plebeians. The south-ern maecenases disappeared or submitted to the Church, which requested them to banish all luxury, including poetry, from their courts. Thus was a new philosophy, a new concept of life, and a rigid intellectual discipline imposed from without. Literature fell into the hands of the clergy, and by the end of the century, as expressed by an authority on the period, Scholasticism had triumphed over *paratge* and the *Gai Saber*. Neither the language nor the literature disappeared completely, but they gradually lost their splendor and dignity, their free and fine demeanour.

While a few troubadours continued to write as if nothing had happened, many introduced a new note in their lyric poems, which at times turned into violent political diatribes against Simon de Montfort and his Crusaders who had come to destroy their civilization. The greatest among these was Peire Cardenal, who, in this respect, has been compared to Agrippa d'Aubigné and Victor Hugo (qq.v.). With him began a new genre, poetry in honor of the Blessed Virgin which soon became very popular and one of the characteristics of the period of decadence. Opposed to Cardenal was Folquet de Marseille, who became bishop of Toulouse and sided with the Crusaders. The prolific Guiraut Riquier, who has been called "the last of the troubadours," lived for several years at the court of the king of Castile, Alphonse X, the Learned. Like him, many 13th-century troubadours went into exile in Spain or in northern Italy, where living conditions were better than in France and where traditions of Provençal poetry had been maintained.

Besides lyric poetry (q.v.), a certain amount of epic (q.v.) and narrative poetry was also written. The earliest Provençal epic that we have, *Girart de Roussillon* (end of 12th century) was probably preceded by others, as suggested by the already mentioned fragment of *Alexander* and a fragment of the *Chanson of Antioche* (beginning of the century). To this must be added the 1437 extant verses of the epic of *Aigar and Maurin* and the 2200 of *Daurel and Beton,* also of the twelfth century. One play, *Sponsus,* a translation of the Latin novel *Philomena,* the Catalan *novas* (novelettes) of Ramon Vidal de Besalú, a few fragments of the life of Saint Amans, and a prose translation of the Gospel belong also to the "Golden Age."

However, it was in the 13th century that religious, intellectual and didactic literature flourished particularly. All the knowledge, aspirations, and ideals of the new era seem to have been summarized in *Lo Breviari d'Amor,* a huge work of 40,000 verses by a Franciscan monk, Matfre Ermengaud. *Lo Breviari* enjoyed a tremendous success until the end of the 14th century. There are at least three 13th-century masterpieces which, even in a short survey, must be named: *Jaufré,* an Arthurian romance, *Flamenca,* acclaimed a perfect jewel among the romances of adventure, and the *Vida de Santa Enimia,* one of the best of the lives of Saints. To these must be added the *Chanson of the Crusade* (6810 verse epic), the *Biographies of the troubadours* (there are 97 of them), and the Provençal works of another Franciscan monk, the Majorcan Ramon Lull (1235-1315). These have been discussed at length during the past few years and given the rank they deserve in the history of modern thought.

The 14th and 15th centuries have little to offer. The most important work produced then is perhaps *Las Leyes d'Amor* (the Rules of Poetry). It is an important treatise written for the Academy known as the Consistory of Gay Science, founded at Toulouse in 1323 for the purpose of encouraging lyric poetry in the vernacular. It codified, instead, all the 13th century ideas which tended to stifle inspiration and destroy free expression. By the time of the Renaissance, Provençal had completely disappeared as a classical and literary language. A dialectal literature had developed at the expenses of the "unity" of the Langue d'Oc, which has never been very great notwithstanding contrary opinions on the subject.

During the second half of the 16th century there was a kind of Renaissance in Provençal literature. The Béarnais catechisms and the Psalms of David rendered into Gascon by Pey de Garros were published in 1565. Encouraged by Salluste du Bartas, were other gascon and southern poets, among them Auger Galhard (approximately 1530-1592) of the Albigense region. In Provence, Bellaud de la Bellaudière (probably 1543-1588), who introduced the sonnet (q.v.) into Provençal poetry, initiated also a renaissance at a time when educated people in southern France were beginning to speak and write in French. But Provençal literature, which in the 12th century was meant for a refined and sophisticated class had now become the property of the common people. Hence the success of such popular genres as the *pastorelas,* the *Nouvé* (or Christmas carols) and other forms of didactic religious literature written for the edification of the people, the popular drama, and burlesque and satirical literature of the 17th, 18th, and part of the 19th centuries.

The following authors deserve to be mentioned here: Guilhem Ader, born in 1578, with his *Lou Gentilome gascoun;* the Provençal Nicolau Saboli (1614-1650) and his *Nouvé;* the Toulousain Goudolin (1579-1649), whose renown became

European through his *Lou Ramelet Moudi;* the dramatists Gaspar Zerbin, author of *La perlo dey musos et coumedies provensales* (1655) and Claude Brueys of Aix-en-Provence with his *Jardin deys Musos provençalos* (1628). In the 18th century, the Languedocian *abbé* Favre (1727-1783) towers far above all other poets with his parodies of the *Odyssey* and the *Eneide,* his picaresque novelette *L'Histouero de Joan-l'anores* and, especially, his mock-heroic poem *Lou siege de Cadaroussa.*

Among the immediate precursors of the 19th-century Renaissance must be named in the first place the Languedocian Fabre d'Olivet (1767-1825), more for his ideas, however, than for his poetry; and Jacques Boe, alias Jasmin (1798-1864), more for his poems than for his ideas. Jasmin, who enjoyed a tremendous popularity, considered himself the last representative of Oc or Provençal literature. Yet he was the chief inspiration for the following generation. We might call him an unconscious forerunner of the movement he professed to despise.

This Provençal renaissance of the nineteenth century was brought about by a combination of circumstances in which political events and social conditions played an important role. It was greatly furthered by individualism, the spirit of Liberty and a longing for self-assertion that prevailed in the provinces after the French Revolution. Also of great importance was the influence of poets and scholars who, during the romantic and preromantic periods, showed interest in the various dialects as well as the languages and literatures of the Middle Ages.

Collections of Provençal poetry and literary periodicals in the vernacular were published, and meetings of regional poets were organized by men who had come to realize the value of joint efforts. However, it was not until 1854 that a few poets from the Avignon region decided to band together and start an association with a definite purpose and a well-defined programme.

Like the founders of the "Consistory de la Gaya Siensa" in 1323, the members of this new pleiad were determined to do their utmost for the maintenance or restoration of the language and literature of the troubadours. To distinguish themselves from the latter and from their contemporaries they called themselves "Felibres," a term whose etymology is still debated. Their association is known as the "Felibrige." The Felibres worked immediately toward the adoption of a common orthography and the purification and enrichment of the Provençal vocabulary.

The movement was given a tremendous impulse in 1859 when Frédéric Mistral (1830-1914), the most famous of the group, published his *Mirèio,* with a French translation on the opposite page. *Mireille* is a poem in twelve cantos, a rustic epic and idyl in which the author depicted and exalted country life in the Rhone valley. It was crowned by the French Academy and it has been translated into all European languages—several times in English. The following year appeared Théodore Aubanel's first collection of lyrics, *La miougrano entre duberto,* which brought the element of pure passion into Provençal lyricism. Meanwhile, the organizer and "father" of the movement, Joseph Roumanille, was publishing his delightful short stories in the *Armana prouvençau,* the organ of the Felibrige since its foundation.

Later the Felibrige, which gave a good deal of attention to various political and social questions, became the most important manifestation of regionalism in France. Twenty years after its foundation it had spread from Provence to Gascony and attracted a large number of Langue d'Oc writers who felt the urge to use their "mother tongue" as a means of literary expression. Many of them were politically minded, fiery advocates of Federalism, but literary masterpieces continued to appear periodically: Mistral published *Calendau* in 1867, *Lou Tresor dóu Felibrige*, his famous dictionary, from 1875 to 1886, the *Pouemo dóu Rose* in 1897. Aubanel's *Li Fiho d'Avignoun* appeared in 1885, and Félix Gras's *Li Rouge dóu Miejour*, whose English translation had several American editions, in 1896. Valère Bernard published his novels *Bagatouni* in 1894 and *Lei Boumian* in 1906-1907; and Charles Rieu, his *Cant dou Terraire* from 1897 to 1911.

Mistral received a Nobel Prize in 1904 for both his literary works and his contributions to philology. Until his death, in 1914, he was recognized as the leading spirit of the movement. Since then the Felibrige has lost a great deal of its former glamor and importance but, considered as a general movement, it still represents the most important aspect of Regionalist thought and literature in southern France.

Among other Provençal or rather Langue d'Oc or "Occitan" poets who have become famous in the wake of Mistral must be named the Languedocian Antonin Perbosc, the Gascons Michel Camelat, Jean Baptiste Chèze, and Philadelphe de Gerde; Arsène Vermenouze from Auvergne, Joseph-Sébastien Pons from Roussillon, Joseph d'Arbeau, Marius Jouveau, Sully-André Peyre, and Pascal Eyssavel from Provence. Although poetry still holds first rank, it is now less concerned with local color and much more with lyrical and musical expression than in the past. Poets of the younger generation—such as Jean Mouzat in Limousin, Ismaël Girard and André Pic in Gascony, Reboul, Galtier, Delavouet and Pierre Millet in Provence—are producing works in which many examples of pure poetry can be found.

We shall not attempt to list authors of the "short short stories." Their name is legion. But the number of novels and novelettes in the vernacular has increased considerably since the First World War. It would be easy to select some forty titles of books ranking in value as high as some of the "best sellers" in the national language during the same period. Some of them, such as d'Arbaud's *La Bestio dóu Vacarés*, have acquired a world-wide reputation.

The drama, especially comedy and farce, has always been a popular genre in southern France. We know from various sources, such as the local press and unpublished repertories sometimes found in municipal archives, that thousand of unpublished plays have been performed in the past, especially in the 16th and 17th centuries. Similarly there are to-day many successful plays (Marquion's *Amour de chato* is a case in point) which remain unpublished. Perhaps the most prolific dramatist of this century has been the Languedocian Emile Barthe. But playwrights are not the only ones unable to publish their works. During the last few years several literary prizes have been awarded for works which are still waiting for the favorable conditions which will allow them to come from the press.

Except in the two periods (12th and 19th centuries) during which it shone most brilliantly, Provençal literature has been hardly noticed by the general public, almost entirely ignored in the very country where it has flourished.

This is mostly due to the fact that it is the literature of a tongue which is not and has never been an official, politically recognized language. And yet Provençal literature possesses this particular characteristic of having developed independently, creating new forms and new themes which have been imitated in all other European literatures; and secondly that of having successfully revived certain genres (with Mistral and Félix Gras particularly) at a time when the attempt would have been doomed to failure in French and other modern languages.

It would be presumptuous to predict the fate of Provençal literature in the near future. Notwithstanding the great activity described above, and in spite of the law of 1950 allowing the teaching of dialects in the French elementary schools, the number of young people determined to write in the vernacular is slowly decreasing as French penetrates deeper into the provinces and the leaders of the renaissance fail to agree on a common orthography for the langue d'Oc dialects. On these two factors rather than on any other political or social development depends the fate of Provençal literature.

Edouard Bourciez, *Éléments de Linguistique romane,* 1923; Joseph Anglade, *Les Troubadours,* 1921; Alfred Jeanroy, *La Poésie occitane*

des origines à la fin du 18ᵉ siècle, 1945; Charles Camproux, *Histoire de la littérature occitane,* 1953; Alphonse V. Roche, *Provençal Regionalism,* 1954.

ALPHONSE V. ROCHE

Provençale, La (1731): See *Regnard.*
Proverbes (1768-1781): See *Carmontelle.*
Psichari, Ernest: (1883-1914) This writer, author of two novels of mystic and patriotic inspiration, *L'Appel des armes* (1912) and *Le Voyage du centurion* (1916), was killed in action during the First World War. He was the grandson of Renan (q.v.).
Pucelle d'Orléans, La (1656-1657): See *Chapelain, Jean.*
puy: A literary society, of which there were many during the Middle Ages, including those at Amiens, Arras and Valenciennes, that produced the *miracles* (q.v.) upon the occasion of some solemn celebration of the Virgin. It also encouraged competition in dramatic performances and in lyric poetry. It was presided over by a prince seated on a pedestal—hence the etymological meaning of the term by extension—who awarded the prize to the winner.
Pyrame et Thisbé (1674): See *Pradon, Jacques.*
Pyrame et Thisbé (1617): See *Viau, Théophile de.*

Q

Quarrel of the Ancients and Moderns: See *Querelle des Anciens et des Modernes.*
Quarrel of the Cid: See *Querelle du Cid.*

Quatre-vingt-treize (1874): See *Hugo.*
Queneau, Raymond: (1903-   ) Philosopher and former surrealist, he has published since 1933 a number of novels, including *Le Chiendent*

(1933), *Pierrot mon ami* (1943), *Loin de Rueil* (1944), *Saint-Glinglin* (1948), and *Le Dimanche de la vie* (1952). The parody in these novels conveyed through his "epic" characters, including concierges, bartenders, junk-dealers, clowns, acrobats, indulging in sport events, carnival scenes and collective rejoicing—insignificant actions that are magnified and given official consecration—assumes the quality of Existentialist (see *Existentialism*) absurdity. Queneau achives his irony and tragic humor through the parody of language: he mingles the written with the spoken language, reproducing the syntax and peculiarities of pronunciation of the latter, relates a stupid story in 99 different ways, and has a concierge, for example, think out the dialectics of existence and non-existence.

Querelle des Anciens et des Modernes: Begun as a literary quarrel stemming from an over-zealous respect, on the part of some writers, for the ancients, it developed later into a controversy centering around the notion of progress. When Desmarets de Saint-Sorlin (q.v.), in his preface to *Clovis* (1657) as well as in other works, defended Christianity as a source of inspiration for French literature, he gave the initial impetus to this quarrel; Boileau (q.v.), an ardent champion of the ancients, in his *Art Poétique* (1674) retorted, condemning the use of religion in literature. The main phase of this quarrel, however, was launched when Charles Perrault (q.v.), in *Le Siècle de Louis le Grand* (1687), a poem he read before the *Académie Française* (q.v.), compared his Age with that of Augustus; the concluding thesis—which he further developed in *Parallèles des Anciens et des Modernes* (1688-1696)—that the moderns were superior to the ancients, led to a veritable battle. Perrault, moreover, was to be aided by Fontenelle (q.v.), who advanced the

philosophical argument, in his *Digression sur les Anciens et les Modernes* (1688), that man's progress and advance in science proves the superiority of the moderns over the ancients. Boileau, however, now supported by La Fontaine and Racine (qq.v.)—whose masterpieces further justified the tendency continued since the time of the *Pléiade* (q.v.) to use the ancients as models of literary perfection—counter-attacked with his *Réflexions sur Longin* (1694); La Bruyère (q.v.), another recruit, pleaded in his *Discours à l'Académie française* (1693) the cause of the ancients. The dispute came to a temporary halt in 1694, when a reconciliation between Perrault and Boileau was effected. The quarrel was resumed twenty years later, however, when Houdard de la Motte (q.v.), in a preface to his *Iliade* (1713)—based on Mme. Dacier's prose translation of the *Iliad* (1699)—tried to discredit the Hellenist scholar, not to mention Homer himself. By 1715 an end was brought—thanks to the intervention of Fénelon (q.v.) and M. de Valincourt—to this quarrel. But a wedge had by now been driven between reason and tradition, between the belief in progress and the respect for the ancients; the quarrel was clearly a victory for the spirit and ideas of the eighteenth century. (cf. *Enlightenment, Age of*) H. Rigault, *Histoire de la Querelle des Anciens et des Modernes*, 1859; H. Gillot, *La Querelle des Anciens et des Modernes*, 1914.

Querelle du Cid: Irritated by the success of *Le Cid* (q.v.) and by Corneille's (q.v.) vainglorious attitude, Georges de Scudéry and Mairet (qq.v.), the former's rivals, began a quarrel by an attack against this play. Included among the *Observations sur le Cid* (1637) were Scudéry's criticisms that *Le Cid* failed to observe the unities (q.v.) and the *bienséances* (q.v.); as proof of the

latter failing, reference is made to the fact that the hero visits the daughter of the man he has just killed and is allowed to see that she still loves him. In addition, it was asserted, its happy ending did not constitute a tragedy (q.v.), and its good parts were plagiarized from the Spanish *Las Mocedades del Cid* (1621) by Guillén de Castro. The question was referred to the newly created *Académie Française* (q.v.) for a decision. An opinion was finally presented in the *Sentiments de l'Académie sur le Cid* (1638) prepared by Chapelain (q.v.). It held that though this play was lacking in verisimilitude (see *Vraisemblance*), it nevertheless bore several merits worthy of recognition. Corneille, who did not accept these criticisms graciously, profited nonetheless from them, as can be seen in his following plays.
A. Gasté, *La Querelle du Cid*, 1898.

Quesnay, François: (1694-1774) Founder of the *physiocrat* school, according to which "all wealth derives from the land," this economist wrote, in addition to his articles for the *Encyclopédie* (q.v.), three important works: *Analyse du Tableau économique* (1760), *Maximes générales du gouvernment économique d'un royaume agricole* (1760) and *La Physiocratie* (1768). Anxious to ameliorate the economic situation in France during the eighteenth century, he attacked many of its abuses.
Y. Guyot, *Quesnay et la Physiocratie*, 1896; H. Higgs, *The Physiocrats*, 1897.

Quête de Joie (1933): See *La Tour du Pin*.

Quietism: Advanced by Molinos (1640-1696), a Spanish theologian, this mystical doctrine, by which man enters into direct communion with God through unspoken prayer and through contemplation of the Divine, was first introduced into France by Mme. Guyon (1648-1717). Attacked by Bossuet (q.v.), intransigent in matters of orthodox Catholicism, this doctrine was defended, however, by Fénelon (q.v.), resulting in a struggle between these two former friends. In the end, after the controversy had been brought to the Pope for his decision, Fénelon was condemned (1699); submitting, he accepted the decision with humility.
A. Bonnel, *De la controverse de Fénelon et de Bossuet sur le quiétisme*, 1850; L. Crouslé, *Fénelon et Bossuet*, 1894-1895; A. Cherel, *Fénelon et la religion du pur amour*, 1935.

Quinault, Philippe: (1635-1688) Ridiculed by Boileau (q.v.) for such sentimental tragedies as *La Mort de Cyrus* (1656) and *Astrate* (1664), this writer is better known for his libretti (*Proserpine*, 1680; *Armide*, 1686; etc.), for which Lulli wrote the music. He also wrote comedies, including *Les Rivales* (1653) and *La Mère coquette* (1665).
E. Gros, *Philippe Quinault*, 1926.

Quinze Joies de Mariage, Les: This anonymous prose work (1st half of 15th century), which was to influence realistic fiction, is a satire on marriage and woman. Each one of the fifteen chapters deals with a joy of marriage; viewed satirically, it represents the different miseries of husbands. Treated with gravity, ridicule and wit, married life with its daily happenings is portrayed in a picturesque manner.
F. Fleuret, ed., *Les Quinze joyes de mariage*, 1936.

R

Rabelais, François: (*c.* 1494-1553) Born in Chinon, he was ordained—after having been a Franciscan friar—a priest. He then entered the Benedictine Order, but soon left to study medicine at Montpellier. In 1532, he was attached as a physician to the main hospital in Lyons. The same year he published, in addition to his Latin translation of Hippocrates, popular humorous *almanachs,* probably with the intention of amusing his patients. When, moreover, a treatment of a popular legend entitled *Grandes et Inestimables Chroniques du grand et énorme géant Gargantua* appeared, he decided to write a better story about Gargantua's son. This work, his *Pantagruel,* also appeared in 1532. In 1534, incorporated into a complete work, *La vie très horrifique du grand Gargantua, père de Pantagruel* formed Book I, and *Pantagruel* became Book II. The *Tiers Livre* appeared in 1546, the *Quart Livre* in 1552, and the posthumous *cinquième et dernier livre des faits et dits héroïques du bon Pantagruel,* probably the work—at least in part—of another writer, in 1564.

This comic prose epic tells of the birth, education and exploits, of Gargantua and his son Pantagruel—both horrific but "part-time" giants—the decision of Pantagruel's scapegrace friend Panurge to get married and the dire results to be expected therefrom, and the voyage both make with Frère Jean and other companions to consult, about this marriage, the Oracle of the "Dive Bouteille." Under the buffoonery of the fantastic, this epic reflects the author's encyclopedic erudition; Rabelais discusses everything, from politics to hygiene, in French, Latin, Greek, *patois* and *argot,* and he makes an important contribution to the development of French prose through his picturesque and prolific vocabulary. A product of the Renaissance (q.v.), Rabelais has a zest for knowledge and respects the culture of the Ancients, their scientific knowledge and philosophy. Rooted in the Middle Ages, moreover, Rabelais never abandoned his religious beliefs, but his ideals of life and education reflect a belief in the goodness of nature and instinct (cf. *Abbaye de Thélème*), and point to the pleasures of life that man can and should enjoy in this world. He also satirized and denounced, in a spirit not dissimilar from that of Erasmus (q.v.), by whom he had been greatly influenced, the corrupt clergy and the imperialistic, warring, ambitious princes of the day.

J. Plattard, *François Rabelais,* 1932; L. Febvre, *Le Problème de l'Incroyance au 16ᵉ siècle. La Religion de Rabelais,* 1942.

Racan, Honorat de Breuil de: (1589-1670) The favorite disciple and biographer of Malherbe (q.v.), this poet follows in the traditions of his master in his odes and in his *Paraphrase des Psaumes* (completed in 1654). In *Arténice ou Les Bergeries* (1618), a pastoral dialogue in five acts, however, his inspiration is basically Italian. His love of nature, as seen in his sentimental and elegiac *Stances à Tirsis,* makes of him an important precursor of La Fontaine (q.v.).

L. Arnould, *Un Gentilhomme de lettres au XVII* siècle, Racan,* 1901.

Racine, Jean: (1639-1699) This dramatist, generally considered the greatest writer of classical tragedy (q.v.), was born at La Ferté-Milon, near Paris. Left an orphan at an early age, he was reared by his paternal grandmother and by an aunt. In accordance with their religious ideas, he was educated at the *Collège de Beauvais* in Picardy (1651-1655) and, during the following four years, at the school of Port-Royal (q.v.). Of these two Jansenist schools, the latter, in particular, stressed—not to the neglect, of course, of the Bible or of Latin—the study of Greek and the Jansenist concept of man's sinful nature. The basic notion, derived from these teachings, that man is a helpless victim of his passions—a kind of inner fate—was to leave its imprint on Racine and was to become a central idea in his plays. Later, in Paris, he showed signs of rebellion against the severity of Jansenist morality. Shocked by the irregular life he was leading, his family sent him to Uzès, in the South of France, where he was to prepare himself for an ecclesiastical post; these plans, however, seemed to have been abandoned, and in 1662 Racine was back in Paris. His *Ode sur la convalescence du Roi* (1663) brought him the patronage of the King; his first play, *La Thébaïde* (1664), produced by Molière (q.v.) and written with the encouragement of his good friend La Fontaine (q.v.), launched him on his dramatic career. His second tragedy, *Alexandre le Grand* (1665), produced by the Hôtel de Bourgogne (q.v.), rivals to Molière's troupe, incurred the enmity of the

latter, and resulted in a break—that was to last until 1677—with his former Jansenist preceptors, who regarded the theater as a force of moral corruption. *Andromaque* (1677; q.v.), written some thirty years after Corneille's (q.v.) *Le Cid,* made Racine the greatest dramatic poet of his time, but, as in the case of the former, brought him criticism from those—including the friends of Corneille—who were jealous of his success. A series of masterpieces—in addition to his Aristophanesque comedy *Les Plaideurs* (1668)—followed. These include *Brittanicus* (1669; q.v.), *Bérénice* (1670)—in whose preface the importance of verisimilitude (see *vraisemblance*) in classical tragedy is stated—*Bajazet* (1672), *Mithridate* (1673), *Iphigénie* (1674) and *Phèdre* (1677; q.v.). Perhaps for personal and other reasons, Racine now renounced the theater, became reconciled with Port-Royal, married, settled down to family life, and accepted the post of royal historian. Only at the insistence of Mme. de Maintenon (q.v.) did Racine return —twelve years later—to the theater. This time it was to write plays of biblical inspiration that were to mark his last contact with the theater. They were *Esther* (1689) and *Athalie* (1691; q.v.), the latter being one of his masterpieces.

Personifying in his tragedies the culmination of the classical ideal, Racine drew his inspiration mostly from Greece. On four different occasions, however,—*Alexandre, Brittanicus, Bérénice* and *Mithridate*— he chose, in an apparent attempt to demonstrate his superiority over Corneille, subjects from Roman history. The simplification of plot in these plays, as compared to those of Corneille, reveals a conception of tragedy that marks Racine's originality. Reducing the action, through an effortless use of the three unities (q.v.), to a minimum,

Plate 15. Jean-Jacques Rousseau at Montmorency

Plate 16. Jean-Paul Sartre

Racine concentrates on psychological analyses of characters experiencing a crisis. These characters, unlike those of Corneille, betray no superhuman qualities; they are helpless victims of their violent passions. Recognizably human in their struggles and in their fateful weaknesses, they leave the illusion of reality. This impression is heightened by Racine's use of a simple, natural and direct language that expresses the depth of feeling of his characters. Added to the precision of his verse is his masterful manipulation of the classical alexandrine (q.v.) line, already popularized by Corneille. The combination renders his tragedy harmonious, musical, perfect in form. His other works, in addition to a number of poems, include his posthumously published *Abrégé de l'histoire de Port-Royal* (1767). J. Lemaître, *Jean Racine*, 1908; Th. Maulnier, *Racine*, 1935; P. Moreau, *Racine, l'homme et l'œuvre*, 1945; G. Brereton, *Jean Racine, a Critical Biography*, 1951; E. Vinaver, *Racine et la poésie tragique*, 1951.

Racine, Louis: (1692-1763) The youngest son of Jean Racine (q.v.), he wrote *La Grâce* (1720) and *La Religion* (1742), sentimental poems of Jansenist (q.v.) inspiration. In addition to these poems, he published *Mémoires* (1747), dealing with the life of his father.

Racines du ciel, Les (1956): See *Gary, Romain*.

Racine et Shakespeare (1825): See *Stendhal*.

Recherches de la France (1560-1621): See *Pasquier, Etienne*.

Radiguet, Raymond: (1903-1923) This young prodigy, discovered by Jean Cocteau (q.v.), wrote two volumes of verse, *Les Joues en feu* (1920) and *Devoirs de vacances* (1921). *Le Diable au corps* (1923) and *Bal du comte d'Orgel* (1924), the two novels for which he is especially

known, contain psychological delineations of character in the classical manner, and reveal the post-war state of mind of that period. Henri Massis, *Raymond Radiguet*, 1927.

raisonneur: or, **porte-parole,** is the character in the play who develops to the final conclusion the arguments and exact thesis of the dramatist. He is especially prominent in the *pièce à thèse* (q.v.) or thesis-play. The use of this character, though not invented by Dumas *fils* (q.v.), was developed by him to its fullest possibilities.

Rambouillet, Hôtel de: See *Hôtel de Rambouillet*.

Ramuntcho (1897): See *Loti*.

Ramuz, Charles Ferdinand: (1878-1947) Because the eight novels and four volumes of poetry he wrote while in Paris from 1902 to 1914 failed to attract much attention, he returned to his native Swiss town, Cully, in the canton of Vaud. There he succeeded in gaining recognition for the twenty-odd novels he began writing in 1914. They not only describe the exact local color, the life and mores of the peasants and simple folk from Vaud, even presenting their peculiarities of speech, but also reveal the universally experienced joys and fears of those living close to nature. Among the more important of these novels are: *La Grande Peur dans la Montagne* (1926), *La Beauté sur la Terre* (1928), and *Si le Soleil ne se levait pas* (1939).

Bernard Voyenne, *C. F. Ramuz ou la sainteté de la terre*, 1948.

Raphaël (1849): See *Lamartine*.

Rapin, René: (1621-1687) Author of poems written in Latin, he also wrote such critical works as *Observations sur les poèmes d'Horace et de Virgile* (1669) and *Réflexions sur la Poétique d'Aristote* (1673), in which he upheld the authority of Aristotle. Consulted by Racine (q.v.), this influential critic was often quoted and invoked even during the 18th century. In his *Histoire du Jansénisme* (p. 1861), he wrote against the Jansenists.

H. Gillot, *La Querelle des anciens et des modernes*, 1914.

Ratés, Les (1920): See *Lenormand*.

Raynal, Guillaume-Thomas-François, Abbé: (1713-1796) Historian and philosopher, he attacked tyranny and the colonial policies of the "civilizing" countries in *Histoire philosophique et politique des établissements et du commerce des Européens dans les deux Indes* (1770), his major work. This attack furthered the cause of the philosophical movement during the eighteenth century.

A. Feugère, *L'Abbé Raynal*, 1922.

Raynal, Paul: (1885-) One of the outstanding dramatists of his generation, he launched his career with *Le Maître de son cœur* (written in 1913, but produced in 1920), a psychological play that depicts a conflict between friendship and love. His next play, *Le Tombeau sous l'Arc de Triomphe* (1924), written after his return from the army, is a poignant study of a soldier in wartime on a furlough which he spends with his fiancée and his father. Cast in the mold of a classical tragedy reminiscent of the tones of Corneille and Racine (qq.v.), containing few characters, oratorical eloquence with sentences which, though composed in prose, have the rhythm of alexandrine (q.v.) lines, this play observes the unities of time, place and action. The tragedy portrayed not only deals with the lack of understanding between the men at the front and the civilians who live in comparative security, but also and most essentially, with the terrible price of all wars, with the sacrifices they demand of the heroic victims, whether they be soldiers or the beloved ones who are left behind. That is why, too, the *première* of this play, which pre-sented characters—those of the soldier, the fiancée, and the father—symbolic in their application, aroused controversy reminiscent of the famous "Bataille d'*Hernani*" of Hugo (q.v.). Although war, as a theme, represents many difficulties for the stage, this play has since been recognized as a masterpiece of psychological analysis. Other plays, including *Au soleil de l'instinct* (1932), *La Francerie* (1933), and *Napoléon unique* (1936), either revert to the psychological drama or deal with war, or combine both. *Le Matériel Humain* (1948) is a more recent achievement.

Raynouard, François-Just Marie: (1761-1836) A noted grammarian and philologist, his chief claim to fame is his *Les Templiers* (1805), one of the best tragedies written during the First Empire. Another tragedy, *Les États de Blois* (1810), was, however, less successful.

Rayons et les Ombres, Les (1840): See *Hugo*.

REALISM: Realism in the arts rests on the premises which are posed by philosophical realism, i.e., that man has the power to perceive external objects and that his cognitions of things about him correspond to real phenomena and furnish real knowledge.

In literature, realism consists in obtaining an aesthetic effect from images which would not affect the reader as pleasant, or would even strike him as unpleasant, if the models they represented were perceived directly by him.

Throughout the history of French literature, realism takes the form of a return to common sense after an over-indulgence in imaginative literature. Furthermore, it often takes the form of a movement of opposition either to a dominant doctrine or to unsatisfactory social conditions.

In the Middle Ages, the *fabliaux* (q.v.) stressed the brutal, coarse and immoral aspects of human behavior, but were made palatable by a constant striving for comic effects. These stories in verse, often crudely written, may be regarded as a deliberate departure from an epic (q.v.) or *poésie courtoise* in which the public no longer recognized life as revealed by experience.

During the 16th century, Rabelais' (q.v.) *Pantagruélisme*, "a kind of cheerfulness steeped in contempt for the fortuitous," stands in opposition to the Platonism (q.v.) of the poets. While the forerunners of of realism *per se* are alleged to have been Bonaventure des Périers (*Cymbalum Mundi*, 1538; q.v.) and Marguerite de Navarre (*Heptaméron*, 1559; q.v.), Noël du Fail has been credited with the introduction of realism in facetious literature (*Propos rustiques et facétieux*, 1547).

During the 17th century, Charles Sorel (q.v.) combines in his novel, *La vraie histoire comique de Francion* (1622), *tableaux* of lower strata of society with moral preoccupations. Later, to the search for *essences* inherent in *préciosité* (q.v.) may be contrasted the *burlesque* (q.v.), exemplified by Paul Scarron's (q.v.) *Roman comique* (1651). Antoine Furetière (q.v.), a lexicographer and a scholar, quite deliberately tried to bring fiction closer to life by choosing for the characters of his *Roman bourgeois* (1666) a variety of representatives of the middle and lower classes of Paris in their authentic settings.

In the 18th century, the successes of Alain Lesage's (q.v.) *Le Diable boiteux* (1707) and *Gil Blas de Santillane* (1731-1735) are examples more of the felicitous adaptation by a French author of the Spanish picaresque novel than of a conscious attempt to recreate life through fiction. It was only with Diderot (q.v.) that the scientific study of nature had a direct effect on the principles of literary composition. In the materialistic pantheism of the author of *Le Rêve de D'Alembert*, thought is a property of life, and life a general property of matter. Since, according to Diderot, the world is governed by physical causes, such causes must function in accordance with laws whose principles could be revealed to man by investigation. The way to move and to instruct the public, therefore, is not for an author to conform to esthetic rules, but rather to familiarize himself through experience with these laws and to reproduce such experiences in literary form as faithfully as possible. This principle entails serious consequences. The logical elimination of certain brute facts is no longer possible under the pretext that they are unsuitable for artistic treatment; the search for guiding principles tends to render the results of experience impersonal; the emphasis upon exactitude brings the author to restrict himself to the study of the present.

If Diderot set realism on the path of experience, lived and felt, the *Idéologues* (q.v.) of the end of the 18th century and the beginning of the 19th furnished it with a philosophical foundation which the positivism of Auguste Comte (q.v.) was to complete. By making the senses the source of ideas, by showing that the functioning of the senses varies according to individual temperaments, by insisting on analysis as a means of research, and by describing the evolution of ideas from generation to generation, they influenced Stendhal and Balzac (qq.v.), the fathers of modern French realism. While by their devotion to fact the *Idéologues* provided Taine (q.v.) with some of the principles of his criticism, by their contempt for the rules of esthetics as such and by the extreme attention which they give to the psychological effects exerted by literature, they anticipate in some measure Zola's (q.v.) *morale en action.* A deliberate lack of discrimination certainly characterizes Restif de la Bretonne's (q.v.) portrayal of the lower classes toward the end of the 18th century. Analysis appears to be one of the basic elements in Choderlos de Laclos's (q.v.) *Liaisons dangereuses* (1782). Both authors claimed to be moralists.

Because of the stress which it placed on the ego, romanticism (q.v.) is sometimes considered an interruption in the development of realism. Yet, some of its elements contributed to the latter's progress, first as a literary theory, then as a method of literary creation. The introduction of the concrete into art, of the familiar into language, of the documentary into exoticism, of the historical method into literary criticism, prepared the terrain for realist authors. Paradoxically, by abandoning accepted rules, the romantics contributed to the establishment and temporary triumph of materialistic determinism in literature.

Stendhal was divided between his dislike for prosaic reality and for the hollowness of the unbridled fantasy which he found in the romantics. He was torn between the scientific exigencies of his mind and a keen esthetic sensitivity, between his materialism and his *espagnolisme.* The solution which brought these elements into harmony was the depiction of man's inner nature through the observation and analysis of his actions. Stendhal's novel *Le Rouge et le Noir* (1831; q.v.) which bore as an epigraph the saying by Danton: "The truth, the harsh truth," was based upon an actual criminal case. *La Chartreuse de Parme* (1839; q.v) was inspired by an Italian chronicle of the 16th century. In both, the combination of dramatic events taken from life or historical facts with the sordid or petty calculations of the protagonists are evoked as if they were seen by cold, penetrating eyes. In addition to his observations, Stendhal soberly formulates the laws which follow from them. And yet, in spite of his faith in a logic which he inherited from the *Idéologues,* he does not suppress the unexpected in the conduct of his characters. The result gives the effect of an hallucination which happened to be true.

Balzac combined in his *Comédie humaine* (q.v.) an apparently inexhaustible store of observation and knowledge with a tireless creative imagination. He was also a disciple of the *Idéologues* and claimed for himself the title of *historien des mœurs.* His admiration for the naturalist Geoffroy Saint-Hilaire (1722-1844) made him conceive the ambitious plan to write a "natural history of man" (*Avant-propos de la Comédie humaine,* 1842). His novels, therefore, are studies of man and his passions observed in their *milieu,* with their causes and results. And yet, he did not permit his taste for precise detail and apparent laws in human behavior to becloud his intuition. He created a world in which setting, period, action, characters, the concrete realities of existence (money, for instance), are indissolubly integrated. An incessant evolution is taking place in this world of his, the characters may seem to be superhuman in their virtues and vices. Still, both evolution and characters follow a logic which impresses the reader as being true to life (*Eugénie Grandet,* 1833, q.v.; *Le Père Goriot,* 1834, q.v.; *La Cousine Bette,* 1846).

Toward the middle of the 19th century, and more specifically from 1848 to 1857, realism, from a literary method, was transformed into an aesthetic formula by Champfleury and Louis Edmond Duranty (qq.v.). Champfleury has been credited with effecting the transition from Balzac to Flaubert (q.v.). As early as 1837 he was oriented toword satire of the middle class by a performance of Henri Monnier's (q.v.) *Scènes populaires*, in which the author was appearing as an actor. In 1849, he published his *Confessions de Sylvius*, a depiction of bohemian life somewhat similar to Henry Mürger's (q.v.) *Scènes de la vie de bohème*, but demonstrating a greater objectivity in the evocation of the sordid aspects of a life with which he was thoroughly familiar. A year earlier, however, Champfleury's ideas on literature had crystallised under the influence of the painter Gustave Courbet, and he passed from the depiction of bohemian life to that of the middle class. In 1855, Courbet's manifesto *Le Réalisme* (probably written in part by Champfleury) marked the official beginning of the campaign. There is little doubt that the provocations of the critics must have contributed toward making Champfleury support an *ism* to which he really preferred the expression *la sincérité dans l'art*. The organs of the newly founded school were Champfleury's *Gazette*, only two issues of which were published (1856), and Duranty's *Réalisme*, a small periodical which appeared for almost a year (1856-1857).

Courbet's manifesto stressed the freedom of the artist to discover his individuality through a thorough study of traditional and modern art and the application of this knowledge to the representation of the true aspects and manners of his time. Champfleury's theories were expounded between 1853 and 1857 in various prefaces, articles and works of polemics. Generally speaking, these theories were limited to questions of aesthetics and advocated a systematic counteraction to the faults of the romantics. His doctrine can be summed up as follows:

a writer's genius consists in a combination of encyclopedic knowledge and a capacity for recording accurately sounds, colors and forms. The author, abandoning his own personality, should introduce himself into each one of his characters and play the rôle as faithfully as he can, in complete forgetfulness of himself. In addition, these characters should always be ordinary people. The necessity of self-effacement on the part of the author should result in a restrained and impersonal style. Narrative prose and dialogue should be the main devices used in the novel, since descriptions of scenery and people show too conscious an effort toward an artistic effect. From 1853 to 1860, Champfleury enjoyed great popular success, but he survived his reputation and was almost forgotten when he died. His best known novels are *Les Aventures de Mlle. Mariette* (1853), *Les Souffrances du Professeur Delteil* (1853), *Les Bourgeois de Molinchart* (1855).

To the theories of Champfleury's, Duranty added another principle. Art, according to him, must not only depict society, but also educate it. The writer, therefore, must demonstrate those qualities of understanding which will lead to the creation of a work from which the public may derive instruction. With this goal in mind, the artist will transcend the realm of aesthetics to attain the practical. He shared the same dislike as Champfleury for the idealism and poetic form of the romantics and inveighed against the historical novel, which, according to him, is a source of lies. His views on a didactic and utilitarian literature put him in direct opposition to the theory of *l'art pour l'art*. In his works, the best-known of which is *Le Malheur d'Henriette Gérard* (1860), Duranty tried to put into practice some of the principles— liberalism, republicanism, anticlericalism—which later on were to be further developed by Zola (q.v.).

Such doctrines were far from being favored by Flaubert as he wrote *Madame Bovary* (1857; q.v.), the novel which has come to be considered the masterpiece of French realism. The book conforms to the tenets of realism to the extent that imagination, if the word is taken as meaning unrestrained fantasy, played a negligible part in the conception and execution of the novel. A deterministic world is presented to us whose every detail is supported by first-hand knowledge or thorough scientific documentation. The main reason for the greatness of *Madame Bovary*, however, resides in a style whose aim was to do justice at once to nature and to art. Flaubert's *L'Éducation sentimentale* (1869) has of late tended to supersede the former novel as a prototype of a realistic novel.

The generation of realists which came to the fore between 1850 and 1870 was directly influenced by pictorial art. The following generation, which became known under the name of naturalists, follow the line of positivist thinking from Diderot to Taine (q.v.), and their leader, Emile Zola (q.v.) founded his theories on the application of the scientific method to literature. The dividing line between the two groups may well be placed in 1865, when Edmond and Jules de Goncourt (q.v.), both artists, although Jules was especially gifted in this respect, claimed in the preface to *Germinie Lacerteux* (1865) that by assuming the scrupulous objectivity of scientists, they had won the right to express the truth without compromise. Although Guy de Maupassant (q.v.) belongs chronologically with the naturalists, his novel *Une vie* (1883), written with Flaubert's example in mind, can be considered a masterpiece of realism.

In fields other than the novel, it is only with great caution that the term "realism" can be used. In poetry, the Parnassian (q.v.) school has been compared to it with limited justification. It is not without reason that Flaubert has been called a Parnassian in prose. Although the Parnassian school took its name in 1866, a number of poets were observing its cult of objectivity and ambition for an impeccable form long before this date. One of these exponents, Théophile Gautier (q.v.), defined himself "a man for whom the external world exists." As he passed from painting to poetry, his experience as an artist taught him to see nature, while his confidence in *le mot juste* and capacity for literary expression enabled him to carry out a faithful rendition of his vision (*España*, 1845; *Emaux et Camées*, 1852). The Parnassian ideal of *l'art pour l'art*, however, scarcely fits in with Champfleury's lack of interest in beauty of style *per se* and the didactic and utilitarian conception of literature of Duranty. Only a detailed study could show to what extent each of the following could be included as tending toward realism: Leconte de Lisle (q.v.), Louis Bouilhet (1822-1869), Sully Prudhomme (q.v.), as well as the other Parnassians.

In the theater, François Ponsard (q.v.) has been called the leader of the school of common sense. His ideal was a theatre "in which events would be plausible, sentiments noble, characters and passions developed truthfully." *Lucrèce* (1843), *Charlotte Corday* (1850), *L'Honneur et l'Argent* (1853) rather show him as counteracting the excesses of the romantics than applying to the stage the concept of realism. Alexandre Dumas *fils* (q.v.) has left a number of *pièces à thèse* (q.v.) which show a strong belief in the moral mission of the theatre, but which certainly do not conform to the principle of the author's self-effacement which the realists advocated. But as his plays, *La Dame aux Camélias* (1852), *Le Demi-Monde* (1855), *Le Fils naturel* (1858), dealt with problems which the author thought were specific to his age, they have that documentary value which is associated with realism. Emile Augier (q.v.) was an excellent craftsman in play writing. His *Le Gendre de Monsieur Poirier* (1854) is still produced on the stage in France nowadays. The exigencies of the stage caused him to accentuate the idiosyncrasies of his characters, to the point of making them types rather than ordinary human beings. Henry Becque (q.v.) fits in better with the realists on account of his frankness without compromise. His main plays, *Les Corbeaux* (1882) and *La Parisienne* (1885), are more in accord with the theories and practice of Flaubert than those of the second generation of realists, then called naturalists, his contemporaries.

While realism as a school came to an end at the same time as its main theorists lost the public's favor, some of the trends which were part of it have been adopted since, taking the forms of *naturalism, populism* and even *unanimism* (qq.v.).

Realism, however, should be understood not as a school, but as a permanent striving on the part of man to reduce the impassable gap which separates art from life, and in this sense it remains a strong aspiration in Western literature.

P. Martino, *Le Roman réaliste sous le Second Empire,* Paris, 1913; G. J. Becker, "Realism: An Essay in Definition," *Modern Language Quarterly,* X, 2, 1949; C. Beuchat, *Histoire du Naturalisme français,* 2 vol., Paris, 1949; A. J. Salvan, "L'Essence du réalisme français," *Comparative Literature,* III, 3, 1951; R. Dumesnil, *Le Réalisme et le Naturalisme,* Paris, 1955.

ALBERT J. SALVAN

Réalisme, Le (1857): See *Champfleury.*
récit: See *Short Story.*
Récits des temps mérovingiens (1840): See *Thierry, Augustin.*
Réflexions sur la Poétique d'Aristote (1673): See *Rapin, René.*
Réflexions sur les divers génies du peuple romain (1663): See *Saint-Évremond.*
Regnard, Jean-François: (1655-1709) The son of a wealthy bourgeois, this Parisian-born dramatist led an adventurous life during his youth. His fantastic experiences while returning from a second trip to Italy served as a basis for his novel *La Provençale* (1731). Returned to Paris, he wrote for his pleasure, without any moralizing intent, comedies that describe the social corruption of his day. Not aiming, moreover, to present a study of manners or character, he is preoccupied with drawing laughter from every possible situation. *Le Joueur* (1696) and *Le Légataire universel* (1708)—his two masterpieces—are, unlike Molière's (q.v.) universal studies, superficial portraits of two characters who offer more fun than sidelights on contemporary society; if, however, his plays are lacking in psychology, they excel in action, plot-construction and style. Written with verve and facility, their versification is brilliant, perhaps superior to Molière's, whose general traditions are followed by this dramatist. Included among his other plays are: *Arlequin homme à bonnes fortunes* (1690), *La Sérénade* (1694), *Attendez-moi sous l'orme* (1694), *Le Distrait* (1697) and *Les Ménechmes* (1705).

H. C. Lancaster, *History of Dramatic Literature in the Seventeenth Century,* IV, 1940.

Régnier, Henri de: (1864-1936) This poet, novelist, and short story writer, evidences in his writings an evolution from Parnassian (q.v.) to Symbolist (see *Symbolism*) and, finally, to neo-classical tendencies. His first collections—*Lendemains*

(1885), *Apaisements* (1886), and *Sites* (1887)—reflect the clarity of technique and perfection of plastic form dear to such a Parnassian as Leconte de Lisle (q.v.). Later, under the influence of Mallarmé (q.v.), his poems in *Poèmes anciens et romanesques* (1890), *Tel qu'en songe* (1892) and *Les Jeux rustiques et divins* (1897), with less obscurity than in Mallarmé, evince the imprecision, mystery, dream element, and musicality common to Symbolism, but with a greater emphasis on the *vers libre* (q.v.), which he uses almost to perfection. In these collections, moreover, as well as in others, most of his imagery is drawn from Greek mythology, pagan in essence. Finally, returning under the influence of Hérédia, his father-in-law (cf. *Gérard d'Houville*), to a neoclassic clarity, and using both the *vers libre* and the classical alexandrine (q.v.) line—he is flexible in the handling of rhymes and rhythms—he published *Les Médailles d'argile* (1900), which contains sonnets, and *La Cité des eaux* (1902), which evokes Versailles, with its preserved beauty of the past. However, he did not abandon the mysterious magic and melancholy of Symbolism.

His short stories may be considered as a transition between his poetry and his novels. The latter consist of those, like *La Double Maîtresse* (1900), *Le Bon Plaisir*, and *Les Rencontres de M. de Bréot* (1904), which have the seventeenth and eighteenth centuries for their settings and which are written in a somewhat archaic style, and others, written in a terse language, like *Le Mariage de minuit* (1903) and *Escales en Méditerranée* (1931), which deal with his contemporary times.

H. Berton, *Henri de Régnier, le poète et le romancier*, 1910; R. Honnert, *Henri de Régnier, son œuvre*, 1923.

Régnier, Mathurin: (1573-1613) Both in his private life, which was undisciplined and libertine despite his theological training, and in his view of poetry, he showed a rebellious spirit. Opposing poetic inspiration to the doctrinaire principles of Malherbe (q.v.), he makes the latter, who had insulted his uncle, the poet Desportes (q.v.), the butt of his anger and sarcasm in one of his satires (*Satire IX, A Rapin*). Continuing the spirit of Villon (q.v.), and more especially, of Rabelais (q.v.) and of the Renaissance, he describes in his sixteen *Satires*, much like Horace and Juvenal, the vices and foibles of his time, and satirizes poets and various social types. His talent for portraying mores and the character of men was recognized by Boileau (q.v.). Régnier also produced three epistles, five elegies, and several odes, sonnets, *stances* and *épigrammes*.

J. Vianey, *Mathurin Régnier*, 1896.

Regrets, Les (1558): See *Du Bellay*.

Relation sur le quiétisme (1698): See *Bossuet*.

Religieuse, La (1760): See *Diderot*.

Remarques sur la langue française (1647): See *Vaugelas*.

RENAISSANCE: The nature, limits, and even validity of the term Renaissance to describe a major period in European history have been the source of constant discussion since Michelet (q.v.) used the term in his *Histoire de France* (1855). It was the most appropriate term he could find to embrace that rich and productive period between 1400 and 1600 approximately, during which man's physical, intellectual, and temporal horizons were extended immeasurably. It was, moreover, a term which the Humanists themselves had suggested in variant forms. In 1524, for example, Guillaume Budé (q.v.) was writing to Pierre Amy of the "renaissance of letters." Five years after Michelet's history the French word was given broad circulation by the appearance of Jacob Burckhardt's *Die Cultur der Renaissance in Italien,* viewing the period as a sustained and uniform movement of the human spirit which broke markedly with the centuries immediately preceding. Other scholars (Burdach, Thode, Haskins, Huizinga, Cohen) have since dedicated themselves to the task of demonstrating that the Renaissance formed only a logical continuum of the Middle Ages or that there existed earlier renaissances than the one heralded by Burckhardt. Since such a complex phenomenon as the Renaissance could be the result of only a series of contributory factors (invention of printing in the West, voyages of exploration, experiments in the physical sciences) it is difficult to assign to it a starting date. Among the dates and motivating events which have been proposed, the most common is the seizure of Constantinople (1453) by the Seljuk Turks, sending many Byzantine scholars as refugees to the West and lending impetus to the Revival of Learning. If the Renaissance was already maturating in Italy by the mid-Quattrocento, it took another half-century to be transplanted in France. Indeed, the somewhat tardy dividing point of 1500-1501 which the Mediaeval Academy and other bodies have established to separate the Middle Ages from the Renaissance is more appropriate to France than to Italy. Similarly, if the sustaining forces of this Humanistic and scientific saltation were more feeble in Italy by the time of the Counter-Reformation and the final Council of Trent (1563), these forces continued unabated in France until the end of the century.

As suggested by the reference to Guillaume Budé above, the Renaissance man was aware that he lived in a new Golden or Saturnian age. This awareness lends support to the Burckhardt conception of the

Renaissance as a conscious revival and break with the immediate past. In Italy Vasari and Lomazzo were speaking of a *rinascita* of the fine arts. Gargantua (q.v.) referred to the recent past as a "tenebrous time" and again refers scornfully to "that thick Gothic night." Indeed, Gargantua, whose education was obtained at the close of the mediaeval period, writes that although he had been reputed one of the sages of the preceding generation, he would now scarcely be admitted to the first grade of school. The writers of the period of Francis I styled themselves "new swans," lineal descendants of the old swans of antiquity. Just as the sixteenth century marked the beginnings of geographical nationalism, it also witnessed the rise of chronological nationalism, which was later to develop into the *Querelle des anciens et des modernes* (q.v.).

Similarly, the broadened horizons of Renaissance man included new dimensions of both space and time. The voyages of Columbus, Vasco da Gama, and Cartier, the scientific discoveries of Copernicus and Galileo, and the restoration of Greco-Roman and Alexandrian science and philosophy brought with them new understanding and the creation of new values. To the socio-economic factors which had already started to weaken feudalism (rise of the towns, overland and overseas trade, centralisation of the monarchies) were added the intellectual objections which would eventually be turned against the monarchy itself. After the St. Bartholomew's Day massacres (1572) the Huguenots made of Etienne de la Boétie's (q.v.) little monograph against tyranny, *Le Contr'un,* a weapon against the monarchy. A commercial aristocracy arose to parallel the feudal hierarchy and to encourage arts and letters: the Briçonnet family builds the lovely chateau of Chenonceaux and the Robortet family protects the poet Ronsard (q.v.).

With the decline of feudalism and the lessening of ecclesiastical authority, a new ideal of man finds its way into contemporary thought and literature. The learned man (*homme instruit*) and the well-rounded gentleman (*homme de bien*) become the goals. It is best of all if these two goals can be realised in the same individual, the "gentleman and scholar" familiar to early American education. As for the scholarly ideal, Gargantua typically wished Pantagruel (q.v.) to learn modern and ancient languages, the seven liberal arts, philosophy, civil law (Rabelais was against canon law, or would probably have listed it as well) geography, astronomy, chemistry, ichthyology, ornithology, horticulture, zoology, mineralogy, petrology, anatomy, talmudic science, the cabbala, and theology. As for the social graces which man must possess to complement his intellectual attainments, he had Castiglione's *Book of the Courtier* (1561) and other courtesy books to spell these out for him.

Italy, viewed by the French Humanists as the seat of the third classicism, was unfortunately the most strife-ridden battleground of the Renaissance. Among the many invasions to which it was subjected were the military sorties by Charles VIII, Louis XII, and Francis I, the latter intent upon restoring Milan to the French. Although these campaigns were relatively short-lived, they succeeded only in further Italianising sixteenth-century France. French literature during the century, like its art, architecture and music, was not merely challenged, but dominated by the Italian models. When the French did not descend into Italy, the Italians (like Luigi Alamanni and Leonardo da Vinci) came to them. During the earlier part of the French Renais-

sance, Italianism was accepted enthusiastically in all phases. Toward the mid-century, however, a reaction set in which is easily perceptible in French literature: Du Bellay's (q.v.) preferring his Loir to the Latin Tiber, Rabelais (q.v.) stirring up sentiment for Gallicanism, Budé decrying the intellectual servility of the French in regard to Italy. It is probable that by the time Italy ceased to be a sustaining force of the Renaissance, the momentum was so strong in France that it could proceed to the "Grand Siècle" unaided and the generations of Malherbe and Boileau (qq.v.) could look down on Dante, Ariosto, and Tasso.

A parallel to (and perhaps a facet of) the reaction to Italianism was the reaction against the authority of Rome. As nationalism grew stronger, obedience to the universal Church and such power-politicians as Julius II was bound to diminish, particularly since the temporal rulers were coming to grips with the Church on matters of taxation, tithes, confiscation of Church property, marriage practices, and the discrepancies between civil and canon law. Rabelais's scathing passages against priests who marry young couples without parental consent show the popular level which anticlerical sentiment could reach. The intensification of orthodoxy during the Counter-Reformation naturally tightened that control over literature which the Sorbonne was already exercising in France. Ecclesiastical tribunals and censorship affected writers and printers alike, and the vicissitudes of each group are symbolised in the persecution of the poet-printer Guillaume Gueroult, the friend of Servetus. The most effective French critic of Rome was of course Jean Calvin (q.v.) of Picardy (1509-64), who influenced the French Reformation so considerably, although

282

Lefèvre d'Étaples (q.v.) had preached Church reform and translated the Scriptures as early as 1523. The new ideas from Germany (where Luther was excommunicated in 1520) infiltrated France and incited "fascheulx debatz" (Marguerite d'Angoulême; q.v.). At first Francis I protected the heretics, encouraged by his sister Marguerite (author of the mystical *Prisons* and *sympathisante* of the Reformation). However, acts of vandalism and the posting of outspoken "placards" caused Francis to decide, as did Charles V, that Protestantism was dangerous to the state. In a sense he was right, since in France as elsewhere, Protestantism was at first popular among the tradesmen and lower classes, for whom a religious reform might promise social and political reform.

Next to the *Institutiones* of Calvin (1536), the French literary work which contributed most to the Reformation within France was Bonaventure des Périers's (q.v.) *Cymbalum mundi* (1538). Des Périers attacked all Church dogma and the Church itself; he even exceeded the position of other Reformational writers by attacking the doctrine of faith itself. The most popular, if indirect, Reformist trend in French literature was the vast number of Scriptural picture books which could be enjoyed even by the unlettered and whose authors in their modest way allowed themselves the privilege of *libre examen* so contested at the time. They formed a counterpart to the Biblical translations and to Guillaume Du Bartas's (q.v.) retelling of stories from *Genesis,* the Apocrypha, and the *Old Testament* in his *Semaines* (1579 —). The nine religious wars within sixteenth-century France did not call forth a great militant Catholic masterpiece (Ronsard's poetic fulminations against Calvin and De Bèze are among his weakest efforts) but did endow France with one stirring masterwork. The *Tragiques* of Agrippa d'Aubigné (1550-1630; q.v.) are a powerful, even satirical cry of protest by a magnificent baroque stylist who belied so convincingly Ronsard's claim that to be a partisan of the Reformation meant that one was an ungrateful and unpatriotic son of France.

In general, the ideals of the Renaissance have persisted as long in France as in any country of Europe. The classical foundations of her education and literature, the freedom of her institutions, the breadth and rationality of her interests, and her high regard for civility and good living attest that Renaissance ideas and ideals still live among Frenchmen.

Jacob Burckhardt, *Die Cultur der Renaissance in Italien,* 1860; Hauser and Renaudet, *Les Débuts de l'Age moderne: La Renaissance et la Réforme,* 1929; J. A. Symonds, *The Renaissance in Italy,* 1935; W. K. Ferguson, *The Renaissance in Historical Thought,* 1948; Louis Batiffol, *Le Siècle de la Renaissance,* n.d.

ROBERT J. CLEMENTS

Renan, Ernest: (1823-1892) Born in Tréguier, Brittany, this philologist, historian and critic, influenced early in his life by a pious mother, and intended for the priesthood, completed his theological studies at the great Seminary of Saint-Sulpice in Paris. As the result of a spiritual crisis, however—the story of which is related in *Souvenirs d'enfance et de jeunesse* (1883)—he soon renounced all plans for the priesthood, and, won over by the scientific spirit of the age as well as by his friendship for the great chemist Berthelot, whom he had met in 1846, he replaced his religious tendency with a zealous devotion to Science. His scientific ardor was to be crowned by his *L'Avenir de la science* (written in 1848; published in 1890). His interest in philology, especially in the field of Semitics (*Histoire générale et Système comparé des Langues sémitiques*, 1855; *Essai sur l'Origine du Langage*, 1858) as a science to be applied to the study of the history of religion, and the inspiration he derived from his archeological mission to Syria and Palestine (1860-1861), gave birth to the idea of a huge work on the history of Christianity. A foreshadowing of an anthropomorphic point of view, the approach used in his *Vie de Jésus* (1863), the first volume of his monumental *Histoire des Origines du Christianisme* (1863-1883), was given in his first lecture at the College de France (1862), to which he was appointed as Professor of Hebrew. As this lecture on Jesus offended orthodoxy, the course was suspended, and Renan was removed from his chair. Although his position was restored to him in 1870, the defeat suffered by France as a result of the Franco-Prussian War shook his faith in German idealism, left him disillusioned and less positive in his convictions and more skeptical regarding the attainment of Truth. This new relativistic attitude, first seen in *Dialogues philosophiques* (1876), and later, in *Drames philosophiques* (including *Caliban*, 1878; *L'Eau de Jouvence*, 1880; *Le Prêtre de Némi*, 1885; and *L'Abbesse de Jouarre*, 1886), was to affect the "dilettantism" of Anatole France (q.v.); his nostalgia for the past and for his own native Brittany anticipated the works of Barrès (q.v.). *Histoire du peuple d'Israël* (1887-1895) may be regarded as a sequel to his epic work on the origins and evolution of Christianity. In the final analysis, his attitude towards Christianity is sympathetic and respectful, even when unorthodox.

J. Pommier, *E. Renan, essai de biographie intellectuelle*, 1923; P. Lasserre, *La Jeunesse de Renan*, 1925-1932; Ph. Van Tiegham, *Renan*, 1948.

Renard, Jules: (1864-1900) Drawing on his own experiences, this writer, in a style that can be called classical—in its economy of words and qualities of precision—describes in his novels characters reminiscent of his family and those whom he knew in Nivernais and in Paris. Provincial life and provincial types are his favorite subjects. *L'Écornifleur* (1892)—his masterpiece—is the story of a parasite; *Poil de Carotte* (1900)—later produced as a play and as a film—describes an unhappy, if ungrateful, child; *La Bigote* (1909) is a caricature of his own mother, while *Le Pain de ménage* (1899) portrays his own peaceful, bourgeois life. His interest in nature and country life is seen in *Histoires naturelles* (1896), which contains portraits of animals.

Henri Bachelin, *Jules Renard, 1864-1910; son œuvre*, 1910; Léon Guichard, *L'Œuvre et l'âme de Jules Renard*, 1935.

René: This semi-autobiographical tale, published separately in 1805, was originally an episode of *Les Natchez* (q.v.), a prose epic on the Indians on which Chateaubriand worked while yet in England. Even before its separate publication, it was incorporated as part of his *Le Génie du Christianisme* (q.v.), as an illustration of his chapter entitled "Du vague des passions." In this story René, exiled among the Natchez in America, recounts to Chactas, following the tale told by the latter (cf. *Atala*), the adventures that led him to leave his native France, explaining to him the origins of his incurable melancholy. Part of the explanation relates the passionate reveries of his youth, the self-consciousness of his solitude among men, and the delirious exaltation he experienced in the company of his sister, Amélie, who decided to withdraw to a convent because of her brother's feelings for her. Although Chateaubriand's intention, far from wishing to present the character of René as a model to be emulated, was to denounce the sentiment of lassitude that characterized his times, his contemporaries, sensitive to his protagonist's charm, psychological analysis, lyricism, and contemplation of sadness, admired him and identified themselves with him.

Renée Mauperin (1864): See *Goncourt.*

"RÉSISTANCE" LITERATURE: The occupation of France by German troops that started with the crushing defeat of the French army in 1940 effected fundamental changes in French literature. Censorship and political pressure silenced many prominent voices in French letters. Only a handful of writers were then able to publish openly in France and these few were able to do so merely because they not only accepted but enthusiastically hailed the German victory. That they were an insignificant minority became more and more evident as the war went on and the German occupation became increasingly unbearable to the French. The most prominent of these "collaborators," Drieu La Rochelle (q.v.), who was to take his own life shortly after the liberation in 1944, frankly admitted that the vast majority of the French intellectuals sided with the cause of the Allies.

The atmosphere of oppression, stifling though it must have appeared to patriotic Frenchmen, paradoxically had the effect of furthering literary activities of all kinds. A new independence was sensed; a realm was discovered into which the invaders and their henchmen could not intrude—thought was as strong and free as ever. As Sartre puts it, looking back to those days: "Never have we been freer than under German occupation . . ." Poets were among the first to score the new form of tyranny. Their verses were loaded with allegorical allusions to historic and biblical precedents of despotism. Between the lines, it was abundantly clear that the new master was the real target of the often brilliant sarcasms to be found in many a poem published in the journals of 1940 and 1941. It must seem amazing, in retrospect, that both German and Vichy French censors allowed such sharp indictments of the fascist regime to be printed. There were several literary periodicals that carried non-conformist poetry. *Confluences, Esprit, Poésie* were among the foremost mouthpieces of patriotic rebellion against the silencing of independent thought. Indignant over the indiscriminate banishing of all values that had been treasured before the downfall of the third republic, poets like Aragon (q.v.) and Jean Tardieu mocked the constant official reference to "French decadence." Aragon's poignant lament *Le Crève-cœur,* published right after the debacle in 1940, had received wide acclaim. It was therefore no wonder that fascist writers should single him out as the scapegoat among non-conformists. Undaunted, Aragon kept sounding the alarm against stultifying self-accusation, as it was preached by the Pétain propaganda. He joined forces at times with Pierre Seghers (q.v.), poet and publisher, around whom a nucleus of rebels had gathered in South-Eastern France. Villeneuve-les-Avignon was a spiritual center in the fight against totalitarianism. From here—despite relentless attacks of the censor and, even worse, denunciation originating with French fascists—the courageous little pamphlets *Poésie 41,* then *Poésie 42, 43* and *44* went out, radiating hope, comfort, and above all stimulation to many avid readers of that suddenly scarce food: thought. Here was poetry unconcerned with the officially praised "return to the soil." Here rang the true voice of France; the real value of *Poésie* lay in its wise blend of pure poetry and ideologically committed articles and poems, even more than in its message of combat. The finest French poets—Pierre Emmanuel (q.v.), Loys Masson, Pierre-Jean Jouve (q.v.), René Char, Guillevic (qq.v.), Jean Marcenac— were the first ones to come out for freedom. Paul Eluard, living in Paris throughout the dark years, wrote his most moving poems in defense of ideals. His "Liberté" became the most popular poem ever circulated in France: this hymn of freedom was copied by hand, mimeographed, printed, memorized by a host of people to whom poetry had not meant anything before.

Prose did not fare quite so well as poetry in the early stages of the occupation, when it was a matter of skill and subtlety to obtain printing privileges. Poetry had a strategic advantage; it was less easy to slip into a short story or an essay cryptic insinuations against dictatorship. A few successful exceptions were noticeable; but long after objectionable prose appeared in certain periodicals, these reviews were suspended: the general public had detected immediately what had passed the censor's scrutiny unhindered.

Meanwhile, after October 1940, there had been systematic attempts at publishing pamphlets and newspapers openly opposing the Germans. The first nucleus of resistance was formed in Paris, at the Musée de l'Homme. After a few months of frantic, and at times not sufficiently cautious activity, practically all the members of the group were arrested and later shot by the

Germans. This and other mass executions, however, did more to harden the will to resist than to discourage it. Gradually everywhere in France clandestine newspapers mushroomed. Initially, these were crude, poorly presented, sporadically appearing sheets of mimeographed material, mostly outcries of revolt. Soon they were to renew a tradition which goes back to the French seventeenth and eighteenth centuries; the preoccupation was more and more with fundamental ideas. The humanistic heritage was strongly felt. While the military Germany and its police forces were denounced, the German people were considered increasingly the victims of their own ruthless masters. To be sure, there still occurred outbursts of hatred, but this was mostly in political leaflets. On the whole, the writings of French men of letters show a marked change from the wholesale condemnation of things German that remains one of the blots on literature during World War I. This phenomenon may be explained by the participation, within the resistance movement, of men from the widest variety of political camps; men of all philosophical or religious backgrounds fought side by side. This wartime harmony doubtless clarified the ideological horizon. Uncompromising in their struggle for the liberation of their country, most French writers showed generosity toward the enemy as a nation. One more explanation of such a change for the better may be that the surplus of emotional energy was absorbed by action: whether they fought with arms in their hands (like Malraux, André Chamson, and René Char; qq.v.) or wrote and circulated illegal literature (like Camus, Vercors, Mauriac (qq.v.), and many others), these writers risked their lives; they also felt themselves a part of that vast community of conspirators for a great cause. This consciousness saved them from cheap and degrading judgments. On the whole, the literature of the French resistance tried to live up to its obligations by maintaining a chivalrous attitude. Many French intellectuals paid with their lives for the endeavour to free their compatriots. Many of the best disappeared: Jean Prévost (q.v.), one of France's outstanding literary hopes, was killed in action, with his Maquis; among the poets who died in Nazi camps and the writers who were shot by the Germans are Max Jacob (q.v.), Robert Desnos, Benjamin Fondane, Andre Chenevière, François Vernet, and Jacques Decour.

As the resistance movement became organized, not only pamphlets and leaflets were printed, but full length books as well. The difficulty of such an endeavour is measured when we remember the total control over all printing presses which the Germans exercised as well as the police and secret police control in streets, trains, even homes everywhere in Europe. The first important clandestine book to appear, Vercors' *The Silence of the Sea,* was deliberately conceived as a piece of ideological writing. Vercors, a pseudonym chosen for its combative connotation, was a newcomer to literature. His book, however, is a masterpiece and has been acclaimed the world over. For it has both beauty and nobility of thought. Vercors showed that it was possible to fight the Germans without indulging in hatred.

Starting in 1943, anthologies of poetry appeared, also clandestinely, in which the patriots sang their hope, their faith, sometimes their indignation, rarely stooping to cries of vengeance. Other volumes followed, with short stories, excerpts from novels, essays. Among the authors already well known were Mauriac, Aveline, Chamson (q.v.), Pierre Bost, Benda (q.v.), Guéhenno (q.v.). Others, like Claude Morgan, Gabriel Audisio, Edith Thomas, Luc Estang (q.v.), achieved a high degree of detachment from the drab, yet gruesome reality. Some authors discovered an entirely new vein, like Jean Cassou (q.v.), already famous as novelist and distinguished critic, who wrote *33 sonnets composed in solitary confinement,* where pure lyrical beauty blends with forceful expression of cultural recollection.

The importance of the literature of the French resistance is that its writers maintained faith in spiritual values, that they refused to submit to conformity dictated by brutal force. The French patriotic writers were conscious of their task. They were not only fighters for the liberation of their country. They were also bearing in mind a far greater obligation: to preserve the cause of mind, in this test where matter seemed so overwhelming. Post-war literature in France, the richness of which is often recognized by its very detractors, owes a definite debt to these pioneers. Resistance literature crystallized characteristics stemming from France's humanistic tradition, and served to develop them further. Writing in spite of seemingly insurmountable odds helped form men of the stature of a Sartre (q.v.), a Camus, a Char. "Intelligence at war" eventually overcame the long-felt barrenness and absence of purpose. If today there is much discussion about the merits and drawbacks of "engagement," it must not be forgotten that poetry received a tremendous impetus from its commitment; that the novel experienced a marked upswing after World War II; that even the theatre gained in more than one way. A sentence coined by the critic Gaëtan Picon (speaking of Paul Eluard; q.v.) fits the whole of resistance literature: "Generosity, the gift of self, is the bond between intimate poetry and civic poetry." Giving their best, the writers of the French resistance may not always have achieved immortality: yet they paved the way for what is certainly one of the richest periods of French literature.

Hannah Josephson & Malcolm Cowley, *Aragon, Poet of the French Resistance*, 1945; Robert Morel, *La Littérature clandestine*, 1945; Louis Parrot, *L'Intelligence en Guerre*. (*Panorama de la Pensée française dans la clandestinité*), 1945; Jean Paulhan & Dominique Aury, *La Patrie se fait tous les jours* (Anthology of Resistance texts), 1945; Gaëtan Picon, *Panorama de la Nouvelle Littérature française*, new ed. 1951; Maurice Nadeau, *La Littérature présente*, 1952; Konrad Bieber, *L'Allemagne vue par les écrivains de la Résistance Française*, 1954; Henri Peyre, *The Contemporary French Novel*, 1955.

KONRAD BIEBER

Restif (or Rétif) de la Bretonne, Nicolas Edmé: (1734-1806) This novelist, called the "Rousseau of the gutter," was the son of a Burgundy-peasant farmer. When he came to Paris, he became a printer, and was to set directly in type many of the more than two hundred volumes of which he was the author. His novels, licentious and depicting the life of the lower classes, whose misfortunes and manners are detailed, offer valuable information about the social and economic life of the masses during the years preceding the French Revolution. At the same time they have moral or didactic pretensions. *Le Paysan perverti* (1775), his first successful work, illustrates, as does *La Paysanne pervertie* (1784), the corrupting effect of city life on virtuous people coming from the country. Country manners are described in *La Vie de mon père* (1778); Parisian life is depicted in *Les Contemporaines* (1780-1785), in which social types from some two hundred trades and professions are drawn. The sordid aspects relating to the life of the people that he describes offer a foreshadowing of the realistic novel during the nineteenth century.

F. Funck-Brentano, *Rétif de la Bretonne*, 1928; A. Bégué, *Rétif de la Bretonne*, 1948.

Retour de Jérusalem, Le (1903): See *Donnay, Maurice*.

Retour de Silbermann, Le (1930): See *Lacretelle, Jacques de*.

Retz, François-Paul de Gondi, Cardinal de: (1614-1679) His *Mémoires* (1671-1675), covering the period of the Fronde (1648-1653), relate the events of his political career. Ordained a priest in 1643, he succeeded through intrigue in obtaining an appointment as cardinal in 1652. His conspiracy against Richelieu and his attempt to overthrow Mazarin, however, resulted in imprisonment and exile; he was eventually granted permission (1662) by Louis XIV to return to France. Despite his personal prejudices, the *Mémoires* have historical importance, for they portray vividly the conditions before and during the Fronde; written, moreover, in a style that is at once clear and concise and that reveals, in a few simple phrases, the leading characters of the day, they are a good example of classical writing. He also published *La Conspiration de Fiesque* (written in 1631), some sermons and letters.

L. Batiffol, *Le cardinal de Retz*, 1927; J. Dussord, *Le Cardinal de Retz, conspirateur né*, 1938.

Reverdy, Pierre: (1889-   ) Commentator upon Braque and Picasso, this poet, born in Narbonne, was hailed at the time of the appearance of *Les Épaves du ciel* (1924), a collection of his early work, as a great poet and as the master among the Surrealists (see *Surrealism*). His poetry, hermetic, making use of subtle analogies, allusions, and half-statements, suggests the strangeness and absurdity of our internal world as well as the spiritual anguish of our times. Cosmic emotions and man's disquietude are frequently expressed in but a few short lines. *Plupart du temps* (1945) is a collection of his earliest poems; *Ferraille* (1937) is one of the most moving collections of our time. Other volumes include *Flaques de verre* (1929), *Plein verre* (1940), and *Sources du Vent* (1945). His aesthetics are explained in *Le Gant de crin* (1926).

Rêveries d'un Promeneur solitaire (1776-1778): See *Rousseau, J. J.*

Rhadamiste et Zénobie (1711): See *Crébillon, Prosper.*

Rhétoriqueurs: are those poets of the fifteenth and early part of the sixteenth century, including Georges Chastelain, Jean Molinet, Jean Meschinot, Guillaume Cretin and Jean Lemaire de Belges (q.v.)—disciples of Alain Chartier (q.v.) who flourished around the court of Burgundy—whose sincerity of thought, feeling and inspiration were replaced by artifices of style and the acrobatics of versification. Their chief aim was to complicate the poetic genres of the twelfth, thirteenth and fourteenth centuries— the *virelai, rondeau, ballade,* and *chant royal* (qq.v.)—and to multiply the technical difficulties of rhyme (for example, *évidente* rhyming with *et vit Dante;* or *à sa corde* immediately followed by *s'accorde*).

H. Guy, *Histoire de la poésie française au XVIᵉ siècle,* t. 1: *L'Ecole des rhétoriqueurs,* 1910.

Richepin, Jean: (1849-1926) This writer, poet, novelist, and dramatist, born in Algeria, is especially important for having continued the romantic tradition. His early work, marked by a romantic defiance, is seen in *La Chanson des gueux* (1876). In this collection, he portrays the *gueux,* reminiscent of Vil-lon (q.v.), while making use of an argot that shocked his contemporaries. *Les Caresses* (1877), another collection, extols physical love. With *Le Chemineau* (1897) he contributed to the revival of the romantic drama in verse; in *Les Truands* (1899) he resuscitated the medieval vagabonds of *Notre-Dame. La Belle au bois dormant* (1908) is a dramatization of the charming tales by Perrault (q.v.). Many other plays give further evidence of a use of rich metaphor and rhyme that almost become bombastic, and of basically impulsive characters in plots that are generally highly imaginative.

Ricochets, Les (1807): See *Picard.*

Rimbaud, Arthur: (1854-1891) At a very early age Rimbaud ran away from home several times, twice to Paris, deserting Charleville, where he was born, and an authoritarian mother, who had become to him intolerable. In 1871 he sent to Verlaine (q.v.) his poem *Bateau ivre,* in which was reflected his intense desire for freedom and his wish to escape from his home life. Soon thereafter the two poets, though separated in years and of incompatible temperaments, began to share together a vagabond existence, going first to England and then to Belgium; there their *liaison* came to an end after a quarrel, in which Rimbaud shot, though not fatally, his older companion. It was then that he wrote and published his "psychologically autobiographical" *Une Saison en enfer* (1873), consisting of prose and some verse. His other important prose-poem, the *Illuminations,* the result of his theory of the "seer," was also composed before 1874. It was to exercise an important influence on the poetic schools of *Symbolism* (q.v.) and *Surrealism* (q.v.). Rimbaud abandoned literature at the age of nineteen, spending the rest of his life travelling. Having contracted an infection while in

Abyssinia, he returned to Marseille, where he died in a hospital. Although Rimbaud at first imitated Hugo, Baudelaire, and the Parnassians (qq.v.), he soon sought a new, personal formula to express his revolt against everything, including his mother, social conventions and morality, literature and art. He accomplished this by exploring in his poetry the invisible and the subconscious, by deliberately introducing hallucination, disorder and the irrational, and by consciously seeking obscurity. Resolved to be a "seer," he invented a mode of expression that was hermetic and correspondent to his visionary world. This quest led him to metrical irregularities to free verse and prose, and ultimately to silence.

P. Berrichon, *La vie de J.-A. Rimbaud*, 1897; Wallace Fowlie, *Rimbaud*, 1946.

rime féminine: Rhyme is said to be "feminine" when the words end in —*e* mute (as in *espérance* and *enfance*); otherwise, the rhyme is "masculine."

rime riche: Rhyme is said to be "rich" when the last two syllables of a word have the same sound (as in *langoureux* and *douloureux*) or when the consonant preceding the last identical vowel sound is the same (as in *apaisées* and *rosées*).

Rivage des Syrtes, Le (1951): See *Gracq, Julien*.

Rivarol, Antoine: (1753-1801) Famous for his reflections and maxims, expressed in language that is at times caustic, at times witty, this moralist is especially known as the author of *Discours sur l'universalité de la langue française* (1784). The latter work, which traces the history of the French language (q.v.) and exposes the reasons for its supremacy in Europe, contains the famous adage of *Ce qui n'est pas clair n'est pas français* ("That which is not clear is not French").

A. Le Breton, *Rivarol, sa vie, ses idées, son talent*, 1895.

Rivière, Jacques: (1886-1925) Critic and long-time editor of the *Nouvelle Revue française*, he wrote in *Études* (1911) penetrating essays on literature, painting, and music. Everywhere, as in *A la Trace de Dieu* (1926), *De la Foi* (1928), and in his *Correspondance* with Paul Claudel and Alain-Fournier (qq.v.) —his brother-in-law—he shows his preoccupation with religion. He also wrote two psychological novels, *Aimée* (1922) and the unfinished *Florence* (1935), published posthumously.

Robe rouge, La (1900): See *Brieux*.

Roblès, Emmanuel: (1914-   ) Born in Oran, this dramatist and novelist is the author of *Travail d'homme* (1942), *Nuits sur le monde* (1944), *Montserrat* (1948)—a tragedy reflecting present-day preoccupations—and *Cela s'appelle l'aurore* (1952). The last-named book, probably his best, achieves high moral qualities, outlining struggles against hypocrisy and cowardice and implying the true values of love and friendship.

Rodogune (1644-1645): See *Corneille, Pierre*.

Roi s'amuse, Le (1832): See *Hugo*.

Rolla (1833): See *Musset*.

Rolland, Romain: (1866-1944) Scholar, historian, novelist, playwright, musicologist, biographer. His dramatic pieces include *Aërt* (1898), *Danton* (1900), *Le Quatorze juillet* (1902), and *Le Jeu de l'amour et de la mort* (1924), and deal with the people and the Revolution (cf. *Théâtre du Peuple*). In addition to his studies in music, including his doctoral thesis, *L'Histoire de l'opéra en Europe avant Lully et Scarlatti* (1895) and his *Vie de Beethoven* (1903), he wrote biographical studies of three geniuses: *Michel-Ange* (1905), *Vie de Tolstoi* (1911) and *Mahatma Gandhi* (1924). His novels include his masterpiece, *Jean-Chris-*

tophe (1903-1912), a *roman-fleuve* (q.v.), *Clérambault; histoire d'une conscience libre pendant la guerre* (1920) and *L'Ame enchantée* (1922-1933).

Under the influences of Tolstoy, whose philosophy of art stressed moral truth and faith in humanity, and Madame Malwida von Meysenbug, the friend of many political and artistic notables, whose personal idealism could not be quelled by the wickedness of life, Rolland shaped the notion that the hero or genius is one who is conquered materially, but who conquers by his willingness to struggle with the adversities of life and by preserving his ideal. This hero-concept is personified by Jean-Christophe, the young musical genius who meets up with discouragement and hostility but who frees himself from sham and hypocrisy by shunning materialistic success. Unlike Barrès (q.v.) with his nationalistic ideas, Rolland is cosmopolitan and "internationalistic," tolerant and full of pity for humanity, as he sweeps across Europe in his study of it and its civilization in *Jean-Christophe*. For this philosophy and for his pacifistic *Au-dessus de la mêlée* (1915), Rolland suffered unpopularity among his compatriots and exile in Switzerland during the First War. In allied countries outside of France, however, his stature was recognized, and, in 1915, he was awarded the Nobel Prize for Literature. With the beginning of the Second World War in 1939, this "citizen of the world" abandoned his pacifist position.

S. Zweig, *Romain Rolland; The Man and His Work* (1921); C. Sénéchal, *Romain Rolland* (1933); W. T. Starr, *R. Rolland and a World at War*, 1956.

Rollin, Charles: (1661-1741) Rector of the University of Paris (1694) and Principal of the Collège de Beauvais (1699), he published *Traité des*

études (1726-1731), a work that includes him among the pedagogues and moralists; exposing a method of teaching and studying, he deals with ancient languages, the French language (q.v.), rhetoric, history and philosophy. He also wrote works of history, the most important among which are *Histoire ancienne* (1730) and *Histoire romaine* (1738).

H. Ferté, *Rollin, sa vie, ses œuvres et l'Université de son temps,* 1902.

Romains, Jules (pseud. of **Louis Farigoule**): (1885-   ) This professor who became one of the twentieth century's most important novelists, as well as dramatist, essayist and poet, was born in a hamlet of the Cévennes Mountains and came to Paris as a youngster. When he was yet a student at the École Normale Supérieure, he conceived the doctrine of *Unanimism* (q.v.), espoused in his early poetry and, more especially, in his publications of *La Vie unanime* (1908) and *Mort de quelqu'un* (1911). After the War, when he gave up his teaching career, he devoted himself completely to writing. His *Psyché* (1922-1929), a trilogy dealing with conjugal love and sex relations, is another illustration of his *unanimistic* doctrines. During the same period, further illustrations of this literary theory were offered in his *Cromedeyre le vieil* (1920), a lyrical tragedy which retraces the history of a village, and in *Donogoo-Tonka* (1920), a farce. *Knock, ou le Triomphe de la médecine* (1923), a farce of Molièresque inspiration, and the comical *M. Le Trouhadec saisi par la débauche* (1923), are good examples of his talents as a dramatist, which are also displayed in his adaptation of Ben Jonson's *Volpone* (1928), done in collaboration with Stefan Zweig.

Unanimism finds its most complete expression in his ambitious and monumental *roman-fleuve* (q.v.) *Les Hommes de bonne volonté*

(1932-1946). In the 27 volumes of this cyclic novel Romains evokes the period in France—with several incursions into other European countries—from October 6, 1908 to October 7, 1933. His procedure is one of juxtaposition; all society, with its most representative personages, from the most humble to the most important, is depicted. The life and soul of a group, linked to that of other groups, or to a landscape, a street, a square, blends around the destinies of the different characters, strangers in the beginning to each other; exceptional individuals like Jallez and Jerphanion, two "normaliens" whose lives, incidentally, lend a semi-autobiographical element to the novel, are of particular interest in this interplay. In the vast frescoes of the first 14 volumes, the masses, despite the efforts of some men of good-will, are seen rushing headlong on to War, the most characteristic episodes of which are seen in *Prélude à Verdun* and *Verdun* (Vols. XV and XVI). The remaining volumes are framed in a spirit of hope and fraternity. The optimism of the last volume, which unfolds some months after Hitler's arrival to power, gives these *men of good will* an unconsciously ironic and paradoxical twist; if Romains has not proven his ability as a political thinker, at least he has shown faith in his refusal to despair of the future. Romains was elected in 1946 to the French Academy.

André Cuisenier, *L'Art de Jules Romains*, 1948.

roman à clef: A novel, like those of Madeleine de Scudéry (q.v.), that pictures contemporary characters, easily recognized, under fictitious names.

roman antique: An epic romance, either historical or legendary, drawing its source from antiquity, that was written by the *clercs* of the Middle Ages. The clercs, who did not often rely on the ancient sources, which they did not always fully comprehend, made adaptations or transpositions that were often fantastic. Full of anachronisms and general travesties, these long romances, of thousands of lines, with settings removed in time and space, excited the curiosity and imagination of the French medieval mind by the strange lands, love stories, customs, costumes, situations and heroes they depicted. Some better-known examples are the *Roman d'Alexandre* (by Lambert le Tort and Alexandre de Bernay; q.v.), the *Roman de Troie* (*c.* 1160, by Benoit de Sainte-More), the *Roman d'Enéas* (*c.* 1170, author unknown) and the *Roman de Thèbes* (*c.* 1150).

E. Faral, *Recherches sur les sources latines des contes et romans courtois du moyen âge*, 1913.

Roman bourgeois, Le (1666): See *Furetière, Antoine*.

roman breton: A romance in verse, popular during the twelfth and thirteenth centuries, which was inspired by the Celtic myths and traditions that still lingered in Wales, Cornwall, Brittany and England. Its legends revolved for the most part round the history of King Arthur (q.v.) and the Knights of the Round Table. They told of the strange adventures of Lancelot, of the quest of the Holy Grail (cf. *Perceval*) and of the loves of Tristan and Iseut (q.v.). Some of these legends had been introduced into French literature through Marie de France's (q.v.) *lais* (q.v.). The conquest of England by William the Conqueror (1066) also had helped to spread these legends to France. The finest tales of these legends are those by Chrétien de Troyes (q.v.). Differing from the *Chansons de geste* (q.v.) in source and in theme, the *romans bretons*, unlike the former, were written to be read, ·

were more imaginative, and gave a predominant place to courtly or chivalrous love. They are an important source of the modern novel. P. Paris, *Les romans de la Table Ronde, mis en français moderne,* 1868-77; M. Lot Borodine, *Le roman idyllique au moyen âge,* 1913; *Les Romans de la Table Ronde* adaptés par J. Boulanger, 1922-23.

Roman comique, Le (1651): See *Scarron, Paul.*

Roman d'Alexandre: A twelfth-century poem of more than 20,000 verses by Lambert le Tort and Alexandre de Bernay. It is the first to be written in the twelve-syllable line; hence the name of *alexandrine* (q.v.) given to such verses. This epic romance, whose theme is the life of the great Alexander, is derived from Latin sources and ultimately from a Greek romance by a certain Callisthenes (*c.* 200 A.D.). It blends fact with fancy, surrounding Alexander the Great with knights and barons, as if he were Charlemagne, and making him go through fantastic lands and enchanted palaces as he performs his wondrous exploits.

Paul Meyer, *Alexandre le Grand dans la littérature du Moyen Age,* 1886.

roman d'aventure: Drawing its subject matter from diverse sources, frequently Byzantine, this genre, developed from the twelfth to the fifteenth centuries, was written, in contrast with the *chansons de geste* (q.v.), to be read and not sung. Its principal themes, of a sentimental nature, deal with woman and love. Among the better-known of these romances are *Parténopeus de Blois, Floire et Blanchefleur*—both of the twelfth century.

Roman de la Momie, Le (1858): See *Gautier.*

Roman de la Rose: The most celebrated allegorical poem of the Middle Ages, consisting of two parts, the first of which, a veritable Art of Love relating in a courtly and somewhat affected manner the poet's dream of his pursuit of the rose, symbolizing his love, was written by Guillaume de Lorris (*c.* 1225), and the second, much longer and more didactic and satiric in tone, was written by Jean de Meung (*c.* 1265). The poem as a whole is representative of the courtly as well as the bourgeois spirit. Among the many translations of this poem is that of Chaucer.

E. Langlois, *Origines et sources du Roman de la Rose,* 1890; A. Mary, *Le Roman de la Rose mis en français moderne,* 1928; A. M. F. Gunn, *The Mirror of Love,* 1952.

Roman de Renart: A collection of many animal tales or fables in verse derived from Aesop that were probably written by different *clercs* beginning with the twelfth and running through the fourteenth century, and distinguished by an absence of moral preoccupation. A veritable animal epic, its principal characters in the many different situations are the fox, given in these poems the proper noun of *Renart* —the name now commonly applied when referring to this animal—and the wolf *Isengrin,* whose physical powers are no match for the ruses and intelligence of *Renart. Renart's* superiority also represents a witty satire upon the powerful social classes of the Middle Ages that exploit the weak.

Léopold Sudre, *Les sources du roman de Renart,* 1892; Gaston Paris, *Le roman de Renart,* 1895; Lucien Foulet, *Le roman de Renart,* 1914.

Roman de Troie (*c.* 1154): See *Benoît de Sainte-Maure.*

Roman d'un jeune homme pauvre, Le (1857): See *Feuillet.*

romanesque: Found in many of the novels of the seventeenth century, and often employed in eighteenth-century French tragedy, its characteristics include such devices as mistaken identities, misconceptions, disguises, and the like, and serve as motivating forces in the development of much of the action.

roman-feuilleton: A serial novel published by a daily newspaper. In 1841, when the *roman-feuilleton* was first inaugurated, the *Journal des Débats* published Frédéric Soulié's *Les Mémoires du diable* as a serial; in the same newspaper appeared the following year Eugene Sue's (q.v.) popular *Les Mystères de Paris.* Other *romans-feuilletons,* written by A. Dumas *père* (q.v.), Xavier de Montépin, and others, appeared in *Le Siècle, Le Constitutionnel* and *La Presse.* The value of the *roman-feuilleton* is that it magnifies the characteristics of the Romantic novel of the forties, dealing as it does with subjects that are more or less historical, whimsical, social and moral.

roman-fleuve: This term, referring to a cyclic novel, is not necessarily synonymous with the long novel, although the *roman-fleuve* does contain numerous personages and does not end abruptly. Its importance is not to be found in the characters, unless they are chroniclers or witnesses of an epoch. For this reason it cannot be said that either Balzac or Zola wrote this kind of novel. Their tales, moreover, even when integrated with the whole, retain their individuality. Although its origins can be traced to other lands, to Tolstoy's *War and Peace,* Thomas Mann's *Buddenbrooks,* and Galsworthy's *Forsyte Saga,* in France it only began to appear in the early twentieth century. Among the most notable examples of the *roman-fleuve* are *A la Recherche du temps perdu* by Marcel Proust (q.v.), *Les Thibault* by Roger Martin du Gard (q.v.), *La Chronique des Pasquier* by Georges Duhamel (q.v.) and *Les Hommes de bonne volonté* by Jules Romains (q.v.).

ROMANTICISM: The pattern of development of French romanticism is a puzzling and exasperating one. Ever since the first days of romanticism, explanations of this phenomenon have been liberally propounded, at first by the writers themselves, later by professors seeking a means of identification useful for students, or writers who felt constrained to establish their own relationship to a great artistic renaissance. Thus, Stendhal (q.v.) called it any literature written to please contemporaries, a definition which Emile Deschanel later rephrased into the paradox that a romanticist was a classicist in the process of succeeding. Hugo (q.v.) considered romanticism a variety of liberalism while Brunetière (q.v.), the Baron Seillière and Irving Babbitt inclined to regard it as a dangerous relaxation of control over the ego. In more modern times, C. M. Bowra has called it "a prodigious attempt to discover the world of spirit through the unaided efforts of the solitary soul," whereas Pierre Moreau pictured its adherents as men inclined to extremes, interested in the relative and the diverse. A wide variation of opinions has produced a wealth of contradictory definitions. Yet each succeeding attempt to discover an explanatory pattern in this tangled skein of lives, events, and books has somehow failed to produce any satisfactory sequence of least common denominators.

Several factors have contributed to the confusion of emphases, above all the insistence that romanticism was the antithesis of classicism (q.v.) and, hence, that each could be defined by opposing lists of the characteristics of the two movements. Such an approach led naturally to the formulation of such dichotomies as: Apollonian versus Dionysian, reason versus imagination, or objectivity versus subjectivity, neat resumés that somehow failed to delimit or to summarize. Secondly, critics fell into the trap of considering romanticism an abstract entity, a thing in itself existing apart from historical reality. It was, consequently, assumed to consist of a series of timeless attitudes, against which any author could be evaluated. These criteria indicated the exact degree of a writer's participation in the movement and established the mixture of classicism and romanticism that differentiated him from all other men.

Complicating the problem, too, is the simplistic approach, a desire to encompass a movement within the confines of a word or a phrase. The romanticists have thus been characterized as more sensitive than their predecessors, haunted by uneasiness, a victim of the "mal du siècle" (q.v.). The romanticist has been variously labelled a humanitarian or an egoist, "l'homme malheureux et solitaire" who is concerned with the personal, the particular, and the concrete. His humor is somber, his personality tormented and proud; he suffers from an inability to adjust to his age, a malaise which his mysticism and wild imagination tend to increase. Freed from religious and social constraints, this "héros fatal" fiercely demands his right to passion, burning and all-consuming.

In a sense, all these seem to describe the romanticist, but with the deceptive and brilliantly thin veneer of the half-truths. On the one hand they have over-simplified a complex social phenomenon and, on the other, they have failed either to characterize the creations of the romanticists or to isolate the movement, to show what is peculiar to romanticism and to no other group. Properly understood, they are helpful terms, but in no sense valid as definitions or summations.

More modern writers, however, have enlarged their critical angle of vision by regarding romanticism as completely different from, and scarcely related to, classicism, a historical phenomenon that occurred shortly after the French Revolution and which had run its course by 1851. During that period a group of men, among them such conflicting personalities as Victor Hugo, Alfred de Vigny, Alfred de Musset, Honoré Balzac, Prosper Mérimée, and Stendhal (qq.v.), proudly accepted the name "romanticist," and worked in the common cause of forcing the acceptance of literary principles they felt necessary for establishing modern art. Though they differed among themselves over the function of art or the merits of the various media they employed, and often engaged in bitter personal feuds, they nonetheless shared a firm belief in the freedom of the artist to create as he pleased.

The concerted efforts of many writers, some famous, many forgotten, were to transform this thesis into the basis of subsequent literature, but their struggle was long and bitter. Superficially, the quarrel seemed to revolve around points of aesthetics, but, in reality, it covered a debate on the nature of literature and its relationship to a society in constant and seething development. And what started as a tempest in a literary teapot developed into a full-fledged revolution as political and philosophical overtones crept into the discussion.

The French Revolution had obliterated the old regime but, understandably, had not immediately affected the principles on which that era had founded a great literature. A long list of famous names and masterpieces kept the hasty architects of a new political world from tampering with the traditional values of art. War and the imperial surge of Bonaparte temporarily relegated literature to the background. Not only did the Emperor frown on deviations from the accepted norm, but so deeply inculcated was the respect for classicism that such boldness was treated as pure lunacy.

Nonetheless, a few intrepid spirits dared express the heresy that a new age deserved a new literature. Mme. de Staël (q.v.) in *De la littérature* (1800), suggested that French taste might be broadened by judicious borrowings from abroad. She was followed by Wilhelm Schlegel and Benjamin Constant (q.v.), both of whom indulged in more pointed remarks on the obsolescence of French literary theory and practice.

So restricted was the quarrel that the word *romantic* was not even used as a name for a literary attitude until 1816. And not until two years later did the debate begin to lose its esoteric character. In 1818, however, the publication of Mme. de Staël's *Considérations sur la révolution française* indicated that the cause of romanticism had now been linked to the Revolution. It became a necessary consequence of the events that had ended the world which had produced classicism.

By this time opinions on romanticism had become clear, and conservatives and revolutionists, literarily speaking, had taken their respective stands. It was apparent to all that a major effect of 1789 had been a shift in the economic, social, and cultural development of France. Young creative artists with few emotional attachments to the literary values of the past sensed the incapacity of the classical theories to cope with their times. They felt the need for new approaches to art, different ways of expressing their reaction to a brave new world. Since they believed the age that had elaborated the principles of classicism to have little in common with their own, they rejected its

principles and struck out boldly in search of an aesthetics tailored to fit the aspirations of the 19th century. Immediately they encountered the strong opposition of the professoriat, the professional critics, and the conservative middle class. The first two held firm allegiance to a doctrine that had given France a Golden Age; the last regarded the youngsters as rebels against the stability of the social order and, hence, a threat to its own security.

At first the neo-classicists succeeded in restraining the romanticists simply through their control of the media of communication: the press, the theaters, and the publishing houses. Therefore, the young writers joined in groups to admire their own work and to plot ways and means of expressing their dissidence and of insuring their success. Those of Catholic, royalist persuasion met at the home of Emile Deschamps, then at Victor Hugo's salon; those of a more liberal political persuasion collected at the homes of Stapfer, Viollet-le-Duc, or Delécluze. To a man they protested against authoritarianism in art and the passive acceptance of the concept of absolutes. They directed bitter challenges at their opponents, and, in so doing, successfully placed in doubt all previously accepted ideas on the nature of art and its place in society.

Meanwhile, the romanticists labored at their work and a series of resounding successes attested to the fact that the public was slowly inclining to their point of view. Lamartine (q.v.) and Hugo won for them the field of poetry; prose fell by default, since the classicists accepted Boileau's (q.v.) opinion of it as a medium beneath consideration.

But the last and most bitter struggle was to be fought over the theater. The classicists marshalled all their forces to keep the romanticists off the stage, because triumph here not only meant fortune for the romanticists, but a general acknowledgment of the justice of their claims. Goaded by the open defiance of the preface to *Cromwell* (q.v.), they used all means to block the acceptance of romantic plays or to sabotage their performance. But first Dumas (q.v.), with *Henri III et sa cour*, then Vigny with *Othello*, paved the way for a great stage success, and with Hugo's *Hernani* (q.v.) it became obvious that the French public had renounced allegiance to the past.

Once victory lay in their grasp, however, the romanticists encountered a series of circumstances that radically changed the character and direction of their revolt. First of all, the unity of the group had been achieved and maintained through a common rejection of classicism. No theory of art united them; in fact, most had not yet arrived at clear conceptions of what they were doing. Hence, once the history of *Hernani* had removed any need for the existence of the group as a coherent, defensive unit, the romantic cénacle dissolved. Its members drifted apart as personal animosities, varying degrees of success, or differences in aesthetic approach snapped the loose bonds that once had joined them. Each now struck out to develop his own literary personality, unhampered by the forms and the necessity of working within the subject matter dictated by another age for another purpose.

But this very freedom might have proved the end of the romanticists had not the development of society presented them with the means to continue their revolution. At the very moment they were facing the problem of what to do with their liberty, they discovered that another phenomenon, of a social and economic nature, had upset the world in which they lived. By 1830 the Industrial Revolution had burst upon France, to change radically the face of the land. Secondly, it was to provide them with an enormous number of topics through its violent impact on every phase of French life. The slums, the plight of the new proletariat, the place of the machine in society, the distribution of wealth, the source of political power, the tragedy of man in an industrial world, alcoholism, illegitimacy, crime, all these and many more similar themes would furnish grist for their mill. Just as important, the Industrial Revolution was to give them technological means to reach a mass audience for the first time in history.

Reaction to this phenomenon, however, was to split romanticism, to reshape it around rejection or acceptance of society as a proper concern for art. Some, a second generation of romantic poets and even more aesthetically pure than their predecessors, refused to compromise with society by making their work reflect the temper of the times; others, mostly the leaders of the original cénacle, adjusted their principles and decided to take art down to the people.

The first group, mostly young men new to the profession of letters, were primarily poets who found their profession of faith in the preface of Hugo's *Orientales* (1829). Fresh on the scene, they found to their amazement that, by 1830, a shift in popular taste made their verse unsaleable. Moreover, the conservative critics attacked these men of no reputation even more vigorously than they had their more famous predecessors. Hurt, bewildered, and angry, the art for art's sake group found its rallying point in a dedication to an exclusive cult of literature that rejected the conventions and utilitarian outlook of the bourgeoisie. For them art became a religion; poetry was their god and prose anathema.

The more they insisted on their right to versify as they pleased, the more suspect they became and the smaller their public. Nonetheless, they continued experimenting, writing for each other, as they exploited the possibilities of their chosen medium. In reaction against the society that rejected them, they took savage and melancholic pleasure in creating the myth of the avant-garde poet, politically to the left, living in Bohemia, anti-religious, anti-social, and completely contemptuous of the sacred values of the middle class. For this most of them would pay the high price of remaining unknown and unpublished. Only a rare member of the troupe, Théophile Gautier (q.v.), achieved fame; the others, Borel, Lassailly, O'Neddy, Forneret, and Bertrand (q.v.) would never know that their work would make possible all later developments in poetry. They had turned their backs on the world which the middle class and the Industrial Revolution had given them, and for this there was no forgiveness.

Not so with the men of the first generation. After *Hernani,* writers like Hugo, Lamartine, George Sand (q.v.), Balzac, and Lamennais (q.v.), succumbed to an overpowering urge to descend into the public arena, to shape the form of society. Before them lay France with all the ailments resultant from the rapid expansion of the machine age, and from a paucity of experience with representative government. This task the romanticists approached with Messianic zeal, firm in the faith that their literary talents could make them function as brilliantly in the realm of politics. They transposed to public affairs the same confidence and beliefs that had led most of them to subscribe to the theory of the divine nature of their genius and mission. Imbued with

the 18th-century notion of progress, these "utilitarians" decided to adapt art to the aims of society, to take advantage of its didactic possibilities for the purpose of directing France toward a realization of the political and social ideals of the Revolution.

Consequently, they seized upon the technological advances offered by the Industrial Revolution as aids to the fulfillment of their purpose. The new presses, the new methods of making paper were utilized to carry their message to the ever-increasing audience which the spread of primary education was presenting them. Since poetry no longer provided a living or appealed to a mass audience, they turned to prose, to the newspaper, or the novel, as better suited to reach large groups with restricted schooling. Some, like Dumas, frankly sought only to please, but Hugo, Lamartine, Sue (q.v.), and Balzac wrote as conscious apostles of a new way of life.

Curiously, it was this aspect of romanticism that brought about the collapse of romanticism as the reigning literary movement. The few dedicated souls were imitated by many who sought only to pander to public taste. Industrial literature brought disrepute to all by its insistence on the necessity of giving the reader what he wanted. Moreover, utilitarian romanticism had tied itself closely to the development of French society, to foreseeing needs or to solving social problems. Romanticism, therefore, faced repudiation unless it could make France change in accordance with its theories. The last happened when the romanticists, given an opportunity in 1848 to govern the nation, vacillated until the coup d'état of Prince Napoleon removed them completely from politics. The lack of a specific program to implement their humanitarianism contributed heavily to their downfall. Both segments of romanticism, however, had left a deep mark on French literature. The first generation had initiated a great poetic revolution, though it abandoned the cause of pure art once the theory had been proposed and its cause had triumphed. These romanticists talked wildly of poetic revolt, but their work was more timid than their manifestoes. Ironically, they would make greater gains in prose, in the novel, for example, while the second generation would continue the revolution and hand it on to the Parnasse (see *Parnassians*).

Romanticism, then, was the movement that expressed France's first literary reaction to that complex phenomenon known as the Industrial Revolution. For some half a century, writers freed of the restraints of classicism experimented in all imaginable directions, in all the genres, creating some, transforming others. Art became pure, or utilitarian. The end result of this turmoil was that the romanticists established a great pool of new ideas as they touched on a multitude of problems, social and artistic, common to men in a modern industrial society. In that sense, the great glory of romanticism lies in the fact that it is the mother lode of all the subsequent literary movements of the 19th and 20th centuries.

Maurice Souriau, *Histoire du romantisme*, 1927; René Bray, *Chronologie du romantisme* (1804-30), 1932; Pierre Moreau, *Le Romantisme*, 1932; Jean Giraud, *L'École romantique française*, 1947; Albert J. George, *The Development of French romanticism*, 1955.

ALBERT J. GEORGE

rondeau: A poem of three stanzas with no uniformity in the number of lines, but in the last two stanzas of which the last line repeats the first line of the first stanza. There are, however, many varieties of the *rondeau*. See *Charles d'Orléans*.

Ronsard, Pierre de: (1524-1585) Although destined by birth for a military and diplomatic career—he had been page at the court, attached to the Duke of Orleans and James V of Scotland, and had later served as secretary to Ambassador Lazare de Baïf (q.v.)—an early deafness caused him to renounce such a career and to turn his interests to study and literature. At the home of Lazare de Baïf, where the young son, Antoine, was being taught by the eminent Hellenistic scholar Daurat (or Dorat), Ronsard zealously studied the Latin and Greek authors. In 1550, a few months after the appearance of the *Défense et Illustration de la langue française*, the manifesto of the group of poets known as the *Pléiade* (q.v.) of which he was to become head, he published his first *Odes*, in which he put into practice the theories of the manifesto by imitating Horace and Pindar. Two years later, replying to the accusation of not knowing how to "sound the sonnet"—very much in vogue because of the Petrarchist tendencies of the age—he published his *Amours*, a collection of 181 sonnets inspired by a certain Cassandre (Salviati) whom he had known and loved. In 1553 forty new sonnets appeared, along with the famous ode (q.v.) *Mignonne, allons voir si la rose*. The evolution that Ronsard was to follow thereafter showed the new poetic inspirations of Anacreon, Horace and Catullus with their more refined lyricism. His poetic output between 1560-1574 is varied; it includes his *Discours*, satirical and patriotic poems, and the incomplete and unsuccessful *La Franciade*, a Homeric epic written in the decasyllabic line. In two collections of poems—in addition to

the previously cited *Amours* (1552)
—Ronsard revealed himself as a
love poet: *Amours de Marie* (1556)
and *Sonnets pour Hélène* (1574),
his last sonnets, one of which begins
with the well-known *Quand vous
serez bien vieille, au soir, à la
chandelle*. His voluminous production, which includes practically
every possible form of poetry, reveals that his true genius lay in his
lyricism and in his mastery of the
ode and the sonnet. In spite of the
oblivion into which he fell during
the seventeenth and eighteenth centuries, the Romantics revived him
as their true predecessor and returned him to his rightful place as
the first of the modern singers of
nature and love, of fleeting time
and death.

Paul Laumonier, *Ronsard poète
lyrique*, 1909; P. de Nolhac, *Ronsard et l'Humanisme*, 1921.

Rostand, Edmond: (1868-1918) Known
more as a dramatist than a poet—he
is the author of the collection *Les
Musardises* (1890)—this writer, born
in Marseille, through a revitaliza-
tion of the romantic drama in verse
of some fifty years before marked a
reaction against the then still popular Naturalistic (see *Naturalism*)
theater. Of all his plays, including
Les Romanesques (1894), *La Princesse lointaine* (1895), *La Samari-
taine* (1897), and *Chantecler* (1910)
—whose crowing, in the most beautiful romantic poetry, nevertheless
does not make the sun rise—
Cyrano de Bergerac (1897) and
L'Aiglon (1900) were the most successful. A feeling of inferiority characterizes the poetic and loving soul
of the ugly Cyrano as well as the
weak eaglet (Napoleon II) deprived
of his wings; this feeling, which adds
to the emotional appeal of these
plays, may, too, in the final analysis,
reflect the true character of the
author's own lack of fulfillment.
Trying to emulate Victor Hugo
(q.v.), Rostand, in verses that have
a wealth of rhythm and rhyme, alternates tragic lyricism with the
grandiloquence of buffoonery; he
resorts to acrobatics in his prosody,
and employs local color. His characters, however, unlike those of
Hugo, are consistent; the historical
sources of his subjects, moreover,
unlike Hugo's, which are drawn
from Spain, Italy, and Germany, are
usually French—the periods of
Louis XIII and Napoleon II; Cyrano and even Chantecler can be
considered as national figures who
incarnate the French spirit. At the
age of 33, Rostand was admitted,
thanks in large part to his fame
obtained as the author of *Cyrano
de Bergerac*, to the French Academy.

Jean Suberville, *Edmond Rostand; son théâtre, son œuvre pos-
thume*, 1921; Rosemonde Gérard,
Edmond Rostand, 1935.

Rotrou, Jean: (1609-1650) Writing for
the Hôtel de Bourgogne (q.v.), as
did Alexandre Hardy (q.v.), this
dramatist, a contemporary of Corneille (q.v.), composed 14 *tragi-
comedies* (q.v.), 13 comedies and 9
tragedies. Of the last, his best are
Saint-Genest (1647)—reminiscent of
Corneille's *Polyeucte* (1643)—and
Venceslas (1647), set in Poland and
drawn from Spanish sources. His
comedies, many of which imitate
Plautus, include *Les Ménechmes*
(1632), *Les Sosies* (1636) and *Les
Captifs* (1638).

H. Chardon, *La Vie de Rotrou*,
1884; H. C. Lancaster, *A History of
French Dramatic Literature in the
17th Century* I, II (1929-1932).

Roucher, Jean Antoine: (1745-1794)
This poet, who was to die on the
scaffold the same day as André
Chénier (q.v.), wrote *Les Mois*
(1779). In this long poem of 12 cantos, he describes the various phases
of country-life and nature through
the course of the year; philosophical
comments are interwoven with the
description.

E. Faguet, *Histoire de la poésie française,* 1935.

Rouget de Lisle, Claude-Joseph: (1760-1836) Prose-writer and dramatist, he is especially known as the author of *La Marseillaise,* the words and music of which he composed on April 25, 1792, while an officer of engineers at Strasbourg. Originally called *Chant de guerre pour l'armée du Rhin,* France's national hymn was named *La Marseillaise* when troops from Marseilles sang it on their way to Paris.

A. Leconte, *Rouget de Lisle, sa vie, ses œuvres, la Marseillaise,* 1892.

Rouge et le Noir, Le: Written by Stendhal (q.v.) in 1831, at a time when the French novel was predominantly historical or lyrical, this novel represents, by its sober and precise style as well as by its contemporary setting, a transition between romanticism and realism. By its penetrating psychological analyses, moreover, it becomes the forerunner of the modern psychological novel. Laid in France during the Restoration, and based on a *cause célèbre* of 1827, it depicts psychologically the character of Julien Sorel, his ambitions, his frustrations.

Realizing the impossibility, since the fall of Napoleon, whom he admired, of rising to power through the army, Julien Sorel, son of a carpenter, believes that the road to success lies in the Church. He becomes, because of his assumed piety and his intelligence, tutor to the children of M. de Rênal. Following the denunciation of his love affair with Mme. de Rênal, Julien is hired, after a short stay at the seminary at Besançon, as the secretary to the Marquis de la Môle. Julien soon succeeds in seducing Mathilde, the proud daughter of the latter. When Mathilde's father learns of her pregnancy, he is ready to let Julien marry her, gives him a fortune, a title, and a commission in the army. A letter, however, which he receives from Mme. de Rênal, who reveals all, ruins the fulfillment of Julien's dreams of glory, power, and happiness; in a fit of rage, Julien, seeking out Mme. de Rênal, shoots her. Although he has not killed Mme. Rênal, Julien is found guilty and is executed. Mme. de Rênal dies shortly thereafter. Mathilde buries with her own hands Julien's severed head.

Rougon-Macquart, Les (1871-1893): See *Zola.*

Rousseau, Jean-Baptiste: (1671-1741) Considered one of the great lyric poets of the eighteenth century, he was forced to spend a good part of his life (1712-1738), after being accused of having written some libellous lines, outside of France. His most celebrated ode—a form in which he excelled—was addressed to his good friend the Comte de Luc. In addition to his *Odes, Cantates, Épigrammes, Épitres* and *Poésies diverses* (1723), he wrote several comedies, including *Le Flatteur* (1696) and *Le Capricieux* (1700).

Voltaire, *Vie de Jean-Baptiste Rousseau,* 1748; H. A. Grubbs, *Jean-Baptiste Rousseau,* 1941.

Rousseau, Jean-Jacques: (1712-1778) Next to Voltaire (q.v.), whom he first admired and then reviled, this writer, a philosopher, political scientist, novelist, teacher and musician, was the most remarkable literary figure of the eighteenth century. Born in Geneva, Switzerland, of a Protestant family, he led an adventurous and abnormal existence during his early years. His mother having died at his birth, he was first raised by his father, a watchmaker, who awakened his young imagination and tender feelings by the reading of sentimental fiction. At the age of sixteen, after having had an unhappy experience as an engraver's apprentice, he left Geneva. His subsequent vagabondage came to an end when, following his wish to be converted to Catholicism, he was sent to the home of Mme. de Warens. Spending the next twelve years (1729-1740) with this woman, who was both mistress and *maman* to him, he had the opportunity to read avidly in philosophy and literature and to study music. Now conscious of his intellectual attainments, and made aware, moreover, that he was no longer welcome, he decided to leave Mme. de Warens and go to Paris. Although his attempt to present his new method of musical notation met with no success, Rousseau, now in his thirties, had the good fortune of being introduced to important personalities in Paris, became associated with the *Encyclopédie* (q.v.), for which he was to write the articles on music, and began a life-long association with Thérèse Levasseur, an uneducated servant girl. The belief, incidentally, that Thérèse Levasseur bore him five children, has been questioned by some scholars.

Fame first came to Rousseau in 1750, when he was awarded a prize by the *Académie de Dijon* for his *Discours* entitled *Si le progrès des sciences et des arts a contribué à corrompre ou à épurer les mœurs.* In this prize essay, the title of which is a modification of the original question proposed—*Si le rétablissement des sciences et des arts a contribué à épurer les mœurs*—Rousseau advances the theory that progress in the sciences and arts, far from improving morals in society, contributes to the corruption of man's innate goodness. This thesis he further developed in a second essay—*Discours sur l'origine et les fondements de l'inégalité parmi les hommes* (1755)—in which he indicts the political state for having created, by its concept of private property, social inequalities and for having perverted the natural goodness of man. Opposing, furthermore, in his *Lettre à d'Alembert sur les spectacles* (1758), the establishment of a theater in Geneva, claiming that it would demoralize the city, he thereby incurred the wrath and animosity of Voltaire (q.v.), a lover of the theater, and of several former friends, including Diderot and d'Alembert (qq.v.), who, together with other Encyclopedists, espoused the ideal of progress in society. Other quarrels, of a more personal nature, caused him to break with Mme. d'Epinay, at whose cottage in the Montmorency forest, near Paris, he had begun several of his most important works. These, including *Le Contrat Social* (1761) and *Émile* (1762), reflect an ideal which, though unacceptable to the eighteenth-century philosophical notion of progress, was not dissimilar in its wish to contribute to man's happiness and to social improvement. The social ills criticized in his second *Discours,* Rousseau attempts to remedy by substituting civil liberty for natural liberty. This can be achieved, as explained in the *Contrat Social,* by re-establishing equality through a society that is founded on the general will of a sovereign people. Such a society, according to the ideas suggested, can guarantee individual liberty. Since society, moreover, has, through the centuries, corrupted the natural goodness of man, Rousseau proposes in *Émile* a system of education which would free the individual from the constraints and traditions of society and, at the same time, allow him to follow his good instincts and the laws of nature. The publication of *Émile,* which contained *La Profession de foi du vicaire savoyard,* a section denying Christian dogma and the necessity of revealed religion, was condemned, and Rousseau was compelled to flee to Geneva. Finding no refuge here, Rousseau accepted the invitation of David Hume, and in 1765 went to England. Quarreling with the philosopher, who, he was convinced, was with other enemies in league against him, he returned in 1767 to France, a victim of a persecution mania. Mostly to justify himself against his enemies, he wrote his autobiographical *Les Confessions* (first begun in 1765; published 1781-1788). During his last years, he also wrote *Rousseau juge de Jean-Jacques* (written 1775-1776), an appeal to win public opinion, and *Les Rêveries d'un Promeneur solitaire* (1776-1778), serene meditations that also become, in the final analysis, a kind of self-justification.

If the political theories in the *Contrat Social* inspired the French Revolution, thus linking Rousseau, despite his basic opposition to the ideas of progress expressed by the *philosophes* (q.v.), with the eighteenth century, the individualism of *Les Confessions* and the stress on imagination, sentiment and love of nature in *La Nouvelle Héloïse* (1761; q.v.)—his only novel—make him the great ancestor of Romanticism.

Included among his other works are *Le Devin du village* (1752), an opera, and the polemical *Lettres écrites de la montagne* (1764).

L. Ducros, *Jean-Jacques Rousseau*, 1908-1918; I. Babbitt, *Rousseau and Romanticism* (1919); A. Schinz, *La pensée de Jean-Jacques Rousseau*, 1929; D. Mornet, *Rousseau, l'homme et l'œuvre*, 1950; J. Guéhenno, *Jean-Jacques*, 1948-1954.

Rousset, David: (1912-   ) Credited with having coined the term *L'Univers concentrationnaire* (1946), the title of a work that describes the experiences of concentration camps, in *Les Jours de notre mort* (1947)—probably the outstanding example of literature dealing with concentration camps—he presents a fresco in which his ideas are set forth with a remarkable sense of dramatic composition. Both books, revealing the tragic situation, have an autobiographical basis.

Roy, Jules: (1907-   ) Following in the tradition of Saint-Exupéry (q.v.), in *La Vallée heureuse* (1946) he recounts bombing expeditions over the Ruhr valley and other parts of Germany. The stoical philosophy implied in the acceptance of one's duty to kill in time of war is seen more clearly in his more recent *Le Métier des Armes* (1948), *Le Navigateur* (1954), as well as in the three-act play *Les Cyclones* (1954).

Rutebeuf: (?—2nd half of 13th century) Like François Villon (q.v.), of whom he is the most significant poetic ancestor, this struggling but important *trouvère* (q.v.) sang, in lyrical verse, of his personal miseries and difficulties. Even more typical of him is his satiric vein, seen in several of his *fabliaux* (q.v.), in his numerous pieces against women, the University and mendicant friars, and in his dramatic monologue, the *Dit de l'Herberie*. He is also the author of the *Miracle du Théophile* (q.v.).

L. Clédat, *Rutebeuf*, 1903.

Ruy Blas: This *drame* (q.v.) in verse, the last dramatic success of Hugo (q.v.), was first presented on November 8, 1838. Set in seventeenth-century Spain, the plot unfolds the base connivings of Don Salluste in his desire for revenge against the Queen, who has banished him for an indiscretion with one of her lady attendants. Ruy Blas, his lackey, becomes the unwitting instrument of his sinister plot when the Queen, in answer to a letter bearing the signature of Don César, whom she has elevated to the rank of Prime Minister, comes at midnight to the secret meeting place designated in the letter. There, she is met by Don Salluste, who, having set the trap, now discloses the fact that the man she has loved and has known as Don César is, in effect, Ruy Blas, his valet, and threatens her, if she refuses to abdicate, with exposure. Revolted, Ruy Blas assassinates Don

Salluste, then poisons himself, dying in the arms of the Queen, who forgives him. This play contains many of the antitheses of which Hugo is so fond, as can be seen in the vile character of the noble Don Salluste and in the noble character of the lackey Ruy Blas, as well as in the mixture of comic and tragic scenes. It also fulfills Hugo's notion of the poet's mission, as is reflected in Ruy Blas' attempt to enlighten the monarch and help the people.

S

Sachs, Maurice: (1906-1945) This critic and translator died mysteriously in Germany. In *Le Sabbat* (written before 1939, published in 1946) he retraces the steps of his own degradation; *La Chasse à courre* (1949) is a diary of his life during the German Occupation. His writings show his concern with the question of individual responsibility.

Sade, Donatien Alphonse François, Marquis de: (1740-1814) The chief claim to fame of this Parisian-born novelist is his sexual perversion, an obsession which led to many years of imprisonment and which is reflected in such novels as *Justine ou les Malheurs de la Vertu* (1791), *Aline et Valcourt* (1793), *La Philosophie dans le Boudoir* (1795), *Juliette* (1797) and *Les 120 Journées de Sodome* (1904). Belonging to the eighteenth century because of the importance he gave to the instincts and to individualism, he is also regarded as a pioneer of modern sexual psychology and as an ancestor of many contemporary French writers and novelists. From his name, incidentally, is derived the term "sadism," applied to the delight, mostly sexual, taken in the sufferings of others.

C. P. Dawes, *The Marquis de Sade*, 1927; G. Gorer, *The Life and Ideas of the Marquis de Sade*, 1953.

Sagan, Françoise: (1935-   ) Probably the youngest of the contemporary French writers of repute, she scored a literary triumph at the age of nineteen with *Bonjour, tristesse* (1954). Containing the story of a girl of seventeen, at once naïve and sophisticated, who is raised by her father in an amoral way, this novel, restrained and classical in style, is a study in female psychology. Many of the same qualities are to be found in her more recent *Un Certain Sourire* (1956).

Saint-Amant, Marc-Antoine de: (1594-1661) His poetic inspiration, like that of Régnier and Théophile de Viau (qq.v.), remained unaffected by the rules set down by Malherbe (q.v.). His poetry shows a great variety in theme and versification. Reacting against preciosity (q.v.), he describes realistically familiar scenes from nature and life, as seen in *La Débauche, Les Cabarets, Le Fromage, Le Melon, La Pluie*, etc. Other poems include the sentimental *Ode sur la solitude* and *Ode du contemplateur* (1623), the heroic-comic *Le Passage de Gibraltar* (1640)—inspired by his numerous experiences as a traveler—the burlesque *Rome ridicule* (1643), and

Plate 17. Voltaire

Plate 18. Émile Zola

the epic *Moïse sauvé* (1653). Verbal exuberance and fantasy, in addition to gay realism, characterize his work.
Durand-Lapie, *Saint-Amant*, 1896; R. Audibert et R. Bouvier, *Saint-Amant, capitaine du Parnasse*, 1946.

Saint-Évremond, Charles de Marguetel, de Saint-Denis de: (1616-1703) This epicurean and *libertin* (q.v.) spent most of his last years in England, after having been exiled as a result of his *Lettre à Monsieur le Marquis de Créqui sur le traité des Pyrénées* (1661), in which he attacked Mazarin. Given the rare honor of being buried in Westminster Abbey, Saint-Évremond was recognized in England as the foremost representative of French criticism during the second half of the seventeenth century. His independence of mind is especially evident in his moral, historical and literary writings. These include *Réflexions sur les divers génies du peuple romain* (1663)—which foreshadows Montesquieu (q.v.)—*De la tragédie ancienne et moderne* (1672) and *Sur les poèmes des Anciens* (1685). He also wrote *Les Académistes* (pub. in 1650), a comedy reminiscent of Molière (q.v.), in which he satirizes the early members of the *Académie Française* (q.v.).
W. M. Daniels, *Saint-Évremond en Angleterre*, 1907; A. M. Schmidt, *Saint-Évremond ou l'humaniste impur*, 1932; K. Spalatin, *Saint-Évremond*, 1934.

Saint-Exupéry, Antoine de: (1900-1944) From the end of the First World War until his tragic disappearance on the Mediterranean front as he was returning from a reconnaissance mission, his life was one of adventure as an aviator; his flights, many of which were almost fatally dangerous, took him to Northwest Africa, South America, and to points of the South Atlantic. His career as a writer—it is difficult to call him a novelist in the accepted sense of the word—was a direct outcome of these experiences. Although *Courrier-Sud* (1929), *Vol de nuit* (1931) and *Terre des hommes* (1939) all concern the establishment of various air-lines, each publication reveals an increasing preoccupation with human problems and an increasing meditation on life and the world. In his meditations, the author-aviator regards his airplane, in the course of its regular struggles with the sea, wind and lightning, as a tool or means with which to come into closer spiritual contact with the human race; away from and above the earth, the aviator is not really alone but is linked, in affection and friendship, with those below, of whom he is thinking and towards whom he feels a sense of moral duty and responsibility. From this notion the author derives an ethic of courage and heroism that exalts the dignity of the human being and that gives meaning to fraternity as well as to life and death. These thoughts Saint-Exupéry expresses in a pure, clear, poetic style free from grandiloquent or facile effects. Other books of his include *Pilote de guerre* (published in New York in 1942) and the posthumous *Citadelle* (1948).
R.-M. Alberès, *Saint-Exupéry*, 1947; Léon Werth, *La Vie de Saint-Exupéry*, 1949.

Saint-Gelais, Mellin de: (1491-1558) Friendly rival of Clément Marot (q.v.), he exercised an Italianizing influence in France. As a poet, he showed great facility with rhyme and excelled in the lighter forms, especially the maxim and the *rondeau* (q.v.). At first disdained by the *Pléiade* (q.v.), who regarded him primarily as a lazy improvising courtier poet, after 1553 he became personally reconciled to them.
H. Molinier, *Mellin de Saint-Gelais*, 1911; Ph. A. Becker, *Mellin de Saint-Gelais*, 1924.

Saint-Genest (1647): See *Rotrou* and *Baroque*.

Saint-Lambert, Jean-François de: (1716-1803) Inspired by the English poem, *The Seasons* (1730), by Thomson, he wrote *Les Saisons* (1769), a descriptive poem that evokes the charm of rustic life. He owes some of his reputation to the fact that he was the close friend of Mme. du Châtelet and Mme. d'Houdetot, companions of Voltaire and Rousseau (qq.v.).

M. Cameron, *L'Influence des 'Saisons' de Thomson sur la poésie descriptive en France*, 1943.

Saint-Marc Girardin: (1801-1873) In his *Cours de Littérature dramatique* (1843), a study of the theater from antiquity to his own times, this critic and professor, also called Marc Girardin, takes to task the *mal du siècle* (q.v.) of the romantic writers who according to him have perverted the great human sentiments; he favors the restoration of the classical traditions with their healthy *morale*.

L. Wylie, *Saint-Marc Girardin— Bourgeois*, 1947.

Saint-Pierre, Bernardin de: (1737-1814) Born at Le Havre, this civil engineer, friend and disciple of Rousseau (q.v.), whom he met in 1772, and with whom he shared ideas of man's natural goodness and love for nature, traveled extensively. In *Études de la Nature* (1784), he expresses the view that Nature is the source of all good and beauty. The setting of *Paul et Virginie* (1787) is the Ile-de-France (Mauritius), where he himself spent more than two years (1768-1771). This popular novel, a detached episode of *Études de la Nature,* and a good illustration of his themes, sets out to prove that happiness consists in living close to nature and in following sentiment. Thus, the tender and innocent love idyl of Paul and Virginie has disastrous consequences when Virginie leaves this distant island to join her aunt in France. For the exotic and picturesque descriptions of tempests and sunsets in this book—which make him a precursor of Chateaubriand (q.v.) and which appealed to a public reacting against the artificial and intellectual life of the eighteenth century—he used a precise and technical vocabulary that was suggestive and that at the same time enriched, in the final analysis, the French language. Included among his other works are the political *Les Vœux d'un solitaire* (1790) and the posthumous *Harmonies de la nature* (1815).

A. Barine, *Bernardin de Saint-Pierre*, 1891; M. Souriau, *Bernardin de Saint-Pierre*, 1905.

Saint-Simon, Louis de Rouvroy, Duc de: (1675-1755) Frustration and bitterness mark the career of this greatest of memoir writers. In 1702 he left the army because he had received no promotion. At the court of Versailles he was piqued because he failed to gain the confidence of Louis XIV; proud of his title of "duke and peer" and insufferably aristocratic, he could not forgive Louis XIV, whom he held chiefly responsible for the success of the *parvenus*—the bourgeois, the parliamentary and judicial families. Although for a while he was politically active under the Regency, his political ambitions were again thwarted when in 1723 his friend the Duc d'Orléans died. His *Mémoires,* written in Paris and on his country estate during the last thirty years of his life, and inspired by his sense of personal frustration, cover the period 1691-1723. Although he had early developed, thanks to his natural gift of observation and curiosity, the habit of jotting down his impressions, and had intended to complete his own Memoirs, he expanded instead Dangeau's *Journal* (covering 1684-1720), which he had read and found unsatisfactory. A penetrating study of the court and of the courtiers, and forming an immense "Human Comedy," the *Mémoires*, written in a style which, in its impetuosity, is "un-classical," contain impressive historical scenes and vivid portraiture of distinct figures. Though they reflect Saint-Simon's personal rancor and are not always objective, they are an invaluable source of information for historians. The *Mémoires* were first published in the nineteenth century, in several different editions. A. Le Breton, *La Comédie humaine de Saint-Simon*, 1914; R. Doumic, *Saint-Simon*, 1919.

Sainte-Beuve, Charles-Augustin: (1804-1869) Probably the greatest of French critics (see *Criticism*), he began his literary career by writing articles for the *Globe;* then a friend of Hugo (q.v.), he identified himself with Romanticism. His early works include *Tableau de la poésie française au XVIᵉ siècle* (1828), a rehabilitation of unknown writers that suggests, at the same time, that Ronsard (q.v.) and his friends were the romanticists of their day; *Vie, Poésies et Pensées de Joseph Delorme* (1829), lyrical poems constituting, in their self-analysis, a moral autobiography of a Saint-Beuve tormented by an inferiority complex; and *Volupté* (1834), a semi-autobiographical novel reflecting his soul-sickness following his *liaison* with Mme. Victor Hugo, which he analyzes psychologically. Finding his true vocation as a critic, he published, among his major works, *Port-Royal* (1840-1859) and *Chateaubriand et son groupe littéraire* (1861), the result of courses taught at the Universities of Lausanne, Berne, and Liège. Other important works of criticism include his series of portraits (*Portraits littéraires*, 1836-1839; *Portraits de Femmes*, 1844; *Portraits contemporains*, 1846) and collections of articles (*Causeries du Lundi*, 1851-1862; *Nouveaux Lundis*, 1863-1870) that had previously appeared in such journals and newspapers as the *Constitutionnel*, *Moniteur*, and *Temps*. His conception of literary criticism, as seen in most of his 48 volumes, amounts to an explanation of a work in terms of the writer's biography, intimate psychology, and individuality of expression. Although after 1830 he gradually detached himself from Romanticism, his final break came toward the end of his life with a more conspicuous tendency toward classical clarity and simplicity in his style, partially a result of his yielding to the generalizing exigencies of science common to the period. L. Séché, *Sainte-Beuve*, 1904; G. Michaut, *Sainte-Beuve*, 1921.

Saisons, Les (1769): See *Saint-Lambert*.

Salacrou, Armand: (1900-   ) One of the most original dramatists of his generation, this former doctor, movie scenarist and surrealist poet, depicts, in his dreamers and other characters constantly in flight, a world in turmoil. Time and memory, in the frequently paradoxical situations of his semi-vaudeville, semi-tragic theater, play an important role in his dramatic technique. His heroes in *Patchouli* (1927) and *Atlas-Hôtel* (1931) are dreamers or visionaries. *Les Frénétiques* (1934), based on his experiences as a scenario writer, is a satire of a man with many irons in the fire who subjects everyone to his personal interests and caprices. Bourgeois *milieux* are portrayed in *Une Femme libre* (1934) and *L'Inconnue d'Arras* (1935); the female protagonist in the first-mentioned play, a play with existentialist (see *Existentialism*) overtones, is twice in flight, once from her fiancé's family, once from the fiancé's brother, to recover her liberty. Miller's *Death of a Salesman* seems to have been influenced by the last mentioned play, in which a man who learns he has been deceived by his wife kills himself. During the minute that elapses after he shoots himself until his death, he reviews, in the course of the three acts, his entire life. In *Un Homme comme les autres* (1936) Salacrou poses the problems of Evil and Destiny. *La Terre est ronde* (1938), his masterpiece, is laid in Florence during the Renaissance. Apart from its denunciation of totalitarian doctrines, evoking at the same time the Nazi period in Germany, it personifies the eternal struggle between the flesh and the spirit. His more recent plays include *Le Soldat et la sorcière* (1945) and *Les Nuits de la colère* (1946), which deals with the Résistance (q.v.).

José Van Den Esch, *Armand Salacrou*, 1947.

Salammbô (1862): See *Flaubert*.

Salons: Flourishing in France especially during the seventeenth and eighteenth centuries, the *salons* were social or literary centers where writers, artists or scientists would gather. The most prominent of the *salons* during the seventeenth century was that of the *Hôtel de Rambouillet* (q.v.), where, in an atmosphere of respect and good taste, writers and members of fashionable society met to discuss, with much wit and refinement, questions dealing with sentiment and literature, grammar and vocabulary. Very different, however, were the *salons* of the eighteenth century, where scholars, writers and thinkers—the *philosophes* (q.v.) or the intellectual aristocracy, contributors to the *Encyclopédie*—gathered together to discuss scientific, political, economic and social questions. Included among these *salons*, during the periods of their greatest influence, are those of: the Duchesse de Maine (1699-1753); Mme. de Lambert (1710-1733), Mme. de Tencin (1726-

1749), Mme. du Deffand (1740-1780), Mme. Geoffrin (1749-1777), Mlle. de Lespinasse (1762-1776), Mme. d'Épinay (1762-1783) and Mme. Necker (1764-1794). It was in these *salons* that the philosophical ideas of the Age of Enlightenment (q.v.) were developed and where their implementation was prepared.

M. Glotz and M. Maire, *Les Salons du XVIII*ᵉ *siècle*, 1945; D. Mornet, *Les Origines intellectuelles de la Révolution française*, 1923.

salut d'amour: A Provençal verse epistle of the Middle Ages beginning with a greeting to the lady for whom the poet writes.

Samain, Albert: (1858-1900) This poet, born at Lille, oscillated between the Parnassian (q.v.) and Symbolist (see *Symbolism*) schools of poetry. Of the latter school he kept the musical and psychological aspects; of the former, he retained the clarity, respect for form and cult of plastic beauty. Both tendencies, which are assimilated, reflect the influences of Baudelaire, Verlaine, Mallarmé, and Hérédia (qq.v.). His collections include *Au Jardin de l'Infante* (1893), personal poems, mostly sonnets, which discreetly express the sadness of a solitary soul, and *Aux Flances du Vase* (1898), little tableaux of graceful idyls, showing his love for Greece. A posthumous collection, *Le Chariot d'or* (1901), contains some of his best poems. He also wrote *Polyphème*, a poetic drama presented at the *Théâtre de l'Œuvre* in 1904.

Albert de Bersaucourt, *Albert Samain; son œuvre*, 1925; Georges Bonneau, *Albert Samain, poète symboliste*, 1925.

Samson (1908): See *Bernstein, Henry*.

Sand, George (Pseud. of **Lucile-Aurore Dupin**): (1804-1876) This novelist, the only great woman writer of the early nineteenth century, was born at Nohant in Berry. She became a writer when, following an unhappy marriage to the Baron Dudevant whom she left in 1830, she had to support herself and her two children in Paris. After a violent love affair with Alfred de Musset (q.v.), which lasted from 1833 to 1835, she returned to Nohant, where she remained most of her subsequent life. The hundred-odd novels, which she wrote with great facility, can be classified into four groups that correspond to four periods in her life. Her unconventional and romantic attitude toward love, in which she sought happiness, can be seen in *Indiana* (1831), *Lélia* (1833), and *Mauprat* (1836). Her interest in the people, influenced by the theories of Lamennais (q.v.) and Pierre Leroux, is affirmed in *Consuelo* (1842) and *Le Meunier d'Angibault* (1845), in which she reveals compassion for the suffering and generally humanitarian tendencies. Her best books evincing her love of nature and her sympathy for peasant life—examples of a type of rural novel whose vogue lasted right up to the twentieth century—include *La Mare au Diable* (1846), *La petite Fadette* (1849), *François le Champi* (1850), and *Les Maîtres Sonneurs* (1853). Although *Elle et lui* (1859) deals with her affair with Musset, her last novels, including *Les beaux messieurs de Boisdoré* (1858) and *Le Marquis de Villemer* (1860), are more serene and less exalted in their depiction of passion and in their setting of nature than her first group of novels. Like Hugo (q.v.), she had, during the Realistic period, much success with her romantic novels, for they contained much idealism and reflected a belief in progress and in man's goodness.

W. Karénine, *G. Sand, sa vie et ses œuvres*, 1899-1926; M. L. Pailleron, *George Sand*, 1938-42; A. Maurois, *Lélia*, 1952.

Sang des autres, Le (1945): See *Beauvoir, Simone de.*

Sang noir, Le (1935): See *Guilloux, Louis.*

Sapho (1884): See *Daudet.*

Sardou, Victorien: (1831-1908) Probably the best disciple of Scribe (q.v.) as regards plot construction and technique, this Parisian-born dramatist, though not so prolific as his master, is more versatile. His plays, several of which have received English and American adaptations, represent a wide variety of types. *La Famille Benoîton* (1856), in the tradition of Dumas *fils* (q.v.), is a social satire of the manners of the Second Empire, depicting as it does the mania of speculation, money-making, and luxury; similar plays of this type include *Nos Intimes* (1860), and *Nos Bons Villageois* (1866). *La Patrie* (1869), one of his best pieces, and *La Haine* (1874) are examples of the historical drama. Political satire is represented by *Rabagas* (1872), and farce by *Divorçons* (1880), one of his masterpieces. *La Tosca* (1887) is an example of those of his plays that have been made into opera libretti, and *Théodore* (1884) remains famous for its magnificent scenic effects. Especially characteristic of Sardou is his successful *Les Pattes de mouche* (1860), wherein he shows his stagecraft and ability to handle intrigue.

H. Rebell, *Victorien Sardou*, 1903.

Sarment, Jean: (1897-   ) The plays of this dramatist, once a member of Jacques Copeau's (q.v.) company of actors in America (1917), reflect a world of disenchantment, of weak-willed and impetuous characters who, when they see their dreams shattered, try in one way or another to escape their lot. The disquietude of a timid, young man, seen in *La Couronne de Carton* (1920), becomes more pronounced in *Le Pêcheur d'ombres* (1921). In this touching and tragic love idyl bathed in a misty and poetic atmosphere of revery, the main protagonist, who has recovered after having suffered from amnesia, upon being told that the girl he loves is not really the one he imagines, but someone else, ends his life. Sarment, who depicts love somewhat in the manner of Musset (q.v.), shows marks of Shakespearean influence in *Le Mariage d'Hamlet* (1922), in which a mob violently snuffs out the life of the protagonist, who is a romantic dreamer. In *Les plus beaux yeux du monde* (1925), the spectator is once again transported into the domain of poetic fantasy and sentimental love. His more recent plays, including *Madelon* (1927), *Léopold le Bien-Aimé* (1927), *Le Plancher des Vaches* (1932), and *Mamouret* (1941), mark a new tendency toward vaudeville and light comedy.

Sartre, Jean-Paul: (1905-   ) This Parisian-born leader of the *Existentialist* (see *Existentialism*) school of literature is at once philosopher, psychologist, essayist, novelist, dramatist, and writer of film scenarios. His psychological studies include *L'Imagination* (1936), *Esquisse d'une théorie des émotions* (1939), *L'Imaginaire* (1940); his major philosophical treatise, *L'Etre et le néant* (1943), contains a systematization of his ideas that, except for the initiated, are better understood in his brief popularization of that work entitled *L'Existentialisme est un humanisme* (1946). The fictionalized world created by Sartre in his novels, plays and cinemas was an attempt—it would seem a dangerous one—to give flesh and spirit to his theses and to his philosophical system. *La Nausée* (1938), his first novel, evokes the real nature of perception and depicts in Roquentin, the main protagonist, the self-conscious, reflective and analytical observer who perceives the absurdity of existence and of the universe. *Le Mur* (1939), a collection of short stories, contains examples of those *inauthentic* beings who refuse to accept their liberty. In 1945 Sartre began publication of a long novel,

Les Chemins de la liberté, the first three volumes of which—*L'Age de raison* (1945), *Le Sursis* (1945), *La Mort dan l'âme* (1949)—have already appeared; the fourth and last volume, *La Dernière Chance,* is yet to see the light in its final finished form. The events of the first-named volume take place in 1938, those of the second deal with the Munich crisis, and those of the third concern the fall of France; however, the entire work is a study of people who, in a variety of ways, assert or deny their freedom to achieve their fullness of *being.* Since indecision is as much a part of liberty as self-commitment, time plays an important part in the lives of the different characters as they work out their *essence;* hence, only at the end of Part I of the third volume does the philosopher, Mathieu Delarue, commit himself heroically during the last fifteen minutes of his life. Sartre the novelist frequently uses in these volumes the technique of such American writers as Hemingway and, more notably, John Dos Passos; the device he borrows from the latter is that of simultaneity.

The dialectic that exalts liberty, responsibility, heroism and the *authentic,* Sartre dramatizes in such plays as *Les Mouches* (1943) (produced, thanks to the delusive setting of ancient Argos under the reign of Aegisthus, at the time of the German occupation), *Huis-Clos* (1944), *Morts sans sépulture* (1946), *La Putain respectueuse* (1946) and *Les Mains sales* (1948). *Le Diable et le Bon Dieu* (1951) has as its theme man's solitude, in a godless universe, of which, however, he is master, as he is of his own destiny. The genius of Sartre in all these works is his lucidity. He has portrayed the metaphysical condition of men. His ideas, born of anguish, in a confused world, have provoked much, frequently passionate discussion. A complete system of ethics, especially as it might reflect itself in his imaginative works, is as yet to be worked out.

R. Campbell, *Jean-Paul Sartre ou une Littérature philosophique* (1945); Francis Jeanson, *Le Problème moral et la pensée de Sartre* (1947); Iris Murdoch, *Sartre Romantic Rationalist* (1953).

satire: A short poem attacking vices or the ridiculous. It has been especially cultivated in France where, since the Middle Ages, the satiric spirit has flourished. Conspicuous in this genre are such writers as Marot, Du Bellay, Aubigné, and Mathurin Régnier (qq.v.). This literary genre was very much in vogue in the 17th century (see *Boileau*). In the 18th century it was best represented by André Chénier (q.v.) in his *Iambes,* and was continued in the 19th century by Hugo (q.v.), especially in his *Châtiments.*

Satire Ménippée: A satirical pamphlet, written in 1593 by several authors, including Jean Leroy, Pierre Pithou, Gilles Durand, Jean Passerat (q.v.), Florent Chrestien, Nicolas Rapin and Jacques Gillot, in derision of the Estates of the ultra-Catholic League, unsuccessfully called together in 1593 to elect a King other than the Huguenot Henri de Navarre (Henri IV). Composed almost entirely in prose, this parody consists primarily of the speeches supposedly delivered in the Louvre by the politically corrupt delegates of the Estates of the League; it is motivated by the spirit of patriotism. The title given to this pamphlet was taken from the Greek philosopher Menippus (*c.* third century B.C.), who also composed his satires in a medley of prose and verse.

F. Giroux, *La composition de la Satire Ménippée,* 1904.

Satires (1666-1705): See *Boileau.*

Saül (1640): See *Du Ryer.*

Saül furieux (1572): See *La Taille, Jean de.*

Scaliger, Joseph-Juste: (1540-1609) Son of Jules-César Scaliger (q.v.), he was an eminent classical scholar, grammarian, and philologist.

Scaliger, Jules-César: (1484-1558) This critic, of Italian origin, became a French subject in 1528. His fame rests essentially on his *Poetics,* written in Latin and first published in 1561, in which he anticipates the strict rules that later applied to French classical tragedy (q.v.). Its rules, which he deduced from Aristotle, he formulated about a century before Boileau (q.v.).

A. Magen, *Documents sur J.-C. Scaliger et sa famille,* 1873.

Scarron, Paul: (1610-1660) The first husband of the future Madame de Maintenon (q.v.), whom he married when he was already physically deformed by disease, he acquired popularity, through his wit and humor, as a poet, dramatist and novelist. In *Énéide travestie* (1648-1653), a parody of an epic poem, he represents the burlesque (q.v.) spirit. In *Le Roman comique* (1651), his best-known novel, he relates, in the tradition of Charles Sorel (q.v.), the odyssey of a strolling troupe of actors, with a satirical picture of provincial life and manners. The realistic portrayal of the life of these comedians, which also helps better understand the life led by Molière (q.v.) and his troupe before arriving in Paris, is part of the same current that attacked and satirized preciosity (q.v.) and the pastoral novel.

M. Morillot, *Scarron et le genre burlesque,* 1888; E. Magne, *Scarron et son milieu,* 1905; M. Magendie, *Le Roman français au XVIIᵉ siècle,* 1932.

Scènes de la vie de Bohème (1851): See *Murger, Henri.*

Scènes de la vie future (1930): See *Duhamel.*

Scève, Maurice: (*c.* 1501-*c.* 1560) One of the principal Lyonese poets who had a great interest in foreign lit-

erature, he believed that a grave he had discovered was that of Laura of whom Petrarch had sung. Steeped, moreover, in Platonic philosophy, he published a collection of difficult poetry, *Délie, objet de plus haute vertu* (1544), consisting of 449 poems composed in decasyllabic lines in varying groupings. In this collection, the title of which is an anagram as well as the pseudonym of the poet's beloved, Pernette du Guillet, the poet's love is carnal as well as spiritual, but primarily idealistic and worshipful. In *Microcosme* (1562), a philosophical and moral poem on man, the history of civilization, philosophy and the sciences is sketched. Regarded by the *Pléiade* (q.v.) as a pioneer in the expression of noble and lofty thought, Scève is the first poet in France to have attempted writing idealistic and philosophical poetry of such high seriousness.
V. L. Saulnier, *Maurice Scève*, 1948.

Schlumberger, Jean: (1877-   ) Together with his friend, Gide (q.v.), he founded in 1909 the *Nouvelle Revue française*. Like Gide, he was deeply concerned with the moral aspects of life; Schlumberger was more reticent when he opposed individualistic ethics to authority. His novels include *Un homme heureux* (1921) and *Saint-Saturnin* (1931). He also wrote many volumes of essays, including *Jalons* (1941) and *Nouveaux Jalons* (1943).
Marie Delcourt, *Jean Schlumberger*, 1945.

Schwob, Marcel: (1867-1905) The scholarship of this essayist, poet, and novelist is seen in his knowledge of certain lesser-known Greek authors, in his interest in such varied subjects as Villon (q.v.), *argot* of the Middle Ages, astrology, the Far East, Anglo-Saxon literature, and in such mystical or philosophical anecdotes as those found in *Le Roi au masque d'or* (1893)

and *La Lampe de Psyché* (1903), his last book. His masterpiece, *Vies imaginaires* (1896), a collection of re-created lives of almost forgotten philosophers of old, and *Mimes* (1894), poems in the ancient manner, testify to his reaction against Naturalism (q.v.) as well as to a dilettantism reminiscent of A. France (q.v.). *Le Livre de Monelle* (1894), a rather cryptic and perplexing novel, is inspired by a personal experience in the life of the author. Schwob also introduced to the French public the English novelists Stevenson and Meredith, whom he knew personally.

Scribe, Eugène: (1791-1861) A contemporary of the Romantic writers, whose theories or doctrines, however, he did not adopt, this Parisian-born dramatist represents a transition between the Romantic and the Social theater of the Realists (see *Realism*). Beginning as a writer of *vaudevilles* (q.v.)—originally short comedies based on contemporary events which had gradually acquired musical interludes—he later gave this *genre* greater breadth and more timely interest, expanding it into the *comedie-vaudeville;* then, by eliminating some of the *vaudeville* features, especially that of music, he turned his plays into the *comédie d'intrigue* type. Although his plays are distinguished neither by style, nor philosophy, nor even by character analysis, they nevertheless had continued popularity, for they portrayed the society of his day and presented bourgeois ideas on bourgeois topics. Moreover—and this explains his originality—Scribe was a master stage craftsman, an exponent of the *pièce bien faite* (q.v.). By concentrating on his plot, whose interest he could skilfully, unlike Hugo (q.v.), for example, suspend or complicate, he spell-bound his audience, robbing it of its logical and reasoning powers while amus-

312

ing it. Though his theater gave orientation to the Comedy of Manners, it is especially as the great technician of plot construction that Scribe was to influence such dramatists as Augier (q.v.), Dumas *fils* (q.v.), and Sardou (q.v.). Among the better known of his 400-odd plays that include comedies, dramas, farces, opera libretti, comic opera, and ballets, are *Bertrand et Raton ou l'art de conspirer* (1833), *La Camaraderie ou la courte-échelle* (1837), *Une Chaîne* (1841), *Le Verre d'eau* (1842), *Adrienne Lecouvreur* (1849), and *Bataille de Dames* (1851).

N. C. Arvin, *Eugène Scribe and the French Theatre*, 1924.

Scudéry, Georges de: (1601-1667) The brother of Madeleine de Scudéry (q.v.), with whom he collaborated in writing novels of adventure that reflect the spirit of preciosity, he is remembered for his *Observations sur le Cid* (1637), in which he criticizes Corneille's (q.v.) play. (Cf. *Querelle du Cid*.) He also wrote some tragedies, including *Le Grand Annibal* (1631) and *La Mort de César* (1635).

C. Clerc, *Un Matamore des lettres, Georges de Scudéry*, 1929.

Scudéry, Madeleine de: (1607-1701) One of the most illustrious *précieuses* (q.v.), whose *salon* after the decline of the Hôtel de Rambouillet (q.v.) became the leading one in Paris (1652-1700), she is also the author, in collaboration with her brother Georges (q.v.), of the ten-volume *Artamène ou le Grand Cyrus* (1649-1653), and of *Clélie, Histoire romaine* (1654-1661), also in ten volumes, which contains the famous *Carte de Tendre* (q.v.). These two novels of adventure, the first one of which deals with a Persian conqueror of the fourth century B.C., and the second one of which is staged in ancient Rome, are examples of the *roman à clef* (q.v.): they portray, in historical

disguise, the contemporary society of the time. The main preoccupation of the characters in these novels, as in *L'Astrée* (see *Honoré d'Urfé*), is love, which, in its *précieux* aspects (see *Préciosité*), becomes the seventeenth-century ideal of politeness and refinement.

Claude Aragonnès, *Madeleine de Scudéry, Reine du Tendre*, 1934.

Sebillet, Thomas: (1512-1589) Despite a certain indulgence he had for the poets of the Middle Ages, he proclaimed in his *Art poétique*, published in 1548—one year before the *Défense et Illustration de la langue française* (q.v.)—the divine character of inspiration and urged the imitation of the Ancients. Concerned, as were many other poets, with the variety and combinations of rhymes, he also promoted the rule of the cesura.

H. de Noo, *Th. Sebillet et son Art poëtique Françoys rapprochés de la Deffence et Illustration de la langue Françoyse de Joachim du Bellay*, 1927.

Secret, Le (1913): See *Bernstein, Henry*.

Sedaine, Michel: (1719-1797) This Parisian-born poet and writer of comic operas and *vaudevilles* (q.v.) is especially remembered for *Le Philosophe sans le savoir* (1765). This play, in which a social problem involving family life is resolved successfully, may be regarded as the best example of the *drame bourgeois* (q.v.). Sedaine is also the author of *La Gageure imprévue* (1768), a one-act comedy.

L. Günther, *L'Œuvre dramatique de Sedaine*, 1908.

Sédécie ou les Juives (1583): See *Garnier, Robert*.

Seghers, Pierre: (1906-) This Parisian-born poet published annually for a number of years the review *Poésie* (1940-1948) which he founded in 1940 at Villeneuve-lès-Avignon, in the south of France, and which was the collective effort

313

of a group of poets that had gathered around him. His own collections of poetry include *Bonne Espérance* (1939), *Le Chien de Pique* (1943) and *Le Domaine Public* (1944); the two last-named were inspired by his war experiences and the Resistance. His more recent *Jeune Fille* (1948) is free of the "involvement" of events, and is more personal in tone.

Segrais, Jean Regnault de: (1624-1701) Author of charming pastoral poems, of *Bérénice* (1648-1651), a novel, and of *Les Nouvelles françaises* (1657), short stories with exotic settings, he was secretary to the Duchesse de Montpensier (1648-1672; q.v.). Although Mme. de La Fayette (q.v.), a close friend of his, signed his name to *Zaïde* (1670), it is not at all certain that he collaborated in it; the suspicion, moreover, that he had a hand in her *La Princesse de Clèves* (1678) is probably also unwarranted.

W. Tipping, *Jean Regnault de Segrais*, 1933.

Semaine, La (1578): *Du Bartas.*

Sénancour, Etienne Pivert de: (1770-1846) The hopelessness, ennui, and melancholy of this Parisian-born writer, caused by disillusionment in love, financial ruin and general inadaptability to social life, are reflected in *Obermann* (1804), written, despite the date of publication, before Chateaubriand's *René* (q.v.). In this autobiographical novel, actually a journal, the author traces the internal experience of his main protagonist, who, like himself, in the search for happiness, is the victim of much suffering. *Obermann* is an important example of the romantic *mal du siècle* (q.v.).

J. Merlant, *Sénancour*, 1907.

Sentiments de l'Académie sur le Cid (1638): See *Chapelain, Jean.*

Séraphita (1832): See *Balzac.*

Serments de Strasbourg: The recorded oaths taken at Strasbourg in 842 by Louis le Germanique and Charles le Chauve against their common enemy, their brother Lothaire. The soldiers of Charles used the tudesque idiom, while those of Louis used the romance idiom, the first example of *popular* French. See *Langues Romanes.*

Servitude et grandeur militaires (1835): See *Vigny.*

Sévigné, Marie de Rabutin-Chantal, Marquise de: (1626-1696) Early a widow as a result of the death of her dissolute husband, killed in a duel (1651), this greatest of letter writers —during the classical period—passionately devoted the rest of her life to her children. When her daughter went to live in Provence, after her marriage to the Comte de Grignan (1668), she found the separation painful; in the great bulk of her fifteen-hundred-odd letters that have been preserved, her love for her daughter, whom she idolized, is prominent. Not only did her letters (written *c.* 1664-1696) serve her as a means of consolation and reflection; they also became a kind of gazette in which she discussed the important events and people of the day, the details of court intrigue and of life in Paris. Written at a time when means of communication were slow and when their arrival was a matter of interest to all, these letters, though composed with much care, reflect a naturalness and unaffected sincerity that are usually found in conversation; their clarity and simplicity of expression give their documentary social interest literary importance. The charm of their style contrasts with the more formal tone in the letters of Guez de Balzac (q.v.) and other contemporaries.

G. Boissier, *Mme de Sévigné*, 1887; J. Aldis, *Mme de Sévigné*, 1907; A. Hallays, *Mme de Sévigné*, 1921.

SHORT STORY:

A. GENERAL SURVEY

The short story in France today occupies a place of honor alongside any other literary type. Though its greatest development is quite recent, it is hardly a now-found literary genre. Its early oral forms are presumably as old as civilization. The Dordogne caveman embroidered his reports of his exploits. The *Bible*, the ancient epics are filled with accounts of adventure, strife, and love. The *chanson de geste* (q.v.) and the Crusade chronicles of Villehardouin and Joinville (qq.v.) are crammed with vivid tales, as are the accounts by Froissart (q.v.) of the English wars in France. The 15th century is specially rich in amusing story developments. It offers the *fabliaux* (q.v.), funny tales for plain people, like *Le vilian mire* used by Molière (q.v.). The animal stories of Reynart the Fox are ironic tales mocking feudal follies. The *Cent nouvelles nouvelles* admit their debt to Boccaccio and freely imitate his lewder models. The following century, the 16th, adds the uproarious Rabelais (q.v.) and his gigantic ribaldry, as well as Marguerite de Navarre's *Heptameron* (q.v.), another imitation of Boccaccio. There is this new element: Marguerite vouches for the veracity of her stories: "n'écrire nouvelle qui ne fût véritable histoire." The 15th and 16th centuries are the early French story's best period, creative, truly Gallic, gaily adventurous with an excess of verbiage that is a mark of the whimsical exuberance of the Renaissance.

Like lyric poetry (q.v.) in the *âge d'or*, the short story is about to wither in the 17th century, when the artistic ideal of control of fancy and emotion discourages personal literary types. Classical discipline in an age of authority is fostered by the new Academy, but it will finally lead to a reaction started by a fairy-story teller, Charles Perrault (q.v.). Thanks to his courageous defiance before the Academy, the musty prose pastoral and the *précieux* (q.v.) novel will in time give way to the rowdy realities of the lowly *Gil Blas* (q.v.). Credit is due also in this century to Sorel (q.v.) in his *Francion*, the clownish adventurer, and to Scarron (q.v.) for his *Roman comique* about two young actors in love. These are burlesques on the pretentious upper-crust longwinded novels of the day with their courtly gallantries. The Cardinal de Retz (q.v.) has some fine character episodes in his *Mémoires,* as has Madame de Sévigné (q.v.) in her *Lettres.* La Fontaine's (q.v.) *Nouvelles en vers* merely promote the old Gallic story to a higher rank by clothing it in verse. The exploits of Fénelon's (q.v.) *Télémaque* are novelistic pedagogy. La Bruyère's (q.v.) *Caractères* have a story trembling at each portrait but he never tells it. The century's only great novelist is a woman, Madame de la Fayette (q.v.), who really gives the *nouvelle* its early promising form in her *Princesse de Clèves* and *Mlle de Montpensier,* although their appeal is in analysis of sentiment rather than in episode.

The 18th century is again a creative period in the story genre. *Gil Blas* has a succession of picaresque adventures, as have Marivaux's (q.v.) *Vie de Marianne* and his *Paysan perverti.* Montesquieu (q.v.) has a vivid Oriental episode in his *Lettres persanes,* and Rousseau's (q.v.) *Confessions* offer his version of experience actually lived. But there are four storytellers who give this medium a new vitality. Prévost (q.v.) in his sentimental *Manon*

315

Lescaut is pathetically biographical. Voltaire (q.v.) in his philosophic tales like *Candide* uses the type to carry on his struggle against the *infâme*. Bernardin de St. Pierre (q.v.) in his *Paul et Virginie* tells a colorful tale of innocent young lovers separated by society. The authentic story genius of this time is Diderot (q.v.) who in his *Neveu de Rameau* and other *nouvelles* traces an accurate satiric portrait of contemporary society. His distinctive free-wheeling dialogue adds a sense of veracity that sweeps the reader along.

The scattered beginnings of the story have now been indicated and Romanticism (q.v.) is about to give the form its push toward full creative existence. This is the time of Hoffman, Scott, Irving, Poe, and of the Romantics in France. The *nouvelle* and the *conte* are natural forms to which are attracted the young authors grouped about Nodier (q.v.) at the Arsenal Library. Even before them Chateaubriand (q.v.) had created models for the *nouvelle* with his despairing *Atala* and his confessional *René*. Constant (q.v.) now follows the master with his tormented *Adolphe*, Lamartine (q.v.) with his elegiac *Graziella*, Hugo (q.v.) with his pathetic *Dernier jour d'un condamné*, Vigny (q.v.) with his dutiful *Servitude et grandeur militaires*, Musset (q.v.) with his *Contes et nouvelles*, Gautier (q.v.) with his *Roman de la momie*, Sand (q.v.) with her *Mare au Diable*. At the same time some of these writers practiced with the *nouvelle* the full-fledged *roman*. The lines between these genres remain clearly set but traversable.

After mid-nineteenth century the short story receives a formidable extension, so that almost all prose writers feel free to practice in it. The great novelists will use the *conte* lavishly like Balzac (q.v.) in his *Episode sous la Terreur,* Méri-mée (q.v.) in his *Tamango,* Flaubert (q.v.) in his *Trois Contes.* With them and others the flood of stories runs at a steady rush and there is hardly an author who does not try his hand. We list: Zola's (q.v.) *Contes à Ninon,* Daudet's (q.v.) *Lettres de mon moulin,* Maupassant's (q.v.) *Boule de suif,* and some-three hundred more. Opposed to Naturalism (q.v.) are Villiers de l'Isle-Adam's (q.v.) *Contes cruels* and works by lesser moralists like Murger (q.v.), Sandeau, Malot, Ohnet. The analysts are mainly France (q.v.) as in *Étui de nacre* and Bourget (q.v.) in *Eau profonde,* and psychologists like Estaunié (q.v.), M. Prévost, Bazin, Bordeaux (qq.v.), Corday, Banville (q.v.), About, Theuriet, Coppée (q.v.), Mendès (q.v.), Arène. The portrayers of manners are legion: The Goncourt (q.v.) and the Rosny brothers, Mirbeau (q.v.), Descaves, Adam, Hermant (q.v.), Hervieu, Lavedan, Lemaître, Régnier, Richepin (qq.v.), Mauclair, Bertrand, Le Braz, Mille, Duvernois. The Erckmann-Chatrian (q.v.) combination for Alsace should be mentioned, as well as writers of tales about children like the Marguerite brothers, Renard (q.v.) in *Poil de Carotte,* Frapié in *La maternelle.* Then there are the writers with foreign scenes, Loti (q.v.) in *Mme Chrysanthème,* Hémon (q.v.) in *Maria Chapdelaine,* Psichari, the Tharaud brothers (qq.v.). The introspectives include Mauriac, Radiguet, Carco, Gide (qq.v.) in *Retour de l'enfant prodigue.* The first world war gave us Duhamel, Maurois, Dorgelès, Romains (qq.v.). Of more recent story writers with a symbolic complex a few of the well-known names are Benoit, Giraudoux, Larbaud, Mac Orlan (qq.v.). Child psychology is a particular domain explored by Crémieux, Obey, Chadourne, Lacretelle (q.v.), Henriot, Thierry, and the feline Colette (q.v.), as well as du Gard (q.v.) in the earlier volumes of his *Thibault* series. The contemporary family of story writers is peculiarly rich in quality with form fully evolved. A partial roster must include at least Bernanos, Malraux, Montherlant, Giono, Saint-Exupéry, Drieu la Rochelle, Jouhandeau, Green, Sartre, Camus, Queneau, Simone de Beauvoir, Bosco, Genet, Delvaux, Gracq, Vercors, Schlumberger, Chamson, Guéhenno, Cassou, Arland, Aymé, Plisnier, and the stealthy Simenon (qq.v.). There is an obvious difference between a novel and a short story. This list has included many writers who are known as novelists but who practice the short story without schizophrenic after effects. As novelists they struggle for long periods perfecting one work to the satisfaction of a guiding artistic sense. As short story writers their prevailing attitude is different, they are likely to reveal more of their character and temperament because the genre encourages greater spontaneity. They have to glance quickly in the short story and convey in one line the meaningful gesture or pose. A fine novel can afford a deeper and richer experience than the most artistic short story. This is the consequence of the requisite tempo in rapid narrative. Some critics have noted that writers of tales make poor novelists, like Maupassant (q.v.), whereas great novelists like Balzac, Flaubert (qq.v.), Turgeniev, Gogol, Tolstoy, Henry James, Maugham, Hemingway, move at ease within the short story form.

B. Its Forms:
conte, nouvelle, récit

Maupassant discusses his art in a famous preface to his novel *Pierre et Jean* (1888). The *conte* is a short story of 150 to 200 lines where chosen essentials create the illusion of the whole. You can't tell everything. "Faire vrai consiste donc à donner l'illusion complète du vrai," and the best artists are those who can impose their special illusion as truth. The *conte* is thus a kind of shorthand using abbreviations to build a concept of the whole. The increasing speed of the 19th century was well served by the *conte* and it fits the convenience today of many who read while running. While our epoch has been marked by thick novels, none has escaped the critics' opinion that it could have been improved by shortening. Our practical hurried times are definitely turned toward the short story as a favored form of art, which, as Maupassant said, uses a few details to convey a total impression of truth.

But the differences between the *nouvelle* and the *conte* are at times hardly perceptible. Larousse defines the *conte* as a short tale of adventure, often imaginary, and the *nouvelle* as a short novel based on recent incident. Most critics would agree that the *conte* is a brief vivid narrative affording a medium for the author's imagination. In its rudimentary form it may be termed a *récit*, recounting a deed. In its more conscious and objective art form it can become a longer composition, a *nouvelle*, just as this genre at a slower pace with more complete developments in depth becomes a *roman*. For the *conte*, the situation or plot is more important since action must be decisive, rapid, unexpected, and composed of few incidents. By these standards, the differences are partly quantitative, with some emphasis on imagination for the *conte* and veracity for the *nouvelle*.

An examination of critical comments on the *nouvelle* may clarify its nature. Thibaudet attributes the creation of the *nouvelle* to Mérimée with a nod to Diderot as a predecessor. Mérimée was indeed a conscious artist with impeccable control of plot and effective style. But Jaloux says that Nodier gave the first model of the *nouvelle* in the 19th century. This would admit to this genre tales of romantic atmosphere, vague nostalgia, and pallid imagination. In general, critical concepts of actuality and realism in the *nouvelle* are not at all recent. In 1657 Segrais (q.v.) published a book of *Nouvelles Françaises* in which one of his ladies says to her fair companions that while the novel follows the dictates of dignity and style, the *nouvelle* should speak more of daily happenings. This was written only a few years before La Fontaine's refusal "de quitter la nature d'un pas," and Molière's famous rule, "peindre d'après la nature." Veracity and clarity were clearly basic for the *nouvelle*. Madame de la Fayette situates the action of her *Mlle de Montpensier* at the court of Charles IX and of her *Princesse de Clèves* at that of Henry II. This concentrated novel on events lived seeks to minimize the fictitious, and tends to destroy the many-volumed romances of the mid-seventeenth century à la Scudéry (q.v.). No doubt the classical principles of the theater contribute to the process when Souhait indicates toward the end of the century that the *nouvelle* takes for its material only one principal event and trims away complicating circumstance. Shades of Racine!

Despite this auspicious beginning, the 18th century is not favorable to the honest *nouvelle* which is gradually replaced by the fantastic *conte*, a more flexible vehicle for ideas that must pass censorship. Perrault's *merveilleux* will be appropriated, with propaganda served by strewing imaginary events along satiric itineraries in the fashion of Rabelais and Cyrano (q.v.). The

conte is adaptable enough to lend itself to this utilitarian use in the guise of a concealed teaching. "A bon entendeur, salut." It is Diderot mainly who will keep the *nouvelle* alive by writing it for his own satisfaction without publication, whereas Lesage and Marivaux will incorporate their *nouvelles* into their long works.

The Goncourts declared of Diderot: "Il a inauguré le roman moderne." A rewarding study could be made of Diderot's art in reporting facial expression for he is a superb portraitist. He comes close to Flaubert and Maupassant in creating the illusion of *le vrai* as he reports the wart on the forehead, the cut lip, and the pox marks near the nose. But he is too fond of strong emotion to exercise restraint. "Vivre sans passions, c'est dormir toute sa vie" he writes, and lets himself go into epic hysterics and gusty dialogue. But the stark realism of his *nouvelle, Le neveu de Rameau,* leaves an indelible impression. Diderot is a *nouvelliste* of first rank.

With Nodier and the Romantics the marvelous manifests itself in vaporous guise in both *nouvelle* and *conte*. It has never been really absent at any time, it resides in religious accounts of miracles, in tales of chivalry, in fables, continues with Perrault and even the satiric fantasy of the *conte philosophique*, creates lunar landscapes in the Romantic mingling of mystery and magic, indeed emerges in our day once more with the symbolist and surrealist writers. The marvelous is so pervasive that it invades the *nouvelle*, formerly the habitat of the *véridique*. Mérimée will be realistic in his *conte, Mateo Falcone*, and use the marvelous in his *Vénus d'Ille*. Balzac and Musset tangle the two genres so that the neat dividing line of historicity becomes blurred. Life is like that, half dream; reality is not so simply distinguished. True that the French logical mind does not accept mystery so easily as the fog-bound English and the sentimental Germans. For the French, the wart on the face looms up out of the mist. Thus André Breton (q.v.), surrealist leader, exclaims finally: "Ce qu'il y a d'admirable dans le fantastique, c'est qu'il n'y a plus de fantastique, il n'y a pas que le réel." Strange things happen to most of us, dreams, premonitions, queer emotions. In our current awareness of the subconscious and its working, there is no longer any perceptible hiatus between inner and outer worlds. As in the play and the novel, the prose narrative of today veers from attention to mere form and attempts to pierce through to some resonant truth that will enrich its readers, a process Thibaudet has called "élargissement et découverte du monde." The merely logical and objective are being superseded by a sort of inner reality seeking the true meaning at the core of living. Gide said: "Mérimée ou la perfection inutile." Balzac in his *nouvelle, Adieu,* is much closer to our modern story concept and infinitely greater in this inner resonance than Mérimée's liquid precision. The secret of their difference lies in their differing proximities to the universal, and the subconscious.

But Maupassant's concept of the short story remains as the guide post, whatever the nature of modern reality. This means brevity, careful selection of the part to suggest the whole, significant detail sending forth echoes from the known to the illimitable till the unexpressed in ourselves awakens and nods knowingly at the familiarity of the mysterious. Here the *conte* and the *nouvelle* shake hands across a non-existent frontier.

André Fage, *Le conte et les conteurs d'aujourd'hui, Anthologie des conteurs d'aujourd'hui,* 1924; F. C.

Green, Preface, *French Short Stories of 19th and 20th centuries,* New York, 1933; Introduction, *Maupassant, Choix de Contes,* 1945; Albert Thibaudet, *Histoire de la littérature française de 1789 à nos jours,* 1936; Daniel Mornet, *Introduction à l'étude des écrivains français d'aujourd'hui,* 1939; Philippe Van Tieghem, *Petite histoire des grandes doctrines littéraires en France de la pléiade au surréalisme,* 1946; Henri Peyre, Introduction, *Contes Modernes,* New York, 1949, Marcel Raymond, *Notes pour une histoire et une poétique de la nouvelle. Anthologie de la nouvelle française,* Lausanne, 1950.

HARRY KURZ

Sidney (1745): See *Gresset.*
Siècle de Louis le Grand, Le (1678): See *Perrault, Charles.*
Siècle de Louis XIV (1751): See *Voltaire.*
Siegfried (1928): See *Giraudoux.*
Siegfried et le Limousin (1922): See *Giraudoux.*
Silbermann (1922): See *Lacretelle, Jacques de.*
Si le grain ne meurt (1926): See *Gide.*
Silvanire (1631): See *Mairet, Jean.*
Simenon, Georges: (1903-) Although a prolific author in a *genre* of writing not always highly regarded, this Belgian-born writer has received the acclaim of such a notable figure as André Gide (q.v.). This can doubtlessly be explained by the fact that his numerous *detective* novels, one of whose main protagonists is Maigret, contain psychological penetration and literary value. Included among them are *Les Fiançailles de M. Hire* and *Monsieur la Souris.*
Simoun, Le (1920): See *Lenormand.*
Six livres de la République (1576): See *Bodin, Jean.*
Sodomme et Gomorrhe (1943): See *Giraudoux.*
Sœur Philomène (1861): See *Goncourt.*
Soirée avec M. Teste (1896): See *Valéry, Paul.*

Soirées de Médan: This collection of naturalistic stories, published in 1880 by the Médan (q.v.) group, had as its central theme the War of 1870. Included in this collection were *L'Attaque du Moulin*, by Zola (q.v.), and *Boule de Suif*, by Maupassant (q.v.), which was to make him famous. The book became a kind of naturalistic (see *Naturalism*) manifesto.

R. Dumesnil, *La publication des Soirées de Médan*, 1933.

Soirées de Saint-Pétersbourg (1821): See *Maistre, Joseph de.*

Solitaires: Also known as the "Messieurs de Port Royal," they are the lay but pious scholars and theologians, including Antoine Arnauld (1612-1694), Nicole (1628-1695), Lancelot (1615-1695) and Pascal (q.v.)—who joined them in 1654—who came to Port-Royal (q.v.) for study and meditation. Here they also founded in 1643 the *Petites Écoles*—where Racine (q.v.) was a student—which stressed the study of Greek and the Bible.

Somaize, Antoine Baudeau de: (1630-?) Remembered mostly for his *Dictionnaire des Précieuses* (1661), in which he offers valuable information concerning preciosity (q.v.), he is also the author of *Les Véritables Précieuses* (1660), a parody of Molière's (q.v.) *Les Précieuses ridicules* (1659).

R. Bray, *La Préciosité et les précieux*, 1948.

Somme de Poésie, Une (1947): See *La Tour du Pin.*

sonnet: A poem of fourteen lines arranged in two quatrains and two tercets. Its origin is attributed to Petrarch, and it enjoyed great popularity during the Italian Renaissance. In France it was introduced by Clément Marot (q.v.), and became the favorite poetic form of the *Pléiade* (q.v.). Although it was held in esteem by Boileau (q.v.), in the 18th century it almost disappeared from French literature.

In the 19th century, however, it flowered again in the poetry of A. de Musset, Sully Prudhomme, Baudelaire, and Hérédia (qq.v.).

M. Jasinski, *Histoire du sonnet en France*, 1903.

Sonnets pour Hélène (1574): See *Ronsard.*

Sophonisbe (1634): See *Mairet, Jean.*

Sorel, Charles: (1599-1674) Reacting against the *précieux* spirit (see *Préciosité*), and representing, much like Molière (q.v.), the realistic current, this novelist ridicules, in his *Le Berger extravagant* (1627), Honoré d'Urfé's (q.v.) *L'Astrée* and other pastoral novels. His main protagonist, a former Parisian turned shepherd as a result of taking too literally the novels he reads, runs into difficulties. In *La vraie Histoire comique de Francion* (1623), written some years before, Sorel portrays realistically, through Francion's journeys and experiences—reminiscent of Lesage's (q.v.) *Gil Blas*—a tableau of Parisian society and of the miserable conditions in which students and unknown authors lived during the seventeenth century. Described with humor and gaiety, this novel reveals keen observation of the bourgeois class.

E. Roy, *La Vie et les œuvres de Charles Sorel*, 1891; G. Regnier, *Le Roman réaliste au XVIIᵉ siècle*, 1914; Ph. Loch, *Ch. Sorel als literarischer Kritiker*, 1934.

sottie: This type of play, which was composed in the fifteenth and sixteenth centuries and of which twenty are extant, differs from the farce (q.v.) essentially because of its political and social satire. The best known, that of Pierre Gringoire (q.v.), *La Sottie du Prince des Sots* (1512), is directed against Pope Julius II.

E. Picot, *La sottie en France*, 1878.

Souffrances du Professeur Delteil, Les (1857): See *Champfleury.*

Soulier de Satin, Le (1930): See *Claudel*.

Soupault, Philippe: (1897-) This poet, novelist, and critic, suffered imprisonment by the Vichy authorities. Following his liberation, he spent some time in the United States. Until 1926 he took an active part in the Surrealist (see *Surrealism*) movement; with André Breton (q.v.) he wrote *Les Champs magnétiques* (1921), an experiment in automatic writing. His novels, including *Le Bon Apôtre* (1923) and *En Joue* (1925), reflect the state of mind of the young of this generation who tried to free themselves through dream, delusion, and adventure. His critical studies, too, are especially of those who sought self-liberation. Included among them are: *Henri Rousseau, le Douanier* (1927), *William Blake* (1928), *Charlot* (1931), *Baudelaire* (1931), *Souvenirs de James Joyce* (1944), and *Labiche* (1946).

Souriante Mme Beudet, La (1921): See *Amiel, Denis*.

Souvenirs d'enfance et de jeunesse (1883): See *Renan*.

Sphinx, Le (1874): See *Feuillet*.

Spire, André: (1868-) The social passion of this intellectual poet appears and reappears in his *Et vous riez!* (1905), *Poèmes juifs* (1908) and other poems of biblical inspiration. Other collections, like *Poèmes de Loire* (1929), reveal his mastery as a lyricist. As a poet, his importance lies in the fact that he sought a scientific basis—one that measured pitch, intensity, and duration—for the rhythm of *vers libre* (q.v.), and that he established his prosodic system exclusively on accent. During the Second World War he lectured on poetry at the École Libre des Hautes Études in New York City.

Stanley Burnshaw, *André Spire and His Poetry*, 1933.

Sponde, Jean de: (1557-1595) This poet was a Protestant converted to Catholicism. His fifty-odd poems on love and death are good examples of baroque verse expressing the anguish of the believer who fears that he is too much in love with life. Also a humanist, he edited Aristotle's *Logic* as well as the works of Homer and Hesiod.

Th. Maulnier et D. Aury, *Poètes précieux et baroques du 17ᵉ siècle*, 1941; M. Arland, *L'Œuvre poétique de Jean de Sponde*, 1943.

Staël, Madame de: (1766-1817) Born in Paris, Germaine Necker, wife of the Baron Staël-Holstein, from whom she was later divorced (1798), was the daughter of the Swiss financier, Jacques Necker, Ambassador from Sweden to France, who became minister of Louis XVI. Her brilliant mind was imbued from her early youth with the ideas of the eighteenth-century "philosophes" (q.v.) discussed in her father's *salon* in Geneva. Later, her intellect attracted, at her own *salon* in Paris, the leading literary and political figures of the day. Her independence and liberalism, which she expressed as a literary critic and novelist, rendered her suspect to Napoleon, who several times exiled her from Paris (cf. *Benjamin Constant*).

Applying the theories of Montesquieu (q.v.) to literature in *De la littérature* (1800), Mme. de Staël concluded that the political and sociological climate of a country explained its peculiar literary characteristics and that only in a free society could French literature progress and develop. Although this work met with little success, its apology for liberty displeased the First Consul. When, therefore, she gave expression to feminist views in her novel *Delphine* (1803) which showed defiance of public opinion and convention, Napoleon ordered her to leave Paris. Her visits to Italy and Germany (1803-1808), following this order, resulted in the publication of *Corinne* (1807) and

De *L'Allemagne,* written in 1810, but first published in 1813. In *Corinne,* the scene of which is laid in Italy, love and passion are glorified with the main protagonist, a poetess of superior intelligence, dying a victim of social constraints. *De L'Allemagne,* on the other hand, reveals to the French the genius of the German people and its literature, art, philosophy, and religion. The chapters on Goethe, Schiller, Lessing, and Schlegel reveal Mme. de Staël's understanding of Romanticism, of which she was an important precursor in France and to whose formation she contributed essential ideas and theories. This book is fundamental to French Romanticism.

Lady Blannerhasset, *Mme de Staël et son temps* (trad. française), 1890; D. G. Larg, *Madame de Staël, la Vie dans l'œuvre,* 1924; G. P. d'Haussonville, *Mme de Staël et l'Allemagne,* 1928.

Stello (1832): See *Vigny.*

Stendhal (pseud. of **Henri Beyle**): (1783-1842) The life of this novelist, born at Grenoble, bears close comparison to his works; in them one finds his personal conception of the world, with his likes and dislikes, ambitions and frustrations. His posthumously published autobiographical works, including his *Journal* (1888), *Vie de Henri Brulard* (1890), and *Souvenirs d'Egotisme* (1892) evoke his unhappy childhood and his later pleasure-seeking existence in Paris (1821-1830). Studies of criticism and esthetics—*Vie de Haydn* (1815), *Vie de Mozart* (1815), *Histoire de la peinture en Italie* (1817)—as well as his *Rome, Naples et Florence* (1817), personal psychological observations on Italian society, appeared during the intervening period in his life, spent in Milan, where he went following the Restoration. The same sensitivity that vibrated before Beauty and that found happiness in Italy—Stendhal wished his epitaph to be *Arrigo Beyle, Milanese*—reacted with hostility to all authority or constraint, whether that of the Church, the legitimist monarchy, or even of a parent, such as his own domineering father. Stendhal's worship of Napoleon, in whose armies he served from 1794 to 1802, and again, from 1806 to 1815, can also be explained by his cult of energy, adventure, conquest, and individualism. In his pursuit of happiness— a life-long objective—love becomes a predominant preoccupation. *De l'amour* (1822), a psychological monograph on the different kinds of love and variations of passion, derives from his experiences and passions; its themes were to be developed in the novels that followed.

Like Stendhal, the main protagonists in his novels, on which his reputation is essentially based, are in search of happiness which they hope to achieve through love; in its pursuit, they are armed, most frequently, with energy, ambition, intelligence, and a spirit of adventure, although, at times, as in *Armance* (1827), his first novel, they betray timidity with women. Their individualism, moreover, is heightened by their struggle with society, which maintains the principles either of the Restoration, as in *Le Rouge et le Noir* (1831; q.v.), or of the finance-ridden politics of the July Monarchy, as in *Lucien Leuwen* (begun in 1834; pub. in 1894), which were denounced by Stendhal. The projection of Stendhal's character or experiences is seen in his heroes and heroines alike; beside Julien Sorel stand Mme. de Rênal and Mathilde, both of *Le Rouge et le Noir;* Sansévérina of *La Chartreuse de Parme* (1839; q.v.); and Lamiel, of the same named work, published in 1889. All of them add to the picture of his ambitions, dreams, and regrets.

It is worthy of note, perhaps, that Stendhal, who began his literary career as a romanticist and contributed in *Racine et Shakespeare* (1825) one of the earliest and most important Romantic manifestoes, soon revealed characteristics that were different from those of his contemporaries. Unlike the sentimental effusions and grandiloquence of the latter, his works reveal much sobriety and the influence of the *Code Civil*, from which he would read regularly. Although he, too, like Mérimée (q.v.), represents a transition between romanticism and realism (q.v.), basing the stories of such masterpieces as the previously-mentioned *Le Rouge et le Noir* and *La Chartreuse de Parme* on facts, and employing details without embellishing on them, his importance is to be found in his penetrating psychological analyses as he dissects the actions, sensations, and motivating forces of his heroes. In the depiction of the human heart he becomes a precursor of the modern psychological novel of Proust (q.v.) and others. It is for this reason essentially that Stendhal was given recognition only towards the end of the 19th century.

E. Rod, *Stendhal*, 1892; P. Hazard, *Vie de Stendhal*, 1927; H. Martineau, *L'Œuvre de Stendhal*, 1932; P. Martino, *Stendhal*, rev. ed., 1934; A. Caraccio, *Stendhal*, 1951.

Suarès, André: (1868-1948) The writings of this essayist, poet, and critic, who was born in the environs of Marseilles, reflect the seclusion into which he withdrew, a solitude motivated by an inner heroic ideal of grandeur and beauty. The subjects he treated, often in aphoristic form, show an overflowing knowledge of the sciences, philology, music, and the arts. His prolific writings include his poems *Images de la grandeur* (1901), literary criticism and portraits, as, for example, *Trois Hommes: Pascal, Ibsen, Dostoïevsky*

(1913), *Goethe le grand Européen* (1932), and *Trois Grands Vivants: Cervantes, Tolstoï, Baudelaire* (1937), and his moralistic meditations in *Voici l'Homme* (1906), *Sur la Vie* (1909-1913), and *Valeurs* (1936).

Sue, Eugène: (1804-1857) After having introduced into France the maritime novel (*Plick et Plock*, 1831; *Atar-Gull*, 1831), which followed the Anglo-Saxon vogue, he wrote, under the influence of the socialistic theories of Fourier (q.v.), *Les Mystères de Paris* (1842-1843)—the first French novel published as a *feuilleton*, a serial in a newspaper—and *Le Juif errant* (1845-1847). The two novels depict, in somber settings and situations, the dregs of Parisian society and the sufferings of the innocent who are the prey of those with evil designs. The powerful imagination of the author in these works appealed to the general public.

N. Atkinson, *Eugène Sue et le roman feuilleton*, 1930.
Sueur de sang (1935): See *Jouve, Pierre Jean.*
Sully-Prudhomme (pseud. of **René François Armand Prudhomme**): (1839-1907) An unhappy love affair and a not-too-happy childhood made this Parisian-born intellectual a poet. The melancholy he expresses in his poetry, unlike that of the Romanticists, however, is discreet and restrained. Nevertheless, his sensitiveness prevented him from being a true representative—despite his cult of beauty and scientific precision—of the Parnassian (q.v.) ideal. Putting truth above beauty, it was natural for this student of Science and Philosophy to make poetry essentially a vehicle for philosophic thought. His philosophy, in the final analysis, is an idealistic one; he believes that happiness is gained through sacrifice; with his sense of human progress, he preaches the doctrine of human solidarity. His

various collections of poetry include *Stances et Poèmes* (1865), *Les Épreuves* (1866), *Les Solitudes* (1869), *Les Vaines Tendresses* (1875), *La Justice* (1878), and *Le Bonheur*. Sully-Prudhomme, a member of the French Academy, received the Nobel Prize in 1901. E. Zyromski, *Sully-Prudhomme*, 1907; E. Estève, *Sully-Prudhomme, poète sentimental et poète philosophe*, 1925.

Supervielle, Jules: (1884-   ) This poet, writer of short stories, novelist, and dramatist, was born in Montevideo, Uruguay, of a French family. In almost all of his works the presence of South America is felt. His poetry, whether it evokes the savage beauty of the pampas, the harmony of a landscape, the grace of an animal, the power of love, or, even the humblest objects, is, despite the frequent identifications of it with Surrealism (q.v.), more melodious, less artificial than Surrealist verse; moreover, it expresses the acceptance, rather than the escape from, the human situation; it lovingly embraces dreams to recapture the reality of the memory. In this manner, his poetry attains a cosmic grandeur. Among his more notable collections are: *Gravitations* (1925), *Le Forçat innocent* (1930), *Les Amis inconnus* (1934), *La Fable du Monde* (1938), and *Poèmes de la France malheureuse* (1941)—poems inspired by the War. His novels include *L'Homme de la Pampa* (1923) and *Le Voleur d'enfants* (1926). His talent as a short story writer is especially seen in *L'Enfant de la haute mer* (1931), *L'Arche de Noé* (1938), and *Le Petit Bois* (1942), in which can be found a mixture of fancy and humor. This mixture also characterizes his plays *Le Belle au bois* (1932), *La Première Famille* (1936), and *Bolivar* (1936). In addition, he wrote an adaptation of Shakespeare: *Comme il vous plaira* (1925).

C. Sénéchal, *Jules Supervielle*, 1939; Claude Roy, *Jules Supervielle*, 1949.

Supplément au voyage de Bougainville (wr. 1769): See *Diderot*.

Suréna (1674): See *Corneille, Pierre*.

SURREALISM: Surrealism, as defined by its founder and chief exponent, André Breton (q.v.), in his First Manifesto (1924) has a twofold meaning. It is considered a form of psychic automatism whereby human expression is liberated from the confines of reason and from established standards of esthetics and morals; in its encyclopedic extension it assumes a metaphysical connotation based on belief in the superior reality of the dream and of those verbal and pictorial associations created by the mind when it is allowed unbridled activity.

The movement was launched in the aftermath of World War I in France by a group of very young intellectual pioneers, versed in the history of literature, esthetics and philosophy, and possessed with an uncompromising passion for liberty. Having first experienced the despair and participated in the nihilistic revolts and exhibitionism of Dadaism (q.v.), they wilfully destroyed Dada, and out of their initial anarchy set out to evolve a positive credo and an affirmative technique. They borrowed the word "surrealist" from Guillaume Apollinaire (q.v.), whom they hailed as the foremost poet of the new century. He had coined the word in his play, *Les Mamelles de Tirésias* to designate a reality above the accepted and obvious one. The surrealists were heterogeneous in national character and temperament, but all Parisians by choice and inspired by the newness of the century. They shared a common faith in the genius of youth and regarded artistic experience not as a professional occupation but as a whole way of life. They brought to a head a gradually intensified indictment of some seventy years' standing in French literature and art, directed at the same time against the otherworldly escapism of the romanticists and against naturalism's (q.v.) close adherence to external reality. In the course of the past century the poet had gained on the French literary scene top rank as intellectual seer. In that capacity he had assumed a militant attitude toward any status quo in man's search for knowledge or his manners of expression. The surrealists considered themselves the twentieth century standard bearers of "the great modern tradition" which Charles Baudelaire (q.v.) had launched in the last two lines of his "Voyage": to find something new in the abysses of the unknown whether the adventure lead to heaven or perdition. As science in the latter part of the nineteenth century had made of the metaphysical or speculative infinite a less satisfactory haven for the seeker of the unknown, the poet was ready to substitute for it what Renan (q.v.) called *l'infini réel* and to illustrate with the writer's use of the word, and the artist's use of the line, the concept of an infinite based on the unconditional acceptance of concrete reality. But the word reality gradually ceased to be identified with the organized forms which physical and human nature had traditionally assumed for the logical mind. Around 1870 works of Lautréamont and Rimbaud, and Mallarmé's (qq.v.) *Igitur* and *Un Coup de dés* had manifested a conscious rejection of natural objects and phenomena and a refusal to reproduce them in imitative style in literature. This materio-mysticism supplied a literary background for surrealism.

There has been much fluctuation in the ranks of the writers and artists who participated with André Breton in the surrealist experience

and in the quasi-scientific experimentation with what might be called the fourth dimension in literature and art. Among the better known of the men of letters who at some time in their careers assumed the surrealist trademark are: Antonin Artaud, Louis Aragon, René Char, René Crevel, Robert Desnos, Paul Eluard, Julien Gracq (qq.v.), Georges Hugnet, E. T. Mesens, Henri Michaux (q.v.), Pierre Naville, Benjamin Péret, Jacques Prevert (q.v.), Raymond Queneau, Philippe Soupault, Tristan Tzara (qq.v.), Roger Vitrac. A host of painters became their associates. Through the artists' more graphic representation of surrealism the international recognition of the movement was accelerated. These included Salvatore Dali, Marcel Duchamp, Max Ernst, Alberto Giacometti, Valentine Hugo, Jean Miro, René Magritte, André Masson, Francis Picabia, Yves Tanguy.

Beginning with *Les Champs magnétiques* (1919), co-authored by André Breton and Philippe Soupault, surrealist production flourished all through the period between the two world wars. The principal journals were: *Littérature*, organized in 1919, about a year before the official advent of surrealism, *Révolution Surréaliste* (1924-30), transformed in 1930 into *Surréalisme au service de la Révolution, Minotaure,* and *Cahiers GLM.*

Surrealism has had its polemics, metaphysics and ars poetica. Its polemics, given free rein in the periodicals and in Breton's two manifestoes, centered primarily around the questions: who is a good and faithful surrealist, and who should be or has been banished from the brotherhood. There are also deifications of spiritual mentors past and present, and rabid attacks on the philistines.

Its metaphysics is best revealed in works such as Breton's *Nadja* (1928),

Aragon's *Le Paysan de Paris* (1926), Crevel's *L'Esprit contre la raison* (1927) and Éluard's *Les Dessous d'une vie, ou la Pyramide humaine* (1926), in which the surrealists crystallized, in a fusion of poetry and prose, their philosophy of reality. In these writings it is the concept of order that is attacked as the arch enemy of the potentials of creative imagination. They refuted not only all forms of *man-conceived* order of things, but Providence, the *mystical* order of things; they accepted instead *hazard* or *chance* as evidence of an inconceivable but existent *disorder* of things. By extracting this "divine" disorder left so long undisturbed in concrete entities, the surrealists hoped to perceive the concrete face of the infinite. "The concrete form of disorder is the outer limit of the mind," said Aragon in *Le Paysan de Paris*, the Bible of the new metaphysics. If the mind can sufficiently free itself from logic to be receptive to this disorder, then it will have overpowered the laws of nature and have risen above what Crevel calls "le bric-à-brac réaliste." The fundamental motivation of surrealist activity was to satisfy both physical and metaphysical thirst by pushing back the frontiers of reality and being able to envisage some of the infinite possibilities of the concrete world.

The ars poetica is clearly stated in Breton's two manifestoes, Aragon's "Traité du style," in Tristan Tzara's "Essai sur la situation de la poésie," and in a number of briefer treatises appearing periodically in the surrealist journals. It precludes first of all imitation of nature as a basis of artistic production. Dealing a radical blow both to newly popularized photography and time-honored descriptive writing, the surrealists attempted to make of art an act of creation rather than of representation, whether it be in terms of

words or objects. Their primary concern was self-fulfillment through a vertiginous freedom of expression; their secondary function, vis-à-vis the public, was not to convey meaning or feeling, but to communicate their own contagious liberation of the imagination.

The creative role of language was strongly stressed in the surrealists' concept of poetry. The poem, no longer an expression of ideas or emotions but the creation of a series of images, need not owe its existence to an *a priori* subject. "Images think for me," says Paul Eluard. It is Breton's belief that the speed of thinking is not superior to that of linguistic expression, which, therefore, need not be subservient to logical thought. Words brought together by creative intuition could explode in a dynamic image much more provocative in result than the impulsion of abstract thoughts groping for words to give them countenance. Words serving as stimuli or irritants to the senses were to produce their own images. Breton compares the spontaneity with which these images offer themselves and their habit forming character to the stupefying state of mind produced by artificial paradises. In this state of subconscious stimulation the poet is alerted to the sensations that words can produce even as the painter is attracted to objects, meaning a different thing to each artist, speaking a different language to each spectator. Words and objects placed on a parallel plane as sensual stimuli draw together the poet's and artist's techniques, and at the same time widen the gap between poetry and the literary forms that continue to have as their aim the expression of ideas.

To discover, then, what might be called the high voltage of words was to be the key to surrealist poetry. But in the composition of the poem, what is even more important than the right word is the happy marriage of words into illuminating (not elucidating) associations, which become the basis of the image. The image thus achieved is no longer based on analogy but on juxtaposition of the far-fetched chance encounter of two realities whose effect is likened to the light produced by the contact of two electrical conductors. While the terms of the ordinary image are chosen on the basis of similarity, the value of the surrealist image depends on the contradiction between one set of associations and another; the greater the disparity the more dynamic the image. Images constructed according to this notion contain a dose of absurdity and that element of surprise, which, in the opinion of Guillaume Apollinaire, is one of the fundamental resources of the modern mind. This type of poetic imagery rises on the same foundation as the "fortuitous meeting," in the words of Max Ernst, of two logically unrelated objects in a surrealist painting. The poet and the artist find themselves in a magnetic field wherein by the attraction of one image to another the objects of reality are deviated from their traditional roles. The result is an incongruous unit, fashioned out of sensory data but in heretofore inconceivable combinations.

To achieve aptitude in surrealist composition, it was deemed necessary to cultivate the irrational qualities of the mind. Breton and his colleagues held in great respect the mentally deranged and felt that the art of the insane contained a great reserve of moral health. In 1928 the surrealists celebrated the fiftieth anniversary of Jean Martin Charcot's publication of studies in hysteria and accepted him as one of their precursors because he had shown scientifically the possibilities of the human mind to conciliate reality with the dream and to experience this conciliation without exterior stimuli or artificial hypnosis. They found even greater support in the more recent investigations of Freud into the inner chambers of the mind. Having become acquainted with the works of Freud personally in 1921, Breton introduced Freudian methods as a rich training ground in preparing the subconscious mind for creative writing or painting.

First among these activities was automatic writing and drawing, which assumed the same importance in the technical equipment of the surrealist as the practice of scales to the musician. It became a form of self-administered psychoanalysis. Placing themselves in a state of quasihypnotic attentiveness, the surrealists tried to shut out all outside disturbances and to let the hand write or draw almost alone, and the pen or pencil transcribe spontaneously the subconscious affiliations which they felt between words and images. These "surrealist texts," as they are called, are not poems. They are a means of developing or enriching poetic consciousness; they also break down traditional word associations which are too deep-set to be warded off consciously, and which the surrealists considered not only ineffective in imagery but detrimental to the component words involved in the tedious alliance.

Séances for collective dreaming and uninhibited recounting and interpretation of dreams constituted another form of Freudian release practiced by the surrealists. Robert Desnos was the greatest dreamer of them all and produced a rich flow of verbal images for his admiring colleagues. In *Les Vases communicants* (1932), dedicated to Freud, André Breton envisaged existence as a composite of two urns, the dream and the state of wakefulness, constantly connected with each other and contributing to each other's intensity. He noted the effect of the dream on imagery and found the same type of displacement of objects and things, and verbal condensations in the poet's dream thoughts worthy of literary transcription as those that Freud had observed in his clinical cases. A third form of Freudian experimentation adopted by the surrealists was the intentional simulation of states of mental abnormality. *L'Immaculée Conception* (1930) was a collaboration between Breton and Eluard which set out: to imitate delirium, artificially assume the various forms of insanity, and thus establish a method of investigating the widest range of mental activity. Breton's Nadja, the most authentic of surrealism's brain children, is presented as mentally deranged, the more gracefully to hide her face behind the heavy, nonexistent feather of her hat and to perceive a blue wind passing in the trees. The author reveals how he overcomes the apparent contradictions caused by the unparallel vision between Nadja and himself.

Out of these theories and experimentations between the two world wars a number of poetic works can already be singled out as surrealist classics. A considerable number of the poems in Breton's collections, provocatively called *Clair de Terre* (1923), *Le Revolver à cheveux blancs* (1932), and *L'Air de l'eau* (1934) illustrate faithfully his precepts: a dazzling originality of subject matter, an unrelenting probing of the sensory world often bordering on hallucination, speculation about the absolute in terms of concrete but incongruous metaphors; his famous "L'Union libre" is a love poem in surrealist style, displaying the virtuosity of the author in the construction of the unusual metaphor. Powerfully endowed with fertile imagery are also the surrealist poems of Paul Eluard, principally those in the collections *Capitale de la douleur* (1926), *L'Amour la poésie* (1929) *La Vie immédiate* (1932). Renewing the romanticists' preoccupation with the themes of love and death, he states them with verbal prowess, considering them on a plane of subjective reality, freed of the limits of perspective, divested of physical laws.

Among the many artists who have exhibited surrealist paintings and in their works demonstrated a veritable crisis of the object, Dali reveals the most successful examples of spontaneous juxtaposition, Max Ernst is notable for his distortions and dehumanizations, Yves Tanguy for his creation of new objects set in horizonless positions.

The effect of the Second World War on the writers who had been connected with surrealism was entirely different from that of the previous one. At the close of the first war, they had assumed an anti-social attitude toward established traditions and institutions, holding them responsible for the existing chaos, and condemning the patriots for bigotry and lack of vision. Under the Nazi occupation the late subversives became fervent patriots, the morale builders of the French people, and their verse the hymns of the Resistance. Particularly prolific in this period were Aragon and Eluard, no longer officially surrealists but retaining in their writing of the disasters of France much of the surrealist technique: the cult of the illogical image, the mystical approach to temporal events, free associations of metaphors with a disregard for logical sequence, a rapprochment of subject and object, a mingling of the physical and spiritual. *Brocéliande* and the majority of the other poems of Aragon collected in 1947 under the telling title of *En Étrange Pays dans mon pays lui-même,* and Eluard's *Poésie ininterrompue* (1946) are in the latter day tradition of surrealism.

André Breton had moved the official seat of surrealism to the western hemisphere, first to New York then to Mexico. While in the U. S. he founded a surrealist periodical VVV which proved short-lived, even as his exile. His war time writing such as *Fata Morgana* (1940) and *Les États généraux* (1943) for all their surrealist point of view, reflect the color of the times: concern over the horrors of war, plea for social justice.

Since the war, the schisms among erstwhile surrealists have grown more serious. As early as 1925 there had been a consensus of opinion that their esthetic ideals bore a definite relation to the social revolution of Lenin and Trotsky because they shared a common drive to transform existing orders. Between the two world wars an attempt had been made at affiliation with the French communist organ, *Clarté.* However, if some of the surrealists found lasting satisfaction in their association with communism, many others, including Breton, realized that their poetic image of revolution was in direct contradiction with the limited sense given to the word by the Stalinists. Even before World War II surrealism veered away from communism and has since broken all ties with those of its former members, principally Aragon and Eluard (until his death in 1952), who had joined the party and fashioned their post war works along partisan lines.

Despite a serious depletion in their ranks, caused by political disruption, André Breton has maintained a nucleus of ever productive faithfuls and strengthened the literary school with the support of new blood and the collaboration of many foreign writers and artists.

Post war surrealist exhibits have been viewed in many countries. In an International Exposition in Paris in 1949 twenty-four nations were represented under the banner of surrealism. In the fall of 1953 a new series of the periodical *Medium* revived the journalistic activity of the surrealists, which had been crippled during and immediately following World War II.

The surrealists have printed without sufficient editing the results of their trial and error methods, confused liberty with license at times, but despite the uneven quality of their output have exercised an undisputable influence, by means of their vociferous rejection of standard styles, on non-surrealist as well as surrealist literature and art. The transformation operating on the French poetic language through their efforts has been inducing similar mutations in the literary language of other countries. Pictorial techniques have been drastically shaken. Surrealist imprint has been felt in the art of decoration, stagecraft, furniture construction, photography, architecture and advertising design. Surrealism's international character, its broad field of radiation are reminiscent of the scope of influence exerted by romanticism in the preceding century.

The surrealists consider their work in the experimental stage, as the beginning of a tremendous upheaval, an unrelenting challenge to man's ability to integrate his perceptions over and above the miscellany of nature. Believing their efforts to run parallel to those of the modern scientists, the surrealists have been trying to give proof that the arts are not lagging behind the sciences in supplying outlets to the inventive capacity of the human mind and to man's unrelenting progression toward knowledge.

Marcel Raymond, *De Baudelaire*

au surréalisme, 1933; Georges Hugnet, "Préface," *Petite Anthologie poétique du surréalisme,* 1934; Herbert Read, *Surrealism,* 1936; Albert Béguin, *L'Ame romantique et le Rêve,* 2 vols., 1937; Georges Lemaître, *From Cubism to Surrealism in French Literature,* 1941; Interview with André Breton, *View,* October-November 1941; Maurice Nadeau, *Histoire du surréalisme,* 1945; Anna Balakian, *Literary Origins of Surrealism,* 1947; Maurice Nadeau, *Documents surréalistes,* 1948; Victor Crastre, "Le Drame du surréalisme," *Les Temps Modernes,* July 1948; Wallace Fowlie, *Age of Surrealism,* 1950.

ANNA BALAKIAN

Sylvie (1853): See *Nerval, Gérard de.*

SYMBOLISM: The Symbolist movement can be viewed today as a development and, in some respects, a fulfillment of the ideals set up by the earlier Romantic generations everywhere in Europe. It seems indeed a part of Romanticism (q.v.), which, in the broad sense of the word, stands for the intuitive as opposed to the rational, the subjective as opposed to the objective, for individuality and liberty. Thus philosophically and esthetically considered, Symbolism is a modern expression of one of the fundamental tempers of man, and, as such, can be properly placed in the line of all mystic, oracular, illuminist, or idealist traditions. This is the broad view. It takes in some of the greatest writers of the nineteenth century in France and includes as well the chief creative geniuses of our own times. But if we take the narrow view, we see merely a swarm of poets loosely called Symbolists grouping and regrouping themselves during the last fifteen years of the nineteenth century into ephemeral schools and cliques. No poet of genius is within the field of our vision, nor, in spite of constant jockeying for position, any single

great leader capable of rallying writers under a clearly defined banner marked Symbolism.

Understood in this very literal and limited sense, the Symbolist movement began in 1886 when Jean Moréas (q.v.), smarting under the accusation that he and his associates were morbid and neurotic, denied the charge in the September 18 issue of the *Figaro* and went on to explain their lofty aims and ambitions. They were seeking, he affirmed, to create beauty through a search for the "pure concept" and the "eternal symbol." Although vague, verbose, and very abstract, Moréas' remarks pleased almost all the new poets. They approved his emphasis upon the positive quality and the grandeur of their aspirations and accepted the article as a manifesto. Symbolism became thereby officially baptized and Jean Moréas was constituted leader of a school so denominated.

The new poets proved themselves more enthusiastic and energetic than disciplined. Individual talents cried for expression, and vied with each other in the numerous little magazines that sprang up following Moréas' manifesto. Poetic circles were in a foment of activity, a general mêlée ensued. Moréas, who had founded a periodical bearing the title, *Le Symboliste,* was challenged by René Ghil (q.v.) through his magazine, *Décadence.* Other leaders and other magazines joined in the fray, with poets and supporters constantly shifting allegiance. Ghil, by 1890, had lost his following and was embarked alone on a course of poetic speculation leading away from Symbolism. The following year Moréas himself stepped down. In another letter to the *Figaro* he announced that Symbolism, only a transitory phenomenon, was dead, and that he was founding the École romane (q.v.) to succeed it. The movement went on without leaders or found new ones. Opposition, at least nominal, increased as new poets established their theory either outside the Symbolist *cadre* or in apparent opposition to it. By 1896 Symbolism had dissolved into a multitude of little chapels calling themselves Paroxysm, Esoterism, Naturism (q.v.), Syntheticism, Humanism, etc. Then, as the century drew to an end, the subject was scarcely discussed. The period of the schools was over.

The self-conscious and self-styled Symbolist poets represent, as has already been suggested, only an articulate and militant phase of a general development in French poetry stemming from the Romantic period and continuing to the present day. Moréas' manifesto did not begin the movement, nor did the ultimate abandonment of all hopes of founding an integrated and enduring Symbolist school alter the trend. Poets of the twentieth century have continued in theory and practice where nineteenth century Symbolists left off. Among them we can count our greatest contemporary poets, far greater than any who wrote and argued in the little magazines of the eighties and nineties. Poets of genius preceded and followed the movement strictly defined, whose chief significance is to have glossed and exploited the genius of the ones and to have thereby made possible the full flowering of the others.

Of the poets of the Romantic period we now distinguish several who, somewhat off the main highway, seem to have followed a byway that would broaden into Symbolism. Among them may be included Aloysius Bertrand (q.v.), who recorded his hallucinations in prose poems; Gérard de Nerval (q.v.), who strove to associate music and transcendental knowledge with poetry; Sainte-Beuve (q.v.), whose poetry struck a rare intimate note; Charles Baudelaire (q.v.), who integrated and gave most complete expression to these early manifestations of the Symbolist spirit.

Baudelaire (1821-1867) is thus the first of the great Symbolist masters. In the words of Hugo (q.v.), this poet had brought a "frisson nouveau" into French poetry, a "frisson" induced by intimate revelation and poetic suggestion of mystery, evil, unhealthy and melancholy beauty. The influence of the *Fleurs du Mal* (1857) operated through successive generations of latter nineteenth century poets. The Parnassian (q.v.) craftsmen, following Gautier (q.v.), were interested primarily in the technical aspect of Baudelaire's verse; Decadents and Symbolists, however, were attracted by its broad implications. A concept of beauty that included the ugly and the evil (the *frisson nouveau*) strongly appealed to the Decadents. Symbolists saw in Baudelaire a poet on the track of a poetic magic that might conjure up, through a blending of rhythm, sound, and image, the veritable face of the universe. In his famous sonnet entitled *Correspondances*, he had suggested that the poet was in moments of perfect evocation capable of perceiving the analogies in nature which bind the universe together, of establishing the symbols which stand for the absolute itself.

From these two aspects of Baudelaire, the artist and the seer, may be traced two traditions that have threaded through poetic history down to the present day. In the line of artists there are the Mallarmés and the Valérys (qq.v.); in that of the seers, Rimbaud (q.v.) and the Surrealists (see *Surrealism*).

Verlaine (1844-1896; q.v.), following his natural inclination, had moved slowly away from the Parnassian ideal toward a concept of poetry that anticipated Symbolism. Even in his earliest collection of verse, the *Poèmes saturniens* (1867), a strong current of Baudelaireanism, running counter to its general Parnassian themes and techniques, indicated the direction which this young poet was going to follow. Not many years later Verlaine formulated his anti-Parnassian notions about poetry in the piece which has become famous, *L'Art poétique.* Verse must be musical, a harmony of sounds inspiring revery. Rime, architecture, must be attenuated; rhetoric must be replaced by suggestion and nuance.

Toward 1885 the young poets discovered poor Lélian. Captivated by the legend that had grown up around Verlaine's name, they saluted him as a leader and sought to imitate his manner. His verses were eagerly sought after by all the Symbolist magazines. He had given in his *Poètes maudits* models for the young poets to follow: Tristan Corbière, the naive bohemian author of *Amours jaunes;* Mallarmé (q.v.); Villiers de l'Isle-Adam (q.v.), whom they called their Chateaubriand (q.v.); Lautréamont (q.v.), poet of Promethean revolt and the prodigious image.

Stéphane Mallarmé (1842-1898) is the third major force in the Symbolist movement. Like Verlaine he proceeded from Baudelaire, like Verlaine he was a guide and teacher to younger poets writing during the latter nineteenth century. Unlike Verlaine, his own poetic production was very limited. But his poetic ambitions exceeded those of Verlaine, and have interested successive generations as much as Verlaine's accomplishments. His poetry stands for the most sublime of all Symbolist dreams, one which has challenged the greatest poets and which is still the object of numerous and voluminous commentaries.

Obsessed by the notion of correspondences, which he had found in the *Fleurs du Mal,* Mallarmé saw everything in the universe bound by subtle analogies which the poet alone could detect. They might lead him beyond the world of appearances into that world of pure ideas whose existence had been affirmed by philosophers from Plato to Hegel. To serve him in his hermetic alchemy Mallarmé deliberately made his verse obscure by omissions, peculiar syntax, and unconventional diction.

Mallarmé was made known to the poets of 1886 by Huysmans' (q.v.) description of him in the celebrated *A Rebours.* Soon he was surrounded by a fervent group who came every Tuesday to the apartment in the Rue de Rome to listen to the master expound his doctrine. As he spoke of the revelatory symbol, of Wagner and the possibility to synthetize poetry with music, Moréas composed his manifesto and René Ghil mapped out his theory of "instrumentation verbale."

Rimbaud (1854-1891) completes the tetrad of the masters of Symbolism. Ten years younger than Mallarmé or Verlaine, Rimbaud nevertheless belonged to their generation. At fifteen he was already a poet. At twenty his career was over. But in three or four years he produced his amazing work and had improvised an aesthetic that would inspire writers for generations to come. The *Alchimie du verbe* proudly and defiantly states his accomplishments: "with instinctive rhythms I have invented a poetry that touches all the senses. I have noted the unexpressable. I have deliberately sought hallucination. I consider sacred the disorder of my mind." Rimbaud's assertions define the poet's rôle as that of a seer, of a *voyant.* As such he acclaimed Baudelaire—"le premier voyant, roi des poètes, un vrai Dieu!"

Rimbaud's sojourn in poetic circles was too brief—moreover, he was too young—to exert the personal influence upon poets that Mallarmé and Verlaine held. His work itself had to wait until recent times to receive its fullest acclaim. But the poets of 1886 used the *Illuminations* to illustrate their new theories and writers like René Ghil were quite patently in Rimbaud's debt.

If Baudelaire, Verlaine, Mallarmé, and Rimbaud were to triumph in the mid-eighties, it is because the youthful rebels against the poetic party then in office had finally gathered enough strength to require leadership for a full scale revolt. The school of Parnasse had ruled officially since 1866. But by the end of the seventies, a decade marked by poetic lethargy, opposition to the values upon which Parnassianism (q.v.) rested or with which it was associated became general enough to indicate a new poetic movement was underway. Positivistic philosophy, bourgeois society, the cult of form in art were under attack by an increasingly large proportion of the younger generation. The Hydropaths, the Hirsutes, and the others sought to outrage the bourgeois by their unconventional ideas and manners. Contemptuous society called the bearded and bohemian revolutionaries the Decadents and they accepted the label with bravado.

The poet who represents the highest achievement of Decadentism is Jules Laforgue (q.v.). To convey his anguish and irony, his cosmic visions and timid complaints, he sought new expressions. Fellow Decadents copied his neologies, the liberties he took with rhythm and rime. He is said to have invented free verse.

When Jean Moréas, in retort to the contemptuous attack upon himself and his colleagues, proposed the name of Symbolist to replace that of Decadent, the latter term soon fell into disuse. For a time there was conflict between poets calling themselves Symbolists and others calling themselves Decadents, but before long their differences were lost in the general Symbolist mêlée. The Decadent period had been one of general revolt and fierce defiance; the new one was in the main more constructive and more exclusively concerned with literature. The differences which soon cropped up among the Symbolists were on purely literary matters.

René Ghil founded a school called "symbolique et harmoniste" to oppose Moréas. Exploiting the implications of Rimbaud's vowel sonnet, Ghil developed his theory of "instrumentation verbale" to reduce the poem to pure music and suggestivity. Several magazines of the times supported Ghil and numerous poets studied with him.

The question of free verse, for some critics, summarizes the entire Symbolist movement. Gustave Kahn (q.v.) declared that it was his invention. He described, defined, and defended it in the *Revue indépendante* in 1888, but his claim for paternity was hotly contested. The entire issue of free verse incited passionate and widespread controversy for years to come. It was the most radical alteration French verse had ever in its entire history undergone. The public was shocked and the poets dazzled by their own daring. But it was the logical step in the direction away from the visual towards the auditory in poetry. Less ambitious than Kahn, Vielé Griffin (q.v.) nevertheless contributed much discussion to the theory of free verse. His own poetry is something between the regular stanza and free verse. The other outstanding vers-librist, Stuart Merrill (q.v.), likewise avoided excessive metrical eccentricities. In 1897 another innovation in poetic forms made a stir: Paul Fort (q.v.) had devised for his ballads a very personal sort of rhythmic prose that accommodated itself easily to the poet's moods. When the critic Brunetière defined Symbolism as simply the "réintégration de l'idée dans la poésie" he was oversimplifying, but less so than those who found Symbolism merely a matter of free verse or music. His statement points out a very fundamental attitude of the poets who followed Mallarmé and accepted the metaphysic of Baudelaire's *Sonnet des Correspondances*. They all sensed the presence of a higher reality behind the world of appearances which they called the world of ideas. Accordingly, all phenomena assumed symbolic value, indications of that higher reality.

Phenomena are linked to the ideas behind them and to each other by the mysterious bonds of analogies which are detected only in the poetic experience. Given this fundamental philosophic assumption and ambition, the matters of poetry-music, of free verse, of suggestion and obscurity take their place as secondary manifestations of the Symbolist thought.

Lying at the heart, therefore, of the Symbolist doctrine is the symbolic image. Each poet sought to translate his aspirations, his thoughts and emotions by its means. Mallarmé had taught that the humblest objects could serve, and many poets attempted to use familiar objects of daily existence. But the pictures tended to conventionalize: fountains and pools of water, moonlight, dawn, twilight, fogs, old parks and dead cities. Antiquity and the Middle Ages were ransacked to build up a common fund of imagery. Greco-Latin lore offered sirens, chimeras, nymphs, satyrs; the recently discovered Middle Ages provided princesses and saints, figures from Celtic and Germanic legends.

Henri Régnier (q.v.) used legendary beasts, all sorts of medieval material, and gardens so dear to Marcel Proust (q.v.). Albert Samain (q.v.) was fond of antique images and great sustained metaphors. Charles Guérin studded his verse with novel images. Francis Jammes (q.v.) had recourse to the quaint charm of bygone years. Verhaeren (q.v.) exploited the modern city.

Symbolist poets were eager to carry their theories into the theater. Wagner's prodigious dream of combining the arts in theatrical presentation had fascinated Mallarmé and continued to inspire his successors. Not that they, any more than Mallarmé, hoped to emulate the German master, but in their modest way they hoped to challenge the monopoly of the Naturalistic play and the *pièce à thèse*. Numerous poets, following Mallarmé's example in *Hérodiade*, composed poems in dramatic form. These could be adapted for the stage. Other poems and prose in dialogue could be recited effectively against scenery and accompanied by music, illustrated by mime or the dance. Lights and even perfumes might prove effective auxiliaries. Audiences, the Symbolists hoped, would become accustomed to this sort of dramatic entertainment just as they went to concerts made up of fragments of operas and symphonies. Between 1890 and 1900 several theaters made such experiments, notably the Théâtre d'art (q.v.) of Paul Fort and the Théâtre de l'Œuvre (q.v.) of Lugné Poe. However interesting these attempts may seem, the only real success that the Symbolist theater could claim is the work of Maurice Maeterlinck (q.v.).

Towards 1900 Symbolism appears to have run its course. It had never presented anything like a completely united front. For fifteen years its history was marked by splits between groups both calling themselves Symbolists and by noisy repudiations such as Jean Moréas' when he founded the École romane. Its greatest exponents—writers like Régnier, Verhaeren, Samain, or Jammes (qq.v.)—moved away from Symbolism in proportion as their native genius declared itself. Now during the last years of the century hostility toward Symbolism could be encountered on every hand. Countless Lilliputian schools hoped to deal it a death blow. Magazines pronounced it already dead and covered it with ridicule. The general public, never vitally concerned, was more interested in the Dreyfus Case than in poetry. Poets themselves turned from their metaphysical speculations to affairs of the day. No champion of any stature would present himself to defend the cause that had been espoused with such pride and confidence.

If Symbolism was dead officially, it has nevertheless lived on in the most significant poets of the twentieth century. Charles Péguy (q.v.) embroidered his medieval themes on Symbolist inspired patterns. Paul Claudel (q.v.) has throughout a long lifetime defended Symbolist theses and illustrated them in the most sumptuous theater of our century. Jean Giraudoux (q.v.), who was hailed as having realized Symbolism in the novel, went on to create a theater that accomplished the Symbolist ambition to discredit Realism (q.v.). The early plays and prose pieces of André Gide (q.v.) were written under Symbolist masters and his style was marked for ever by the Symbolist associations of his youth. His ethic, too, one might say. Proust's aesthetic and metaphysic derive quite clearly from the great nineteenth century poets. Paul Valéry is Mallarmé's successor. Dadaism and Surrealism (qq.v.), the chief poetic movement of the between-wars period, pushed Symbolist theories to their ultimate conclusion. It is not too much to say that the French poetry of the twentieth century comes almost exclusively out of Symbolism, and that from Baudelaire to the poets of the present age we can trace an almost unbroken line.

Nor has Symbolism's influence been restricted to France. Poets from all over the world have received inspiration from Symbolists, and carried into their own countries the ideas and techniques they found in France. Throughout Europe, America, and even in Asia, Symbolism has stimulated great poetic revivals and oriented native geniuses. France, once described by Emerson as that country "where poets were never born," has thereby acquired a prestige and importance that can scarcely be challenged.

A. Van Bever et Léautaud, *Poètes d'aujourd'hui, morceaux choisis,* 1910; T. Visan, *L'Attitude du lyrisme contemporain,* 1911; P. Martino, *Parnasse et Symbolisme,* 1925; J. Charpentier, *Le Symbolisme,* 1927; M. Raymond, *De Baudelaire au surréalisme,* 1933; A. Schmidt, *La Littérature symboliste, 1870-1900,* 1942; Guy Michaud, *Message poétique du symbolisme,* 1947; *La Doctrine symboliste,* 1947; K. Cornell, *The Symbolist Movement,* 1951; M. Jones, *The Background of Modern French Poetry,* 1951.

LAURENT LESAGE

Symphonie pastorale, La (1919): See *Gide.*

Système de la nature, Le (1770): See *Holbach.*

T

Taciturne, Un (1931): See *Martin du Gard.*

Taine, Hippolyte: (1828-1893) Unorthodox views caused this brilliant scholar, born in Vouziers, to fail his *agrégation* in philosophy; eventually, however, his monographs brought him fame. In *La Fontaine et ses Fables* (1853 and 1860)—his doctoral thesis that was finally accepted by the Sorbonne—and in his *Histoire de la littérature anglaise* (1863), he expressed a mechanistic or deterministic theory. According to this doctrine, three factors—*race, milieu, moment* (heredity, environment, and the historical moment)—resulting in a "faculté maitresse," determine the character of a writer and his works. Applying the method of the natural sciences not only to literary criticism but to art—he was for about twenty years (1864-1883) professor at the École des Beaux-Arts —he wrote *La Philosophie d l'Art* (1865). History, too, Taine explained in terms of the same invariable laws. *Les Origines de la France contemporaine* (1875-1894), consisting of three parts—one on the *Ancien Régime,* another on the Revolution, and a third on the *Régime moderne*—was undertaken as the result of his wish to know the causes of the evils brought about by the Franco-Prussian War and the Civil War that followed. Such a rigorously dogmatic and systematic application of his doctrine to all moral and human phenomena made Taine the prime theorist of Naturalism (q.v.); his influence was especially felt in the works of Zola and Brunetière (qq.v.). Other important works by Taine include *Essai sur Tite-Live* (1856), *Essais de Critique et d'Histoire* (1858-1865-1894), and *De l'Intelligence* (1870), a treatise on experimental psychology.

V. Giraud, *Essai sur Taine,* 1901; A. Chevrillon, *Taine; formation de sa pensée,* 1932; M. Leroy, *Taine,* 1933; K. de Schaedryver, *Taine; essai sur l'unité de sa pensée,* 1938.

Tallemant des Réaux, Gédéon: (1619-1692) Author of memoirs, his *Historiettes* (completed *c.* 1657) have much the same importance that Mme. de Sévigné's (q.v.) letters do; containing anecdotes about the celebrated men and women of the time, they are considered among the most interesting sources for gaining a knowledge of seventeenth-century society.

E. Magne, *La joyeuse existence de Tallemant des Réaux,* 1921.

Tartuffe: Called also *L'Imposteur,* this play by Molière (q.v.), though written in 1664 was not performed before the public until five years later because of the attack on religion which the Church saw in it. Tartuffe, a religious impostor and hypocrite, has so succeeded in ingratiating himself with Orgon, a religious fanatic, that the latter has offered him hospitality and the deed to his house, entrusted him with confidential matters, and promised him the hand of his daughter Mariane. Because of Tartuffe, Orgon's family is disunited. Aided by his equally fanatic mother, Mme. Pernelle, Orgon will not heed the warnings of those members of his family who suspect the true character of Tartuffe. It is not long before Orgon turns his son Damis out of the house for expressing his true feelings concerning Tartuffe; despite, moreover, Mariane's love for young Valère, Orgon is intent on forcing her to marry Tartuffe, whom she detests. Only when Orgon is finally persuaded to hide under a table while his wife Elmire, who is aware that she is secretly desired by Tartuffe, cleverly leads the latter to reveal his true nature, does Orgon begin to realize how he has been taken in. The analysis, in this connection, of Tartuffe's sensuality—his basic human weakness—is of psychological interest and explains, in part, why this play is regarded as the first perfect example of a *comédie de caractère* (q.v.). Although disabused, Orgon is now at the mercy of Tartuffe; the latter warns Orgon that the house, thanks to the deed previously given him, is his. Only the direct intervention of the King—an example of the *deus ex machina*—leads to Tartuffe's imprisonment for fraud and saves Orgon and his family from a possibly tragic end.

tearful comedy: See *comédie larmoyante*.

Télémaque (1699): See *Fénelon*.

Templiers, Les (1805): See *Raynouard*.

Temps difficiles, Les (1934): See *Bourdet, Édouard*.

Temps du mépris, Le (1935): See *Malraux*.

tençon: A form of poetry of Provençal origin, popular during the Middle Ages, consisting of a casuistic discussion between two poets upon some point of love.

Tentation de Saint-Antoine, La (1874): See *Flaubert*.

Terre, La (1887): See *Zola*.

Testament, Le (1461): See *Villon, François*.

Têtes de rechange (1926): See *Pellerin, Jean-Victor*.

Thaïs (1890): See *France, Anatole*.

Tharaud, Jérôme (1874-1953) and **Jean** (1877-1952): The work of these two brothers from Limousin who travelled together, collaborated together, became members of the French Academy—Jérôme in 1940, Jean in 1946—was awarded in 1919 the *Grand Prix de Littérature*. Always alert and curious, they drew from their journeys as well as from various events—political or otherwise—their literary inspiration. *Dingley* (1902), their first important novel, draws a portrait of Rudyard Kipling and is based upon the newspaper accounts of the Boer War (1899). *L'Ombre de la Croix* (1917) and *Un royaume de Dieu* (1920) are novels that deal with Jewish life in Central Europe and Hungary, while *Marrakech ou les Seigneurs de l'Atlas* (1920) is a record of their mission to Morocco. Their well-written novels have a journalistic and documentary interest.

J. Bonnerot, *Jérôme et Jean Tharaud; leur œuvre*, 1927.

Théâtre d'Art: See *Paul Fort* and *Lugné-Poe*.

Théâtre de l'Œuvre: See *Lugné-Poe*.

Théâtre du Marais: A rival theater of the Hôtel de Bourgogne (q.v.) founded *c.* 1600, it became firmly established around 1637. In that year, Corneille's *Le Cid* (q.v.) was here produced. Disbanded in 1673, it was consolidated in 1680 with Molière's and the Hôtel de Bourgogne's theaters, forming the Comédie Française (q.v.).

S. W. Holsboer, *Le Théâtre du Marais.* Vol. I: *La période de gloire et de fortune, 1634(1629)-1648,* 1954.

Théâtre du Peuple: This theater "from the people, and for the people" was started at the end of the nineteenth

century by Maurice Pottecher (1867-
). In a small village in the
Vosges, he presented, in his open-
air theater, plays that he had written. These plays, including *Le
Diable marchand de goutte* (1895)
and *Liberté* (1898), represented the
attempt to blend proletarian with
bourgeois elements, the legendary
with the historical. On his aesthetics Pottecher wrote the essay *Le
Théâtre du peuple, renaissance et
destinée du théâtre populaire*
(1899). Other such ventures were
started throughout France, including that of the group *Le Théâtre
de la Coopération des Idées* (1899).
The endeavor was resumed by Romain Rolland (q.v.), who explained
his aesthetics in *Le Théâtre du
peuple, essai d'esthétique d'un
théâtre nouveau* (1903). His aim
was to create an art that is both
artistic and social, that reflects the
political and social struggles of
modern times, and that reveals the
individual conflicts of freedom
versus social discipline and abne-
gation. His plays, which constitute
a kind of history of the French
Revolution, that is, in its broad
psychological spirit, consist of two
cycles, *Tragédies de la Foi* and
Tragédies de la Révolution, which
include *Les Loups* (1898), *Danton*
(1900), *Le Jeu de l'Amour et de la
Mort* (1924), *Robespierre* (1938),
and *Le Quatorze Juillet* (1902)—
accepted enthusiastically in 1936 by
the workers at a moment when they
were engaged in their own struggles. His is the theater that best
personifies the broad human appeal, but despite him, France does
not possess a proletarian stage;
French dramatists have not succeeded in producing such plays.
Théâtre du Vieux-Colombier: See *Copeau, Jacques.*
Théâtre-Français: See *Comédie-Française.*
Théâtre-Libre: This theater (1887-
1894), founded by Antoine (q.v.),
which produced 124 new plays, introduced greater realism in subject
matter and simplicity and naturalness in acting and staging. It represented an attack against the artificial play-making of Scribe, Augier,
and Dumas *fils* (qq.v.). Its traditions
were later continued by Antoine
at his own playhouse, the Théâtre
Antoine (1897-1906).
Théâtre National Populaire: See *Vilar,
Jean.*
Thébaïde, La (1664): See *Racine.*
Théories de la terre (1749): See *Buffon.*
Thérèse Raquin (1867): See *Zola.*
Thibaudet, Albert: (1874-1936) This
professor, a versatile critic, perhaps
the most important between the
two World Wars, shows marked
traces of Bergsonian influence (see
Bergson). His monographs include
studies on Mallarmé, Maurras,
Barrès, Flaubert, Valéry (qq.v.), and
Bergson. His predilection for surveys, comparisons, and classifica-
tions—especially in terms of *generations*—is seen in his unfinished
*Histoire de la littérature française
de 1789 à nos jours* (1936), edited
by Bopp and Paulhan (q.v.). He
displays in his criticism much intelligence and a truculent style of
great originality.
Thibault, Les (1922-1940): See *Martin
du Gard.*
Thibaut IV de Champagne: (1201?-1253)
First the enemy, then the ally of
Blanche of Castille, he sang of her
in delicate verses written in a
courtly vein. One of the finest lyric
poets of his century, he is the author of *Jeux partis* as well as of
several *tençons* (q.v.) and *pastourelles* (q.v.), all of which have a
remarkable elegance of form.
Thierry, Augustin: (1795-1856) Influenced by Chateaubriand (q.v.),
through whom he found his vocation, this historian saw conquest as
the basis of all national history and
racial hostility as the cause of the
Anglo-Norman war. To prove this

theory he wrote *Histoire de la conquête de l'Angleterre par les Normands* (1825). Some years later, in his *Récits des Temps Mérovingiens* (1840), he restored, through an imaginative interpretation based on the study of chronicles and original documents, the early Middle Ages in France. His narrative gift and use of a high literary standard of expression, his emphasis on local color and on the medieval past, stamp him as a Romantic.
F. Valentin, *Augustin Thierry*, 1895.

Thomas d'Angleterre: (?-?) A twelfth-century Anglo-Norman poet, whose version of the legend of *Tristan et Iseut* (q.v.) (*c.* 1170) is the most interesting one.
J. Bédier, *Le Roman de Tristan par Thomas*, 1902-1905.

Thomas l'Imposteur (1929): See *Cocteau*.

Thomas l'obscur (1941): See *Blanchot, Maurice*.

Timocrate (1656): See *Corneille, Thomas*.

Tinayre, Marcelle: (1872-1948) This novelist is preoccupied with religious and social questions, and particularly with feminism. Her liberal theses and her description of passion are somewhat reminiscent of George Sand (q.v.). Included among her novels are: *La Maison du péché* (1902), *La Rebelle* (1905), *La Vie amoureuse de François Barbazanges* (1905), and *Perséphone* (1920).

Tocqueville, Alexis de: (1805-1859) As a result of his visit to America (1831), this historian wrote *La Démocratie en Amérique* (1835-1840), a study of this country's institutions. Although, like many other historians of the Romantic period, he showed in his *L'Ancien Régime et la Révolution* (1856) an interest in the period of the French Revolution, unlike them he saw in it not a clear-cut dividing-line, but a continuation of the *ancien régime*.

In the final analysis, he is more of a philosopher of history than an historian; his basic interest in general principles calls to mind Montesquieu's (q.v.) *Esprit des Lois*. He exercised an influence on the generation of Renan and Taine (qq.v.).
G. d'Eichthal, *A. de Tocqueville*, 1897; J. P. Mayer, *Prophet of the Mass Age*, 1939.

Tombeau sous l'Arc de Triomphe, Le (1924): See *Raynal, Paul*.

Topaze (1928): See *Pagnol, Marcel*.

Tosca, La (1887): See *Sardou*.

Tour du monde en 80 jours, Le (1873): See *Verne, Jules*.

Tour de Nesle, La (1832): See *Dumas* PÈRE.

Tovaritch (1934): See *Deval, Jacques*.

TRAGEDY: The noun "tragedy" may be applied to all action, real or fictitious, in which the character or characters are led, by an inevitable chain of circumstances, to a fated catastrophe, while remaining superior to it. In literature, all works based on this principle are considered tragic. However, French "tragedy" refers more precisely to a dramatic genre written principally in the XVIth, XVIIth and XVIIIth centuries, and may be defined as follows: a tragedy is a play in verse, composed of five acts, in which the entire action develops in a single setting, in which the fictional duration is never longer than twenty-four hours and in which the heroes are great historical or mythical figures presented to the spectator in the last moments of their adventure—that is to say, at the time of the inevitable climax, a climax which ends in a catastrophe, generally the death of one or many of the characters.

If one considers the works themselves, it can also be said that: (1) the heroes, generally borrowed from Greco-Latin antiquity, may also be taken from a biblical source (Racine's *Esther*, 1689, and *Athalie*, 1691) or from the history of distant

339

countries (Racine's *Bajazet*, 1672; Voltaire's *Alzire*, 1736); (2) these heroes are sometimes supported by a chorus (XVIth century tragedies; Racine's *Esther* and *Athalie*); (3) the dénouement, generally catastrophic, may also be a reconciliation or a compromise (especially in Corneille's tragedies: *Cinna*, 1640; *Nicomède*, 1651); (4) there are some examples of tragedies written in prose; (5) free verse appears in the choruses or in certain monologues (for instance, in Corneille's *Polyeucte*, 1643).

Although primarily concerned with form and dramatic impact, the writers also considered the moral significance of their tragedies. Tragedy was meant to provoke not only sentiments of terror and pity, as in Aristotle's definition, but was also meant to inspire horror of vice (that is to say: excesses of passion). In this manner, the idea of *catharsis* (purification), which gave moral significance to Greek tragedy, was revived on a more elementary level.

French tragedy came into being during the XVIth century. It was largely inspired by Greco-Latin tragedy, which was revived along with other ancient genres by the poets and theoreticians of the Renaissance. *Cléopâtre* (1550), by Jodelle (q.v.), is considered the first French tragedy. In the tragedies of Robert Garnier (*Antigone*, 1579; *Les Juives*, 1580; q.v.), the scenes of conflict, foreshadowing the style of Corneille, alternate with long lyric lamentations on the cruelty of fate.

The influence of the Spanish drama directed the new French theater towards the baroque (q.v.) genre of "tragi-comedy." In 1636, Corneille's (q.v.) *Le Cid* provoked severe criticism from the French Academy (q.v.), and the "rules" of tragedy were reaffirmed. Among these numerous and varied rules—the most famous being that of the

"three unities" (place, time and action)—were the rules of dramatic probability, propriety (according to which it was advisable to avoid the effects of blood on stage) and unity of tone and style (according to which tragedy was to be constantly maintained on a high and noble level, leaving no place for an easing of tension or any humor whatever).

It is said that after *Le Cid*, Corneille, of almost Elizabethan temperament, was hindered by these demands. Nevertheless, in spite of an occasional distortion of the rules, his were the most elevated tragedies of French literature. Corneille's tragic art in general consists of the intransigence of his heroes who, having passionately chosen a value (honor, patriotic duty, power, religious faith, *etc.*), rationalize their choice and through many varied and painful conflicts sacrifice other values or passions.

Although Corneille is considered to be "classical," the term is more suitable to the theater of Racine (q.v.). As to form, Racine had no difficulty in respecting the unities, and a maximum of dramatic or poetic effect was produced with an apparent minimum of means. Even more than in Corneille, the action takes place on an inner level. Since it is not the act itself (battle, murder, *etc.*) which counts, but its psychological effect, the act is not shown but recounted (the murder of Pyrrhus by Oreste in *Andromaque*, 1667; the appearance of the sea monster and the death of Hippolyte in *Phèdre*, 1667). As a result, everything is translated into words, and almost every scene is an explanation, an attempt at becoming aware, or merely a rationalization. Moreover, the principle of fatality appears neither as an exterior force nor in the form of the hero's unyielding choice, but as an inner necessity of which the hero is the victim: the fatality of passion. Dominated by passion, Racine's characters, despite their qualms or even their remorse, are irresistibly led to murder or to suicide.

The XVIIIth century writers of tragedy imitated their illustrious predecessors, Racine in particular. Voltaire (q.v.), according to his contemporaries, was the great tragic writer of the century. He sought to modify the genre somewhat, especially by putting "philosophical" remarks into the mouths of his characters, by making his plays into "lessons," in the style of the century, and also by trying—in imitation of the English—to write "national" tragedies (*Adélaïde Du Guesclin*, 1734) or by cautiously imitating certain of Shakespeare's techniques (in *Zaïre*, 1732, and *La Mort de César*, 1735).

Despite the appearance and development of the bourgeois theater and the romantic drama, Racinianlike tragedies continued to be written all during the XVIIIth and XIXth centuries. In the XXth century, the revival of classical mythology in the theater has often caused critics to apply the term "tragedy" to such plays as Cocteau's (q.v.) *La Machine Infernale* (1934) or Giraudoux' (q.v.) *La Guerre de Troie n'aura pas lieu* (1935).

E. Faguet, *Essai sur la tragédie française au XVIᵉ siècle*, 1883; F. H. d'Aubignac, *La Pratique du Théâtre*, 1657, edited by Pierre Martino, 1927; G. Lanson, *Esquisse d'une histoire de la tragédie française*, 1927; J. Racine, *Principes de la Tragédie, en marge de la Poétique d'Aristote*, edited by Eugène Vinaver, 1944; J. Schérer, *La Dramaturgie classique en France*, 1950; R. Lebègue, *La Tragédie française de la Renaissance*, 1954.

JACQUES GUICHARNAUD

tragi-comedy: Flourishing from *c.* 1592 to *c.* 1640, when it was dis-placed by tragedy (q.v.), this type of play contains a happy ending to a series of adventurous events that threaten to become tragic. A kind of melodrama (q.v.), it deals with the loves of heroes from legend or history as well as with those of the contemporary period. The novels of La Calprenède and Madeleine de Scudéry (qq.v.) may be considered its counterpart. Representative of this kind of play are Garnier's (q.v.) *Bradamante* (1592), Théophile de Viau's (q.v.) *Pyrame et Thisbe* (1617), and several of the dramatic pieces by A. Hardy and Corneille (qq.v.).

H. C. Lancaster, *The French Tragi-Comedy (1551-1621)*, 1907.

tragi-comédie pastorale: This type of play, an example of which is Mairet's *Silvanire* (1630)—in whose preface the unities (q.v.) of time, place and action were set forth—contains elements of both the *tragi-comedy* and the *pastorale* (qq.v.). Like the latter dramatic forms, it, too, was displaced (*c.* 1630) by the tragedy (q.v.).

Tragiques, Les (1616): See *Aubigné, Agrippa d'*.

Trahison des clercs, La (1927): See *Benda, Julien*.

Traité de l'amour de Dieu (1616): See *François de Sales*.

Traité de la conformité du français avec le grec (1565): See *Estienne, Henri [II]*.

Traité de l'éducation des filles (1687): See *Fénelon*.

Traité de politique tirée des Écritures (1709): See *Bossuet*.

Traité des études (1726-1731): See *Rollin*.

Traité des passions, Le (1649): See *Descartes*.

Traité des Sensations (1754): See *Condillac*.

Traité du verbe (1886): See *Ghil, René*.

tranche de vie: Coined by Jean Jullien (q.v.), this term designates a play that has neither exposition nor dénouement, one that begins or stops at points inconclusive. Such a play becomes, theoretically, at least, a faithful mirror of life, and presents characters in a scene or scenes in which they act only as they are acted upon by heredity and environment. This type of play was advocated by Jullien and was frequently seen at the Théâtre-Libre (q.v.).

Travailleurs de la mer, Les (1866): See *Hugo.*

Trilby (1822): See *Nodier, Charles.*

Tristan et Iseut: Five different versions of this *roman breton* (q.v.) within a half century—three of them by Frenchmen, Béroul (*c.* 1150; q.v.), Thomas (*c.* 1170; q.v.) and Chrétien de Troyes (1160? now lost; q.v.), and two by Germans, Eilhart von Oberge (1190-1200) and Gottfried von Strassburg (*c.* 1200) —give ample testimony to the importance of this great tragedy of love in literature. The legend of this romance tells of Tristan's expedition to Ireland where he was sent by his uncle, King Mark of Cornwall, in order to bring back with him the blond-haired Iseut, whom the King is to marry. During the voyage back to Cornwall, Tristan and Iseut make the fatal mistake of unintentionally drinking the love-philter intended for the bridal pair, and they become irretrievably enamored of each other. The sequel and dénouement of this guilty passion vary from version to version, but that of Thomas is the most interesting: Tristan leaves Cornwall to go to Brittany where he marries another Iseut—she of the White Hands—partly because her name and beauty remind him of the one he reluctantly had to leave. Later, on one of his adventures, he is wounded by a poisoned weapon and can only be cured by Iseut of Cornwall. A messenger is dispatched to Cornwall with the order to hoist a white sail upon his return if he has succeeded in bringing her back, and a black one if he has failed. When the vessel is in sight and displays a white sail, Iseut of the White Hands who has learned the secret, announces out of jealousy that the sail is black, and Tristan expires. Iseut, his beloved, dies also, at the sight of the dead body of her lover. This version of the story forms the basis of Wagner's opera *Tristan und Isolde* (1865). The *Tristan et Iseut* of Béroul and Thomas (qq.v.) has been preserved only in fragments. Joseph Bédier has based his remarkable version on these fragments.

Le Roman de Tristan et Iseut, traduit et restauré par J. Bédier, 1900.

Tristan L'Hermite (pseud. of François L'Hermite): (1601-1655) In addition to his melancholy love poetry, he wrote his *Le Page disgracié* (1643), essentially an autobiographical novel, and several tragedies—including his successful *Mariane* (1636?)—that are reminiscent of Corneille's (q.v.) Roman tragedies. Quinault (q.v.) was influenced by him.

N. M. Bernadin, *Un Précurseur de Racine, Tristan L'Hermite,* 1895.

Trois Filles de M. Dupont, Les (1897): See *Brieux.*

Trois Mousquetaires, Les (1844): See *Dumas* PÈRE.

Trophées, Les (1893): See *Hérédia.*

troubadour: Poet and singer of Southern France, especially Provence, who used the *langue d'oc* (q.v.) as his idiom, he would go from castle to castle singing the perennial theme of love. His poetry exercised a considerable influence upon northern French poetry during the thirteenth century. About the beginning of the fourteenth century, his role is ended. Among the most celebrated troubadours were Bernard de Ventadour, Jofroy Rudel and Arnaud Daniel. Cf. *trouvère.*

trouvère: Poet of Northern France,

especially Picardy, who used the *langue d'oïl* (q.v.) as his idiom. The preferred themes of the *trouvère* were lyric and satiric. Some of the *trouvères* even composed *miracles* (q.v.). Their role does not extend beyond the fourteenth and fifteenth centuries. Some of the better known *trouvères* were Jean Bodel (q.v.), Conon de Béthune, Blondel de Nesles, Colin Muset (q.v.) and Thibaut IV de Champagne (q.v.). Cf. *troubadour.*

Turcaret (1709): See *Lesage.*

Turgot, Anne-Robert-Jacques, Baron de l'Aulne: (1727-1781) Like Quesnay (q.v.), a leader of the *physiocrat* school, he was also a minister of finance under Louis XVI (1775-1776) and a writer of several articles for the *Encyclopédie* (q.v.). To combat many of the economic abuses that existed during the eighteenth century, this economist, one of the first to found the science of political economy, wrote *Réflexions sur la formation et la distribution des richesses* (1766), a work in which he expounds the doctrine that "all wealth derives from the land."

G. Schelle, *Turgot*, 1909; E. C. Lodge, *Sully, Colbert and Turgot*, 1931.

Tyard (or **Thiard**) **Pontus de:** (1521-1605) One of the group of Lyonese poets, and a disciple of Maurice Scève (q.v.), he influenced Du Bellay (q.v.) by the first book of his *Erreurs amoureuses* (1549) and was accepted by the *Pléiade* (q.v.) as one of them. Later, under the auspices and banner of Ronsard (q.v.), he published the second book (1551) and third book (1553) of his *Erreurs.* In addition to his poetry, he wrote many philosophical dialogues, published in 1587 under the title of *Discours Philosophiques.* In 1578 he became Bishop of Châlon-sur-Saône.

Abel Jeandet, *Pontus de Tyard*, 1860.

Tzara, Tristan: (1896-) This Rumanian-born poet founded in Zurich, in 1916, the *Dada* (see *Dadaism*) movement, of which he was the theoretician. Three years later his group joined the literary vanguard of Paris. After having waged war on language and on logic in his incoherent poems, he evolved toward a less violent lyricism. His major work, *L'Homme approximatif* (1936), is a kind of epic poem; *L'Antitête* expresses his theory of poetic art. More recently, he has been trying to reconcile Surrealism (q.v.) with Marxism.

U

Ubu roi (1896): See *Jarry, Alfred.*

Unanimism: Although this literary theory emerged largely from Duhamel's (q.v.) sympathies, it was systematized and crystallized by the head of the movement, Jules Romains (q.v.), to whom it had first appeared as a revelation. Essentially, this doctrine, the forerunners of which seemingly include Verhaeren (q.v.), Whitman, Zola (q.v.), Durkheim (q.v.), and whose first adherents include René Arcos, Georges Chennevière, Charles Vildrac (q.v.) and Jules Romains himself—most of whom were of the

Abbaye de Créteil (q.v.) group—represents a reaction against the individualism, the dilettantism of art for art's sake, and the loss of the humanitarian tradition of the nineteenth century. Its espousal of collective themes and of group psychology results in a kind of social mysticism. The mission of the poet following its tenets is to confer upon all groups everywhere, as those, for example, in the street, village or theater, a solidarity of soul and sentiment that would transcend all individual emotions. Included in this kind of poetry are the early publications of Jules Romains: *L'Ame des hommes* (1904), *La Vie unanime* (1908), and *Odes et prières* (1913). This doctrine, formulated in his *Manuel de déification* (1910) into a credo and manifesto, was also extended to such tales and novels as *Le Bourg régénéré* (1906) and *Mort de quelqu'un* (1911), his masterpiece, in which the death of an obscure worker unites his neighbors into a new kind of fraternity. Romains shows his preoccupation with Unanimism in his plays and novels, the culminating example of which is his *roman-fleuve* (q.v.), *Les Hommes de bonne volonté*, begun in 1932. Unanimism can be credited with having invented a new lyricism and style in poetry, the drama and the novel.

André Cuisenier, *Jules Romains et l'unanimisme*, 1935.

Unités, les trois: This rule, based on certain passages in Aristotle's *Poetics*, and applied to French Classical tragedy (q.v.), maintains that there should be but one principal action (*unité d'action*); that it should be completed in one day (*unité de temps*); and that it should

take place within a restricted area, often in one room (*unité de lieu*).

Unities: See *Unités, les trois.*

Uranus (1948): See *Aymé, Marcel.*

Urfé, Honoré d': (1567-1625) Inspired by the Spanish *Amadis*, novels of chivalry, and by Spanish and Italian pastoral novels, including Montemayor's *Diana* (1542), Tasso's *Aminta* (1581) and Guarini's *Pastor Fido* (1585), he wrote *L'Astrée* (1607-1627), a pastoral novel, also considered to be the first French novel (q.v.). The last volume of this immensely long novel—consisting of more than 5000 pages and arranged in five volumes, each one of which is divided into twelve books—was published posthumously. Apart from the numerous incidental stories, the main theme, a relatively simple one, concerns the love of the shepherd Céladon for the shepherdess Astrée and the various obstacles that beset them. This love has semi-autobiographical undertones. The events are staged in Merovingian times, on the banks of the Lignon near Le Forez, a town between Lyons and Auvergne where the author was born. Supplying endless subjects of conversation for the Hôtel de Rambouillet (q.v.) and other *salons*, the constant preoccupation with and analysis of love in this work suggest one of the principal themes of seventeenth-century literature; its emphasis on gallantry and Neo-Platonic love, expressed in *précieux* (see *Préciosité*) or refined language, represents a reaction against the vulgarity of the sixteenth century.

O. C. Reure, *La Vie et les œuvres d'H. d'Urfé*, 1910; M. Magendie, *L'Astrée*, 1929.

Ursule Mirouet (1841): See *Balzac.*

V

Vagabonde, La (1910): See *Colette*.

Valéry, Paul: (1871-1945) Probably the greatest of French poets of the twentieth century, he was born in Sète, near Montpellier, of a French father and an Italian mother. When, at the age of 21, he came to Paris, he was introduced, through his friend Pierre Louÿs (q.v.), to Mallarmé (q.v.) and to his circle. After writing verses in the symbolist (see *Symbolism*) tradition for *avant-garde* magazines—verses which he was to publish later under the title of *Album de vers anciens* (1920)—he turned from poetry to prose. In *Soirée avec M. Teste* (1896)—a kind of narcissistic portrait—and *Introduction à la Méthode de Léonard de Vinci* (1895), in which the combination of artist, scholar, engineer and architect represented by the genius he studied appealed to his intellectual ideal, Valéry sought principles of knowledge and reflection; these works are meditations on the means and ends of all intellectual activity. Hoping thereby to penetrate into Being, whose fundamental activity is disguised by the personality, he ceased writing for some twenty years to devote himself to mathematics and philosophy and to the problems of the dance and architecture, in order to see the relationships that help explain the mind at work. His silence was broken when he published *La Jeune Parque* (1917), a long and difficult poem written as an "exercise" or as an application of his intellectual "method," which

was to have been his *adieu* to poetry. Other publications followed, including *Charmes* (1922)—which gained him admittance to the French Academy—and one of his poetic masterpieces, *Le Cimetière marin* (1920). The techniques used in these poems—those of ellipses, mixed suggestions, and musical combinations—are very much like those of Mallarmé; unlike the latter, however, whose main concern is with pure beauty, Valéry unfolds the *genesis* of meditations on man's consciousness, on his anguish and despair, caused by his conflict between intelligence and sensibility. Moreover, Valéry continues the Classical tradition of imposing upon himself the rigid rules of versification exemplified by Malherbe and Boileau (qq.v.). In a word, for Valéry poetry is an intellectual feast in which all the oranaments of language and resources of music are made use of.

After his publication of the previously cited *Charmes*, Valéry returned to the writing of prose, as seen in his two Platonic dialogues, *L'Ame et la Danse* (1923)—in which Socrates assigns to art the function of antidote to the boredom of living—and *Eupalinos* (1923), a long discussion on the genius of the artist in which admiration is shown for the artist's ability to assemble, organize and create his masterpiece, as well as, more particularly, for the god-like quality of intelligence. In his five volumes of essays entitled *Variétés* (from 1924 to 1944),

Valéry demonstrates his ability as a literary critic and his concern with the problems of his time. *Mon Faust* (1946) is a posthumous and incomplete work.

Albert Thibaudet, *Paul Valéry*, 1923; Aimé Laffont, *Paul Valéry, l'homme et l'œuvre*, 1943; J. Hytier, *La poétique de Valéry*, 1953; F. Scarfe, *The art of Paul Valéry*, 1954; N. Suckling, *Paul Valéry and the Civilized Mind*, 1954. **Vallée heureuse, La** (1946): See *Roy, Jules.*

VAUDEVILLE: The word "vaudeville" originally described a form of satiric song of the 15th century, possibly created in the Val de Vire in Normandy. Another theory suggests that it comes from the expression "voix de ville," or street calls sung in the cities.

Subsequently, the term "pièces en vaudevilles," or vaudeville plays, was applied to plays which included songs, with original lyrics, related to the plot, and music borrowed from popular melodies. It was thus a form of light, satiric and popular opera, but a form which might also designate more literary plays such as Beaumarchais' (q.v.) *Le Mariage de Figaro* (1784). However, it was mainly in the second half of the 19th century that vaudeville became a truly independent genre— a comedy, with or without songs, in which the light and complicated intrigue undoubtedly evolved from the former "pièces en vaudevilles," but principally characterized by its mechanical aspect, innumerable surprises, and consistent gaiety.

Most of the "vaudevilles" of Labiche (*Un chapeau de paille d' Italie*, 1851; *Le Voyage de Monsieur Perrichon*, 1860; q.v.) and his collaborators seem to use the techniques of the "pièce bien faite" (q.v.) as applied to the farce. The end of the 19th and beginning of the 20th century witnessed the de-

velopment of a kind of vaudeville characterized primarily by its frequent use of risqué and salacious situations (adultery, unfaithfulness, illegitimate love). The master of this genre was Georges Feydeau (1862-1921; q.v.), whose major plays, often immoral but constructed with mathematical precision (*Le Dindon*, 1896; *Occupe-toi d'Amélie*, 1908), were revived during the 1940's and 1950's at the Comédie-Française (q.v.) and in the principal theaters of Paris.

Now, in the mid-20th century, vaudeville is played each year on the stages of the Boulevard. The plays of this genre are often pure, somewhat vulgar bedroom farces. Yet, André Roussin (*La Petite Hutte*, 1948; *Lorsque l'Enfant paraît*, 1951; *Bobosse*, 1950), while remaining faithful to the genre, has succeeded in enriching it with either poetry or tenderness and has given consistency to the traditionally sketchy characters, sometimes using Pirandello-like effects.

Several Paris theaters specialize in the production of vaudeville, in particular the Théâtre du Palais Royal, founded in 1821, and still considered the temple of vaudeville.

Auguste Font, *Favart: L'Opéra comique et la comédie vaudeville aux 17ᵉ et 18ᵉ siècles*, 1894; Jules Lemaître, *Impressions de théâtre*, 1888-1898.

JACQUES GUICHARNAUD

Vaugelas, Claude Favre: (1595-1650) A member of the *Académie Française* (q.v.) since its inception, he assumed in 1638 the editorship of its dictionary for a period of ten years. In 1647 he published his *Remarques sur la langue française*, in which, as arbiter of correct French, he condemned popular and provincial terms, and, in contrast to Malherbe (q.v.), approved, as a standard of good usage, the language (q.v.) used at the court, the *salons* of Paris, and by the best writers of his period.

Vauquelin de la Fresnaye, Jean: (1536-1608) Finding inspiration in Horace's *Satires*, this poet and theorist, still maintaining the principles of Ronsard (q.v.), wrote an interesting *Art poétique* (1605), in which he also exposed some new ideas relating to the introduction of Christianity in literature. He also wrote sonnets, idylls and epigrams.

Lemercier, *Étude littéraire et morale sur les poésies de Jean Vauquelin de la Fresnaye*, 1889.

Vauvenargues, Luc de Clapiers, Marquis de: (1715-1747) Born in Aix-en-Provence, this moralist turned to literature after suffering disappointment, as a result of illness, in his military career. Despite his physical ailments and his failure to realize his ambitions, in his *Introduction à la connaissance de l'esprit humain, suivie de réflexions et maximes* (1747), consisting of maxims, *portraits*, reflections on writers, and sundry thoughts, he reveals, unlike La Rochefoucauld (q.v.), a generally optimistic view of life and faith in the goodness of human nature. His doctrine, expressed in a clear and serious style, links him to the eighteenth-century ideal (cf. *Enlightenment, Age of*); but he presages Rousseau (q.v.) by the importance he ascribes to emotion and instinct, and Stendhal (q.v.) by his cult of action and energy.

G. Lanson, *Le Marquis de Vauvenargues*, 1930; F. Vial, *Une philosophie et une morale du sentiment, Vauvenargues*, 1938.

Venceslas (1647): See *Rotrou*.

Ventres dorés, Les (1905): See *Fabre, Emile*.

Vercors (pseud. of **Jean Bruller**): (1902-) A former printer and illustrator, he founded, during the German occupation, the clandestine *Les Éditions de Minuit* press, which published his famous *Silence de la mer* (1942), a tale whose humanitarian ideal was decidedly anti-Hitlerian. Other writings of his, collections of essays or short stories, include *Le Sable du temps* (1945) and *Les Yeux et la Lumière* (1948).

Verhaeren, Émile: (1855-1916) The work of this writer, the greatest poet of Belgium and one of the greatest French poets of his time, is varied and full. In his early collection, *Les Flamandes* (1883), written in the conventional alexandrine (q.v.), he describes, much like the Parnassians (q.v.), scenes or landscapes of his native Flemish province. *Les Moines* (1886) represents his mystic penchant. After a personal crisis of despair and gloom—during which time his collections, *Les Soirs* (1887) and *Les Flambeaux noirs* (1890) appeared, written in freer verse and varying rhythms—he discovered, thanks to a happy marriage, a new faith and hope, especially for a different social order. It is then that the real, original Verhaeren—who has often been compared to Walt Whitman—reveals himself, exalting, unlike his contemporary Symbolists (see *Symbolism*), the victory of modern man, or civilization, over rustic life.

His *Campagnes hallucinées* (1893) and *Villes tentaculaires* (1895) depict, on the one hand, the sad spectacle of the country abandoned, and on the other, the monstrous but magnificent progress of civilization spread by the city. Victory and faith in a life of energy and action—sung in a free verse of dynamic and violent rhythm—are seen in his *Forces tumultueuses* (1902) as well as in other collections. Apologist of industrial life, he is inspired by the ever-onward march of humanity, by its progress and by its search for a better destiny. Verhaeren, who died in Rouen as a result of a railway accident, is the national poet of his country, but is representative of two civilizations, Flemish and French, of two worlds, agricultural and industrial, realistic and mystical. A. Mockel, *Émile Verhaeren*, 1923; P. M. Jones, *Émile Verhaeren*, 1957.

verisimilitude: See *vraisemblance*.

Verlaine, Paul: (1844-1896) Despite the early salutary influences of a good family background and fine upbringing, followed by a fortunate marriage, he succumbed to his weakness for drink and led an existence which, in its errant and criminal phases, calls to mind the life of François Villon (q.v.). In 1871 the evil genius of the young Rimbaud (q.v.), whose acquaintance he had recently made, cast its spell on the weak-willed and melancholy character of Verlaine. Soon thereafter Verlaine abandoned his wife and lived with Rimbaud, at different intervals, in England and Belgium. After a quarrel one day he shot Rimbaud; the next sixteen months of his stay in Belgium were spent in prison, where, given to serious meditation, he was converted to Catholicism. However, once released and back in Paris, he reverted to a vagabond existence until his death.

The poetry of Verlaine, evolving from Parnassian (q.v.) tendencies to Symbolism (q.v.), of which he is one of the most important forerunners, is in large part a confession of his desires, faults and repentance, and reflects the various periods of his life. Although he contributed to *Le Parnasse contemporain* (1866) and identified himself thereby with the Parnassian School, the publication the same year of his *Poèmes saturniens* already indicated the melancholy, vague and musical characteristics of his poetry found in such later volumes as the Watteau-inspired *Les Fêtes galantes* (1869) and *La Bonne Chanson* (1870), which he composed out of love for

his fiancée. *Romances sans paroles* (1874), as the title suggests, shows the poet's concern with the musical value and the power of suggestion of the words in the poems. His "Art poétique" (written in 1874, but published ten years later in *Jadis et Naguère*), expresses his poetic credo as well as his opposition to the Parnassian ideal. Removing himself from the plastic objectivity of the latter, he stressed, after music, a poetry that would include the odd-number syllable line, new rhymes, the union of the vague with the precise, the nuance, and that would evoke or suggest, but not describe, sensations, sentiments and dreams. E. Delahaye, *Verlaine*, 1919; P. Martino, *Verlaine*, 1924.

Verne, Jules: (1828-1905) Under the influence of the scientific spirit of the Sixties, his novels, including *Voyage au centre de la terre* (1864), *Vingt mille lieues sous les mers* (1869), and *Le tour du monde en 80 jours* (1873), have, in many ways, proven strangely accurate in their prophecy. They are still popular with young people. Allotte de la Fuye, *Jules Verne*, 1928; B. Frank, *Jules Verne et ses voyages*, 1941.

Verneuil, Louis: (1893-1952) Actor and playwright, many of whose plays were staged on Broadway, he excelled in the comical intrigue, in caricature, and in the depiction of contemporary manners. His plays include *La Charrette anglaise* (1916), a *comédie-vaudeville* written in collaboration with Georges Berr, *Pile ou Face* (1924), *Le Mariage de maman* (1925), and *La Banque Némo* (1931), a caricature of a former newsboy who becomes a financial Titan. In 1950, after a stay of eleven years in the United States, he produced in New York the highly successful *Affairs of State*, a play, however, he never saw fit to produce in Paris. He died, in Paris, a suicide.

Verre d'eau, Le (1842): See *Scribe.*

verset: A kind of free verse, it has its origins in some of the poems by Rimbaud (q.v.), and its main exponent is Paul Claudel (q.v.). Not unlike a Biblical verse, it is more like poetic prose modelled on the spoken word, whose rhythm is determined by the feelings or the emotions expressed.

vers libre: "Invented" by Gustave Kahn and Jules Laforgue (qq.v.) and adopted by such symbolist poets (see *Symbolism*) as Vielé-Griffin, Stuart Merrill, and Henri de Regnier (qq.v.), this form of poetry tends to replace the conventional rules of caesura, hiatus, number of syllables, rhythm, and alternation of rhymes by a psychological rhythm, one that expresses most adequately the personal feelings of each poet. In other words, this form of verse is governed by the emotional stress of the phrase, and consequently, by the impulse of the poet's personal rhythm. Written for the ear, and not the eye, it allowed for assonance (q.v.), alliteration, and rhyme—or lack of it—in any combination. The *vers libre* of La Fontaine (q.v.), it should be noted, although emancipated from many of the classical prescriptions, nevertheless had based itself on a mathematical syllabic system.

E. Dujardin, *Les Premiers poètes du vers libre,* 1922.

Vert-Vert (1734): See *Gresset.*

Viau, Théophile de: (1596-1626) For his irreverence and free-thinking utterances, this poet, born to Huguenot parents, suffered imprisonment, banishment, and almost death. An adversary, like Régnier, of Malherbe (qq.v.), to whose technique, however, he rendered homage in his *Élégie à une dame,* he refused to submit, because of his belief in poetic inspiration, to literary rules or doctrine. Many poems, like *Le Matin* and *La Solitude,* show a feeling for nature and charming lyric qualities. In addition to *Pyrame et Thisbé* (1617), a *tragi-comedy* (q.v.), he wrote odes, elegies and satires. His reputation as a poet was rehabilitated in the nineteenth century by the romantics.

C. Garrison, *Théophile et Paul de Viau, étude historique et littéraire,* 1899; A. Adam, *Théophile de Viau et la libre pensée française en 1620,* 1936.

Vie, Une (1883): See *Maupassant.*

Vie de Henri Brulard (1890): See *Stendhal.*

Vie de Jésus (1863): See *Renan.*

Vie de Marianne, La: Written by Marivaux (1731-1741; q.v.), this book, also known as *Les Aventures de la Comtesse de* . . . , is, if not the first, certainly one of the great psychological novels in French literature. Not only does it analyze fully the character of this young girl, at first desperate to secure a place in society; more important, it concentrates on the motives, emotions and caprices of Marianne as she tries to keep the love of Valville. At the same time, it reflects the manners of French contemporary society as Marianne, ruthless in her self-analysis, recounts autobiographically the adventures and vicissitudes in her life. Left an orphan in Paris, Marianne, exposed to the dangers of society, undergoes trying and humiliating experiences. Mme. Dutour the seamstress, in whose employ she finds herself, is good to her; the advances made to her by the hypocritical Climal, however, compromise her in the eyes of Valville, his nephew, whom she loves. Seeking refuge in a church, she meets Mme. de Miran, Valville's mother. The latter, won over to her, is sympathetic and encourages her love for her son, whom Marianne is willing to give up, however, because of the objections raised as a result of social inequalities. The twelfth part of this incomplete novel, written by Mme. Riccobini, unites Marianne in wedlock with Valville.

Vie de Saint Alexis: (c. 1050) This anonymous poem, written before the *Chanson de Roland* (q.v.), consists of 625 assonanced lines (see *assonance*) divided into 125 stanzas of 5 lines each. It relates the life of this Saint who, on the day of his marriage—which he holds in detestation—flees to Syria where he leads a miserable existence. After several years, he returns to his paternal home, where he is not recognized and where he lives for seventeen years. Only after his death is he recognized by his parents and venerated as a saint.

Vie de Saint Léger: One of the oldest monuments of the French language (c. 10th century), this anonymous poem, consisting of 240 assonanced (see *assonance*) lines which are divided into 40 stanzas of 6 lines each, relates the struggle and martyrdom of this Bishop.

Vie de Saint Louis (1309): See *Joinville*.

Vies des dames illustres: See *Brantôme*.

Vies des hommes illustres de Plutarque (1559): See *Amyot, Jacques*.

Vie des martyrs (1917): See *Duhamel*.

Vie et aventures de Salavin (1920-1932): See *Duhamel*.

Viélé-Griffin, Francis (1863-1937) Born in Norfolk, Virginia, this symbolist poet (see *Symbolism*) transplanted himself to France where he remained the rest of his life. His love in particular for Touraine, the garden of France, and for its charms of country life on the banks of the Loire, can be seen in his first collection, *Cueille d'avril* (1886). After the publication of *Joies* (1888)—the title typifies his optimistic belief in the goodness of nature and man, an attitude maintained in *Poèmes et poésies* (1886-1893)—he adopted the *vers libre* (q.v.), of which he became the indisputable master. In addition to this verse, which expresses his whole personality, he uses the technique of popular song —one common to the Symbolist poets—in *Clarté de vie* (1897).

Vie secrète, La (1908): See *Estaunié, Edouard*.

Vigny, Alfred de: (1797-1863) The life of this poet, dramatist and novelist, born in Loches, is marked by disillusionment. Vigny was born too late to earn glory in the Napoleonic campaigns and knew only the austere and monotonous army life of peacetime for almost fourteen years, finally resigning in 1827 with a captain's commission. The feeling of his uselessness and of the futility of life —a kind of *mal du siècle* (q.v.) that afflicted the Romanticists—was not alleviated by a marriage that required nursing an invalid wife, nor by his *liaison* with the actress Marie Dorval, which ended disastrously. Even becoming a member of the *Académie Française* (q.v.) in 1845 gave him little joy, for he was received most unenthusiastically. His Romanticism, however, unlike that of Lamartine (q.v.), for example, is not, despite his personal sufferings, lyrical or confidential. Before 1830, he published: *Cinq Mars* (1826), the first historical novel in France, which deals with a conspiracy against Richelieu and which, drawing a favorable portrait of nobility humiliated by absolute monarchy, mirrors his own personal attachment to the prerogatives of his own caste; the first edition of *Poèmes Antiques et Modernes* (1826), which includes the poem *Moïse*—a fine example of the symbolical transmutation that is the essential characteristic of Vigny's poetry—and which is a symbolical portrait of the genius or superior person who of necessity remains alone and unhappy; and adaptations of several of Shakespeare's plays, including *Roméo et Juliette* (1827), *Othello* (1829)—produced at the Comédie-Française (q.v.)—and *Le Marchand de Venise* (1830).

After 1830, Vigny's philosophical thinking becomes more clearly delineated. Moreover, whether it be in the novel, drama, or poetry, he expresses his ideas in symbolical form. *Stello* (1832), relating the unfortunate fate of three different poets, Gilbert, Chatterton and André Chénier, shows symbolically the lack of recognition that society bestows upon genius, while *Servitude et grandeur militaires* (1835), consisting of three stories that are written in a restrained and sober style, reveals the self-abnegation, the sense of honor, and the blind obedience to duty that are typical of the soldier. Genius misunderstood is once again the symbolical theme in *Chatterton* (1835), a play in prose which, in its psychological action, minimum plot, and observance of the three unities (q.v.), resembles more a classical tragedy than a romantic *drame* (q.v.). The success of this play, however, is due more to the tone of sincerity found in the depiction of the love between young Chatterton, who in the end commits suicide, and Kitty Bell, than to its philosophy. The pessimism of Vigny's poetry, the work of a profound thinker, can neither be entirely explained by the incidents in his personal life nor viewed as his entire philosophy. A complete philosophical system that concludes, not on a note of pessimism, but with a kind of optimism, can be disengaged from the poems making up the two meager collections of the definitive edition of *Poèmes antiques et modernes* (1837) and of the posthumous *Les Destinées* (1846). Although Vigny, unlike Lamartine (q.v.), finds no solace in Nature (see his "Maison du Berger"), nor, for that matter, in Woman (see his "Colère de Sam-

son") or in God (see his "Mont des Oliviers"), he adopts a stoic attitude, in his "La mort du Loup," that consists in suffering without complaining. Moreover, suffering, common to Man, brings all men together in love, pity, and sacrifice [see his "Eloa" (1824), a poem, incidentally, that anticipates Lamartine's (q.v.) *La Chute d'un ange*, Hugo's (q.v.) *Fin de Satan*, and, to a certain degree, Baudelaire's (q.v.) *Les Fleurs du Mal*]. In the end, there is a ray of hope and faith in the future and in the ultimate triumph of the Idea (see "La Bouteille à la mer"). The furtherance of these sentiments becomes, in the final analysis, the function of the poet as he leaves his message to a hostile world.

M. Citoleux, *Alfred de Vigny*, 1924; F. Baldensperger, *Alfred de Vigny*, 1929; B. de la Salle, *Alfred de Vigny*, 1939; E. Lauvrière, *Alfred de Vigny*, 1946.

Vilar, Jean: (1912-   ) This young Parisian *metteur-en-scène* has produced not only T. S. Eliot's *Murder in the Cathedral*, but also several spectacles, given every summer, at the *Palais des Papes* in Avignon. His staging, much like the theater of antiquity, without footlights or curtain, finds, in the vast scenic spaces, direct contact with the crowd. His theatrical and poetic frescoes are stagings of Shakespeare, Von Kleist, Corneille (q.v.), and Musset (q.v.). He has also given an opportunity to young authors, including Maurice Clavel.

Just a few years ago, the French government created a national popular theater under the direction of Vilar. The purpose of the Théâtre National Populaire, which produces its dramatic pieces at the Palais de Chaillot in Paris, is to renew the vigor of the theater in an atmosphere of communion between the actors and the crowd, in the hope that a wide public would be reached. Its repertoire includes classical and contemporary plays, both French and foreign.

Vildrac, Charles (pseud. of **Charles Messager):** (1882-   ) This Parisian-born writer, brother-in-law of Duhamel (q.v.), began by writing poetry that shows the influence of Whitman in form and ideas. His first volume of verse, *Images et mirages* (1908), was printed by the press of the Abbaye de Créteil (q.v.). But he soon transferred his interest to the stage. In *Le Paquebot Tenacity* (1920), a play practically without plot, he portrays two friends whose characters become sharply delineated in a love situation resulting from their forced stay at an inn when their boat remains in port to be repaired. Although both friends fall in love with the girl at the inn, the realist of the two goes away to settle down with her, while the dreamer, seeking freedom, is left in the end to go alone. Human character responding to love is also depicted in other plays, including *Michel Auclair* (1922), where an idealist becomes the guardian angel of the girl he loves when she marries someone else. Friendship, a favorite theme with Vildrac, as already evidenced in the first mentioned play, is again studied in *La Brouille* (1930), where opposing attitudes, one realistic, one idealistic, towards business relations, almost cause a permanent rift. Other important plays include *Madame Béliard* (1925) and *Le Pèlerin* (1926). In all his plays, Vildrac shows a predilection for psychological character portrayal; he brings to the boards humble sailors and workmen, whose daily lives, in moments of intimate crisis, reveal the highest kind of nobility, in their hidden, poetic souls.

Villehardouin, Geoffroy de: (1165?-1213?) Knight of Champagne, he played an important part in the Fourth Crusade (1202-1204), having accompanied the Venetians to Constantinople, which was to be captured by them. This campaign, which also led to the founding of the so-called Latin Kingdom, serves as the subject of his historical memoirs, *La Conquête de Constantinople* (*c.* 1205-1213), the earliest example of important French prose writing. Its tone is aristocratic, the whole work revealing restraint in statement and nobility of purpose, in spite of which it is probably an attempted justification of the deflection of the Crusade.

A. Debidour, *Les chroniqueurs,* I, 1888; E. Faral, *Villehardouin, La Conquête de Constantinople éditée et traduite,* 1938-39.

Villemain: (1790-1870) The founder of historical and comparative criticism, he was convinced, as was Madame de Staël (q.v.), that a close relationship exists between literature and society. He therefore studied the influence exercised by environment on the writer and that of the writer on his contemporaries. He also sought to establish the relationship between other literatures and French literature. His method can be seen in such works as *Tableau de la Littérature au Moyen Age* and *Tableau de la Littérature au XVIII*ᵉ *siècle* (1828-1829). His method paved the way for Sainte-Beuve (q.v.).

Villiers de l'Isle-Adam, Jean Marie Mathias Philippe Auguste, comte de: (1838-1889) Descendant of an old noble family, this poet, novelist, and dramatist, a friend of Baudelaire (q.v.), Mallarmé (q.v.), and Richard Wagner, found refuge from the political cares of his century in his glorious and chivalric heritage, in romantic reflections, and in self-contemplation. His early writings consist of *Premières poésies* (1859), a collection of verses, *Isis* (1862), a philosophical novel of love in which his antagonism to the scientific materialism of his age is already made manifest, and two dramas of love—*Elën* (1865) and *Morgane* (1866)—that are crowned by death. After his first two novelettes, *Claire Lenoir* (1867) and *l'Intersigne* (1868), he collected, under the title of *Contes cruels* (1883), tales of terror, mystery, and fantasy, previously published in newspapers and magazines, which reveal symbolically a genuine antipathy to the values of his day —money, democracy, equality, and science. This general hatred is further personified in *Tribulat Bonhomet* (1887), that *pseudo-savant* who is the archetype of his century, and in *Ève future* (1886), a novel which adumbrates, in a humorous as well as idealistic manner, a machine age into which love and the spirit cannot enter. As Villiers de l'Isle-Adam, who exercised an important influence on Symbolistic (see *Symbolism*) writers, sought refuge in occultism and supernatural visions, so do his hero and heroine in *Axël* (1890) —a posthumous poetic drama—relinquish wealth, earthly treasures, and even love, for an Eternity which they could only find in death.

Max Daireaux, *Villiers de l'Isle-Adam; l'homme et l'œuvre*, 1936.

Villon, François: (1431-1463?) The real name of this poet was either François des Loges or François de Montcorbier; the name by which he is known today he adopted from Guillaume de Villon, his benefactor. This University of Paris scholar, with the degrees of Bachelor and Master of Arts (1452), led an erratic life, becoming embroiled, together with other ruffians, in all sorts of criminal acts, including theft and murder. Imprisoned several times, he would also have been hanged had it not been for the amnesties granted him by Louis XI. His poetry, not voluminous, includes *Le Petit Testament* (1456), also known as *Les Lais* or *Legs* (not to be confused with the narrative *lais* of the

romans bretons, q.v.), consisting of 40 stanzas, in which he leaves to his friends—in a spirit of buffoonery or mockery—such diverse things as his renown and heart, and *Le Testament* (1461), consisting of 173 stanzas and of about 200 *ballades* (q.v.) and *rondeaux* (q.v.). In the latter collection, the principal themes are concerned with his imprisonment, his dissipated youth, fleeting time and death, by which he was constantly haunted. Its interest lies in the personal and moral reflections of the poet, which are touching, sensitive and sincere in their lyrically human qualities. The human foibles, of which he repents but which he is ready to repeat, are expressed with naturalness and force, explaining in part Villon's originality and reputation as the greatest French poet of the Middle Ages. Included among the better known poems of Villon are his *Ballade des dames du temps jadis* (q.v.), *Ballade des pendus* and his *Ballade pour prier Notre-Dame*, which also reflects his religious sentiments and makes of him a true representative of his period.

F. Villon, *Œuvres complètes,* ed. Aug. Longnon, 1911; P. Champion, *F. Villon, sa vie et son temps,* 1914; *L'Œuvre de Fr. Villon, édition en vieux français et version en français moderne,* par Raoul Mortier, 1937.

Vingt mille lieues sous les mers (1869): See *Verne, Jules.*

Vipère au poing (1947): See *Bazin, Hervé.*

virelai (or **vireli**): A type of lyric poem —like the *rondeau* (q.v.)—consisting of three stanzas with a popular dance refrain. The *virelais* are found in number from the 12th through the 15th centuries.

Visionnaires, Les (1637): See *Desmarets de Saint-Sorlin.*

Voiture, Vincent: (1598-1648) Thanks to his wit and intelligence he occupied for almost twenty years an important rôle at the *Hôtel de*

Rambouillet (q.v.) gatherings. Wishing to please and to entertain, he always sought to express himself in polite and elegant language. His poetry, consisting of *rondeaux, sonnets* and *chansons* (qq.v.), Renaissance and pre-Renaissance genres that he revived, is light and witty. In other genres, too—*stances, madrigaux* and *épigrammes*—he tries to please his elegant society with gallant, if not always sincere, compliments. Known chiefly for his Letters, which he wrote during his travels to his friends in Paris, he displays therein the same badinage that characterizes his verses. Much of his *Correspondence* reflects the *précieux* (see *Préciosité*) spirit, with its affectation. As a stylistic model, his prose represents a self-conscious attitude towards style, a preoccupation with correctness and urbanity that contributed to the development of the French language (q.v.) during the seventeenth century.

E. Magne, *Voiture et l'Hôtel de Rambouillet*, 1929-30.

Voix intérieures, Les (1837): See *Hugo.*

Voltaire (pseud. of **François-Marie Arouet**): (1694-1778) The preëminent literary figure of the eighteenth century, he dominated, as perhaps no single writer did, the intellectual life of his time. His prolific literary output, universal in scope and consisting of almost every conceivable genre, influenced the social institutions of his country. If, moreover, he gained fame during his lifetime as a poet and dramatist, though failing to be recognized as France's Shakespeare, to posterity he is known essentially as a prose writer; in the *conte* (q.v.) and in his historical writings, not to mention his correspondence, he exposes clearly and simply the most complicated questions involving man's destiny and his political, social and religious life. The ideals of tolerance, liberty and progress, which he relentlessly pursued, derive their inspiration, in part at least, from his turbulent career, marked by successes, quarrels and persecutions. His qualities of intelligence, wit and cynicism—qualities which not only contributed to his reputation as a writer, but also won him the friendship of illustrious personalities and thinkers as well as entry into the courts of Europe—no doubt contributed to most of his unhappy experiences as well.

Born in Paris, the son of a prosperous notary, he studied at the Jesuit *Collège Louis-le-Grand*. His brilliance and independence of mind, which impressed his teachers and soon won him the admiration of the *Société du Temple*, a group of free-thinkers that he frequented, demanded an outlet. Although this need was soon to be satisfied, as he launched his literary career, satiric verses attributed to him and aimed at the Regent resulted in a short period of imprisonment (1717) at the Bastille. The following year he gained success as a dramatist for his tragedy *Œdipe* (1718), which he conceived while in prison. Some years later, however, he was once again imprisoned (1725), after he had challenged the Duc de Rohan, following a quarrel, to a duel. Bitter, though wiser as a result of this experience, which taught him the effects of injustice and of social inequality, he was happy to accept the condition imposed upon him for his liberation from prison. Exiled to England, where he was to spend the next three years (1726-1729), he could not help being impressed by its intellectual climate of political and religious freedom, especially as it contrasted with conditions in France. Not only did liberty of thought and expression thrive in this relatively democratic government, but science, too, had progressed. In this atmosphere Voltaire, after having been exposed to the scientific theories of Newton and

Locke and to the philosophical notions of Swift, Pope, Bolingbroke and Walpole, composed his *Lettres philosophiques* (also known as *Lettres Anglaises*), in which he embodies his discoveries of English civilization; he found it most fitting, at the same time, to publish the epic poem *La Henriade* (1728)—previously known under the title of *La Ligue* (1723)—in which he portrays Henri IV as a tolerant king and as an adversary of fanaticism. Back in France, Voltaire continued to write poetry and tragedies, among them *Brutus* (1730) and *Zaïre* (1732)—his masterpiece—inspired by Shakespeare's *Othello*. When, however, his *Lettres philosophiques* (1734; q.v.) appeared, reflecting most unfavorably upon France, he was forced to leave Paris. Finding refuge in Cirey, in eastern France, at the home of Mme. du Châtelet, where he was to chiefly spend the next fifteen years, he devoted himself mostly to writing history, an earlier interest he now resumed with greater enthusiasm. In *Histoire de Charles XII* (1731), *Siècle de Louis XIV* (1751) and *Essai sur les mœurs* (1756)—his three principal historical works—he gives evidence of much careful, scientific documentation, of an approach that overlooks no phase of human life and that no longer views history as only political or military. As these works, moreover—models of conciseness and clarity, and examples, too, of his narrative ability—reflect man's progress, Voltaire, unlike Bossuet (q.v.), does not see the hand of Providence; rather he gives further testimony to the belief that progress itself, aided by reason, and revealing the lesson of tolerance and of human brotherhood, has been impeded by superstition and fanaticism.

In his war against intolerance, Voltaire discovered the great resources of the *conte*, in which he revealed his true genius. Within the framework of the short, fantastic tale, composed in a simple and clear language, he made use of his mordant wit and irony, of humor and ridicule, in order to open the minds of those whose ideas were clouded by prejudice and falsehood. Thus, *Zadig* (1747) is at once a social and religious satire; *Micromegas* (1752) offers the lesson of relativity; and *Candide* (1759; q.v.), his most important and best-known short philosophical novel, is a reply, in the catastrophes that befall its protagonist, to Leibnitz's philosophy of optimism. All these philosophical tales suggest a kind of wisdom: if man can but eliminate the evils of intolerance, he will attain happiness. The same spirit, it should be added, animates the *Dictionnaire philosophique* (1764). Written, like most of the *contes* and the historical works, after his visit to Prussia at the invitation of Frederick the Great, it is a work of maturity; consisting of encyclopedic articles, it is marked by skepticism, rationalization and a critical method of derogatory insinuation, aiming to teach the relativity of truth.

A *philosophe* (q.v.) without a systematized philosophy, Voltaire did not believe in remaining above the battle. Placing his talents at the service of humanity, he defended or rehabilitated such victims of intolerance or injustice as Calas, Sirven and Lally-Tolendal. Living like a "patriarch" at Ferney, on French territory near Geneva, Voltaire was visited during the last years of his life (1758-1778) by sovereigns, intellectuals, poets and victims of tyranny. Maintaining his correspondence, which, throughout his lifetime, amounted to more than ten thousand letters, he wrote during this last period of his life polemics against his enemies and pamphlets in behalf of the dis-

tressed. In 1778, the year of his
death, he returned to Paris to receive, during the performance of
Irène, one of his tragedies, a final
ovation.

Champion of reason, tolerance
and progress, Voltaire was the incarnation of the eighteenth-century
ideal. Though not a revolutionist,
he destroyed many of the existing
social abuses of the time. Contributing, through his encyclopedic output, to the philosophic movement,
he undermined respect for authority and tradition, and thereby prepared the spirit of the French Revolution.

Of his many notable works, in
addition to his important literary
criticism, special mention should be
made of such *contes* as *Jeannot et
Colin* (1764), *L'Ingénu* (1767) and
La Princesse de Babylone (1768).
Included among his more representative works in verse are: *Le
Mondain* (1736), a satire; *Sept discours sur l'homme* (1738), *Poème sur
le désastre de Lisbonne* (1755) and
Religion naturelle (1755)—all philosophical poems. Of his dramatic
output, *La Mort de César* (1735),
Mahomet (1741), *Mérope* (1743) and
Tancrède (1760) are his more representative tragedies, while *Nanine*
(1749) and *L'Écossaise* (1760) are
his more significant comedies.

S. G. Tallentyre, *Life of Voltaire*,
1903; G. Lanson, *Voltaire*, 1906; R.
Aldington, *Voltaire*, 1925; H. N.
Brailsford, *Voltaire*, 1935; F. Vial,
Voltaire, sa vie, ses œuvres, 1953.

Volupté (1834): See *Sainte-Beuve*.

Voulez-vous jouer avec moâ (1923): See
Achard, Marcel.

Voyage au bout de la Nuit, Le (1932):
See *Céline.*

Voyage de M. Perrichon, Le (1860): See
Labiche.

Voyage en Orient (1835): See *Lamartine.*

Voyageur, Le (1923): See *Amiel,
Denis.*

Voyageurs de l'impériale, Les (1943): See
Aragon.

Voyageur sans bagages, Le (1936): See
Anouilh.

Vraie Histoire comique de Francion, La
(1623): See *Sorel, Charles.*

vraisemblance: An important principle or criterion in French classical
tragedy (q.v.), it stressed the "plausible" or the illusion of reality. Corneille (q.v.) did not completely
subscribe to a narrow conception of
vraisemblance, and his rivals
pointed to this failing in *Le Cid*
(q.v.).

#

Wace: (1100?-1174?) Probably the
greatest vernacular chronicler of the
twelfth century, he is the author of
Brut (q.v.) and of the *Roman de
Rou* (begun in 1160). In the latter
work, also a verse chronicle, the
author begins with the fall of Troy,
and continues up to the invasion of
England (1066), which he narrates
in detail.

B. F. Carpenter, *The Life and
Writings of Maistre Wace*, 1930.

Y

Yvain ou Le Chevalier au lion: See *Chrétien de Troyes*.

Z

Zadig (1747): See *Voltaire*.
Zaïde (1670): See *La Fayette, Mme. de*.
Zaïre (1732): See *Voltaire*.
Zimmer, Bernard: (1893-   ) Before devoting himself in 1932 to scenario writing, this dramatist composed two farces dealing with two forms of bourgeois hypocrisy. *Le Veau gras* (1924), a satire of post-war manners, reveals the hypocritical methods of exploitation used to extract money from an old duchess; *Le Coup de deux décembre* (1928), satirizes women of respectable society who offer themselves to a young adolescent because of his ill-merited reputation as a lover. *Bava l'africain* (1925), more psychological, is a satirical analysis of the power of myth, of the admiration attached to anyone recounting his fantastic exploits, once credence is placed in them. The cynical and credulous, those who here attack or defend this weaver of imaginary expeditions, are presented humorously; the situations, moreover, in these three plays testify to this dramatist's gift for the comical.

Zola, Emile: (1840-1902) A romantic by temperament, the head of the Naturalistic School (see *Naturalism*), as he was to be known, was born in Paris, where he was to spend most of his life, of a French mother and an Italian engineer who became a naturalized Frenchman. To his father and the early environment of Aix-en-Provence, where he remained most of the first eighteen years of his life, he owed the romantic tendency that was to permeate, despite his aesthetics, much of his work. The hard realities of life, the early experiences of poverty, help explain the change from the sentimental *Contes à Ninon* (1864), his first published work, to *Thérèse Raquin* (1867), his first "naturalistic" novel, in which remorse is studied like an "organic disorder." The influences, moreover, of Positivism (q.v.), of Taine's (q.v.) determinism, of Claude Bernard's *Introduction à l'étude de la médecine expérimentale* (1865), not to mention those of Stendhal, Balzac, the Goncourt brothers, and Flaubert (qq.v.), were to be reflected in his new approach to the novel. Much like Balzac (q.v.), who had depicted in his *Comédie Humaine* the Restoration and the July Monarchy, Zola, in his projected *Rougon-Macquart* (1871-1893) series, was going to portray the society of the period of the Second Empire. More than Balzac, however, Zola, like a scientist in the laboratory performing a controlled experiment, an experiment he did not realize was "scientifically" impossible because of his *a priori* ideas and conclusions, was going to trace, from novel to novel, the hereditary (biological and physiological) effects, in varying circumstances and environments, on five successive generations. The "experiment," carried through the twenty volumes, and applied to the progeny of this family tainted by drunkenness and neurasthenic tendencies, proved to be less successful, as was to be expected, in producing memorable individual character studies, despite the carefully-prepared dossiers for each of them; as symbols of group-life, they are much more effective. Seen as the "Human Comedy" of the Second-Empire, the thousand-odd characters who appear in the *Rougon-Macquart* cycle become, in the final analysis, a portrait of the different social classes, *milieux,* places seen, visited, and studied, for documentary purposes, by Zola. Provincial life is seen in *La fortune des Rougon* (1871); demi-monde society is viewed in *Nana* (1880); the business world is depicted in *Le ventre de Paris* (1873), a picture of the central markets, and in *Au bonheur des dames* (1883), a portrait of the department store; the world of finance is described in *La Curée* (1871) and in *L'Argent* (1891). The

hero or central figure in *La Bête humaine* (1890) is the railroad, while in *L'Assommoir* (1877)— which established his reputation as the head of the Naturalistic School —the saloon and alcohol are seen in their deteriorating effects on man. Probably his best novel is *Germinal* (1885; q.v.), a study of miners and the mine; *La Terre* (1887) is an ugly picture of the peasantry. Because of its scandalous nature, the latter work resulted in the "Manifeste des Cinq," a protest by some of the previous disciples of Zola. *La Débâcle* (1892), next to the last volume in the entire cycle, is a vivid portrait of the Franco-Prussian war.

Naturalism, as seen in the *Rougon-Macquart* series, includes the characteristics of scientific determinism, a mechanistic and pessimistic view of humanity, emphasis on the vulgar, sordid, and pathological, with a predilection for the lower classes. As for his aesthetics, Zola formulated his naturalistic theories in such works as *Le Roman Expérimental* (1880), *Les Romanciers naturalistes* (1881), and *Le Naturalisme au théâtre* (1881). In the latter work, his dramatic theories are clearly delineated.

Won over to social humanitarianism toward the latter part of his life, Zola wrote two other cycles, no longer naturalistic in perspective. *Les trois villes* (1894-1898), including *Lourdes, Rome,* and *Paris,* is anti-clerical, while the unfinished *Les quatre évangiles* (1899-1903), which consists only of *Fécondité, Travail,* and *Vérité* (*Justice* never appeared) expresses a humanitarian view. The same generous love of humanity and devotion to truth caused him to champion the cause of the innocent Captain in the famous Dreyfus case (cf. *Anatole France*). Although Zola did not have the good fortune of being admitted to the *Académie Française* (q.v.), his remains were transferred to the Panthéon.

H. Massis, *Comment Zola composait ses romans*, 1906; F. Doucet, *L'Esthétique de Zola*, 1923; M. Josephson, *Zola and His Time*, 1928; A. Wilson, *Emile Zola, an Introductory Study*, 1952; F. W. J. Hemmings, *Emile Zola*, 1953.

LIST OF TERMS AND TOPICS OTHER
THAN TITLES AND AUTHORS

Abbaye de Créteil
Abbaye de Thélème
Académie Française
Académie Goncourt
alexandrine
Aristotle (Influence of)
Art for Art's sake
assonance
Athénée
Atelier
aube
ballade
Baroque
Basoche
bestiaire
bienséance
"Bohême"
bovarysme
burlesque
cantilène
casuistry
chanson courtoise
chanson de geste
chanson de geste (Origins of)
chanson de mal mariée
chanson de toile
chant royal
Cinema
Classicism
Collège de France
comédie à ariettes
Comédie des Champs-Elysées
Comédie-Française
Comédie humaine
Comédie-Italienne
comédie larmoyante
comédie rosse
Comedy
comedy of character
comedy of manners
commedia dell'arte
Compagnons de la Chimère, Les
Compagnie Madeleine
  Renaud—Jean-Louis Barrault
Compagnie Pitoëff
Confrérie de la Passion
conte

courtly love
Criticism
Crusades
Cubism
cry
Dadaism
débat
dit
Drama
drama, liturgical
drame
drame bourgeois
École Romane
écriture artiste
églogue
élégie
Enfants-sans-souci
enjambement
Enlightenment, Age of
Epic
épigramme
épître
esprit gaulois
Essay
Existentialism
fabliau
farce
Felibres
Felibrige
Foire, théâtres de la
Franco-American Literary Relations
Grail (or Holy Grail)
Grand Guignol
Hernani ("battle" of)
honnête homme
Hôtel de Bourgogne
Humanism
Idéologues
Illustre Théâtre
Impressionism
Jansenism
jeu
jongleur
lai
Language
langue d'oc
langue d'oïl

361

Langues Romanes
lapidaire
libertins
libertinage
Lyric Poetry (Origins of)
mal du siècle
Marivaudage
Mathurins, Les
Médan (group of)
Melodrama
miracle
moralité
mystère
Naturalism
Naturisme
nouvelle
Novel
ode
Opéra-Comique
Palais des Papes
Pantagruelism
Parnassianism
Parnassians
pastorale
pastourelle
Personnalisme
Petrarchism (Influence of)
philosophes
pièce à thèse
pièce bien faite
Platonism (Influence of)
Pléiade
Poetry
Populism
Port-Royal
Positivism
précieuses
précieux
preciosity
Prix Goncourt
Provençal (language and literature)
puy
Quarrel of the Ancients and Moderns
Quarrel of the Cid
Quietism
raisonneur
Rambouillet, Hôtel de
Realism
récit
Renaissance
"Résistance" Literature
Rhétoriqueurs
rime féminine
rime riche
roman à clef
roman antique
roman breton
roman d'aventure
romanesque
roman-feuilleton
roman-fleuve
Romanticism
rondeau
salut d'amour
satire
Short Story
Solitaires
sonnet
sottie
Surrealism
Symbolism
tençon
Théatre d'Art
Théâtre-Français
Théatre-Libre
Théatre National Populaire
Théatre de l'Œuvre
Théâtre du Marais
Théâtre du Peuple
Théâtre du Vieux-Colombier
Tragedy
tragi-comédie pastorale
tragi-comedy
tranche de vie
troubadour
trouvère
Unanimism
unities
Vaudeville
verset
vers libre
virelai
vraisemblance